The
Zohar

by
Rabbi Shimon bar Yochai

with
The Sulam commentary

of
Rabbi Yehuda Ashlag

The First Ever Unabridged
English Translation with Commentary

from the press of
Yeshivat Kol Yehudah
Dean Rav S. P. Berg Shlita

Edited and compiled by
Rabbi Michael Berg

בהוצאת ישיבת "קול יהודה"
ללמודי הנגלה והנסתר
Published by the Press of the
"Yeshivat Kol Yehuda"
Dean Rav Berg
For the study of Kabbalah

14 Ben Ami Street, Tel Aviv, Israel 63342
And
155 E. 48th St., New York City, NY 10017

שנת ה' תשס"א לפ"ק

First Edition
ISBN: 1-57189-197-8

Printed in Canada

מציאת בני זוג, בריאות ואושר

גיטל בת הלן ומשה

רחל בת גיטל

דוד בן גיטל

בריאות הנפש והגוף ואור

שאול בן משה והלן

איילין בת משה והלן

למשה והלן

APPLYING THE POWER OF THE ZOHAR

The Zohar is a book of great mystical power and wisdom. It is Universally recognized as the definitive work on the Kabbalah – and it is also so Much more.

The Zohar is a wellspring of spiritual energy, a fountainhead of metaphysical power that not only reveals and explains, but literally brings blessing, protection, and well-being into the lives of all those who read or peruse its sacred texts. All that is required is worthy desire, the certainty of a trusting heart, and an open and receptive mind. Unlike other books, including the great spiritual texts of other traditions, The Zohar is written in a kind of code, through which metaphors, parables, and cryptic language at first conceal but ultimately reveal the forces of creation.

As electrical current is concealed in wire and cable before disclosing itself as an illuminated light bulb, the spiritual Light of the Creator is wrapped in allegory and symbolism throughout the Aramaic text of the Zohar. And while many books contain information and knowledge, the Zohar both expresses and embodies spiritual Light. The very letters on its pages have the power to bring spiritual wisdom and positive energy into every area of our lives.

As we visually scan the Aramaic texts and study the accompanying insights that appear in English, spiritual power is summoned from above – and worlds tremble as Light is sent forth in response.

It's primary purpose is not only to help us acquire wisdom, but to draw Light from the Upper Worlds and to bring sanctification into our lives. Indeed, the book itself is the most powerful of all tools for cleansing the soul and connecting to the Light of the Creator. As you open these pages, therefore, do not make understanding in the conventional sense your primary goal.

Although you may not have a knowledge of Aramaic, look first at the Aramaic text before reading the English. Do not be discouraged by difficulties with comprehension. Instead, open your heart to the spiritual transformation the Zohar is offering you.

Ultimately, the Zohar is an instrument for refining the individual soul – for removing darkness from the earth – and for bringing well being and blessing to our fellow man.

Its purpose is not only to make us intellectually wise, but to make us spiritually pure.

Glossary of Hebrew words

Torah

Also known as the Five Books of Moses, the Torah is considered to be the physical body of learning, whereas the Zohar is the internal soul. The literal stories of the Torah conceal countless hidden secrets. The Zohar is the Light that illuminates all of the Torah's sublime mysteries.

Beresheet	Genesis
Shemot	Exodus
Vayikra	Leviticus
Bemidbar	Numbers
Devarim	Deuteronomy

Prophets

Amos	Amos
Chagai	Haggai
Chavakuk	Habakkuk
Hoshea	Hosea
Malachi	Malachi
Melachim	Kings
Michah	Micah
Nachum	Nahum
Ovadyah	Obadiah
Shmuel	Samuel
Shoftim	Judges
Tzefanyah	Zephaniah
Yechezkel	Ezekiel
Yehoshua	Joshua
Yeshayah	Isaiah
Yirmeyah	Jeremiah
Yoel	Joel
Yonah	Jonah
Zecharyah	Zechariah

Writings

Daniel	Daniel
Divrei Hayamim	Chronicles
Eicha	Lamentations
Ester	Esther
Ezra-Nechemiah	Ezra-Nehemiah
Iyov	Job
Kohelet	Ecclesiastes
Mishlei	Proverbs
Rut	Ruth
Sir Hashirim	Songs of Songs
Tehilim	Psalms

The Ten Sfirot – Emanations

To conceal the blinding *Light* of the Upper World, and thus create a tiny point into which our universe would be born, ten *curtains* were fabricated. These ten *curtains* are called Ten Sfirot. Each successive Sfirah further reduces the emanation of *Light*, gradually dimming its brilliance to a level almost devoid of *Light* – our physical world known as *Malchut*. The only remnant of Light remaining in this darkened universe is a *pilot light* which sustains our existence. This Light is the life force of a human being and the force that gives birth to stars, sustains suns and sets everything from swirling galaxies to busy ant hills in motion. Moreover, the Ten Sfirot act like a prism, refracting the Light into many *colors* giving rise to the diversity of life and matter in our world.

The Ten Sfirot are as follows:

Keter	Crown
Chochmah	Wisdom
Binah	Understanding
Da'at	Knowledge
Zeir Anpin	Small Face,

(includes the next six Sfirot):

Chesed	Mercy (Chassadim - plural)
Gvurah	Judgment (Gvurot - Plural)
Tiferet	Splendor
Netzach	Victory (Eternity)
Hod	Glory
Yesod	Foundation
Malchut	Kingdom

The Partzufim - Spiritual forms

One complete structure of the Ten Sfirot

creates a *Partzuf* or Spiritual Form. Together, these forces are the building blocks of all reality. As water and sand combine to create cement, the Ten Sfirot combine to produce a Spiritual Form *[Partzuf]*. Each of the Spiritual Forms below are therefore composed of one set of Ten Sfirot.

These Spiritual Forms are called:

Atik	Ancient
Atik Yomin	Ancient of Days
Atika Kadisha	Holy Ancient
Atik of Atikin	Anceint of Ancients
Aba	Father
Arich Anpin	Long Face
Ima	Mother
Nukva	Female
Tevunah	Intelligence
Yisrael Saba	Israel Grandfather
Zachar	Male

These names are not meant to be understood literally. Each represents a unique spiritual force and building block, producing a substructure and foundation for all the worlds make up reality.

The Five Worlds

All of the above Spiritual Forms *[Partzufim]* create one spiritual world. There are Five Worlds in total that compose all reality, therefore, five sets of the above Spiritual Forms are required.

Our physical world corresponds to the world of: Asiyah – Action

Adam Kadmon	Primordial Man
Atzilut	Emanation
Briyah	Creation
Yetzirah	Formation
Asiyah	Action

The Five Levels of the soul

Nefesh	First, Lowest level of Soul
Ruach	Second level of Soul
Neshamah	Third level of Soul
Chayah	Fourth level of Soul
Yechidah	Highest, fifth level of Soul

Names of God

As a single ray of white sunlight contains the seven colors of the spectrum, the one Light of the Creator embodies many diverse spiritual forces. These different forces are called *Names of God.* Each Name denotes a specific attribute and spiritual power. The Hebrew letters that compose these Names are the interface by which these varied Forces act upon our physical world. The most common Name of God is the Tetragrammaton (the four letters, *Yud Hei Vav Hei* יהוה.) Because of the enormous power that the Tetragrammaton transmits, we do not utter it aloud. When speaking of the Tetragrammaton, we use the term *Hashem* which means, *The Name.*

Adonai, El, Elohim, Hashem, Shadai, Eheyeh, Tzevaot, Yud Hei Vav Hei

People

Er	The son of Noach
Rabbi Elazar	The son of Rabbi Shimon bar Yochai
Rabbi Shimon bar Yochai	Author of the Zohar
Shem, Cham, Yefet	Noach's children
Shet	Seth
Ya'akov	Jacob
Yishai	Jesse (King David's father)
Yitzchak	Isaac
Yosef	Joseph
Yitro	Jethro
Yehuda	Judah

Angels

Angels are distinct energy components, part of a vast communication network running through the upper worlds. Each

unique Angel is responsible for transmitting various forces of influence into our physical universe.

Adriel, Ahinael, Dumah (name of Angel in charge of the dead), Gabriel, Kadshiel, Kedumiel, Metatron, Michael, Rachmiel, Raphael, Tahariel, Uriel

Nations

Nations actually represent the inner attributes and character traits of our individual self. The nation of Amalek refers to the doubt and uncertainty that dwells within us when we face hardship and obstacles. Moab represents the dual nature of man. Nefilim refers to the sparks of Light that we have defiled through our impure actions, and to the negative forces that lurk within the human soul as a result of our own wrongful deeds.

Amalek, Moab, Nefilim

General

Aba	Father

Refers to the male principle and positive force in our universe. Correlates to the proton in an atom.

Chayot	Animals
Chupah	Canopy (wedding ceremony)
Et	The
Avadon	Hell
Gehenom	Hell
Sheol	Hell

The place a soul goes for purification upon leaving this world.

Ima	Mother

The female principle and minus force in our universe. Correlates to the electron in an atom.

Kiddush	Blessing over the wine
Klipah	Shell (negativity)
Klipot	Shells (Plural)
Kriat Sh'ma	The Reading of the Sh'ma
Mashiach	Messiah

Mishnah	Study
Mochin	Brain, Spiritual levels of Light
Moed	A designated time or holiday
Negev	The south of Israel
Nukva	Female
Partzuf	Face
Shamayim	Heavens (sky)
Shechinah	The Divine presence, The female aspect of the Creator
Tefilin	Phylacteries
Tzadik	Righteous person
Zion	Another name for Jerusalem
Yisrael	The land of Israel
	The nation of Israel or an individual Israelite
Zohar	Splendor

The Hebrew vowels

Chirik א, Cholam אוֹ א, Kamatz א, Patach א, Segol א, Sh'va א, Shuruk אוּ א, Tzere א

The Twelve Tribes

Asher, Dan, Ephraim, Gad, Issachar, Judah, Levi, Menasheh, Naphtali, Reuben, Shimon, Zebulun

Jewish Holidays

Rosh Hashanah	The Jewish New Year
Yom Kippur	Day on Atonement
Sukkot	Holiday of the Booths
Shmini Atzeret	The day of Convocation
Simchat Torah	Holiday on which we dance with the Torah
Pesach	Passover
Shavout	Holiday of the Weeks

כרך טו

פנחס חלק ב׳, מטות

Vol. XV

Pinchas B, Matot

A Prayer from The Ari

To be recited before the study of the Zohar

Ruler of the universe, and Master of all masters, The Father of mercy and forgiveness, we thank You, our God and the God of our fathers, by bowing down and kneeling, that You brought us closer to Your Torah and Your holy work, and You enable us to take part in the secrets of Your holy Torah. How worthy are we that You grant us with such big favor, that is the reason we plead before You, that You will forgive and acquit all our sins, and that they should not bring separation between You and us.

And may it be your will before You, our God and the God of our fathers, that You will awaken and prepare our hearts to love and revere You, and may You listen to our utterances, and open our closed heart to the hidden studies of Your Torah, and may our study be pleasant before Your Place of Honor, as the aroma of sweet incense, and may You emanate to us Light from the source of our soul to all of our being. And, may the sparks of your holy servants, through which you revealed Your wisdom to the world, shine.

May their merit and the merit of their fathers, and the merit of their Torah, and holiness, support us so we shall not stumble through our study. And by their merit enlighten our eyes in our learning as it stated by King David, The Sweet Singer of Israel: "Open my eyes, so that I will see wonders from Your Torah" (Tehilim 119:18). Because from His mouth God gives wisdom and understanding.

"May the utterances of my mouth and the thoughts of my heart find favor before You, God, my Strength and my Redeemer" (Tehilim 19:15).

PINCHAS

Name of the Articles

Page No.

76. "Take from among you an offering," not from
    among the mixed multitude   4
77. Mem of Mavet flying in the air   10
78. The Yud that Pinchas earned was the Yud of Shadai   13
79. Yisrael are the body parts of the Shechinah   18
80. "Let Us make man in Our image, after Our likeness"   22
81. What is 'Yesh' – Chochmah   27
82. "Whatever the Elohim does, it shall be forever"   31
83. "According to the lot"   36
84. The sacrifices   41
85. Additional Nefesh, additional Ruach, additional Neshamah 69
86. Arvit (the evening prayer)   76
87. Moses, the two Messiahs, the rainbow and Malchut   78
88. "I have gathered my myrrh... Drink, drink deep,
    O loving companions"   86
89. He that treats lightly bread crumbs   89
90. Olive-size and egg-size   92
91. The twelve Challot   102
92. The things one should observe at the Shabbat table   104
93. Three who harm themselves   117
94. Three Yud's in the Yud Hei Vav Hei fully spelled
    with Yud amounting to 63   120
95. As a flame connected to a burning coal   123
96. Fine flour for an offering   129
97. "Mingled with...beaten oil"   132
98. Zarka, Makaf, Shofar Holech, Segolta   137
99. Bring an atonement over Me   139
100. The moon has contracted itself   142
101. The Yud Hei Vav Heis in the middle   144
102. A he-goat to Azazel   146
103. "And in the beginnings of your new moons"   150
104. The hind of dawn   155
105. The holiday of Pesach (Passover)   162
106. "Rebuke the wild beast of the reed grass"   186
107. Four redemptions   191
108. "A bird's nest"   194

109. The four passages in the Tefilin and the reading of Sh'ma   196
110. The shewbread which is the twelve faces   198
111. "My offering, the provision of My sacrifices made by fire"   202
112. Fine flour, average flour and waste matter   203
113. Shavuot (Holiday of the Weeks)   206
114. "But you shall surely let the mother go"   215
115. Yisrael know how to hunt good game   216
116. "A bird's nest"   220
117. Moses' bride   223
118. "And you shall offer a sacrifice made by fire for
     a burnt offering"   227
119. "Also on the day of the firstfruits"   231
120. Yom Kippur (Day of Atonement)   234
121. The holiday of Sukkot (Holiday of the Booths)   239
122. Shmini Atzeret (the Eighth day of Assembly)   251
123. Explanations about Malchut   253
124. Explanations of the Holy Names and appelations   265
125. The reading of Sh'ma Yisrael and the Tefilin   273
126. Two arrangements of the four passages of the Tefilin   275
127. Shavuot   280
128. Rosh Hashanah (the Jewish New Year)   282
129. Sukkot   284
130. The water libation   286

76. "Take from among you an offering," not from among the mixed multitude

76. "Take from among you an offering," not from among the mixed multitude

A Synopsis

Rabbi Shimon and Rabbi Elazar discuss the question of whether the offering was to be taken only from the children of Yisrael or from the mixed multitudes as well. They also determine that Yisrael did not in fact worship Baal Pe'or.

471. קְחוּ מֵאִתְּכֶם תְּרוּמָה. ת״ח, בְּקַדְמֵיתָא כְּתִיב, מֵאֵת כָּל אִישׁ אֲשֶׁר יִדְּבֶנּוּ לִבּוֹ. כֹּלָּא בִּכְלָל. כֵּיָן דְּאִינּוּן עֵרֶב רַב עָבְדוּ דָא, וּמִיתוּ מִנַּיְיהוּ אִינּוּן דְּמִיתוּ, בָּעָא קוּדְשָׁא בְּרִיךְ הוּא לְאִתְפַּיְּיסָא בַּהֲדַיְיהוּ דְּיִשְׂרָאֵל, אָמַר לוֹן, אִתְחַבְּרוּ כֻּלְּכוּ לְסְטַר חַד, הֲדָא הוּא דִכְתִּיב וַיַּקְהֵל מֹשֶׁה אֶת כָּל עֲדַת בְּנֵי יִשְׂרָאֵל בִּלְחוֹדַיְיהוּ, אָמַר לוֹן, בְּנַי, בְּכוֹן אֲנָא בָּעֵי לְמִשְׁרֵי, עִמְכוֹן תְּהֵא דִּיּוּרָא דִּילִי. וְע״ד, קְחוּ מֵאִתְּכֶם תְּרוּמָה, מֵאִתְּכֶם, וְלָא מֵאַחֲרָא, לָא בָּעֵינָא דִּתְהֵא שׁוּתָּפָא לְאַחֲרָנִין בַּהֲדִי, וְלָא בַּהֲדַיְיכוּ, וּבְג״כ כֻּלְּהוּ אִשְׁתְּצִיאוּ. אוּף הָכָא הָא אִינּוּן מֵאִינּוּן גִּזְעָא בִּישָׁא הֲווֹ, וַיִּהְיוּ הַמֵּתִים. הַמֵּתִים, וַדַּאי מֵתִים, וְלָא מִיִּשְׂרָאֵל. וּבְג״כ מָנָה לוֹן, דִּכְתִּיב שְׂאוּ אֶת רֹאשׁ בְּנֵי יִשְׂרָאֵל, אֲרִימוּ רֵישַׁיְיהוּ.

471. "Take from among you an offering" (Shemot 35:5). Come and see, in the first instance it is written: "of every man whose heart prompts him to give" (Shemot 25:2). That is, from absolutely anyone, EVEN THE MIXED MULTITUDE. Since the mixed multitude had made THE GOLDEN CALF, and some of them who had died, the Holy One, blessed be He, wanted to be reconciled with Yisrael. He said to them: 'Join yourselves together, all of you, to one side,' as it is written: "And Moses gathered all the congregation of the children of Yisrael" (Shemot 35:1) by themselves. He said to them: 'My children, I want to rest upon you; My dwelling shall be amongst you. And so it is written: "Take from among you an offering" from you and not from anyone else. I do not want the others to have any connection with Me nor with you.' And this is why all OF THE MIXED MULTITUDE were destroyed. And so also here. All those about whom it is written "And those that were dead..." (Bemidbar 25:9) were of a bad stock, NAMELY THEY WERE THE OFFSPRING OF THE MIXED MULTITUDE WHO HAD

INTERMARRIED WITH THE TRIBE OF SHIMON, AS ABOVE. Those dead were certainly ALREADY dead, FOR THEY WERE OF THE MIXED MULTITUDE WHO ARE CALLED 'DEAD' EVEN DURING THEIR LIFETIME, AS ABOVE, and not from Yisrael. And this is why he counted them, as it is written: "Take the sum of the congregation of the children of Yisrael" (Bemidbar 26:2), WHICH MEANS LITTERALLY, raise up their heads.

472. א"ר אֶלְעָזָר, אַבָּא, כַּמָּה יָאוּת הוּא, אִי לָא אַשְׁכַּחְנָא פְּלוּגְתָּא עַל דָּא. אָמַר לֵיהּ בְּרִי אֵימָא. א"ל וְהָא כְּתִיב וַיִּצָּמֶד יִשְׂרָאֵל לְבַעַל פְּעוֹר, וְתָנֵינָן דְּאִתְחַבָּרוּ יִשְׂרָאֵל בַּהֲדֵיהּ, כְּצַמִּידָא דָא דְּאִתְחַבָּר בב"ן בְּקִשּׁוּטוֹי, הָכִי אִתְחַבָּרוּ יִשְׂרָאֵל בְּבַעַל פְּעוֹר. א"ל אֶלְעָזָר, הָכִי הוּא, וַיִּצָּמֶד יִשְׂרָאֵל לְבַעַל פְּעוֹר, אֶלָּא אֲנָא לָא אֲמָרִית דְּאִתְדְּכוּ יִשְׂרָאֵל מֵהַהוּא חוֹבָה, אֶלָּא דְּאִתְדְּכוּ מִמּוֹתָא, דְּלָא שַׁרְיָא עֲלֵיהוּ מוֹתָא.

472. Rabbi Elazar said, Father, WHAT YOU HAVE SAID would have been most beautiful if there had not been an internal contradiction. He said to him, My son, please tell me. And he replied, It is written: "And Yisrael joined himself to Baal Pe'or" (Bemidbar 25:3), and we have learnt that Yisrael were joined to Baal Pe'or as a bracelet is joined to a bejeweled person. THAT IS: YISRAEL ALSO SINNED, AND NOT ONLY THE MIXED MULTITUDE. He said to him: So it is indeed, Elazar, that "Yisrael joined himself to Baal Pe'or," but I did not say that Yisrael were innocent of that sin. All I said was that they were cleared of death, that death did not rest on them.

473. א"ל וְהָא כְּתִיב, קַח אֶת כָּל רָאשֵׁי הָעָם וְהוֹקַע אוֹתָם. א"ל רָאשֵׁי הָעָם וַדַּאי, וְלָא רָאשֵׁי בְּנֵי יִשְׂרָאֵל. וּמִן הָעָם אִית לָן לְמֵילַף, כְּתִיב הָכָא הָעָם, וּכְתִיב הָתָם וַיִּרָא הָעָם. וַיִּקָּהֵל הָעָם. וַיִּפּוֹל מִן הָעָם. אֲבָל ת"ח, וַיִּצָּמֶד יִשְׂרָאֵל לְבַעַל פְּעוֹר, וְלָא פַּלְחוּ לֵיהּ, אֲבָל מִן סֵיפֵיהּ דִּקְרָא אוֹכַח, דִּכְתִיב וַיֹּאכַל הָעָם וַיִּשְׁתַּחֲווּ, וְלָא כְּתִיב וַיֹּאכַל וַיִּשְׁתַּחוּ יִשְׂרָאֵל. אֶלָּא הָעָם, כֵּיוָן דִּכְתִיב וַיִּצָּמֶד יִשְׂרָאֵל, מַאי וַיֹּאכַל הָעָם. אֶלָּא הַהוּא זַרְעָא בִישָׁא, הֲווֹ חוֹבָה דְּיִשְׂרָאֵל.

473. He said to him: But it is also written: "Take all the chiefs of the people and hang them" (Ibid. 4), WHICH MEANS THEY WERE OF YISRAEL. He said

to him, It does indeed specifically say "the chiefs of the people," NAMELY THE MIXED MULTITUDE WHO ARE CALLED 'PEOPLE' WITHOUT FURTHER EPITHET. IT DOES not SAY 'the chiefs of the children of Yisrael'. And from the use of the term "the people" we can learn THAT WHEREVER SCRIPTURE USES "THE PEOPLE" THE REFERENCE IS TO THE MIXED MULTITUDE. In this verse it is written "the people," and elsewhere it is written: "And when the people saw that Moses delayed" (Shemot 32:1) and: "the people gathered themselves together" (Ibid.), and: "And there fell of the people..." (Ibid. 28). IN ALL THESE CASES, "THE PEOPLE" MEANS THE MIXED MULTITUDE. But come and see: All that is written is "And Yisrael joined himself to Baal Pe'or" (Bemidbar 25:3). It does not say that they worshipped, as understood from the end of the verse, as is written: "and the people ate, and bowed down to their Elohim" (Ibid. 2). Scripture does not say that Yisrael ate and bowed down, but IT IS WRITTEN, "the people." And since it is written "And Yisrael joined...," what is the meaning of "and the people ate"? SCRIPTURE SHOULD HAVE SAID: 'AND YISRAEL ATE'. However, it was that bad stock, NAMELY THE MIXED MULTITUDE WHO MARRIED WOMEN OF YISRAEL, which was the sin of Yisrael.

474. מַהוּ דִּכְתִיב וַיִּצָּמֶד יִשְׂרָאֵל לְבַעַל פְּעוֹר. ת״ח, וַיִּצָּמֶד יִשְׂרָאֵל בְּבַעַל פְּעוֹר לָא כְּתִיב, אֶלָּא לְבַעַל פְּעוֹר. קְשׁוּטִין וְתוּקְפָּא יָהֲבוּ לְבַעַל פְּעוֹר, בְּלָא דַּעְתָּא, בְּגִין דְּפוּלְחָנָא דִּפְעוֹר הוּא, לְמִפְרַע גַּרְמֵיהּ, וּלְאַפָּקָא קַמֵּיהּ צוֹאָה רוֹתַחַת. וְהַהוּא עֲבִידְתָּא אַהֲנֵי לֵיהּ, וְאִתְתְּקַף מִנֵּיהּ. וְיִשְׂרָאֵל כֵּיוָן דְּחָמוּ דָּא, חֲשִׁיבָא דְּזִלְזוּלָא דִּילֵיהּ אִיהוּ, וְקִלְקוּלָא דִּילֵיהּ, דְּהָא בע״ז כְּתִיב, צֵא תֹּאמַר לוֹ. וְאִינּוּן בְּגִין זִלְזוּלָא דַּעֲבוֹדָה זָרָה, פַּרְעוּ גַּרְמַיְיהוּ בְּלָא יְדִיעָה, וְעַל הָנֵי כְּפַר פִּנְחָס, וּבָטַל מוֹתָנָא, דִּכְתִיב וַיְכַפֵּר עַל בְּנֵי יִשְׂרָאֵל.

474. ANOTHER COMMENT. Take the verse: "And Yisrael joined himself to Baal Pe'or." Come and see: 'And Yisrael joined himself within Baal Pe'or' is not written, but rather "to Baal Pe'or." This is so because they gave ONLY embellishment and strength to Baal Pe'or, without awareness, because the worship of Pe'or consisted of uncovering oneself and depositing in front of him hot feces, which worship used to give him pleasure and Baal Pe'or grew strong from it. Yisrael, when they saw this, thought that they were thereby

scorning him and disgracing him, for about idolatry it is written: "You shall say to it: Get you hence (Heb. *tze*)" (Yeshayah 30:22), AND THE WORD FOR FECES (HEB. *TZO'AH*) COMES FROM THE SAME ROOT. So they, YISRAEL, uncovered themselves in order to deride the idolatry, without awareness. And it was for these that Pinchas made atonement and stopped the plague FROM THEM, as it is written: "And he made atonement over the children of Yisrael" (Bemidbar 25:13).

A Synopsis

The Faithful Shepherd confirms that the offering was not taken from the mixed multitude. He says that the rule of the mixed multitude over Yisrael causes Yisrael to come under the jurisdiction of the stars and planets rather than God.

רעיא מהימנא

475. אָמַר רַעְיָא מְהֵימָנָא, הֵשִׁיב אֶת חֲמָתִי, מַאי הֵשִׁיב אֶת חֲמָתִי. אֶלָּא ג׳ מְמוּנִים דְּגֵיהִנָּם, חַד עַל שְׁ״ד, וְחַד עַל גִּ״ע, וְחַד עַל עַ״ז. וְאִינּוּן: מַשְׁחִית, אַף, וְחֵימָה. הוּא חֵימָה דַּהֲוָה טָאס בְּעָלְמָא. אָמַר הֵשִׁיב אֶת חֲמָתִי מֵעַל בְּנֵי יִשְׂרָאֵל, וְלָא אָמַר מֵעַל הָעָם, דְּאִינּוּן עֵרֶב רַב, דְּאִתְּמַר וַיִּפּוֹל מִן הָעָם בַּיּוֹם הַהוּא כִּשְׁלֹשֶׁת אַלְפֵי אִישׁ, דְּהָכִי אוֹקִימְנָא וְשָׁאִילוּ לְבוּצִינָא קַדִּישָׁא.

Ra'aya Meheimna (the Faithful Shepherd)

475. The Faithful Shepherd said, IT IS WRITTEN: "turned away My wrath" (Ibid. 11). What is the meaning of "turned away My wrath?" AND HE ANSWERS THAT this refers to three officials over Gehenom. One is over bloodshed, another over sexual transgressions, and the third over idolatry, and they are CALLED 'Destruction', 'Anger' and 'Wrath'. And the latter, Wrath, was flying through the world, AND ABOUT HIM IT SAID: "TURNED AWAY MY WRATH." He said, "turned away My wrath from the children of Yisrael," but He did not say 'from the people', which WOULD REFER TO the mixed multitude. For it is said, "And there fell of the people that day about three thousand men" (Shemot 32:28), WHERE THE MEANING OF "THE PEOPLE" IS THE MIXED MULTITUDE. BUT HERE IT DOES NOT SAY 'TURNED AWAY MY WRATH FROM THE PEOPLE,' BUT RATHER "FROM

THE CHILDREN OF YISRAEL." THIS IS TO TEACH THAT HE DID NOT TURN THE WRATH AWAY FROM THE MIXED MULTITUDE. For this is how we explained it, and we asked the holy luminary, THAT IS, RABBI SHIMON.

476. וּמַה כְּתִיב, קְחוּ מֵאִתְּכֶם תְּרוּמָה לַיְיָ׳, וְלָא מֵעֵרֶב רַב, דְּלָא אִתְקְרִיאוּ קְהִלָּה וְחִבּוּר, עַד דְּאִתְעֲבָר מִנְּהוֹן עֵרֶב רַב, כְּבִיכוֹל בְּזִמְנָא דְּמִתְעָרְבִין בֵּינַיְיהוּ, כְּאִילוּ לָא הֲווֹ גּוֹי אֶחָד. וּבְגִ״ד קְחוּ מֵאִתְּכֶם תְּרוּמָה, וְלָא מִשּׁוּתְּפוּ אַחֲרָא, דְּלָא בָּעֵינָא לְשַׁתְּפָא אַחֲרָנִין בֵּינֵי וּבֵינַיְיכוּ.

476. What is written? "Take from among you an offering to Hashem" (Shemot 35:5), "FROM AMONG YOU" and not from the mixed multitude, for YISRAEL was not called 'a community' and 'a union' until the mixed multitude had been removed from them. When THE MIXED MULTITUDE was intermingled amongst them, as it were, it was as though they were not one people. That is why it says, "Take from among you an offering" and not from any other partnership, NAMELY NOT FROM THE MIXED MULTITUDE, for I do not want to involve others between Me and you.

477. וְלָא עוֹד, אֶלָּא כַּד עֵרֶב רַב אִינּוּן מְעוּרָבִין בְּיִשְׂרָאֵל, מַה כְּתִיב הָיוּ צָרֶיהָ לְרֹאשׁ. וְיִשְׂרָאֵל בָּתַר דְּמִתְעַבְרֵי מִנַּיְיהוּ אֵלֵין מַה כְּתִיב, שְׂאוּ אֶת רֹאשׁ כָּל עֲדַת בְּנֵי יִשְׂרָאֵל. וְלָא עוֹד, אֶלָּא דְּאָמַר קוּדְשָׁא בְּרִיךְ הוּא, אֲנָא בָּעֵי לְדַיְירָא עִמְּכוֹן. הֲדָא הוּא דִכְתִיב, וְעָשׂוּ לִי מִקְדָּשׁ וְשָׁכַנְתִּי בְּתוֹכְכֶם.

477. And not only that, but when the mixed multitude were intermingled with Yisrael, what is written? "Her adversaries have become the chief" (Eichah 1:5). And after THE MIXED MULTITUDE have been removed from Yisrael, what is written? "Take the sum (lit. 'lidt up the head') of all the congregation of the children of Yisrael" (Bemidbar 26:2). And not only that, but the Holy One, blessed be He, said: 'I want to dwell with them,' this being what is meant by: "and let them make Me a sanctuary; that I may dwell among you" (Shemot 25:8).

‏478. וְלֹא עוֹד, אֶלָּא כַּד בְּנֵי יִשְׂרָאֵל בְּגָלוּתָא, עָלַיְיהוּ אִתְּמַר מִי מְעַכֵּב
‏שְׂאוֹר שֶׁבָּעִסָּה, וְהָא אוֹקְמוּהָ מָארֵי מַתְנִיתִין, בְּזִמְנָא דְּעֵרֶב רַב אִינּוּן
‏רָאשִׁים עַל יִשְׂרָאֵל, כִּבְיָכוֹל כְּאִילּוּ עַבְרִין שׁוּלְטָנֵי דְּקוּדְשָׁא בְּרִיךְ הוּא,
‏וְיֵיעָלוּן בְּמִשְׁפָּטֵי כּכְבַיָּא וּמַזָּלֵי. ובג"ד צַוְוחִין וְאַמְרִין, יְיָ' אֱלֹהֵינוּ
‏בְּעָלוּנוּ אֲדוֹנִים זוּלָתֶךָ.

478. And not only that, but when the children of Yisrael are in exile it is said about them: What prevents? The yeast in the dough, for the sages of the Mishnah have taught: When the mixed multitude are the heads over Yisrael, as it were, it is as though the rule of the Holy One, blessed be He, was removed and they had come under the rule of the jurisdiction of the stars and constellations. This is why they cry out, saying, "Hashem our Elohim, other masters beside You have had dominion over us" (Yeshayah 26:13).

77. Mem of Mavet flying in the air

A Synopsis

Rabbi Shimon says that Elijah (Elijah being Pinchas in reincarnation) snatched the letters Mem and Vav from the word mavet, which means death, by means of the great pity he had for Yisrael and his determination that they should not be lost because of the sins of Zimri and Cozbi – this is how and why he killed the two sinners with a spear. Rabbi Shimon concludes by saying that whenever there is a righteous man in the world, the patriarchs come to help him.

479. ד"א, פִּנְחָס וְגוֹ'. קוּם בּוּצִינָא קַדִּישָׁא, וְאַפְתַּח מִלֵּי קַמֵּי שְׁכִינְתָּא. קָם בּוּצִינָא קַדִּישָׁא, וְאָמַר, בְּחַבּוּרָה קַדְמָאָה אִתְּמַר הָכִי. תָּא חֲזֵי, פִּינְחָס קָאִים קַמֵּי דִּינָא תַּקִּיפָא דְּיִצְחָק, וְקָם קַמֵּי פִּרְצָה, דִּכְתִיב וַיַּעֲמוֹד פִּינְחָס וַיְפַלֵּל וַתֵּעָצַר הַמַּגֵּפָה, בְּגִין לְאַגָּנָא עֲלַיְיהוּ דְּיִשְׂרָאֵל, וּבְגִין דָּא כָּלִיל דָּא וְדָא בְּחוּשְׁבָּנָא, פִּינְחָס כְּמִנְיַן יִצְחָק, וְהָכָא צָרִיךְ לְחַדְתָּא מִלִּין.

479. Another explanation of the verse, "Pinchas..." (Bemidbar 25:11): Arise, holy luminary, and say things in the presence of the Shechinah. The holy luminary, THAT IS RABBI SHIMON, arose and said, In the first section it was said: Come and see, Pinchas arose before the strong Judgment of Isaac and stood in the breach, NAMELY THE OUTBREAKS OF THE PLAGUE, as it is written: "Then Pinchas stood up, and executed judgment: and so the plague was stayed" (Tehilim 106:30). AND THIS HE DID in order to protect Yisrael. This is the reason why Pinchas and Isaac have the same numerical value. And now new things have to be said here.

480. פָּתַח וְאָמַר, אֵלִיָּהוּ רְחִימָא דְּמַלְכָּא עִלָּאָה, חָזָא מֶ"ם מִן מָוֶת טָאס בַּאֲוִירָא, חָטַף לָהּ, וְשִׁתֵּף לָהּ עִם ר"ח, דְּאִיהוּ יִצְחָק, וְאִיהוּ בְּחוּשְׁבַּן פִּינְחָס, וְאִשְׁתְּלִים בָּהּ רמ"ח. לְבָתַר חָזָא ו' מִן מָוֶ"ת טָס בִּרְקִיעָא, וְחָטַף לֵיהּ, וְשַׁוֵּי לֵיהּ בְּרַמַ"ח, וְאִשְׁתְּלִים רוֹמַ"ח. הֲדָא הוּא דִכְתִיב, וַיִּקַּח רוֹמַח בְּיָדוֹ.

480. He began by saying, Elijah, the beloved of the Supernal King, NAMELY PINCHAS, FOR ELIJAH IS PINCHAS, saw the letter Mem from the word *mavet* (Eng. 'death') flying in the air, snatched it down and joined it to Resh Chet, which is the numerical value of both Isaac and Pinchas, and WITH THE MEM completed the combination Resh Mem Chet. Subsequently, he saw the letter Vav from the word *mavet* flying in the sky, and he snatched it down also and placed it with the Resh Mem Chet, thus completing the word: Resh Vav Mem Chet (Heb. *romach*), a spear in the fuller spelling, as it is written: "and he took a spear in his hand" (Bemidbar 25:7).

481. וְאִיהוּ, בַּמֶּה יָכִיל לַחֲטוֹף תְּרֵין אַתְוָון אִלֵּין. בִּתְרֵין רוּחִין דְּאִשְׁתְּמָרוּ לְעֵילָא, דְּאִשְׁתְּתָפוּ בְּפִנְחָס. פְּנֵ"י חָ"ס. בִּתְרֵין פָּנִים אִלֵּין, חָס עַל יִשְׂרָאֵל דְּלָא אִתְאֲבִידוּ, בְּחֵילָא דְּתַרְוַוייְהוּ, וַיִּדְקוֹר אֶת שְׁנֵיהֶם, בִּתְרֵין אַתְוָון מ"ו. וְהַיְינוּ בְּקַנְאוֹ אֶת קִנְאָתִי בְּתוֹכָם.

481. And with what was he able to snatch down these two letters, MEM AND VAV? He used the two spirits that were preserved for him on high, for they make up Pinchas, namely *Pnei Chas* (Eng. 'the countenance of pity'), for with these two countenances he had pity on Yisrael that they should not be lost because of those two, ZIMRI AND COZBI, "and he thrust both of them through" (Ibid. 8) with the two letters, Mem and Vav, as is written: "in that he was zealous for My sake among them" (Ibid. 11).

482. וְאַמַאי אִשְׁתַּתַּף בְּיִצְחָק. בְּגִין דְּיִצְחָק מָסַר גַּרְמֵיהּ לְמִיתָה. וּבְגִין דָּא אִשְׁתַּתַּף לֵיהּ לְיִצְחָק, לְמֶהֱוֵי לֵיהּ עֵזֶר. דְּמִסִּטְרָא דִּתְרֵין עִזְלֵי דְּאַיַּילְתָּא, אִשְׁתַּתְּפֵי בֵּיהּ אַבְרָהָם וְיַעֲקֹב, דְּאַבְרָהָם דַּרְגֵּיהּ חֶסֶד אִשְׁתַּתַּף בַּח"ס דְּפִנְחָ"ס. יַעֲקֹב אִיהוּ פְּנֵ"י דְּפִנְחָס בְּגִין דְּאִתְמַר בֵּיהּ, כַּאֲשֶׁר עָבַר אֶת פְּנִיאֵל, פְּנֵ"י אֵ"ל. בְּגִין דְּכַד עָלְמָא אִיהוּ בְּדוֹחֲקָא, וְאִית צַדִּיק בְּעָלְמָא מְקַנֵּי עַל בְּרִית, אֲבָהָן אִשְׁתַּתְּפוּ בֵּיהּ, וּבְגִינַייְהוּ אָמַר מֹשֶׁה בְּדוֹחֲקָא דְּיִשְׂרָאֵל, זְכֹר לְאַבְרָהָם לְיִצְחָק וּלְיִשְׂרָאֵל עֲבָדֶיךָ. וּבְתִלַת אַתְוָון יה"ו מִן אֵלִיָּהוּ, זָכָה לֵהּ מִן הַנָּבִיא, וְדָא אִיהוּ אֵלִיָּהוּ, ה' נָבִיא, וְאִשְׁתְּלִים בֵּיהּ יְדֹו"ד.

482. Why did Pinchas associate himself with Isaac? It was because Isaac gave himself over to death, which is why he joined himself to Isaac, that he could help him. For from the side of the two fawns of the doe, Abraham and Jacob participated in him, for Abraham, whose level is that of Chesed, participated in Chet Samech of Pinchas, while Jacob is Pnei of Pinchas, because it is said about him (about Jacob): "And as he passed over Peniel" (Beresheet 32:32), WHICH CAN BE READ AS: Pnei El, the face of El. For, whenever the world is in trouble, but there is a righteous man in the world, who is zealous for the covenant, then the patriarchs join him. And for their sake, Moses said, when Yisrael were in trouble, "Remember Abraham, Isaac and Yisrael, Your servants" (Shemot 32:13). And with the three letters Yud-Hei-Vav of Elijah, WHICH ARE THE SECRET OF ABRAHAM, ISAAC AND JACOB, he earned the Hei, WHICH IS MALCHUT, of *hanavi* (Eng. 'the prophet') – and this is Elijah the prophet, and thus Yud Hei Vav Hei was completed in him.

78. The Yud that Pinchas earned was the Yud of Shadai

A Synopsis

The Zohar expounds upon the meaning of the lower Yud and the upper Yud in terms of the covenant. The Yud of Shadai prevents the evil inclination from harming a person. We hear that Pinchas was zealous for the covenant both in thought and in deed.

483. י׳ דְּזָכָה פִּנְחָס בֵּיהּ, בְּגִין דְּקַנֵּי עַל בְּרִית, זָכָה לִבְרִית. וּתְרֵין יוֹדִין אִינּוּן, יוֹד עִלָּאָה מִן יְדֹנָ״ד, דִּכְרַת בָּהּ לְאַבְרָהָם, בֵּין י׳ אֶצְבְּעָוֹת דִּיָדִין. יוֹ״ד זְעֵירָא אִיהִי מִן אֲדֹנָי, דִּכְרַת בָּהּ בֵּין י׳ אֶצְבְּעָאן דְּרַגְלִין וְאִיהִי אָת קַדִּישָׁא, דְּמִתְעַטְּרָא בִּרְשִׁימוּ עִלָּאָה.

483. The Yud that Pinchas earned, WHERE HIS NAME IS WRITTEN OUT IN FULL WITH A YUD, was because he was zealous for the covenant, and thus merited the covenant, FOR THE YUD THAT WAS ADDED TO HIS NAME IS AN INDICATION OF THE COVENANT. There are two Yuds, upper Yud from Yud Hei Vav Hei, with which He made the covenant with Abraham between the Yud (ten) fingers of the hands, and small Yud which is from Adonai, with which He made the covenant between the Yud toes of the feet. And it is a holy letter that is adorned as a the supernal imprint.

484. וְדָא אִתְרְשִׁים תָּמִיד לְעָלְמִין, אִיהִי אוֹת דְּשַׁבָּת, אוֹת דִּתְפִלִּין, אוֹת דְּיוֹמִין טָבִין, אוֹת דְּשַׁדַּי דְּרָשִׁים עַל מְזוּזוֹת בֵּיתֶךָ וּבִשְׁעָרֶיךָ. לְמֶהֱוֵי בָּהּ רְשִׁימִין יִשְׂרָאֵל בִּרְצוּעַיְיהוּ, בִּבְרִית דִּלְהוֹן, דְּאִינּוּן בְּנוֹי דְּמַטְרוֹנִיתָא, בְּנוֹי דְּהֵיכָלָא דְּמַלְכָּא קַדִּישָׁא, וּבְאוֹרַיְיתָא, אִינּוּן רְשִׁימִין בְּאָת י׳ עִלָּאָה, דְּאִינּוּן בְּנֵי מַלְכָּא עִלָּאָה, כְּמָה דְּאוּקְמוּהָ. וְהָא אִתְּמַר בָּנִים אַתֶּם לַיְיָ׳ אֱלֹהֵיכֶם.

484. This SMALL YUD is always ever recorded, THAT IS TO SAY THAT IT IS MARKED UPON ALL THE GRADES OF MOCHIN, FOR WITHOUT IT NO GRADE IS REVEALED. It is the sign of Shabbat, the sign of the Tefilin, the sign of the festival days, the sign of Shadai that is recorded "on the doorposts of your house and on your gates" (Devarim 6:9), WHICH IS THE SECRET OF THE YUD OF SHADAI (SHIN DALET YUD), so that Yisrael will be impressed

with it on their straps, NAMELY ON THE KNOT OF THE HAND TEFILIN WHICH HAS THE SHAPE OF THE LETTER YUD, and on their covenant, NAMELY THE CIRCUMCISED MEMBER, SO THEY WILL BE MARKED THROUGH IT as the children of Malchut, the household of the palace of the Holy King, WHICH IS MALCHUT CALLED 'PALACE'. THIS MEANS THAT THEY SHOULD RECEIVE THE MOCHIN OF LOWER CHOCHMAH, WHICH ARE DRAWN DOWN FROM MALCHUT, AND THIS THEY MERIT BY KEEPING GUARD OVER THE COVENANT and BY ENGAGING IN the Torah. They are marked with the upper Yud OF YUD HEI VAV HEI, NAMELY THEY MERIT UPPER CHOCHMAH, for they are the children of the Supernal King. It is as we have taught, and so it is said: "You are the children of Hashem your Elohim" (Devarim 14:1) IN THE SECRET OF THEIR RECEIVING FROM YUD OF YUD HEI VAV HEI, WHICH IS FROM ZEIR ANPIN, WHO IS CALLED YUD HEI VAV HEI.

485. וְאוֹת יוֹד דְּשַׁדַּי, אִיהוּ חוּלְיָא דְּשַׁלְשֶׁלֶת, עַל קוּדְלָא דְּשֵׁד יֵצֶר הָרָע, דְּלָא לְנַזְיק לֵיהּ לִבְּ״נ. דְּעֲלֵיהּ אָמַר דָּוִד, הַצִּילָה מֵחֶרֶב נַפְשִׁי מִיַּד כֶּלֶב יְחִידָתִי. אִיהוּ נָחָשׁ, אִיהוּ כֶּלֶב, אִיהוּ אַרְיֵה. דְּעֲלֵיהּ אָמַר דָּוִד, יֶאֱרוֹב בַּמִּסְתָּר כְּאַרְיֵה בְּסֻכֹּה. וְהַנְּבִיא קָרָא לֵיהּ דּוֹב, הֲהַ״ד דּוֹב אוֹרֵב הוּא לִי אֲרִי בְּמִסְתָּרִים. נִמְשַׁל כַּבְּהֵמוֹת, נִמְשַׁל לְכָל חֵיוָן מְסָאֲבָן, דְּאִינוּן דּוֹרְסִין, אִתְמְתִיל לְכָל בְּ״נ, כְּפוּם חוֹבוֹי, וְהָא אִתְּמַר.

485. And the letter Yud of Shadai (Shin Dalet Yud) THAT IS THE SIGN OF THE COVENANT is a ring halter that is lowered onto the neck of the demon, which is the Evil Inclination, FOR THE LETTERS OF SHADAI MAKE TWO WORDS *SHED* (LIT. 'A DEMON' - SHIN DALET), AND *YUD*, to prevent it from harming people. And this is as David said: "Deliver my life from the sword; my only one from the power of the dog" (Tehilim 22:21), FOR THE EVIL INCLINATION is a serpent, a dog and a lion, about which David said, "He lies in wait secretly like a lion in his den" (Tehilim 10:9), or, in the words of the prophet, a bear, as it is written: "He is to me a bear lying in wait, and like a lion in secret places" (Eichah 3:10). And IT is likened to all the animals, namely is likened to all the beasts of prey, and the likeness is drawn for each person according to his sins. THAT IS, ACCORDING TO A PERSON'S SINS SO IS THE EVIL INCLINATION CALLED 'LION' OR 'BEAR' AND SO ON but this has already been clarified.

486. וְהַאי אִיהוּ כֶּלֶב וְנָחָשׁ וַחֲמוֹר נוֹעֵר, דְּמַרְכִּיבִין עָלֵיהּ נַפְשָׁא. וּמִיַּד דְּאִשְׁתְּמוֹדַע הַהוּא דִּרְכִיב עָלֵיהּ דְּאִיהוּ חַיָּיבָא, עָלֵיהּ כְּתִיב, וַיִּפּוֹל רוֹכְבוֹ אָחוֹר. וְרָזָא דְּמִלָּה, כִּי יִפּוֹל הַנּוֹפֵל מִמֶּנּוּ. וּבְגִין דָּא אָמַר אִיּוֹב, לֹא נוֹפֵל אָנֹכִי מִכֶּם. וְצַדִּיק דִּרְכִיב עָלֵיהּ, קָשִׁיר לֵיהּ בְּקִשּׁוּרוֹ דִּרְצוּעִין דִּתְפִלִּין. אוֹת תְּפִלִּין דְּאִיהוּ אוֹת יוֹד. דְּשַׁדַּי, חוּלְיָא עַל קְדָלֵיהּ. שׁ דִּתְפִלִּין, שַׁלְשֶׁלֶת עַל קְדָלֵיהּ.

486. And this, THE EVIL INCLINATION, is a dog, a serpent and a braying donkey, onto which the soul is mounted, and, as soon as it is known that its rider is wicked it is written about it: "his rider shall fall backward" (Beresheet 49:17), and the secret of the matter is: "If any (falling) man fall from it" (Devarim 22:8). And for this reason, Job said: "I am not inferior to you" (Iyov 12:3). (The literal rendering of this verse is: 'I do not fall from you'). But the righteous person who rides on it binds it with the knot of the Tefilin straps, the sign of the Tefilin, which is the letter Yud of Shadai, being the ring, the halter on its neck, while the Shin of the Tefilin is a chain on its neck.

487. וּבֵיהּ רָכִיב אֵלִיָּהוּ, וְסָלִיק לִשְׁמַיָּא. הה"ד, וַיַּעַל אֵלִיָּהוּ בַּסְעָרָה הַשָּׁמָיִם. וּבֵיהּ וַיַּעַן יְדֹנָ"ד אֶת אִיּוֹב מִן הַסְּעָרָה. וּבְגִין דָּא, אוֹקְמוּהָ רַבָּנָן דְּמַתְנִיתָא עָלֵיהּ, אֵיזֶהוּ גִּבּוֹר הַכּוֹבֵשׁ אֶת יִצְרוֹ. וְאִית לְמַאן דְּמִתְהַדָּר לֵיהּ חֲמוֹר, דְּלָאו אִיהוּ מְצַטַּעֵר רוֹכְבוֹ. וְאִלֵּין אִינּוּן דְּמִשְׁתַּדְּלִין בְּקַל וָחוֹמֶר. וּבְגִין דָּא אִתְּמַר בְּאַבְרָהָם, וַיַּחֲבֹשׁ אֶת חֲמוֹרוֹ. וּבְגִינֵיהּ אִתְּמַר עַל מָשִׁיחַ, עָנִי וְרוֹכֵב עַל חֲמוֹר.

487. And Elijah rode on it when he ascended into heaven, as it is written: "And Elijah went up by a storm of wind into heaven" (II Melachim 2:11). And through it: "Then Hashem answered Job out of the storm wind" (Iyov 38:1). And this is why the sages of the Mishnah taught: Who is mighty? He that subdues his inclination. And there are those for whom it becomes a donkey (Heb. chamor) that causes no trouble for its rider, and they are the ones who make efforts at exposition by inference from minor to major (Heb. chomer). And this is why it is written about Abraham: "and saddled his ass" (Beresheet 22:3). And this is also why it is said about Messiah: "humble and riding upon an ass" (Zecharyah 9:9).

488. וּבְגִין דָּא י' מָן שַׁדַּ"י, דְּאִיהוּ חוּלְיָיא דְּשַׁלְשֶׁלֶת, מִינָּהּ מְפַחֲדִין כָּל שֵׁדִין וּמַזִּיקִין, וּמִיַּד דְּחַזְיָין לֵיהּ בַּמְזוּזוֹת דְּתַרְעִין, בַּרְחִין, דְּבָהּ אִתְּמַר, לֶאֱסוֹר מַלְכֵיהֶם בְּזִיקִים וְנִכְבְּדֵיהֶם בְּכַבְלֵי בַרְזֶל. כ"ש כַּד חַזְיָין לָהּ בְּאוֹת תְּפִלִּין עַל דְּרוֹעִין, וּרְשִׁימִין בָּהּ בְּאוֹת בְּרִית בְּבִשְׂרֵיהוֹן, וְהַזָּר הַקָּרֵב יוּמָת, לֵית זָר, אֶלָּא יֵצֶר הָרָע, דְּדַמְיָא לְכָל חֵיוָן וְעוֹפִין דּוֹרְסִין.

488. And for this reason, all demons and spirits are fearful of the Yud of Shadai (Shin Dalet Yud), NAMELY THE SIGN OF THE COVENANT, which is the noose ring from the chain, and immediately on seeing THE YUD OF SHADAI on the doorposts of the gates they flee, for about THE YUD OF SHADAI it is said: "to bind their kings with chains, and their nobles with fetters of iron" (Tehilim 149:8). And even more DO THEY FLEE AWAY when they see it on the Tefilin that are on the arms, NAMELY IN THE KNOT OF THE HAND TEFILIN. And of those who are marked with this sign of the covenant on their own flesh, ABOUT THEM IT IS SAID: "and the stranger that comes near shall be put to death" (Bemidbar 1:51); NAMELY THE EVIL INCLINATION THAT IS CALLED 'STRANGER' SHALL BE PUT TO DEATH, for stranger is none other than the Evil Inclination, that is similar to all the beasts and birds of prey, AS ABOVE.

489. וּבְגִין דָּא, זְכוֹר נָא מִי הוּא נָקִי אָבָד, דָּא פִּנְחָס, דְּקַנֵּי עַל בְּרִית, וְאִתְרְשִׁים בֵּיהּ, דְּאִיהוּ בְּרָא דְּמַלְכָּא וּמַטְרוֹנִיתָא. קַנֵּי בְּמַחֲשָׁבָה, וְזָכֵי לְאָת י' מָן יְהוֹ"ה. וְקַנֵּי בְּעוֹבָדוֹי, וְזָכָה לְאוֹת י' מָן אֲדֹנָי. וְהַאי אִיהוּ חָכְמָה בְּרֹאשׁ. וְחָכְמָה בַּסּוֹף. וּבְגִין דְּאָדָם קַדְמָאָה הֲוָה רָשׁוּם בִּתְרַוְוייהוּ, אוֹקְמוּהָ עֲלֵיהּ רַבָּנָן, דְּאִיהוּ רִאשׁוֹן לַמַּחֲשָׁבָה, אַחֲרוֹן לְמַעֲשֶׂה. אַדְהָכִי דְּאָמַר מִלִּין אִלֵּין אִתְכַּסֵּי מְנַיְיהוּ. אָמַר ר' אֶלְעָזָר, זַכָּאָה חוּלָקָנָא, דְּזַכֵינָא לְמִשְׁמַע מִלִּין מִבְּנֵי עָלְמָא דְּאָתֵי.

489. And for this reason, "Recall now, who that was innocent ever perished?" (Iyov 4:7). This refers to Pinchas, who was zealous for the covenant, SINCE THE LETTERS OF THE WORD INNOCENT (Heb. NAKI), WHEN REARRANGED, SPELL KANI (ARAMAIC FOR ZEALOUS). And it is

recorded upon him that he is the son of the King and the Queen, for when he was zealous in thought, he earned the letter Yud of Yud Hei Vav Hei, WHICH IS THE SECRET OF SUPERNAL CHOCHMAH, AND HE BECAME THE SON OF THE KING. And when he was zealous in deed, he earned the letter Yud of Adonai, WHICH IS LOWER CHOCHMAH, AND BECAME THE SON OF THE QUEEN. And this is the meaning of Chochmah at the beginning OF THE COMBINATION YUD-ALEPH-HEI-DALET-VAV-NUN-HEI-YUD, WHICH IS YUD OF YUD HEI VAV HEI, and Chochmah at the end OF THE COMBINATION YUD-ALEPH-HEI-DALET-VAV-NUN-HEI-YUD, WHICH IS THE YUD OF ADONAI. And since Adam was marked with THESE two YUDS, the sages taught about him that he is the first in thought but the last in deed. FOR YUD HEI VAV HEI IS THE SECRET OF THOUGHT AND ADONAI IS THE SECRET OF DEED. And while he was still saying these things, he disappeared from their sight. Rabbi Elazar said, Happy is our portion that we have been privileged to hear these matters from those of the World to Come.

490. וּבְחִבּוּרָא קַדְמָאָה. לָכֵן אֱמֹר, בְּאוֹמָאָה עֲלָךְ, אִם הוּא בִּרְעוּתָךְ, וְאִי לָאו, אֵימָא. ר' פִּנְחָס בֶּן יָאִיר. הַהוּא טוּלָא בָּטַשׁ בְּעֵינוֹי דר' אַבָּא, וְכִי לָא הֲוָה יָדַע קוּדְשָׁא בְּרִיךְ הוּא, אִי הֲוָה בִּרְעוּתֵיה, אִם לָאו. א"ל, אִם לֵיהּ גָּלוּי, מִי גָּלוּי לְאַחֲרִינֵי, וּבג"ד לָכֵן אֱמוֹר.

490. And in the first section, HE SAID, "Wherefore, say" (Bemidbar 25:12), NAMELY THIS BEING WHAT THE HOLY ONE, BLESSED BE HE, SAID TO MOSES: 'An oath upon you: Whether you want TO SAY TO HIM "BEHOLD, I GIVE TO HIM MY COVENANT OF PEACE" (IBID.), or whether you don't want TO SAY IT TO HIM, say it.' THIS WAS WHAT Rabbi Pinchas ben Yair SAID, FOR 'WHEREFORE' IS USED IN OATHS. That shadow CAME AND smote Rabbi Aba in the eyes AND SAID TO HIM, Did the Holy One, blessed be He, really not know if Moses wanted to say this or not? DID HE REALLY HAVE TO SAY IT TO HIM WITH SOME DOUBT: EITHER WAY…SAY! He said to him, Even if it is apparent to the Holy One, blessed be He, who says that it is obvious to others? Therefore HE SAID TO HIM: "Wherefore, say" VIS-A-VIS THE OTHERS.

79. Yisrael are the body parts of the Shechinah

A Synopsis

The Faithful Shepherd talks about the Shechinah giving testimony about Yisrael, as the Shechinah is their help from heaven. People take strength from the study and teaching of Halachah and Mishnah, and in this study the Shechinah has a home. We learn that those who bring others to righteousness are like the stars forever and ever.

491. וְתוּ אִתְּמַר בְּחִבּוּרָא קַדְמָאָה, מִכְתָּם לְדָוִד, סִימָנָא דְּאַחְזִיאוּ לֵיהּ לְדָוִד, כַּד שָׁדַר לְיוֹאָב לַאֲרַם נַהֲרַיִם וּלְאֲרַם צוֹבָה לְאַגָּחָא בְּהוּ קְרָבָא. אָמַר רַעְיָא מְהֵימָנָא, שׁוּשַׁן עֵדוּת: דָּא סַהֲדוּתָא דִּשְׁכִינְתָּא, דְּאִיהוּ שׁוּשַׁן עֵדוּת. דְּאִיהִי סַהֲדוּתָא דְּקַיְּימָא עֲלָן, וְסָהִידַת עֲלָן קַמֵּי מַלְכָּא, וְדַרְגִּין עִלָּאִין קַדִּישִׁין בַּהֲדָהּ, וְסִיַּיעְתָּא קַדִּישָׁא לְתוּשְׁבַּחְתָּא. אָמַר ר"מ, שׁוּשַׁן עֵדוּת דְּאִינוּן סָהֲדִין עַל יִשְׂרָאֵל, דְּאִינוּן אֵבָרִים, וְאִיהִי נִשְׁמָתָא עֲלַייהוּ. אִיהוּ סִיַּיעְתָּא דִּשְׁמַיָּא. דְּאִתְּמַר בָּהּ, וְאַתָּה תִּשְׁמַע הַשָּׁמַיִם. אִיהִי סִיַּיעְתָּא קַדִּישְׁתָּא, דְּאִתְּמַר עֲלָהּ תַּנְיָא דִּמְסַיֵּיעַ לָךְ.

491. And it was also said in the compilation of the first part: "TO THE CHIEF MUSICIAN UPON SHUSHAN-EDUT, a *michtam* of David" (Tehilim 60:1). David was shown a sign IN A ROSE (HEB. *SHOSHANAH*) THAT HE WOULD WIN THE WAR when he sent Joab to Aram Naharaim (Mesopotamia) and Aram Tzovah to make war against them. The Faithful Shepherd said, Shushan Edut is the *Edut* (Eng. 'testimony') of the Shechinah, which is CALLED 'Shushan Edut' because she testifies, standing over us and testifying on us before the King, and the holy upper levels are with her, and she is holy help for US TO OFFER praises; THEREFORE, SHE IS CALLED 'SHUSHAN EDUT'. The Faithful Shepherd said, IT IS CALLED 'Shushan Edut' because THE SHECHINAH gives *Edut* (Eng. 'testimony') about Yisrael, that they are its parts and she is their soul over them. She is help from heaven, about which is written: "then hear You in heaven" (I Melachim 8:32). She is holy assistance, about which it has been said: Here is *Tanya* (Eng. 'support') to help you, FOR THE SHECHINAH IS CALLED '*TANYA*'.

492. אֵיתָן מוֹשָׁבֶךָ וְשִׂים בַּסֶּלַע קִנֶּךָ. אֵיתָ"ן: תַּנְיָ"א. תַּמָּן קִנָּא דְּנִשְׁרָא

עִלָּאָה, וְאִיהִי שְׁכִינְתָּא. וְעָלָה אִתְּמַר, כְּנֶשֶׁר יָעִיר קִנּוֹ עַל גּוֹזָלָיו יְרַחֵף, דְּאִינּוּן שׁוֹנֵי הֲלָכוֹת וּמִשְׁנָיוֹת. וְכָל דִּבּוּר וְדִבּוּר דְּנָפִיק מִפּוּמוֹי דְּהַהוּא תַּנְיָ"א, דְּאַפִּיק בֵּין לִשְׁמָא דִּידוֹד, בֵּין בְּאוֹרַיְיתָא, בֵּין בִּצְלוֹתָא, בֵּין בְּבִרְכָה, בֵּין בְּכָל פִּקוּדָא וּפִקוּדָא, מַה כְּתִיב בֵּיהּ. יִפְרוֹשׂ כְּנָפָיו, הַהוּא נִשְׁרָא דְּהוּא דִּבּוּר, דְּבֵיהּ יְהֹוָ"ה.

492. "Strong (Heb. *eitan*) is your dwelling-place, and you put your nest in a rock" (Bemidbar 24:21). *Eitan* (Aleph Yud Tav Nun) is SPELLED WITH the letters of *tanya* (Tav Nun Yud Aleph), NAMELY MISHNAH AND BARAITHA. There, IN THE MISHNAH AND BARAITHA, is the nest of the upper eagle, which is the Shechinah, and about it is said: "As an eagle stirs up her nest, broods over her young" (Devarim 32:11). And those who study Halachah and Mishnah ARE CALLED 'THE YOUNG OF THE EAGLE'. And each speech that emerges out of the mouth of that *tanya*, NAMELY FROM THE STUDENTS OF MISHNAH, whether for the sake of the Name Yud Hei Vav Hei and whether in Torah, prayer, blessing, or in any one of the precepts; what is written about it? "spreads abroad her wings" (Ibid.), namely that same eagle that is speech, FOR THE SHECHINAH IS CALLED 'SPEECH', with which is Yud Hei Vav Hei, NAMELY ZEIR ANPIN WHO IS CALLED 'VOICE', THAT EAGLE WILL SPREAD ITS WINGS.

493. יִקָּחֵהוּ יִשָּׂאֵהוּ עַל אֶבְרָתוֹ, מַאי עַל אֶבְרָתוֹ. עַל הַהוּא אֵבֶר דב"ן, דְּבֵיהּ מִצְוָה יְדוֹ"ד, אִתְקְרֵי אֵבֶר דִּשְׁכִינְתָּא. וּבג"ד יִשָּׂאֵהוּ עַל אֶבְרָתוֹ. יִשָּׂאֵהוּ: כְּגוֹן יִשָּׂא יְדוֹ"ד פָּנָיו אֵלֶיךָ.

493. "takes them, bears them on her pinion (Heb. *ever*)" (Devarim 32:11). HE ASKS, What is the meaning of "her pinion"? AND HE ANSWERS: On that part (Heb. *ever*) of man, with which he performed a precept of Hashem, called 'a body part of the Shechinah'. Thus: "bears them on her pinion." And the meaning of "bear (Heb. *yisa*)" is as in the verse: "Hashem lift up (Heb. *yisa*) His countenance to you" (Bemidbar 6:25).

494. וּמַאי וְשִׂים בַּסֶּלַע קִנֶּךָ. אֶלָּא אָמַר דָּוִד עָלֶיהָ, יְיָ' סַלְעִי וּמְצוּדָתִי. אוֹף הָכִי תָּנָא, דְּאִיהוּ בֵּיהּ הֲלָכָה תַּקִּיפָא כַּסֶּלַע, דְּלֵית פַּטִּישׁ יָכִיל

לְפַצְצָא יָתָה בְּכָל קוּשְׁיָין דְּעָלְמָא. בְּהַאי אִיהוּ מְקַנְּנָא נִשְׁרָא, וְכָל
תַּנָּאִים אִתְקְרִיאוּ קִנִּים דִּילָהּ. וּבְגִין דָּא, כִּי יִקָּרֵא קַן צִפּוֹר לְפָנֶיךָ,
בְּאֹרַח מִקְרֶה, זִמְנָא חֲדָא כְּאוּשְׁפִּיזָא וְאַכְסְנָאִי, דְּאִזְדְּמַן לְפוּם שַׁעֲתָא
בְּבֵי אוּשְׁפִּיזֵיהּ.

494. And what is the meaning of "and you put your nest in a rock"? But David said about THE SHECHINAH, "Hashem is my rock, and my fortress" (II Shmuel 22:2). So also for the Tanna, NAMELY HE WHO STUDIES MISHNAH, in which the Halachah is as firm as a rock that no hammer can break with all the objections in the world. It is here that the eagle, NAMELY THE SHECHINAH, makes its nest. And all the Tannaim are called 'nests of THE SHECHINAH'. Therefore, "If a bird's nest chance to be before you..." (Devarim 22:6), THAT IS THE SHECHINAH THAT IS CALLED 'A BIRD', namely that comes by pure chance, once, as a visitor, as a wayfarer who just happens to come to the inn.

495. וְאִית דְּאִינּוּן בְּמַתְנִיתָא דִּלְהוֹן דִּירָה לִשְׁכִינְתָּא, הה״ד וְשָׁמְרוּ
בְנֵי יִשְׂרָאֵל אֶת הַשַּׁבָּת וְגוֹ', לְדוֹרוֹתָם, לְדֹרֹתָם חָסֵר, לָשׁוֹן דִּירָה. וְאִית
מָארֵי מִשְׁנָה דְּתוֹרָתָם אוּמָנוּתָם, דְּלָא זָזַת שְׁכִינְתָּא מִנְּהוֹן כָּל יוֹמֵיהוֹן.
אֲבָל אִלֵּין, כִּי יִקָּרֵא קַן צִפּוֹר לְפָנֶיךָ, בְּהוֹן שְׁכִינְתָּא בְּאֹרַח מִקְרֶה,
זִמְנִין שַׁרְיָיא עֲלַיְיהוּ וְאִשְׁתְּכָחַת עִמְּהוֹן, וְזִמְנִין לָא אִשְׁתְּכָחַת עִמְּהוֹן.

495. And there are Tannaim, STUDENTS OF THE MISHNAH, in whose study of the Mishnah the Shechinah has A PERMANENT home, as it is written: "Wherefore the children of Yisrael shall keep the Shabbat, to observe the Shabbat throughout their generations (Heb. dorotam)" (Shemot 31:16). 'dorotam' is written in the abbreviated spelling, derived from 'apartment (Heb. dirah)'. And indeed, there are sages of the Mishnah, whose study of Torah is their craftsmanship; in such cases the Shechinah does not move from them all their days. But those ABOUT WHOM THE SCRIPTURE SPEAKS IN THE VERSE "If a bird's nest chance to be before you" are those to whom the Shechinah comes by chance, at one time resting on them and being with them and at another time not being with them.

496. וְרָזָא דְּמִלָּה, זִמְנִין דְּאִשְׁתְּכָחַת עִמְּהוֹן, לֹא תִקַּח הָאֵם. וְזִמְנִין

דְּלָא אִשְׁתְּכַחַת עִמְּהוֹן, שַׁלֵּחַ תְּשַׁלַּח אֶת הָאֵם. אֶפְרוֹחִים אָלֵּין מָארֵי
מִשְׁנָה. אוֹ בֵּיצִים, מָארֵי מִקְרָא בְּאָלֵּין דְּלָא קַבְעִין לְמוֹדַיְיהוּ, שַׁלֵּחַ
תְּשַׁלַּח אֶת הָאֵם. אֲבָל בְּאָלֵּין דְּקַבְעִין לְמוֹדַיְיהוּ, לֹא תִקַּח הָאֵם עַל
הַבָּנִים. וְאִית מָארֵי הֲלָכוֹת, דְּדַמְיָין לְכֹכְבַיָּא, הַה"ד וּמַצְדִּיקֵי הָרַבִּים
כַּכֹּכָבִים לְעוֹלָם וָעֶד. לָאו כַּכֹּכָבִים, דְּאִתְּמַר בְּהוֹן וְכָל צְבָאָם יִבּוֹל.
אֶלָּא כְּאִינּוּן כֹּכְבַיָּא דְּעָלְמָא דְּאָתֵי, דְּאִינּוּן לְעוֹלָם וָעֶד קַיְימֵי תָּדִיר.

496. And the secret of the matter is: The occasional times when THE SHECHINAH is with them is WHEN IT IS SAID: "You shall not take the mother BIRD OVER THE YOUNG" (IBID.), BUT ONE DOES NOT LET THE MOTHER BIRD, WHICH IS THE SHECHINAH, GO. And the times when THE SHECHINAH is not with them IS WHEN IT IS SAID: "but you shall surely let the mother go" (Ibid. 7), FOR THEY ARE NOT FITTING TO BE WITH HER. "The young" are the sages of the Mishnah; "or eggs" (Ibid. 6) are the sages of the Bible. About those who do not study regularly IT IS SAID: "You shall surely let the mother go," while about those who do study regularly IT IS SAID: "You shall not take the mother bird together with the young"; BUT ONE DOES NOT LET HER GO. And there are sages of Halachah (lit. 'legal tradition') who are like the stars, as it is written: "and they who turn many to righteousness like the stars for ever and ever" (Daniel 12:3). They are not as the stars, about which it is written: "and all their host shall fall down" (Yeshayah 34:4), but rather as though they were the stars of the World to Come that remain always for ever and ever, AND TO WHICH IS APPLIED THE VERSE: "LIKE THE STARS FOREVER AND EVER."

80. "Let Us make man in Our image, after Our likeness"

A Synopsis

The Faithful Shepherd tells us that God's last act of creation was to make man, and by 'man' is meant Yisrael and not the idolaters. Rabbi Shimon talks about the tradition given to Moses at Sinai, and how Moses illuminates all of Yisrael with the light of the Torah. As the Faithful Shepherd and Rabbi Shimon discuss the creation of man, Moses clarifies that man was indeed created from all of the angels and other creatures and he was made to rule over the creatures. He goes on to say that the holy Malchut is the image of everything including all the inhabitants of the three worlds, and that God looked into it before He created everything. Lastly we are told that man depends solely on God for his punishment or reward, and not on an angel or seraph or any other creature.

497. וַיֹּאמֶר אֱלֹהִים נַעֲשֶׂה אָדָם, בָּתַר דְּאַשְׁלִימוּ לַעֲבִידְתַּיְיהוּ כָּל אוּמָן וְאוּמָן, אָמַר לוֹן קוּדְשָׁא בְּרִיךְ הוּא, אוּמָנוּתָא חֲדָא אִית לִי לְמֶעְבַּד, דִּיהֵא שׁוּתָּפָא דְּכֻלָּנָא. אִתְחַבָּרוּ כֻּלְכוּ כַּחֲדָא, לְמֶעְבַּד בֵּיהּ כָּל אֶחָד וְאֶחָד מֵחוּלָקָא דִּילֵיהּ, וַאֲנָא אֶשְׁתַּתַּף עִמְּכוֹן, לְמֵיהַב לֵיהּ מֵחוּלָקָא דִּילִי. וְהַיְינוּ נַעֲשֶׂה אָדָם בְּצַלְמֵנוּ כִּדְמוּתֵנוּ. וְאוֹקְמוּהָ רַבָּנָן, דְּלֵית אָדָם אֶלָּא יִשְׂרָאֵל, הה"ד וְאַתֵּן צֹאנִי צֹאן מַרְעִיתִי אָדָם אַתֶּם. אַתֶּם אָדָם, וְלָא עכו"ם. ובג"ד יִשְׂמַח יִשְׂרָאֵל בְּעוֹשָׂיו.

497. "And Elohim said: Let Us make man in Our image, after Our likeness" (Beresheet 1:26). After each craftsman had completed his work, the Holy One, blessed be He, said to them: 'One craft remains for Me to undertake, and all of us shall be partners in it. Let all join together, and let each one do its share, and I shall join in partnership with you, to give it My share.' For this is what is written: "Let Us make man in Our image, after Our likeness." And the sages taught that only the people of Yisrael are referred to as man, as it is written: "But you My flock, the flock of My pasture, are men" (Yechezkel 34:31). That is: You are men, but the idolators are not, and therefore it is written: "Let Yisrael rejoice in his Maker" (Tehilim 149:2).

498. אָמַר בּוּצִינָא קַדִּישָׁא, וַדַּאי הַהוּא תָּנָא דְּאִתְּטְמַר בְּסֶלַע דִּחֲוְיָא

אָמַר דָּא, דִּכְתִיב בֵּיהּ אֵיתָן מוֹשָׁבֶךָ וְשִׂים בַּסֶּלַע קִנֶּךָ. דִּתְלַת אֲבָהָן
נִקְרְאוּ אֵיתָנִים, וּרְבִיעָאָה אֵיתָן מוֹשָׁבֶךָ. דְּבֵיהּ מִתְיַשְּׁבָא הֲלָכָה,
דְּאִתְּמַר בָּהּ הֲלָכָה לְמֹשֶׁה מִסִּינַי. דְּאִיהוּ אִתְפַּשַּׁט עַל שִׁתִּין רִבּוֹא
דְיִשְׂרָאֵל, וְנָהִיר לוֹן בְּאוֹרַיְיתָא, כְּשִׁמְשָׁא דְּאִתְכַּסֵּי בְּלֵילְיָא, וְנָהִיר לְכָל
כֹּכְבַיָּא וּמַזָּלֵי. וְלֵית לֵילְיָא אֶלָּא גָּלוּתָא, וְאִיהִי שׁוֹמֵר מַה מִּלֵּילָה
שׁוֹמֵר מַה מִּלֵּיל. וְאִתְגַּלְיָא בִּימָמָא, דְּאִתְּמַר הַבֹּקֶר אוֹר, בֹּקֶר דְּאַבְרָהָם,
דְּאִתְּמַר בֵּיהּ וּבֹקֶר וּרְאִיתֶם אֶת כְּבוֹד יְיָ'. חַי יְיָ' שִׁכְבִי עַד הַבֹּקֶר.

498. Said the holy luminary, THAT IS, RABBI SHIMON, This must certainly
have been said by that same Tanna who hid in the rock of the Serpent, about
whom it is written: "Strong (Heb. *eitan*) is your dwelling-place, and you put
your nest in a rock" (Bemidbar 24:21). For the three patriarchs are called
'the strong ones', and the fourth one, THAT IS, MOSES, is "Strong is your
dwelling place" for in him the Halachah, WHICH IS THE SHECHINAH, takes
shape, as in the expression 'A tradition given to Moses from Sinai'. And he
spreads over the six hundred thousand of Yisrael and gives them light with
the Torah as the sun which is hidden by night but gives light to all the stars
and constellations. SO IT IS WITH MOSES: HAD HE NOT HIDDEN IN THAT
ROCK, HE WOULD HAVE BEEN UNABLE TO GIVE LIGHT TO YISRAEL. And
night always refers to the exile, as in "Watchman, what of the night?
Watchman, what of the night?" (Yeshayah 21:11). THIS REFERS TO THE
EXILE, FOR THEN MOSES HIDES IN THE ROCK and appears by day, AT
THE TIME OF THE REDEMPTION, about which it is said: "As soon as the
morning was light" (Beresheet 44:3), which is the morning of Abraham,
about which is said: "and in the morning, you shall see the glory of Hashem"
(Shemot 16:7), and: "As Hashem lives, lie down until the morning" (Rut 3:13).

499. אַדְּהָכִי, הָא רַעְיָא מְהֵימְנָא נָפִיק מֵהַהוּא סֶלַע, וְאָמַר, בּוֹצִינָא
קַדִּישָׁא, מַה מוֹעִיל לִי לְאִתְטַמְּרָא מִקַּמָּךְ, דְּהָא לָא שְׁבַקְנָא אֲתָר דְּלָא
עָלִית לְאִתְטַמְּרָא מִנָּךְ, וְלָא אַשְׁכַּחְנָא, אִי הָכִי לֵית לִי לְאִתְכַּסְּיָיא
מִנָּךְ.

499. While he was yet speaking, behold, the Faithful Shepherd came out
from that rock AND APPEARED TO RABBI SHIMON. He said to him, holy

luminary, what good did it do me to hide from you, for I have not left a place that I did not enter to hide from you, and I could not HIDE FROM YOU IN IT. That being so, there is no sense in my continuing to hide from you.

‏500. א״ל בּוּצִינָא קַדִּישָׁא, בָּתַר דְּאָמַר נַעֲשֶׂה אָדָם בְּצַלְמֵנוּ כִּדְמוּתֵנוּ, מַאי נִיהוּ דְּאָמַר לְבָתַר וַיִּבְרָא אֱלֹהִים אֶת הָאָדָם בְּצַלְמוֹ. א״ל, מַה דְּאוֹקְמוּהָ עַל דָּא מָארֵי מַתְנִיתִין, דְּמִנְּהוֹן הֲווֹ אַמְרִין יִבָּרֵא, וּמִנְּהוֹן אַמְרִין לָא יִבָּרֵא, קוּדְשָׁא בְּרִיךְ הוּא בָּרָא לֵיהּ, דִּכְתִיב וַיִּבְרָא אֱלֹהִים אֶת הָאָדָם בְּצַלְמוֹ. אָמַר לֵיהּ, אִי הָכִי אִיהוּ, לָא יָהִיב חוּלָקָא בֵּיהּ חַד מִנַּיְיהוּ, וְלָא אִתְעֲבֵיד בְּדִיּוּקְנָא דִּלְהוֹן, אֶלָּא בְּאִיקוּנִין דְּמַלְכָּא בְּצַלְמוֹ כִּדְמוּתוֹ, דְּאִיהוּ צֶלֶם דְּמוּת תַּבְנִיתוֹ. אָמַר הָכִי אִשְׁתְּמוֹדַע.

500. The holy luminary said TO THE FAITHFUL SHEPHERD: After it is said: "Let Us make man in Our image, after Our likeness" (Beresheet 1:26), what is the meaning of that which is written later: "So Elohim created man in His own image" (Ibid. 27)? He replied: This is what the sages of the Mishnah taught: HE ASKED THE MINISTERING ANGELS WHETHER TO CREATE MAN OR NOT. Some said: Let him be created, while others urged: Let him not be created. And the Holy One, blessed be He, created him, as it is written: "So Elohim created man in His own image." He said to him: If that is so, then He did not place in him one part FROM THE MINISTERING ANGELS, and he was not made after their form, but after the form of the King, in His image, in His likeness, which is the image of the likeness of His form ALONE. He noted: That is the seeming meaning OF WHAT YOU SAY.

‏501. אָמַר ח״ו. אֶלָּא אֲנָא אֲמֵינָא לָךְ, דְּאִתְבְּרֵי בְּכֹלָּא, וְאַשְׁלְטֵיהּ עַל כֹּלָּא. וְאִי הֲוָה יָהִיב כָּל חַד בֵּיהּ חוּלָקֵיהּ, בְּזִמְנֵיהּ דַּהֲוָה כַּעֲסֵיהּ עֲלֵיהּ, כָּל חַד, הֲוָה נָטִיל חוּלָקֵיהּ מִנֵּיהּ, כִּי בַמֶּה נֶחְשָׁב הוּא.

501. THE FAITHFUL SHEPHERD Said: Heaven forbid. I HAVE NOT SAID THAT HE IS NOT MADE UP OF ANY OF THE ANGELS AND CREATURES. What I said to you was that he was created from all THE ANGELS AND CREATURES, and was made to rule over all the creatures. Had each one given his share TO MAN, THEN, when he would have been angry with him,

each one could have come back and taken his share away from him. "For in what is he to be accounted of" (Yeshayah 2:22).

502. אֶלָּא קוּדְשָׁא בְּרִיךְ הוּא בָּרָא לֵיהּ בְּדִיוּקְנֵיהּ, דָּא מַלְכוּת קַדִּישָׁא, דְּאִיהִי תְּמוּנַת כֹּל. דְּבָהּ אִסְתַּכַּל קוּדְשָׁא בְּרִיךְ הוּא, וּבָרָא עָלְמָא, וְכָל בִּרְיָין דְּבָרָא בְּעָלְמָא, וְכָלַל בָּהּ עִלָּאִין וְתַתָּאִין, בְּלָא פֵּרוּדָא כְּלַל, וְכָלַל בָּהּ עֲשַׂר סְפִירָן, וְכָל שְׁמָהָן וְכִנּוּיִין וַהֲוָיָין. וְעָלַת עַל כֹּלָּא, דְּאִיהוּ אָדוֹן עַל כֹּלָּא, וְלֵית אֱלָהָא בַּר מִנֵּיהּ, וְלָא יִשְׁתְּכַח בְּעִלָּאִין וְתַתָּאִין פָּחוֹת מִינָהּ. בְּגִין דְּאִיהִי קֶשֶׁר דְּכֻלְּהוּ, שְׁלִימוּ דְּכֻלְּהוּ, לְקַיְּימָא בֵּיהּ וּמַלְכוּתוֹ בַּכֹּל מָשָׁלָה. וּבְגִין דְּלָא אִשְׁתְּכַח עָלַת עַל כֹּלָּא בְּעִלָּאִין וְתַתָּאִין פָּחוֹת מִנָּהּ, אֲפִילוּ בְּחַד מִנַּיְיהוּ, אִתְקְרִיאַת אֱמוּנַת יִשְׂרָאֵל. וּמִסִּטְרָא דְּעָלַת עַל כֹּלָּא, אִתְּמַר בָּהּ, כִּי לֹא רְאִיתֶם כָּל תְּמוּנָה, אֲבָל מִסִּטְרָא דִּשְׁאַר בִּרְיָין. אִתְּמַר בָּהּ, וּתְמוּנַת יְיָ' יַבִּיט.

502. But the Holy One, blessed be He, created him in His image, which is the holy Malchut THAT IS CALLED 'IMAGE', which is the picture of everything, FOR ALL THE INHABITANTS OF THE WORLDS OF BRIYAH, YETZIRAH AND ASIYAH ARE INCLUDED IN IT. And the Holy One, blessed be He, looked into it and created the world and all the creatures that He created in the world, and He included in it the upper grades and the lower grades without any separation whatsoever, and He included in it ten Sfirot and all the names and appellatives and Yud Hei Vav Hei's. And the Supreme Cause, who is Master of all, and there is no Elohim beside Him, is not to be found in upper and lower grades less than it, for it is the connection among all of them, the perfection of all of them, to establish in it: "and His kingdom rules over all" (Tehilim 103:19). And there is no Cause of all to be found in even one of the upper and lower grades less than it, IT IS NOT INCLUDED IN HIM. And it is called 'the Faith of Yisrael'. From the point of view of the Supreme Cause, it is said: "For you saw no manner of form" (Devarim 4:15), but from the point of view ACCORDING TO WHICH IT IS INCLUSIVE of the other creatures, it is said: "And the similitude of Hashem does he behold" (Bemidbar 12:8).

503. אָתָא בּוּצִינָא קַדִּישָׁא וּשְׁאַר חַבְרַיָּיא, וְאִשְׁתְּטָחוּ קַמֵּיהּ, וְאָמְרוּ, וַדַּאי כְּעַן לֵית מַאן דְּיָכִיל לְמֵיטַל מִנֵּיהּ חוּלָקֵיהּ, דְּלָא יָהִיב בֵּיהּ

חוּלָקָא חַד בְּעָלְמָא, אֶלָּא בּוֹרֵא עָלְמִין, עַלַּת עַל כֹּלָּא, וּבֵיהּ תַּלְיָא עָנְשֵׁיהּ, אוֹ אַגְרֵיהּ, וְלָא בְּמַלְאָךְ וְשָׂרָף, וְלָא בְּשׁוּם בְּרִיָּה דְּעָלְמָא. וּבְגִין דָּא אוּקְמוּהָ רַבָּנָן דְּמַתְנִיתִין, הַמְשַׁתֵּף שֵׁם שָׁמַיִם וְדָבָר אַחֵר, נֶעֱקַר מִן הָעוֹלָם. מִיַּד דְּשָׁמַע מִלִּין אִלֵּין דְּאר״ש בּוּצִינָא קַדִּישָׁא חַדֵי ר״מ. וְכָל חַבְרַיָּיא בָּרִיכוּ לֵיהּ, וְאָמְרוּ, ר״מ, אִי לָא הֲוָה אָתֵי ב״נ בְּעָלְמָא אֶלָּא לְמִשְׁמַע דָּא דַּיֵּי.

503. The holy luminary came with the other companions, and they prostrated themselves before him, saying, certainly there is now none that can take from him, FROM MAN, his portion, FOR not EVEN one in the world contributed to him a part, except the Creator of the World, the Supreme Cause ALONE. And on Him depends his punishment or reward and not on an angel nor a Seraph nor any other creature in the world. Thus the sages of the Mishnah taught: Anyone who combines the Name of Heaven and something else is uprooted from the world. Immediately on his hearing what Rabbi Shimon, the holy luminary, said, the Faithful Shepherd rejoiced. And all the companions blessed him, THE FAITHFUL SHEPHERD, and said: O, Faithful Shepherd, if a man were to have come into the world just to hear this, it would be enough for him.

81. What is 'Yesh'- Chochmah

A Synopsis

We learn that those people are happy who, in the last exile, make a great effort to know the Shechinah, to suffer for her and to keep the precepts. We are told that Yesh is Chochmah, substance out of nothing, that is drawn from Keter; this means that those who love God will inherit wisdom.

504. זַכָּאָה אִיהוּ, מַאן דְּאִשְׁתַּדַּל בְּגָלוּתָא בַּתְרָאָה, לְמִנְדַע לִשְׁכִינְתָּא, לְאוֹקִיר לָהּ בְּכָל פִּקוּדִין, וּלְמִסְבַּל בְּגִינָהּ כַּמָה דּוֹחֲקִין. כְּמָה דְּאִתְּמַר, אַגְרָא דְכַלָּה דּוֹחֲקָא. וַיִּשְׁכַּב בַּמָּקוֹם הַהוּא, אִם יֵשׁ כ״ב אוֹתִיּוֹת דְּאוֹרַיְיתָא, אִיהִי שְׁכִיבַת עֲמֵיהּ.

504. Happy is he who makes an effort in the last exile to know the Shechinah, to honor Her with all the precepts and to suffer for Her a number of exigencies, as they said: The wages of attending the bride lies in the crush AND THE SORROW. THAT IS TO SAY: ACCORDING TO THE SUFFERING SO IS THE REWARD. "And he lay down (Heb. *vayishkav*) in that place" (Beresheet 28:11). 'VAYISHKAV' CAN BE READ AS TWO WORDS: VEYESH, CAF BET, (MEANING: AND THERE ARE 22.) That is, if there are the 22 letters of the Torah, NAMELY THAT HE IS PERFECT IN TORAH, then the Shechinah lies with him.

505. מַאן יֵ״שׁ. חָכְמָה מֵאַיִן. דְּבַאֲתַר דִּשְׁכִינְתָּא עִלָּאָה תַּמָּן, חָכְמָה תַּמָּן. וּבְגִינָהּ אִתְּמַר, לְהַנְחִיל אוֹהֲבַי יֵשׁ. וְהַיְינוּ וְעָשָׂה חֶסֶד לַאֲלָפִים לְאוֹהֲבָי. מִסִּטְרָא דְּאַהֲבַת חֶסֶד. וְיֵשׁ דְּאִיהִי חָכְמָה לִימִינָא, דְּהָכִי אוֹקְמוּהָ הָרוֹצֶה לְהַחְכִּים יַדְרִים. וּבְגִין דָּא, לְהַנְחִיל אוֹהֲבַי יֵשׁ.

505. HE ASKS, What is the meaning of *'yesh'* (Eng. 'there is')? HE ANSWERS THAT it refers to Chochmah, which is SUBSTANCE out of nothing, THAT IS TO SAY THAT IT IS DRAWN DOWN FROM KETER, WHICH IS CALLED 'NOTHING'. For in the place where the upper Shechinah is, WHICH IS BINAH, there is Chochmah, FOR CHOCHMAH IS REVEALED ONLY IN BINAH, and for it is said, "That I may cause those that love Me to inherit substance (Heb. *yesh*)" (Mishlei 8:21). FOR CHOCHMAH THAT IS IN BINAH

ILLUMINATES ONLY IN CHESED, AND THOSE THAT CLEAVE TO CHESED ARE CALLED 'THE LOVERS OF HASHEM', AND IT IS ONLY THEY WHO CAN INHERIT *YESH*, WHICH IS CHOCHMAH, BECAUSE THEY HAVE CHESED. AND THIS IS THE MEANING OF: "but showing mercy to thousands of generations of those that love Me" (Shemot 20:6), NAMELY from the side of the love of Chesed, FOR THOUSANDS IS THE SECRET OF CHOCHMAH, AND HE SHOWS MERCY (CHESED) SO AS TO ATTIRE CHOCHMAH WITH CHASSADIM. And this *yesh*, which is Chochmah, is on the right, THAT IT ILLUMINATES ONLY WHEN ATTIRED IN CHESED OF THE RIGHT, as has been taught: He who wants to grow wise should turn to the south. And that is why IT IS WRITTEN: "That I may cause those that love Me to inherit substance (Heb. *yesh*)," SINCE THEY HAVE CHESED, WHICH IS THE RIGHT.

506. תָּא חֲזֵי בְּרָזִין סְתִימִין, בְּמִדּוֹת דְּקוּדְשָׁא בְּרִיךְ הוּא, הַהִיא מִדָּה דְּמִשְׁתַּדְּלִין בָּהּ, וְדַכְרִין בָּהּ, עָלָהּ אִתְּמַר, בַּמִּדָּה שֶׁאָדָם מוֹדֵד בָּהּ מוֹדְדִין לוֹ. וְשַׁבְעִין אַנְפִּין לְאוֹרַיְיתָא, וְהַאי אִיהוּ בְּכָל הַמָּקוֹם אֲשֶׁר אַזְכִּיר אֶת שְׁמִי, תַּזְכִּיר אֶת שְׁמִי מִבָּעֵי לֵיהּ. אֶלָּא בְּהַהִיא מִדָּה דְּאַזְכִּיר אֶת שְׁמִי, בְּהַהִיא מִדָּה אָבֹא אֵלֶיךָ וּבֵרַכְתִּיךָ.

עד כאן רעיא מהימנא

506. Come and see into the hidden secrets, in the attributes of the Holy One, blessed be He, for about the same quality over which people make an effort, and which they mention, it is said: With the same measure that a man metes out, so is it measured to him, FOR HE IS TREATED WITH THE SAME ATTRIBUTE THAT HE MENTIONS. And there are seventy aspects to the Torah BASED ON THE PRINCIPLE OF THE SEVENTY ATTRIBUTES, FOR THERE ARE THE SEVEN ATTRIBUTES: CHESED, GVURAH, TIFERET, NETZACH, HOD, YESOD AND MALCHUT, EACH OF WHICH IS COMPOSED OF TEN SFIROT, MAKING SEVENTY, THIS BEING THE SECRET OF: THERE ARE SEVENTY ASPECTS TO THE TORAH. Thus "in all places where I cause My name to be pronounced, I WILL COME TO YOU, AND I BLESS YOU" (Shemot 20:21). Should Scripture not have said: 'you cause My name to be pronounced, I WILL COME TO YOU AND BLESS YOU'? NO, FOR THE

MEANING IS RATHER: With the same attribute that I uttered My name, with that very same attribute I will come to bless you.

End of Ra'aya Meheimna

A Synopsis
Rabbi Shimon tells Rabbi Yehuda that God brings true craftsmanship out of chaos, that has no substance at all, and His creation is perfected properly, in actuality, and He never again has to change it.

507. עַל פִּי הַגּוֹרָל תֵּחָלֵק נַחֲלָתוֹ בֵּין רַב לִמְעָט. ר' יְהוּדָה פָּתַח וְאָמַר, יָדַעְתִּי כִּי כָּל אֲשֶׁר יַעֲשֶׂה הָאֱלֹהִים הוּא יִהְיֶה לְעוֹלָם עָלָיו אֵין לְהוֹסִיף וּמִמֶּנּוּ אֵין לִגְרוֹעַ וְגוֹ'. שְׁלֹמֹה מַלְכָּא, דְּחָכְמָתֵיהּ יַתִּיר עַל כָּל בְּנֵי עָלְמָא, לָא יָדַעְנָא כִּי כָּל אֲשֶׁר יַעֲשֶׂה הָאֱלֹהִים הוּא יִהְיֶה לְעוֹלָם, וְאִיהוּ אָמַר יָדַעְתִּי, מַה דְּלָא יָדַע ב"נ אַחֲרָא.

507. "According to the lot shall their inheritance be divided between many and few" (Bemidbar 26:56). Rabbi Yehuda began by quoting: "I know that, whatever the Elohim does, it shall be forever; nothing can be added to it, nor anything taken from it" (Kohelet 3:14). This was said by King Solomon, whose wisdom exceeded that of all the inhabitants of the world. I, MYSELF, did not know that whatever Elohim does, it shall be forever, UNTIL he said: "I know." FOR HE KNEW what no one else knows.

508. אֶלָּא וַדַּאי שְׁלֹמֹה מַלְכָּא חָכְמָתֵיהּ סַלְקָא עַל כָּל בְּנֵי עָלְמָא, וּמַה דְּאִיהוּ יָדַע לָא יַדְעֵי כָּל שְׁאָר בְּנֵי עָלְמָא. ת"ח, שְׁאָר אוּמָנֵי דְּעָלְמָא, כַּד אִיהוּ עָבֵיד עֲבִידְתָּא, אַשְׁגַּח בֵּיהּ, וְאִסְתָּכַּל זִמְנָא וּתְרֵין זִמְנִין וְעָבֵיד לֵיהּ, וּלְבָתַר אוֹסִיף עֲלֵיהּ, אוֹ גָּרַע מִנֵּיהּ. וְקוּדְשָׁא בְּרִיךְ הוּא לָאו הָכִי, אַפִּיק עֲבִידְתָּא לַאֲמִתּוּ מִתֹּהוּ, דְּלֵית בָּהּ מַמָּשׁוּת כְּלָל, וְאִיהוּ מַמָּשׁ אִתְתְּקַן כַּדְקָא יָאוּת, וְלָא אִצְטְרִיךְ לְאוֹסָפָא וּלְאַגְרָעָא מִנֵּיהּ. בְּגִין כָּךְ כְּתִיב, וַיַּרְא אֱלֹהִים אֶת כָּל אֲשֶׁר עָשָׂה וְהִנֵּה טוֹב מְאֹד.

508. HE ANSWERS: the explanation of this is that of course King Solomon's wisdom was greater than that of other men, and he knew what was not

known to other people. Come and see, Any other craftsman in the world, when he has something to make, looks at it and considers it once and twice and then makes it. Later he adds to it or takes away from it. With the Holy One, blessed be He, it is not like that: He brings true craftsmanship out of chaos, that has no substance at all, and it is perfected properly, in actuality, and He does not need to add or take anything away from it. That is why it is written: "And Elohim saw everything that He had made, and, behold, it was very good" (Beresheet 1:31). AND IT WAS ABOUT THIS THAT SOLOMON SAID, "I KNOW THAT WHATEVER ELOHIM DOES, IT SHALL BE FOREVER; NOTHING CAN BE ADDED TO IT, NOR ANYTHING TAKEN FROM IT."

82. "Whatever the Elohim does, it shall be forever"

A Synopsis

Rabbi Shimon explains about the tree that is Zeir Anpin and that is
the Torah on which faith is suspended. He says that God is, was,
and will be – nothing can be added to Him or taken from Him. He
then talks about a lower tree that is Malchut, that is nourished from
the upper tree, and concludes by saying that only those who are fit
should come close to God, and that all others should be afraid.

509. תּוּ כָּל אֲשֶׁר יַעֲשֶׂה הָאֱלֹהִים, לְתִקּוּנָא דְּעָלְמָא, וַדַּאי הוּא יִהְיֶה
לְעוֹלָם. ר' יִצְחָק אָמַר, אִי הָכִי מַהוּ וְהָאֱלֹהִים עָשָׂה שֶׁיִּירְאוּ מִלְּפָנָיו.
אֶלָּא הַאי קְרָא הָכִי אוֹלִיפְנָא, וְהוּא רָזָא עִלָּאָה בֵּין חַבְרָנָא, הַאי קְרָא
הָכִי מִבְּעֵי לֵיהּ, כִּי כָּל אֲשֶׁר עָשָׂה הָאֱלֹהִים הוּא יִהְיֶה לְעוֹלָם, מַהוּ כָּל
אֲשֶׁר יַעֲשֶׂה, וְהָא כְּתִיב מַה שֶׁהָיָה כְּבָר הוּא וַאֲשֶׁר לִהְיוֹת כְּבָר הָיָה,
וְאַתְּ אַמְרַת כָּל אֲשֶׁר יַעֲשֶׂה.

509. "whatever the Elohim does" (Kohelet 3:14). A further explanation is
THAT WHATSOEVER HE DOES to correct the world, will surely be forever,
BUT THE DEMONS AND THE OTHER SIDE WILL BE NULLIFIED AT THE
END OF CORRECTION, AND ARE NOT ETERNAL. Rabbi Yitzchak said, If
that is so, what is THE MEANING OF: "and the Elohim does it, so that men
should fear before Him" (Ibid.)? WHICH IS UNDERSTOOD TO ALLUDE TO
THE OTHER SIDE, WHO CAST FEAR ON THE WORLD. It is not so, for we
have learned that the verse, and this is a divine secret amongst the
companions, should be read as follows: Whatever the Elohim did, it shall be
forever. But what is meant by: "whatever the Elohim does (lit. 'will do')" for
is it not written "That which is, already has been; and that which is to be has
already been" (Ibid. 15)? Yet you say: "whatever the Elohim will do"?

510. אֶלָּא מִקְרָא אַחֲרָא אִשְׁתְּמַע, כְּתִיב עַיִן לֹא רָאֲתָה אֱלֹהִים זוּלָתְךָ
יַעֲשֶׂה לִמְחַכֵּה לוֹ. יַעֲשֶׂה, עָשִׂיתָ מִבְּעֵי לֵיהּ. לִמְחַכֵּה לוֹ, לְךָ מִבְּעֵי לֵיהּ.
אֶלָּא אֲתָר עִלָּאָה הוּא, דְּנָגִיד וְנָפִיק וְאַדְלִיק בּוֹצִינִין כֻּלְּהוּ לְכָל עִיבָר,
וְאִקְרֵי עוֹלָם הַבָּא. וּמִנֵּיהּ נָפִיק חַד אִילָנָא, לְאִתְשַׁקְיָא וּלְאִתַּתְקְנָא.
וְהַאי אִילָנָא עִלָּאָה וְיַקִּירָא הוּא עַל כָּל שְׁאָר אִילָנִין, וְהָא אוֹקִמוּהָ.

וְהַהוּא עוֹלָם הַבָּא דְּנָגִיד וְנָפִיק, אַתְקִין לֵיהּ לְהַאי אִילָנָא תָּדִיר, אַשְׁקֵי
לֵיהּ, וּמְתַקֵּן לֵיהּ בַּעֲבִידְתֵּיהּ, מְעַטֵּר לֵיהּ בְּעִטְרִין, לָא פָּסִיק מַבּוּעֵי
מִנֵּיהּ לְעָלַם לְעָלְמֵי עָלְמִין.

510. HE ANSWERS, we can understand the matter from another verse. It is written: "Neither has the eye seen that an Elohim, beside You, should do such a thing for him who waits for Him" (Yeshayah 64:3). It should have said 'have done' instead of "should do" and 'for him who waits for You' instead of "for Him." HE ANSWERS, rather, it is an upper place that is drawn down and emerges and kindles all the lights, NAMELY ALL THE SFIROT OF ZEIR ANPIN AND MALCHUT, in all directions, BOTH TO THE RIGHT AND TO THE LEFT, and is called 'the World to Come', NAMELY BINAH. And from it emerges a tree, WHICH IS ZEIR ANPIN, to be watered and corrected. And this tree is more sublime and more precious than all other trees, and we have already learned about this. And that World to Come, WHICH IS BINAH, which comes out and emerges, corrects this tree continuously, and waters it, NAMELY IT EMANATES MOCHIN TO IT, and improves it in its work; NAMELY BINAH IMPROVES THE VESSELS OF ZEIR ANPIN WITH ITS OWN VESSELS SO THAT IT SHOULD BE FITTED TO RECEIVE MOCHIN FROM IT; and crowns it with diadems, WHICH IS THE SECRET OF THE FIRST THREE SFIROT, and none of the fountains ceases to flow from it forever and ever.

511. בְּהַהוּא אִילָנָא תַּלְיָא מְהֵימְנוּתָא, בֵּיהּ שַׁרְיָא מִכָּל שְׁאַר אִילָנִין,
קִיּוּמָא דְּכֹלָּא בֵּיהּ. וְעַל דָּא כְּתִיב, כָּל אֲשֶׁר יַעֲשֶׂה הָאֱלֹהִים הוּא יִהְיֶה
לְעוֹלָם. וַדַּאי הוּא הָיָה הוּא הֹוֶה וְהוּא יְהֵא. עָלָיו אֵין לְהוֹסִיף, וּמִמֶּנּוּ
אֵין לִגְרוֹעַ. וְעַל דָּא בְּאוֹרַיְיתָא כְּתִיב, לָא תּוֹסְף עָלָיו וְלָא תִגְרַע מִמֶּנּוּ.
דְּאִילָנָא דָּא, דְּאוֹרַיְיתָא הוּא. וַאֲתָר דָּא אַתְקִין הָאֱלֹהִים תָּדִיר.
הָאֱלֹהִים סְתָם, דָּא גְּבוּרָה מֵאֵין סוֹף וּמֵאֵין חֵקֶר. כד"א, אֵין חֵקֶר
לִתְבוּנָתוֹ, הָאֱלֹהִים, וְלָא אֱלֹהִים. וע"ד עָשָׂה יַעֲשֶׂה תָּדִיר, כְּמַבּוּעַ דְּלָא
פָּסְקָן מֵימוֹי לְדָרֵי דָּרִין.

511. On that tree, WHICH IS ZEIR ANPIN, Faith is suspended, WHICH IS MALCHUT THAT IS CALLED 'FAITH', which rests on it, rather than all the other trees, IN THE SECRET OF THE VERSE: "LIKE THE APPLE TREE

AMONG THE TREES OF THE WOOD, SO IS MY BELOVED AMONG THE SONS" (SHIR HASHIRIM 2:3). The existence of everything is to be found in it, INASMUCH AS IT IS THE CENTRAL COLUMN THAT GIVES EVERYTHING ITS EXISTENCE. And therefore it is written: "whatever the Elohim does, it shall be forever." Specifically, He was, He is, and He will be. "Nothing can be added to Him, nor anything taken from Him" (Ibid.). And thus it is written in the Torah: "you shall not add thereto, nor diminish from it" (Devarim 13:1). For this tree is the Torah, SINCE ZEIR ANPIN IS CALLED 'TORAH'. And the Elohim, WHO IS BINAH, establishes this place always. And the Elohim, unless specified otherwise, is Gvurah from the Infinite and Unfathomable One, NAMELY BINAH THAT IS CALLED 'GVURAH', IN THE SECRET OF THE VERSE: "I AM UNDERSTANDING (BINAH); I HAVE STRENGTH (GVURAH)" (MISHLEI 8:14). As it is written: "there is no searching for His understanding" (Yeshayah 40:28), NAMELY THERE IS NO FATHOMING TO HIS BINAH. This is why 'the Elohim' is written and not just 'Elohim', FOR ELOHIM WITHOUT THE DEFINITE ARTICLE REFERS TO MALCHUT. Thus He 'will do' always, as constant as a spring whose waters will not cease for all generations.

512. בְּגִין כַּךְ כְּתִיב, וְהָאֱלֹהִים עָשָׂה שֶׁיִּירְאוּ מִלְּפָנָיו. אַתְקִין לֵיהּ לְהַאי אִילָנָא, בְּתִקּוּנָא שְׁלִים, דְּאָחִיד לְכָל סְטַר עֵילָא וְתַתָּא, בְּגִין דְּיִירְאוּ מִלְּפָנָיו. וְלָא יַחְלְפוּן לֵיהּ בְּחִלּוּפָא אַחֲרָא לְדָרֵי דָרִין.

512. For this reason it is written: "And the Elohim has so made it, that men should fear before Him" (Kohelet 3:14). THIS MEANS THAT He established that tree, WHICH IS ZEIR ANPIN, in complete perfection, until it is attached to all sides, RIGHT AND LEFT, above and below, NAMELY TO BINAH AND MALCHUT, so that they should "fear before Him" and not replace it with any substitute for all generations.

513. א"ר אַבָּא, וַדַּאי שַׁפִּיר קָא אֲמָרַת, אֲבָל תּוּ אִית לְאִסְתַּכְּלָא, בְּקַדְמֵיתָא יַעֲשֶׂה, וּלְבָתַר וְהָאֱלֹהִים עָשָׂה, מַה בֵּין הַאי לְהַאי. אֶלָּא וַדַּאי יַעֲשֶׂה וְאַתְקִין לְהַאי אִילָנָא, דְּלָא פַּסְקִין מֵימוֹי לְדָרֵי דָרִין. וּלְבָתַר עָשָׂה, מַהוּ עָשָׂה. אֶלָּא עָשָׂה הָאֱלֹהִים אִילָנָא אַחֲרָא לְתַתָּא מִנֵּיהּ. וְלָא יַעֲשֶׂה כְּהַאי. דְּהַאי אִילָנָא תַּתָּאָה, עָבִיד לֵיהּ וְאַתְקִין לֵיהּ,

בְּגִין דְּמַאן דְּיֵיעוֹל לְאִילָנָא עִלָּאָה, יֵיעוֹל בִּרְשׁוּ, וְיִשְׁכַּח לְאִילָנָא
תַּתָּאָה, וְיִדְחַל לְמֵיעָאל, אֶלָּא כַּדְקָא חָזֵי.

513. Rabbi Aba said: What you have said is indeed nice, but one has to look into it even further. At the beginning of the verse IT SAYS "does (lit. 'will do')," and later "and Elohim does (lit. 'made') it." Why this difference? HE ANSWERS, surely because He "will do" and establish this tree, ZEIR ANPIN, so that its waters should not cease for all generations, SINCE THE WATERS OF BINAH DO NOT CEASE FOR ALL GENERATIONS AS THEY ARE DRAWN DOWN FROM SUPERNAL ABA AND IMA, WHOSE UNION IS NEVER INTERRUPTED. And then, IT IS WRITTEN "made." What did He make? Rather, the Elohim, WHICH IS BINAH, made another tree, WHICH IS MALCHUT, below it, but He will not make IT like this one, LIKE ZEIR ANPIN. THAT IS TO SAY: BINAH WILL NOT BESTOW UPON IT A NEVER CEASING BOUNTY, WHICH IS CHASSADIM FROM SUPERNAL ABA AND IMA, AS IT BESTOWS UPON ZEIR ANPIN. Therefore it is written "made" and not "will make," for this lower tree, WHICH IS MALCHUT, He made it and establishes it BY THE ASPECT OF THE LEFT, WHICH IS JUDGMENT so when one enters the upper tree, WHICH IS ZEIR ANPIN, one will so enter with permission OF THE LOWER TREE, WHICH IS MALCHUT, and, on finding the lower tree, he will be afraid to enter THE UPPER TREE other than in a proper way.

514. ת"ח, דְּהַאי, נָטִיר פִּתְחָא הוּא. וְעַל דָּא אִקְרֵי שׁוֹמֵר יִשְׂרָאֵל וְדָא אִילָנָא תַּתָּאָה עָשָׂה, אִתְשַׁקְיָא וּמִתְזָן מֵאִילָנָא דִּלְעֵילָּא. וע"ד לָא כְּתִיב יַעֲשֶׂה, אֶלָּא עָשָׂה. מ"ט. שֶׁיֵּירָאוּ מִלְּפָנָיו בְּנֵי עָלְמָא, וְלָא יִקְרְבוּן לֵיהּ, אֶלָּא אִינּוּן דְּיִתְחֲזוּן לְקָרְבָא, וְלָא אַחֲרָא, וְיִסְתַּמְּרוּן בְּנֵי נָשָׁא אָרְחֵי דְּאוֹרַיְיתָא, וְלָא יִסְטוּן לִימִינָא וְלִשְׂמָאלָא.

514. Come and see that this one, THE LOWER TREE WHICH IS MALCHUT, is the doorkeeper OF ZEIR ANPIN, AND MALCHUT is therefore called "He who keeps Yisrael" (Tehilim 121:4), FOR IT KEEPS ZEIR ANPIN, WHO IS CALLED 'YISRAEL'. And it is this lower tree that THE ELOHIM, WHICH IS BINAH, made, that it should be watered and nourished from the upper tree, WHICH IS ZEIR ANPIN. And it is therefore not written 'will make' but "made," FOR HE HAD MADE IT TO BE A KEEPER AND SO THAT IT SHOULD

BE NOURISHED FROM ZEIR ANPIN. What was the reason FOR HIS MAKING IT A KEEPER? It was so that men should be fearful of Him, and not draw close to Him, except for those who are fitted to come close, and not any others, and that men should keep the ways of the Torah and not deviate to the right nor the left, BUT SHOULD CLEAVE TO THE CENTRAL COLUMN.

83. "According to the lot"

A Synopsis

Rabbi Shimon begins by telling us that the lot to which David was attached is the tree, Malchut. Rabbi Aba talks about the voice from the firmament, saying that this firmament is nourished from the voice. We learn about the stone of Yisrael that descended from its place under the divine Throne, and upon which the lot is written. Rabbi Elazar concludes by saying that those who follow righteousness are the ones who seek God.

515. ת״ח, עַל הַאי אִילָנָא דְּכָל חֵילוֹי בֵּיה שַׁרְיָא, אָמַר דָּוִד, אַתָּה תּוֹמִיךְ גּוֹרָלִי. מַהוּ גּוֹרָלִי. דָּא עַדְבָא דְּאָחִיד בֵּיה דָּוִד מַלְכָּא. וע״ד, ע״פ הַגּוֹרָל כְּתִיב. וְכֵן הוּא ע״פ יְיָ. וַיָּמָת שָׁם ע״פ יְיָ. הַגּוֹרָל כְּתִיב. זַכָּאָה חוּלָקֵהוֹן דְּאִינּוּן דְּמִשְׁתַּדְּלִין בְּאוֹרַיְיתָא יְמָמָא וְלֵילֵי, וְיַדְעֵי אָרְחוֹי. וְאִינּוּן אַכְלֵי בְּכָל יוֹמָא מְזוֹנָא עִלָּאָה. כד״א, הַחָכְמָה תְּחַיֶּה בְעֶלֶיהָ. דְּהָא אוֹרַיְיתָא דִּלְעֵילָּא מֵאֲתָר דָּא אִתְּזָן, וְהָא אִתְּמַר עָלַיְיהוּ, הִנֵּה עֲבָדַי יֹאכֵלוּ.

515. Come and see: About this tree, MALCHUT, on which rest all of the hosts of the worlds OF BRIYAH, YETZIRAH AND ASIYAH, David said: "You maintain my lot" (Tehilim 16:5). What is the meaning of "my lot?" It is the lot to which David is attached, WHICH IS MALCHUT, and it is therefore written: "According to the lot" (Bemidbar 26:56) (where the Hebrew for 'according to' is, literally: 'On the mouth of'). THIS ALLUDES TO MALCHUT, WHICH IS CALLED 'MOUTH.' And the same expression is used in the verse: "So Moses the servant of Hashem died there in the land of Moab, according to the word (lit. 'mouth') of Hashem" (Devarim 34:5), WHICH IS MALCHUT. CONSEQUENTLY, "the lot" is written, WITH THE DEFINITE ARTICLE (HEI), TO REFER TO MALCHUT. Happy are the portions of those who engage in the study of Torah day and night and who know its ways, and each day they eat the divine food OF THE FLOWING BOUNTY OF CHOCHMAH, as it is written: "For wisdom gives life to those who have it" (Kohelet 7:12), for the Torah on high, NAMELY ZEIR ANPIN, is nourished from this place, FROM CHOCHMAH. And it is said about them: "Behold, My servants shall eat" (Yeshayah 65:13).

516. רִבִּי אַבָּא פָּתַח וְאָמַר, וַיְהִי קוֹל מֵעַל לָרָקִיעַ. דָּא קוֹל דְּאָחִיד
לְהַאי רָקִיעַ, וְאִשְׁתְּתַּף בַּהֲדֵיהּ. וְדָא הוּא זֵכֶר עָשָׂה לְנִפְלְאוֹתָיו. וְהַהוּא
רְקִיעָא קָאֵים עָלַיְיהוּ, עַל אִינּוּן חֵיוָון. וְדָא הוּא דְּאִבְרֵי בַּשֵּׁנִי, לְהַבְדִּיל
בֵּין מַיִם לָמָיִם.

516. Rabbi Aba started by quoting: "And there was a voice from above the firmament" (Yechezkel 1:25). About this voice, ZEIR ANPIN, which is attached to this firmament (YESOD OF ZEIR ANPIN) and participates with it, it is said: "He has made His wonderful works to be remembered" (Tehilim 111:4), WHICH REFERS TO THE FIRMAMENT WHICH IS YESOD THAT IS CALLED 'REMEMBRANCE'. And this firmament stands over those living creatures, AS IT IS SAID: "AND THERE WAS A VOICE FROM ABOVE THE FIRMAMENT THAT WAS OVER THEIR HEADS." And this is THE FIRMAMENT that was created on the second day OF THE WORKS OF CREATION, ABOUT WHICH IT IS SAID: "divide water from water" (Beresheet 1:6), THE UPPER WATERS AND THE LOWER WATERS.

517. וְהָא אוּקְמוּהָ, דְּשִׁבְעָה רְקִיעִין לְעֵילָּא לְעֵילָּא. וַדַּאי וִילוֹן אֵינוֹ
מְשַׁמֵּשׁ, דְּהָא לֵית לֵיהּ מִדִּילֵיהּ, אֶלָּא מַה דְּיָהֲבִין לֵיהּ. וּמִסְכְּנֵי בֵּיהּ
אִתְאַחֲדוּ, דָּא הוּא רָזָא דִּכְתִּיב, וּבְעָנְיִי הֲכִינוֹתִי לְבֵית אֱלֹהַי. וְדָא
מַכְנִיס שַׁחֲרִית וּמוֹצִיא עַרְבִית. דְּהָא בְּלֵילְיָא, אַפִּיק חַיְלוֹי לְכָל סִטְרִין,
וְשַׁלְטָא עַל אִינּוּן חַיָּילִין וְאֻכְלוֹסִין. וּבְשַׁחֲרִית כָּנִישׁ לְכֻלְּהוּ, וְאָעֵיל
לְנַקְבַּיְיהוּ, וְלָא שַׁלְטִין. דְּהָא בֹּקֶר כָּלִיל כֻּלְּהוּ. כד"א לְהַגִּיד בַּבֹּקֶר
חַסְדֶּךָ וֶאֱמוּנָתְךָ בַּלֵּילוֹת. וְהָא אוּקְמוּהָ.

517. It has been taught: There are seven firmaments higher on high, CORRESPONDING TO CHESED, GVURAH, TIFERET, NETZACH, HOD, YESOD AND MALCHUT THAT ARE IN YESOD. Certainly 'Curtain', WHICH IS PARALLEL TO MALCHUT THAT IS IN IT, serves no purpose, for MALCHUT has nothing of her own, apart from what ZEIR ANPIN gives her. And the poor take hold of her, this being the inner meaning of the verse: "Now, behold, in my trouble (poverty) I have prepared for the house of Hashem" (I Divrei Hayamim 22:14) INASMUCH AS DAVID WAS ATTACHED TO MALCHUT, WHICH IS POOR, AS ABOVE. HENCE HE SAID, "IN MY

POVERTY." And this FIRMAMENT, CURTAIN, WHICH IS MALCHUT, introduces the morning and ushers out the evening, for at night MALCHUT brings out her hosts in all directions, TO THE RIGHT AND TO THE LEFT, and has control over these hosts and regiments, FOR THEN IS THE RULE OF MALCHUT. And in the morning, she collects together all its hosts, and brings them into their hole (Heb. *nekev*), THAT IS TO SAY TO THEIR ASPECT OF THE FEMALE (NUKVA), and they have no power, for the morning includes them all, as it is written: "to relate Your steadfast love (Heb. *Chesed*) in the morning, and Your faithfulness every night" (Tehilim 92:3). But this has already been taught.

518. וְקוֹל אִית עַל הַאי רָקִיעַ, מִנֵּיהּ אִתְזָן הַאי רָקִיעַ, בְּשַׁעֲתָא דְּהַאי קוֹל אִתְּעַר, כֻּלְּהוּ אַכְלוּסִין לָא נַטְלִין, וְלֵית בְּהוּ רְשׁוּ, אֶלָּא לְמֵיקָם בְּדוּכְתַּיְיהוּ, וְאַקְרְבֵי חֵילֵיהוֹן וּמְחַכָּאן, לְהַהוּא טִיבוּ דְּנָגִיד לְהַהוּא רָקִיעַ, וְיִתְבָּרְכָן בְּגִינֵיהּ, וע״ד אִיהוּ מֵעַל לָרָקִיעַ אֲשֶׁר עַל רֹאשָׁם.

518. And there is a voice, WHICH IS ZEIR ANPIN, that is above this firmament, for from it this firmament is nourished, SINCE YESOD RECEIVES FROM ZEIR ANPIN. When this voice awakens, none of the hosts are in motion, and they have no permission to do anything but stand still where they are. AND THIS IS THE SECRET OF THE VERSE: "AND THERE WAS A VOICE FROM ABOVE THE FIRMAMENT THAT WAS OVER THEIR HEADS; WHEN THEY STOOD STILL, THEY LET DOWN THEIR WINGS" (YECHEZKEL 1:25); NAMELY WHEN THE VOICE STIRS OVER THEIR HEADS, THEN THEY STAND STILL. And the hosts draw near and wait for that goodness which is drawn down FROM THE VOICE, WHICH IS ZEIR ANPIN, to that firmament, WHICH IS YESOD, and they are blessed because of it, NAMELY THAT THEY RECEIVE FROM THE FIRMAMENT. And therefore, ZEIR ANPIN is above the firmament that is over their head, AND THEY CAN RECEIVE ONLY FROM THE FIRMAMENT, WHICH IS YESOD.

519. ת״ח וּמִמַּעַל לָרָקִיעַ אֲשֶׁר עַל רֹאשָׁם כְּמַרְאֵה אֶבֶן סַפִּיר דְּמוּת כִּסֵּא, כְּמַרְאֵה אֶבֶן סַפִּיר, דָּא אֶבֶן יִשְׂרָאֵל. וְדָא הוּא רָזָא דִכְתִיב, וְגָלְלוּ אֶת הָאֶבֶן וְגוֹ׳. חַד אֶבֶן נַחְתָּא מִלְּעֵילָא, כַּד בָּעוּ יִשְׂרָאֵל לְמֵירַת אַרְעָא, וּכְתִיב בֵּיהּ גּוֹרָל. וְאִיהוּ אָמַר, דָּא לִפְלַנְיָא, וְדָא לִפְלַנְיָא. וְדָא

אֶבֶן הוּא מִתְחוֹת כֻּרְסְיָיא דְּמַלְכָּא נַחְתָּא. וַדַּאי מִשָּׁם רוֹעֶה אֶבֶן יִשְׂרָאֵל כְּתִיב. וּבְגִינֵי כָּךְ ע״פ הַגּוֹרָל וַדַּאי תֵּחָלֵק נַחֲלָתוֹ.

519. Come and see, "And above the firmament that was over their heads was the likeness of a Throne, in appearance like a sapphire stone" (Ibid. 26). "in appearance like a sapphire stone" refers to the stone of Yisrael, WHICH IS MALCHUT. And this is the inner meaning of what is written: "and they rolled the stone" (Beresheet 29:3). From on high descended a certain stone, WHICH IS MALCHUT, when Yisrael wanted to inherit the Land (of Yisrael), and on it the lot is written, NAMELY "ACCORDING TO THE LOT," and THE LOT would say: This part for so-and-so, this part for so-and-so. And this stone descended from under the King's Throne, NAMELY MALCHUT, WHICH IS THE SECRET OF THE THRONE OF ZEIR ANPIN. Surely it is written "from thence, from the Shepherd, the Stone of Yisrael" (Beresheet 49:24), FOR THIS IS THE STONE OF ZEIR ANPIN THAT IS CALLED 'YISRAEL'. And for this reason: "According to the lot (WHICH IS MALCHUT) shall their inheritance be divided" (Bemidbar 26:56).

520. רִבִּי יִצְחָק וְרִבִּי יְהוּדָה הֲווֹ אַזְלֵי מֵאוּשָׁא לְלוֹד, פָּגַע בְּהוּ ר׳ אֶלְעָזָר, רָהֲטוּ אֲבַתְרֵיהּ. אָמְרוּ, וַדַּאי נַרְהִיט אֲבַתְרֵיהּ דִּשְׁכִינְתָּא. עַד דִּמְטוּ לְגַבֵּיהּ, אָמְרוּ וַדַּאי נִשְׁתַּתֵּף בַּהֲדָךְ, וְנִשְׁמַע מִלָּה חַדְתָּא.

520. Rabbi Yitzchak and Rabbi Yehuda were walking from Usha to Lod. Rabbi Elazar encountered them and they ran after him, saying, Surely we shall run after the Shechinah. When they caught up with him, they said, Let us now certainly join you and hear a new matter.

521. פָּתַח וְאָמַר, שִׁמְעוּ אֵלַי רוֹדְפֵי צֶדֶק מְבַקְשֵׁי וְגו׳. שִׁמְעוּ אֵלַי רוֹדְפֵי צֶדֶק, אִינּוּן דְּאַזְלִין בָּתַר מְהֵימְנוּתָא, רוֹדְפֵי צֶדֶק, וַדַּאי אִינּוּן מְבַקְשֵׁי ה׳. אִי בָּעִיתוּ לְמִנְדַּע מְהֵימְנוּתָא, וּלְאַחֲדָא לְהַאי צֶדֶק, לָא תִסְתַּכְּלוּן בָּהּ בִּלְחוֹדָהָא כִּשְׁאַר בְּנֵי עָלְמָא, דְּגַרְמוּ מִיתָה לְגַרְמַיְיהוּ עַל דָּא. אֲבָל הַבִּיטוּ אֶל צוּר חֻצַּבְתֶּם וְאֶל מַקֶּבֶת בּוֹר נֻקַּרְתֶּם.

521. He began by quoting, "Hearken to me, you that follow after righteousness, you that seek Hashem" (Yeshayah 51:1). "Hearken to me, you

that follow after righteousness" refers to those who follow AND PURSUE AFTER the Faith, WHICH IS MALCHUT, THAT IS CALLED 'RIGHTEOUSNESS', for those who follow righteousness are CERTAINLY the ones who "seek Hashem." If you want to know the Faith and to take hold of this righteousness, then do not look at it on its own WITHOUT ZEIR ANPIN, as do other people WHO CLEAVE TO MALCHUT WITHOUT ZEIR ANPIN, THIS BEING THE SECRET OF LEFT WITHOUT RIGHT, and for which reason they bring death to themselves. But "look to the rock whence you were hewn, and to the hole of the pit from which you were dug out" (Ibid.), NAMELY TO UNITE IT WITH ZEIR ANPIN, AND ABA AND IMA.

84. The sacrifices

A Synopsis
Rabbi Elazar says that the perfect offering is one made without sin, i.e. the peace offering. Anyone who sins draws upon himself an unclean spirit that controls him; the function of the sacrifice is to break that spirit and make atonement. We hear that God loves a broken and contrite heart. Rabbi Elazar says he learned in the Book of Enoch that all sacrifices when they ascend go first to the Garden of Eden, and we learn why animals are sacrificed. Rabbi Shimon offers a deeper explanation, saying that the secret of the sacrifices is the secret of the Holy Beasts, and he elaborates with many details about ox, eagle, lion and man. He says that man's prayer is similar to the sacrifices. We learn from this section that no one is allowed to eat before the Supreme King does. Rabbi Shimon tells Elijah how it could be possible for the Supreme King to eat, since it seems that there is no eating or drinking above.

522. צַו אֶת בְּנֵי יִשְׂרָאֵל וְאָמַרְתָּ אֲלֵיהֶם אֶת קָרְבָּנִי לַחְמִי וְגו'. כְּתִיב הַחֵפֶץ לַיְיָ' בְּעוֹלוֹת וּזְבָחִים כִּשְׁמוֹעַ בְּקוֹל יְיָ' וְגו'. לֵית רְעוּתָא דְּקוּדְשָׁא בְּרִיךְ הוּא, דְּיֵחוּב בַּר נָשׁ, וְעַל חוֹבֵיה יַקְרִיב קָרְבָּן. אֶלָּא קָרְבָּן דְּאִיהוּ בְּלִי חוֹבָה, דָּא אִיהוּ קָרְבָּן שָׁלִים, וְאִקְרֵי שְׁלָמִים, וְקָרְבָּן תָּמִיד אוּף הָכִי, וְאע"ג דִּמְכַפֵּר עַל חוֹבִין.

522. "Command the children of Yisrael, and say to them: My offerings, the provisions of My sacrifices made by fire" (Bemidbar 28:2). It is written: "Has Hashem as great a delight in burnt offerings and sacrifices, as in obeying to the voice of Hashem?" (I Shmuel 15:22). The Holy One, blessed be He, does not desire that a man sin and then offer a sacrifice because of his sin; but a sacrifice that is without any iniquity is the perfect sacrifice (Heb. *shalem*). And it is called "peace-offerings" (Heb. *shelamim*). The daily offering is also PERFECT, for although THE DAILY SACRIFICE atones for sins, IT IS NEVERTHELESS A PERFECT SACRIFICE.

523. רִבִּי אַבָּא פָּתַח, זִבְחֵי אֱלֹהִים רוּחַ נִשְׁבָּרָה וְגו'. הַאי קְרָא אוּקְמוּהָ, דִּרְעוּתָא דְּקוּדְשָׁא בְּרִיךְ הוּא, לָא אִתְרְעֵי בְּקָרְבָּן דב"נ עַל חוֹבוֹי, אֶלָּא רוּחַ נִשְׁבָּרָה. וּבְנֵי נָשָׁא לָא יַדְעֵי מַאי קָאמְרֵי, וְהָכִי

שְׁמַעְנָא מִבּוּצִינָא קַדִּישָׁא, דְּכַד אָתֵי בַּ"נ לְאִסְתַּאֲבָא בְּחוֹבוֹי, אַמְשִׁיךְ עֲלֵיהּ רוּחַ, מִסִּטְרָא דִמְסָאֲבָא, וְאִתְגָּאֵי עַל בַּ"נ, וְשַׁלִּיט עֲלֵיהּ לְכָל רְעוּתָא. וְהַהוּא סִטְרָא מְסָאֲבָא, אִתְגַּבָּר בְּחֵילֵיהּ וְאִתְתַּקַּף, וְשַׁלִּיט עֲלֵיהּ לִרְעוּתֵיהּ. אָתֵי בַּ"נ וְשַׁלִּיט עֲלֵיהּ לְאִתְדַּכָּאָה, מְדַכְּאִין לֵיהּ.

523. Rabbi Aba began by quoting: "The sacrifices of Elohim are a broken spirit" (Tehilim 51:19). This verse has been interpreted to mean that the Holy One, blessed be He, does not want a man to bring a sacrifice for his sin, but, rather, HE WANTS a broken spirit. People do not know what they say. From the holy luminary I heard as follows: When a man becomes impure in his iniquities, he draws down onto himself a spirit from the side of uncleanliness, and THE SPIRIT dominates that person and controls him at will. The aspect of uncleanliness, FROM WHICH THE SPIRIT IS DRAWN DOWN, grows stronger with his strength and becomes more powerful and controls him to its wish. When a man comes and takes control over it, in order to become pure, he is helped to be purified FROM ABOVE.

524. בְּזִמְנָא דַּהֲוָה בֵּי מַקְדְּשָׁא קַיָּים, אַקְרִיב קָרְבְּנֵיהּ, כָּל כַּפָּרָה דִּילֵיהּ תַּלְיָיא עֲלֵיהּ, עַד דְּאִתְחֲרַט, וְתָבַר לְהַהוּא רוּחַ מִגּוֹ גֵּאוּתָא דִּילֵיהּ, וּמָאִיךְ לֵיהּ. וְדָא הוּא תְּבִירוּ, דְּהַהוּא דַּרְגָּא דִּמְסָאֲבָא. וְכַד אִתְבַּר הַהוּא רוּחַ מְסָאֲבָא, וְקָרִיב קָרְבְּנֵיהּ, דָּא אִיהוּ דְּאִתְקַבֵּל בִּרְעֻוָא כַּדְקָא יָאוּת.

524. In the period when the Temple was still standing, THE SINNER would offer his sacrifice, his whole atonement being dependent on it, until he feels remorse and breaks down that spirit FROM THE SIDE OF UNCLEANLINESS THAT HE DREW TO HIMSELF WITH HIS SIN, from its pride, and humiliates it. And it is this that is meant by the breaking down of that grade of uncleanliness, FROM WHICH THE SPIRIT IS DRAWN, and when that spirit of uncleanliness is broken, and he offers his sacrifice, this is an acceptable and proper SACRIFICE.

525. וְאִי לָא אִתְבַּר הַהוּא רוּחַ, לָאו קָרְבְּנֵיהּ כְּלוּם, וּלְכַלְבֵּי אִתְמְסַר, דְּהָא קָרְבְּנָא דָּא לָאו דְּקוּדְשָׁא בְּרִיךְ הוּא, אֶלָּא מְכַלְבֵּי. וּבְג"כ זִבְחֵי

אֱלֹהִים כַּדְקָא יָאוּת, הוּא רוּחַ נִשְׁבָּרָה, דְּיִתְבַּר הַהוּא רוּחָא מְסָאֲבָא,
וְלָא יִשְׁלוֹט. וְעַל דָּא מַאן דְּיִתְבַּר לֵיהּ כַּדְקָא יָאוּת, עֲלֵיהּ כְּתִיב, רוּחַ
הוֹלֵךְ וְלֹא יָשׁוּב. לֶיהֱוֵי הַהוּא גַּבְרָא בְּאַבְטָחוּתָא, דְּלָא יְתוּב לְגַבֵּיהּ
לְעָלְמִין. הֲדָא הוּא דִכְתִיב, וְלֹא יָשׁוּב. לֵב נִשְׁבָּר וְנִדְכֶּה, הַהוּא גַּבְרָא
דְּלָא אִתְגָּאֵי, וְלָא אִתְעַנַּג בְּעֹנוּגִין דְּעָלְמָא, אֱלֹהִים לֹא תִבְזֶה, בִּיקָרָא
אִיהוּ לְגַבֵּיהּ.

525. But if that spirit OF UNCLEANLINESS is not broken, then his sacrifice is worth nothing and is given to the dogs, for this is a sacrifice not for the Holy One, blessed be He, but for the dogs. And this is why Scripture says that the proper sacrifices of Elohim are a broken spirit, for that spirit of uncleanliness has to be broken so that it will not be in control. Consequently, about the one who breaks it as it should be broken, it is written: "A wind (or spirit) that passes away, and comes not again" (Tehilim 78:39). And that man can be assured that it will not ever come to him again. Hence "and comes not again." "A broken and a contrite heart" (Tehilim 51:19). This is a man who is not proud and does not take pleasure in the delights of the world. And "Elohim, You will not despise" (Ibid.), for He has a place of honor with him.

526. צַו אֶת בְּנֵי יִשְׂרָאֵל. מַאי צַו. דָּא ע"ז. בְּגִין דְּלָא יֵיעוֹל גַּרְמֵיהּ
לְאִסְתַּאֲבָא בְּרוּחַ מְסָאֲבָא, דְּאִיהוּ ע"ז מַמָּשׁ.

526. "Command the children of Yisrael." To what does 'command' refer? It refers to idolatry, that is, he should not bring himself in to become impure in the spirit of uncleanliness, for this would be real idolatry.

527. ר' אֶלְעָזָר פָּתַח. בָּאתִי לְגַנִּי אֲחוֹתִי כַלָּה וְגוֹ'. הַאי קְרָא אוֹקְמוּהָ,
אֲבָל אִית סְתָרִים בְּקָרְבְּנָא הָכָא, וְכֹלָּא אִתְּמַר. א"ל ר"ש, יָאוּת הוּא,
דְּשָׁרִית מִלָּה, וְסָתַמְתְּ, אֵימָא. אָמַר, בְּגִין דַּחֲמֵינָא בְּסִפְרָא דְּחֲנוֹךְ
מִלָּה, וְאוֹלִיפְנָא. אָמַר, אֵימָא הַהִיא מִלָּה דְּחָמִית וְשָׁמַעַת.

527. Rabbi Elazar began by quoting: "I am come into my garden, my sister, my bride" (Shir Hashirim 5:1). We have already learned this verse, yet it

contains secrets concerning the sacrifices. But then we have already learned it all. Rabbi Shimon said to him, It is good that you have started the discussion on these matters, BUT why have you concealed them? BECAUSE HE SAID THAT EVERYTHING HAS BEEN SAID. Tell us WHAT YOU KNOW ABOUT THE SACRIFICES. RABBI ELAZAR replied, It was because I saw something in the Book of Enoch and learned it THAT I SAID THAT EVERYTHING HAS BEEN SAID. Rabbi Shimon said, Tell us that matter that you have seen and heard.

528. אָמַר כֹּלָּא חַד מִלָּה, קוּדְשָׁא בְּרִיךְ הוּא אָמַר דָּא, בָּאתִי לְגַנִּי, בְּגִין דְּכָל קָרְבְּנִין דְּעָלְמָא כַּד סַלְקִין, כֻּלְּהוּ עַיְילִין לְגוֹ גִּנְתָּא דְעֵדֶן בְּקַדְמֵיתָא, רָזָא דכ״י. וְהֵיאַךְ בְּקַדְמֵיתָא וְשֵׁירוּתָא דְּקָרְבְּנָא, בְּשַׁעֲתָא דב״נ אוֹדֵי חַטָאוֹי עֲלָה, וּנְכִיסוּ וְזָרִיקוּ דְּדָמֵיהּ עַל מַדְבְּחָא.

528. He said: It is all really just one matter. The Holy One, blessed be He, said "I am come into my garden" because all the sacrifices that are made in the world, when they ascend AS MAYIN NUKVIN (LIT. 'FEMALE WATERS') first enter into the Garden of Eden, which is the secret of The Congregation of Yisrael, WHICH IS MALCHUT. But initially how is it at the beginning of the sacrifice? FOR I HAVE SAID THAT THEY FIRST COME INTO THE GARDEN OF EDEN, MEANING when a man confesses his sins over THE SACRIFICE, at the time of the slaughtering and the scattering of the blood over the altar, THEN THE SACRIFICE ASCENDS AS MAYIN NUKVIN, TO T THE GARDEN OF EDEN. AND THEN, SAYS THE HOLY ONE, BLESSED BE HE, WHO IS ZEIR ANPIN: "I AM COME INTO MY GARDEN" WHICH IS THE GARDEN OF EDEN, MALCHUT, FOR THE MAYIN NUKVIN OF THE SACRIFICE AWAKEN THE UNION.

529. הַשְׁתָּא אִית לְאִסְתַּכְּלָא, הֵיאַךְ אִינּוּן רוּחִין קַדִּישִׁין אִתְהֲנוּן מֵהַאי. ומ״ט דְּקָרְבְּנָא דִּבְהֵמָה, וְהָא יַתִּיר הֲוָה סַגְיָא, לְתַבְרָא ב״נ הַהוּא רוּחָא, וּלְאָתָבָא בִּתְיוּבְתָּא מ״ט נְכִיסוּ דִּבְהֵמָה, וּלְאוֹקְדָא לֵיהּ בְּנוּרָא דְּמַדְבְּחָא.

529. Now one has to concentrate to understand how these holy spirits benefit from this, FROM THE ASCENT OF MAYIN NUKVIN OF THE SACRIFICE.

Also, what is the reason that the sacrifice has to be of an animal, when it is more important that a man should break that spirit THAT HE HAS DRAWN DOWN BY HIS SIN, and return in repentance? What is the reason for the ritual slaughtering of the animal, and the burning of it by fire on the altar?

530. אֶלָּא רָזָא הוּא, בְּגִין דְּאִית בְּהֵמָה דִּרְבִיעָא עַל אֶלֶף טוּרִין, וְאֶלֶף טוּרִין אַכְלַת בְּכָל יוֹמָא, וְכֻלְּהוּ אִקְרוּן בְּהֵמוֹת בְּהַרְרֵי אָלֶף. וְעַל דָּא תְּנֵינָן, דְּאִית בְּעִירָא אָכִיל בְּעִירֵי. וּמִמַּה הֲווֹ. מֵאֶשָּׁא. וְכֻלְּהוּ לָחִיךְ לוֹן הַהִיא בְּהֵמָה בִּלְחִיכָא חֲדָא, הה"ד כִּי יְיָ' אֱלֹהֶיךָ אֵשׁ אֹכְלָה הוּא אֵל קַנָּא. וְכָל מַיָּא דְּיַרְדֵּן, דְּאַמְלָא בְּשִׁית שְׁנִין, הִיא עַבְדַת לֵיהּ גְּמִיעָה חֲדָא, הה"ד, יִבְטַח כִּי יָגִיחַ יַרְדֵּן אֶל פִּיהוּ.

530. HE ANSWERS, It is a mystery. There is an animal that lies on a thousand hills, WHICH IS THE SECRET OF MALCHUT, WHICH IS THE ASPECT OF YUD HEI VAV HEI, FULLY SPELLED WITH HEI'S, WHOSE NUMERICAL VALUE IS THE SAME AS THAT OF ANIMAL (HEB. *BEHEMAH* = 52). And it devours a thousand hills each day, ALL OF THE THOUSAND BEING THE SECRET OF THE GRADES OF CHOCHMAH THAT ARE DRAWN DOWN FROM THE LEFT, FOR CHOCHMAH IS TERMED A THOUSAND (HEB. *ELEF*) IN THE SECRET OF THE VERSE: "AND I SHALL TEACH (HEB. *A'ALFECH*) YOU WISDOM" (IYOV 33:33), and they are called: "and the cattle upon a thousand hills" (Tehilim 50:10). And we have already learned about this, that there is an animal that devours animals. And what do THE ANIMALS consist of? They are of fire, and this animal, WHICH IS MALCHUT, consumes all of them with one gulp, as it is written: "For Hashem your Elohim is a consuming fire, a jealous El" (Devarim 4:24). And all the waters of the Jordan, WHICH IS YESOD OF ZEIR ANPIN, that is filled within six years, WHICH IT RECEIVES FROM CHESED, GVURAH, TIFERET, NETZACH, HOD AND YESOD OF ZEIR ANPIN, THAT ARE CALLED 'SIX YEARS', are made into one gulp, NAMELY ONE SWALLOW, by it, MALCHUT, as it is written: "he trusts that river will thrust some food into his mouth" (Iyov 40:23).

531. סִתְרָא דְּמִלָּה, חֲמִירָא דְּכָל הָנֵי, עִקָּרָא וִיסוֹדָא לְהָנֵי בְּעִירֵי דִּלְתַתָּא. בְּגִין דְּרוּחָא מִנַּיְיהוּ מִתְפַּשְּׁטָא לְתַתָּא, וְאִתְצַיָּיר הַהוּא רוּחָא

לְתַתָּא בִּבְעִירֵי. וְכַד חָב ב"נ, אַיְיתֵי בְּעִירָא לְקָרְבְּנָא, וְהַהוּא רוּחָא
דִּבְעִירָא דָא, סַלְקָא וְתָב לְאַתְרֵיה, וּמִתְפָּשַׁט הַהוּא רוּחָא בְּכֻלְּהוּ. וְכָל
אִינּוּן דְּזִינָא דָא, מִתְקַרְבִין וְאַתְיָין וְאִתְהַנְיָין מֵהַהוּא חֶלְבָּא וְדָמָא,
דְּהַהוּא לְבוּשָׁא דְּרוּחָא דָא, דְּהָא מִסְטְרָא דִּלְהוֹן הֲוָה הַהוּא רוּחָא.
וְכֻלְּהוֹן אִתְהֲנוּ וְאִתְזָנוּ, וְאִתְעֲבָדוּן סַנֵּיגוֹרִין עַל הַהוּא ב"נ. וְעָאל דֶּרֶךְ
וֶשֶׁט, כְּמָה דְּאִתְּמַר. וּבְג"כ קָרְבְּנָא מִן הַבְּהֵמָה.

531. And the secret of the matter is that the yeast of those ANIMALS ON A THOUSAND HILLS, WHICH ARE THE SECRET OF THE ILLUMINATION OF CHOCHMAH THAT IS ON THE LEFT, is the principle and basis for those animals below, for the spirit spreads downwards from them, and this spirit is formed in the animals below, THAT IS TO SAY, IT BECOMES THE SPIRIT OF THE ANIMAL BELOW. And when a sinner brings an animal for sacrifice, then that spirit of the animal ascends and returns to its place, TO THE UPPER ANIMAL, WHICH IS MALCHUT, and this spirit spreads through all THE ANIMALS THAT ARE ON A THOUSAND HILLS, AS ABOVE. And all those that are of this sort, NAMELY, THE OTHER SIDE THAT ARE DRAWN DOWN FROM THE LEFT, approach and enjoy that fat and blood that are the raiment of this spirit. And this spirit is from their side, NAMELY FROM THE LEFT SIDE, and they all benefit and are nourished and become advocates of that person, FOR THE PROSECUTOR BECOMES DEFENSE COUNSEL, AND MAYIN NUKVIN OF THE SACRIFICE enter by way of the esophagus, as we have learned. This is why the sacrifice is taken from an animal.

532. אר"ש, בְּרִיךְ בְּרִי לְקוּדְשָׁא בְּרִיךְ הוּא, עֲלָךְ אִתְּמַר יִשְׂמַח אָבִיךְ
וְאִמֶּךְ וְתָגֵל יוֹלַדְתֶּךָ. יִשְׂמַח אָבִיךְ, דִּלְעֵילָּא. וְאָמֵר, דָּא כְּנֶסֶת יִשְׂרָאֵל.
וְתָגֵל יוֹלַדְתֶּךָ, דָּא בְּרַתֵּיה דר' פִּנְחָס בֶּן יָאִיר חֲסִידָא. אֶלְעָזָר בְּרִי
אֵימָא, הָא קוּרְבָּנָא דִּבְהֵמָה, קָרְבְּנָא דְּעוֹפֵי מַאי. דִּכְתִיב וְאִם מִן הָעוֹף
עוֹלָה קָרְבָּנוֹ. א"ל, לָא חֲמֵינָא, אֲבָל אִסְתַּכְּלָנָא מֵהַאי מִלָּה דִּבְהֵמָה,
מִלָּה דְּעוֹפֵי. וְלָא אֵימָא, בְּגִין דְּלָא חֲמֵינָא, וְעַד כְּעַן לָא שְׁמַעְנָא.

532. Rabbi Shimon said, Blessed is my son to the Holy One, blessed be He. About you it is said: "Let your father and your mother be glad, and let her who bore you rejoice" (Mishlei 23:25). Let your father on high be glad,

THAT IS ZEIR ANPIN, and your mother is the Congregation of Yisrael, WHICH IS MALCHUT. And let her that bore you rejoice, namely the daughter of the pious Rabbi Pinchas ben Ya'ir, THE MOTHER OF RABBI ELAZAR. Elazar, my son, what you have said is CORRECT regarding the sacrifice of an animal, BUT what is the reason for the offering of fowls? For it is written: "And if the burnt sacrifice for his offering to Hashem be of birds" (Vayikra 1:14). He said to him: I have not seen, but I draw an analogy from what is said about animals to what is said about fowl. Nevertheless, I will not speak, because I have not seen it nor, until now, have I heard it.

533. א״ל אֶלְעָזָר, יָאוֹת אֲמַרְתְּ. אֲבָל רָזָא דְקָרְבְּנִין סִתְרִין סַגִּיאִין תַּמָּן, וְלָא אִתְמְסָרוּ לְגַלָּאָה, בַּר לְזַכָּאֵי קְשׁוֹט, דְּרָזָא דְמָארֵיהוֹן לָא אִתְכַּסֵּי מִנַּיְיהוּ. סִתְרָא דְקָרְבְּנִין, דָּא אִיהוּ סִתְרָא, לְאִינוּן חֵיוָן קַדִּישִׁין. ד׳ דְּיוּקְנִין חֲקוּקִין בְּכֻרְסַיָּא, וְדָא אִיהוּ כּוּרְסְיָיא דְמַלְכָּא קַדִּישָׁא. פְּנֵי שׁוֹר. פְּנֵי נֶשֶׁר. פְּנֵי אַרְיֵה. פְּנֵי אָדָם. פְּנֵי אָדָם דְּכָלִיל לְכֻלְּהוּ. וְכָל אַנְפִּין מִסְתַּכְּלִין אִלֵּין לְאִלֵּין, וְאִתְכְּלִילָן אִלֵּין בְּאִלֵּין, וּמִנַּיְיהוּ מִתְפַּשְׁטָן לְכַמָּה סִטְרִין וְרִבְוָון, עֵילָא וְתַתָּא, דְּלֵית לוֹן שִׁיעוּרָא וּמִנְיָינָא וְחֻשְׁבּוֹן.

533. Rabbi Shimon said: Elazar, what you have said is good, but there are many secrets among the secrets of the sacrifices, and they have not been handed down to be revealed, except to the truly righteous, from whom their Master's secret is not hidden. The secret of the sacrifices is the secret of the holy living creatures, the four forms engraved on the Throne, this being the Throne of the Holy King, NAMELY MALCHUT, WHICH IS A THRONE FOR ZEIR ANPIN, AND THESE FOUR ARE: The face of an ox, the face of an eagle, the face of a lion, the face of a man. The face of a man includes all of them, FOR LION, OX, AND EAGLE ARE THE SECRET OF THE THREE COLUMNS, AND THE FACE OF A MAN IS MALCHUT THAT RECEIVES THEM AND THEREFORE INCLUDES ALL OF THEM. And all FOUR faces look at each other and are included in each other, and from them they spread out in many directions, and tens of thousands, above and below, without measure, number, or account.

534. פְּנֵי שׁוֹר, אִתְפְּשַׁט לְבְעִירֵי רוּחָא מִנֵּיהּ, לְאַרְבְּעָה זַיְינִין,

וְאִתְכְּלִילָן בְּחַד, וְאִלֵּין אִינּוּן: פָּרִים, וּכְבָשִׂים, וְעַתּוּדִים, וְעִזִּים. וְאִלֵּין
קַיְימִין לְקָרְבְּנָא. וּבְגִין דְּמִנְהוֹן הֲווֹ, אִינּוּן חַיָּילִין קַדִּישִׁין דְּמִתְפַּשְּׁטֵי
מֵהַהוּא פְּנֵי שׁוֹר, מִתְקָרְבִין לִיסוֹדָא דִּלְהוֹן, וְאִתְהֲנוּן מֵהַהוּא יְסוֹדָא
וּלְבוּשָׁא דִּלְהוֹן. וְאִי לָא דַּהֲווֹ לְהוּ יְסוֹדָא דְּהַאי עָלְמָא, לָא מִתְקָרְבִין
תַּמָּן.

534. From the face of an ox, WHICH IS THE SECRET OF THE LEFT, spreads a spirit to the animals, to four species, that are included in each other, as one, namely; oxen, sheep, rams and goats, and these serve for the sacrifices. And since THE SACRIFICE is from them, these holy hosts that spread out from the face of that ox, and draw close, BY THE ACT OF SACRIFICE, to their element, WHICH IS THE FACE OF AN OX, and benefit from that element and their apparel. And were it not that they contain the element of this world, WHICH IS THE SACRIFICE THAT ASCENDS TO THEM, they would not draw close there, TO THEIR ELEMENT, WHICH IS THE FACE OF AN OX.

535. כְּגַוְונָא דַּהֲוֵי נַיְיחָא לִשְׁכִינְתָּא קַדִּישָׁא, מֵרוּחֵיהוֹן דְּצַדִּיקַיָּיא, וְאִתְקְרִיבַת לְקַבְּלָא רוּחָא דְּהַהוּא זַכָּאָה, וְאִתְהֲנָאַת מִנֵּיהּ, בְּגִין דְּמִנָּהּ הֲוָה הַהוּא רוּחַ. כַּךְ אִלֵּין אִתְהֲנוּן מִסִּטְרָא דִּיסוֹדָא דִּלְהוֹן, וְאִתְהֲנוּן מֵהַהוּא לְבוּשָׁא דְּמִתְקָרְבֵי לֵיהּ, דְּהָא רוּחַ מַלְבּוּשָׁא דְּרוּחָא דִּלְהוֹן הֲוָה. ובג"כ אִתְהֲנוּן מִנַּיְיהוּ.

535. And just as the Holy Shechinah takes pleasure in the spirits of the righteous THAT ASCEND HER AS MAYIN NUKVIN, and She draws her to welcome the spirit of a righteous person, and enjoys it because that spirit is drawn from her, so is it also with those HOSTS THAT SPREAD FORTH FROM THE FACE OF AN OX. They benefit from the aspect of their element, WHICH IS THE FACE OF AN OX, and from that raiment that is offered TO THEIR ELEMENT, WHICH IS THE SACRIFICE, for the spirit OF THE SACRIFICE is from the raiment of their spirit, which is why they enjoy it.

536. פְּנֵי נֶשֶׁר אִתְפָּשַׁט לְעוֹפָא רוּחַ מִנֵּיהּ. וְנֶשֶׁר בִּתְרֵין סִטְרִין אִיהוּ. וְרָזָא דָּא וְעוֹף יְעוֹפֵף, תְּרֵין רוּחִין. וּבְגִין כַּךְ אִתְפָּשַׁט וְנַחְתָּא מִימִינָא

וּמִשְׂמָאלָא קָרְבְּנָא דְעוֹפֵי.

536. From the face of an eagle spreads a spirit to the fowl, FOR THE SPIRIT THAT IS IN THE FOWL IS DRAWN FROM THE FACE OF AN EAGLE. And an eagle is on two sides, ON THE RIGHT AND ON THE LEFT, FOR EAGLE IS TIFERET, THE CENTRAL COLUMN THAT INCLUDES THE RIGHT AND THE LEFT. And this is the secret of "And let birds fly" (Beresheet 1:20) WHICH INDICATES two spirits. For this reason, the sacrifice of fowl spreads out and descends from the right and from the left. WHILE THE SACRIFICE OF CATTLE IS ONLY FROM THE FACE OF AN OX, WHICH IS THE LEFT, AS ABOVE, THE SACRIFICE OF FOWL IS FROM THE FACE OF AN EAGLE THAT INCLUDES THE TWO COLUMNS.

537. מִכָּל סְטָר דַּכְיָא, לָא אִתְקְרִיב אֶלָּא יוֹנָה וְתוֹרִים, דְּאִינּוּן בְּקִשּׁוֹט לְזִוּוּגַיְיהוּ, מִכָּל שְׁאַר עוֹפִין. וְהֵם נִרְדָּפִין, וְלָא רוֹדְפִין. וּמְהֵימְנָא דָא לְדָא, נוּקְבָּא לְבַר זוּגוֹ. וע״ד קָרְבְּנָא מִנַּיְיהוּ. וְנַחְתֵּי וּמִתְקָרְבֵי אִינּוּן רוּחִין קַדִּישִׁין, וְאִתְהַנְיָין מִיְּסוֹדָא וְעִקָרָא דִּלְהוֹן.

537. Of all the pure aspects OF FOWL, only a dove and turtle-doves are sacrificed, because they are true to their partners more than all the other fowl. And they are preyed upon but do not prey; they are faithful to each other, the female to her partner, and therefore the sacrifice is of them. And those holy spirits descend and draw near and enjoy their element and essence, AS ABOVE.

538. וְאִי תֵּימָא, הֵיךְ אִתְפְּשַׁט זְעֵיר מֵהַאי יוֹנָה, אוֹ מִשַּׁפְנִינָא דָּא, לְכַמָּה סִטְרִין חַיָּילִין דְּלֵית לוֹן שִׁיעוּרָא. אוֹ מִן בְּעִירָא חֲדָא אוֹף הָכִי. ת״ח. חַד שְׁרָגָא דָּקִיק דָּלִיק, אִתְמַלְיָיא מִנֵּיהּ כָּל עָלְמָא. תּוּ אָעָא דָּקִיק, אַדְלִיק לְרַבְרְבָא.

538. And you might well ask: How can the little that ascends from the dove or from the turtledove spread out in the number of directions to the hosts on high who are without measure? AND THE SAME QUESTION CAN BE ASKED ABOUT WHAT ASCENDS of the single animal. HE ANSWERS: Come and see,

the whole world fills with light from one thin burning candle. Again: One thin piece of wood enkindles a large piece.

539. עַד הָכָא קָרְבְּנָא מִתְּרֵין סִטְרִין דְּחָקִיקִין בְּכֻּרְסְיָיא. הַשְׁתָּא אִית לְמִשְׁאַל, ד' דְּיוֹקְנִין אִינּוּן, דְּחָקוּקִין בְּכֻרְסְיָא, מ"ט לֵית קָרְבְּנִין מֵאַחֲרָנִין. אֶלָּא וַדַּאי מִכֻּלְּהוּ אִית קָרְבְּנָא. אַרְיֵה חָקוּק בְּכֻרְסְיָיא, בְּשַׁעֲתָא דְּקָרְבְּנָא שְׁלִים, אַרְיֵה נָחִית וְעָאל בְּאֶשָּׁא, וְאָכִיל וְאִתְהֲנֵי מִתַּמָּן. אָדָם חָקוּק בְּכֻרְסְיָיא, אָדָם עִקָּרָא דְּכֹלָּא, וּמַקְרִיב תַּמָּן רוּחֵיהּ וְנִשְׁמָתֵיהּ, וְאָדָם עִלָּאָה אִתְהֲנֵי מֵאָדָם תַּתָּאָה, וְכָל זִינָא אִתְקְרִיב לְזִינֵיהּ, וְאִתְהֲנֵי מִנֵּיהּ מִדִּילֵיהּ מַמָּשׁ, וּמִיסוֹדָא דִּילֵיהּ.

539. So far the sacrifice HAS BEEN CLARIFIED from two sides engraved on the Throne, NAMELY FROM THE FACE OF AN OX FOR CATTLE, AND FROM THE FACE OF AN EAGLE FOR FOWL. Now the question has to be put: There are four shapes that are engraved on the Throne, so what is the reason for there being no sacrifice from shapes of the other FORMS? HE ANSWERS, There is certainly sacrifice from all of them. The lion that is engraved on the Throne: When the sacrifice is perfect, the lion descends and enters the fire, eats and has enjoyment from there. And as for the man that is engraved on the Throne: Man is the essence of all of them, and he sacrifices there TO THE FACE OF A MAN, WHICH IS MALCHUT, his spirit and his soul, and upper man benefits from lower man. And each species draws near to its own and benefits from it, from that which is really its own, and from its own element.

540. וְאִי תֵּימָא, הָא אַרְיֵה דְּלֵית לֵיהּ יְסוֹדָא לְתַתָּא בְּהַהוּא קָרְבְּנָא. אַרְיֵה כָּלִיל בְּכֻלְּהוּ, דְּהָא לִימִינָא הֲוֵי, וּבְג"כ אָכִיל בְּכֻלְּהוּ, וְכָל שְׁאַר לָא אָכְלִין מִזִּינֵיהּ, בְּגִין דִּימִינָא הוּא. הָא כָּל ד' דְּיוֹקְנִין דְּחָקוּקִין בְּכֻרְסְיָא, מִתְקָרְבִין לְקָרְבְּנָא, וּבְג"כ הֲוֵי קָרְבְּנָא שְׁלִים. וְכַד אִתְהֲנוּן מֵעִקָּרָא וִיסוֹדָא דִּלְהוֹן, כְּדֵין נַחַת רוּחַ לְאַדְלְקָא בּוּצִינִין עִלָּאִין.

540. You might well ask: But lion has no basis below in the sacrifice, WHILE THE FACE OF AN OX HAS A BASIS BELOW, IN THE ANIMALS; THE FACE OF AN EAGLE HAS A BASIS BELOW, IN THE BIRDS; THE FACE OF A MAN

HAS A BASIS BELOW, IN THE SPIRIT AND SOUL OF THE MAN OFFERING THE SACRIFICE, BUT THE LION HAS NO BASIS BELOW AT ALL. AND HE ANSWERS, lion is included in all of them, for it is on the right, WHICH IS CHESED, AND CHESED INCLUDES ALL OF THEM. For this reason, it eats from all of them THAT ARE BELOW IT, while the others, OX, EAGLE, AND MAN, do not eat from its species, because it is to the right AND HIGHER THAN THEY. Thus, all four of the forms that are engraved on the Throne come close to the sacrifice, which is why it is a perfect sacrifice. And when they enjoy their principle and element, then a spirit descends to kindle the upper candles, NAMELY THE UNION IS MADE BETWEEN ZEIR ANPIN AND MALCHUT.

541. כַּהֲנֵי וְלֵיוָאֵי וְיִשְׂרָאֵלִי, יָהֲבֵי יְסוֹדָא וְעִקָּרָא לְאִינּוּן דַּרְגִּין עִלָּאִין דִּלְהוֹן. וְכָל דַּרְגָּא יָהִיב לִיסוֹדֵיהּ ד' דְּיוּקְנִין דְּכוּרְסַיָּיא בְּקַדְמֵיתָא. כִּדְאָמַרָן זִינָא לָקֳבֵל זִינֵיהּ, וּמִתְקָרְבֵי אִינּוּן בְּקַדְמֵיתָא זִינָא לְזִינֵיהּ. פְּנֵי שׁוֹר כֻּלְּהוּ פָנִים דְּמִתְפַּשְּׁטָן לְאִינּוּן זִינִין כִּדְקָאֲמָרָן, כֻּלְּהוּ מִתְקָרְבֵי לְעִקָּרָא וְיִסוֹדָא דִּלְהוֹן. פְּנֵי נֶשֶׁר, כִּדְאָמַרָן. פְּנֵי אַרְיֵה, כִּדְאָמַרָן. פְּנֵי אָדָם, דְּמַקְרִיב רוּחֵיהּ וְנִשְׁמָתֵיהּ מִתְקְרִיב לְגַבֵּי אָדָם עִלָּאָה.

541. Priests, Levites and Yisrael give a basis and principle to the upper grades from which THEY ARE DRAWN, and each grade gives to its element ON HIGH. First, the four shapes of the Throne, as we have said IN THE PRECEDING PARAGRAPH, each species unto its like, are they first to draw near, like unto like. The face of an ox, all the faces, NAMELY THE HOSTS AND CAMPS, that spread out to those species, as we have noted, all of them draw near to their principle and element, THE FACE OF AN OX. AND SIMILARLY FOR THE face of an eagle it is as we have noted. SO, TOO, WITH the face of a lion it is as we have noted AS WELL AS the face of a man who offers a sacrifice, his spirit and soul approaching to the upper man, WHICH IS MALCHUT.

542. כַּהֲנָא דִּמְיַחֵד שְׁמָא קַדִּישָׁא, מִתְקְרִיב לְגַבֵּי כַּהֲנָא עִלָּאָה. הַהוּא דְּעָאל לְבֵית קֹדֶשׁ הַקֳּדָשִׁים. וְאִתְקְרִיב דָּא, וְאַדְלִיק בְּתִקּוּנֵיהּ בִּנְהִירוּ דְּאַנְפִּין, לְקַדְמוּת כַּהֲנָא דִּלְתַתָּא. לֵיוָאֵי דִי מְנַגְּנֵי בְּחֶדְוָה, הַהוּא סִטְרָא דִּלְהוֹן חַדֵי, וְאַנְהִיר אַנְפִּין. יִשְׂרָאֵל דְּקָרִיב, דְּקַיְימוּ עַל קָרְבְּנָא

בִּצְלוֹתָא, דְּהָא צְלוֹתָא עַל כֹּלָּא הֲוָה. אִתְּעַר לְגַבַּיְיהוּ יִשְׂרָאֵל סָבָא, סְתָמָא קַדִּישָׁא, וְאַנְהִיר אַנְפִּין.

542. The priest who pronounces the unity of the Holy Name OVER THE SACRIFICE is himself approaching to the upper priest, WHICH IS CHESED OF ZEIR ANPIN, the same that enters the house of the Holy of Holies, WHICH IS YESOD OF MALCHUT, and he draws close to the latter and kindles THE CANDLES OF MALCHUT by his being complete with a shining countenance, corresponding to the priest below WHO OFFERS THE SACRIFICE. When the Levites play their instruments happily WHEN THE SACRIFICE IS MADE, their side, WHICH IS GVURAH OF ZEIR ANPIN, rejoices and illuminates the faces. Yisrael, who bring the sacrifices – who begin to pray over the sacrifice, for prayer was ordained for all THE SACRIFICES – awakens Yisrael-Saba, the Holy Indefinite, towards them and Yisrael-Saba welcomes them.

543. כָּל זִינָא לְזִינֵיהּ, וְכָל מִלָּה בָּתַר יְסוֹדָא דִּילֵיהּ אַזְלָא וְאִתְּעֲרוּ דַּרְגִּין תַּתָּאִין לְדַרְגִּין עִלָּאִין, וְאע"ג דְּכֻלְּהוּ מִתְעָרִין, וְאִתְּעֲרוּ דַּרְגִּין דְּחָקִיקִין בְּכֻסָּא, לְגַבֵּי דַּרְגִּין דְּאַרְעָא, יְסוֹדָא דִּלְהוֹן. וְאִינּוּן דַּרְגִּין עִלָּאִין דְּמִטַּמְרָן, כֻּלְּהוּ מִתְעָרֵי וּמִתְקָרְבֵי לִסְעוּדָתָא, וּמִתְעַדְּנֵי. אֲבָל לֵית רְשׁוּ לְחַד מִנַּיְיהוּ לְמֵיכַל, לָא לְדַרְגֵּי עִלָּאֵי, וְלָא לְדַרְגֵּי תַּתָּאֵי, וּלְמִתְהֲנֵי שׁוּם הֲנָאָה, וְלָא לְאוֹשִׁיט יְדָא בְּקָרְבָּנָא, עַד דְּמַלְכָּא עִלָּאָה אָכִיל וְאִתְהֲנֵי, וִיהִיב לוֹן רְשׁוּ.

543. And each species is sacrificed to its own kind, and everything follows its element ON HIGH. The lower grades awaken the higher grades, and although all of them awaken, and the grades that are engraved on the Throne, WHICH ARE THE FOUR LIVING CREATURES, awaken towards the grades that are on earth, being their basis, NAMELY THE FACE OF AN OX FOR ANIMALS, THE FACE OF AN EAGLE FOR FOWL, AS ABOVE, and also those upper hidden grades, they all stir and come close for the meal OF THE SACRIFICE and find pleasure; yet none of them has permission to eat, neither the higher grades nor the lower grades, and not to enjoy it, nor to put out a hand to the sacrifice, until after the Supernal King, WHO IS ZEIR ANPIN, has eaten and enjoyed it, and given them permission.

544. לְבָתַר דְּיָהַב לוֹן רְשׁוּ, כָּל חַד וְחַד אִתְהֲנֵי וְאָכִיל. וְהַיְינוּ דִּכְתִיב אֲרִיתִי מוֹרִי עִם בְּשָׂמִי, אִלֵּין אִינּוּן דַּרְגִּין עִלָּאִין. מוֹרִי עִם בְּשָׂמִי, אָכְלֵי וְאִתְהֲנֵי כְּדְקָא יָאוּת. דָּא דְּרוֹעָא יְמִינָא, בִּירַכָא שְׂמָאלָא. אָכַלְתִּי יַעֲרִי עִם דִּבְשִׁי, דָּא יַעֲקֹב בְּרָחֵל, דָּא אֲכִילָה כְּדְקָא יָאוּת. שָׁתִיתִי יֵינִי עִם חֲלָבִי, דָּא דְּרוֹעָא שְׂמָאלָא, בִּירַכָא יְמִינָא. הָא כֻּלְּהוּ דַּרְגִּין עִלָּאִין, דְּאִתְהֲנֵי בְּהוּ מַלְכָּא קַדִּישָׁא בְּקַדְמֵיתָא. וְדָא מֵיכְלָא דִּילֵיהּ וַהֲנָאָה דִּילֵיהּ. עַד הָכָא מֵיכְלָא דְּמַלְכָּא עִלָּאָה בְּקַדְמֵיתָא.

544. After He gives them permission, each one of them enjoys it and eats, this being as it is written: "I have gathered my myrrh with my spice" (Shir Hashirim 5:1). These are the upper grades OF ZEIR ANPIN; "my myrrh and my spice" – that eat and enjoy as is fitting, and this is THE UNITY OF the right arm, WHICH IS CHESED, with the left leg, WHICH IS HOD. "I have eaten my honeycomb with my honey": This is Jacob with Rachel, NAMELY THE UNITY OF TIFERET WITH MALCHUT. And this is eating proper, FOR ONLY HERE IS THE WORD "EAT" USED. "I have drunk my wine with my milk." This is the unity of the left arm with the right leg, NAMELY GVURAH WITH NETZACH. And these are all the upper grades from which the Holy King has enjoyment first. AND THIS IS HIS EATING AND HIS PLEASURE. So far we have discussed the food of the Supernal King, who eats first.

545. מִכָּאן וּלְהָלְאָה, יָהִיב רְשׁוּ לְד' דְּיוֹקְנִין דְּחָקִיקִין בְּכוּרְסַיָּיא, וּלְכָל אִינּוּן דְּמִתְפַּשְּׁטָן מִנַּיְיהוּ, לְאִתְהֲנֵי וּלְמֵיכַל. הה"ד, אִכְלוּ רֵעִים שְׁתוּ וְשִׁכְרוּ דּוֹדִים. אִכְלוּ רֵעִים, אִלֵּין אִינּוּן אַרְבַּע דְּיוֹקְנִין דְּאֲמָרָן. שְׁתוּ וְשִׁכְרוּ דּוֹדִים, כָּל אִינּוּן דְּמִתְפַּשְּׁטֵי מִנַּיְיהוּ, וְכֻלְּהוּ אָכְלֵי וּמִתְפַּשְּׁטֵי, וְאִתְהֲנוּן כְּדְקָא יָאוּת, וְאַנְהִירוּ אַנְפִּין, וְעָלְמִין כֻּלְּהוּ בְּחֶדְוָה, וְכָל חַד וְחַד, בֵּין דַּרְגִּין עִלָּאִין, וּבֵין דַּרְגִּין תַּתָּאִין, בִּיסוֹדָא דִּלְהוֹן מִתְקָרְבִין וּמִתְהֲנִין. דָּא אִיהוּ רָזָא וְסִתְרָא דְּקָרְבְּנָא כְּדְקָא חֲזֵי.

545. From this point on, THE King, WHO IS ZEIR ANPIN, gives permission to the four forms that are engraved on the Throne, and to all those that spread out from them, to enjoy and eat. For the verse continues: "Eat, O dear ones; drink, drink deep, loving companions" (Ibid.). "Eat, O dear ones"

are four forms that we have mentioned: LION, OX, EAGLE, MAN. "Drink, drink deep, loving friends" meaning all those who spread out from them, and they all eat, stretch out and enjoy as is fitting, and their faces shine. And all the worlds rejoice, and each one, whether at the upper levels or at the lower levels, draws closer to its element, NAMELY EACH ONE TO ITS PARALLEL ASPECT: CHESED TO THE FACE OF A LION; GVURAH TO THE FACE OF AN OX..., and they enjoy. This is the secret and mystery of the sacrifices in a proper manner.

546. אָתוּ ר' אֶלְעָזָר וְר' אַבָּא וּשְׁאָר חַבְרַיָּיא, וְאִשְׁתְּטָחוּ קַמֵּיהּ. א"ר אַבָּא, אִלְמָלֵא לָא אִתְמְסַר אוֹרַיְיתָא בְּטוּרָא דְּסִינַי, אֶלָּא דְּאָמַר קוּדְשָׁא בְּרִיךְ הוּא, הָא בַּר יוֹחָאי אוֹרַיְיתָא וְסִתְרִין דִּילִי, דַּיֵּי לְעָלְמָא. וַוי כַּד תִּסְתְּלַק מִן עָלְמָא. מָן יַנְהִיר בּוּצִינִין דְּאוֹרַיְיתָא, בְּלָא יִתְחֲשַׁךְ מֵהַהוּא יוֹמָא. דְּהָא עַד דְּיֵיתֵי מַלְכָּא מְשִׁיחָא, לָא לֶיהֱוֵי דָּרָא כְּדָרָא דָּא, דר"ש שָׁרֵי בְּגַוֵּויהּ.

546. Rabbi Elazar and Rabbi Aba, together with the other companions, came and prostrated themselves before him, BEFORE RABBI SHIMON. Rabbi Aba said, Had the Torah not been given at Mount Sinai, but instead the Holy One, blessed be He, had said: 'Here is the son of Yochai TO GIVE YOU the Torah and My secrets, it would have sufficed for the world'. Woe for when you depart from the world! Who will then kindle the lights of the Torah? Everything will be in darkness from that day! For until the arrival of King Messiah there will be no generation such as this generation, in whose midst is Rabbi Shimon!

547 אָמַר ר"ש, עַל רָזָא דָּא, אָסִיר לֵיהּ לב"נ לִטְעוֹם כְּלוּם, כַּד דְּיֵיכוּל מַלְכָּא עִלָּאָה, וּמַה אִיהוּ. צְלוֹתָא. צְלוֹתָא דב"נ, כְּגַוְונָא דָּא, בְּקַדְמֵיתָא, מְזַמְּנִין לְדִיוּקְנִין דְּחָקִיקִין בְּכוּרְסְיָיא, עַל אִינּוּן בִּרְיָין, דְּמִתְפַּשְּׁטֵי רוּחִין דִּלְהוֹן, עַל עוֹפֵי וּבְעִירֵי, לְקָרְבְּנָא בִּרְיָין דְּרוּחָא דִּלְהוֹן יְסוֹדָא בְּהַאי עָלְמָא מִנַּיְיהוּ, וְהַיְינוּ מָה רַבּוּ מַעֲשֶׂיךְ יְיָ', דְּהָא בִּרְיָין דְּאִתְחֲזָון לְקָרְבְּנָא רוּחָא דִּילְהוֹן, מִתְפַּשְּׁט עֲלַיְיהוּ אַרְבַּע דִּיוּקְנִין, מְזַמְּנָן עַל קָרְבְּנִין אִלֵּין. וְהַיְינוּ דְּקָאַמְרָן, וְהָאוֹפַנִּים וְחַיּוֹת

הַקֹּדֶשׁ, וְכָל אִינּוּן חַיָּילִין אַחֲרָנִין דְּקָא מִתְפַּשְּׁטֵי מִנַּיְיהוּ.

547. Rabbi Shimon said concerning THE ABOVE MENTIONED secret, a man is forbidden to taste anything until the Supreme King has eaten. And what is meant by HIS EATING? This means prayer, WHICH IS IN THE STEAD OF SACRIFICES. A man's prayer is similar in respect TO WHAT WE SAID ABOVE ABOUT THE SACRIFICES. First the four forms that are engraved on the Throne are invited, THAT THEY SHOULD DWELL over these creatures, over the fowl and the animals, for the spirits OF THE FOUR LIVING CREATURES spread out over them so that they should be sacrifices, FOR THEY ARE creatures the basis of whose spirit in this world is of them, OF THE FOUR LIVING CREATURES, and that is: "Hashem, how manifold are Your works" (Tehilim 104:24). For over the creatures whose spirit is suitable for sacrifice spread out the four forms THAT ARE IN THE THRONE, which are come over these sacrifices. And it is to this that we refer when we say 'The wheels and holy living creatures'. FOR THIS IS THE SECRET OF THE FOUR LIVING CREATURES THAT ARE IN THE THRONE, and all those other hosts who spread out from them, TO WHICH ARE JOINED THE SPIRIT OF ANIMALS AND FOWL THAT ARE FIT FOR OFFERING AS SACRIFICES.

548. וּלְבָתַר כַּהֲנָא רַבָּא דְּקָא מְיַיחֵד שְׁמָא קַדִּישָׁא, הַיְינוּ אַהֲבַת עוֹלָם אֲהַבְתָּנוּ וְכוּ'. יִחוּדָא דְּקָא מְיַיחֵד, הַיְינוּ שְׁמַע יִשְׂרָאֵל יְיָ' אֱלֹהֵינוּ יְיָ' אֶחָד. וּלְבָתַר לֵיוָאֵי, דְּקָא מִתְעָרֵי לְנַגּוּנָא, הַיְינוּ וְהָיָה אִם שָׁמוֹעַ וְגוֹ', הִשָּׁמְרוּ לָכֶם פֶּן יִפְתֶּה וְגוֹ'. דָּא נִגּוּנָא דְּלֵיוָאֵי, בְּגִין לְאִתְעָרָא סִטְרָא דָּא, בְּקוֹרְבָּנָא דָּא. וּלְבָתַר יִשְׂרָאֵל, דָּא אֱמֶת וְיַצִּיב וְנָכוֹן, יִשְׂרָאֵל סָבָא דְּקַיְימָא עַל קָרְבְּנָא, דְּאִיהִי יְ' דַּרְגִּין עִלָּאִין פְּנִימָאִין דְּכֹלָּא, קַיְימָא עַל פָּתוֹרָא.

548. And afterwards the High Priest proclaims the unity of the Holy Name, namely 'With abounding love', WHERE LOVE IS CHESED, THE ATTRIBUTE OF THE PRIEST. The unity THAT THE PRIEST PROCLAIMS IS: "Hear, O Yisrael, Hashem our Elohim, Hashem is one" (Devarim 6:4). And afterwards the Levites arise to play the music, which is: "And it shall come to pass, if you hearken diligently to My commandments..." (Devarim 11:13). "Take heed to yourselves, that your heart be not deceived..." (Devarim 16-21)

WHICH PORTION PARALLELS THE LEFT WHICH IS GVURAH. For this is the melody of the Levites, THAT IS TO SAY THAT THE SIGNING OF THE LEVITES IS FROM THE LEFT, in order to awaken this side, THE SIDE OF THE LEFT with this sacrifice, NAMELY, WITH THE PRAYER THAT IS IN PLACE OF THE SACRIFICE. And then come Yisrael with: 'True and firm, established and enduring', WHICH ALLUDES TO Yisrael-Saba, who stands over the sacrifice. For He, the ten upper inner levels to everything, NAMELY THE TEN SFIROT, is at the table WHILE THEY ARE, TRUE AND FIRM AND ESTABLISHED AND ENDURING.

549. אֲבָל לֵית רְשׁוּ לְחַד מִנַּיְיהוּ לְמֵיכַל, וּלְאוֹשִׁיט יְדָא לְקָרְבְּנָא, עַד דְּמַלְכָּא עִלָּאָה אָכִיל. וְהַיְינוּ ג׳ רִאשׁוֹנוֹת, וְג׳ אַחֲרוֹנוֹת. כֵּיוָן דְּאִיהוּ אָכִיל, יָהִיב רְשׁוּ לְד׳ דִּיוּקְנִין, וּלְכָל אִינּוּן סִטְרִין דְּמִתְפָּרְשָׁן מִנַּיְיהוּ, לְמֵיכַל.

549. But not one of them has permission to eat and to stretch a hand out to the sacrifice, NAMELY THE PRAYER, until the Supernal King, WHO IS ZEIR ANPIN, has eaten, by which is meant the first three blessings and the last three blessings OF THE AMIDAH PRAYER, WHICH IS WHERE THE UNION OF ZEIR ANPIN AND MALCHUT TAKES PLACE, AND THIS IS THE SECRET OF THE KING'S EATING. After He has eaten, He grants permission to the four forms, NAMELY THE FOUR LIVING CREATURES IN THE THRONE, and to all those parties that spread out from them, to eat.

550. כְּדֵין אָדָם, דְּאִיהוּ דִּיוּקְנָא דְּכָלִיל כָּל שְׁאַר דִּיוּקְנִין, מָאִיךְ וְנָפִיל עַל אַנְפּוֹי, וּמָסִיר גַּרְמֵיהּ וְרוּחֵיהּ לְגַבֵּי אָדָם דִּלְעֵילָא, דְּקַיְימָא עַל אִינּוּן דִּיוּקְנִין, דְּכָלִיל כָּל דִּיוּקְנִין, לְאִתְעָרָא לֵיהּ עֲלֵיהּ כַּדְקָא חֲזֵי, וְהַיְינוּ אֵלֶיךָ יְיָ׳ נַפְשִׁי אֶשָּׂא, לְאִתְעָרָא דִּיוּקְנִין אַחֲרָנִין, וְכָל אִינּוּן דְּמִתְפַּשְׁטֵי מִנַּיְיהוּ. וְהַיְינוּ יַבִּיעוּ. יְרַנְּנוּ. יֹאמְרוּ. יְדַבֵּרוּ. וְכֻלְּהוּ אַכְלִין וְאִתְהַנְיָין כָּל חַד וְחַד כַּדְקָא חֲזֵי לֵיהּ.

550. And then man, who is the form that includes all the other forms, lowers himself, and throws himself on his face and gives himself and his spirit to Supernal Man who stands over these forms and who includes all the forms,

that he should awaken towards him as is fitting. And this is what is meant by SAYING: "To You, Hashem, do I lift up my soul" (Tehilim 25:1), namely in order to awaken other forms and all those who spread out from them. And this is what is meant WHEN SAYING IN "A PRAISE OF DAVID" (TEHILIM 145): "They shall utter...and shall sing" (Ibid. 7); and "They shall speak...and talk" (Ibid. 11). And they all eat and enjoy THE PRAYER, each one as is fitting for him.

551. מִכָּאן וּלְהָלְאָה לֵימָא ב״נ עָאקוּ דְּלִבֵּיהּ, הה״ד יַעַנְךָ יְיָ׳ בְּיוֹם צָרָה. כְּעוּבַּרְתָּא דְּיַתְבָא בְּעָאקוּ, לְאִתְהַפְּכָא כֻּלְּהוֹן סַנֵּיגוֹרִין עָלֵיהּ דב״נ. וע״ד כְּתִיב אַשְׁרֵי הָעָם שֶׁכָּכָה לוֹ וְגוֹ׳.

551. From here on a man may mention the troubles that are in his heart, as it is written: "May Hashem hear you in the day of trouble" (Tehilim 20:2), for example, a pregnant woman in labor, so that they should all become advocates for the person. Therefore, it is written: "Happy is the people that is in such a case" (Tehilim 144:15).

552. ר״ש הֲוָה אָזִיל לִטְבֶרְיָא, פָּגַע בֵּיהּ אֵלִיָּהוּ, א״ל שְׁלָמָא עָלֵיהּ דְּמַר. א״ל ר״ש, בְּמַאי קָא עָסִיק קוּדְשָׁא בְּרִיךְ הוּא בִּרְקִיעָא. א״ל בְּקָרְבְּנוֹת עָסִיק, וְאָמַר מִלִּין חַדְתִּין מִשְׁמָךְ, זַכָּאָה אַנְתְּ, וַאֲתֵינָא לְאַקְדְּמָא לָךְ שְׁלָם, וּמִלָּה חֲדָא בָּעֵינָא לְמִשְׁאַל מִנָּךְ, לְאַסְבְּמָא. בְּמְתִיבְתָּא דִּרְקִיעָא שְׁאֶלְתָּא שָׁאִילוּ, עָלְמָא דְּאָתֵי לֵית בֵּיהּ אֲכִילָה וּשְׁתִיָּה, וְהָא כְּתִיב בָּאתִי לְגַנִּי אֲחוֹתִי כַלָּה וְגוֹ׳, אָכַלְתִּי יַעְרִי עִם דִּבְשִׁי וְגוֹ׳. מַאן דְּלֵית בֵּיהּ אֲכִילָה וּשְׁתִיָּה, אִיהוּ אָמַר אָכַלְתִּי יַעְרִי עִם דִּבְשִׁי שָׁתִיתִי יֵינִי עִם חֲלָבִי.

552. Rabbi Shimon was on his way to Tiberias when Elijah met him and said, Greetings, sir. Rabbi Shimon said to him: With what is the Holy One, blessed be He engaged in the firmament? Elijah replied: He is occupied with the sacrifices, and saying new things in your name. Happy are you! And I came to welcome you with greetings, and there is one thing that I wanted to ask you to settle for me. A question has been asked in the Yeshivah of the firmament: In the World to Come there is no eating and drinking, yet it is

written: "I am come into my garden, my sister, my bride; I have gathered my myrrh with my spice; I have eaten my honeycomb with my honey..." (Shir Hashirim 5:1). Would one for whom there is no eating nor drinking say: "I have eaten my honeycomb with my honey; I have drunk my wine with my milk?"

553. אר"ש, וְקוּדְשָׁא בְּרִיךְ הוּא מַאי קָא אָתִיב לוֹן. א"ל, אָמַר קוּדְשָׁא בְּרִיךְ הוּא, הָא בַּר יוֹחָאי יֵימָא. וַאֲתֵינָא לְמִשְׁאַל מִנָךְ. אר"ש, כַּמָה חֲבִיבוּ חֲבַב קוּדְשָׁא בְּרִיךְ הוּא לִכְנֶסֶת יִשְׂרָאֵל, וּמִסַגִיאוּ דִּרְחִימוּ דִּרְחִים לָה, שַׁנֵּי עוֹבָדוֹי מִמַּה דְהוּא עָבִיד. דאע"ג דְּלָאו אוֹרְחוֹי בְּמֵיכְלָא וּמִשְׁתַּיָּיא, בְּגִין רְחִימוּתָא, אָכִיל וְשָׁתָה. הוֹאִיל וְאָתֵי לְגַבָּה, עָבֵיד רְעוּתָה. כַּלָּה עַיֶּילַת לַחוּפָּה, וּבָעַת לְמֵיכַל, לֵית דִּין דְּיֵיכוּל חַתְנָה בַּהֲדָה, אע"ג דְּלָאו אָרְחֵיה לְמֶעְבַּד הָכִי. הה"ד בָּאתִי לְגַנִּי אֲחוֹתִי כַלָּה. הוֹאִיל וְאֲתֵינָא לְגַבָּה, וּלְמֵיעַל בַּהֲדָה לַחוּפָּה, אָכַלְתִּי יַעְרִי עִם דִּבְשִׁי וְגוֹ'.

553. Said Rabbi Shimon: And what did the Holy One, blessed be He, reply to them? Elijah answered: The Holy One, blessed be He, said, 'There IS the son of Yochai. Let him tell you!' So I came to ask you. Rabbi Shimon said: In what great affection did the Holy One, blessed be He, hold the Congregation of Yisrael, and out of the intense love with which He loved her, He altered his deeds from the way He had been NORMALLY doing. For, although He does not usually eat and drink, NEVERTHELESS, because of the love of her, He ate and drank. Since He had come to her, He did as she wanted. If a bride just entering the wedding canopy wants to eat, does it not follow that her bridegroom will eat with her, even if he is not used to doing so? This is what is written: "I have come into my garden, my sister, my bride." Since I have come to her, to go with her into the wedding canopy, "I have eaten my honeycomb with my honey; I have drunk my wine with my milk."

554. וְיַלְפֵינָן מִדָּוִד, דְּזַמִּין לְקוּדְשָׁא בְּרִיךְ הוּא, וְשַׁנֵּי עוֹבָדוֹי מִמַּה דְאָרְחוֹי דְקוּדְשָׁא בְּרִיךְ הוּא, וְקוּדְשָׁא בְּרִיךְ הוּא קַבִּיל וְעָבֵיד רְעוּתֵיה. זַמִּין לְמַלְכָּא וּמַטְרוֹנִיתָא בַּהֲדֵיה, הֲדָא הוּא דִכְתִיב קוּמָה יְיָ' לִמְנוּחָתֶךָ אַתָּה וַאֲרוֹן עוּזֶּךָ. מַלְכָּא וּמַטְרוֹנִיתָא כַּחֲדָא, בְּגִין דְּלָא לְאַפְרָשָׁא לוֹן,

שָׁנֵּי מָאנִין, וְשָׁנֵּי עוֹבָדִין דְּמַלְכָּא.

554. And we can learn this also from David, who invited the Holy One, blessed be He, and changed his actions from the way the Holy One, blessed be He, was accustomed, and the Holy One, blessed be He, accepted it and did as he wanted, for he (David) invited the King, together with the Queen, as it is written: "Arise, Hashem, to Your resting place; You and the ark of Your strength" (Tehilim 132:8), namely the King together with the Queen. And in order not to make any separation between them, he changed the vessels, and he altered the customs of the King.

555. הה״ד, כֹּהֲנֶיךָ יִלְבְּשׁוּ צֶדֶק וַחֲסִידֶיךָ יְרַנֵּנוּ בַּעֲבוּר דָּוִד וְגוֹ', כֹּהֲנֶיךָ יִלְבְּשׁוּ צֶדֶק, לְוִיֶּיךָ מִבָּעֵי לֵיהּ, דְּהָא צֶדֶק מִסִּטְרָא דִּלְוָאֵי אִיהוּ. וַחֲסִידֶיךָ יְרַנֵּנוּ, לְוִיֶּיךָ יְרַנֵּנוּ מִבָּעֵי לֵיהּ, דְּהָא רִנָּה וְזִמְרָה בִּלְוָאֵי נִינְהוּ, וְאִיהוּ שָׁנֵּי וְאָמַר, כֹּהֲנֶיךָ וַחֲסִידֶיךָ, דְּאִינּוּן מִסִּטְרָא דִּימִינָא.

555. This is what is written: "Let Your priests be clothed with righteousness; and Your pious ones shout for joy. For Your servant David's sake, turn not away the face of Your anointed" (Ibid. 9). It should have said: 'Let Your Levites be clothed with righteousness', and not: "Let Your priests be clothed with righteousness," since righteousness is from the side of the Levites; NAMELY MALCHUT FROM THE ASPECT OF THE LEFT IS CALLED 'RIGHTEOUSNESS', AND THE LEFT IS THE ASPECT OF THE LEVITES. Similarly, it should have said: 'and Your Levites shout for joy', and not: "and Your pious ones shout for joy," since joyous melody and song are from the side of the Levites, NAMELY FROM THE LEFT SIDE. But he changed things and said: "Your priests" and "Your pious ones," who are from the right side.

556. א״ל קוּדְשָׁא בְּרִיךְ הוּא, דָּוִד לָאו אוֹרַח דִּילִי הָכִי. אָמַר דָּוִד, בַּעֲבוּר דָּוִד עַבְדְּךָ אַל תָּשֵׁב פְּנֵי מְשִׁיחֶךָ. תִּקּוּנָא דַּאֲנָא תַקִּינַת, לָא תְשַׁנֶּה לֵיהּ. א״ל, דָּוִד, הוֹאִיל וְזַמִּינַת לִי, אִית לִי לְמֶעְבַּד רְעוּתָךְ, וְלָאו רְעוּתִי. וְיָלְפִינָן מֵהַאי, אוֹרְחָא דְּעָלְמָא, דְּמַאן דִּמְזַמֵּן לְאַחֲרָא, הַהוּא דְּאָתֵי לְגַבֵּיהּ, אִית לֵיהּ לְמֶעְבַּד רְעוּתֵיהּ, אע״ג דְּלָאו אוֹרְחֵיהּ בְּכָךְ.

556. The Holy One, blessed be He, said to him: 'David, this is not the way I do things.' David replied: "For Your servant David's sake, turn not away the face of Your anointed" (Ibid. 10). Do not alter the correction that I have instituted. THE HOLY ONE, BLESSED BE HE said to him, 'David, since you have invited Me, I have to do what you want and not what I want.' From this we learn that if one invites another, the guest has to do as the host wishes, even if that is not his usual way.

557. כָּךְ וַיִּקַּח מֵאַבְנֵי הַמָּקוֹם וְגוֹ', הוֹאִיל וְאָתָא חָתָן לְגַבֵּי כַּלָּה, אע"ג דְּלָאו אוֹרְחֵיהּ לְמִשְׁכַּב. אֶלָּא בְּכָרִים וּכְסָתוֹת, וְאִיהִי יָהֲבָה לֵיהּ אֲבָנִין לְמִשְׁכַּב, כֹּלָּא יְקַבֵּל בִּרְעוּתָא דְּלִבָּא. הה"ד, וַיִּשְׁכַּב בַּמָּקוֹם הַהוּא, עַל אִינּוּן אֲבָנִין, אע"ג דְּלָאו אוֹרְחֵיהּ בְּכָךְ.

557. Thus: "And he took of the stones of the place" (Beresheet 28:11). When the bridegroom comes to the bride, FOR JACOB IS THE SECRET OF TIFERET AND PLACE IS THE SECRET OF MALCHUT, WHERE TIFERET AND MALCHUT ARE THE SECRET OF THE BRIDEGROOM AND BRIDE, although it is not his custom to lie down without pillows and cushions, when she gave him stones to lie on, he accepts it all willingly, as it is written: "and lay down in that place" (Ibid.), on those stones, although that was not what he was used to.

558. אוֹף נָמֵי הָכָא, אָכַלְתִּי יַעְרִי עִם דִּבְשִׁי אע"ג דְּלָאו אָרְחוֹי בְּכָךְ, בְּגִין רְחִימוּ דְּכַלָּה. ועכ"ד בְּבֵיתָא דְּכַלָּה וְלָא בַּאֲתַר אַחֲרָא. בְּאַתְרַיֵּיה לָא אָכִיל וְלָא שָׁתֵי, בַּאֲתַר דִּילָהּ אָכִיל וְשָׁתֵי. הה"ד, בָּאתִי לְגַנִּי. מַלְאָכִין דְּשָׁדַר קוּדְשָׁא בְּרִיךְ הוּא לְאַבְרָהָם, לָא אַכְלוּ וְלָא שָׁתוּ בְּאַתְרַיְיהוּ, בְּגִין אַבְרָהָם אַכְלוּ וְשָׁתוּ. א"ל, ר'. חַיֶּיךְ, מִלָּה דָּא בָּעֵי קוּדְשָׁא בְּרִיךְ הוּא לְמֵימַר, וּבְגִין דְּלָא לְמֶחֱזַק טִיבוּ לְגַרְמֵיהּ, קַמֵּי כְּנֶסֶת יִשְׂרָאֵל, סָלִיק מִלָּה לְגַרְמָךְ, זַכָּאָה אַנְתְּ בְּעָלְמָא, דְּמָארָךְ מִשְׁתַּבַּח בָּךְ לְעֵילָּא. וְעָלָךְ כְּתִיב, צַדִּיק מוֹשֵׁל יִרְאַת אֱלֹהִים.

558. This same applies in our case: "I have eaten my honeycomb with my honey." Although this was not His way, HE NEVERTHELESS DID IT because

of love of the bride. And this ONLY happens in the house of the bride and not anywhere else. In His own place He neither eats nor drinks, but in her place He both eats and drinks, as it is written: "I have come into my garden," NAMELY THE GARDEN OF EDEN, WHICH IS THE PLACE OF MALCHUT. SIMILARLY, the angels whom the Holy One, blessed be He, sent to Abraham neither ate nor drank in their own place, but for the sake of Abraham they both ate and drank. ELIJAH said to him: Master, upon your life! The Holy One, blessed be He, wanted to relate this matter, but in order not to pay Himself a compliment before the Congregation of Yisrael He raised it to you. Happy are you in this world, that your Master on high is praised through you. About you is it written: "just, ruling in the fear of Elohim" (II Shmuel 23:3).

559. אֶת קָרְבָּנִי לַחְמִי לְאִשַּׁי וְגוֹ', ר' יוֹדָאי אָמַר, בְּקָרְבָּנָא אִית עָשָׁן, וְאִית רֵיחַ, וְאִית נִיחֹחַ. עָשָׁן: אִינּוּן מָארֵי דְּרוּגְזָא. דִּכְתִיב, כִּי אָז יֶעְשַׁן אַף יְיָ'. אִינּוּן אִתְהֲנוּן מֵעָשָׁן. וְעָשָׁן רוּגְזָא, בְּחוֹטָמָא אִיהוּ. רֵיחַ: אִינּוּן דְּאִקְרוּן תַּפּוּחִין. אָמַר ר' אַבָּא, כְּתַפּוּחִים. הה"ד, וְרֵיחַ אַפֵּיךְ כַּתַּפּוּחִים.

559. "My offerings, the provisions of My sacrifices made by fire" (Bemidbar 28:2). Rabbi Yudai said, In sacrifices there is smoke, there is smell, and there is sweet savor. Smoke is those with a temper, as it is written: "but then the anger (lit. 'nose') of Hashem…shall smoke" (Devarim 29:19). And those WITH A TEMPER enjoy smoke, smoke MEANING anger in the nose. Smell refers to those who are called 'apples'. Rabbi Aba said, They are like apples, as it is written: "the scent of your nose like apples" (Shir Hashirim 7:9).

560. אֶת הַכֶּבֶשׂ אֶחָד תַּעֲשֶׂה בַבֹּקֶר. מַאי בַבֹּקֶר. דָּא בֹּקֶר דְּאַבְרָהָם. דִּכְתִיב, וַיַּשְׁכֵּם אַבְרָהָם בַּבֹּקֶר. מְנָלָן דְּהַאי בֹּקֶר דְּאַבְרָהָם הוּא. א"ר אֶלְעָזָר, מֵהָכָא, הַבֹּקֶר אוֹר. בֹּקֶר אוֹר לָא כְּתִיב, אֶלָּא הַבֹּקֶר אוֹר, וְדָא אוֹר קַדְמָאָה, דְּבָרָא קוּדְשָׁא בְּרִיךְ הוּא בְּעוֹבָדָא דִּבְרֵאשִׁית, וְע"ד תַּעֲשֶׂה בַבֹּקֶר, בַּבֹּקֶר דְּאִשְׁתְּמוֹדְעָא. וּלְקַבֵל בֹּקֶר דְּאַבְרָהָם, אִתְקְרִיב קָרְבָּנָא דָּא. קָרְבָּן דְּבֵין הָעַרְבַּיִם, דָּא יִצְחָק, וּלְקַבֵל עֶרֶב דְּיִצְחָק אִתְקְרִיב. מְנָלָן. דִּכְתִיב וַיֵּצֵא יִצְחָק לָשׂוּחַ בַּשָּׂדֶה לִפְנוֹת עָרֶב. וְעֶרֶב

דְּיִצְחָק הוּא, וְהָא אוּקִימְנָא.

560. "The one lamb shall you offer in the morning" (Bemidbar 28:4). What is meant by morning? This refers to the morning of Abraham, NAMELY THE LIGHT OF CHESED, as it is written: "And Abraham rose up early in the morning" (Beresheet 22:3). How do we know that this morning is that of Abraham? Rabbi Elazar answered: From here, WHERE IT IS WRITTEN: "As soon as the morning was light" (Beresheet 44:3). Not 'morning' but "the morning" is written, WITH THE DEFINITE ARTICLE (HEI), for this was the first light that the Holy One, blessed be He, created in the Work of Creation. Thus IS IT WRITTEN: "shall you offer in the morning," namely on the particular morning, for this sacrifice is offered corresponding to the morning of Abraham. The lamb that is offered as a sacrifice at dusk is CORRESPONDING TO Isaac, paralleling the evening of Isaac, WHICH IS THE LIGHT OF GVURAH, WHICH IS JUDGMENT. How do we know this? Because it is written: "And Isaac went out to meditate in the field at eventide" (Beresheet 24:63), which is the evening of Isaac. And we have already learned this.

A Synopsis

Moses talks about the precepts of sacrifice and prayer, and says that offerings are sent to Zeir Anpin via Malchut, the Shechinah. We learn which prayers are optional and which obligatory. Moses says that Messiah son of Ephraim will come from the line of Joseph, the Righteous. Rabbi Shimon explains when one should bow and when one should stand upright during prayers, and he ends with some information about the time of redemption.

רעיא מהימנא

561. פִּקּוּדָא דָא לְהַקְרִיב מִנְחָה בְּכָל יוֹם, וּלְהַקְרִיב קָרְבָּן מוּסַף שַׁבָּת. וַאֲבַתְרֵיהּ לְהַסְדִּיר לֶחֶם הַפָּנִים וּלְבוֹנָה. וְקָרְבָּן מוּסַף בְּרֹאשׁ חֹדֶשׁ. בּוּצִינָא קַדִּישָׁא, בְּכָל יוֹמָא צָרִיךְ לְשַׁדּוּרֵי דּוֹרוֹנָא לְמַלְכָּא בִּידָא דְמַטְרוֹנִיתָא. אִי אִיהִי בִּרְשׁוּ בַּעְלָהּ, צָרִיךְ תּוֹסֶפֶת, כְּגוֹן מוּסַף בְּשַׁבָּת וּבְרֹאשׁ חֹדֶשׁ, וּמוּסַף דְּכָל יוֹמִין טָבִין.

Ra'aya Meheimna (the Faithful Shepherd)

561. It is a precept to offer the afternoon sacrifice each day, and the additional sacrifice on the Shabbat. And after it, to arrange the shewbread and the frankincense and the additional sacrifice on the first day of the month. holy luminary, each day a gift has to be sent to the King, to ZEIR ANPIN, in the hands of the Queen. And if she is in her husband's domain, a supplement has to be given, namely the additional sacrifice of the Shabbat, the first day of each month and of all the festivals.

562. דְּאִיהִי רְשׁוּת הַיָּחִיד דִּילֵיהּ וְעַמּוּדָא דְּאֶמְצָעִיתָא אִיהוּ בַּעֲלָה דְּהַאי רְשׁוּת. וְיַעֲקֹב דְּתִקֵן צְלוֹתָא דְעַרְבִית, אִיהוּ דַּרְגָּא דִּילֵיהּ דְּעַמּוּדָא דְּאֶמְצָעִיתָא. בְּגִין דָּא אוֹקְמוּהָ מָארֵי מַתְנִיתִין, תְּפִלַּת עַרְבִית רְשׁוּת, דְּאַף עַל גַּב דִּבְגָלוּתָא דְּדוֹמֶה לְלַיְלָה, דְּשַׁלְטִין תַּמָּן סָמָאֵל וְנָחָשׁ, וְכָל מְמָנָן דְּאֻכְלוּסִין דִּילֵיהּ, וּשְׁכִינְתָּא נַחְתַּת בְּגָלוּתָא עִם יִשְׂרָאֵל, אִיהִי בִּרְשׁוּ דְּבַעֲלָהּ אִשְׁתַּכְּחַת, הֲדָא הוּא דִכְתִיב, אֲנִי יְיָ' הוּא שְׁמִי וּכְבוֹדִי לְאַחֵר לֹא אֶתֵּן.

562. For she, MALCHUT, is his, ZEIR ANPIN's private property, and the Central Column, ZEIR ANPIN, is the owner of this property. And the level of Jacob, who instituted the evening prayers, is that of the Central Column, WHICH IS ZEIR ANPIN. For this reason, the sages of the Mishnah taught: The evening prayer is optional (Heb. *reshut*), FOR THE PRAYER, WHICH IS MALCHUT, IS IN THE DOMAIN (HEB. *RASHUT*) OF HER HUSBAND. For although being in exile, which is like the night-time, WHICH IS THE TIME FOR THE EVENING PRAYERS, and where Samael and Serpent and all those appointed over his regiments have control, and although the Shechinah goes into exile with Yisrael, NEVERTHELESS she is to be found in the domain of her husband, as it is written: "I am Hashem, that is My name, and My glory I will not give to another" (Yeshayah 42:8).

563. וּבְגִין דָּא וַיִּפְגַּע בַּמָּקוֹם, לֵית פְּגִיעָה, אֶלָּא פִּיוּסָא. בְּגִין אַל תִּפְגְּעִי בִי. כ"י פַּיִּיסַת לֵיהּ, דְּלָא יְזוּז מִינָהּ, דְּקוּדְשָׁא בְּרִיךְ הוּא אִיהוּ מְקוֹמוֹ שֶׁל עוֹלָם. מַאי עוֹלָם. דָּא שְׁכִינְתָּא. תַּרְגוּם עוֹלָם, עָלְמָא, לִישָׁנָא דְּעוּלֵימָא, כד"א הָעַלְמָה. וּמַה כְּתִיב בֵּיהּ, וַיָּלֶן שָׁם, אִתְפַּיֵּיס

עִמָּהּ, לְמֵיבַת תַּמָּן בְּגָלוּתָא עִם שְׁכִינְתָּא. וְאִי תֵּימָא דְּיַעֲקֹב פַּיֵּיס לָהּ,
שַׁפִּיר. וּבְגִין דְּאִיהִי בְּכָל לֵילְיָא, דְּאִיהוּ גָלוּתָא, בִּרְשׁוּ בַּעֲלָהּ, אוֹקְמוּהָ
תְּפִלַּת עַרְבִית רְשׁוּת. וּפֵירוּשָׁא אַחֲרִינָא, אִיהוּ תֶּבֶן לְמֵיכַל לִבְעִירָן
חוֹמְרִיִּים בק"ו. נַחְתּוּ מָארֵי מַתְנִיתִין, וְאִשְׁתְּטָחוּ קַמֵּיהּ, וְחַדֵּי בְּהַאי
מִלָּה, וְקַשְׁרוּ לָהּ בְּכַמָּה קִשְׁרִין דְּרָזִין סְתִימִין. וְאַעֲטָרוּ לָהּ, וּסְלִיקוּ לָהּ
לְגַבֵּי חַבְרַיָּיא דְּאִשְׁתָּאֲרוּ תַּמָּן.

563. Because of this IT IS WRITTEN: "And he lighted (Heb. *vayifga*) on a certain place" (Beresheet 28:11); which is reconciliation AND APPEASEMENT, as in: "Neither make intercession (Heb. *tifgei*) to Me" (Yirmeyah 7:16). The Congregation of Yisrael appeased ZEIR ANPIN, that He should not leave her, for the Holy One, blessed be He, ZEIR ANPIN, is the Place of the world. What is meant by world? The Shechinah. For the Aramaic word for 'world' is *alma*, which is derived from youth, as in the verse: ."..the maid (Heb. *almah*)..." (Beresheet 24:43), NAMELY MALCHUT THAT IS A MAIDEN. And what is written about him? "and tarried there all night" (Beresheet 28:11); THAT ZEIR ANPIN made peace with her, to stay there in the exile with the Shechinah. And should you suggest THAT THE MEANING OF "AND HE LIGHTED ON A CERTAIN PLACE" IS that Jacob appeased MALCHUT, that is fine. BUT IT CAN ALSO BE TAKEN TO MEAN THAT MALCHUT APPEASED JACOB, WHO IS ZEIR ANPIN, SO THAT HE SHOULD NOT LEAVE HER IN THE EXILE, AS ABOVE. And because every night, which is THE ASPECT OF exile, she is in the domain (Heb. *rashut*) of her husband, AS ABOVE, the sages taught that the evening prayers are optional (Heb. *reshut*). FOR PRAYER IS MALCHUT AND EVENING IS EXILE, SO THAT SAYING EVEN THEN IN THE DOMAIN (HEB. *RASHUT*) OF HER HUSBAND. And the other, LITERAL, explanation of the saying, NAMELY THAT THE EVENING PRAYERS ARE OPTIONAL AND NOT OBLIGATORY, is but straw for the fodder of material animals, by inference from minor to major (Heb. *chomer*); IT IS EASY FOR ONE WHO IS MATERIAL (HEB. *CHOMER*) TO UNDERSTAND, BUT NOT FOR ONE OF INTELLIGENCE. The sages of the Mishnah came down to him, prostrated themselves before him, and were happy over this matter, and they bound him with a number of knots of mysterious secrets, NAMELY THEY EXPOUNDED THAT MATTER IN A NUMBER OF WAYS WITH TORAH SECRETS. And they crowned him and raised him up to the other friends who had remained there.

564. אָמַר רַעְיָא מְהֵימָנָא, בּוּצִינָא קַדִּישָׁא, בְּגִין דָּא בִּשְׁאַר צְלוֹתִין אִיהוּ חוֹבָה, דְּשַׁטַר חוֹב עָלַיְיהוּ, לְסַמְכָא לָהּ בְּצַדִּיק חַי עָלְמִין, דְּבֵיהּ כָּל הַסּוֹמֵךְ גְּאוּלָה לַתְּפִלָּה, אֵינוֹ נִזּוֹק בְּכָל אוֹתוֹ יוֹם. וּבְמַאי סְמִיכַת עַל יְסוֹד. בִּדְרוֹעָא יְמִינָא. הה"ד, חַי יְיָ' שִׁכְבִי עַד הַבֹּקֶר.

564. The Faithful Shepherd said TO RABBI SHIMON: holy luminary, this is why it is obligatory with the remaining prayers, imposed on them as a promissory note, to bring near MALCHUT to the Righteous, the life of the worlds, WHICH IS YESOD. For in this connection THE SAGES TAUGHT: One who joins ge'ulah (Eng. 'Redemption') to the Amidah Prayer, will meet with no mishap for the whole of the day WHERE GE'ULAH IS YESOD AND TEFILAH IS MALCHUT. And how is she joined to Yesod? By the right arm, WHICH IS CHESED, as it is written: "As Hashem lives; lie down until the morning" (Rut 3:13), NAMELY UNTIL CHESED THAT IS CALLED 'MORNING' SHALL GIVE LIGHT.

565. כַּד מָטֵי זְמַן צְלוֹתָא דְּמִנְחָה, בָּעֶרֶב הִיא בָאָה. הה"ד, וַתָּבֹא אֵלָיו הַיּוֹנָה לְעֵת עֶרֶב. בְּגִין דְּמִנְחָה שְׁלוּחָה הִיא לַאֲדוֹנִי, בְּגָלוּתָא דְּעֵשָׂו, וְהִנֵּה גַם הוּא אַחֲרֵינוּ. וְעוֹד לַאֲדוֹנִי, דָּא אִיהוּ אֲדוֹן כָּל הָאָרֶץ, וְדָא צַדִּיק, מִתַּמָּן יוֹסֵף הַצַּדִּיק, בְּכֹר שׁוֹרוֹ הָדָר לוֹ. דְּעָתִיד לְנָפְקָא מִנֵּיהּ מָשִׁיחַ בֶּן אֶפְרַיִם. וּבְגִינֵיהּ אִתְּמַר וְהִנֵּה קָמָה אֲלֻמָּתִי וְגַם נִצָּבָה וְהִנֵּה תְסֻבֶּינָה אֲלֻמֹּתֵיכֶם וַתִּשְׁתַּחֲוֶינָה לַאֲלֻמָּתִי. וּבַצַדִּיק, כָּל הַכּוֹרֵעַ כּוֹרֵעַ בְּבָרוּךְ.

565. The arrival time of Minchah (the afternoon prayer) IS THE SECRET OF "in the evening she would go" (Ester 2:14), NAMELY THE UNIFICATION JUST BEFORE DUSK, as it is written: "and the dove came unto him in the evening" (Beresheet 8:11), FOR THE DOVE IS MALCHUT, because "it is a present (Heb. minchah) sent to my lord" in the exile of "Esau" (Beresheet 32:19), FOR EVENING IS THE SECRET OF EXILE. "and, behold, also he is behind us" (Ibid.), NAMELY ZEIR ANPIN IS COMING AFTER US TO REDEEM HER FROM EXILE. Furthermore, "to my lord" refers to the lord of all the land, which is the Righteous, NAMELY YESOD. For from there, FROM THE ASPECT OF THE UNION, AT MINCHAH THAT IS AT EVENTIME, IT IS

SAID ABOUT Joseph, the Righteous: "The firstling of his herd, grandeur is his" (Devarim 33:17). FOR THE UNIFICATION OF MINCHAH COMES FROM THE CONTROL OF THE LEFT THAT IS CALLED 'EVENING', AND SINCE THE MINCHAH IS "SENT TO MY LORD," NAMELY TO YESOD, WHICH IS JOSEPH, THEREFORE JOSEPH ALSO BECOMES THE ASPECT OF "FIRSTLING OF HIS HERD," WHICH IS THE LEFT COLUMN. And in the future Messiah the son of Efraim will issue from him, FOR MESSIAH THE SON OF DAVID IS THE ASPECT OF THE RIGHT AND MESSIAH THE SON OF EFRAIM IS THE ASPECT OF THE LEFT. And for his sake, FOR THE SAKE OF MESSIAH THE SON OF EFRAIM, it is said: "and, lo, my sheaf (Heb. *alumah*) arose, and also stood upright; and, behold, your sheaves came round about, and bowed down to my sheaf" (Beresheet 37:7), FOR MESSIAH THE SON OF EFRAIM IS CALLED 'MUTE' (HEB. *ILEM*) IN THE EXILE. And about the Righteous IT WAS SAID: Everyone who bows should do so at the word 'Blessed'. AND IT WAS THEREFORE SAID FOR HIS PART: "AND BOWED DOWN TO MY SHEAF," WHICH IS MESSIAH.

566. אָמַר בּוּצִינָא קַדִּישָׁא, רַעְיָא מְהֵימְנָא, בָּךְ אִתְּמַר וַיִּקַּח מֹשֶׁה אֶת עַצְמוֹת יוֹסֵף. בְּגִין דְּגוּף וּבְרִית חֲשַׁבֵינָן חַד. וּבג"ד עָלָךְ אִתְּמַר, וְהִנֵּה קָמָה אֲלוּמָתִי וְגַם נִצָּבָה. דְּכַךְ תְּפִלָּה מְעוֹמָד. וְכֵן כָּל הַזּוֹקֵף זוֹקֵף בְּשֵׁם. וּבַצַּדִיק, כָּל הַכּוֹרֵעַ כּוֹרֵעַ בְּבָרוּךְ, וְהַיְינוּ וַתִּשְׁתַּחֲוֶינָה לַאֲלֻמָּתִי. דְּאַנְתְּ אָחִיד בִּימִינָא וּבִשְׂמָאלָא, בְּגוּף וּבְרִית. וּלְבָתַר תִּסְתַּלַּק עֲלַיְיהוּ לַבִּינָה, לְמִפְתַּח בָּהּ חַמְשִׁין תַּרְעִין דְּחֵירוּ לְיִשְׂרָאֵל. לְקַיְּימָא, כִּימֵי צֵאתְךָ מֵאֶרֶץ מִצְרַיִם אַרְאֶנּוּ נִפְלָאוֹת, וּבג"ד צְלוֹתָא דְּשַׁחֲרִית חוֹבָה, דְּעַרְבִית רְשׁוּת.

566. Said the holy luminary, THAT IS RABBI SHIMON: Faithful Shepherd, it is said about you: "And Moses took the bones of Joseph" (Shemot 13:19). SINCE MOSES IS TIFERET, WHICH IS CALLED 'BODY', AND JOSEPH IS YESOD, THAT IS CALLED 'COVENANT', AND we consider body and covenant to be one, it is therefore said about you: "And, lo, my sheaf arose, and also stood upright," NAMELY MALCHUT THAT IS CALLED 'EL' IN EXILE, for so is the Amidah prayer, said while standing upright, WHERE PRAYER IS THE SECRET OF MALCHUT. Likewise: Everyone who returns to an upright position, should do so at the mention of the Name, WHICH IS TIFERET, NAMELY MOSES, AND THEREFORE IT IS SAID ABOUT HIM: "MY

SHEAF AROSE." And regarding the Righteous everyone who bows, should do so at the word 'Blessed'; and thus it is said "and bowed down to my sheaf." THE RISING UP, FROM THE POINT OF VIEW OF TIFERET, IS TO MALCHUT, WHILE THE BOWING DOWN, FROM THE POINT OF VIEW OF YESOD IS TO MALCHUT. For you are attached to the right and to the left, to the body and covenant, WHICH ARE TIFERET AND YESOD, AND TIFERET INCLINES TO THE RIGHT, AND YESOD INCLINES TO THE LEFT. Subsequently, you will ascend on them to Binah, to open there fifty gates of freedom for Yisrael, NAMELY TO DRAW DOWN THE GREAT MOCHIN OF FREEDOM, to fulfill the verse: "As in the days of your coming out of the land of Egypt, I will show to him marvelous things" (Michah 7:15). For this reason the morning prayer is obligatory and the evening PRAYER is optional.

567. בְּעַרְבִית אִיהוּ הַשְׁכִּיבֵנוּ, דְּשְׁכִיבַת בֵּין דְּרוֹעֵי מַלְכָּא בְּגָלוּתָא. כַּד יֵיתֵי צַפְרָא, פֶּסַח אָחִיד בֵּיהּ בִּימִינָא. אֲבָל בִּדְרוֹעָא שְׂמָאלָא דְּיִצְחָק, תִּשְׁרֵי. וַיְהִי הוּא טֶרֶם כִּלָּה לְדַבֵּר וְהִנֵּה רִבְקָה יוֹצֵאת, מִן גָּלוּתָא. וּבְגִין דְּלָא נַפְקֵי מִסִּטְרָא דְּדִינָא, יַעֲקֹב שִׁכֵּל אֶת יָדָיו, וְשַׁוֵּי שׁוֹר בִּימִינָא, אַרְיֵה בִּשְׂמָאלָא. וּבְג"ד נָאֵם יְיָ' לַאדוֹנִי שֵׁב לִימִינִי, דָּא צַדִּיק, לְקַבְּלֵיהּ מָשִׁיחַ בֶּן יוֹסֵף, וְאָמַר לֵיהּ שֵׁב לִימִינִי, דְּרוֹעָא דְּאַבְרָהָם, בְּגָלוּתָא דְּיִשְׁמָעֵאל, עַד אָשִׁית אוֹיְבֶיךָ הֲדוֹם לְרַגְלֶיךָ.

567. In the evening prayer, MALCHUT is *Hashkivenu* (Eng. 'Cause us to lie down'), NAMELY she lies between the arms of the King in exile, FOR SHE LIES DOWN AND DOES NOT STAND UPRIGHT, SINCE NIGHT-TIME IS THE ASPECT OF EXILE. When the morning, WHICH IS THE ASPECT OF REDEMPTION, comes, THE HOLIDAY OF PESACH (Passover,) WHICH IS THE SECRET OF RIGHT, NAMELY CHESED OF ZEIR ANPIN, hold her on the right, NAMELY BESTOWS CHASSADIM TO HER. But IT IS SAID about the left arm of ZEIR ANPIN, THAT IS CALLED 'Isaac', WHICH IS THE ASPECT OF Tishrei, "And it came to pass, before he had done speaking, that, behold, Rivkah came out" (Beresheet 24:15) from the exile, FOR THE REDEMPTION COMES FROM THE CORRECTION OF THE LEFT SIDE, WHICH IS ISAAC. And so that MALCHUT should not emerge FROM THE EXILE from the side of Judgment, FOR THE LEFT IS JUDGMENT, THEREFORE, Jacob, WHO IS ZEIR ANPIN, "changing his hands" (Beresheet 48:14), placed ox, WHICH IS LEFT, on his right, WHICH IS CHESED, and lion, WHICH IS RIGHT, he

placed on the left, WHICH IS JUDGMENT, for which reason: "Hashem says to my master: Sit at My right hand" (Tehilim 110:1). This is the Righteous, WHICH IS YESOD, that parallels Messiah the son of Joseph, WHICH IS JUDGMENT; and He said to him: "Sit at My right hand," which is the arm of Abraham, WHICH IS CHESED AT THE TIME of the exile of Ishmael. THAT IS, BECAUSE JACOB, "CHANGING HIS HANDS," SAID "TO MY MASTER," WHICH IS THE LEFT OF YESOD, WHICH IS MESSIAH THE SON OF EFRAIM, WHICH IS JUDGMENT, THAT HE SHOULD SIT AT THE RIGHT, WHICH IS CHESED, "until I make your enemies your footstool" (Ibid.).

85. Additional Nefesh, additional Ruach, additional Neshamah

A Synopsis

At the time of redemption, the Zohar tells us, an additional spirit will awaken over Yisrael, and they will have rest from their enemies. For each individual, the extra spirit is allocated according to his deeds or level. If a person is completely perfect, having all ten of the qualities that are in Malchut, he is given the crown, Keter, as written in, "I will pour out My spirit upon all flesh." There there is then no rule left for Samael or his adherents. Moses concludes by saying that on Shabbats and festivals the prayers are more important to God than all sorts of spices.

568. בְּהַהוּא זִמְנָא, יִתְעַר רוּחַ יְתֵירָה תּוֹסֶפֶת עַל יִשְׂרָאֵל, הה״ד אֶשְׁפּוֹךְ אֶת רוּחִי עַל כָּל בָּשָׂר, וְיֶהֱוֵי נַיְיחָא לְיִשְׂרָאֵל מֵאוּמִין דְּעָלְמָא, וְנוֹחַ מֵאוֹיְבֵיהֶם. כְּגַוְונָא דְּשַׁבָּת, דְּאִתּוֹסַף בב״נ נֶפֶשׁ יְתֵירָה בְּשַׁבָּת, וְאִית לוֹן בָּהּ נַיְיחָא, אִי בְּנֶפֶשׁ יְתֵירָה אִית לוֹן נַיְיחָא, דְּאִיהִי נוּקְבָּא, כָּל שֶׁכֵּן בְּרוּחָא דְּאִיהוּ דְּכוּרָא.

568. At that time an extra spirit will awaken, THAT IS, AN additional SPIRIT, over Yisrael, as it is written: "I will pour out My spirit upon all flesh" (Yoel 3:1), and Yisrael will have rest from the nations of the world, "rest from their enemies" (Ester 9:16). And it will be as on the Shabbat when an extra Nefesh is added to a person, and he obtains rest therein. And if he has rest with an extra Nefesh, which is feminine, how much more WILL HE HAVE REST with the spirit, which is masculine.

569. וְתַנָּאִים וַאֲמוֹרָאִים, נֶפֶשׁ יְתֵירָה בְּשַׁבָּת לְכָל יִשְׂרָאֵל כַּחֲדָא, חַד אִיהִי. אֲבָל לְכָל ב״נ, אִיהוּ כְּפוּם עוֹבָדוֹי. וְאֶלִיפְנָא מק״ו דְּתִיוּבְתָּא, דְּכָל יִשְׂרָאֵל כַּחֲדָא, בְּכָל זִמְנָא דְּחַזְרִין כֻּלְּהוּ, מִתְקַבְּלֵי. הה״ד, בְּכָל יְיָ' אֱלֹהֵינוּ בְּכָל קָרְאֵנוּ אֵלָיו, דְּשֵׁם יְיָ' מוּכְתָּר עֲלַיְיהוּ בְּכִתְרֵיהּ, דְּאִיהוּ כֶּתֶר עֶלְיוֹן. וְהַאי אִיהוּ נִשְׁמָה יְתֵירָה דְּכָל יִשְׂרָאֵל, בְּשַׁבָּת וְיוֹמִין טָבִין. ובג״ד תַּקִּינוּ בְּכָל יוֹמִין, לְמִחְתַּם בְּשֵׁם יָדוֹד, דְּאִיהוּ חוֹתָם דְּכָל בִּרְכָאן דִּצְלוֹתִין, וְלָא אַמְרִין מוּסָף בְּלָא כֶּתֶר. וּבְשַׁבָּת, תַּקִּינוּ לְמֵימַר בְּמוּסָף,

כֶּתֶר יִתְּנוּ לְךָ יְיָ׳ אֱלֹהֵינוּ.

569. And, Tannaim and Amoraim, HEAR: the extra Nefesh on Shabbat, which is for the whole of Yisrael together, is but one, WHICH IS THE SECRET OF KETER, but for each person it is allocated according to his deeds, NAMELY FOR EACH ONE ACCORDING TO HIS LEVEL. And this we have learned from repentance by inference from minor to major. For all of Yisrael together, whenever making repentance, are all accepted, as it is written: "as Hashem our Elohim is in all things that we call upon Him for" (Devarim 4:7), THIS BEING THE REASON FOR IT BEING FOR ALL YISRAEL TOGETHER. They are crowned with the Name of Yud Hei Vav Hei, with His crown, which is Upper Keter. And this UPPER KETER is an additional Neshamah for all Yisrael together on Shabbatot and festival days. For this reason it was decreed that THE BLESSINGS be sealed, NAMELY CONCLUDED, with the Name of Yud Hei Vav Hei, which indeed concludes each blessing of the Amidah prayer, but no additional service is said without the ILLUMINATION OF Keter, FOR KETER OF THE NAME OF YUD HEI VAV HEI DOES NOT ILLUMINATE EVERY DAY, AND THE BLESSINGS ARE THEREFORE CONCLUDED WITH YUD HEI VAV HEI, WHICH IS ZEIR ANPIN, WHILE NO ADDITIONAL SERVICE, WHICH IS THE KETER OF ZEIR ANPIN, IS RECITED. But on the Shabbat, it was decreed that 'A crown will be given to You, Hashem our Elohim' is recited, BECAUSE ON SHABBAT THE KETER OF ZEIR ANPIN ILLUMINATES, AND THE ADDITIONAL SERVICE IS THEREFORE RECITED. AND THIS KETER OF ZEIR ANPIN IS THE SECRET OF THE ADDITIONAL NESHAMAH THAT GIVES LIGHT FOR THE WHOLE OF YISRAEL TOGETHER, AS ABOVE.

570. אֲבָל לְכָל חַד מִיִשְׂרָאֵל, הָכִי נָחִית לֵיה נֶפֶשׁ יְתֵירָה, כְּפוּם דַּרְגָּא דִּילֵיה. אִי הוּא חָסִיד, יָהֲבִין לֵיה נֶפֶשׁ יְתֵירָה מִמִּדַּת חֶסֶד, כְּפוּם דַּרְגָּא דִּילֵיה. אִי אִיהוּ גִּבּוֹר, יְרֵא חַטְא, יָהֲבִין לֵיה נֶפֶשׁ יְתֵירָה, מִמִּדַּת גְּבוּרָה. וְאִי אִיהוּ אִישׁ תָּם, יָהֲבִין לֵיה נֶפֶשׁ יְתֵירָה, מִמִּדַּת אֱמֶת. וְנֶפֶשׁ יְתֵירָה דָּא מַלְכוּת, דְּאִיהִי כְּלִילָא מֵעֲשַׂר סְפִירָאן, וּכְפוּם מִדָּה דב"נ. אִם נְשִׂיא יִשְׂרָאֵל, אוֹ חָכָם, אוֹ מֵבִין בְּחָכְמָה, אוֹ בַּתּוֹרָה, דְּאִתְּמַר בֵּיה, לְהָבִין מָשָׁל וּמְלִיצָה. אוֹ בַּנְּבִיאִים, אוֹ בַּכְּתוּבִים. הָכִי יָהֲבִין לֵיה נֶפֶשׁ יְתֵירָה, דְּאִתְקְרִיאַת כֶּתֶר מַלְכוּת.

570. For each individual of Yisrael, however, an additional Nefesh descends to him according to his level. If he is pious (Heb. *chasid*), he is given an additional Nefesh from the attribute of Chesed, according to his level. If he is a mighty man, fearful of sin, he is given an additional Nefesh from the attribute of Gvurah. If he is an honest man, he is given an additional Nefesh from the attribute of truth. For the additional Nefesh is Malchut, and is made up of the ten Sfirot, AND THEREFORE a person RECEIVES FROM A SFIRAH OF MALCHUT according to his character. THAT IS: If he is a chief in Yisrael, or a sage or one who has understanding in wisdom or Torah, about which is said: "to understand a proverb, and a figure" (Mishlei 1:6) or the Prophets or the Writings, is he given an additional Nefesh accordingly, which is called 'Keter of Malchut', IF HE IS A CHIEF IN YISRAEL.

571. וְאִי חָכָם, כְּמָה דְּאוֹקִימְנָא הַמַּחְכִּים לְכָל אָדָם, דְּאִתְּמַר כֻּלָם בְּחָכְמָה עָשִׂיתָ, יָהֲבִין לֵיהּ נֶפֶשׁ יְתֵירָה מִתַּמָּן. וְאִם הוּא מֵבִין דָּבָר מִתּוֹךְ דָּבָר בְּאוֹרַיְיתָא, יָהֲבִין לֵיהּ נֶפֶשׁ יְתֵירָה מִבִּינָה. וְאִם הוּא חָכָם בַּנְּבִיאִים וּבַכְּתוּבִים, יָהֲבִין לֵיהּ נֶפֶשׁ יְתֵירָה מִנֶּצַח וְהוֹד. וְאִי אִיהוּ צַדִּיק גָּמוּר דְּנָטַר אוֹת בְּרִית, אוֹת שַׁבָּת, אוֹת יוֹמִין טָבִין, אוֹת תְּפִילִין, יָהֲבִין לֵיהּ נֶפֶשׁ יְתֵירָה מִצַּדִּיק, וּבְכָל אֲתָר, נֶפֶשׁ יְתֵירָה מִמַּלְכוּת.

571. CONTINUING THE EXPLANATION OF HIS WORDS, If he is a wise man, as we have learned: WHO IS A WISE MAN? He who adds wisdom to every man, as it is written: "in wisdom have You made them all" (Tehilim 104:24). He is given an extra Nefesh from there. And if he understands one matter from another in the Torah, he is given an extra Nefesh from Binah. And if he is a scholar in the Prophets and the Writings, he is given an extra Nefesh from Netzach and Hod. And if he is completely righteous, keeping the sign of the covenant, the sign of the Shabbat, the sign of the festivals, and the sign of the Tefilin, he is given an extra Nefesh from the Righteous, WHICH IS YESOD. And in every case, the extra Nefesh THAT THE INDIVIDUAL RECEIVES is from Malchut. AND IF HE IS SAID TO BE YESOD, FOR EXAMPLE, THEN THIS MEANS THE SFIRAH YESOD OF MALCHUT, AND SO WITH THE OTHER SFIROT.

572. וְאִי אִיהוּ ב"נ מִכָּל מִדּוֹת אִלֵּין, יָהֲבִין לֵיהּ כֶּתֶר בְּשֵׁם יְדֹוָד, כַּיְדֹוָד אֱלֹהֵינוּ בְּכָל קָרְאֵנוּ אֵלָיו. אֵין קָדוֹשׁ כַּיְדֹוָד. מֵעָלְמָא דִּדְכוּרָא,

דְּאִיהוּ תִּפְאֶרֶת, מֶלֶךְ מוכְתָּר בְּכֶתֶר עִלָאָה, דְּבָהּ יִמְלוֹךְ בִּשְׁכִינָתֵיהּ,
דְּאִיהִי נֶפֶשׁ יְתֵירָה. וְכֶתֶר נִשְׁמָה יְתֵירָה, יְהֹוָ"ה, רוּחַ, דְּאִתְּמַר אֶשְׁפּוֹךְ
אֶת רוּחִי עַל כָּל בָּשָׂר, וְאִיהוּ כָּלִיל י' סְפִירָאן מֵעֵילָא לְתַתָּא, כְּגַוְונָא
דָא: י' חָכְמָה. ה' בִּינָה. ה' כָּלִיל שִׁית סְפִירָאן, מֵחֶסֶד עַד יְסוֹד. ה'
מַלְכוּת. כ' מִן כַּיְדֹוָד אֱלֹהֵינוּ, כֶּתֶר עַל רֵישֵׁיהּ. וְהַאי אִיהוּ נִשְׁמָה
דְּאִתּוֹסְפָא בְּיוֹם שַׁבָּת.

572. And if he is a person who has all the above-mentioned qualities and IS COMPARABLE AND SIMILAR TO THE WHOLE OF YISRAEL TOGETHER, he is given Keter in the Name of Yud Hei Vav Hei. AND THIS IS IN THE SECRET OF THE VERSES: "as Hashem our Elohim is in all things that we call upon Him for" and "There is none holy as Hashem" (I Shmuel 2:2). 'As (HEB. CAF)' THAT IS PREFIXED TO HASHEM IS THE SECRET OF KETER OF ZEIR ANPIN. AND THIS IS AN EXTRA NESHAMAH from the world of the Male, which is Tiferet, AND IS NOT AS THE EXTRA NEFESH OF AN INDIVIDUAL, WHICH IS ONLY FROM THE SFIROT OF MALCHUT. For He is a King crowned with an upper crown FROM BINAH, in which He rules with His Shechinah, which is the extra Nefesh. And Keter is the extra Neshamah THAT IS RECEIVED FROM Yud Hei Vav Hei, which is Ruach, about which it is said: "I will pour out My spirit upon all flesh." AND THIS SPIRIT, WHICH IS YUD HEI VAV HEI is composed of the ten Sfirot, downwards from above, as follows: Yud is Chochmah, Hei is Binah, Vav incorporates the six Sfirot, from Chesed to Yesod, Hei is Malchut. And the Caf, (as) in "as Hashem our Elohim" is the crown on the head OF YUD HEI VAV HEI. And this is the Neshamah that is added on the Shabbat day EITHER TO ALL OF YISRAEL TOGETHER OR TO AN INDIVIDUAL WHO HAS ALL THE TEN QUALITIES IN MALCHUT.

573. וּבְגִין דְּעִלַּת הָעִלּוֹת, מוּפְלָא וּמְכוּסֶּה בְּהַאי כֶּתֶר, וְאִתְפָּשַׁט בְּשֵׁם
יְהֹוָה בְּשַׁבָּתוֹת וְיָמִים טוֹבִים, לֵית שׁוּלְטָנוּתָא לְסָמָאֵל וּלְנָחָשׁ וּלְכָל
מְמָנָן דִּילֵיהּ, וְלֵית לֵיהּ שַׁלְטָנוּתָא לַגֵּיהִנָּם, נוּקְבָּא בִּישָׁא דְּסָמָאֵל, וְלָא
לְמַשִׁרְיָין דִּילֵיהּ, כֻּלְּהוּ מִתְטַמְּרִין מִן קֳדָם מַשִׁרְיָיתָא דְּמַלְכָּא, כְּגַוְונָא
דְּיִתְטַמְּרָן אוּמִין עכו"ם דְּעָלְמָא, כַּד יִתְגְּלֵי מְשִׁיחָא, הה"ד וּבָאוּ
בִּמְעָרוֹת צוּרִים וּבִנְקִיקֵי הַסְּלָעִים.

573. And because the Prime Cause is wonderful and covered with this crown, and on the Shabbat days and festivals THE CROWN (Heb. *KETER*) spreads in the Name Yud Hei Vav Hei, there is, therefore, no rule THEN for Samael and Serpent and all his officials, nor does Gehenom, which is the wicked female of Samael, have any rule, nor his camps, for all of them take cover before the camps of the King, just as the idolatrous nations of the world will hide when Messiah is revealed, as it is written: "And they shall go into the holes of the rocks" (Yeshayah 2:19); "and in the holes of the rocks" (Yeshayah 7:19).

574. קָמוּ תַּנָּאִין וַאֲמוֹרָאִין, וְאָמְרוּ, רַעְיָא מְהֵימָנָא, אַנְתְּ הוּא שָׁקִיל לְכָל יִשְׂרָאֵל, מְמוּלָּא מִכָּל מִדּוֹת טָבִין, וַדַּאי בָּךְ שַׁרְיָיא, הַהוּא דְּאִתְּמַר בֵּיהּ, אֵין קָדוֹשׁ כַּיְדֹוָד אֱלֹהֵינוּ. אַנְתְּ כֶּתֶר עַל כָּל חַד וְחַד מִיִּשְׂרָאֵל, כִּי אֵין בִּלְתֶּךְ ב״ן, דְּיֵהֵא כֶּתֶר עָלָךְ, לָא נָשִׂיא, וְלָא חָכָם, וְלָא מֵבִין, וְלָא חָסִיד, וְלָא גִּבּוֹר, וְלָא תָם, וְלָא נָבִיא, וְלָא צַדִּיק, וְלָא מֶלֶךְ. אַנְתְּ הוּא בְּדִיּוּקְנָא דְּקוּדְשָׁא בְּרִיךְ הוּא, בְּרָא בְּדִיּוּקְנָא דַּאֲבוּהִי, כְּגַוְונָא דְיִשְׂרָאֵל, דְּאִתְּמַר בְּהוֹן, בָּנִים אַתֶּם לַיְיָ' אֱלֹהֵיכֶם. אַשְׁלִים פְּקוּדִין דְּמָארָךְ, דְּלֵית פְּקוּדִין מֵאִלֵּין דִּילָךְ, דְּלָא יִתְעַטֵּר בֵּיהּ קוּדְשָׁא בְּרִיךְ הוּא וּשְׁכִינְתֵּיהּ עֵילָא וְתַתָּא, בְּכֶתֶר עִלָּאָה, בְּכָל מִדָּה וּמִדָּה.

574. The Tannaim and the Amoraim arose and said, Faithful Shepherd, you are equivalent to all of Yisrael, filled with all good qualities, and certainly in you rests He about whom it is said: "There is none holy as Hashem our Elohim," NAMELY THE CAF (= AS) THAT IS PREFIXED TO YUD HEI VAV HEI WHICH ALLUDES TO KETER OF YUD HEI VAV HEI. You are a crown (keter) on each and every one of Yisrael, for there is no man who can be a crown over you, not a chief, nor sage, nor a man of understanding, not a pious man, not a mighty one, nor an honest man, not a prophet, not a righteous person, nor a king. FOR THESE ARE THE TEN SFIROT OF MALCHUT, FROM WHICH EACH INDIVIDUAL ONE OF YISRAEL TAKES. But you are in the form of the Holy One, blessed be He, NAMELY ZEIR ANPIN, WHICH IS THE SECRET OF THE WORLD OF THE MALE, AS ABOVE, the son being in the form of his father, FOR MOSES IS THE SON OF ZEIR ANPIN, just as is Yisrael AS A WHOLE, about whom it is written: "You are the children to Hashem your Elohim" (Devarim 14:1). Complete the precept of

your Master, for there is no PRECEPT of those precepts that you perform with which the Holy One, blessed be He, and His Shechinah will not be adorned above and below, with upper Keter in every attribute.

575. פָּתַח וְאָמַר, תַּנָּאִין וַאֲמוֹרָאִין, דְּכַד הֲוָה קָרֵי לְכֻלְּהוּ, לר"ש בְּכְלַל עִמְהוֹן בְּכָל זִמְנָא, אָמַר לוֹן, אֲנָא מְשַׁבַּחְנָא לְכוּ, כְּפוּם נְדִיבוּת דִּלְכוֹן, דְּאַתּוּן בְּנֵי נְדִיבִים אַבְרָהָם יִצְחָק וְיַעֲקֹב. לֵית מַאן דְּיָכִיל לְשַׁבְּחָא לְכוֹן, אֶלָּא מָרֵי עָלְמָא, דַּאֲפִילוּ אוֹרַיְיתָא כֻּלָּהּ עַד אֵין סוֹף, בְּכוּ הִיא תַּלְיָא. כְּגַוְונָא דְּאִתְּמַר בְּאוֹרַיְיתָא, אֲרוּכָּה מֵאֶרֶץ מִדָּה וּרְחָבָה מִנִּי יָם, הָכִי שֶׁבַח דִּילְכוּ. אֲבָל יִתְקַיֵּים בְּכוּ, מַה דְּאִתְקַיֵּים בִּי, דַּחֲדֵינָא בִּיקָרָא דְּאַהֲרֹן אָחִי, כְּמָה דְּאוֹקְמוּהָ, הַלֵּב שֶׁשָּׂמַח בִּגְדוּלַת אָחִיו, יִלְבַּשׁ אוּרִים וְתוּמִים.

575. THE FAITHFUL SHEPHERD opened and said: Tannaim and Amoraim, LISTEN. AND THE ZOHAR EXPLAINS that every time that THE FAITHFUL SHEPHERD called all the friends, with Rabbi Shimon among them, BY THE TITLE 'TANNAIM AND AMORAIM,' he said to them: I praise you according to your munificence, for you are the sons of princes, NAMELY: Abraham, Isaac, and Jacob. No one but the Master of the Universe can praise you, for even the whole of the Torah in its infinite extension is dependent on you. As it is said in the Torah: "Its measure is longer than the earth, and broader than the sea" (Iyov 11:9), so is your praise. But may what was fulfilled in me be fulfilled in you also, for I rejoiced in the honor of Aaron, my brother, as we have learned ABOUT AARON: The heart that rejoiced at the greatness of his brother shall put on the Urim and Tumim.

576. וְתַנָּאִין וַאֲמוֹרָאִין, כָּל מוּסָפִין דְּשַׁבָּתוֹת וְיָמִים טוֹבִים, כָּל מוּסָף דְּאַמְרֵינָן בֵּיהּ כֶּתֶר, מֵהָכָא אִשְׁתְּמוֹדְעִין. וְכָל צְלוֹתִין דְּיִשְׂרָאֵל, רֵיחָא דִּלְהוֹן, כְּרֵיחָא דְּמֹר וּלְבוֹנָה וְכָל אַבְקַת רוֹכֵל, בִּשְׁאַר יוֹמִין. אֲבָל בְּשַׁבָּתוֹת וְיָמִים טוֹבִים, חָשִׁיב עֲלֵיהּ מִכָּל מִינֵי בְּשָׂמִים.

576. And LISTEN, Tannaim and Amoraim, all the additional prayers of Shabbatot and festivals, every additional service in which Keter is recited, are

known from here, NAMELY KETER OF ZEIR ANPIN, ABOUT WHICH IS SAID: "THERE IS NONE HOLY AS HASHEM." And the smell of all the prayers of Yisrael is as the smell of "myrrh and frankincense, with all the powders of the merchant" (Shir Hashirim 3:6). This is the case of weekdays, but on Shabbatot and festivals, WHEN THE KETER OF ZEIR ANPIN ILLUMINATES, AS ABOVE, the prayer is much more valuable for the Holy One, blessed be He, than all sorts of spices.

577. בְּגִין דְּבְיוֹמִין טָבִין, סַלְקִין מִכָּל אַבְקַת רוֹכֵל, דְּאִתְּמַר בֵּיה, וַיֵּאָבֵק אִישׁ עִמּוֹ. דְּצְלוֹתָא דְּאִיהִי פְּגִימָה, אִתְאָבָק עִמָּה סָמָאֵל, לְאַגָּחָא עִמֵּה בְּהַהוּא פְּגִימוּ דַּעֲבֵירָה, בְּהַהוּא אָבָק דְּדָא, וְדָא סָלִיק עַד שְׁמַיָּא.

577. For on festival days THE PRAYERS are more sublime AND VALUABLE than all "the powders (Heb. avkah) of the merchant," about which it is said: "and there wrestled (Heb. ye'avek) a man with him" (Beresheet 32:25), for Samael wrestles with faulty prayer, using it to fight AND DENOUNCE by means of that fault of a transgression IN THE PRAYER; namely with that dust (Heb. avak) OF THE PRAYER, HE ASCENDS AND DENOUNCES, and this rises up to the heavens.

86. Arvit

A Synopsis

The Faithful Shepherd talks about the evening prayer, calling it Jacob's ladder on which the prayers ascend and merits descend. He says that those who teach merit are the defenders in the war of the Torah, and he talks about the war of the evening prayer that continues until dawn.

578. אֲבָק דְּיַעֲקֹב, לְאוֹלְפָא זְכוּתָא עַל צְלוֹתָא, בְּכַמָּה מַשְׁרְיָין דְּזַכְוָון דְּאִינּוּן חַיָּלִין וּמַשְׁרְיָין, דְּמִתְכַּנְּשִׁין עִמֵּיהּ, לְאוֹלְפָא זְכוּ עָלַהּ. וַאֲבָק דַּרְגָּא דְּסָמָאֵל, סָלִיק בְּכַמָּה מַשְׁרְיָין דְּחוֹבִין, לְאוֹלְפָא חוֹבִין עָלַהּ, וְדָא צְלוֹתָא דְּעַרְבִית, דְּאִקְרֵי סֻלָּם דְּיַעֲקֹב, דְּבַהּ וְהִנֵּה מַלְאֲכֵי אֱלֹהִים עוֹלִים וְיוֹרְדִים בּוֹ. אִלֵּין דְּסַלְּקִין חוֹבִין, וְנַחְתֵּי זַכְוָון תְּחוֹתַיְיהוּ, וְאִלֵּין סַלְּקִין זַכְוָון, וְנַחְתִּין חוֹבִין תְּחוֹתַיְיהוּ. וּמַשְׁפִּילִין לוֹן בְּכַמָּה קְרָבִין.

578. AND THERE ARE TWO SORTS OF DUST, for the dust of Jacob, NAMELY HIS WAR, comes to teach merit about prayers, in a number of hosts of merits that are regiments and camps that gather with him to teach merit ABOUT THE PRAYER. And the dust from the level of Samael ascends in a number of camps of debt, teaching guilt ABOUT THE PRAYER. And this prayer of Arvit is called 'Jacob's Ladder', in which: "And behold the angels of Elohim ascending and descending on it" (Beresheet 28:12). These are THE PRAYERS that ascend WHEN THEY ARE liabilities, and merits descend in their place. FOR THE CAMPS OF THE TEACHERS OF MERIT OF JACOB OVERCAME THE CAMPS OF THE TEACHERS OF LIABILITY OF SAMAEL. And there are those that ascend as merits and liabilities descend in their stead. IN THIS CASE, THE CAMPS OF THE TEACHERS OF LIABILITY OF SAMAEL HAVE OVERCOME THE OTHERS, FOR THESE CAMPS humiliate them in a number of wars.

579. דְּאִינּוּן מָארֵי תְּרִיסִין, בְּמִלְחַמְתָּא שֶׁל תּוֹרָה, עַד דְּיִשְׁתְּמַע קְרָבָא לְטוּרִין רַבְרְבִין, דְּאִינּוּן אַבְרָהָם יִצְחָק וְיַעֲקֹב, הה״ד, שִׁמְעוּ הָרִים אֶת רִיב יְיָ׳. רִיב דִּצְלוֹתָא. רִיב דְּאוֹרַיְיתָא. וְהַאי קְרָבָא דִּצְלוֹתָא דְּעַרְבִית, עַד עֲלוֹת הַשַּׁחַר. דְּרַבָּן גַּמְלִיאֵל אוֹקְמָהּ, עַד עֲלוֹת הַשַּׁחַר. דִּתְפִלַּת

עַרְבִית זְמַנָּה כָּל הַלַּיְלָה, אֶלָּא דְּחַכְמִים עָבְדוּ גְּדֵר עַד חֲצוֹת.

579. For they, WHO TEACH MERIT, are the defenders in the war of the Torah, until the war becomes audible to the great mountains, that is to Abraham, Isaac, and Jacob, as it is written: "Hear, O mountains, Hashem's controversy" (Michah 6:2). This is the controversy of prayer, the controversy of Torah, NAMELY THE CONTROVERSY OF THOSE WHO TEACH MERIT AND OF THOSE WHO TEACH LIABILITY OVER MAN'S STUDY OF TORAH AND PRAYER. And this war of Arvit continues until sunrise, for Rabban Gamliel determined it as until the rise of dawn, for Arvit may be said at any time during the night, but the sages erected a boundary around it AND DETERMINED IT as until midnight.

580. ובג״ד וַיֵּאָבֵק אִישׁ עִמּוֹ עַד עֲלוֹת הַשַּׁחַר, מַאן שָׁחַר. צְלוֹתָא דְּעַרְבִית. דְּשִׁיעוּרָה עַד בֹּקֶר דְּאַבְרָהָם, דְּאִיהִי אַרְבַּע שָׁעוֹת וַיַּשְׁכֵּם אַבְרָהָם בַּבֹּקֶר. בְּרֵישׁ שַׁעֲתָא קַדְמָאָה, בְּסוֹף הַשַּׁחַר, דְּאִיהוּ נֶצַח יַעֲקֹב, דְּתַמָּן לַמְנַצֵּחַ עַל אַיֶּלֶת הַשַּׁחַר, לְנַטְלָא נוּקְמָא מִסָּמָאֵל, דְּנָגַע בְּיָרֵךְ שְׂמָאלָא דְּיַעֲקֹב, דְּאִיהוּ הוֹד, דְּבֵיהּ אִתְמַר נְתָנַנִי שׁוֹמֵמָה כָּל הַיּוֹם דָּוָה, הוֹד, מִסִּטְרָא דְּהוֹד, אֶלֶף חֲמִישָׁאָה, אִשְׁתְּאָרַת בֵּי מַקְדְּשָׁא חֲרֵבָה וִיבֵשָׁה.

580. And because THE DUTY OF RECITING ARVIT IS UNTIL THE RISE OF DAWN, IT IS SAID: "and there wrestled a man with him until the breaking of the day" (Beresheet 32:24). What is meant by the dawn? It refers to Arvit, NAMELY THE SHECHINAH, whose limit is until the morning of Abraham, WHOSE TIME IS the fourth hour. "And Abraham rose up early in the morning" (Beresheet 22:3), namely at the beginning of the first hour at the end of the dawn, which is Netzach of Jacob, for there "To the chief musician (Heb. *menatze'ach*) upon the morning star" (Tehilim 22:1), to wreak vengeance on Samael for having touched Jacob's left thigh, which is Hod, of which it is said: "he has made me desolate and faint (Heb. *davah* - Dalet Vav Hei) all the day" (Eichah 1:13), WHERE THE LETTERS OF THE WORD *DAVAH*, REARRANGED, SPELL Hod. From the side of Hod, which is the fifth millenium, the Temple remained destroyed and barren.

87. Moses, the two Messiahs, the rainbow and Malchut

A Synopsis

Rabbi Shimon talks to Moses about two dawns and two Messiahs that come from two kingdoms. He says that Messiah son of David parallels Netzach, Messiah son of Ephraim parallels Hod, and Moses is the Central Column between them because his level is Tiferet and Yesod. We learn about the covenant of the rainbow, and about the three colors in it. We are told of the 39 types of work that are prohibited on the Shabbat, and the four kinds of 'going out' on that day.

581. אָמַר ר"ש, דָּא הוֹד דִּילָךְ רַעְיָא מְהֵימָנָא, דְּבֵיהּ אַנְתְּ חָרֵב, מִנְבוּאָה דִּילָךְ מִשְׂמָאלָא, וּבְגִין דְּאַנְתְּ מוֹלִיךְ לִימִין מֹשֶׁה דְּאִיהוּ נֶצַח, רֵישָׁא דִּשְׁחָרִין, אַיֶּלֶת אֲהָבִים, פָּתַח דָּוִד לַמְנַצֵּחַ עַל אַיֶּלֶת הַשַּׁחַר, דְּבֵיהּ יֵיתֵי מָאֲרֵי נַצְחָן קְרָבַיָּיא. וּבְגִין דְּנֶצַח וְהוֹד תְּרֵין שַׁחֲרִין, אוּקְמוּהָ בְּמַתְנִיתִין מֵאֵימָתַי קוֹרִין אֶת שְׁמַע בִּשְׁחָרִין, וְלָא אָמַר בַּשַּׁחַר. אֶלָּא בִּשְׁחָרִין תְּרֵין.

581. Rabbi Shimon said: Faithful Shepherd, this is your Hod, in which your prophecy is dried up on the left, and because you "caused... to go at the right hand of Moses" (Yeshayah 63:12), which is Netzach, which is the head of the dawns, "A loving hind" (Mishlei 5:19), THEREFORE David opened: "To the chief musician upon the morning star (hind)" (Tehilim 22:1), for the victors (Heb. *menatzchim*) in the wars will come through NETZACH. And since Netzach and Hod are two dawns, it was taught in the Mishnah: From what time may one recite the Sh'ma in the mornings? It does not say, 'in the morning', but 'in the mornings', two of them.

582. וּתְרֵין מְשִׁיחִין יִתְעָרוּן לְגַבַּיְיהוּ, מָשִׁיחַ בֶּן דָּוִד, לָקֳבֵל נֶצַח, וְאִתְקְשַׁר בַּבֹּקֶר דְּאַבְרָהָם, הֲדָא הוּא דִכְתִיב, נְעִימוֹת בִּימִינְךָ נֶצַח. הוֹד בִּגְבוּרָה, דְּבֵיהּ מָשִׁיחַ בֶּן אֶפְרַיִם אָחִיד. אַנְתְּ בְּאֶמְצָעִיתָא, דְּדַרְגָּא דִּילָךְ תִּפְאֶרֶת, דְּאִתְקְשַׁר בָּךְ עַמּוּדָא דְּאֶמְצָעִיתָא. וִיסוֹד חַי עָלְמִין בְּדַרְגָּא דִּילָךְ. וְחָכְמָה בְּיָמִין, הָרוֹצֶה לְהַחְכִּים יַדְרִים. וּבִינָה לִשְׂמָאלָא, הָרוֹצֶה לְהַעֲשִׁיר יַצְפִּין.

582. And two Messiahs, COMING FROM TWO MALCHUTS (LIT. 'KINGDOMS') awaken before them, NETZACH AND HOD. Messiah son of David parallels Netzach and is connected with the morning of Abraham, which is as is written: "at Your right hand are pleasures for evermore (Heb. *Netzach*)" (Tehilim 16:11). Hod IS CONNECTED to Gvurah, since to it, TO HOD, is attached Messiah the son of Efraim. You, MOSES, THE FAITHFUL SHEPHERD, are in the center, for your level is Tiferet, for the Central Column, WHICH IS TIFERET, is connected with you, and also Yesod, the life of the Worlds, is in your level. And Chochmah is on the right; let him who wants to be wise turn south. And Binah is on the left; let him who wants to be rich turn to the north.

583. אִיהִי הַקֶּשֶׁת גַּבָּךְ, וְהַאי אִיהוּ לְבוּשָׁא דִּשְׁכִינְתָּא. לְבוּשָׁא דְּצַדִּיק, דְּאִתְקְרֵי בְּרִית הַקֶּשֶׁת. וְאִיהוּ אוֹת שַׁבָּת, וְאוֹת י״ט, וְאוֹת תְּפִילִין, וְאוֹת בְּרִית מִילָה. וְאָמַר קוּדְשָׁא בְּרִיךְ הוּא, מַאן דְּלָאו אִיהוּ רָשִׁים בְּהַאי אוֹת, לָא יֵיעוּל בְּמַרְאָה דָּא, בְּחֶדֶר דָּא. וְהַאי אִיהוּ מַטֶּה, דְּעַמּוּדָא דְּאֶמְצָעִיתָא מַטֶּה בֵּיהּ כְּלַפֵּי חֶסֶד לַצַדִּיקִים גְּמוּרִים, לְמֵיהַב לוֹן זַכְוָון, בח״י בִּרְכָאן דִּצְלוֹתָא. וּמַטֶּה כְּלַפֵּי חוֹבָה לְרַשִׁיעַיָּא, לְמֵידָן לוֹן בִּגְבוּרָה לְדִינָא, כְּפוּם עוֹבָדֵיהוֹן. וּבְעַמּוּדָא דְּאֶמְצָעִיתָא מַאֲרִיךְ עַל בֵּינוֹנִים. וְהַאי אִיהוּ ש׳.

583. She, MALCHUT, is a rainbow with you, FOR MALCHUT RECEIVES FROM HIM THE THREE COLORS OF THE RAINBOW, WHICH ARE THE SECRET OF THE THREE COLUMNS. And this RAINBOW is the apparel of the Shechinah and the apparel of the Righteous, WHICH IS YESOD, that is called 'the covenant of the rainbow'. And it is the sign of the Shabbat and the sign of a festival, and the sign of Tefilin, and the sign of circumcision. And the Holy One, blessed be He, said: 'One who is not marked with the sign shall not enter into this vision, into this room,' WHICH IS MALCHUT. And MALCHUT is a staff (Heb. *mateh*), for the Central Column, WHICH IS ZEIR ANPIN, inclines (Heb. *mateh*) on it towards Chesed, WHICH IS THE SECRET OF THE RIGHT COLUMN, for the completely righteous, to accord them merits with the eighteen blessings of the Amidah prayer, and inclines towards liability, WHICH IS THE SECRET OF THE LEFT COLUMN, for the wicked, to judge them with Gvurah as guilty according to their deeds. And in the Central Column it is lenient to those who are mediocre. And this is the form

of the letter Shin, THAT HAS THREE HEADS, CORRESPONDING TO THESE THREE COLUMNS.

584. תְּלַת גְּוָונִין דְּקֶשֶׁת, אוֹת בְּרִית הַקֶּשֶׁת, בַּת יְחִידָה, שַׁבָּת מַלְכְּתָא. וְאִית לָהּ שִׁית דַּרְגִּין, תְּחוֹת שׁוּלְטָנוּתָא, דְּאִינוּן שֵׁשֶׁת יְמֵי הַמַּעֲשֶׂה, דְּכְלִילָן בִּמְטַטְרוֹן. דְּעָלַיְיהוּ אִתְּמַר, שֵׁשֶׁת יָמִים תַּעֲשֶׂה מַעֲשֶׂיךָ. אֲבָל בַּת יְחִידָה, שַׁבָּת לַיְדוָֹד, הָעוֹשֶׂה בָהּ מְלָאכָה יוּמָת.

584. The three colors of the rainbow, WHITE, RED AND GREEN, WHICH ARE THE SECRET OF THE THREE COLUMNS, are a sign of the covenant, NAMELY OF YESOD. The rainbow ITSELF IS an only daughter, the Queen Shabbat, WHICH IS MALCHUT THAT RECEIVES THE THREE COLORS OF THE RAINBOW FROM YESOD. And she, MALCHUT, has six grades, CHESED, GVURAH, TIFERET, NETZACH, HOD AND YESOD OF METATRON, under her control, which are the six days of Creation that are included in Metatron, about which it is said: "Six days you shall do your work" (Shemot 23:12), but the only daughter, MALCHUT OF ZEIR ANPIN, is Shabbat to Yud Hei Vav Hei: "whoever does work on it shall be put to death" (Shemot 35:2).

585. יְדוָֹד אִתְקְרֵי בְּאוֹת ה'. וּמִסְטְרָא דָא, יד"ו לִימִינָא. דְּאִיהוּ ה' שְׁלִימוּ דִּילֵיהּ. וְהָכִי לְכָל סְטְרָא בְּשִׁית סְטְרִין, ידו, דוי, ויד, יוד, דיו, ודי. אִינוּן ח"י אַתְוָון, דְּכְלִילָן בְּצַדִּיק חַי עָלְמִין. וְאִיהִי רְבִיעִית הַהִין בְּכָל סְטְרָא.

585. Yud Hei Vav Hei is called by the letter Hei, THAT IS TO SAY THE LETTER HEI COMPLETES THE NAME YUD HEI VAV HEI. FOR ZEIR ANPIN IS YUD HEI VAV, AND THE FINAL HEI IS MALCHUT, and from this side to the right, Yud-Hei-Vav, where the Hei is its completion. And so it is with each of the six extremities OF ZEIR ANPIN, THE HEI IS HIS COMPLETION. FOR THERE ARE SIX COMBINATIONS OF THE LETTERS YUD HEI VAV IN THE SIX EXTREMITIES OF ZEIR ANPIN, NAMELY: Yud Hei Vav; Hei Vav Yud; Vav Yud Hei; Yud Vav Hei; Hei Yud Vav; and Vav Hei Yud. This comes to a total of eighteen letters that are included in the Righteous, the life (Heb. *chai* = eighteen) of the worlds, WHICH IS YESOD.

MALCHUT is the fourth part of a hin on each side. THAT IS TO SAY MALCHUT IS THE FOURTH LETTER, THAT IS THE FINAL HEI THAT COMPLEMENTS EACH OF THE ABOVE SIX COMBINATIONS. THUS IT IS CALLED 'THE FOURTH PART OF A HIN' BECAUSE IT IS THE FOURTH LETTER AND THEREFORE THE FOURTH PART, AND IT IS OF A HIN BECAUSE IT IS THE LETTER HEI.

586. וְאִיהִי הֵ"א, מִסִּטְרָא דִשְׁמָא מְפֹרָשׁ, יוֹ"ד הֵ"א וָא"ו. יוֹ"ד בְּחֶסֶד, הֵ"א בִּגְבוּרָה, וָא"ו בְּתִפְאֶרֶת. כַּד שַׁלְטָא הַאי ט"ל, אָסָרוּ חֲכָמִים אַרְבָּעִים מְלָאכוֹת חָסֵר אַחַת. וְאִתְקְרִיאוּ אָבוֹת מְלָאכוֹת, ע"ש דְּאִינּוּן לָקֳבֵל אֲבָהָן, דְּשַׁלִּיט עֲלַיְיהוּ ט"ל, דְּאִיהוּ אַרְבָּעִים חָסֵר אַחַת.

586. And she, MALCHUT, is Hei FULLY SPELLED WITH ALEPH, from the point of view of the explicit Name Yud-Vav-Dalet, Hei-Aleph, Vav-Aleph Vav. Yud-Vav-Dalet is in Chesed; Hei-Aleph is in Gvurah; Vav Aleph Vav is in Tiferet, WHILE THE FINAL HEI-ALEPH IS IN MALCHUT. And when these 39 are in control, the sages prohibited forty save one types of work that are called 'the main classes' (lit. 'fathers') of work, because they correspond to the patriarchs who control them, NAMELY CHESED, GVURAH AND TIFERET THAT ARE CALLED 'PATRIARCHS'. FOR YUD-VAV-DALET, HEI-ALEPH, VAV-ALEPH-VAV ARE CHESED, GVURAH AND TIFERET, AS ABOVE, AND THEIR NUMERICAL VALUE IS 39, namely forty save one.

587. וּבְאִלֵּין אַרְבָּעִים מְלָאכוֹת חָסֵר חַד, לָקָה עֲשָׂרָה מַלְקִיּוֹת לְאָדָם. וַעֲשָׂרָה לְחַוָּה. וַעֲשָׂרָה לַנָּחָשׁ. וְתִשְׁעָה לְאַרְעָא. וּבְגִין דְּט"ל שַׁלְטָא, בְּשַׁבָּת, דְּאִיהוּ ה' אֵין לוֹקִין בְּשַׁבָּת. וְהַאי ט"ל לָאו אִיהוּ כט"ל דְּחוֹל, מִסִּטְרָא דְּעֶבֶד מְטַטְרוֹן. וְאַרְבָּעִים מְלָאכוֹת חָסֵר אַחַת, הֵם הַזּוֹרֵעַ וְהַחוֹרֵשׁ וְכוּ'.

587. And with these forty save one types of work THAT ARE PERMITTED ON WEEKDAYS, lashes were administered, ten to Adam, ten to Eve, ten to the serpent, and nine to the land, MAKING A TOTAL OF 39 CURSES. And because these 39, NAMELY YUD-VAV-DALET, HEI-ALEPH, VAV-ALEPH VAV, rule on Shabbat, which is Hei-ALEPH, no lashes are administered on Shabbat. And these 39 are not the same as the 39 TYPES OF WORK

PERMITTED on a weekday, for the former are from the side of the servant Metatron, while the forty save one types of work are sowing and ploughing, etc.

588. סָבָא סָבָא, שְׁכִינְתָּא אִתְקְרֵי אֶרֶ"ץ דְּקוּדְשָׁא בְּרִיךְ הוּא. הֲהַ"ד וְהָאָרֶץ הֲדוֹם רַגְלָי. מִסִּטְרָא דְּחֶסֶד אִתְקְרִיאַת מַיִם. וּמִסִּטְרָא דִּגְבוּרָה אִתְקְרִיאַת אֵשׁ. וּמִסִּטְרָא דְּעַמּוּדָא דְּאֶמְצָעִיתָא אֲוִיר. וְאִיהִי אֶרֶץ, קַרְקַע לְכֻלְּהוּ.

588. THE FAITHFUL SHEPHERD SAID TO RABBI SHIMON: Old man, old man, the Shechinah is called 'the earth of the Holy One, blessed be He', as it is said: "and the earth is My footstool" (Yeshayah 66:1). From the point of view of Chesed, THE SHECHINAH is called 'water', and from the point of view of Gvurah, she is called 'fire', while from the point of view of the Central Column, WHICH IS TIFERET, IT IS CALLED 'air'. But IN HERSELF, the SHECHINAH IS CALLED 'earth', ground for all of them, NAMELY SHE ACCEPTS ALL OF THEM.

589. וּבְגִין דְּנִשְׁמָתָא יְתֵירָה אִתְפַּשְּׁטָא בִּשְׁכִינְתָּא, דְּאִיהִי שַׁבָּת מַלְכְּתָא, דְּאִתְּמַר בָּהּ וּמַלְכוּתוֹ בַּכֹּל מָשָׁלָה, מִשָּׁם אִיהִי מַלְכוּת, דְּשַׁלְטָנוּתָהָא עַל אַרְעָא, וְעַל אִילָנִין וְזַרְעִין. וּבְגִין דְּאִילָנָא דְּחַיֵּי, דְּהִיא נִשְׁמָתָא יְתֵירָה דְּבְשַׁבָּת, בָּהּ תּוֹלְדִין דִּילָהּ, אִית נַיְיחָא לְאַרְעָא, דְּאִיהִי שְׁכִינְתָּא.

589. And whereas the extra Neshamah spreads in the Shechinah, which is the Shabbat Queen, about which is said: "and His kingdom rules over all" (Tehilim 103:19), from there is Malchut, whose rule is over the earth and over the trees and the seeds. And since the Tree of Life, WHICH IS ZEIR ANPIN, which is the extra Neshamah that comes on the Shabbat, contains all her offspring, the earth, which is the Shechinah, has rest.

590. וּבְגִין דִּשְׁכִינְתָּא עִלָּאָה אִתְפַּשְׁטַת בְּאַרְעָא, דְּאִתְּמַר בָּהּ פָּרָה אֲדֻמָּה תְּמִימָה אֲשֶׁר אֵין בָּהּ מוּם אֲשֶׁר לֹא עָלָה עָלֶיהָ עֹל, אָסוּר

לַחֲרוֹשׁ בְּשַׁבָּת חֲרִישָׁה בַּשּׁוֹר. דְּאִתְּמַר עַל גַּבִּי חָרְשׁוּ חוֹרְשִׁים. וּשְׁכִינְתָּא תַּתָּאָה אִיהִי פָּרָה אֲדוּמָה מִסִּטְרָא דִּגְבוּרָה. תְּמִימָה, מִסִּטְרָא דְּחֶסֶד, דְּאִיהוּ דַּרְגָּא דְּאַבְרָהָם, דְּאִתְּמַר בֵּיהּ הִתְהַלֵּךְ לְפָנַי וֶהְיֵה תָמִים. אֲשֶׁר אֵין בָּה מוּם, מִסִּטְרָא דְּעַמוּדָא דְּאֶמְצָעִיתָא. אֲשֶׁר לֹא עָלָה עָלֶיהָ עוֹל, מִסִּטְרָא דִּשְׁכִינְתָּא עִלָּאָה דְּאִיהִי חֵירוּ, בַּאֲתָר דְּאִיהִי שַׁלְטָא וְהַזָּר הַקָּרֵב יוּמָת, לֵית רְשׁוּ לְסִטְרָא אַחֲרָא לְשַׁלְטָאָה, לֹא שָׂטָן, וְלֹא מַשְׁחִית, וְלֹא מַלְאַךְ הַמָּוֶת, דְּאִינּוּן מִסִּטְרָא דְּגֵיהִנָּם.

590. And since the upper Shechinah, WHICH IS BINAH, spreads in the land, WHICH IS MALCHUT, and about MALCHUT, it is said: "a red heifer without defect, in which there is no blemish, and upon which never came a yoke" (Bemidbar 19:2), it is forbidden to plough with an ox on the Shabbat, as it is written: "The ploughers ploughed upon my back" (Tehilim 129:3), NAMELY THE JUDGMENTS OF THE LEFT, FOR IT IS THEREFORE SAID ABOUT MALCHUT "UPON WHICH NEVER CAME A YOKE." And the lower Shechinah, WHICH IS MALCHUT, is a red heifer from the aspect of Gvurah, perfect from the point of view of Chesed, which is the level of Abraham, about whom it is said: "Walk before Me and be perfect" (Beresheet 17:1). "in which there is no blemish" is from the side of the Central Column, WHICH IS TIFERET. "and upon which never came a yoke" is from the side of the upper Shechinah, WHICH IS BINAH, which is freedom, for where she is in control, "the stranger that comes near shall be put to death" (Bemidbar 1:51), since permission to control is not granted to the Other Side, not to the Satan nor to the Destroyer nor to the Angel of Death, for they are from the side of Gehenom.

591. וּבְגִין דָּא, בְּיוֹמִין דְּחוֹל, אַמְרִין יִשְׂרָאֵל, וְהוּא רַחוּם יְכַפֵּר עָוֹן וְלֹא יַשְׁחִית וְהִרְבָּה לְהָשִׁיב אַפּוֹ וְגו'. בְּגִין דְּבְיוֹמִין דְּחוֹל, שְׁכִינְתָּא תַּתָּאָה אִתְלַבְּשַׁת בְּאִלֵּין קְלִיפִין דְּמִיתָה דְּדִינָא. וּבְשַׁבָּת אִתְפַּשְּׁטַת מִנַּיְיהוּ, בְּגִין דְּאִילָנָא דְּחַיֵּי דְּאִיהוּ בֶּן י"ד, יד"ו, אִתְחַבָּר בְּהֵ"א. בְּהַהוּא זִמְנָא נַיְיחָא אִשְׁתְּכַחַת לְהֵ"א, וְכָל מַה דְּאִיהוּ תְּחוֹתָהּ, וְלָא צָרִיךְ לְמֵימַר בֵּיהּ וְהוּא רַחוּם. וּמַאן אִינּוּן תְּחוֹתָהּ. יִשְׂרָאֵל. וְכָל אֲתָר דְּיִשְׂרָאֵל מִשְׁתַּכְּחִין, נְטִירוּ אִשְׁתְּכַח וְנַיְיחָא.

591. For this reason, on weekdays Yisrael say: "But He was full of compassion, forgiving iniquity, and He did not destroy them: often He turned away His anger, not stirring up all His wrath" (Tehilim 78:38). On weekdays the lower Shechinah puts on these Klipot of death and Judgment, but on the Shabbat She sheds them, because of the Tree of Life, which is the son of Yud-Hei, THAT IS, IT HAS THE MOCHIN OF YUD-HEI, WHICH ARE CHOCHMAH AND BINAH, BEING Yud-Hei-Vav, AS ZEIR ANPIN IS VAV AND HAS THE MOCHIN OF YUD-HEI. ON SHABBAT, it joins with Hei, WHICH IS MALCHUT. At the time there is rest for the Hei and everything that is under it, WHICH IS WHY it is not necessary, on the Shabbat, to say: "But He was full of compassion..." And who are they who are under it? Yisrael. And wherever Yisrael are to be found, keeping and rest are to be found.

592. וּבְג"ד, אָסוּר לְמֶחֱרַשׁ בְּאַרְעָא, וּלְמֶעֲבַד בָּהּ גּוּמוֹת, דַּהֲוֵי כְּאִילּוּ עָבֵיד פְּגִימוּ בְּאַרְעָא קַדִּישָׁא, דְּאִיהִי שְׁכִינְתָּא. וְאָסוּר לְאִשְׁתַּמְּשָׁא בְּכֵלִים דְּאַרְעָא בְּשַׁבָּת. וַאֲפִילוּ לְטַלְטֵל אֶבֶן. וְלָא כְּלִי בְּעָלְמָא. דִּיהֵוֵי נַיְיחָא לוֹן בְּזָכוּ דִּשְׁכִינְתָּא דְּאִתְקְרִיאַת אַבְנָא, דִּכְתִיב בָּהּ וְהָאֶבֶן הַזֹּאת אֲשֶׁר שַׂמְתִּי מַצֵּבָה, בִּצְלוֹתָא. עֲמִידָה אִיהִי לְיִשְׂרָאֵל, דִּבְגִינָהּ אִית לוֹן קִיּוּמָא בְּעָלְמָא. וְעֲלֵיהּ אִתְּמַר, מִשָּׁם רוֹעֶה אֶבֶן יִשְׂרָאֵל. עַל אֶבֶן אַחַת שִׁבְעָה עֵינַיִם, אֶבֶן מָאֲסוּ הַבּוֹנִים.

592. And this is why it is forbidden to plough the land or to make ditches in it, FOR THE LAND ALLUDES TO MALCHUT, and it is like one who makes a defect in the holy land, which is the Shechinah. And it is forbidden to use the tools of the land, even to move a stone, or any tool, so that they should have rest in the merit of the Shechinah that is called 'stone', about which is written, "and this stone, which I have set up for a pillar" (Beresheet 28:22), in the prayer. AND SHE IS CALLED 'A PILLAR' BECAUSE she stands up for Yisrael, and for her sake Yisrael exist in the world. And it is said about her: "from thence from the shepherd, the Stone of Yisrael" (Beresheet 49:24); and "Upon one stone are seven eyes" (Zecharyah 3:9); and "The stone which the builders rejected" (Tehilim 118:22).

593. וּבְג"ד וְשָׁמְרוּ בְנֵי יִשְׂרָאֵל אֶת הַשַּׁבָּת לַעֲשׂוֹת אֶת הַשַּׁבָּת לְדֹרֹתָם

בְּרִית עוֹלָם. צָרִיךְ לְנַטְרָא לָהּ בְּדִירָתָם, דְּלָא יִפְּקוּן מרה"י לרה"ר. וְהַאי אִיהוּ דְּאוּקְמוּהָ מָארֵי מַתְנִיתִין, יְצִיאוֹת הַשַּׁבָּת שְׁתַּיִם שֶׁהֵן אַרְבַּע, הוֹצָאָה מֵרְשׁוּת לִרְשׁוּת, וְהַכְנָסָה נָמֵי יְצִיאָה קָרֵי לָהּ. וְאִינּוּן סָמָאֵל וְנָחָשׁ, צְרִיכִין יִשְׂרָאֵל לְנַטְרָא לוֹן, דְּלָא יֵיעֲלוּן לְדִירָה דִּשְׁכִינְתָּא, דְּאִיהִי רְשׁוּת הַיָּחִיד. מַאן רְשׁוּת הָרַבִּים. חֲלָלָה שִׁפְחָה זוֹנָה נִדָּה גּוֹיָה, רְשׁוּת דְּסָמָאֵל וְנָחָשׁ, וְשַׁבְעִין מְמָנָן דְּעַמִּין.

ע"כ רעיא מהימנא

593. And for this reason: "Wherefore the children of Yisrael shall keep the Shabbat, to observe the Shabbat throughout their generations (Heb. *dorotam*), for a perpetual covenant" (Shemot 31:16), which they have to keep in their homes (Heb. *diratam*). That is, they must not leave the private domain for the public domain, and this is what the sages of the Mishnah taught: There are two, which are, indeed four, kinds of 'going out' on the Shabbat, namely transfer from one domain on to another; also, bringing in is considered going out. And as for Samael and Serpent, Yisrael have to guard against their entering the dwelling of the Shechinah, which is the private domain. What is the public domain? It is: a daughter to a priest's illegitimate connection, a bondwoman, a prostitute, a menstruating woman, a gentile woman, who are in the domain of Samael and Serpent and the seventy appointees over the peoples.

End of Ra'aya Meheimna

88. "I have gathered my myrrh... Drink, drink deep, O loving companions"

A Synopsis

Rabbi Shimon analyzes the title verse to show the secret of the sacrifices, and he tells us the significance of Jacob's name being changed to Israel.

594. פָּתַח וְאָמַר, בָּאתִי לְגַנִּי וְכוּ', וּבְחֲבוּרָא קַדְמָאָה, אָרִיתִי מוֹרִי עִם בְּשָׂמִי, דְרוֹעָא יְמִינָא בְּיַרְכָא שְׂמָאלָא. אָכַלְתִּי יַעְרִי עִם דִּבְשִׁי, יַעֲקֹב בְּרָחֵל. שָׁתִיתִי יֵינִי עִם חֲלָבִי, דְרוֹעָא שְׂמָאלָא בְּיַרְכָא יְמִינָא. דְרוֹעָא יְמִינָא בְּיַרְכָא שְׂמָאלָא, אִינּוּן חֶסֶד עִם הוֹד. יַעֲקֹב בְּרָחֵל, עַמּוּדָא דְאֶמְצָעִיתָא בַּמַלְכוּת. דְרוֹעָא שְׂמָאלָא בְּיַרְכָא יְמִינָא גְּבוּרָה בְּנֶצַח.

594. He began by quoting: "I am come into my garden..." (Shir Hashirim 5:1). And in the first compilation HE SAYS: "I have gathered my myrrh with my spice" refers to the right arm over the left leg. "I have eaten my honeycomb with my honey" refers to Jacob with Rachel. "I have drunk my wine with my milk" refers to the left arm on the right leg. THE EXPLANATION OF THIS IS: The right arm on the left leg are Chesed with Hod. Jacob with Rachel are the Central Column, WHICH IS TIFERET, along with Malchut. Left arm with right leg are Gvurah with Netzach.

595. וְאַמַּאי שְׁנֵי מִדּוֹת מִדּוֹת דִּילֵיהּ הָכִי. אֶלָּא רָזָא דִנֵימָא הָכָא, דָּוִד אָמַר הָכָא, כֹּהֲנֶיךָ יִלְבְּשׁוּ צֶדֶק וַחֲסִידֶיךָ יְרַנֵּנוּ. וְאִתְּמַר הָתָם, וּלְוִיֶּךָ מִבָּעֵי לֵיהּ לְמֵימַר. אָמַר קוּדְשָׁא בְּרִיךְ הוּא לָאו אֹרַח לְשַׁנּוֹת מִדּוֹתַי, אֶלָּא בָּתַר דְּזַמֵּינַת לִי, אִית לִי לְמֶעְבַּד רְעוּתָךְ. וּמֵהָכָא אוֹלִיפְנָא, דְּבַעַל הַבַּיִת דִּמְזַמֵּין אֲפִילוּ לְמַלְכָּא, אִית לֵיהּ לְמֶעְבַּד רְעוּתֵיהּ. וּבְג"ד אוֹקְמוּהָ, כָּל מַה שֶׁאוֹמֵר לָךְ בַּעַל הַבַּיִת עֲשֵׂה חוּץ מִצֵּא. וְעִם כָּל דָּא דְּרָזָא דָא דָא שַׁפִּיר אִיהוּ, הָא כְּתִיב אֲנִי יְיָ' לֹא שָׁנִיתִי, וּבְכָל קַרְבְּנִין לָא כְּתִיב בְּהוֹן אֶלָּא לַיְדוָֹד, אֵיךְ יָכִיל לְמֶהֱוֵי דְּיִשַׁנֵּי דַרְגִּין דִּשְׁמֵיהּ בְּקָרְבְּנָא.

595. HE ASKS: Why did He so change His attributes? AND HE ANSWERS, the secret that is here stated is because David said here: "Let Your priests be clothed with righteousness; and let Your pious ones shout for joy" (Tehilim 132:9). And we learned there that he should have said 'Your Levites'. The Holy One, blessed be He, said: 'It is not my way to change my attributes, but since you have invited Me, I have to do your will.' And we further learned that even when a householder invites the king, the latter has to do the will of the former. It was thus taught: 'Whatever the host tells you to do, do, except 'leave''. Nevertheless, for all that this secret is beautiful, it is still written: "For I am Hashem, I do not change" (Malachi 3:6), and indeed in respect of all the sacrifices, it is written of them for Hashem only, IN WHICH THERE IS NO CHANGE, and how could it indeed be that He would change the levels of His name with the sacrifices?

596. אֶלָּא, אָרִיתִי מוֹרִי: יוֹצֵר אוֹר. עִם בְּשָׂמִי: אַהֲבַת עוֹלָם. אָכַלְתִּי יַעְרִי: שְׁמַע יִשְׂרָאֵל. עִם דִּבְשִׁי: בָּרוּךְ שֵׁם כְּבוֹד מַלְכוּתוֹ לְעוֹלָם וָעֶד. שָׁתִיתִי יֵינִי: וְהָיָה אִם שָׁמוֹעַ, עַד וַיֹּאמֶר. עִם חֲלָבִי: מִן וַיֹּאמֶר, עַד אֱמֶת. אִכְלוּ רֵעִים: ג' רִאשׁוֹנוֹת, וְג' אַחֲרוֹנוֹת. שְׁתוּ וְשִׁכְרוּ דּוֹדִים: שְׁאַר בִּרְכָאן דִּצְלוֹתָא.

596. HE ANSWERS, "I have gathered my myrrh" REFERS TO THE BLESSING OF 'who forms light'; "with my spice" REFERS TO 'everlasting love'. "I have eaten my honeycomb" IS THE Sh'ma Yisrael, and "with my honey" IS 'Blessed be the name of the glory of His kingdom forever and ever'. "I have drunk my wine" REFERS TO "And it shall come to pass, if you hearken" (Devarim 11:13-21) up to "And Hashem spoke," and "with my milk" refers to from "And Hashem spoke" (Bemidbar 15:37-41) up to 'True.' "Eat, O dear ones" REFERS TO the first three blessings and the last three blessings OF THE AMIDAH PRAYER, while "and drink, drink deep, O loving companions" refers to all the remaining blessings of the prayer.

597. וּבְחַבּוּרָא קַדְמָאָה, סִתְרָא דְּקָרְבְּנָא, פָּרִים וּכְבָשִׂים וְעַתּוּדִים וְעִזִּים, אִינּוּן, ד' פְּנֵי שׁוֹר. פְּנֵי נֶשֶׁר וְגוֹ', שְׁתֵּי תוֹרִים אוֹ שְׁנֵי בְּנֵי יוֹנָה, וְצָרִיךְ לְפָרְשָׁא. אַרְיֵה נָחִית לְגַבֵּי שׁוֹר, דְּאִיהוּ שְׂמָאלָא, לְאִתְקַשְּׁרָא חֶסֶד בִּגְבוּרָה. אָדָם נָחִית לְגַבֵּי נֶשֶׁר. דַּרְגָּא דְּיַעֲקֹב. וּבְג"ד אוֹקְמוּהָ

מָארֵי מַתְנִיתִין, שׁוּפְרֵיהּ דְּיַעֲקֹב שׁוּפְרֵיהּ דְּאָדָם קַדְמָאָה הֲוָה. וּמַאן
גָּרִים לְאִסְתַּלְּקָא לְאִתְקְרֵי יִשְׂרָאֵל, דִּכְתִיב לֹא יַעֲקֹב יֵאָמֵר עוֹד שִׁמְךָ
כִּי אִם יִשְׂרָאֵל יִהְיֶה שְׁמֶךָ, דִּיהֵוֵי יִשְׂרָאֵל עִקָּר לְאִתְפְּרְשָׁא בֵּינַיְיהוּ.

597. And in the first section, HE SAID: The secret of the sacrifices is that cattle and sheep and rams and goats are the four COUNTENANCES OF the face of an ox. The face of an eagle, etc. ARE two turtledoves or two young doves, but this matter is in need of further clarification. Lion, WHICH IS CHESED, descends to the ox, which is left, WHICH IS GVURAH, in order to link Chesed with Gvurah, NAMELY THAT THEY SHOULD BE INCORPORATED WITHIN EACH OTHER. Man, WHICH IS MALCHUT, descends to the eagle, WHICH IS TIFERET, which is the level of Jacob, SO THAT TIFERET AND MALCHUT WILL UNITE WITH EACH OTHER. This is why the sages of the Mishnah taught that Jacob's beauty was that of Adam. And who caused his ascendancy so that he should be called 'Israel'? THE HOLY ONE, BLESSED BE HE, as it is written: "Your name shall be called no more Jacob, but Israel" (Beresheet 32:29) will be your name, THE MEANING OF WHICH IS that Yisrael should be the primary name to spread among them.

89. He that treats lightly bread crumbs

A Synopsis

Rabbi Shimon says that anyone who throws bread on the ground will be assured of poverty, for only God has dominion over the five kinds of grain.

598. וַעֲשִׂירִית הָאֵיפָה, אֲמַאי. אֶלָּא עֲשִׂירִית הָאֵיפָה, לָקֳבֵל כ"י. דְּאִיהִי עֲשִׂירָאָה דְּדַרְגִּין, וְאִצְטְרִיכָא לְאִתְיַיהֲבָא בֵּין תְּרֵין דְּרוֹעִין, וְאִיהִי סֹלֶת נָהֲמָא, וְאִיהִי נָהֲמָא. וּבְגִין דְּאִיהִי נָהֲמָא, לָא אִתְפְּקַד עַל נָהֲמָא דַּחֲמֵשֶׁת מִינִין, דְּאִיהִי חִטָּה, וּשְׂעוֹרָה, וְשִׁיפוֹן וְכוּ', מְמָנָא דְּעָלְמָא. וְלָא שַׁוֵּי מְמָנָא עֲלַייהוּ, אֶלָּא קוּדְשָׁא בְּרִיךְ הוּא בִּלְחוֹדוֹי.

598. Why "the tenth part of an efah" (Bemidbar 28:5)? HE ANSWERS, the tenth part of an efah parallels the Congregation of Yisrael, which is the tenth grade, NAMELY MALCHUT, and it has to be placed between the two arms, WHICH ARE CHESED AND GVURAH OF ZEIR ANPIN, SO THAT IT SHOULD BE MADE UP OF CHOCHMAH OF THE LEFT AND CHASSADIM OF THE RIGHT. AND THEN it is fine flour for the baking of bread, and it is bread. And because MALCHUT is THE SECRET OF bread, no official in the world is appointed over bread made of the five kinds of grain, that are wheat, barley, rye, oats, and spelt, and no one is appointed over them, but the Holy One, blessed be He, alone.

599. וּבג"ד, מַאן דִּמְזַלְזֵל בְּנַהֲמָא, וְזָרִיק לֵיה בְּאַרְעָא, עֲנִיוּתָא רָדִיף אֲבַתְרֵיה. וְחַד מְמָנָא אִתְפְּקַד עַל דָּא, וְאִיהוּ רָדִיף אֲבַתְרֵיה, לְמֵיהַב לֵיה עֲנִיוּתָא, וְלָא יִפּוּק מִן עָלְמָא, עַד דְּיִצְטְרִיךְ לִבְרִיָּין. וַעֲלֵיה כְּתִיב, נוֹדֵד הוּא לַלֶּחֶם אַיֵּה. נוֹדֵד הוּא, וְיֵהַךְ מִטַּלְטֵל, וְגָלֵי מֵאֲתָר לַאֲתָר, לַלֶּחֶם אַיֵּה הוּא. וְלֵית מַאן דְּיַשְׁגַּח עֲלֵיה, הה"ד אַיֵּה. מַאן דִּירַחֵם עֲלֵיה, בְּגִין דְּלָא יִשְׁכַּח.

599. And therefore poverty follows anyone who shows contempt to bread and throws it on the ground. And an angel that is appointed over this matter follows after him to assure him poverty. And he will not depart from this world until he has been in need of assistance from others. And it is written

about such a one: "He wanders abroad for bread, saying, Where is it?" (Iyov 15:23), THE MEANING OF WHICH IS THAT HE shall wander abroad, going from place to place, IN HIS SEARCH for bread: 'Where is it?' And no one will have any regard for him, as it is written: "Where is it?" WHERE IS the one who will have mercy on him? For such a one will not be found.

A Synopsis

Moses leads the discussion into the foolishness of those who treat lightly the crumbs of the Torah – the secrets in the crowns of the letters. As these unwise people will perish, so will those who transmit secrets of the Torah and Kabbalah to people who are dishonest or who have an evil inclination.

רעיא מהימנא

600. וּבְחִבּוּרָא קַדְמָאָה אָמַר רַעְיָא מְהֵימָנָא, מַאן דִּמְזַלְזֵל בְּפֵרוּרִין דְּנַהֲמָא. וְזָרִיק לוֹן בַּאֲתַר דְּלָא אִצְטְרִיךְ. הַאי כָּל שֶׁכֵּן מַאן דִּמְזַלְזֵל בְּפֵירוּרִין דְּמוֹחָא, דְּאִינּוּן טִפִּין דְּזֶרַע, דְּזָרִיק לוֹן בְּאַרְעָא, דְּאִתְּמַר בְּהוֹן כִּי הִשְׁחִית כָּל בָּשָׂר אֶת דַּרְכּוֹ עַל הָאָרֶץ. אוֹ דְּזָרִיק לוֹן בְּנִדָּה, אוֹ בְּבַת אֵל נֵכָר, אוֹ בְּשִׁפְחָה אוֹ בְּזוֹנָה. וכ"ש וכ"ש מַאן דִּמְזַלְזֵל בְּפֵירוּרִין דְּנַהֲמָא דְּאוֹרַיְיתָא, דְּאִינּוּן קוֹצֵי אַתְוָון, וְתָגֵי אַתְוָון, דְּאִתְּמַר עֲלַיְיהוּ כָּל הַמִּשְׁתַּמֵּשׁ בְּתָגָא חָלָף.

Ra'aya Meheimna (the Faithful Shepherd)

600. And in the first part, the Faithful Shepherd said: Whoever treats lightly crumbs of bread and throws them where they should not be, and even more so one who treats lightly pieces of marrow, that are drops of seed, and throws them on the ground, it is said about them: "for all flesh had corrupted its way upon the earth" (Beresheet 6:12). Or he who throws them to a menstruating woman, or the daughter of an idolater, or a bondwoman or a prostitute, and much more so one who treats lightly the crumbs of the bread of the Torah, which are THE SECRETS THAT ARE IN the tips of the letters and the crowns of the letters, about these it is said: He that makes worldly use of the crown shall perish.

601. כ"ש מַאן דְּמָסַר רָזִין דְּאוֹרַיְיתָא, וְסִתְרֵי קַבָּלָה, וְסִתְרֵי מַעֲשֵׂה בְרֵאשִׁית, אוֹ סִתְרֵי אַתְוָון דִּשְׁמָא מְפֹרָשׁ, לַאֲנָשִׁים דְּלָאו אִינּוּן הֲגוּנִים, דְּשָׁלִיט עָלַיְיהוּ יֵצֶר הָרָע, אִשָּׁה זוֹנָה, דְּאִתְּמַר עֲלָה, כִּי בְעַד אִשָּׁה זוֹנָה עַד כִּכַּר לָחֶם. וְלֵית לֶחֶם אֶלָּא כ"ב אַתְוָון דְּאוֹרַיְיתָא. וְלֵית כִּכָּר, אֶלָּא אֲפִילוּ הֲלָכָה אַחַת.

601. And how much more so whoever transmits secrets of the Torah and the secrets of the Kabbalah and the secrets of the Works of Creation or secrets of the letters of the explicit Name to people who are not worthy, who are in the control of the Evil Inclination, a harlot, about whom it is written: "For by means of a harlot a man is brought to a piece of bread" (Mishlei 6:26). And whenever bread is mentioned the meaning is the 22 letters of the Torah, and whenever 'piece' is mentioned the meaning is even a single Halachah.

602. וּבְחִבּוּרָא קַדְמָאָה, לָא גַּלֵּי רָזָא בְּאִלֵּין פְּרוּרִין, אֶלָּא בְּאֹרַח פְּשָׁט, וְלָא יָהִיב בְּהוֹן שִׁיעוּרָא. אֲבָל אוֹקְמוּהָ מָארֵי מַתְנִיתִין, דְּשִׁיעוּרָא דְּפִירוּרִין כַּזַּיִת לְפָחוֹת, כָּל שֶׁכֵּן אִי אִינּוּן כַּבֵּיצָה. דְּמָארֵי מַתְנִיתִין דְּקַדְקוּ עָלַיְיהוּ, עַד כַּזַּיִת עַד כַּבֵּיצָה לְבָרְכָא עָלַיְיהוּ.

602. And in the first part, he revealed the secret of these crumbs, only according to the literal meaning, nor did he determine the amounts. But the sages of the Mishnah taught: The amount of the crumbs is not less than the size of an olive. And how much more so if they are of a quantity the size of an egg, for the sages of the Mishnah were stringent about them: How much should one eat to have to say the Blessing AFTER THE MEAL? An olive's size, an egg's size.

90. Olive-size and egg-size

A Synopsis

Moses tells the esoteric meaning of the amount of the crumbs, and he asks God and the Shechinah to give everyone perfect food for the correction of the World to Come. Next the Faithful Shepherd engages in a dialogue with Great-grandfather, upper Chochmah, who descends to him and talks about who is the host and who the guest that break the bread and distribute it and bless it. Rabbi Shimon and the other friends join the discussion and bring up the topic of levirate marriage and reincarnation. The Faithful Shepherd invites all those present to gather round for the banquet of the King, and while talking about the breaking of the bread into an egg-size and an olive-size he explains the secret and importance of 'amen'.

603. וְאֹרַח רָזָא, א״ח הוּא ט׳ פְּרוּרִין, שָׁלֹשׁ לְכָל סְטָר, תְּלַת מִן ד׳, תְּרֵין עֲשַׂר. רְבִיעִית אִיהוּ שְׁלִימוּ, לְאַשְׁלְמָא בֵּיהּ עֲשַׂר. וּלְאַשְׁלְמָא ד׳, דְּאִינּוּן יְדֹוָד. מַאי עֲשַׂר. אִינּוּן: יוּ״ד הֵ״א וָא״ו הֵ״א. קוֹצָא דְּאָת ד׳ מִן אֶחָד, שִׁיעוּרָא כַּזַיִת. י׳ מִן יְדֹוָד, שִׁיעוּרָא דִּילֵיהּ כַּבֵּיצָה.

603. And according to the esoteric meaning: Aleph Chet (= nine) OF THE WORD 'ONE' (*HEB. ECHAD - ALEPH CHET DALET*) make nine crumbs, three in each direction. And with the three of the Dalet (= four) OF ECHAD, we have a total of twelve CRUMBS. Again, the fourth OF THE DALET OF *ECHAD* completes to ten. And this completes the four, which are THE FOUR LETTERS of Yud Hei Vav Hei. What are the ten? They are THE TEN LETTERS IN Yud-Vav-Dalet, Hei-Aleph, Vav-Aleph-Vav, Hei-Aleph. Now the tip of the letter Dalet of *Echad* is the size of an olive-size. The Yud of Yud Hei Vav Hei is the measure of an egg-size.

604. אִיהִי ד׳, שְׁלִימוּ דְּמֶרְכַּבְתָּא דְּאָדָם, וּשְׁלִימוּ דְּאַרְבַּע אַנְפִּין דְּאָדָם. וּבַג״ד, יִשָּׂא יְדֹוָד פָּנָיו אֵלֶיךָ. וְאוֹקְמוּהָ מָארֵי מַתְנִיתִין, וְהָכְתִיב אֲשֶׁר לֹא יִשָּׂא פָּנִים. אֶלָּא אָמַר הַקּוּדְשָׁא בְּרִיךְ הוּא, וְלֹא אָמַרְתִּי לָהֶם וְאָכַלְתָּ וְשָׂבָעְתָּ, וְהֵם דְּקַדְקוּ עֲלֵיהֶם, עַד כַּזַיִת אוֹ עַד כַּבֵּיצָה, וְאֵיךְ לֹא אֶשָּׂא לָהֶם פָּנִים. וְרַבָּנָן דְּמַתְנִיתִין וַאֲמוֹרָאִין, כָּל תַּלְמוּדָא דִּלְהוֹן, עַל רָזִין דְּאוֹרַיְיתָא סָדְרוּ לֵיהּ.

604. This fourth LIVING CREATURE THAT IS THE SECRET OF "THE FACE OF A MAN" (YECHEZKEL 1:10), which is the completion of the Chariot of Man, WHICH IS ZEIR ANPIN THAT IS CALLED 'MAN', IN THE SECRET OF YUD HEI VAV HEI, FULLY SPELLED WITH ALEPHS, WHOSE NUMERICAL SUM IS THE SAME AS THAT OF MAN (HEB. *ADAM*). And it is also the completion of the four faces that are in the face of a man, FOR THE FACE OF A MAN IS MALCHUT, WHICH ITSELF HAS FOUR FACES: LION, OX, EAGLE, AND MAN, AND IS THE FOURTH FACE WHICH IS THE SECRET OF MALCHUT THAT IS IN MALCHUT. For this reason, IT IS WRITTEN: "Hashem lift up His countenance to you" (Bemidbar 6:26). And the sages of the Mishnah taught: Is it not written: "who favors no person" (lit. 'Who does not lift up countenance') (Devarim 10:17)? But the Holy One, blessed be He, said: 'Did I not command them: "And you shall eat and be satisfied AND BLESS HASHEM YOUR ELOHIM" (Devarim 8:10)? And they are very particular about SAYING THE BLESSING AFTER THE MEAL even if the quantity is but that of an olive-size or an egg-size. How then should I not lift up My countenance to them?' And not only that but the sages of the Mishnah and the Amoraim arranged their whole study according to the secrets of the Torah.

605. קָם רַעְיָא מְהֵימָנָא, וְסָלִיק יְדוֹי קַמֵּי קוּדְשָׁא בְּרִיךְ הוּא וּשְׁכִינְתֵּיה, וְאָמַר הָכִי, קוּדְשָׁא בְּרִיךְ הוּא יְהֵא רַעֲוָא דִילָךְ, לְמֵיהַב לוֹן מְזוֹנָא שְׁלֵימָתָא, לְתַקְנָא לְגַבָּךְ, וּלְגַבֵּי מַטְרוֹנִיתָא עִלָּאָה עָלְמָא דְּאָתֵי, דְּאִתְּמַר עָלָהּ, כִּי לַיְיָ' הַמְּלוּכָה וּמוֹשֵׁל בַּגּוֹיִם. וּלְגַבֵּי מַטְרוֹנִיתָא תִּנְיָינָא, דְּאִתְּמַר בָּהּ זִמְנָא תִּנְיָינָא, וְהָיְתָה לַיְיָ' הַמְּלוּכָה. לְתַקְנָא פָּתוֹרָא שְׁלֵימָתָא, מִכָּל עִדּוּנִין, וּמִכָּל מַאֲכָלִין.

605. The Faithful Shepherd rose, spread out his hands before the Holy One, blessed be He and His Shechinah, and spoke thus: O Holy One, blessed be You, may it be Your will to give us perfect food for correction to You and to the heavenly Queen, that is the World to Come, NAMELY BINAH, about which it is said: "For the kingdom is Hashem's: and He is ruler over the nations" (Tehilim 22:29), and regarding the second Queen, WHICH IS MALCHUT, it is said a second time: "and the kingdom shall be Hashem's" (Ovadyah 1:21), and a whole table is set with all delicacies and dishes.

606. וַאֲנָא מְזַמֵּן עִמָּךְ, לְכָל מָארֵי מַתְנִיתִין, וּלְמָארֵי מִקְרָא, וּלְמָארֵי

תַּלְמוּד, וכ״ש לְמָארֵי סִתְרֵי תוֹרָה דִּילָךְ, כַּלָּה דִּילָךְ, מַטְרוֹנִיתָא
קַדִּישָׁא דִּילָךְ, עִלָּאָה וְתַתָּאָה, וְכֹלָּא בִּרְשׁוּת דְּעִלַּת כָּל עִלָּאִין, אָדוֹן
כָּל הָאֲדוֹנִים, מֶלֶךְ עַל כָּל הַמְּלָכִים דְּעֵילָא וְתַתָּא, דְּאִיהוּ יָחִיד בְּלָא
תִּנְיָינָא, וְלֵית אָת וּנְקוּדָה דְּמִשְׁתַּתֵּף בַּהֲדֵיהּ, וְלָא שְׁנוּי גְּווֹנִין דְּאֵינָשָׁא.
דְּאִיהוּ מָארֵי כָּל מַפְתְּחָאן, דְּרָזִין דְּהַוָּויוֹת, וּשְׁמָהָן וְכִנּוּיִין, וְכָל רָזִין
גְּנִיזִין דְּחָכְמְתָא, דְּתִפְתַּח לוֹן כֻּלְּהוּ לִיקָרָא דִּילָךְ, עִלַּת עַל כָּל עִלּוֹת.
אֲנָא מִתְחַנֵּן קֳדָמָךְ, דְּתִתְפְּתַּח לוֹן לִיקָרָא דִּילָךְ, דִּיקָרָא דִּילָךְ אִיהוּ
מֵאָבִי וְאִמִּי דִּשְׁמַיָּא, וְאָב דְּכָל יִשְׂרָאֵל, וְאֵם דִּלְהוֹן, דְּאִתְּמַר בָּהּ וְאַל
תִּטּוֹשׁ תּוֹרַת אִמֶּךָ, וְעִמָּךְ לֵית שׁוּתָּפוּ דְּאֵם בְּעָלְמָא.

606. And I invite with You, all the sages of the Mishnah, the scholars of the Bible and the sages of the Talmud, and especially the masters of the secrets of Your Torah, and Your bride, WHO IS Your Holy Queen, both the upper one, WHICH IS BINAH, and the lower one, WHICH IS MALCHUT, everything being with the permission of the Cause who is above all supernal beings, the Lord of all lords, King over all the kings who are above or who are below, for He is unique without a second, no letter nor vowel sign that will join with Him, and no variations as is customary with man, for He is the Master of all the keys to all the secrets of Yud Hei Vav Hei's and names and appellations and all the hidden secrets of wisdom, so that You open them all for us, for the sake of Your glory, O Cause over all causes. I beseech You to open for us Your glory, for Your glory is of my Father and my Mother of the heavens, NAMELY CHOCHMAH AND BINAH, WHICH ARE FATHER AND MOTHER OF ZEIR ANPIN, WHO IS CALLED 'HEAVENS'. And the Father of all of Yisrael IS ZEIR ANPIN, and their Mother IS MALCHUT, about which it is said: "and do not forsake the Torah of your mother" (Mishlei 1:8), and with Yourself no connection exists with any mother in the world.

607. קָם זִמְנָא תִּנְיָינָא, וְאָמַר מָארֵי מַתְנִיתִין, נִשְׁמָתִין וְרוּחִין וְנַפְשִׁין
דִּלְכוֹן, אִתְעֲרוּ כְּעַן כּוּלְּהוּ, וְאַעְבָּרוּ שֵׁינָתָא מִנְּכוֹן, דְּאִיהִי וַדַּאי מִשְׁנָה,
אֹרַח פְּשָׁט דְּהַאי עָלְמָא. דַּאֲנָא לָא אִתְעַרְנָא בְּכוּ, אֶלָּא בְּרָזִין עִלָּאִין
דְּעָלְמָא דְּאָתֵי, דְּאַתּוּן בְּהוֹן הֲנֵה לָא יָנוּם וְלֹא יִישָׁן.

607. He rose a second time and said: O sages of the Mishnah, your Neshamah and Ruach and Nefesh wake up now in all of you, and remove the sleep from yourself, for this certainly is Mishnah, the literal explanations of this world. But I woke you only with heavenly secrets of the World to Come, for you are involved with them, and in this respect it is said there: "Behold, He who keeps Yisrael shall neither slumber nor sleep" (Tehilim 121:4).

608. פָּתַח וְאָמַר, הָא אוֹקְמוּהָ מָארֵי מַתְנִיתִין, בעה"ב בּוֹצֵעַ וְאֹרֵחַ מְבָרֵךְ. וְעוֹד אוֹקְמוּהָ, צָרִיךְ לְדַקְדֵּק בְּה' מִן הַמּוֹצִיא. וּתְרֵין הֵהִין אִינּוּן, לְקַבֵּל שְׁתֵּי הַלֶּחֶם. שְׁתֵּי כִּכְּרוֹת דְּשַׁבָּת. י', אִיהִי כַּבֵּיצָה לְכָל חַד וְחַד. וּמַאן אִיהוּ בעה"ב דְּבוֹצֵעַ. דָּא ו'.

608. He opened with the words, The sages of the Mishnah taught: The host breaks bread and the guest says the Blessing after the meal. And they also taught: one must pronounce clearly the Hei of Hamotzi. And the two Heis OF YUD HEI VAV HEI WHICH ARE BINAH AND MALCHUT, stand for the two loaves of bread, the two Challot of the Shabbat. The Yud OF YUD HEI VAV HEI is A SLICE OF BREAD equal in measure to the size of an egg THAT IS GIVEN to each one. And who is the host that breaks bread? This is the Vav OF YUD HEI VAV HEI, AND SO ALL THE FOUR LETTERS OF IT ARE HERE ALLUDED TO.

609. אַדְהָכִי, הָא סָבָא דְּסָבִין קָא נָחִית לְגַבֵּיה, וְאָמַר, רַעְיָא מְהֵימָנָא חֲזוֹר בָּךְ. דְּהָא לֶחֶם אִיהוּ ו', שְׁתֵּי כִּכְּרוֹת דִּילֵיה, כְּמָה דְּאָמְרַת אִינּוּן ה' ה'. וַדַּאי ו' אִיהוּ לָקֳבֵל יַעֲקֹב. ה' ה' לָקֳבֵל לֵאָה וְרָחֵל. י', כַּבֵּיצָה לְכָל חַד.

609. While they were still having this discourse, behold, a very old sage, WHICH IS SUPERNAL CHOCHMAH, descended to him and said: Faithful Shepherd, take back what you have just said, for bread is the Vav. Its two loaves of bread are, as you have said, Hei Hei. AND HE EXPLAINS, Vav is surely parallel to Jacob, WHO IS ZEIR ANPIN, while the two Heis parallel Leah and Rachel. AND THEREFORE BREAD IS IN GENERAL THE SECRET OF VAV, WHICH IS ZEIR ANPIN, THAT HAS TWO MATES. ONE MATING IS WITH LEAH, WHO IS HIS FEMALE FROM THE CHEST AND UP, WHILE THE

SECOND MATING IS WITH RACHEL, WHO IS HIS FEMALE FROM THE CHEST AND DOWN, AND THIS IS WHY THE BREAD IS DIVIDED INTO TWO LOAVES. The Yud OF YUD HEI VAV HEI IS THE SECRET OF THE SLICE THAT IS GIVEN TO EACH ONE, as the size of an egg for each, FOR EGG IS THE SECRET OF YUD OF YUD HEI VAV HEI, WHICH IS CHOCHMAH, WHICH IS THE PLENTY THAT IS DRAWN DOWN BY THE VAV AND THE TWO HEIS OF YUD HEI VAV HEI.

610. א״ל, סָבָא סָבָא, וְהָא בְּכַמָּה אַתְרִין אוּקְמוּהָ, דְּיַעֲקֹב אִיהוּ בַּעַל הַבַּיִת, וְיוֹסֵף אוֹרֵחַ, דְּדַרְגֵּיהּ יְסוֹד חַי עָלְמִין, כָּלִיל ח״י בִּרְכָאן דִּצְלוֹתָא, וּבְגִין דָּא אוּקְמוּהָ עָלֵיהּ, בִּרְכוֹת לְרֹאשׁ צַדִּיק. א״ל הָכִי הוּא, וְכֹלָּא קְשׁוֹט. כָּל רָזָא בְּאַתְרֵיהּ, מַה דַּאֲנָא אֲמָרִית, וּמַה דְּאַתְּ אֲמָרְתְּ. אֲבָל הַהוּא דְּפָלִיג נַהֲמָא מַאן הוּא.

610. He said to him: old, old sage, in how many places is it taught that Jacob is the host, WHICH IS ZEIR ANPIN, and Joseph is a guest whose level is Yesod, the life (Heb. *chai* = eighteen) of the worlds, which incorporates the eighteen blessings of the Amidah prayer, for which reason it was taught about it: "Blessings are upon the head of the righteous" (Mishlei 10:6). THEREFORE THEY SAID THAT THE HOST, WHO IS ZEIR ANPIN, BREAKS THE BREAD, WHILE THE GUEST, WHICH IS YESOD, RECITES THE BLESSING AFTER THE MEAL, BUT NOW YOU SAY THAT ZEIR ANPIN IS THE SECRET, NOT OF THE HOST, BUT OF THE BREAD. THE OLD SAGE replied to him: That is how it is, and everything is true. Each secret has its rightful place, BOTH what I said and what you said. And now, ACCORDING TO MY OPINION THAT ZEIR ANPIN IS THE BREAD, who is THEN the one WHO BREAKS the bread and distributes it?

611. א״ל, סָבָא אַנְתְּ בְּדִיּוּקְנֵיהּ, וְדָא יוּ״ד הֵ״א וָא״ו הֵ״א, וְדָא אָדָם דְּמֶרְכַּבְתָּא עִלָּאָה, דְּאַנְפִּין דִּילֵיהּ יְהֹוָ״ה. וּבְגִין דָּא, ו׳ לֶחֶם, דְּאִינוּן ה׳ ה׳. וְשִׁעוּרָא דְּאוּקְמוּהָ כַּזַּיִת וְכַבֵּיצָה, הָא אִתְּמַר כַּזַּיִת בְּאָן שְׁמָא מְשַׁעֲרִין, דְּהָא אוּקְמוּהָ רַבָּנָן דְּאֵין עוֹשִׂין מִצְוֹת חֲבִילוֹת, אוּף הָכִי, לָא יַהֲבִינָן תְּרֵין שִׁעוּרִין בְּאָת י׳, לְמֶהֱוֵי כַּזַּיִת וְכַבֵּיצָה. אֶלָּא תְּרֵי אַלְפָא בֵּיתוֹת אִינוּן, אִית י׳ עִלָּאָה, וְאִית י׳ זְעֵירָא, י׳ מִן יְדוֹד, עִלָּאָה. י׳ מִן

אֲדֹנָי, זְעֵירָא. וְאִלֵּין תְּרֵין, חַד בְּכַזַּיִת, וְחַד בְּכַבֵּיצָה, בְּרָזָא דָא
יְאֲהֹדֹוָנֹהי. אָתָא סָבָא וְנָשִׁיק לֵיהּ.

611. THE FAITHFUL SHEPHERD said to him: Old sage, you have his
likeness; NAMELY THE OLD SAGE HIMSELF, WHICH IS THE SECRET OF
CHOCHMAH, IS IN THE FORM OF THE HOST WHO BREAKS THE BREAD,
which is Yud-Vav-Dalet, Hei-Aleph, Vav-Aleph-Vav, Hei-Aleph, WHOSE
NUMERICAL SUM IS 45, WHICH IS THE SECRET OF CHOCHMAH (CHET
CAF MEM HEI), WHOSE LETTERS SPELL OUT, *KOACH* (ENG. STRENGTH -
CAF CHET) OF MEM HEI, which is man, WHICH IS MEM HEI IN
NUMERICAL VALUE. HE IS of the upper Chariot, the face of which, NAMELY
CHOCHMAH, is the Yud Hei Vav Hei SPELLED OUT FULLY WITH ALEPHS,
THE NUMERICAL VALUE OF WHICH IS MEM HEI. And for this reason, Vav
is bread, which consists of TWO LOAVES, two Heis, and the amount OF
PLENTY, as taught, is the size of an olive and the size of an egg. And we have
already learned in which name it is measured as an olive, NAMELY IN THE
YUD, but the sages have taught: One does not make precepts into bundles,
BUT EACH PRECEPT MUST STAND ON ITS OWN. Here also, we do not
ascribe two quantities to the letter Yud, that BOTH an olive-size nad an
egg-size SHOULD BE YUD, but there are two alphabets, WHERE THE LARGE
ALPHABET IS IN BINAH AND THE SMALL ALPHABET IS IN MALCHUT.
THEREFORE, there is an upper Yud and a smaller Yud. The Yud WHICH IS
THE YUD of Yud Hei Vav Hei is the upper YUD WHICH IS THE SECRET OF
SUPERNAL CHOCHMAH, while the Yud of Adonai is a small YUD, WHICH IS
THE SECRET OF CHOCHMAH OF THE LEFT. And of these two YUDS, one is
an olive-size, NAMELY THE SMALL YUD OF ADONAI, and the other is an
egg-size, NAMELY THE UPPER YUD OF YUD HEI VAV HEI. And they are in
the secret of Yud-Aleph-Hei-Dalet-Vav-Nun-Hei-Yud, NAMELY THE
COMBINATION OF YUD HEI VAV HEI AND ADONAI, WHERE THE INITIAL
YUD IS THE SECRET OF AN EGG-SIZE, AND THE FINAL YUD IS THE
SECRET OF AN OLIVE-SIZE. The old sage came and kissed him.

612. אַדְהָכִי קָם בּוּצִינָא קַדִּישָׁא, פָּתַח וְאָמַר, וַדַּאי כְּעַן מִתְחַבְּרִין מַה
שְׁמוֹ וּמַה שֵּׁם בְּנוֹ, חָדוּ חַבְרַיָּיא וְאָמְרוּ, זַכָּאָה הוּא מַאן דְּזָכֵי לְמֵיכַל
מֵהַאי נָהֲמָא, דְּאִתְּמַר בֵּיהּ לְכוּ לַחֲמוּ בְּלַחֲמִי. וְזַכָּאָה נַפְשָׁא, דְּאִתְּמַר

בָּהּ מִלֶּחֶם אָבִיהָ תֹּאכֵל. וְכָל זָר לֹא יֹאכַל בּוֹ. דְקוּדְשָׁא בְּרִיךְ הוּא בֵּיהּ
אִתְּמַר, הֲלֹא אָב אֶחָד לְכֻלָּנוּ. וְנַפְשָׁא דְאִתְעַסְקַת בְּאוֹרַיְיתָא, מִלֶּחֶם
אָבִיהָ תֹּאכֵל.

612. While they were still considering this, the holy luminary, THAT IS
RABBI SHIMON, arose, and opened by saying: "what (Heb. *Mah* - Mem Hei)
is His name and what (Mem Hei) is His son's name" (Mishlei 30:4) come
together, FOR CHOCHMAH IS THE SECRET OF YUD HEI VAV HEI FULLY
SPELLED WITH ALEPHS, WHOSE NUMERICAL VALUE IS MEM HEI. AND
THE SON OF CHOCHMAH, WHICH IS TIFERET, IS ALSO YUD HEI VAV HEI
FILLED IN WITH MEM HEI. AND IT FOLLOWS THAT MAH IS THE NAME OF
CHOCHMAH AND MAH IS THE NAME OF ITS SON, WHICH IS TIFERET.
AND THE OLD SAGE, WHO IS CHOCHMAH, JOINED WITH THE FAITHFUL
SHEPHERD, WHO IS TIFERET. The friends rejoiced and said: Happy is the
one who was privileged to eat of this bread, WHICH IS VAV OF YUD HEI
VAV HEI, about which it is said: "Come, eat of my bread" (Mishlei 9:5). And
happy is the Soul of whom it is said: "she shall eat of her father's bread: but
no stranger shall eat of it" (Vayikra 22:13), for about the Holy One, blessed
be He, it is said: "Have we not all one father?" (Malachi 2:10), and the soul
that occupied itself with the Torah "shall eat of her father's bread."

613. וּמָאן גָּרִים לָהּ דְּאָכְלַת מִלֶּחֶם אָבִיהָ. בְּגִין דְּתָבַת בְּתִיוּבְתָּא
וְאִתְאַחֲדַת כִּנְעוּרֶיהָ. הֲה"ד, וְשָׁבָה אֶל בֵּית אָבִיהָ כִּנְעוּרֶיהָ, כְּגוֹן וְיָשׁוּב
לִימֵי עֲלוּמָיו. כְּגַוְונָא דְאִילָנָא דְקָצִיצוּ לֵיהּ, וְאִתְחַדָּשׁ בְּשָׁרְשׁוֹי. וְהַאי
אִיהוּ רָזָא, דְּמָאן דְּמִית בְּלָא זֶרַע.

613. And who is the cause FOR THE SOUL to eat of her father's bread? This
is because she returned in repentance and united WITH THE HOLY ONE,
BLESSED BE HE, as in her youth, as it is written: " and has returned to her
father's house, as in her youth" (Vayikra 22:13). AND THE MEANING OF
THIS IS THE SAME as: "he shall return to the days of his youth" (Iyov
33:25), just like a tree that has been cut down and has grown again from its
roots. And this is a secret for one who dies childless, THAT BY LEVIRATE
MARRIAGE HE REINCARNATES AND IS RENEWED.

614. וְעוֹד אִית רָזָא אַחֲרָא, דִּלְבָתַר יֵיתֵי בְּגִלְגּוּלָא, וְיִתְחַדָּשׁ

כְּמִלְקַדְמִין. וְהַיְינוּ אַלְמָנָה וּגְרוּשָׁה, דְּאִתְתָּרְכַת מִגִּנְתָּא דְּעֵדֶן, וּבְגִין דָּא אִתְקְרִיאַת גְּרוּשָׁה, כְּגוֹן וַיְגָרֶשׁ אֶת הָאָדָם. וּמַאן גָּרִים לָהּ. בְּגִין דְּזֶרַע אֵין לָהּ, דְּמִית בְּלָא בְּנִין. וְשָׁבָה אֶל בֵּית אָבִיהָ כִּנְעוּרֶיהָ, דְּתָבַת בְּהַאי עָלְמָא בְּהַהוּא נַעַר בֶּן יָבָם, וְהַיְינוּ וְשָׁבָה אֶל בֵּית אָבִיהָ כִּנְעוּרֶיהָ. וּלְבָתַר דְּזַכָּת לְזֶרַע מִלֶּחֶם אָבִיהָ תֹּאכֵל. וְכָל זָר לֹא יֹאכַל בּוֹ וְגוֹ'. לֹא תִהְיֶה אֵשֶׁת הַמֵּת הַחוּצָה, לְאִישׁ זָר.

614. And there is a further secret, FOR A MAN WHO DIES CHILDLESS will later reincarnate and be renewed again, as it is written: "...be a widow or divorced" (Ibid.), as HIS SOUL is driven out of the Garden of Eden. Hence it is called 'divorced' (Heb. *grushah*) as in: "So He drove (Heb. *vayegaresh*) out the man..." (Beresheet 3:24). And what was the reason for this? It was because "she had no child" (Vayikra 22:13), for he died childless. "and has returned to her father's house, as in her youth," that is, returns to this world, AND INCARNATES in the son of the levirate marriage. This is the meaning of "and has returned to her father's house, as in her youth." And after it has been privileged to have offspring, "she shall eat of her father's bread: but no stranger shall eat of it." THIS IS WHAT IS WRITTEN: "the wife of the dead man shall not be married abroad to a stranger" (Devarim 25:5). FOR IF SHE DOES NOT MARRY THE KINSMAN, SHE WILL FALL INTO THE HANDS OF A STRANGER, NAMELY THE OTHER SIDE.

615. אָמַר ר"מ, הַלֵּל וְשַׁמַּאי, דְּאַתּוּן, חַד מִסִּטְרָא דְּרַחֲמֵי, וְחַד מִסִּטְרָא דְּדִינָא, דְּאִינּוּן חֶסֶד וּגְבוּרָה, דַּרְגִּין דְּאַבְרָהָם וְיִצְחָק. וְאַתּוּן מִגִּזְעַיְיהוּ, אִתְכְּנָשׁוּ הָכָא, אַתּוּן וְתִמְנִין תַּלְמִידִים דַּהֲווֹ לֵיהּ לְהַלֵּל. וְאוֹף הָכִי תַּלְמִידֵי בֵּית שַׁמַּאי, לִסְעוּדָתָא דְּמַלְכָּא.

615. The Faithful Shepherd said, Hillel and Shammai: That is, you two, one of whom is of the side of Mercy, NAMELY HILLEL, while the other is of the side of Judgment, NAMELY SHAMMAI, are Chesed and Gvurah, the levels of Abraham and Isaac, and you are of their stock: gather round here, you and the eighty pupils that Hillel had, as well as the pupils of the House of Shammai, gather around for the banquet of the King.

616. הָא אוֹקַמְתּוּן, אַתּוּן וְחַבְרַיָּיא דְּעִמְּכוֹן, מָארֵי דְהוֹרָאוֹת, דְּאוֹקַמְתּוּן, אֵין הַבּוֹצֵעַ רַשַּׁאי לְמֵיכַל, עַד שֶׁיַּעֲנוּ אָמֵן מָארֵי סְעוּדָתָא, וְלֵית מָארֵי סְעוּדָתָא רַשָּׁאִין לְמֵיכַל, עַד שֶׁיֹּאכַל הַבּוֹצֵעַ. וַדַּאי כַּד בָּצַע בַּעַל הַבַּיִת, וּבָצַע לְאִינוּן מָארֵי סְעוּדָתָא, לָאו לְכֻלְּהוּ מְשַׁעֵר שְׁעוּרָא חֲדָא, דְּלָאו אֹרַח אֵלֵּין בּוֹצְעִין, לִבְצוֹעַ בְּשָׁוֶה, דִּלְזִמְנִין יָהִיב לְדָא כְּבֵיצָה, וּלְדָא כַּזַּיִת. וְכַד עוֹנִין אָמֵן עַל הַאי בְּצִיעָא, קֹדֶם דְּיֵיכוּל בַּעַל הַבַּיִת, מְחַבְּרִין תְּרֵין שִׁעוּרִין כַּחֲדָא, בְּכַזַּיִת וְכַבֵּיצָה, וְאַהְדּוֹנָהִי, אָמֵן, דָּא לָאו אִיהוּ עַל הָאֲכִילָה, אֶלָּא עַל הַבְּצִיעָה, לְבָתַר דְּאִינוּן שִׁעוּרִין מִצְטָרְפִין בְּאָמֵן, יֵיכוֹל בַּעַל הַבַּיִת. וְהַיְינוּ אָרִיתִי מוֹרִי עִם בְּשָׂמִי אָכַלְתִּי יַעְרִי עִם דִּבְשִׁי, וּלְבָתַר אִכְלוּ רֵעִים שְׁתוּ וְשִׁכְרוּ דּוֹדִים. אִכְלוּ רֵעִים, מָארֵי סְעוּדָתָא. דְּיֹהוֹן בְּנִין בְּדִיּוּקְנָא דְּאֲבוּהוֹן.

616. You have taught, you and those with you who give legal and ethical instructions, you have taught: He who breaks bread may not eat until the diners have answered 'amen,' and: The guests may not eat anything until the one who breaks the bread has eaten. Obviously, when the host breaks the bread and gives it to the guests, he does not measure out the same amount for each person, for those who break bread do not usually break it into equal parts, and he could give to one an egg-size and to another an olive-size. And when they respond 'amen' over this breaking of the bread, before the host eats, they join together the two quantities, the egg-size and the olive-size, WHERE THE EGG-SIZE QUANTITY IS DRAWN DOWN FROM THE YUD OF YUD HEI VAV HEI AND THE OLIVE-SIZE QUANTITY IS FROM THE YUD OF ADONAI, AS ABOVE, AND THUS THE JOINING OF THE EGG-SIZE AND THE OLIVE-SIZE IS THE SECRET OF THE COMBINATION OF Yud-Aleph-Hei Dalet-Vav-Nun-Hei-Yud, WHICH IS THE SECRET OF 'amen'. And this UNIFICATION is not over the eating but over the breaking of the bread. AND THEREFORE, after these quantities, THE EGG-SIZED AND THE OLIVE-SIZED, have joined together IN THE UNIFICATION OF YUD-ALEPH-HEI DALET-VAV-NUN-HEI-YUD, by SAYING 'amen,' then the host may eat. And this is: "I have gathered my myrrh with my spice; I have eaten my honeycomb with my honey; I have drunk my wine with my milk," after which comes: "Eat, O dear ones, and drink, drink deep, O loving companions" (Shir Hashirim 5:1). "Eat, O dear ones" refers to the guests, so that the children, who are the guests, should be as their father, WHO IS THE HOST

WHO BREAKS THE BREAD, WHICH IS THE SECRET OF SUPERNAL CHOCHMAH, THAT IS CALLED 'FATHER'.

617. הָא הָכָא לֶחֶם בִּשְׁתֵּי כִכְּרוֹת, וְשִׁיעוּרוֹ כַּזַיִת וְכַבֵּיצָה. מַאי נִיהוּ לֶחֶם הַפָּנִים דְּפָתוֹרָא דְּמַלְכָּא. אֶלָּא הָא אוֹקְמוּהָ, דְּאִית לֵיה תְּרֵיסָר אַנְפִּין. וּמַאי נִיהוּ. אֶלָּא אִינּוּן ד' אַנְפֵּי אַרְיֵה. ד' אַנְפֵּי שׁוֹר. ד' אַנְפֵּי נֶשֶׁר. וְאִינּוּן יְבָרֶכְךָ יְדֹוָד. יָאֵר יְדֹוָד. יִשָּׂא יְדֹוָד.

617. And here we have bread in two loaves, WHERE BREAD IS VAV, AND EACH OF THE LOAVES IS HEI, and the amount OF THE EATING IS an olive-size and an egg-size, WHICH IS THE SECRET OF THE UNIFICATION YUD-ALEPH-HEI-DALET-VAV-NUN-HEI-YUD, AS ABOVE. HE ASKS: What is the shewbread that is on the King's table, NAMELY THE TWELVE CHALLOT THAT WERE ARRANGED ON THE TEMPLE TABLE? HE ANSWERS: Have we not already learned that THE BREAD, WHICH IS ZEIR ANPIN, has twelve countenances? And what are they? They are the four faces of a lion, the four faces of an ox, the four faces of an eagle, FOR THE LION, OX, AND EAGLE ARE THE SECRET OF THE THREE COLUMNS, IN EACH ONE OF WHICH ARE CHESED, GVURAH, TIFERET AND MALCHUT AND FOUR TIMES THREE COMES TO TWELVE, AND THEY ARE THE SECRET OF THE THREE YUD HEI VAV HEI'S, namely: "Hashem bless you... Hashem make His face shine... Hashem lift up..." (Bemidbar 6:24-26), WHERE EACH YUD HEI VAV HEI HAS FOUR LETTERS, AND THREE TIMES FOUR MAKES TWELVE LETTERS.

91. The twelve Challot

A Synopsis

This section tells us about the Shewbread and why there are four loaves in each Shabbat meal. We also hear about the six Sfirot from the light downwards and the six Sfirot from the light upwards, and the six steps in the upper Throne and the six steps in the lower Throne. The lesson from this is that from a certain place secrets are hidden and from another place secrets are revealed.

618. וּמְנָלָן דְּלֶחֶם הַפָּנִים אִיהוּ מִפָּתוֹרָא דְּמַלְכָּא. דִּכְתִיב, וַיְדַבֵּר אֵלִי זֶה הַשֻּׁלְחָן אֲשֶׁר לִפְנֵי יְדֹוָד. ז"ה: י"ב אַנְפִּין. וְאוֹף הָכִי, מַאן דְּאִית לֵיהּ, בָּעֵי לְתַקְנָא וּלְסַדְּרָא עַל פָּתוֹרֵיהּ, אַרְבַּע כִּכָּרוֹת בְּכָל סְעוּדָתָא דְּשַׁבַּת, לִתְלַת סְעוּדָתֵי תְּרֵיסָר אַנְפִּין.

618. And how do we know that the shewbread comes from the King's table? Because of what is written: "and he said to me: This (Heb. *Zeh*) is the table that is before Hashem" (Yechezkel 41:22), AND THE NUMERICAL VALUE OF 'this' (Heb. *zeh*) refers to the twelve countenances. Moreover, whoever can do so, should arrange and establish on his table four loaves in each Shabbat meal, which at three meals MAKE TWELVE LOAVES, WHICH ARE the twelve countenances.

619. וְאִי תֵּימָא לָאו אִינּוּן אֶלָּא שִׁית מִדְּאוֹרַיְיתָא, מִשּׁוּם לֶחֶם מִשְׁנֶה. אֶלָּא לָא נֵיכוּל לְמִדְכַּר ו', בְּלָא חַבְרֵיהּ, ו' ו', שִׁית מִלְּעֵילָא לְתַתָּא, וְשִׁית מִלְּתַתָּא לְעֵילָא. לָקֳבֵל שִׁית דַּרְגִּין דְּכֻרְסְיָיא עִלָּאָה. וְשִׁית דַּרְגִּין דְּכֻרְסְיָיא תַּתָּאָה. שִׁית בְּאִתְכַּסְיָיא. וְשִׁית בְּאִתְגַּלְיָיא. הַנִּסְתָּרוֹת לַידֹוָ"ד אֱלֹהֵינוּ וְהַנִּגְלֹת לָנוּ וּלְבָנֵינוּ עַד עוֹלָם.

619. And you might wish to suggest that from the Torah we learn about six CHALLOT, as only double the bread WAS REQUIRED FOR EACH OF THE THREE MEALS, MAKING A TOTAL OF SIX ONLY, NOT TWELVE. HE ANSWERS, we cannot mention Vav (= six), without also mentioning its companion Vav namely Vav Vav, THE SOUND OF THE PRONOUNCED VAV, the six from above downwards, and the six from below upwards. AND they

parallel the six steps that are in the upper Throne and the six steps of the lower Throne, SIX OF THE UPPER THRONE are concealed, while six are in the open. AND THIS IS THE SECRET OF THE VERSE: "The secret things belong to Hashem our Elohim: but those things which are revealed belong to us and to our children for ever" (Devarim 29:28).

92. The things one should observe at the Shabbat table

A Synopsis

We are told of the parallel between all the breads prescribed at Shabbat and the four faces of the Holy Beasts. We learn of all the deep meanings of the ten preparations for the meal. Lastly the bread of the Torah is said to be the Shechinah.

620. וְלַחֲמֵי תוֹדָה אִינוּן מ׳ חַלּוֹת, י׳ רְקִיקִין. י׳ רְבוּכִין. י׳ שֶׁל חָמֵץ. י׳ שֶׁל מַצָּה. הָא אִינוּן מ׳. לָקֳבֵל י׳ מִן יְדֹוָ"ד. ד׳ אַנְפֵּי אָדָם. י׳ מִן יְדֹוָ"ד, ד׳ אַנְפֵּי אַרְיֵה. י׳ מִן יְדֹוָ"ד, ד׳ אַנְפֵּי שׁוֹר. י׳ מִן יְדֹוָ"ד, ד׳ אַנְפֵּי נֶשֶׁר. הַאי אִיהוּ תִּקּוּנָא קַדְמָאָה דְּפָתוֹרָא דְּמַלְכָּא, דְּאִינוּן י׳ דְּבָרִים דְּצָרִיךְ בַּר נָשׁ לְאַנְהָגָא בְּפָתוֹרָא דְּשַׁבָּת.

620. The breads of thanksgiving are forty Challot, ten wafers, ten mixed with hot water and oil, ten of leavened bread, ten of unleavened bread, making a total of forty, PARALLELING THE FOUR YUD'S THAT ARE IN THE FOUR YUD HEI VAV HEI'S THAT ARE IN THE FOUR FACES, NAMELY paralleling the Yud of Yud Hei Vav Hei of the four faces of a man, AND PARALLELING the Yud of the Yud Hei Vav Hei of the four faces of a lion, AND PARALLELING the Yud of Yud Hei Vav Hei of the four faces of an ox, AND PARALLELING the Yud of the Yud Hei Vav Hei of the four faces of an eagle. And this is the first preparation for the King's table, for there are ten things that a person must observe at the Shabbat table.

621. חַד, לְתַקְּנָא פָּתוֹרָא כְּמַאן דְּאָכִיל קַמֵּי מַלְכָּא. הה"ד זֶה הַשֻּׁלְחָן אֲשֶׁר לִפְנֵי יְדֹוָ"ד. תִּנְיָינָא, נְטִילַת יָדַיִם, עַד שִׁעוּרָא דְּגָזְרוּ רַבָּנָן, דְּאִינוּן חָמֵשׁ קְשָׁרִין, דִּבְהוֹן יָ"ד פִּרְקִין. וְאוֹף הָכִי יַ"ד פִּרְקִין אִינוּן, דִּיָד שְׂמָאלָא. וְאִינוּן כ"ח פִּרְקִין. לָקֳבְלַיְיהוּ כ"ח יְדֹוָ"ד, דְּאִינוּן כ"ח אַתְוָון דִּקְרָא קַדְמָאָה דְּעוֹבָדָא דִּבְרֵאשִׁית. דְּאִתְּמַר בְּהוֹן, וְעַתָּה יִגְדַּל נָא כֹּחַ יְדֹוָד.

621. The first THING TO OBSERVE FOR THE SHABBAT TABLE IS to prepare the table, as for one who eats in the presence of a King, as it is written: "This

is the table that is before Hashem" (Yechezkel 41:22). The second PREPARATION is to wash the hands to the extent that the sages decreed, namely five knots, THAT IS THE FIVE FINGERS OF THE RIGHT HAND, which contain fourteen joints, FOR EACH FINGER HAS THREE JOINTS, AND THE THUMB ONLY TWO, TOTALING FOURTEEN JOINTS. Similarly there are fourteen joints in the left, making A TOTAL OF 28 joints. And corresponding to these 28 JOINTS IS THE SECRET OF "the power of Hashem" (where the word for 'power' is *koach* = 28), and these are the 28 letters of the first VERSE in the Works of Creation: "IN THE BEGINNING ELOHIM CREATED THE HEAVEN AND THE EARTH" (BERESHEET 1:1). THERE ARE 28 LETTERS IN THE verse, and about them it is written: "And now, I pray you, let the power (Heb. *koach*) of Hashem be great" (Bemidbar 14:17).

622. וַעֲשַׂר אֶצְבְּעָן, רְמִיזֵי לַעֲשַׂר אֲמִירָן דְּעוֹבָדָא דִּבְרֵאשִׁית. וּבְגִין דָּא אוּקְמוּהָ מָארֵי מַתְנִיתִין, מַאן דְּמְזַלְזֵל בִּנְטִילַת יָדַים, נֶעֱקַר מִן הָעוֹלָם. אֲמַאי. בְּגִין דְּאִית בְּהוֹן רָזָא דַּעֲשַׂר אֲמִירָן, וכ״ח אַתְוָון, דִּבְהוֹן אִתְבְּרֵי עָלְמָא.

622. The ten fingers correspond to the ten sayings at the creation of the world. For this reason, the sages of the Mishnah taught: Whoever is careless over the washing of the hands is uprooted from the world. Why is this? It is because the ten fingers of the hands and the 28 joints of the fingers contain the secret of the ten sayings and the 28 letters with which the world was created.

623. תְּלִיתָאָה, כּוֹס דִּבְרָכָה, דְּתָקִינוּ בֵּיהּ עֲשָׂרָה דְּבָרִים. הַדָּחָה. שְׁטִיפָה. עֶטּוּר. עֶטּוּף. חַי. מָלֵא. מְקַבְּלוֹ בִּשְׁתֵּי יָדָיו. וְנוֹתְנוֹ בַּיָּמִין. וְנוֹתֵן עֵינָיו בּוֹ. וּמַגְבִּיהוֹ מִן הַקַּרְקַע טֶפַח. וּמְשַׁגְּרוֹ בְּמַתָּנָה לְאַנְשֵׁי בֵּיתוֹ.

623. The third thing to observe is the cup of benediction, for which ten things were ordained: It requires washing, rinsing, adorning, wrapping, and must be undiluted, full, taken up with both hands, and placed in the right hand; he who says the blessing must look at it, it must be raised a handbreadth from the surface, and he must send it around to those members of his household as a present.

‏624. וְאוֹרַח רָזָא, כּוֹס מָלֵא בִּרְכַּת יְיָ'. כּוֹס בְּגִי' אֱלֹהִי"ם. וּמִתַּמָּן נִשְׁמָתָא, דְּאִיהִי עַל שְׁמֵיהּ כּוֹס. הַהָ"ד כּוֹס יְשׁוּעוֹת אֶשָּׂא. מַאן יְשׁוּעוֹת. ה' אֶצְבְּעָן. דְּאִינּוּן לְקַבֵּל ה' סְפִירָן דְּכוֹס. דְּאִיהוּ אֱלֹהִים חַיִּים בִּינָה מִתְפַּשְּׁטָא בְּהוֹן, לְחַמְשִׁין תַּרְעִין. ה' זִמְנִין עֶשֶׂר. בָּאת י', דְּאִיהוּ י' דְּבָרִים דְּתָקִינוּ רַבָּנָן בְּכוֹס, דְּאִיהוּ אֱלֹהִים חַיִּים, ה' אַתְוָון, בְּחֻשְׁבַּן ה'.

624. And according to the esoteric meaning, IT IS THE SECRET OF the cup "full with the blessing of Hashem" (Devarim 33:23), for the numerical value of the word cup (Heb. *kos*) is the same as Elohim, WHICH IS BINAH, NAMELY MALCHUT ENCLOTHING IN BINAH. And from there comes the Neshamah that is named after it, cup, as it is written: "I will raise the cup of salvation" (Tehilim 116:13). What is the meaning of "salvation"? It is the five fingers THAT HOLD THE CUP, which correspond to the five Sfirot: CHESED, GVURAH, TIFERET, NETZACH, HOD AND YESOD, that are in the cup, which is the living Elohim which is Binah, that spreads THROUGH THE FIVE SFIROT to fifty gates, which are five times ten. That is, the letter Yud stands for the ten things that the sages ordained for the cup, which is the living Elohim, and the five (Hei) letters OF THE WORD ELOHIM, which are five in number, AND TEN TIMES FIVE COMES TO FIFTY GATES.

‏625. וְאוּקְמוּהָ בְּכוֹס, שֶׁצָּרִיךְ הַדָּחָה וּשְׁטִיפָה. הַדָּחָה מִבַּחוּץ, וּשְׁטִיפָה מִבִּפְנִים. וְרָזָא דְּמִלָּה, שֶׁיְּהֵא תּוֹכוֹ כְּבָרוֹ. מַאן דְּזָכֵי לְנִשְׁמָתָא מֵהַאי כּוֹס, לְמֶהֱוֵי נִשְׁמָתָא דַּכְיָא מִלְּגוֹ וּמִלְּבַר. וְרָזָא דְּמִלָּה, וְטַהֲרוּ וְקִדְּשׁוֹ, טַהֲרָה מִבִּפְנִים, וּקְדוּשָׁה מִבַּחוּץ. וּמַה כּוֹס לָאו טַהֲרָתֵיהּ וּקְדוּשָׁתֵיהּ מִלְּגוֹ וּמִלְּבַר בְּלָא מַיָּא. אוֹף הָכִי נִשְׁמָתָא, לָאו טַהֲרָתָה וּקְדוּשָׁתָה מִלְּגוֹ וּמִלְּבַר בְּלָא אוֹרַיְיתָא. וּבְגִין דָּא אָמַר רַבָּן גַּמְלִיאֵל, מִי שֶׁאֵין תּוֹכוֹ כְּבָרוֹ לֹא יִכָּנֵס לְבֵית הַמִּדְרָשׁ. בְּגִין דְּלָאו אִיהוּ מִסִּטְרָא דְּאִילָנָא דְּחַיֵּי, אֶלָּא מֵעֵץ הַדַּעַת טוֹב וָרָע.

625. And they taught about the cup that it needs washing and rinsing, where washing refers to the outside, rinsing to the inside. And the secret of the matter is that the inside and the outside OF THE CUP should be the same, for

whoever has been privileged to receive a Soul from this cup, WHICH IS BINAH, SUCH A SOUL MUST be pure both within and without. And the secret of the matter is: "and cleanse it, and hallow it" (Vayikra 16:19) with purification on the inside and sanctification on the outside. And just as the cup, whose purification and sanctification both inside and outside is only with water, so the purification and sanctification of the soul, both inside and outside, is only with the Torah. And this is why Rabban Gamliel said: No one whose inside does not correspond to his exterior may enter the academy house. This is because such a person is not from the Tree of Life, but from the Tree of Knowledge of Good and Evil, FOR WHOEVER IS LACKING HOLINESS ON THE OUTSIDE OR PURITY ON THE INSIDE IS A MIXTURE OF GOOD AND EVIL.

626. עֲטוּר, אוֹקְמוּהָ מְעַטְּרוֹ בַּתַּלְמִידִים. וְאָרַח רָזָא, ה' אִיהוּ כּוֹס, מְעַטְּרוֹ בַּתַּלְמִידִים בְּאָת י', דְּאִיהוּ עֲטֶרֶת עַל ה'. עָטוּף, צָרִיךְ לְאַעֲטְפָא רֵישֵׁיהּ בְּגִין דִּשְׁכִינְתָּא עַל רֵישֵׁיהּ. דְּהָכִי אוֹקְמוּהָ מָארֵי מַתְנִיתִין, אָסוּר לְתַלְמִיד חָכָם לְמֵיהַךְ ד' אַמּוֹת בְּגִלּוּי הָרֹאשׁ. מִשּׁוּם מְלֹא כָל הָאָרֶץ כְּבוֹדוֹ. כָּל שֶׁכֵּן בִּבְרָכָה, וּבְאַדְכָּרַת שְׁמָא קַדִּישָׁא, לְמֶהֱוֵי בְּגִלּוּי הָרֹאשׁ.

626. The adornment THAT IS STATED IN RESPECT OF THE CUP, has been explained thus: He crowns it with pupils. And the secret is that Hei is the cup, NAMELY BINAH, and it is crowned with pupils, with the letter Yud, which is a diadem on the Hei, FOR THE PUPILS MULTIPLY AND DRAW DOWN CHOCHMAH. The wrapping THAT IS MENTIONED IN RESPECT TO THE CUP refers to the need to wrap the head, NAMELY TO COVER IT, because the Shechinah is over his head. For this is what the sages of the Mishnah taught: A scholar of the Law is forbidden to walk four cubits with his head uncovered because, "the whole earth is full of His glory" (Yeshayah 6:3). And even more so IS IT FORBIDDEN to go with uncovered head during a blessing or the mention of the Holy Name!

627. דְּאָת י' מִן יְדוֹד, אִיהִי אִתְעַטָּף בָּאוֹר, וְאִתְעֲבֵיד אֲוִיר. בְּגִין דְּאָת י' דְּאִיהִי חָכְמָה בַּאֲוִיר, וְהַיְינוּ אוֹר דְּאִתְעֲטָּף בֵּיהּ כַּד בָּרָא עָלְמָא, הה"ד עוֹטֶה אוֹר כַּשַּׂלְמָה. וְהַאי אִיהוּ יְהִי אוֹר יְהִי אֲוִיר. וְאוֹקְמוּהָ

מָארֵי סִתְרֵי תּוֹרָה, בְּטֶרֶם נִתְהֲוָוה כָּל דָּבָר, נִתְהֲווּ הָהַוָּיוֹת. וּבְגִין דָּא יְהִי אוֹר וַיְהִי אוֹר, דַּהֲוָה מִקַּדְמַת דְּנָא.

627. AND THE REASON FOR THE PROHIBITION OF GOING WITH UNCOVERED HEAD IS that the letter Yud of Yud Hei Vav Hei, WHICH IS CHOCHMAH, is enveloped in light (Heb. *or* - Aleph Vav Resh) and becomes air (Heb. *avir* - Aleph Vav Yud Resh), since the letter Yud, which is Chochmah, is in the air. And this is the light with which He enveloped Himself when He created the world, as it is written: "Who covers Himself with light as with a garment" (Tehilim 104:2). Thus "Let there be light" (Beresheet 1:3) is 'Let there be air'. And the sages of Sitrei Torah taught: Before anything else was formed, the existences were formed. Thus: "Let there be light, and there was light" REFERS TO LIGHT that had existed previously.

628. חַ"י אוּקְמוּהָ, חַי מִן הֶחָבִית. וְאֹרַח רָזָא, שְׁכִינְתָּא עִלָּאָה אִיהִי תְּמִינָאָה דִּסְפִירָן מִתַּתָּא לְעֵילָא, וּבְגִין דָּא אִתְקְרִיאַת ח', וְאִתְּמַר בָּהּ בְּחָכְמָה יִבָּנֶה בָּיִת. וְהַיְינוּ חָבִית: ח' בַּיִ"ת. וּבְגִין דְּאִיהִי חַיִּים, דִּכְתִיב עֵץ חַיִּים הִיא לַמַּחֲזִיקִים בָּהּ, יַיִן מִתַּמָּן אִיהוּ חַ"י. וְדָא אִיהוּ יֵינָא דְּאוֹרַיְיתָא. מַאן דְּאִשְׁתְּדַל בָּהּ, אִקְרֵי חַ"י. וְעוֹד, צַדִּיק חַ"י. אִיהוּ חַי מִן הֶחָבִית.

628. AND REGARDING the 'undiluted' IN RESPECT TO THE CUP OF BLESSING, they taught: Undiluted from the barrel, WHICH MEANS THAT IT SHOULD NOT BE MIXED WITH ANY WATER THERE. And the secret is: The upper Shechinah, WHICH IS BINAH, is the eighth Sfirah OF THE TEN SFIROT, WHEN ONE STARTS TO COUNT from the below upwards, and is for that reason called 'Chet' (whose numerical value is eight). And this is alluded to in the verse: "Through wisdom a house (Heb. *bayit*) is built" (Mishlei 24:3). Hence a barrel (Heb. *chavit* - Chet Bet Yud Tav) IS THE LETTERS CHET AND *BAYIT* (Bet Yud Tav). FOR THIS SHOWS THAT THE WINE, WHICH IS THE SECRET OF GVURAH OF ZEIR ANPIN, IS TO BE DRAWN DOWN FROM BINAH, THAT IS CALLED 'BARREL', NAMELY CHET BAYIT. And because BINAH is life, as it is written, "She is a tree of life to those who lay hold on her" (Mishlei 3:18) therefore, the wine that is DRAWN DOWN

from there, FROM BINAH, is undiluted (lit. 'live'). And this is the wine of the Torah, for whoever engages in it is called 'live'. And furthermore, the Righteous, WHICH IS YESOD, is CALLED 'live' and is undiluted from the barrel, BECAUSE ITS LIGHTS ARE DRAWN FROM BINAH, THAT IS CALLED 'BARREL', AS ABOVE.

629. יַיִן אִית מִנֵּיהּ תְּרֵין גַּוְונִין, חִוָּור וְסוּמָק. יַיִן, ע' אַנְפִּין. הָא ע"ב. וְלָקֳבֵל תְּרֵין גַּוְונִין דְּיַיִן, אִיהִי זָכוֹר וְשָׁמוֹר דְּשַׁבָּת, וְעַ' תֵּיבִין דְּקִדּוּשׁ וַיְכֻל"וּ, הָא ע"ב.

629. Wine comes in two colors, white and red. THE NUMERICAL VALUE OF WINE IS seventy facets, this makes 72, AND THIS ALLUDES TO THE FACT THAT THE LIGHTS OF THE 72-LETTER NAME ILLUMINATE IN WINE. And corresponding to the two colors of the wine are 'Remember' and 'Keep', referring to the Shabbat, AND THESE, TOGETHER WITH the seventy words of the SHABBAT EVE Kiddush, make 72.

630. מָלֵא, הה"ד כּוֹס מָלֵא בִּרְכַּת יְיָ'. וְאוֹף דְּאִיהוּ מָלֵא מְיֵינָא דְּאוֹרַיְיתָא. בַּר נָשׁ הָכִי צָרִיךְ לְמֶהֱוֵי שְׁלִים, כמד"א אִישׁ תָּם: גְּבַר שְׁלִים. כְּמוֹ וַיָּבֹא יַעֲקֹב שָׁלֵם, הָכִי צָרִיךְ לְמֶהֱוֵי נִשְׁמְתָא שְׁלֵימָתָא, וְלֹא יְהֵיְה בָּהּ פְּגַם, דְּכֹל אֲשֶׁר בּוֹ מוּם לֹא יִקְרָב. אוֹף הָכִי אִלֵּם עִם יָ"ה, הוּא אֱלֹהִים, כְּחוּשְׁבָּן כּוֹס. אִיהוּ מָלֵא, וַהֲפוֹךְ אִלֵּם וְתִמְצָא מָלֵא. אֵימָתַי. כַּד אִית תַּמָּן יָ"ה. וְהַיְינוּ כִּי יַד עַל כֵּס יָ"ה. אֲדֹנָ"י חוּשְׁבָּנֵיהּ ו"ה. עַמּוּדָא דְּאֶמְצָעִיתָא מָלֵא מִן תַּרְוַויְיהוּ. וּבְגִין דָּא שַׁרְיָא עֲלֵיהּ אָדָם, דְּהוּא שְׁמָא מְפֹרָשׁ.

630. AND THE CUP OF BENEDICTION MUST BE full, as it is written: A cup "full with the blessing of Hashem" (Devarim 33:23); and also he HAS TO BE full of the wine of the Torah, and so must a person be perfect, as it is written: "a plain man" (Beresheet 25:27). THE MEANING OF THIS IS a perfect (Heb. *shalem*) man, as in the verse: "And Jacob came to Shalem" (Beresheet 33:18), NAMELY JACOB IS HERE CALLED 'PERFECT'. So also must the Soul be perfect, without any fault being in it, because "For whatever man he be that has a blemish, he shall not approach" (Vayikra 21:18). So also here, THE

LETTERS OF Elohim: (Aleph-Lamed-Hei-Yud-Mem) can be re-written as Aleph-Lamed-Mem with Yah (Yud-Hei). And IT HAS the numerical value of cup (Heb. *kos*), WHICH IS 86. THUS THE CUP HAS to be full (Heb. *male*), for Aleph- Lamed-Mem in reverse order is *male*: (Mem Lamed Aleph). FOR THE NUMERICAL VALUE OF THE LETTERS OF THE WORD CUP IS THE SAME AS 'FULL OF YAH' (MALE YAH). For when is it full? When there is Yah there. And that is: "Because Yah has sworn by His throne" (Shemot 17:16), WHERE THE NAME IS NOT COMPLETE, BUT LACKS VAV HEI. The numerical value of Adonai, TREATING ALL TENS AS UNITS, Vav-Hei. The Central Column is full from both of them, OF YUD-HEI AND THE VAV-HEI. And therefore THE NAME OF *Adam* (Eng. 'man') dwells upon it, which is the explicit Name, YUD-VAV-DALET, HEI, HEI-ALEPH, VAV-ALEPH-VAV, HEI-ALEPH; WHICH HAS THE NUMERICAL VALUE OF 'ADAM'.

631. מְקַבְּלוֹ בִּשְׁתֵּי יָדָיו, כְּגַוְונָא דְּאוֹרַיְיתָא, דַּהֲוָה בִּתְרֵין לוּחִין, ה'
דִּבְרָן בְּלוּחָא חֲדָא, לָקֳבֵל ה' אֶצְבְּעָאן דִּיד יְמִינָא. וְה' בְּלוּחָא תִּנְיָינָא,
לָקֳבֵל ה' אֶצְבְּעָן דִּיד שְׂמָאלָא. וְאִתְיְיהִיבוּ בִּימִינָא דְּהַיְינוּ בְּיַד יָמִין.
וּבְגִין דָּא, שְׁנֵי לוּחוֹת אֲבָנִים הוֹרִיד בְּיָדוֹ, וְלָא בִּיְדָיו. וְהַאי אִיהוּ
דְּאַסְהִיד קְרָא, מִימִינוֹ אֵשׁ דָּת לָמוֹ.

631. REGARDING THE CUP OF BENEDICTION, THAT must be taken up with both hands, corresponding to the Torah which was written on two tablets. Five commandments on the one tablet correspond to the five fingers of the right hand, and five commandments on the second tablet correspond to the five fingers of the left hand, that were given with the right, that is, the right hand, THAT IS TO SAY THAT THE FIVE OF THE LEFT WERE INCLUDED IN THE FIVE OF THE RIGHT. And for this reason IT IS WRITTEN: "and took in his hand the two tablets of stone" (Shemot 34:4), and not 'in his hands,' NAMELY IN ONLY ONE HAND, WHICH WAS THE RIGHT, and this is as Scripture testifies: "from His right hand went a fiery law for them" (Devarim 33:2).

632. וְנוֹתֵן עֵינָיו בּוֹ, בְּגִין דְּהַאי כּוֹס, דְּאִיהוּ לָקֳבֵל אַרְעָא דְּיִשְׂרָאֵל,
דְּאִתְּמַר בָּהּ, תָּמִיד עֵינֵי יְיָ' אֱלֹהֶיךָ בָּהּ. וְעַיְינִין דִּלְעֵילָּא, אִינוּן שַׁבְעִין
סַנְהֶדְרִין, וּמֹשֶׁה וְאַהֲרֹן עֲלַיְיהוּ. תְּרֵין עַיְינִין עִלָּאִין. חַד עַיִן יָמִין, וְחַד

עַיִן שְׂמָאלָא, וְאִינוּן ע״ב, כְּמִנְיָן בַּיַּיִן. וְהַאי אִיהוּ רָזָא דְּנוֹתֵן בַּכּוֹס עֵינוֹ.

632. REGARDING THE INSTRUCTION THAT HE WHO SAYS THE BLESSING must look at the cup of benediction, this is because it corresponds to the Land of Yisrael, WHICH IS MALCHUT ENCLOTHING BINAH, about which it is said: "the eyes of Hashem your Elohim are always upon it" (Devarim 11:12); and the eyes of heaven are the seventy (numerical value of the letter Ayin, which, as a word, means 'eye') members of the Sanhedrin, with Moses and Aaron over them, they being the two upper eyes, NAMELY, CHOCHMAH AND BINAH, being one right eye and one left eye, amounting to 72, the same numerical value as the expression 'with wine' (Heb. *beyayin*). FOR THE SEVENTY MEMBERS OF THE SANHEDRIN CORRESPOND TO THE SEVEN SFIROT: CHESED, GVURAH, TIFERET, NETZACH, HOD, YESOD AND MALCHUT, EACH ONE BEING COMPOSED OF TEN. AND OVER THEM ARE CHOCHMAH AND BINAH, WHICH ARE MOSES AND AARON, AND THIS IS THE SECRET OF HIS LOOKING AT IT, TO DRAW DOWN CHOCHMAH AND BINAH TO THE CUP, WHICH IS MALCHUT, and this is the secret of why he who says the blessing must look at the cup.

633. וּמַגְבִּיהוּ מִן הַקַּרְקַע טֶפַח, בְּגִין דְּאַת ה׳ אִיהִי כוֹס, בָּעֵי לְסַלְּקָא לָהּ בְּאָת י׳, דְּאִיהִי טֶפַח, דְּבֵיהּ אִתְפַּתְּחַת ה׳ בַּה׳ אֶצְבְּעָאן. וּמְשַׁגְּרוֹ לְאַנְשֵׁי בֵּיתוֹ בְּמַתָּנָה, בְּגִין דְּיִתְבָּרַךְ דְּבֵיתְהוּ, דְּאִיהִי נֶפֶשׁ, דְּאִתְּמַר בָּהּ נַפְשֵׁנוּ יְבֵשָׁה אֵין כֹּל, וְאִתְבָּרְכַת וְאִתְעֲבֵידַת פֵּרִין, הה״ד תַּדְשֵׁא הָאָרֶץ דֶּשֶׁא.

633. AND THE CUP OF BENEDICTION must be raised a handbreadth from the surface. Since the letter Hei OF YUD HEI VAV HEI is a cup, it has to be raised up to the letter Yud OF YUD HEI VAV HEI, which is CALLED 'a handbreadth', for the Hei is opened up in it with the five (Hei) fingers, WHICH IS THE SECRET OF THE FIFTY GATES OF BINAH. And he must send THE CUP OF BENEDICTION round to members of his household as a present, NAMELY in order that his wife should be blessed, for she is THE SECRET OF the Nefesh, about which it is said: "but now our soul (Heb. Nefesh) is dried away: there is nothing at all" (Bemidbar 11:6), and she is blessed and bears fruits, as it is written: "Let the earth bring forth grass" (Beresheet 1:11).

634. רְבִיעָאָה, לְמֶהֱוֵי עַל פָּתוֹרֵיהּ דִּבְרֵי תוֹרָה, דְּלָא יִתְקַיַּים בֵּיהּ כְּגַוְונָא דְעַמֵּי הָאָרֶץ, דְּאִתְּמַר עֲלַיְיהוּ כִּי כָּל שֻׁלְחָנוֹת מָלְאוּ קִיא צוֹאָה. אֲבָל בְּסִתְרֵי תוֹרָה אוֹקְמוּהָ, הָרוֹצֶה לְהַעֲשִׁיר יַצְפִּין, יִתֵּן שֻׁלְחָן לַצָּפוֹן, הֲרֵי שֻׁלְחָן לִשְׂמָאלָא, דְּאִיהוּ דִּין, בָּעֵי לְקַשְׁרָא בֵּיהּ יְמִינָא, דְּאִיהוּ אוֹרַיְיתָא, דְּאִתְיְהִיבַת מֵחֶסֶד, דְּאִיהוּ רַחֲמֵי, יָמִין ה'.

634. And the fourth THING TO OBSERVE AT THE TABLE is that matters of Torah should be discussed over the table so that the verse "For all tables are full of vomit and filth" (Yeshayah 28:8) should not be fulfilled in him as it is with the ignorant. But it was taught in Sitrei (lit. 'hidden') Torah: let him who wants to grow rich turn to the north; namely he should place the table northwards, for the table is left, which is Judgment. He has, THEREFORE, to connect it to the right, which is the Torah that was given out of Chesed, which is Mercy, which is the right hand of Hashem.

635. חֲמִישָׁאָה, אוֹקְמוּהָ מָארֵי מַתְנִיתִין, דְּצָרִיךְ לְהַאֲרִיךְ עַל פָּתוֹרֵיהּ, בְּגִין עֲנִיִּים. וְרָזָא דְמִלָּה, בְּגִין דִּצְדָקָה יַאֲרִיךְ יוֹמוֹי, דְּלָא יִתְקַצְרוּן. כְּגַוְונָא דְאוֹרַיְיתָא אִיהוּ אֲרִיכוּת יוֹמִין, בִּתְרֵין עָלְמִין, בְּעָלְמָא דֵין וּבְעָלְמָא דְאָתֵי לְנִשְׁמָתָא. אוֹף הָכִי צְדָקָה, אִיהִי אֲרִיכוּת יוֹמִין לְגוּפָא, בִּתְרֵין עָלְמִין, הה"ד כִּי הוּא חַיֶּיךָ וְאוֹרֶךְ יָמֶיךָ. כִּי הוּא חַיֶּיךָ בְּעוֹלָם הַזֶּה וְאוֹרֶךְ יָמֶיךָ בָּעוֹלָם הַבָּא. דְּעָלְמָא דְאָתֵי לְגוּפָא לְתְחֲיַית הַמֵּתִים, דִּלְבָתַר דְּיֵיקוּם לָא יָמוּת. וּכְגַוְונָא דְעָלְמָא דְאָתֵי יְהֵא קַיָּים, הָכִי עָלְמָא דֵין יְהֵא קַיָּים.

635. And the fifth THING TO OBSERVE AT THE TABLE was taught by the sages of the Mishnah: The meal must be lengthened for the sake of the poor, THAT HE WILL BE ABLE TO GIVE THEM SOMETHING TO EAT. And the secret of the matter is that charity should lengthen his days, that he should not die young, just as does the Torah which is longevity for the Soul in two worlds: this world and the World to Come. Charity, likewise, is longevity for the body in two worlds, as it is written: "for He is your life, and the length of your days" (Devarim 30:20), which is interpreted to mean: 'your life' in this world, and 'the length of your days' in the World to Come. AND THE

MEANING OF the World to Come for the body is at the resurrection of the dead, that after it rises at the resurrection of the dead, it will not die. And just as it will be in the World to Come so will it be in this world.

636. שְׁתִיתָאָה, שֶׁלֹּא יְהֵא גַּרְגְּרָן וּבַלְעָן עַל פָּתוֹרֵיהּ דְּמַלְכָּא, כְּגַוְונָא דְּעֲשׂוּ דְּאָמַר הַלְעִיטֵנִי, אֹרַח הַלְעָטָה, אֶלָּא בְּאֹרַח טְחִינָה. אוּף הָכִי, מַאן דְּאַפִּיק מִלִּין דִּצְלוֹתִין אוֹ דְּאוֹרַיְיתָא מִפּוּמוֹי, בָּעֵי לְאַפָּקָא לוֹן בְּהַטְחָנָה שְׁלֵמִים, וְלָא בְּהַלְעָטָה חֲסֵרִים. וְלֹא עוֹד, אֶלָּא בְּגִין סַכְּנָה דִּשְׁמָא יַקְדִים קָנֶה לַוֵּשֶׁט.

636. And the sixth THING TO OBSERVE is that he should not be a voracious glutton at the King's table, as was Esau, who said: "Give me to swallow" (Beresheet 25:30), by gulping it down, but by way of mastication, GRINDING THE FOOD WITH HIS TEETH. So, too, one who produces words of prayer or words of Torah from his mouth, should bring them out, chewed over, and complete; NAMELY, HE SHOULD CONSIDER THEM AND GO OVER THEM, AS THOUGH CHEWING THEM OVER, and not in a gulping fashion, imperfectly. And furthermore, because of the danger that the food might enter his trachea instead of his esophagus, HE MUST EAT BY WAY OF MASTICATING AND NOT GULPING.

637. שְׁבִיעָאָה, מַיִם אַחֲרוֹנִים. וְאוֹקְמוּהָ. וּמַיִם רִאשׁוֹנִים מִצְוָה. וְאַחֲרוֹנִים חוֹבָה. וְאֶמְצָעִיִּים רְשׁוּת. מַיִם רִאשׁוֹנִים צָרִיךְ לְסַלְּקָא אֶצְבְּעָן, בְּגִין דְּלָא יְהַדְרוּן מַשְׁקִין וִיטַמְּאוּ אֶת הַיָּדַיִם. וְאִית מֵרַבָּנָן דְּאָמְרֵי, דְּאַחֲרוֹנִים מִשּׁוּם מֶלַח סְדוֹמִית, שֶׁלֹּא תְּסַמֵּא אֶת הָעֵינַיִם. וְאִי הָכִי אַפְּקִין לוֹן מֵחוֹבָא. וְסִתְרֵי מִילִין, אִלֵּין דְּאָמְרוּ עֲלַיְיהוּ חוֹבָה, וְלָאו אֹרַח אַרְעָא לְסִתְרָא גְּאוֹנִים מִלִּין, אֶלָּא דְּאִתְקְרֵי עֲלַיְיהוּ, עַל פִּי הַתּוֹרָה אֲשֶׁר יוֹרוּךָ.

637. And the seventh PREPARATION is water at the end of the meal, as it has been taught: Water to wash the hands at the beginning of the meal is a precept and at the end of the meal is an obligation, while WATER in between (courses) optional. With the water at the beginning of the meal, he has to

raise his fingers up so that the dirty water will not run back and defile the hands. And there are sages who held the opinion that the water at the end of the meal is because of Sdomite salt, lest it blind the eyes. They thereby removed from us the obligation, FOR TO WASH THE HANDS AT THE END OF THE MEAL IS NO MORE THAN GOOD ADVICE, IN ORDER NOT TO BLIND THE EYES, AND IS NOT OBLIGATORY. And there are secret matters with those who held that WATER TO WASH THE HANDS AT THE END OF THE MEAL is obligatory. And it is not good practice to contradict the words of the great, but to them may be applied the verse: "according to the sentence of the Torah which they shall teach you" (Devarim 17:11).

638. וְלֹא עוֹד, אֶלָּא דְּאָמְרוּ עֲלַיְיהוּ ג' קְדוּשׁוֹת, הֲדָא הוּא דִכְתִיב, וְהִתְקַדִּשְׁתֶּם וִהְיִיתֶם קְדוֹשִׁים. וְהִתְקַדִּשְׁתֶּם אֵלּוּ מַיִם רִאשׁוֹנִים. וִהְיִיתֶם קְדוֹשִׁים אֵלּוּ מַיִם אַחֲרוֹנִים. כִּי קָדוֹשׁ, זֶה שֶׁמֶן עָרֵב. אֲנִי יְיָ', זוֹ בְּרָכָה. וְאֶמְצָעָיִים, בֵּין גְּבִינָה לְבָשָׂר. וּבְג"ד, וְהִתְקַדִּשְׁתֶּם וִהְיִיתֶם קְדוֹשִׁים כִּי קָדוֹשׁ אֲנִי יְיָ'. זַכָּאִין עַמָּא, דְּמָארֵיהוֹן יְשַׁוֵּי לוֹן לְגַבֵּיהּ.

638. And furthermore, three sanctifications were stated in this connection, as it is written: "you shall therefore sanctify yourselves, and you shall be holy; for I am holy" (Vayikra 11:44). "sanctify yourselves" refers to the water for washing the hands at the beginning of the meal. "and you shall be holy" refers to the water at the end of the meal. "for...holy" is pleasant oil TO REMOVE THE DIRT FROM THE FINGERS. "I am Hashem" is a blessing. And the water in the middle is between cheese and meat, and this is why it is written: "you shall therefore sanctify yourselves, and you shall be holy; for I am holy." Happy is this people whose Master places them near to Him, AND WHO IMBUES THEM WITH HIS HOLINESS!

639. אוֹף הָכִי וְהִתְקַדִּשְׁתֶּם, בְּשַׁעֲתָא תַשְׁמִישׁ. מַיִם רִאשׁוֹנִים דְּזָרַע בַּר נָשׁ, מִצְוָה. אַחֲרוֹנִים דְּנוּקְבָּא, חוֹבָא. וְאֶמְצָעָיִים קָא רָמִיז, וְכַגְּבִינָה תַקְפִּיאֵנִי. הֲדָא הוּא דִכְתִיב, הֲלֹא כֶּחָלָב תַּתִּיכֵנִי וְכַגְּבִינָה תַקְפִּיאֵנִי. וְהַאי אִיהוּ דְּקָא רָמִיז, בֵּין גְּבִינָה לְבָשָׂר, דְּאִתְּמַר בֵּיהּ עוֹר וּבָשָׂר תַּלְבִּישֵׁנִי.

639. So, too, COULD BE SAID, "sanctify yourselves" refers to the time of sexual intercourse. The initial emission of a man's seed is a precept, NAMELY, KEEPING OF THE COMMANDMENT TO BE FRUITFUL AND MULTIPLY, while the latter is THE SEED of the female, which is obligatory, THAT IS TO SAY: THE SEED OF THE MALE OBLIGATES HER TO PRODUCE SEED. And THE WATER in between is hinted at in "and curdled me like cheese" (Iyov 10:10), NAMELY, THE HOLY ONE, BLESSED BE HE, WHO GIVES SOLID FORM TO THE SEED FOR THE BUILDING UP OF THE EMBRYO, as it is written: "Have You not poured me out like milk, and curdled me like cheese?" And this is the allusion TO THE WATER THAT IS IN THE MIDDLE, between cheese and meat, for it is said about Him, ABOUT THE HOLY ONE, BLESSED BE HE: "You have clothed me with skin and flesh" (Ibid. 11).

640. תְּמִינָאָה, לְשַׁלְשָׁה צָרִיךְ כּוֹס. אֲמַאי. בִּינָה אִיהִי תְּלִיתָאָה מֵעֲשַׂר סְפִירָאן, מֵעֵילָא לְתַתָּא. וּבְגִין דָּא פָּחוּת מִשַּׁלְשָׁה לָא צָרִיךְ כּוֹס. לְשַׁלְשָׁה צָרִיךְ כּוֹס, קָא רָמִיז קְדוּשָׁה לָךְ יְשַׁלֵּשׁוּ. וְלֹא עוֹד, אֶלָּא דְּאוֹרַיְיתָא לָא נַחְתָּא פָּחוּת מִג', כֹּהֲנִים, לְוִיִם, יִשְׂרְאֵלִים. תּוֹרָה, נְבִיאִים, וּכְתוּבִים. בְּיֶרַח תְּלִיתָאי, בְּיוֹם תְּלִיתָאי. וְדָא בִּינָה, יְד"וּ. וּבְגִינָהּ אִתְּמַר, שָׁלֹשׁ מִשְׁמָרוֹת הֲוֵי"י הַלַּיְלָה. מַלְכוּת ה' רְבִיעִית, עָלָהּ אִתְּמַר אַרְבָּעָה מִשְׁמָרוֹת הֲוֵי הַלַּיְלָה. וְשׁ' דְּתַלָת עַנְפִין לְקַבֵל תְּלַת מִשְׁמָרוֹת. וְשׁ' דְּאַרְבַּע עַנְפִין, לְקַבֵל אַרְבָּעָה מִשְׁמָרוֹת.

640. The eighth THING TO OBSERVE is that at least three men must be present for the cup of benediction. Why? BECAUSE THE CUP ALLUDES TO BINAH, and Binah is the third of the ten Sfirot, WHEN COUNTING THEM from the top downwards, NAMELY, KETER, CHOCHMAH AND BINAH. For this reason, if less than three men are present, the cup is not required. ANOTHER EXPLANATION WHY at least three men must be present for the cup of benediction is that it refers to 'They call You thrice holy'. Furthermore, the Torah did not state less than three, NAMELY: Priests, Levites and Yisrael, WHICH ARE the Torah, Prophets and the Writings, AND IT WAS GIVEN in the third month, on the third day. And this Binah is Yud-Hei-Vav OF YUD HEI VAV HEI, WHICH IS THE SECRET OF THE THREE COLUMNS. And in its regard it was said: The night has three watches. And Malchut is the fourth Hei, WHICH RECEIVES ALL THREE COLUMNS, and

about her it was said: The night has four watches, CORRESPONDING TO THE THREE COLUMNS AND MALCHUT THAT RECEIVES THEM. And the letter Shin with the three branches corresponds to the three watches, while the letter Shin with four branches, corresponds to the four watches.

641. תְּשִׁיעָאָה, כּוֹס שֶׁל בְּרָכָה, רְבִיעִית לוֹג, וְשִׁיעוּרָא דִּילֵיהּ, לָקֳבֵל ה', רְבִיעָאָה דְּשֵׁם יְדֹנָ"ד. עֲשִׂירָאָה, בַּעֲשָׂרָה אוֹמֵר נְבָרֵךְ לֵאלֹהֵינוּ. וּשְׁכִינְתָּא תַּתָּאָה, אִיהִי רְבִיעִית, וַעֲשִׂירִית. רְבִיעִית לְשֵׁם יְדֹוָד. עֲשִׂירִית לַעֲשַׂר סְפִירִין. דְּאִינּוּן יֹו"ד הֵ"א וָא"ו הֵ"א. וְכַמָּה צָרִיךְ ב"נ לְנַטְרָא גַּרְמֵיהּ, דְּלָא לְזָרוֹק מִלִּין אִלֵּין בַּאֲתָר דְּלָא אִצְטְרִיךְ. כְּמוֹ מַאן דְּזָרִיק נָהֲמָא. כ"ש מַאן דְּזָרִיק נָהֲמָא דְּאוֹרַיְיתָא, לְבַר מִפָּתוֹרֵיהּ, דְּאִיהִי שְׁכִינְתָּא. דְּאִתְּמַר בָּהּ, זֶה הַשֻּׁלְחָן אֲשֶׁר לִפְנֵי יְיָ'.

ע"כ רעיא מהימנא

641. And the ninth THING TO OBSERVE is the cup of benediction, that is one-quarter of a log, the amount corresponding to the letter Hei, WHICH IS the fourth LETTER of the Name Yud Hei Vav Hei. And the tenth THING TO OBSERVE is that when there are ten men present, he WHO SAYS GRACE adds 'let us bless our Elohim'. THE REASON FOR THIS IS THAT the lower Shechinah, WHICH IS MALCHUT, is both fourth and tenth – the fourth letter of the name Yud Hei Vav Hei, and the tenth in the count of the ten Sfirot – WHICH ARE THE SECRET OF THE TEN LETTERS Yud-Vav-Dalet, Hei-Aleph, Vav-Aleph-Vav, Hei-Aleph. AND THEREFORE THE PRESENCE OF TEN PERSONS IS REQUIRED IN ORDER TO MENTION THE NAME 'OUR ELOHIM.' And a man must be very careful not to throw these matters in a place where he shouldn't, like one who throws away bread, and how much more so one who throws out from his table the bread of the Torah, for it is the Shechinah, about which it is said: "This is the table that is before Hashem" (Yechezkel 41:22).

End of Ra'aya Meheimna

93. Three who harm themselves

A Synopsis
Rabbi Shimon tells about the three ways a person can harm himself:
by cursing himself, by throwing bread on the ground, and by
kindling a light before the doxology is finished on Shabbat. He who
commits the last of these three transgressions is considered to have
profaned the Shabbat, and a special place in Gehenom is reserved
for him.

642. וּבְחַבוּרָא קַדְמָאָה, תְּלַת אִינּוּן דְּגַרְמִין בִּישׁ לְגַרְמַיְיהוּ. תְּרֵין
בְּהַאי עָלְמָא, וְחַד בְּעָלְמָא אַחֲרָא, וְאִלֵּין אִינּוּן: מַאן דְּלָיֵיט גַּרְמֵיהּ,
דִּתְנֵינָן חַד מְמָנָא אִתְפְּקַד קַמֵּיהּ דב״נ, וּבְשַׁעֲתָא דְּלָיֵיט גַּרְמֵיהּ הַהוּא
ב״נ, הַאי מְמָנָא, וְשַׁבְעִין אַחֲרָנִין דִּמְמָנָן תְּחוֹתֵיהּ, נַטְלִין הַהִיא מִלָּה,
וְאַמְרֵי אָמֵן, וְסַלְקֵי לָהּ לְעֵילָּא, וְדַיְיִנִין לָהּ, וְאִיהוּ רָדִיף אֲבַתְרֵיהּ, עַד
דְּעָבֵיד לֵיהּ, וְאַשְׁלִים לֵיהּ הַהוּא מִלָּה.

642. And in the first composition, HE SAYS: There are three who cause harm
to themselves, two of whom are in this world, and one in another world. And
these are: The one who curses himself, as we have learned; one official is
appointed before man, and when a man curses himself this official together
with his seventy appointed subordinates take that word and respond 'amen,'
and they raise it up on high and judge him. And THE OFFICIAL follows him
until he does something and then he puts into effect for him THE CURSE OF
that word THAT HE UTTERED.

643. מַאן לָךְ רַב מִמֹּשֶׁה, דְּאָמַר וְאִם אַיִן מְחֵנִי נָא מִסִּפְרְךָ אֲשֶׁר
כָּתַבְתָּ, וְאָמַר לְצוֹרֶךְ, וְאע״ג דְּקוּדְשָׁא בְּרִיךְ הוּא עָבֵיד רְעוּתֵיהּ, עִם כָּל
דָּא לָא אִשְׁתְּזִיב מֵעוֹנְשָׁא, וְהָא אִתְּמַר דְּלָא אִדְכַּר בְּפָרָשַׁת וְאַתָּה
תְּצַוֶּה, וְאִתְמְחֵי מִתַּמָּן. וְהָא אוֹקְמוּהָ. מַאן לָךְ רַב מִדָּוִד מַלְכָּא, דְּאָמַר
אָמַרְתִּי אֶשְׁמְרָה דְרָכַי מֵחֲטוֹא בִלְשׁוֹנִי אֶשְׁמְרָה לְפִי מַחְסוֹם בְּעוֹד רָשָׁע
לְנֶגְדִּי, מַאי בְּעוֹד רָשָׁע לְנֶגְדִּי. הַהוּא מְמָנָא דְּאִתְפְּקַד עַל דָּא, וְנָטִיל
הַהִיא מִלָּה לְאַבְאָשָׁא לֵיהּ לב״נ.

643. Who do we have that is greater than Moses, who said: "and if not, blot me, I pray you, out of Your book which You have written" (Shemot 32:32). This he said for the sake OF YISRAEL, and although the Holy One, blessed be He, did his wish AND FORGAVE YISRAEL, nevertheless he was not spared punishment, for it has already been noted that HIS NAME is not mentioned in the portion of Tetzaveh, but has been blotted out from there. And this has already been taught. And who do we have that is greater than King David, who said: "I said: I will take heed to my ways, that I sin not with my tongue: I will keep a curb on my mouth, while the wicked is before me" (Tehilim 39:2). What is the meaning of "while the wicked is before me"? This refers to that official who was appointed over the one WHO CURSES HIMSELF, and takes that word to harm a man, AS ABOVE.

644. וְחַד מַאן דְּזָרִיק נַהֲמָא, אוֹ פֵּירוּרִין דְּנַהֲמָא בְּאַרְעָא, וְקָא עָבֵיד בֵּיהּ זִלְזוּלָא, כְּמָה דְּאִתְּמַר. הָנֵי תְּרֵי בְּהַאי עָלְמָא. וְחַד בְּהַהוּא עָלְמָא, מַאן דְּאוֹקִיד שְׁרַגָּא בְּמוֹצָאֵי שַׁבָּת, עַד לָא מָטוּ יִשְׂרָאֵל לִקְדוּשָׁא דְּסִדְרָא, בְּגִין דְּקָא מְחַלֵּל שַׁבְּתָּא, וְגָרִים לְנוּרָא דְּגֵיהִנָּם לְאִתּוֹקְדָא, עַד לָא מָטָא זִמְנֵיהּ.

644. And one WHO DOES HARM TO HIMSELF is the person who throws bread, or crumbs of bread, onto the ground, having no respect for it, as we have learned. And these are the two WHO RECEIVE THEIR PUNISHMENT in this world. And the one WHO DOES HARM TO HIMSELF in another world is the person who kindles a light at the end of the Shabbat, before Yisrael recite the doxology after the daily portion, DURING THE PASSAGES "OF VEATA KADOSH" AT THE END OF SHABBAT. And such a one is considered as a profaner of the Shabbat because he causes the fire of Gehenom to be kindled before its time.

645. חַד דּוּכְתָּא אִית בְּגֵיהִנָּם, לְאִינוּן דְּקָא מְחַלְּלֵי שַׁבְּתָּא. כֵּיוָן דְּאִיהוּ אוֹקִיד שְׁרַגָּא עַד לָא מָטָא זִמְנֵיהּ, חַד מְמָנָא אִית בְּגֵיהִנָּם בְּמ"ש, וְאוֹקִיד בְּקַדְמֵיתָא לְהַהוּא דּוּכְתָּא, וְאָמַר הַאי דּוּכְתָּא דִּפְלַנְיָא. וְכָל חַיָּיבִין דְּגֵיהִנָּם, מְסַיְּיעֵי לְאוֹקְדָּא הַהוּא דּוּכְתָּא. הַהוּא מְמָנָא קָארֵי וְאָמַר, הִנֵּה יְיָ' מְטַלְטֶלְךָ טַלְטֵלָה גֶּבֶר וְעֹטְךָ עָטֹה. חַיָּיבִין דְּגֵיהִנָּם

אַמְרֵי, כַּדּוּר אֶל אֶרֶץ רַחֲבַת יָדַיִם שָׁמָּה תָמוּת וְגוֹ'. בְּגִין דְּאִיהוּ גָּרִים
לוֹן לְאִתּוֹקְדָא, עַד לָא מָטָא זִמְנַיְיהוּ. הָא לָן תְּלָתָא, דְּגַרְמֵי בִּישׁ
לְגַרְמַיְיהוּ, כְּמָה דְּאִתְּמַר.

645. There is a special place in Gehenom for those who profane the Shabbat. And since he kindles the light before its time, there is a certain official in Gehenom at the end of Shabbat, and he first lights that place and says: This spot is for so-and-so. And all the wicked ones who are in Gehenom help him to light up that spot, and that official calls out, saying: "Behold, Hashem will thrust you about with a mighty throw, and will seize you firmly" (Yeshayah 22:17). And the wicked who are in Gehenom respond: "He will violently roll and toss you like a ball into a large country: there shall you die" (Ibid. 18). And this is because he caused them to be kindled before time and this makes three who cause harm to themselves, as we have learned.

94. Three Yud's in the Yud Hei Vav Hei fully spelled with
Yud amounting to 63

A Synopsis
Rabbi Shimon tells Moses that in the future he will be exalted
above all creatures because he ascended to the Name Yud Hei Vav
Hei fully spelled out.

רעיא מהימנא

646. ד"א וַיַּחֲלוֹם וְהִנֵּה סֻלָּם, רַעְיָא מְהֵימְנָא, מַה ל' אִסְתַּלִּק עַל כָּל
אַתְווֹן, הָכִי אַתְּ עָתִיד לְאִסְתַּלְּקָא עַל כָּל בִּרְיָין. בְּגִין דְּאִסְתְּלַק לִשְׁמָא
דְיוֹ"ד הֵ"י וָא"ו הֵ"י. דְּבֵיה יי"י, דְּחוּשְׁבְּנֵיה ל'. דִּבְקַדְמֵיתָא הֲוֵית בְּשֵׁם
יוֹ"ד הֵ"א וָא"ו הֵ"א, דְּאִיהוּ יאאא, בִּ"ג מְכִילָן דְּרַחֲמֵי, דְּאִינּוּן אֶחָד.
כְּעַן תִּסְתְּלַק בְּאֵל, דְּאִיהוּ ייא"י. דִּתְרֵין שְׁמָהָן סַהֲדִין, הֲלֹא אֵל אֶחָד
בְּרָאָנוּ. הה"ד, הֲלֹא אָב אֶחָד לְכֻלָּנוּ הֲלֹא אֵל אֶחָד בְּרָאָנוּ.

Ra'aya Meheimna (the Faithful Shepherd)

646. Another explanation: "And he dreamed, and behold a ladder"
(Beresheet 28:12). Faithful Shepherd, just as the letter Lamed rises alone all
the other letters, BECAUSE THE LAMED ALLUDES TO BINAH, so will you in
the future be exalted above all creatures because you ascended to the name
Yud-Vav-Dalet, Hei-Yud, Vav-Aleph-Vav, Hei-Yud, WHOSE NUMERICAL
VALUE IS 63, WHICH IS BINAH. And in it THERE ARE THREE YUDS, Yud
Yud Yud, the numerical value of them making Lamed (= thirty). For initially
you were in the name Yud-Vav-Dalet, Hei-Aleph, Vav-Aleph-Vav, Hei-
Aleph, WHICH HAS THE NUMERICAL VALUE OF 45, WHICH IS ZEIR
ANPIN. It contains Yud-Aleph-Aleph-Aleph, THE NUMERICAL VALUE OF
WHICH IS THIRTEEN, which stands for the thirteen attributes of Mercy, AND
HAS THE SAME NUMERICAL VALUE AS THE WORD One (Heb. echad -
Aleph Chet Dalet = thirteen). And now you have ascended with El (= 31),
which is Yud Yud Aleph Yud OF THE FULL SPELLING OF 63. And both of
these Names are witnesses, "has not one El created us?" (Malachi 2:10).

FOR THE YUD-YUD-ALEPH-YUD OF YUD HEI VAV HEI, FULLY SPELLED OF THE NUMERICAL VALUE OF 63 HAS THE NUMERICAL VALUE OF THE WORD EL, AND THE ALEPH-FILLING OF THE YUD HEI VAV HEI, YUD-ALEPH-ALEPH-ALEPH IS THE NUMERICAL VALUE OF THE WORD ONE (Heb. ECHAD).. Hence it is written: "Have we not all one father? has not one El created us?"

647. וּבג' יוֹדִין אִלֵּין, יִתְקַיֵּים בָּךְ, יָרוּם וְנִשָּׂא וְגָבַהּ מְאֹד, בְּמַ"ה. דְּהָכִי סָלִיק מְאֹ"ד, לְחֻשְׁבַּן אָדָ"ם. וּבְהִפּוּךְ אַתְוָון, מְאֹד הוּא אָדָם. יָרוּם: בְּאַרְבַּע אַנְפִּין דְּאַרְיֵה, דְּאִינּוּן יְבָרֶכְךָ יְדֹנָ"ד. וְנִשָּׂא: בְּאַרְבַּע אַנְפִּין דְּשׁוֹר, דְּאִינּוּן יִשָּׂא יְדֹנָ"ד בִּשְׂמָאלָא. וְגָבַהּ מְאֹד: יָאֵר יְדֹנָ"ד, בְּאֶמְצָעִיתָא. וְדָא יוֹד הֵי וָאו הֵי, יִשָּׂא יְדֹנָ"ד פָּנָיו אֵלֶיךָ וְיָשֵׂם לְךָ שָׁלוֹם. רְבִיעָאָה יְדֹנָ"ד, וְשָׂמוּ אֶת שְׁמִי עַל בְּנֵי יִשְׂרָאֵל וַאֲנִי אֲבָרֲכֵם.

647. And with these three Yud's OF THE 63 NUMERIC VALUE-LETTER NAME may the verse be established in you: "He shall be exalted and extolled, and be very high" (Yeshayah 52:13). "VERY (HEB. ME'OD) HIGH" REFERS TO YUD HEI VAV HEI OF THE NUMERICAL VALUE OF 45, which is the numerical value of the word me'od (Mem Aleph Dalet), which is the same as man (Heb. adam - Aleph Dalet Mem), 45, and in fact the letters of the word 'very' are the same as those of the word 'man', written in a different order. "He shall be exalted" is in the four faces of the lion, WHICH IS CHESED THAT RISES TO CHOCHMAH, which is the secret of "Hashem bless you" (Bemidbar 6:24), THIS BEING THE SECRET OF YUD HEI VAV HEI FULLY SPELLED TO THE NUMERICAL VALUE OF 72, THUS: YUD-VAV-DALET, HEI-YUD, VAV-YUD-VAV, HEI-YUD; WHICH IS THE NUMERICAL VALUE OF CHESED, AND THIS IS CHOCHMAH OF THE RIGHT. "and extolled" is through the four faces of ox, WHICH IS GVURAH THAT RISES TO BINAH, namely: "Hashem lift up" (Ibid. 26), AND THIS IS BINAH of the left. "and be very high" is "Hashem make His face shine" (Ibid. 25), WHICH IS ZEIR ANPIN, AND IS in the middle, AND IS YUD HEI VAV HEI, FULLY SPELLED TO THE NUMERICAL VALUE OF 45. And this Yud Vav Dalet, Hei Yud, Vav Aleph Vav, Hei Yud, WHICH IS YUD HEI VAV HEI, FULLY SPELLED TO THE NUMERICAL VALUE OF 63, is, "Hashem lift up His countenance to you, and give you peace" (Ibid. 26). The fourth Yud Hei Vav Hei, NAMELY, THAT FILLED WITH HEIS OF THE NUMERICAL VALUE OF 52 IS MALCHUT,

94. Three Yud's in the Yud Hei Vav Hei fully spelled with Yud amounting to 63

AND THIS is: "And they shall put My name upon the children of Yisrael: and I will bless them" (Ibid. 27), FOR MALCHUT IS CALLED 'NAME.'

95. As a flame connected to a burning coal

A Synopsis

We hear of the waters of the Torah emerging from the smooth precious stones that were derived from the stone called Malchut. The further explanation is that the Torah is actually the secret of Light because it consists of both Chassadim and Chochmah. From the right-hand side Malchut is called a stone, but from the left it is called a burning coal, and this appellation speaks to the vengeance that will be taken against the enemies of Yisrael. Rabbi Shimon talks about the events that will happen at the end of the Exile, when the two Messiahs will be connected with the Faithful Shepherd. At that time the Klipot that surround the Shechinah will be shattered into pieces and one of the three stones will be revealed. We are told that the Faithful Shepherd issues from upper Ima and spreads throughout the six Sfirot to the Righteous, and from there it waters the Garden that is the Shechinah.

648. מִסְטְרָא דִּימִינָא, אִתְקְרִיאַת אֶבֶן. וְכַמָּה אֲבָנִין מְפוּלָמִין יַקִּירִין אִשְׁתְּכָחוּ מִנָּהּ, דְּמִנַּיְיהוּ מַיָּא דְּאוֹרַיְיתָא נָפְקִין. וּבְגִינֵיהוֹן אִתְּמַר, אָמַר ר' עֲקִיבָא לְתַלְמִידָיו כְּשֶׁתַּגִּיעוּ לְאַבְנֵי שַׁיִשׁ טָהוֹר אַל תֹּאמְרוּ מַיִם מַיִם שֶׁמָּא תִסְתַּכְּנוּ בְּנַפְשְׁכֶם. לָא תֵּימְרוּן דְּאִינּוּן מַיִם, מַיִם מַמָּשׁ. מִשּׁוּם דּוֹבֵר שְׁקָרִים לֹא יִכּוֹן לְנֶגֶד עֵינָי. דְּאַלֵּין מַיִם, דָּא אוֹרַיְיתָא, דְּאִתְּמַר בָּהּ וְתוֹרָה אוֹר. וּבְגִין דְּהַאי נְהוֹרָא נְבִיעַ בְּמַבּוּעָא דְּמַיָּא, אֲשֶׁר לֹא יְכַזְבוּ מֵימָיו, אִתְקְרֵי מַיִם.

648. From the right-hand side, MALCHUT is called 'a stone'; and a number of smooth precious stones, NAMELY, STONES THAT ISSUE WATER, are to be derived from it. From them issue the waters of the Torah, about which we have learned: Rabbi Akiva said to his disciples, When you reach stones of pure marble, do not say: Water, water, lest you endanger your souls. THE MEANING OF THIS IS: Do not say that these waters OF MALCHUT are real waters, NAMELY, ONLY CHASSADIM, because "he that tells lies shall not remain in My sight" (Tehilim 101:7). For these waters THAT ARE IN MALCHUT are Torah; THAT IS TO SAY THAT THEY ARE DRAWN DOWN FROM ZEIR ANPIN, WHICH IS CALLED 'TORAH', AND IS COMPOSED OF CHOCHMAH AND CHASSADIM TOGETHER, AND IS THEREFORE THE

SECRET OF LIGHT AND NOT OF WATER, WHICH INDICATES CHASSADIM
WITHOUT CHOCHMAH, for it is said about it: "and Torah is light" (Mishlei
6:23). And since this light stems from a spring "whose waters fail not"
(Yeshayah 58:11), FOR ZEIR ANPIN RECEIVES THIS LIGHT FROM
SUPERNAL ABA AND IMA WHOSE UNION IS NEVER ENDING, AND THERE,
IN ABA AND IMA, IT IS CHASSADIM, it is therefore called 'water', WHICH
IS CHASSADIM. HOWEVER, WHEN THE CHASSADIM COME TO ZEIR
ANPIN, THEY ARE COMPOSED OF CHOCHMAH AS WELL, AND ARE
CALLED 'LIGHT'. AND THIS IS THE SECRET OF "AND TORAH IS LIGHT."

649. וּמִסִּטְרָא דִשְׂמָאלָא, הַאי אֶבֶן דְּאִיהִי י', אִתְקְרֵי גַּחֶלֶת. וּמִתַּמָּן
עֲשַׂר סְפִירָן כְּשַׁלְהֶבֶת קְשׁוּרָה בַּגַּחֶלֶת. וְאִית לָהּ ד' גְּוָונִין, וְעַשְׂרָה
אִינּוּן, יוֹד הֵא וָאו הֵא. יְדוָ"ד. וְאִיהִי יַד הַגְּדוֹלָה בִּימִינָא, יַד הַחֲזָקָה
בִּשְׂמָאלָא, עַמּוּדָא דְּאֶמְצָעִיתָא, מִתַּמָּן אִיהִי יַד רָמָה, כָּלִיל ממ"ב
גְּוָונִין.

649. And from the left-hand side, this stone, which is Yud, NAMELY,
MALCHUT, is called 'a burning coal', NAMELY, BY MEANS OF THE
JUDGMENTS OF THE LEFT THAT BURN IN IT, whence the ten Sfirot ARE
REFERRED TO as a flame joined to a burning coal. And it has four hues,
NAMELY, THE FOUR LETTERS OF THE SIMPLE YUD HEI VAV HEI, and
they are ten, NAMELY, THE TEN LETTERS OF YUD HEI VAV HEI FULLY
SPELLED WITH ALEPHS: Yud-Vav-Dalet, Hei-Aleph, Vav-Aleph-Vav, Hei-
Aleph. TOGETHER THIS MAKES FOURTEEN LETTERS. And it is the great
hand (= fourteen) FROM THE POINT OF VIEW OF the right WHICH IS
CHESED, the mighty hand FROM THE POINT OF VIEW of the left WHICH IS
GVURAH, WHILE FROM THE POINT OF VIEW of the Central Column it is an
upraised hand. It is thus composed of 42 hues, THIS BEING THE SUM OF
THREE TIMES FOURTEEN.

650. וּבְגִין דְּאִיהִי מִסִּטְרָא דְּיְמִינָא אֶבֶן, וּמִסִּטְרָא דִשְׂמָאלָא גַּחֶלֶת, בָּהּ
נָטִיל קוּדְשָׁא בְּרִיךְ הוּא נוּקְמָא, מִיִּשְׁמָעֵאל וֶאֱדוֹם, דְּאִינּוּן אִישִׁין
נוּכְרָאִין, וּמַיִם הַזֵּדוֹנִים. וּמְמַנָּן דִּלְהוֹן סָמָאֵל וְנָחָשׁ. סָמָאֵל אֶשָׁא
דְּגֵיהִנָּם, מְמוּנֶה עַל אוּמָּה דְּעֵשָׂו. נָחָשׁ מְמוּנֶה עַל אוּמָּה, דְּיִשְׁמָעֵאל
וְאִיהוּ רָהָב דִּמְמַנָּא עַל מַיָּא.

650. And since from the point of view of the right it is a stone, and from the point of view of the left it is a burning coal, the Holy One, blessed be He, takes vengeance with it from Ishmael and Edom, WHO ARE DERIVED FROM THE WASTE MATTERS OF RIGHT AND LEFT. For they are strange fires OF, OTHER SIDE and the proud waters, WHERE ISHMAEL IS PROUD WATERS AND EDOM IS STRANGE FIRES, and their appointed officials are Samael and Serpent. Samael, who is the fire of Gehenom, is appointed over the nation of Esau, and Serpent is appointed over the nation of Ishmael, and this is THE ANGEL Rahav, who is in charge of the waters.

651. בִּימִינָא דְּאַבְרָהָם, דְּדַרְגֵּיהּ חֶסֶד, נָטִיל נוּקְמָא מִיִּשְׁמָעֵאל, וּמְמָנָא דִּילֵיהּ. וּבִשְׂמָאלָא דְּיִצְחָק, דְּדַרְגֵּיהּ פַּחַד, נָטִיל נוּקְמָא מֵעֵשָׂו, וּמְמָנָא דִּילֵיהּ. בִּתְרֵין מְשִׁיחִין, דְּאִינּוּן חַד מִימִינָא, מָשִׁיחַ בֶּן דָּוִד. וְחַד מִשְּׂמָאלָא, מָשִׁיחַ בֶּן יוֹסֵף. וּבְדַרְגָּא דְּיַעֲקֹב, דְּאִיהִי לְקָבְלֵיהּ, בְּרָזָא דְּשִׁכֵּל אֶת יָדָיו. אַרְיֵה לִשְׂמָאלָא. שׁוֹר לִימִינָא, דְּיִשְׁמָעֵאל. בְּגִין דִּיהוּדָה גָּלָה בְּעֵשָׂו, אִשְׁתְּכַח יְמִינָא דִקְדוּשָׁה, עִם שְׂמָאלָא דְּעֵשָׂו. וּשְׂמָאלָא דִּקְדוּשָׁה עִם יְמִינָא מְסָאֲבָא דְּיִשְׁמָעֵאל, עַד כִּי יָבֹא שִׁילֹה, רַעְיָא מְהֵימָנָא, בְּדַרְגֵּיהּ תִּפְאֶרֶת יִשְׂרָאֵל, נָטִיל נוּקְמָא מֵעֵרֶב רַב.

651. From the right of Abraham, whose level is Chesed, He takes vengeance on Ishmael and his official, and from the left of Isaac, whose level is Fear, NAMELY, GVURAH, He takes vengeance on Esau and his appointed official by means of two Messiahs, one of whom, Messiah son of David, is from the right, while the other, Messiah son of Joseph, is from the left. And the level of Jacob, WHICH IS TIFERET, IS THE CENTRAL COLUMN, that corresponds to them, in the secret of "changing his hands" (Beresheet 48:14) – the lion, to the left, CORRESPONDING TO ESAU, and the ox to the right, CORRESPONDING to Ishmael. And since Judah was exiled in Esau, it follows that the right of holiness is with the left of Esau, and likewise IN THE EXILE OF ISHMAEL the left of holiness is TO BE FOUND with the impure right of Ishmael. ACCORDINGLY, IT FOLLOWS THAT MESSIAH SON OF DAVID, WHICH IS RIGHT, WILL TAKE VENGEANCE ON ESAU, WHILE MESSIAH SON OF JOSEPH, WHICH IS LEFT, WILL TAKE VENGEANCE ON ISHMAEL. "Until Shiloh come (lit. 'comes')" (Beresheet 49:10), WHERE THE NUMERICAL VALUE OF SHILOH IS THE SAME AS THAT OF MOSES, WHO IS the Faithful Shepherd, whose level is Tiferet Yisrael, WHICH IS THE

CENTRAL COLUMN. He will take vengeance from the mixed multitude, FOR THE MIXED MULTITUDE IS COMPOSED OF THE RIGHT AND LEFT OF IMPURITY, AND SO THE CENTRAL COLUMN, WHICH IS COMPOSED OF THE RIGHT AND LEFT OF HOLINESS, WILL BE AVENGED ON THEM.

652. בִּתְלַת דַּרְגִּין אָלֵין, יִפְקוֹד כֹּהֲנִים לְוִיַם וְיִשְׂרָאֵלִים, מִן גָּלוּתָא. וּבְהוֹן נָטִיל נוּקְמָא, מֵעֵשָׂו וְיִשְׁמָעֵאל וְעֵרֶב רַב. כְּגַוְונָא דְּעֵרֶב רַב מְעוּרְבִין בְּעֵשָׂו וְיִשְׁמָעֵאל, הָכִי יַעֲקֹב מְעוֹרָב בְּאַבְרָהָם וְיִצְחָק, עָרוּב דִּתְרַוְויְיהוּ. וְהָכִי מִתְעָרַב שִׁילֹה, עִם מָשִׁיחַ בֶּן דָּוִד וּמָשִׁיחַ בֶּן יוֹסֵף, וִיהֵא שַׁלְשֶׁלֶת דְּתַרְוַויְיהוּ, כְּהַהוּא זִמְנָא דְּחָזָא בִּלְעָם בַּנְּבוּאָה דִּילֵיהּ, דְּהָכִי מִתְקַשְּׁרֵי תְּרֵין מְשִׁיחִין בְּרַעְיָא מְהֵימָנָא, בִּתְלַת אֲבָהָן, בְּגָלוּתָא בַּתְרָאָה.

652. In these three grades, RIGHT, LEFT AND CENTER, AS ABOVE, the priests, Levites, and Yisrael will be recalled from the Exile, FOR THEY ARE DRAWN DOWN FROM THESE THREE COLUMNS. And in them, IN THE THREE COLUMNS, He takes vengeance upon Esau, Ishmael, and the mixed multitude, for just as the mixed multitude is intermixed with Esau and Ishmael, NAMELY, CONTAINING RIGHT AND LEFT OF IMPURITY, so Jacob, WHO IS THE CENTRAL COLUMN, is composed of Abraham and Isaac, WHO ARE RIGHT AND LEFT, for he is a mixture of the two of them. And so, too, Shiloh, WHICH IS MOSES, WHO IS ALSO THE CENTRAL COLUMN, AS ABOVE, is intermixed with Messiah son of David, WHO IS THE RIGHT SIDE, and WITH Messiah son of Joseph, WHO IS THE LEFT SIDE, and he will be the chain THAT INCORPORATES AND CONNECTS the two of them, as at the time that Bilaam saw in his prophecy, NAMELY, "UNTIL SHILOH COME." For thus the two Messiahs are connected with the Faithful Shepherd, THIS BEING THE SECRET OF the three patriarchs, NAMELY, THE THREE COLUMNS, AS ABOVE, in the final exile. AND THEY WILL THUS HAVE THE POWER TO WIN AND DESTROY ALL THE KLIPOT THAT CORRESPOND TO THE THREE COLUMNS OF HOLINESS, AS ABOVE.

653. פָּתַח וְאָמַר, לֹא הִבִּיט אָוֶן בְּיַעֲקֹב וְלֹא רָאָה עָמָל בְּיִשְׂרָאֵל יְיָ' אֱלֹהָיו עִמּוֹ וּתְרוּעַת מֶלֶךְ בּוֹ. וְכֹלָּא לְקַיְּימָא קְרָא, וּבְרַחֲמִים גְּדוֹלִים אֲקַבְּצֵךְ. בְּהַהוּא זִמְנָא מִתְבָּרִין קְלִיפוֹת, דַּהֲווֹ מְסַחֲרִין לִשְׁכִינְתָּא. מִיַּד

אִתְגַּלְיָיא אַבְנָא חֲדָא מִתְּלַת אֲבָנִין, דְּאִינּוּן סְגוֹלְתָּא. דְּעָלַיְיהוּ אִתְּמַר,
וַיְהִי בִּשְׁלֹשִׁים שָׁנָה, וְאִינּוּן יי"י בָּרְבִיעִי, אַבְנָא רְבִיעָאָה. בַּחֲמִשָׁה
לַחֹדֶשׁ, אַבְנָא חֲמִשָׁאָה. לְקַבְלַיְיהוּ, וַיִּקַּח דָּוִד חֲמִשָׁה חַלּוּקֵי אֲבָנִים מִן
הַנַּחַל. וְאִינּוּן לְקַבְלַיְיהוּ חָמֵשׁ תֵּיבִין, דְּאִינּוּן שְׁמַע יִשְׂרָאֵל יְדֹוָ"ד
אֱלֹהֵינוּ יְדֹוָ"ד.

653. He opened by quoting: "He has not beheld iniquity in Jacob, neither has He seen perverseness in Yisrael; Hashem his Elohim is with him, and the trumpet blasts of the King is among them" (Bemidbar 23:21). And all this is to fulfill the verse: "But with great compassion will I gather you" (Yeshayah 54:7). And at that time, the Klipot that surround the Shechinah will be shattered into pieces, and immediately one of the three stones will be revealed. And the three stones are Segolta THAT IS THE SECRET OF MALCHUT, WHICH IS THE APEX OF THE SEGOLTA IN THE TONAL NOTES, and about these THREE POINTS, it is said: "Now it came to pass in the thirtieth year" (Yechezkel 1:1). THIS IS THE SECRET OF THE THREE YUD'S, Yud, Yud, Yud, WHERE EACH OF THE THREE POINTS THAT MAKE UP THE SEGOLTA IS A YUD, AND THE NUMERICAL SUM OF THREE YUDS IS THIRTY. "in the fourth month" (Ibid.) refers to the fourth stone, WHICH IS NETZACH. "on the fifth day of the month" refers to the fifth stone, WHICH IS HOD. Corresponding to them is: "and chose five smooth stones out of the brook" (I Shmuel 17:40), THESE BEING THE SECRET OF CHESED, GVURAH, TIFERET, NETZACH AND HOD, THAT ARE TAKEN FROM YESOD THAT INCORPORATES ALL OF THEM, AND IS CALLED 'BROOK'. And corresponding to them are the five words: "Hear O Yisrael, Hashem our Elohim, Hashem" (Devarim 6:4).

654. וַאֲנִי בְּתוֹךְ הַגּוֹלָה, דָּא שְׁכִינְתָּא, בָּהּ קוּדְשָׁא בְּרִיךְ הוּא אֶחָד. ו'
בְּתוֹסֶפֶת וַאֲנִי, הוּא נָהָר, צַדִּיק חַי עָלְמִין. וְנָהָר יוֹצֵא מֵעֵדֶן לְהַשְׁקוֹת
אֶת הַגָּן, מַאי עֵדֶן. דָּא בִּינָה, נָהָר דְּנָפִיק מִנָּהּ, דָּא ו', בֶּן י"ה, דַּרְגָּא
דִּרְעֲיָא מְהֵימְנָא, ור"מ, נָפִיק מֵאִימָּא עִלָּאָה, וְאִתְפַּשַּׁט בְּשִׁית סְפִירָאן
עַד צַדִּיק, וּמִנֵּיהּ אַשְׁקֵי לְגִנְתָּא, דְּאִיהִי שְׁכִינְתָּא.

654. "as I was among the exiles" (Yechezkel 1:1). This is the Shechinah, WHICH IS CALLED 'I', in which the Holy One, blessed be He, is One (Heb.

Echad), BECAUSE ZEIR ANPIN IS ALEPH CHET OF *ECHAD* (ALEPH CHET DALET), AND THE SHECHINAH IS DALET OF *ECHAD*. The Vav (lit. 'as') added to 'I', FOR IT IS WRITTEN 'AS I', is the river, which is the Righteous, life of the worlds, NAMELY, YESOD. AND HE EXPLAINED HIS WORDS: "And a river went out of Eden to water the garden" (Beresheet 2:10). What is meant by Eden? This is Binah (Bet Yud Nun Hei). The river that went out OF BINAH WHICH IS EDEN is Vav, the son (Heb. *ben* - Bet Nun) of Yud Hei, NAMELY, ZEIR ANPIN, which is the level of the Faithful Shepherd. And the Faithful Shepherd, WHICH IS ZEIR ANPIN, issues from supernal Ima, WHICH IS THE SECRET OF EDEN, and spreads throughout the six Sfirot: CHESED, GVURAH, TIFERET, NETZACH, HOD AND YESOD, to the Righteous, WHICH IS YESOD. And from there, FROM YESOD, it waters the Garden, which is the Shechinah, AND SO THE VAV (LIT. 'AS') OF 'I' THEREFORE ALLUDES TO YESOD THAT WATERS IT.

655. מַאי כְּבָ״ר. כ׳, כֶּתֶר. ב׳, בִּינָה. ר׳, רֵאשִׁית חָכְמָה. כֶּתֶר בִּימִינָא, חָכְמָה בִּשְׂמָאלָא, בִּינָה בְּאֶמְצָעִיתָא. רֶכֶב לְעֵילָא לְעָלַת הָעִלּוֹת. י׳ סְפִירָאן כֻּלְּהוּ, אִתְכָּלְלוּ בְּנָהָר, דְּאִיהוּ אִתְפְּשָׁט עַד צַדִּיק, דְּאִיהוּ כָּל, כָּלִיל כֹּלָּא. וּבְגִינֵיהּ אוּקְמוּהָ, אִילָנָא רַבָּא וְתַקִּיף, וּמְזוֹן לְכֹלָּא בֵּיהּ. מִנֵּיהּ תַּלְיָא כֹּלָּא. כַּד חָמָא שְׁכִינְתָּא מִגּוֹ קְלִיפִין, חָזָא עִמָּה עֲשַׂר סְפִירָן.

ע״כ רעיא מהימנא

655. IT IS WRITTEN: "BY THE RIVER KEVAR" (YECHEZKEL 1:1). What is *Kevar* (Caf Bet Resh)? HE ANSWERS THAT Caf ALLUDES TO Keter, Bet TO Binah, AND Resh TO the beginning of (Heb. *reshit*) Chochmah. Keter is on the right side; Chochmah is on the left side; Binah is in the center. And they form a Chariot (Heb. *rechev* - Resh Caf Bet) on high for the Prime Cause, INFINITY. All ten of the Sfirot are included in the river, WHICH IS ZEIR ANPIN, which spreads as far as the Righteous, WHICH IS YESOD, that IS CALLED 'All', AS it is all inclusive, containing WITHIN IT all THE SFIROT, and about it was it said: "The tree grew, and was strong... and on it was food for all" (Daniel 4:8-9). Everything depends on it. When EZEKIEL saw the Shechinah among the Klipot, he saw ten Sfirot with her.

End of Ra'aya Meheimna

96. Fine flour for an offering

A Synopsis

We learn that the fine flour should be composed of both the right and left side.

656. סֹלֶת לְמִנְחָה, לְאַעֲלָאָה לְהַאי סֹלֶת, קַמֵּי מַלְכָּא עִלָּאָה לְמִנְחָה. בֵּין תְּרֵין דְּרוֹעִין.

656. IT IS WRITTEN: "fine flour for a meal offering" (Bemidbar 28:5); that is, that this fine flour, WHICH IS MALCHUT, should be brought before the Supernal King for a meal offering between the two arms; THAT IS TO SAY THAT IT SHOULD BE COMPOSED OF THE TWO ARMS, WHICH ARE CHESED AND GVURAH, THE RIGHT SIDE AND THE LEFT SIDE.

A Synopsis

Moses explains the flour by talking about Isaac, the left hand of Zeir Anpin, and Abraham, the right hand of Zeir Anpin. He says the fine flour is the lower Shechinah, as it has no connotation of darkness. Just as the chaff and straw have to be removed from the grain during threshing, Yisrael must remove any dark ones that become intermingled with them. Moses says that darkness is the Evil Inclination.

רעיא מהימנא

657. וּבְחִבּוּרָא קַדְמָאָה, אָמַר רַעְיָא מְהֵימָנָא, מֵהַאי אִשְׁתְּמוֹדַע, הָנֵי מִילִין סְתִימִין אִינּוּן, וְצָרִיךְ לְמִפְתַּח לוֹן קַמֵּי חַבְרַיָּיא, אַבְרָהָם יִצְחָק דְּתִקִּינוּ שַׁחֲרִית וּמִנְחָה, אִתְּמַר עֲלַיְיהוּ, אַף יְדֵי יָסְדָה אֶרֶץ, דָּא יִצְחָק. וִימִינִי טִפְּחָה שָׁמַיִם, דָּא אַבְרָהָם. דְּדַרְגִּין דִּלְהוֹן חֶסֶד וָפַחַד. דְּאִתְּמַר עֲלַיְיהוּ נִשְׁבַּע יְיָ' בִּימִינוֹ, וּבִזְרוֹעַ עֻזּוֹ, אִינּוּן תְּרֵין דְּרוֹעִין דְּמַלְכָּא, דְּאִיהוּ יְדֹוָ"ד, עַמּוּדָא דְּאֶמְצָעִיתָא. סֹלֶת דִּילֵיהּ, דָּא שְׁכִינְתָּא תַּתָּאָה, נְהוֹרָא דִּילֵיהּ, סֹלֶת נְקִיָּיה מִסְטְרוֹי בְּלָא פְּגִימוּ דַּחֲשׁוֹכָא, וּבְלָא תַּעֲרוֹבֶת חֲשׁוֹכָא כְּלָל. דְּהָכִי אִינּוּן חֲשׁוֹכִין עִם נְהוֹרִין, כְּבַר קֶדָם מוֹץ וְתֶבֶן.

Ra'aya Meheimna (the Faithful Shepherd)

657. And in the first composition, the Faithful Shepherd said: From this, FROM WHAT THE ZOHAR SAYS ABOUT "THE FINE FLOUR FOR A MEAL OFFERING" BEING BETWEEN THE TWO ARMS, it must be understood that these are hidden matters that have to be explained to the friends. It is said about Abraham and Isaac, who instituted the morning and afternoon prayers: "My hand also has laid the foundation of the earth" (Yeshayah 48:13), which refers to Isaac, WHO IS THE LEFT HAND OF ZEIR ANPIN, "and My right hand has spanned the heavens" (Ibid.) refers to Abraham, WHO IS THE RIGHT HAND OF ZEIR ANPIN. Their levels are Chesed and Fear, as it is said about them: "Hashem has sworn by His right hand, and by the arm of His strength" (Yeshayah 62:8), which are the two arms to the King, which is Yud Hei Vav Hei, NAMELY, ZEIR ANPIN, the Central Column. And His fine flour is the lower Shechinah, NAMELY, MALCHUT, which is His light, THAT IS OF ZEIR ANPIN, and is clean fine flour from His sides, NAMELY, WHEN CLEAVING TO HIS RIGHT AND LEFT SIDES, without blemish of darkness, and without any implication of contaminated darkness. For such is the relationship of light to darkness, as clean grain is to chaff and straw. MALCHUT IS THEREFORE TERMED FINE FLOUR WHEN SHE IS WITHOUT ANY INTIMATION OF DARKNESS.

658. וּבְחוֹבֵיהוֹן דְּיִשְׂרָאֵל, מִתְעָרְבִין חֲשׁוֹכִין בִּנְהוֹרִין, וּכְגַוְונָא דְּדָשׁ בְּ"ן תְּבוּאָה, וּלְבָתַר אִיהוּ בּוֹרֵר לָהּ, כְּבוֹרֵר אוֹכֶל מִתּוֹךְ פְּסוֹלֶת. כָּךְ יִשְׂרָאֵל, צָרִיךְ לְמֶעְבַּד בְּרוּחֵיהוֹן, כַּד אִתְעָרַב בְּהוֹן חֲשׁוֹכִין. וְרָזָא דְמִלָּה, זִבְחֵי אֱלֹהִים רוּחַ נִשְׁבָּרָה וְגוֹ'. דִּבְהָכִי אִתְבַּר חֲשׁוֹכָא, דְּאִיהוּ יֵצֶר הָרָע, דִּמְכַסֵּי עַל רוּחָא, כְּמוֹץ דִּמְכַסֶּה עַל חִטָּה. אוֹ כְּעָנָן, דִּמְכַסֶּה עַל שִׁמְשָׁא, וְלָא מָנַח לֵיהּ לְאַנְהָרָא.

658. But in the iniquities of Yisrael, dark ones become mixed up with the luminous ones. And just as a man threshes the grain and then makes his selection OF THE WHEAT FROM THE CHAFF AND STRAW, like one picking out food from amongst rubbish, so it is with Yisrael that, when dark ones become intermingled with them, they have to make AND CORRECT their spirits. And the secret of the matter is contained in the verse: "The sacrifices of Elohim are a broken spirit" (Tehilim 51:19). For darkness – which is the

Evil Inclination that covers the spirit as the chaff that covers the grain or as the cloud that covers the sun not allowing it to give light – is broken.

659. וּבְזִמְנִין דְּחֹשֶׁךְ, דְּאִיהוּ יצה״ר, מְכַסֶּה עַל יֵצֶר הַטּוֹב, דְּאִיהוּ אוֹר. אִיהוּ כְּמַאן דְּתָפִיס בְּבֵית הָאֲסוּרִין דִיצה״ר. וְאוּף הָכִי, כַּד יֵצֶר הַטּוֹב אִיהוּ תָּפִיס בִּרְשׁוּ דִיצה״ר, הָכִי אִינּוּן תְּפִיסִין חַיָּילִין דְּיֵצֶר הַטּוֹב, בִּרְשׁוּ דְּחַיָּילִין דְּיֵצֶר הָרָע. וּבְזִמְנָא דְּיִתְבַּר ב״נ רוּחֵיהּ, בְּכָל אֵבָרִין דִּילֵיהּ, קֳדָם יְדֹוָ״ד, מַה כְּתִיב. לֵאמֹר לַאֲסוּרִים צֵאוּ וְלַאֲשֶׁר בַּחֹשֶׁךְ הִגָּלוּ.

659. And in the time when darkness, which is the Evil Inclination, covers the Good Inclination, the latter, which is light, is like one who is imprisoned in the prison of the Evil Inclination. And so, too, when the Good Inclination is imprisoned in the domain of the Evil Inclination, the hosts of the Good Inclination are also imprisoned in the domain of the hosts of the Evil Inclination. And when a person breaks his spirit in all his limbs before Hashem, what does Scripture say? "That you may say to the prisoners, Go forth; to them that are in darkness, Show yourselves" (Yeshayah 49:9).

660. אֲבָל שְׁכִינְתָּא אִיהִי סֹלֶת נְקִיָּיה, דְּלֵית חֲשׁוֹכָא וְקַבְלָא יָכִיל לְאִתְעָרְבָא בָּהּ. אִיהִי כַּגֶּפֶן, דְּלָא מְקַבְּלָא הַרְכָּבָה מִמִּין אַחֲרָא, דְּלָאו אִיהִי מִינָהּ. וְהַאי סֹלֶת בֵּין דְּרוֹעֵי מַלְכָּא אִיהִי יָתְבָא, בְּלוּלָה בְּשֶׁמֶן כָּתִית.

ע״כ רעיא מהימנא

660. But the Shechinah is pure fine flour, in which darkness and gloom can not become mixed up. And she is as a vine that rejects a graft of another sort, that is not of its type. And this fine flour dwells between the arms of the King, NAMELY CHESED AND GVURAH, "mingled with...beaten oil" (Bemidbar 28:5).

End of Ra'aya Meheimna

97. "Mingled with...beaten oil"

A Synopsis

Rabbi Shimon asks for an explanation of the word "beaten" in the
title verse, and he is told that it has to do with drawing an
emanation down from above. The Righteous is the one who crushes
the holy olives for the anointing oil with his perfect longing for
Malchut.

661. בְּלוּלָה בְשֶׁמֶן כָּתִית, בְּשֶׁמֶן, בְּהַהוּא שֶׁמֶן דְּנָגִיד וְנָפִיק מִלְעֵילָּא.
אֲרֵ"שׁ, יָאוּת אֲמַרְתְּ. אֲבָל מַאי כָּתִית. אֶלָּא רָזָא עִלָּאָה אִיהוּ. דְּכֵיוָן
דְּאִיהוּ שֶׁמֶן, מַאי כָּתִית. אֶלָּא רֶמֶז הוּא דְּקָא רָמִיז לְשִׁמּוּשָׁא בְּנוּקְבָא,
לְאַנְגְּדָא לְגַבָּהּ שֶׁמֶן כָּתִית כַּדְקָא יָאוּת לָהּ, לָא הֲוֵי אֶלָּא כָּתִית
לְאַפָּקָא מִזֵּיתִים, דְּאִינּוּן שַׁיְיפִין דְּגוּפָא, וּלְאַמְשָׁכָא הַהוּא נְגִידוּ
מִלְעֵילָּא, בְּכָל שַׁיְיפָא וְשַׁיְיפָא.

661. "Mingled with...beaten oil" (Bemidbar 28:5). Oil refers to that oil that
is poured out and issues from on high, FROM CHOCHMAH OF THE RIGHT
SIDE. Rabbi Shimon said: What you have said is good, but how do you
explain "beaten"? HE ANSWERS, it is a divine secret. Since we are talking
about oil, what is "beaten"? It is an allusion to the mating with the Female,
NAMELY, MALCHUT, to draw down to her beaten oil as is fitting for her,
FROM SUPERNAL CHOCHMAH, which is none other than beaten in order to
extract OIL from the olives, which are the limbs of the body, NAMELY, THE
SFIROT OF ZEIR ANPIN, TERMED BODY, and to draw that emanation down
from above, FROM SUPENRAL CHOCHMAH, with each and every limb.

662. וְצַדִּיק אִיהוּ דְּכָתִישׁ כְּתִישִׁין, וְאַפִּיק מִכָּל אִינּוּן שַׁיְיפִין עִלָּאִין,
דְּאִינּוּן זֵיתִין קַדִּישִׁין, מְשַׁח רְבוּ בִּתְיאוּבְתָּא שְׁלִים, לְגַבֵּי נוּקְבֵיהּ. וְאִי
לָא כָּתִישׁ, לָא יִפּוּק הַהוּא מִשְׁחָא, אֶלָּא בְּלָא תִּיאוּבְתָּא דְּשַׁיְיפִין,
וְהַהוּא נְגִידוּ, לָא אִתְהֲנֵי מִנֵּיהּ נוּקְבָא, וְלָא הֲוֵי כַּדְקָא יָאוּת, עַד
דְּתְהֵא בְּלוּלָה מִנֵּיהּ מִכָּל שַׁיְיפִין. וְעַ"ד בְּלוּלָה בְשֶׁמֶן כָּתִית,
לְאִתְהֲנָאָה וּלְאִתְזָנָא מִנֵּיהּ.

662. And the Righteous, WHICH IS YESOD, is the one who crushes with pestles and extracts from all those upper limbs, FROM THE SFIROT of ZEIR ANPIN, that are holy olives, anointing oil, with a perfect longing for the Female, WHICH IS MALCHUT. But if he does not crush them, that oil will issue forth only without the longing of the limbs, and the Female will have no enjoyment from that emanation, AND THE OIL, WHICH IS THE LIGHT OF CHOCHMAH, will not be fitting until it is a blend of all the limbs. Therefore it is written: "mingled with...beaten oil," IN ORDER to enjoy it and be nourished from it.

A Synopsis

Moses furthers the explanation of the same topic, and he gives information about the three brains – of memory, of thought, and of imagination. He says that imagination and memory ascend from the heart and the thoughts descend to them to the heart, where they are welcomed as a king. Moses also brings in the factor of the four faces of the Holy Beasts.

רעיא מהימנא

663. אָמַר רַעְיָא מְהֵימָנָא, בּוּצִינָא קַדִּישָׁא, כַּמָּה מְתִיקִין מִילָךְ, וַדַּאי אִתְּמַר הָכָא, בְּלוּלָה בְּשֶׁמֶן כָּתִית. וְאִתְּמַר הָתָם, בְּאוֹרַיְיתָא דבע״פ, בְּלוּלָה בַּמִּקְרָא, בַּמִּשְׁנָה, בַּתַּלְמוּד. וְעוֹד אִית רָזָא תִּנְיָינָא, בְּלוּלָה בְּשֶׁמֶן כָּתִית. וַדַּאי לָאו אוֹרַיְיתָא אִיהִי בְּלוּלָה. אֶלָּא לְמַאן דְּסָבִיל כַּמָּה מַכְתָּשִׁין בְּגִינָה. כְּמָה דְּאוּקְמוּהָ מָארֵי מַתְנִיתִין, דְּלֵית אוֹרַיְיתָא מִתְקַיְּימֶת, אֶלָּא בְּמִי שֶׁמֵּמִית גַּרְמֵיה עָלָה. וְעוֹד אָמְרוּ, בִּזְמַן שֶׁאַתָּה מְכַתֵּת רַגְלֶיךָ מִמְּדִינָה לַמְּדִינָה, תִּזְכֶּה לִרְאוֹת פְּנֵי שְׁכִינָה.

Ra'aya Meheimna (the Faithful Shepherd)

663. The Faithful Shepherd said TO RABBI SHIMON: holy luminary, how sweet are your words! It is certainly said here "mingled with...beaten oil," and it says there, in the Oral Law, that it is blended in Bible, Mishnah, and Talmud. And there is yet a second secret here in "mingled with...beaten oil." It is certainly not the Torah that is mingled IN BIBLE, MISHNAH, AND TALMUD, but only for the person who suffers a number of chastisements for

its sake, as the sages of the Mishnah taught: The Torah is only upheld by one who kills himself for it. And they said further: When you trudge from county to county TO LEARN TORAH, you will be privileged to see the face of the Shechinah.

664. וְעוֹד בְּלוּלָה בְּשֶׁמֶן כָּתִית, דָּא הוּא דִּמְקַיֵּים פַּת בַּמֶּלַח תֹּאכַל, וּמַיִם בַּמְּשׂוּרָה תִּשְׁתֶּה. וְעוֹד בְּלוּלָה בְּשֶׁמֶן כָּתִית, הַה"ד, וְהוּא מְחוֹלָל מִפְּשָׁעֵינוּ מְדוּכָּא מֵעֲוֹנוֹתֵינוּ. וְעוֹד בְּלוּלָה בְּשֶׁמֶן כָּתִית, דָּא צַדִּיק חַי עָלְמִין, דְּנָגִיד טִפִּין קַדִּישִׁין, דְּאִינּוּן פֵּירוּרִין כַּזֵּיתִים, מִמּוֹחָא עִלָּאָה, דְּאִינּוּן חַד עִשָּׂרוֹן לָקֳבֵל י'. וּשְׁנֵי עֶשְׂרוֹנִים, י' י'. וּשְׁלֹשָׁה עֶשְׂרוֹנִים לַפָּר, י' י' י'. וְאִינּוּן עִשָּׂרוֹן לַכֶּבֶשׂ, וּב' עֶשְׂרוֹנִים לָאַיִל, וּשְׁלֹשָׁה עֶשְׂרוֹנִים לַפָּר.

664. Again: "mingled with...beaten oil": This refers to one who keeps the injunction: You shall eat bread with salt, "You shall drink also water by measure" (Yechezkel 4:11). Again, "mingled with...beaten oil" corresponds to "But he was wounded because of our transgressions, bruised because of our iniquities" (Yeshayah 53:5). And again, "mingled with...beaten oil" refers to the Righteous, life of the worlds, WHICH IS YESOD, that draws down holy drops that are olive-sized crumbs from the upper brain, WHICH IS SUPERNAL CHOCHMAH, which are one tenth measure corresponding to Yud, two tenth measures to Yud Yud, and three tenth measures to Yud Yud Yud. And these are: a tenth measure for a lamb and two tenth measures for the ram and three tenth measures for a bullock.

665. וְרָזָא דְּמִלָּה אָמְרוּ בְּתַעֲנִיּוֹת, אֵין טִפָּה יוֹרֶדֶת מִלְמַעְלָה, שֶׁאֵין עוֹלִין כְּנֶגְדָּהּ טְפַיִּים. וְאִינּוּן בְּרָזָא דָּא וְרְמִיזוּ דִּלְהוֹן לָקֳבֵל תְּלַת מוֹחִין. חַד מוֹחַ הַזִּכָּרוֹן. תִּנְיָינָא מוֹחַ הַמַּחֲשָׁבָה. תְּלִיתָאָה מוֹחַ הַדִּמְיוֹן. הַדִּמְיוֹן וְהַזִּכָּרוֹן סַלְקִין מִן לִבָּא, הַמַּחֲשָׁבוֹת נַחְתָּא עֲלַיְיהוּ לְלִבָּא, וּמְקַבְּלִין לָהּ עֲלַיְיהוּ, כְּמַלְכָּא. בְּגִין דְּהַאי אָדָם דְּאִיהוּ מַחֲשָׁבָה, דְּרָכִיב וְשָׁלִיט עַל חֵיוָא תְּלִיתָאָה, וְנַחִית עֲלָהּ לְגַבֵּי תְּרֵין חַיָּין, וּפַתְחִין גַּדְפַּיְיהוּ לְקַבְּלָא לָהּ, כְּגוֹן חוֹלָם עַל צֵרֵי, אִתְעֲבֵיד סְגוֹלְתָּא. וְדָא כֶּתֶר עֶלְיוֹן עַל חָכְמָה וּבִינָה.

665. And the secret of the matter is as they said in Tractate Ta'anit: Not one drop (of rain) descends from above without two drops coming up to meet it FROM BELOW. And they are in this secret∴ : And their allusion corresponds to three brains: of memory, of thought, and of imagination. Imagination and memory ascend from the heart, the thoughts descend to them to the heart, AND THE IMAGINATION AND THE MEMORY welcome them as a king, because this man, which is thought, mounts and controls the third living creature, descending on it to the two living creatures that open their wings to receive it, just as a Cholam placed over a Tzere becomes a Segolta. And this is upper Keter over Chochmah and Binah.

666. עִשָּׂרוֹן וּשְׁנֵי עֶשְׂרוֹנִים, רְמִיזִין לִתְלַת חֵיוָן דְּמֶרְכַּבְתָּא עִלָּאָה. דְּאִינּוּן: גְּדוּלָה, גְּבוּרָה, תִּפְאֶרֶת. שְׁלֹשָׁה עֶשְׂרוֹנִין, רְמִיזִין: לְנֶצַח, הוֹד, יְסוֹד. מֶרְכֶּבֶת הַמִּשְׁנֶה. רְבִיעִית הַהִין: דָּא מַלְכוּת קַדִּישָׁא, ה' רְבִיעָאָה מִן שֵׁם יְדֹוָ"ד. דְּאִיהוּ אַרְבַּע אַנְפֵּי אָדָם.

ע"כ רעיא מהימנא

666. One tenth measure and two tenth measures allude to the three living creatures of the upper Chariot, that are Greatness, WHICH IS CHESED, Gvurah, and Tiferet. Three tenth measures allude to Netzach, Hod and Yesod, in which is the second, LOWER, Chariot. The fourth part of a hin is holy Malchut, which is Hei, the fourth letter of the Name Yud Hei Vav Hei, in which are the four faces of a man. FOR IN CHESED THERE ARE FOUR FACES OF A LION; IN GVURAH THERE ARE FOUR FACES OF AN OX; AND IN TIFERET THERE ARE FOUR FACES OF AN EAGLE; WHILE IN MALCHUT ARE THE FOUR FACES OF A MAN.

End of Ra'aya Meheimna

A Synopsis
We are told that Malchut is a continual burnt offering that rises to God every single day, ascending to the Divine Thought that has no end. This is why a burnt offering is only required for sinful meditation of the heart, which is thought.

667. רְבִיעִית הַהִין, רַגְלָא רְבִיעָאָה לְכֻרְסְיָיא עִלָּאָה, וְאִיהוּ עוֹלָה

תָּמִיד לְגַבֵּיהּ בְּכָל יוֹמָא וְיוֹמָא, עַד מַחֲשַׁבְתָּא עִלָּאָה, דְּלֵית לָהּ סוֹף. וּבג״ד, עוֹלָה קָא אַתְיָא עַל הִרְהוּר הַלֵּב.

667. "a fourth part of a hin" (Bemidbar 28:14) refers to the fourth leg of the divine Throne, WHICH IS BINAH, THAT HAS FOUR LEGS, NAMELY: CHESED, GVURAH AND TIFERET OF ZEIR ANPIN AND MALCHUT. AND MALCHUT "is a continual burnt offering (Heb. *olah*)" (Ibid. 6) to Him every single day, AND IT ASCENDS (HEB. *OLAH*) to the Supernal Thought that has no end; and therefore a burnt offering SACRIFICE is due only for sinful contemplation of the heart, WHICH IS THOUGHT.

98. Zarka, Makaf, Shofar Holech, Segolta

A Synopsis
Moses talks about the three beasts that are twelve tribes.

רעיא מהימנא

668. וּבְחִבּוּרָא קַדְמָאָה אָמַר, רַעְיָא מְהֵימָנָא, הַהִיא תָּגָא דְּזַרְקָא, אִיהִי יוֹד, רְבִיעִית. אוֹף הָכִי בַּחַיָּה דִּשְׁמָהּ אָדָם, דְּאַרְבַּע אַנְפִּין דִּילֵיהּ דְּאִינּוּן יְדֹנָ"ד, מַקָּף שׁוֹפָר הוֹלֵךְ סְגוֹלְתָּא. תְּלַת חֵיוָן, דְּאִינּוּן תְּרֵיסַר שְׁבָטִין.

ע"כ רעיא מהינמא

Ra'aya Meheimna (the Faithful Shepherd)

668. And in the compilation of the first part, the Faithful Shepherd said: "This crown that is called Zarka is Yud, which is the fourth SFIRAH TO CHESED, GVURAH AND TIFERET, NAMELY, MALCHUT. AND IT IS CALLED 'ZARKA' BECAUSE IT IS CAST (HEB. *NIZREKET*) AS FAR AS THE SUPERNAL THOUGHT THAT HAS NO END, AS ABOVE IN THE PRECEDING PARAGRAPH. So also the living creature whose name is man, WHICH IS MALCHUT, and its four faces, which are THE FOUR LETTERS OF Yud Hei Vav Hei, ARE Makaf, Shofar Holech, Segolta, for it is three living creatures which are twelve tribes.

End of Ra'aya Meheimna

A Synopsis
We are told that the continual burnt offering is on each of the six Days of Creation, with a double offering on the Shabbat that adds light and perfection to it.

669. וּבְחִבּוּרָא קַדְמָאָה, עוֹלַת תָּמִיד, אִיהִי רֶגֶל רְבִיעָאָה לְכֻרְסַיָּיא עִלָּאָה, דָּא עוֹלָה תָּמִיד בְּכָל יוֹם, מֵאִינּוּן יוֹמִין שִׁית דִּבְרֵאשִׁית. בְּשַׁבָּת עַל חַד תְּרֵין, בְּגִין דְּיִתּוֹסַף בָּהּ נְהִירוּ וּשְׁלֵימָא כַּדְקָא יָאוּת, וְהָא אִתְּמַר.

669. The continual burnt offering is the fourth leg of the Supernal Throne, NAMELY, MALCHUT. It rises (Heb. *olah*) continually on each one of the six Days of Creation, NAMELY: CHESED, GVURAH, TIFERET, NETZACH, HOD AND YESOD OF ZEIR ANPIN, while on the Shabbat it is a double portion offering (or: 'doubly rises'), so that light and perfection should be added to it, as is fitting, and this we have already learned.

A Synopsis

The Faithful Shepherd tells why "A crown they shall give You" is recited in the additional service, the Musaf.

רעיא מהימנא

670. אָמַר רַעְיָא מְהֵימָנָא, מַלְכוּ. בְּשִׁית סְפִירָן אִיהִי עוֹלָה תָּמִיד לְגַבֵּי ו', דְּאָחִיד בְּהוֹן. בֶּן יָ"ה, גְּנִיז בַּבִּינָה. וּבְאָן סְפִירָה מֵאִינוּן שִׁית סְלִיקַת לְגַבֵּיהּ. בְּיוֹמָא תְּלִיתָאָה, דְּאִקְרֵי תִּפְאֶרֶת. דְּבַיוֹם הַשַּׁבָּת אִתּוֹסַף עֲמֵיהּ נֶפֶשׁ יְתֵירָה, דְּאִיהִי בִּינָה. ה' עִלָּאָה. י' אוֹת בְּשַׁבָּת, חָכְמָה עִלָּאָה. מֶלֶךְ מְעוּטָּר בְּכֶתֶר, וּבְג"ד, בִּתְפִלַת מוּסַף כֶּתֶר יִתְּנוּ לְךָ.

Ra'aya Meheimna (the Faithful Shepherd)

670. In the first part, the Faithful Shepherd said: In six Sfirot Malchut ascends continually to the Vav, WHICH IS ZEIR ANPIN, that is attached to them. It is the son of Yud Hei, WHICH IS ZEIR ANPIN, HAVING THE MOCHIN OF YAH, which is hidden in Binah. And in a certain Sfirah of the six SFIROT THAT ARE IN MALCHUT, NAMELY, TIFERET OF MALCHUT THAT INCLUDES ALL SIX OF ITS SFIROT, she ascends to ZEIR ANPIN. This is on the third day, NAMELY, WITH HIS THIRD SFIRAH, that is called 'Tiferet', WHICH IS ALSO COMPOSED OF ALL SIX OF HIS SFIROT. BUT on the Shabbat day, an extra Nefesh added to him is which is Binah, namely, the upper Hei OF THE YUD HEI VAV HEI, AND THEN HE ALSO HAS Yud, which is the sign of the Shabbat, NAMELY, supernal Chochmah; AND ALSO the King, WHICH IS ZEIR ANPIN, is adorned with a crown, NAMELY, KETER, CHOCHMAH AND BINAH OF BINAH. And for this reason 'A crown they shall give You' IS RECITED in the additional service (Musaf).

99. Bring an atonement over Me

A Synopsis

We hear about the two points of the Segol that are two kings, and we learn that both the burnt offering and the sin offering are the secret of Malchut. The essential thrust of this section has to do with the attributes of Judgment and Mercy.

671. וּבְרָאשֵׁי חָדְשֵׁיכֶם, וְכִי כַּמָה רֵישִׁין אִית לָה לְסִיהֲרָא. אֶלָּא אִינוּן תְּרֵין נְקוּדִין , כְּגַוְונָא דָּא נְקוּדָה תַּתָּאָה סִיהֲרָא, תְּרֵין רֵישִׁין דִּילָה, תְּרֵין נְקוּדִין דְּאִינוּן עָלָה, סָגוֹל. בְּקַדְמֵיתָא הֲוָה כֶּתֶר עֲלֵי תְּרֵי מַלְכִין כְּגַוְונָא דָּא, וַהֲוַת סְגוֹלְתָּא. וּלְבָתַר דְּאַמְרַת אִי אֶפְשָׁר לִשְׁנֵי מְלָכִים לְהִשְׁתַּמֵּשׁ בְּכֶתֶר אֶחָד, א״ל הַקוּדְשָׁא בְּרִיךְ הוּא, לְכִי וּמַעֲטִי אֶת עַצְמֵךְ. וּנְחִיתַת לְרַגְלוֹי דִּתְרֵין מַלְכִים, כְּגַוְונָא דָּא וְהַיְינוּ סָגוֹל, מַה דַּהֲוַת סְגוֹלְתָּא, אִתְהַדְּרַת סָגוֹל.

671. "And in the beginning (lit. 'heads') of your moons" (Bemidbar 28:11). HE ASKS: How many heads does the moon have, THAT YOU SAY, "IN THE HEADS OF YOUR MOONS"? AND HE ANSWERS: There are two points, thus: •.• Segol, where the lower dot is the moon, NAMELY, MALCHUT. Its two heads are the two dots over and ABOVE IT, AND TOGETHER THEY ARE CALLED 'Segol'. Initially it was a crown over two kings, NAMELY, NETZACH and HOD OF ZEIR ANPIN, thus: •ᵒ•, which is the form of the Segolta AS A TONAL CANTILLATION SIGN; and afterwards, when it said that it is not possible for two kings to use one crown, the Holy One, blessed be He, said to it: 'Go and contract yourself,' it descended to the feet of those two kings, NAMELY, BELOW NETZACH AND HOD, thus •.• becoming a Segol. And where it had been a Segolta, it became a Segol.

672. וְרָזָא דְּמִלָּה, לָקֳבֵל תְּרֵין נְקוּדִין, דְּאִינוּן תְּרֵין מַלְכִים, קָא רָמִיז פָּרִים בְּנֵי בָקָר שְׁנַיִם, וְלָקֳבֵל נְקוּדָה עֲטָרָה עַל רֵישַׁיְיהוּ, אָמַר, וְאַיִל אֶחָד, כְּמוֹ כֶּתֶר אֶחָד. בָּתַר דְּאַמְרַת אִי אֶפְשָׁר לִשְׁנֵי מְלָכִים שֶׁיִשְׁתַּמְּשׁוּ בְּכֶתֶר אֶחָד, אַזְעִירַת גַּרְמָהּ אוֹף הָכִי, וּשְׂעִיר עִזִּים אֶחָד לְחַטָּאת. אַיִל דְּיִצְחָק, אִתְהַדָּר שָׂעִיר. אִתְהַפָּךְ מֵרַחֲמֵי לְדִינָא, וְאִתְזְעִיר.

-139-

672. And the secret of the matter is that corresponding to the two points, which are the two kings, NAMELY, NETZACH AND HOD OF ZEIR ANPIN, is the allusion to "two young bullocks" (Ibid.); and corresponding to the one point which is the diadem on the head OF THE TWO POINTS, the Scripture said "and one ram" (Ibid.), like a crown, which is just one. AND THIS IS ACCORDING TO THE SHAPE OF THE SEGOLTA, WHERE MALCHUT IS A CROWN OVER NETZACH AND HOD. And after she said: It is impossible for two kings to use one crown, and contracted herself, it also CONTRACTED "And one kid of the goats for a sin offering" (Ibid. 15), for the ram of Isaac, WHICH IS THE LEFT COLUMN OF BINAH, became a he-goat, for it changed from Mercy to Judgment and contracted.

673. וּבְגִין דָּא שָׂעִיר עִזִּים אֶחָד לְחַטָּאת, וְלֹא אָמַר לְעוֹלָה, לְמֶהֱוֵי כֶּתֶר. וּמְנָלָן דְּאִית יְרִידָה בַּחַטָּאת, שֶׁנֶּאֱמַר וַיֵּרֶד מֵעֲשׂוֹת הַחַטָּאת. וְאַמַּאי שָׁתַּף עוֹלָה עִם חַטָּאת בַּיְרִידָה. אֶלָּא לְאוֹלְפָא, דְּעוֹלָה הֲוַת בְּקַדְמֵיתָא מִדַּת הָרַחֲמִים, וּלְבָתַר אִתְהַפְּכַת לְדִינָא בַּיְרִידָה, וְאִתְקְרִיאַת חַטָּאת, וְכֹלָּא חַד.

673. And this is why THE SCRIPTURE SAYS: "And one kid of the goats for a sin offering," and not for a burnt offering (lit. 'ascent'), WHICH WOULD HAVE MEANT THAT IT ASCENDS to be a crown OVER NETZACH AND HOD. And how do we know that there is descent in a sin offering? From the verse: "and came down from offering the sin offering" (Vayikra 9:22). And why did he combine the sin offering with the burnt offering in the descent? This is to teach that initially there was a burnt offering, which is the attribute of Mercy, NAMELY, FROM THE CHEST AND UPWARDS OF ZEIR ANPIN, WHICH IS THE PLACE OF MERCY, and later it became Judgment in the descent TO BELOW THE CHEST OF ZEIR ANPIN, WHICH IS THE PLACE OF JUDGMENT, and is called 'a sin offering'. And it is all one, FOR BOTH THE BURNT OFFERING AND THE SIN OFFERING ARE THE SECRET OF MALCHUT.

674. וּבְגִין דָּא, הָבִיאוּ עָלַי כַּפָּרָה, עָלַי הֲוַת סִיהֲרָא כֶּתֶר וַדַּאי, כְּגַוְונָא דָּא וּלְבָתַר אִתְמְעִיטַת, וְנַחְתַּת לְרַגְלִין דִּילֵיהּ, כְּגַוְונָא דָּא וּבְזִמְנָא דָּא הָבִיאוּ עָלַי כַּפָּרָה, אִיתְּמַר בָּהּ, הִיא הָעוֹלָה, סְלִיקַת מֵרַגְלוֹי. דְּאִתְּמַר

בָּה, וְהָאָרֶץ הֲדֹם רַגְלָי. לְמֵימַר בָּה, הַשָּׁמַיִם כִּסְאִי. וְהַאי אִיהוּ רָזָא, צַדִּיק מוֹשֵׁל יִרְאַת אֱלֹהִים. דִּמְהַפֵּךְ דִּינָא לְרַחֲמֵי. וְרָזָא דְּמִלָּה, אֶבֶן מָאֲסוּ הַבּוֹנִים הָיְתָה לְרֹאשׁ פִּנָּה. כְּגַוְונָא דָּא, דּוֹד"י. יְדֹוָד.

674. And this is why THE HOLY ONE, BLESSED BE HE, WHO IS ZEIR ANPIN, SAID: 'Bring atonement over Me, for the moon was certainly a crown over Me,' PRIOR TO THE CONTRACTION, NAMELY, A CROWN ABOVE NETZACH AND HOD OF ZEIR ANPIN, thus: •ᵒ• and subsequently it contracted and descended to His feet, NAMELY, BENEATH NETZACH AND HOD, THAT ARE CALLED 'LEGS', thus: •ₒ•. And at the time OF 'bring over Me atonement', NAMELY, WHEN THE HE-GOAT OF THE NEW MOON IS SACRIFICED TO ATONE FOR THE CONTRACTION OF THE MOON, it is said about it, "It is the burnt offering (lit. 'ascent')" (Vayikra 6:3), for it ascends from His feet, and it is THEN said about it: "and the earth is My footstool" (Yeshayah 66:1), WHERE THE EARTH IS MALCHUT. NOW IT RISES TO BE A THRONE FOR BINAH, TOGETHER WITH ZEIR ANPIN, WHO IS CALLED 'HEAVEN', so that it can be said about it: "The heaven is My throne" (Ibid.), FOR THE HEAVENS, WHICH IS ZEIR ANPIN TOGETHER WITH MALCHUT, BECOME A THRONE FOR BINAH. And this is the secret of the verse "just, ruling in the fear of Elohim" (II Shmuel 23:3). For He turns Judgment into Mercy. And the secret of the matter is contained in the verse: "The stone which the builders rejected has become the head stone of the corner" (Tehilim 118:22). And likewise THERE IS THE COMBINATION: Hei Vav Hei Yud, WHICH INDICATES THE ATTRIBUTE OF JUDGMENT, AND THERE IS THE COMBINATION: Yud Hei Vav Hei, THAT INDICATES THE ATTRIBUTE OF MERCY.

100. The moon has contracted itself

A Synopsis
The Faithful Shepherd says that the lambs of the sacrifice correspond to the Sfirot and to the seven days of the moon.

675. וְעוֹד, כֶּבֶשׂ א' וּשְׁנֵי כְבָשִׂים בְּנֵי שָׁנָה תְּמִימִים, לְקָבֵל תְּלַת סְפִירָן. שִׁבְעָה כְבָשִׂים בְּנֵי שָׁנָה, לָקֳבֵל שְׁבַע סְפִירָן. שִׁבְעָה כְּבָשִׂים, אִינּוּן ז' יוֹמִין דְּסִיהֲרָא. בְּנֵי שָׁנָה, בְּנוֹי דְּסִיהֲרָא, דְּאִקְרֵי שָׁנָה. דְּאִיהִי חֲדָא מֵאִינּוּן שָׁנִים קַדְמוֹנִיּוֹת.

ע"כ רעיא מהימנא

675. Furthermore, the one lamb and "two lambs of the first year without blemish" (Bemidbar 28:9) correspond to the UPPER three Sfirot. Seven lambs of the first year correspond to the seven LOWER Sfirot. The seven lambs are seven days, NAMELY, SEVEN SFIROT, of the moon, WHICH IS MALCHUT, for they are "of the first year (lit. 'sons of a year')," namely, the sons of the moon which is called 'a year', this being one of those primordial years.

End of Ra'aya Meheimna

A Synopsis
Rabbi Shimon tells how the renewal of Jacob and Joseph every month to illuminate the moon must be done via the sacrifices.

676. וּבְרָאשֵׁי חָדְשֵׁיכֶם וְגוֹ'. וְכִי כַּמָה רָאשִׁין אִינּוּן לְסִיהֲרָא. וְהָא לֵית רֵישָׁא לְסִיהֲרָא, אֶלָּא שִׁמְשָׁא, דְּאִיהוּ רֵישָׁא לְגַבָּהּ. אֶלָּא רָאשֵׁי תְּרֵין בְּכָל יַרְחָא וְיַרְחָא. וְאִינּוּן יַעֲקֹב וְיוֹסֵף, דְּמִתְחַדְתֵּי עַל סִיהֲרָא. וְע"ד בָּעוּ לְחַדְתָּא לָהּ.

676. "And in the beginnings (lit. 'heads') of your new moons" (Ibid. 11). HE ASKS: How many heads does the moon have, since there exists no head to

the moon, but the sun, WHICH IS ZEIR ANPIN, that is a head for it? HE ANSWERS: There are two heads in every month, namely, Jacob and Joseph, WHICH ARE ZEIR ANPIN AND YESOD, and they are renewed to ILLUMINATE the moon, WHICH IS MALCHUT. And it has, therefore, to be renewed, NAMELY, WITH THE SACRIFICES.

677. פָּרִים בְּנֵי בָקָר שְׁנַיִם, אַלֵּין אִינוּן דְּאָמְרָה סִיהֲרָא, דְּהֵיךְ יִשְׁתַּמְּשׁוּן בָּה כַּחֲדָא, וְאַזְעֵירַת גַּרְמָה תְּחוֹתַיְיהוּ. וְאַיִל אֶחָד, דָּא אַיִל דְּיִצְחָק. וְכִי אַבְרָהָם לְאָן אָזִיל. אֶלָּא בְּגִין דְּאִתְּעַר תַּמָּן עֵשָׂו, אִתְכְּנִישׁ אַבְרָהָם, דְּלָא יֶחֱמֵי לֵיהּ, וּמַאן אִיהוּ שָׂעִיר דר"ח. יִצְחָק, אִשְׁתְּכַח תַּמָּן, דִּרְחִימוּ דִּילֵיהּ לְגַבֵּיהּ, כְּחַמְרָא עַל דּוּרְדְּיֵיהּ. יַעֲקֹב אִשְׁתְּכַח תַּמָּן, לְתַבְרָא אַנְפּוֹי. יוֹסֵף דְּאִיהוּ שׁוֹר דִּילֵיהּ, לְגַבֵּי רָחֵל.

677. "Two young bullocks" (Ibid.): These are they about whom the moon said: How can TWO KINGS use one CROWN, NAMELY, ZEIR ANPIN AND MALCHUT FROM THE ASPECT OF THE TWO GREAT LIGHTS; AND AFTERWARDS it contracted itself beneath them "and one ram" (Ibid.) refers to the ram of Isaac, WHICH IS GVURAH. HE ASKS: Where did Abraham go? NAMELY, WHY IS THE QUALITY OF ABRAHAM, WHICH IS CHESED, NOT MENTIONED HERE? AND ANSWERS it is because Esau awoke there. And who is that? That is the he-goat (Heb. seir) of the new moon, WHICH CONTAINS A PART FOR THE OTHER SIDE AND IS CALLED 'SEIR', JUST AS ESAU WAS "A HAIRY (HEB. SA'IR) MAN" (BERESHEET 27:11). Therefore Abraham, WHO IS THE LIGHT OF CHESED, was gathered up, that he should not be seen, THAT IS TO SAY THAT THERE SHOULD BE NO NOURISHMENT FOR THE OTHER SIDE FROM THE LIGHT OF CHESED. BUT Isaac, WHO IS THE LEFT COLUMN, was there because his love for him was as wine with its sediment. FOR ESAU IS THE REFUSE OF THE LEFT COLUMN, AND THE LIGHT OF THE LEFT IS CALLED 'WINE', AND THE REFUSE IS CALLED 'SEDIMENT'. Jacob, WHO IS ZEIR ANPIN, THE CENTRAL COLUMN, was there in order to break the face OF ESAU. Joseph, NAMELY, YESOD, which is the ox OF ZEIR ANPIN, THAT IS TO SAY WHICH IS DRAWN FROM THE LEFT COLUMN OF ZEIR ANPIN THAT IS CALLED 'OX', WAS THERE for Rachel, NAMELY, TO BESTOW ON MALCHUT, THAT IS CALLED 'RACHEL'.

101. The Yud Hei Vav Heis in the middle

A Synopsis

The Faithful Shepherd tells how the earth was founded by wisdom and the heavens were established by understanding.

רעיא מהימנא

678. אָמַר ר"מ, וַדַּאי בְּנֵי שָׁנָה אִתְקְרִיאוּ עַל שֵׁם חַמָּה, אִימָּא קַדִּישָׁא, דְּאִתְּמַר בָּהּ פְּנֵי מֹשֶׁה כִּפְנֵי חַמָּה. שָׁנָה אִית בָּהּ שס"ה יוֹמִין, כְּחוּשְׁבַּן שס"ה לֹא תַעֲשֶׂה. וְאִיהוּ ע"ד לִשְׂמָאלָא. אִימָּא עִלָּאָה, סִיהֲרָא בִּימִינָא. אֲסוּרָה בְּרַתָּא לְאַבָּא דְּאִיהוּ לִימִינָא חֶסֶד. וְאִיהִי כְּלִילָא מרמ"ח פִּקּוּדִין. אִשְׁתְּכַח ו' עִם אִימָּא לִשְׂמָאלָא. בְּרַתָּא עִם אַבָּא לִימִינָא דְּחֶסֶד. וְרָזָא דְּמִלָּה, בְּחָכְמָה יָסַד אֶרֶץ. חָכְמָה אַבָּא. אֶרֶץ בְּרַתָּא. כּוֹנֵן שָׁמַיִם דְּאִיהוּ בְּרָא, עִם אִימָּא דְּאִיהוּ תְּבוּנָה, וְהַאי אִיהוּ ידד"ו, הַוָיוֹת בְּאֶמְצַע.

Ra'aya Meheimna (the Faithful Shepherd)

678. The Faithful Shepherd said: Certainly the one-year-old LAMBS are named after the sun, which is Holy Ima, NAMELY, BINAH, for it is said about it: The face of Moses is as that of the sun. A year contains 365 days, THAT IS, TOGETHER WITH THE THE DAYS FROM ROSH HASHANAH TO YOM KIPPUR. This is the same number, 365, as that of the negative precepts. And this is a witness to the left, and is supernal Ima. The moon, WHICH IS MALCHUT, is on the right side, for the daughter is joined to Aba, which is Chesed, on the right side. And she, MALCHUT, is composed of the 248 positive precepts. It follows that the Vav, WHICH IS ZEIR ANPIN, is with Ima on the left side, IN THE SECRET OF THE 365 NEGATIVE PRECEPTS, and the daughter is with Aba on the right side, which is Chesed. And the secret of the matter is in the verse: "by wisdom founded the earth" (Mishlei 3:19). Wisdom refers to Aba, NAMELY, CHOCHMAH OF THE RIGHT WHICH IS CHESED. Earth is the daughter, NAMELY, MALCHUT, AND THUS THE DAUGHTER IS JOINED WITH ABA. "BY UNDERSTANDING HE ESTABLISHED THE HEAVENS" (IBID.). "He established the heavens," which

is the son, NAMELY, ZEIR ANPIN, with Ima, which is Tevunah. And this results in THE PERMUTATION OF Yud Hei Hei Vav, which is the secret of the Yud Hei Vav Heis in the middle.

102. A he-goat to Azazel

A Synopsis

Moses says that the goat for Azazel is a bribe to assuage Samael's anger and to prevent him from drawing near the Temple and making accusations against Yisrael. He also tells us why the goat is sent by the hand of a crippled man, and how the goat bears all of Yisrael's iniquities.

679. וְעוֹד וּשְׂעִיר עִזִּים אֶחָד, תְּרֵין שְׂעִירִין אִינוּן, דְּאִתְּמַר עֲלַיְיהוּ וְלָקַח אֶת שְׁנֵי הַשְּׂעִירִים וְגוֹ' גּוֹרָל אֶחָד לַיְיָ' וְגוֹרָל אֶחָד לַעֲזָאזֵל. שָׂעִיר לַיְיָ', בְּגִין מִיעוּט סִיהֲרָא, וְאִיהוּ שָׂעִיר אֶחָד לַיְדֹנָ"ד לְחַטָּאת. אֶחָד: מִסִּטְרָא דְּיִחוּדָא. אֲבָל שָׂעִיר דַּעֲזָאזֵל, לָא כְּתִיב בֵּיה אֶחָד, לָא קָרְבָּן, וְלָא אִשֶּׁה, וְלָא עוֹלָה. אֶלָּא וְשִׁלַּח בְּיַד אִישׁ עִתִּי הַמִּדְבָּרָה. וְשִׁלַּח, כִּדְאָמַר יַעֲקֹב מִנְחָה הִיא שְׁלוּחָה לַאדֹנִי לְעֵשָׂו. אוֹף הָכִי שׁוֹחַד, לְתַבְרָא רוּגְזָא דְּסָמָא"ל, דְּלָא יִתְקְרִיב לְמַקְדְּשָׁא לְקַטְרְגָא.

679. Again: "one kid of the goats" (Bemidbar 29:11). There are two goats, about which it is said: "And he shall take the two goats... one lot for Hashem, and the other lot for Azazel" (Vayikra 16:7-8). The goat that is for Hashem IS AN ATONEMENT over the contraction of the moon and is "And one kid of the goats for a sin offering to Hashem" (Bemidbar 28:15). It is therefore referred to as 'one' BECAUSE IT IS from the side of unity. But the goat for Azazel is not referred to as 'one,' neither is it called 'a sacrifice', 'a fire offering', nor 'a burnt offering', but "shall send him away by the hand of an appointed man into the wilderness" (Vayikra 16:21). "And shall send away" is the same term used by Jacob: "it is a present sent to my lord Esau" (Beresheet 32:19). Likewise, THE GOAT FOR AZAZEL is a bribe, in order to break Samael's anger that he should not draw near the Temple, to denounce IT.

680. לְכַלְבָּא דְּאִיהוּ רָעֵב, וּמַאן דְּבָעֵי דְּלָא נָשִׁיךְ לֵיה, יָהִיב לֵיה בִּשְׂרָא לְמֵיכַל, אוֹ נַהֲמָא, וְיַשְׁקֵי לֵיה מַיָּא. וְרָזָא דְּמִלָּה, אִם רָעֵב שׂוֹנַאֲךָ הַאֲכִילֵהוּ לֶחֶם וְגוֹ'. וּבְדָא יִתְהַדָּר רְחִימוּ דב"ן, דְּלָא דַּיי דְּלָא נָשִׁיךְ לֵיה בְּכַמָּה יִסּוּרִין, אֶלָּא אִתְהַדָּר לְמֶהֱוֵי לֵיה סַנֵּיגוֹרָא, וְאִתְהַדָּר רְחִימוֹי.

680. IT IS LIKE a hungry dog: whoever does not want to be bitten by it gives it meat or bread to eat and water to drink. And the secret of the matter is contained in the verse: "If your enemy be hungry, give him bread to eat; and if he be thirsty, give him water to drink" (Mishlei 25:21). He thereby becomes friendly towards the person, and not only does not bite him, with a number of tribulations, but becomes an advocate for him and loves him.

681. וְאֲמַאי הֲווֹ שַׁלְחִין לֵיהּ בְּיַד אִישׁ עִתִּי, פָּגִים. בְּגִין דְּסִטְרִין אַחֲרָנִין כֻּלְּהוּ מָאֲרֵי מוּמִין, וְאִתְקְרִיאוּ שְׂעִירִים, דִּכְתִּיב וּשְׂעִירִים יְרַקְדוּ שָׁם. וְאִתְּמַר בְּהוֹן, וְלֹא יִזְבְּחוּ עוֹד אֶת זִבְחֵיהֶם לַשְּׂעִירִים. דְּעֲלַיְיהוּ אִתְּמַר, יִזְבְּחוּ לַשֵּׁדִים לֹא אֱלוֹהַּ. וּבְשָׂעִיר דָּא, אִתְפְּרַשׁ מִכֹּלָּא, וְנוֹשֵׂא כָּל חוֹבִין דְּיִשְׂרָאֵל עָלֵיהּ, כד"א, וְנָשָׂא הַשָּׂעִיר עָלָיו אֶת כָּל עֲוֹנוֹתָם. וְעוֹד, בָּתַר דְּנָטִיל אִיהוּ וְנָשָׂא. קוּדְשָׁא בְּרִיךְ הוּא נוֹשֵׂא עָוֹן. מַאי בֵּין נוֹשֵׂא לְנָשָׂא. נָשָׂא: מָטוּלָא. נוֹשֵׂא: סְלִיקוּ דְּמָטוּלָא.

עד כאן רעיא מהימנא

681. HE ASKS, Why is THE GOAT sent TO AZAZEL by the hand of an appointed man who is crippled? HE ANSWERS, because all of the Other Sides are defective, and are called 'goats' (Heb. *seirim*), as it is written: "and goats (Heb. *seirim*) shall dance there" (Yeshayah 13:21). And about them it is said: "And they shall no more offer their sacrifices to the demons (Heb. *seirim*)" (Vayikra 17:7); and also: "They sacrificed to powerless spirits" (Devarim 32:17). And with this goat TO AZAZEL, SAMAEL IS separated from everything and bears all the transgressions that are in Yisrael upon him, as it is written: "and the goat shall bear upon it all their iniquities" (Vayikra 16:22). And furthermore, after that AZAZEL takes all THE TRANSGRESSIONS and bears them, NAMELY, THAT THE HOLY ONE, BLESSED BE HE, SHALL BEAR AND FORGIVE, the Holy One, blessed be He, is called "forgiving (bearing) iniquity" (Shemot 34:7), AND ABOUT THE GOAT FOR AZAZEL IT IS WRITTEN: "AND THE GOAT SHALL BEAR UPON IT ALL THEIR INIQUITIES." What is the difference between these two types of bearing? HE ANSWERS, "bear" means CARRYING a burden, while "bearing" MEANS the removal of the burden, NAMELY, THAT HE ATONES FOR THE INIQUITIES. AND ALL OF THIS IS EXPLAINED ABOVE.

End of Ra'aya Meheimna

102. A he-goat to Azazel

A Synopsis
We hear that were it not for the monthly contraction of the moon no offering would ever be given to Samael.

682. וּשְׁלֹשָׁה עֶשְׂרוֹנִים, תְּלַת דַּרְגִּין קַדְמָאִין דִּילָהּ, דְּכָל חַד וְחַד עֲשַׂר, כְּגַוְונָא דִּלְעֵילָא עֶשְׂרוֹנִים, חַד מֵעֲשָׂרָה. וּשְׂעִיר חַטָּאת אֶחָד, אֲמַאי אִקְרֵי חַטָּאת. בְּגִין דְּאִיהוּ חַטָּאת, וּמִסְּטְרָא דְּחַטָּאת הוּא. א״ר אֶלְעָזָר, וְהָא כְּתִיב לַיְיָ׳. אֶלָּא לַיְיָ׳ אִתְקְרִיב וַדַּאי, דִּכְתִיב לְכַפֵּר. לְתַבְרָא אַנְפִּין, וְכֹלָּא יִתְקְרִיב לְמַקְדְּשָׁא, אֶלָּא יָהֲבֵי חוּלָקָא חֲדָא לְסָמָאֵל, וְאָכִיל לֵיהּ, וְלָא אָחִיד בִּשְׁאַר קָרְבָּנִין. וְדָא אִיהוּ לְחוֹדֵיהּ, דְּלָא אִשְׁתְּתַּף אַחֲרָא עִמֵּיהּ לְמֵיכַל בֵּיהּ.

682. And: "three tenth measures" (Bemidbar 29:9) namely, it is her three first grades, NAMELY KETER, CHOCHMAH AND BINAH, each one of which is MADE UP of ten, as it is above, WITH ZEIR ANPIN; and by tenth measures IS MEANT one part in ten, FOR MALCHUT IS ONE OF THE TEN SFIROT OF ZEIR ANPIN, AND EACH INDIVIDUAL SFIRAH OF HERS CORRESPONDS TO ONE OF TEN IN ZEIR ANPIN, AND THEY ARE THEREFORE CALLED 'TENTH MEASURES'. And one goat for a sin offering: HE ASKS why it is called 'a sin offering'? AND ANSWERS, because it is a sin and is from the side of sin, THAT IS TO SAY: A PORTION OF IT IS FOR THE OTHER SIDE, AND IT IS THEREFORE FROM THE SIDE OF SIN. Rabbi Elazar said, But it is written: "To Hashem (Bemidbar 28:15)!" HOW THEN CAN YOU SAY THAT IT IS FROM THE SIDE OF SIN?! AND ANSWERS, it is certainly sacrificed to Hashem, for it is written: "to make atonement" (Ibid. 21), namely, to break the face OF THE OTHER SIDE, so everything will be sacrificed to the Sanctuary, but one portion is also given to Samael, and he eats it, AND FOR THIS REASON does not take hold of the other sacrifices. This sacrifice alone IS FOR HIM TO EAT, and no other sacrifice is joined with him for him to eat.

683. אִיהוּ אִתְהֲנֵי בְּגוֹ סְעוֹדָתָא דְּמַלְכָּא בְּחוּלָקָא דָּא, וְעַל דָּא חַדֵּי, וְאִתְפְּרַשׁ מִיִּשְׂרָאֵל, וְלָא מְקַטְרְגָּא עֲלַיְיהוּ. וְאִי לָאו דַּהֲוָה מִיעוּטָא דְּסִיהֲרָא, לָא הֲווֹ יָהֲבֵי לֵיהּ בִּסְעוֹדָתָא דְּמַלְכָּא כְּלוּם. וְכִי בְּמִיעוּטָא דְּסִיהֲרָא מַאי קָא עָבֵיד. אֶלָּא בְּגִין דְּקָרִיב וְיָנִיק, וְנָטִיל חֵילָא לְעַמֵּיהּ,

מִגּוֹ סְטַר שְׂמָאלָא דְּסִיהֲרָא, וְאִתְתְּקַף בֵּיהּ. וּבִשְׂעִיר דָּא אִתְפְּרַשׁ
מִכֹּלָּא, וְאִתְהֲנֵי בְּהַאי. וּבְגִין דְּקוּדְשָׁא בְּרִיךְ הוּא אַזְעִיר לָהּ לְסִיהֲרָא,
מְקָרְבִין לֵיהּ לְהַאי שָׂעִיר, בְּגִין דְּיִתְפְּרַשׁ מִנָּהּ, וְלָא יִתְקְרִיב לְמַקְדְּשָׁא.
וע״ד תָּנֵינָן, הָבִיאוּ עָלַי כַּפָּרָה. עָלַי: בְּגִינִי, דְּאַזְעִירַת לָהּ, בְּגִין סִבַּת
דִּילִי אַתּוּן צְרִיכִין דָּא.

683. He, SAMAEL, enjoys the banquet of the King with this portion THAT HE TAKES FROM THE GOAT FOR A SIN OFFERING and he therefore rejoices and leaves Yisrael alone and does not accuse them. And were it not for contraction of the moon, NAMELY, MALCHUT, nothing at all would be given TO SAMAEL from the King's banquet. HE ASKS: And what does he do in the contraction of the moon? AND ANSWERS: Because he comes close and suckles FROM THE VACATED PLACE IN MALCHUT, and takes power for his people from the side of the left of the moon, WHICH IS MALCHUT, and grows strong in it, and in this goat, A PORTION OF WHICH IS GIVEN TO HIM, he abandons everything and gains his enjoyment from this. And because the Holy One, blessed be He, contracted the moon, FOR HE SAID TO IT 'GO AND CONTRACT YOURSELF', therefore this goat is sacrificed, so that SAMAEL will depart from it and not come close to the Sanctuary, WHICH IS MALCHUT. And thus we learned THAT THE HOLY ONE, BLESSED BE HE, SAID: 'Bring an atonement over me', FOR I HAVE CONTRACTED THE MOON. 'Over Me', namely, for Me, for I contracted it, and it is because of Me, SINCE I CONTRACTED IT, that you need this, THAT YOU NEED TO SACRIFICE A GOAT IN ORDER TO SEPARATE HIM FROM THE PLACE OF THE CONTRACTION OF MALCHUT.

103. "And in the beginnings of your new moons"

A Synopsis

The Faithful Shepherd says that just as on the new moon a portion must be given to the Other Side, a woman must give her fingernails and a little of her hair to the Other Side; this protects her from evil. The sages of the Mishnah had said that in previous times when the people were sanctifying the new moon they would kindle flares on the tops of the mountains so that God could see the moon and sanctify it. Malchut is sometimes a crown for God, sometimes a throne for Him to sit on, and sometimes a footstool for His feet. Moses explains why the moon is called 'white'; he says that the moon is from the side of the Tree of Knowledge of Good and Evil, so it changes from dark to light and back again.

רעיא מהימנא

684. וּבְרָאשֵׁי חָדְשֵׁיכֶם, אִינּוּן יַעֲקֹב וְיוֹסֵף. אֵלֶּה תּוֹלְדוֹת יַעֲקֹב יוֹסֵף, דִּמְחַדְּתֵּי עַל סִיהֲרָא. אַשְׁכַּחְנָא בְּסִפְרָא דַּחֲנוֹךְ דְּאָמַר, כְּמָה דְּבִרְאֹשׁ חֹדֶשׁ, דְּאִתְדַּכִּיאַת סִיהֲרָא לְאִתְקָרְבָא בְּבַעְלָהּ, אִצְטְרִיךְ לְמֵיהַב לְסִטְרָא אַחֲרָא חוּלָקָא חֲדָא, בְּהַהוּא זִינָא דִּילָהּ. אוֹף ה"נ אִצְטְרִיכַת לְאִתְּתָא, בְּשַׁעֲתָא דְּאִתְדַּכִּיאַת לְאִתְקָרְבָא בְּבַעְלָהּ, לְמֵיהַב חוּלָקָא חֲדָא לְס"א, בְּהַהוּא זִינָא דִּילֵיהּ.

Ra'aya Meheimna (the Faithful Shepherd)

684. "And in the beginnings (lit. 'heads') of your new moons" (Bemidbar 28:11). THE WORD 'HEADS' IS WRITTEN IN THE PLURAL, referring to Jacob and Joseph, NAMELY, ZEIR ANPIN AND YESOD, AS IT IS WRITTEN: "These are the generations of Jacob. Joseph..." (Beresheet 37:2) that renew the moon, WHICH IS MALCHUT. I have found in the Book of Enoch that he said that just as on the first day of the month, the moon, WHICH IS MALCHUT, is purified to come close to her husband, ZEIR ANPIN, so must one portion be given to the Other Side and from the same type AS THE OTHER SIDE, NAMELY, A GOAT; so also the woman when she is purified for her husband, one portion must be given to the Other Side, and from its own type.

685. וּמַאן אִיהוּ. הַהוּא חוּלָקָא טוּפְרָהָא בְּטִנּוּפָא דִּלְהוֹן. וּזְעֵיר מֵרִישׁ

דְּשַׁעֲרָא, בְּגִין דְּבָעֵי לְאַסְרְקָא רֵישָׁא, וּלְאַבְרְכָא לוֹן דָּא בְּדָא, וְלָא יֵזִיל אֲבַתְרָה הַהוּא סִטְרָא בִּישָׁא, לְאַבְאָשָׁא לָהּ, וְאִתְפְּרַשׁ מִנָּהּ בְּכָל סִטְרִין. וּמַה תַּעֲבִיד, מֵהַהוּא שַׂעֲרָא וְטוּפְרִין. לְבָתַר דְּתַכְרִיךְ לוֹן כַּחֲדָא, אִצְטְרִיךְ לְאַנָּחָא לוֹן בַּאֲתָר דְּלָא עַבְרִין תַּמָּן בְּנֵי נָשָׁא, אוֹ בְּגוֹ חוֹרִין תַּתָּאִין דְּחָצֵרָא, וְתַגְנִיז לוֹן תַּמָּן.

685. And what is that portion THAT THE WOMAN HAS TO GIVE TO THE OTHER SIDE? It is the fingernails with their dirt and a little of the ends of her hair, for she has to comb her head and tie them together, TO GIVE THEM TO THE OTHER SIDE, and then that Evil Side will not go after her to harm her, but will leave her alone from all sides. And what does she do with those hairs and nail clippings? After she has bound them together, she has to place them where people do not pass by, or in holes in the bottom of the yard, and conceal them there.

686. וְעוֹד וּבְרָאשֵׁי חָדְשֵׁיכֶם אָמְרוּ רַבָּנָן דְּמַתְנִיתִין, דְּכַד הֲווֹ מְקַדְּשִׁין יַרְחִין עַל פִּי בֵּית דִּין, הֲווֹ מַשִּׂיאִין מַשּׂוּאוֹת בְּרָאשֵׁי הֶהָרִים, וַהֲווֹ אַמְרִין כָּזֶה רְאֵה וְקַדֵּשׁ. לְזִמְנִין סִהֲרָא הֲוַת כְּגַוְונָא דָּא. הֲוָה מִסְתַּכְּלָא לְעֵילָא בְּקַרְנָהָא. וּלְזִמְנָא מִסְתַּכְּלָא לְתַתָּא כְּגַוְונָא דָּא. לְזִמְנִין מִסְתַּכְּלָא בְּמִזְרָח, כְּגַוְונָא דָּא. לְזִמְנִין לְמַעֲרַב, כְּגַוְונָא דָּא. לְזִמְנִין לְדָרוֹם. וּלְזִמְנִין לְצָפוֹן. וְהַאי אִיהוּ אִסְתַּכְּלוּתָא דִּילָהּ לְשִׁית סִטְרִין, דְּכָלִיל לוֹן תִּפְאֶרֶת, דְּאִיהוּ ו'. גְּדוּלָה, גְּבוּרָה, תִּפְאֶרֶת, נֶצַח, וְהוֹד, יְסוֹד.

686. Again: "And in the beginnings of your new moons." The sages of the Mishnah said: When the new moon used to be sanctified according to the court, flares used to be kindled on the tops of the mountains and they used to say: Sanctify it the way you see it. The moon would be shaped thus ∪, sometimes with the beams facing upwards, and sometimes so ∩, facing downwards, sometimes to the east thus ⊂, and sometimes to the west, thus ⊃ sometimes to the south and sometimes to the north. And this is its facing in six directions that Tiferet, which is a large Vav, encompasses, NAMELY: Greatness, Gvurah, Tiferet, Netzach, Hod and Yesod. GREATNESS, WHICH

IS CHESED, IS FACING THE SOUTH, AND ITS LOOKING TO THE NORTH IS GVURAH, TO THE EAST IS TIFERET, AND TO THE WEST IS YESOD.

687. נְקוּדָא דְּנָגִיד עֲלֵיהּ מִלְּגוֹ, הִיא חָכְמָה. וְהַהִיא חוּט דְּאַסְחַר עֲלָהּ, אִיהוּ כֶּתֶר. וְהַהִיא נְקוּדָא אִיהוּ לְזִמְנִין עֲטָרָה, וּלְזִמְנִין כֻּרְסְיָיא, לְמֵיתַב עֲלֵיהּ, לְזִמְנִין שַׁרְפְּרַף לַהֲדוֹם רַגְלָיו.

687. The point that is drawn IN THE MOON, WHICH IS MALCHUT, from the inside, is Chochmah, and the line that circumvents the moon is Keter. AND AS A RULE that point, WHICH IS MALCHUT, is sometimes a crown FOR ZEIR ANPIN, IN THE SECRET OF THE VERSE: "A VIRTUOUS WOMAN IS A CROWN TO HER HUSBAND" (MISHLEI 12:4), and sometimes a throne FOR ZEIR ANPIN to sit upon, and at yet other times a footstool for his feet OF ZEIR ANPIN.

688. וְאַמַאי אִתְקְרִיאַת לְבָנָה. עַל שֵׁם לִבּוּן הַהֲלָכָה, דְּאִיהִי מִלְּגוֹ, כָּל כְּבוּדָּהּ בַּת מֶלֶךְ פְּנִימָה. וּבְאֶשָּׁא דְּבִינָה דְּנָחִית עֲלָהּ אִיהִי מִתְלַבְּנַת. וְרָזָא דְּמִלָּה, אִם יִהְיוּ חֲטָאֵיכֶם כַּשָּׁנִים כַּשֶּׁלֶג יַלְבִּינוּ. וּמַאי דַּהֲוַת אֲדֹנָי דִּינָא, סוּמָקָא בִּגְבוּרָה, דְּתַמָּן בִּינָה. אִתְלַבְּנַת מִסִּטְרָא דְּחֶסֶד, דְּתַמָּן חָכְמָה, וְאִתְהַדְּרַת יְדֹוָד.

688. HE ASKS, Why is MALCHUT called 'moon' (lit. 'white')? HE ANSWERS, it is named after the clarification (whitening) of the Halachah, NAMELY, IT IS NAMED AFTER CHOCHMAH OF THE RIGHT SIDE THAT CLARIFIES THE HALACHAH, WHICH IS MALCHUT THAT IS CALLED 'HALACHAH'. FOR CHOCHMAH is from within MALCHUT, IN THE SECRET OF THE VERSE: "The king's daughter is all glorious within" (Tehilim 45:14) and she is whitened in the fire of Binah that descends upon her. And the secret of the matter is to be found in the verse: "though your sins be like scarlet, they shall be as white as snow" (Yeshayah 1:18). And whereas she was called 'Adonai', THE LETTERS OF WHICH, REARRANGED, SPELL 'Dina' (Eng. 'Judgment'), which is red with Gvurah, NAMELY, WITH THE LEFT COLUMN where Binah is, she becomes whitened by the side of Chesed where Chochmah is, and returns to THE NAME OF Yud Hei Vav Hei, WHICH IS MERCY.

689. וּמַה גָּרִים לְאִתְהַפְּכָא מִדִּינָא לְרַחֲמֵי צַדִּיקִים גְּמוּרִים דְּסִיהֲרָא מִסִּטְרָא דְּעֵץ הַדַּעַת טוֹב וָרָע, אִיהִי קְלִיפָא דִּילֵיהּ חֲשׁוֹכָא, אִם בַּהֶרֶת שְׁחוֹרָה, הִיא יֵצֶר הָרָע, שִׁפְחָה. וּשְׁפָלָה אֵינֶנָּה וְהִיא כֵּהָה, וְלֵית לָהּ מִדִּילָהּ, אֶלָּא הַהוּא חוּט דְּנָהִיר בָּהּ, דְּאִיהוּ לָוֵי לָהּ בְּלֵילְיָא, דְּאִיהִי גָּלוּתָא. וְאִתְעַבָּר מִנָּהּ בִּימָמָא, דְּאִיהוּ עָלְמָא דְּאָתֵי, דְּבֵיהּ וְזָרְחָה לָכֶם יִרְאֵי שְׁמִי שֶׁמֶשׁ צְדָקָה וּמַרְפֵּא בִּכְנָפֶיהָ.

689. And what is the cause of MALCHUT's changing from Judgment to Mercy? This is the completely righteous, for the moon, WHICH IS MALCHUT is from the side of the Tree of Knowledge of Good and Evil. Its Klipah is darkness THAT IS, if it is a bright black spot, which is the Evil Inclination, which is a handmaid, ABOUT WHOM IT IS SAID: "and it be lower...but be somewhat dimmer" (Vayikra 13:21). And MALCHUT has nothing of her own, but only that thread that gives her light, THIS BEING THE SECRET OF A THREAD OF CHOCHMAH OF THE LEFT SIDE WITHOUT CHASSADIM, WHICH IS HER MAIN STRUCTURE, BUT ITS LIGHT IS AS THIN AS A THREAD BECAUSE IT CANNOT ILLUMINATE WITHOUT CHASSADIM. For it accompanies it during the night-time, which is the Exile, IN THE SECRET OF THE VERSE: "SHE RISES ALSO WHILE IT IS YET NIGHT" (MISHLEI 31:15) and leaves it during the day. FOR THE DAY IS THE TIME OF THE RULE OF THE CHASSADIM OF ZEIR ANPIN, AND CHOCHMAH OF THE LEFT SIDE IS UNABLE TO RULE BY DAY. FOR DAYTIME is THE LIGHT OF CHESED OF the World to Come, WHICH IS BINAH, in which "But to you who fear My name the sun of righteousness shall arise with healing in its wings" (Malachi 3:20).

690. אֲבָל סִיהֲרָא דְּעֵץ הַחַיִּים, הַהִיא נְקוּדָה דִּלְגוֹ מִנָּהּ, אִיהִי כְּמַבּוּעָא דְּלֵית לֵיהּ פְּסָק, דִּכְתִּיב בָּהּ, וּכְמוֹצָא מַיִם אֲשֶׁר לֹא יְכַזְּבוּ מֵימָיו. וְאִתְקְרִיאַת אַיֶּלֶת אֲהָבִים מִסִּטְרָא דְּחֶסֶד, דְּהַיְינוּ אַהֲבַת עוֹלָם אֲהַבְתִּיךְ עַל כֵּן מְשַׁכְתִּיךְ חֶסֶד. וּתְרֵין קַרְנִין אִית לָהּ מִן נְהוֹרָא, כְּגַוְונָא דָּא לְזִמְנִין הָאַחַת גָּבוֹהַּ מִן הַשֵּׁנִית, כְּגַוְונָא דָּא, לְזִמְנִין קַרְנִים אִינוּן שָׁוִין.

ע"כ רעיא מהימנא

690. But that point that is within the moon, WHICH IS MALCHUT, that is from the side of the Tree of Life, WHICH IS ZEIR ANPIN, IS THE SECRET OF CHOCHMAH OF THE RIGHT SIDE, WHICH IS CHESED, and is as a never ceasing spring, BECAUSE IT IS DRAWN DOWN FROM SUPERNAL ABA AND IMA BY WAY OF ZEIR ANPIN, WHOSE UNION IS NEVER ENDING, and about which it is written: "like a spring of water, whose waters fail not" (Yeshayah 58:11), and it is called 'a loving hind' from the side of Chesed, WHICH IS LOVE, this being as is written: "I have loved you with an everlasting love: therefore I have remained true to you" (Yirmeyah 31:2), LOVE BEING THE SECRET OF CHESED; and it has two beams from the light, thus: ∪ and sometimes "but one was higher than the other" (Daniel 8:3), thus: ⊔ and at other times they are equal.

End of Ra'aya Meheimna

104. The hind of dawn

A Synopsis

Rabbi Aba brings up the difficulty that in the verse "As the hart pants after the water brooks," "hart" is masculine and yet the verb, which should agree with the noun, is feminine. Rabbi Shimon then talks about the hind of the dawn, that refers to the merciful Malchut who brings nourishment for everyone else. The hind suffers the pangs of exile in the morning, and when the morning brings light she is no longer visible. Rabbi Shimon speaks about the hind becoming a hart and giving birth with great pain.

691. וּבַחֹדֶשׁ הָרִאשׁוֹן וְגוֹ'. רִבִּי אַבָּא פָּתַח, כְּאַיָּל תַּעֲרוֹג עַל אֲפִיקֵי מָיִם כֵּן נַפְשִׁי תַעֲרוֹג אֵלֶיךָ אֱלֹהִים. הַאי קְרָא אוּקְמוּהָ, וְאע״ג דְּאִית דְּכַר וְנוּקְבָּא, כּוֹלָּא חַד. הַאי אַיָּל, אִיהוּ אִקְרֵי דְּכַר. וְאִיהוּ אִקְרֵי נוּקְבָּא. הה״ד כְּאַיָּל תַּעֲרוֹג וְלָא כְּתִיב יַעֲרוֹג. וְכֹלָּא חַד.

691. "And on...the first month" (Bemidbar 28:16). Rabbi Aba opened, "As the hart pants after the water brooks, so pants my soul after You, Elohim" (Tehilim 42:2). We have already learned this verse, and although it contains masculine and feminine FORMS, it is all one, for the word hart *ayal* is masculine, while the verb *ta'arog* (Eng. 'she pants') is feminine, and although the subject and the verb should agree in gender, *ya'arog* (Eng. 'he pants') is not written IN THE MASCULINE, because it is all one.

692. אַיֶּלֶת הַשַּׁחַר מַאי אַיֶּלֶת הַשַּׁחַר. אֶלָּא דָּא אִיהִי חַיָּה חֲדָא רַחֲמָנִית, דְּלֵית בְּכָל חֵיוָן דְּעָלְמָא רַחֲמָנִית כְּוָותָהּ. בְּגִין דְּבְשַׁעֲתָא דִּדְחִיקַת לָהּ שַׁעֲתָא, וְאִצְטְרִיכַת לִמְזוֹנָא לָהּ וּלְכָל חֵיוָן. אִיהִי אַזְלַת לְמֵרְחִיק לְאֹרַח רְחִיקָא. וְאַתְיַאת וְאוֹבִילַת מְזוֹנָא. וְלָא בָּעָאת לְמֵיכַל, עַד דְּתֵיתֵי וְתִתְהַדַּר לְאַתְרָהָא. אֲמַאי. בְּגִין דְּיִתְכַּנְּשׁוּן לְגַבָּהּ שְׁאַר חֵיוָן, וּתְחַלֵּק לוֹן מֵהַהוּא מְזוֹנָא. וְכַד אָתַת, מִתְכַּנְּשִׁין לְגַבָּהּ כָּל שְׁאַר חֵיוָן, וְהִיא קַיְימָא בְּאֶמְצָעִיתָא, וּפַלְגַּת לְכָל חַד וְחַד. וְסִימָן, וַתָּקָם בְּעוֹד לַיְלָה וַתִּתֵּן טֶרֶף לְבֵיתָהּ וְגוֹ'. וּמִמַּה דִּפְלִיגַת לוֹן, אִיהִי שַׂבְעָה, כְּאִלּוּ אָכְלָה יַתִּיר מֵיכְלָא מִכֹּלָּא.

692. What is "the morning star (lit. 'the hind of the dawn')" (Tehilim 22:1)? AND HE ANSWERS: This is a certain merciful animal, NAMELY, MALCHUT, and among all the animals of the world there is none merciful like her, for when time is pressing and she needs nourishment for herself and for all the animals, WHICH ARE ALL THE HOSTS OF THE WORLDS OF BRIYAH, YETZIRAH, AND ASIYAH, she goes to a distant place, far away, and comes, bringing food, but does not herself want to eat until she returns to her place. Why is this so? So that all the other animals will collect together by her, and she distributes from that food to them. And when she comes, all the other animals do indeed collect around her, and she stands in the middle, and allocates to each one of them. And this you may derive from the verse: "She rises also while it is yet night, and gives food to her household, and a portion to her maidens" (Mishlei 31:15). And from what she gives to them she is herself satiated, as if she had eaten more food than all of them.

693. וְכַד יֵיתֵי צַפְרָא דְּאִקְרֵי שַׁחַר. יֵיתֵי לָהּ חֲבָלִים דְּגָלוּתָא. וּבְגִין דָּא, אִתְקְרִיאַת אַיֶּלֶת הַשַּׁחַר. עַל שֵׁם קַדְרוּתָא דְּצַפְרָא. דַּחֲבָלִים לָהּ כְּיוֹלֵדָה. הה״ד, כְּמוֹ הָרָה תַּקְרִיב לָלֶדֶת תָּחִיל תִּזְעַק בַּחֲבָלֶיהָ וְגוֹ'.

693. And when the morning, which is called 'dawn', arrives, the pangs of the Exile come to her, and this is why she is called 'the hind of the dawn', after the blackness of the morning, for she THEN has pangs as a woman giving birth, as it is written: "Like as a woman with child, that draws near the time of her delivery, is in pain, and cries out in her pangs" (Yeshayah 26:17).

694. אֵימָתַי פַּלְגַת לְהוֹן. כַּד צַפְרָא בָּעֵי לְמֵיתֵי. בְּעוֹד דְּאִיהִי לֵילְיָא, וְקַדְרוּתָא סְלִיקַת לְאַנְהָרָא. כד״א, וַתָּקָם בְּעוֹד לַיְלָה וַתִּתֵּן טֶרֶף לְבֵיתָהּ וְגוֹ'. כֵּיוָן דְּאַנְהִיר צַפְרָא, כֻּלְּהוּ שַׂבְעִין בִּמְזוֹנָא דִּילָהּ.

694. When does she distribute to them? This is when the morning is just about to come, but it is still night, and the blackness departs for the illumination, as it is written: "She rises also while it is yet night, and gives food to her household." But by the time it is morning, they are all satiated with her food.

695. כְּדֵין, קָלָא חַדָא אִתְּעַר בְּאֶמְצָעִיתָא דִּרְקִיעַ, קָארֵי בְּחַיִל וְאָמַר,

קְרִיבִין עוּלוּ לְדוּכְתַּיְיכוּ. רְחִיקִין. פּוּקוּ. כָּל חַד וְחַד לִיכְנָשׁ לְאַתְרֵיהּ
דְּאִתְחֲזֵי לֵיהּ. כֵּיוָן דְּאַנְהִיר שִׁמְשָׁא, כָּל חַד וְחַד אִתְכְּנִישׁ לְאַתְרֵיהּ.
הה״ד תִּזְרַח הַשֶּׁמֶשׁ יֵאָסֵפוּן וְגוֹ׳. וְאִיהִי אַזְלַת בִּימָמָא, וְאִתְגַּלְיָא
בְּלֵילְיָא. וּפַלְגָּא בְּצַפְרָא. וּבג״כ אִקְרֵי, אַיֶּלֶת הַשַּׁחַר.

695. And then a certain voice awakens in the midst of the firmament and calls out aloud, saying: Let those who are near, go to their places; let those who are far, leave. Let each one gather to his rightful place. And by the time the sun shines, each one is gathered to its place, as it is written: "The sun rises, they slink away" (Tehilim 104:22). And she departs during the day, and is revealed at night, and distributes FOOD in the morning, which is why she is called 'the hind of the dawn'.

696. לְבָתַר אִתְתְּקַפַת כְּגִיבָּר וְאַזְלַת, וְאִקְרֵי אַיִל. לְאָן אֲתַר אַזְלַת.
אַזְלַת שִׁתִּין פַּרְסֵי מֵהַהוּא אֲתַר דְּנַפְקָא, וְעָאלַת לְגוֹ טוּרָא דַּחֲשׁוֹכָא.
אַזְלַת בְּגוֹ הַהוּא טוּרָא דַּחֲשׁוֹכָא, אָרַח לְרַגְלָהּ חִוְיָא חֲדָא עֲקִימָא,
וְאָזִיל לְרַגְלָהּ. וְאִיהִי סַלְקָא מִתַּמָּן, לְגַבֵּי טוּרָא דִּנְהוֹרָא. כֵּיוָן דְּמָטַת
תַּמָּן, זַמִּין לָהּ קוּדְשָׁא בְּרִיךְ הוּא חִוְיָא אַחֲרָא, וְנָפִיק וּמְקַטְרְגָא דָּא
בְּדָא, וְאִיהִי אִשְׁתְּזִיבַת. וּמִתַּמָּן נַטְלַת מְזוֹנָא, וְתָבַת לְאַתְרָהּ, בְּפַלְגוּת
לֵילְיָא. וּמִפַּלְגוּ לֵילְיָא, שַׁרְיָא לְפַלְגָּא, עַד דְּסָלִיקַת קַדְרוּתָא דְּצַפְרָא.
כֵּיוָן דְּאַנְהִיר יְמָמָא, אַזְלַת, וְלָא אִתְחֲזִיאַת, כְּמָה דְּאִתְּמַר.

696. Subsequently, she grows stronger and leaves, and is called 'a hart', NAMELY, A MASCULINE FORM. Where does she go? HE ANSWERS, she goes sixty pharasangs from the place that she left and she enters into the mountain of darkness. As she goes into the mountain of darkness, a certain labyrinthine serpent sniffs at her feet and follows her, and she ascends from there to the mountain of light. When she reaches there, the Holy One, blessed be He, arranges for her another serpent, who goes forth and they fight each other, and she is saved. And from there she takes food, and returns to her place by midnight. And from midnight on, she begins the distribution, until the blackness of the morning arises. And when the morning gives light, she goes from there and is no longer visible, as we have learned.

697. וּבְשַׁעֲתָא דְעָלְמָא אִצְטְרִיךְ לְמִטְרָא, מִתְכַּנְּשִׁין לְגַבָּה כָּל שְׁאָר חֵיוָן, וְהִיא סְלִיקַת לְרֵישׁ טוּרָא רָמָאָה, וְאִתְעַטְּפַת רֵישָׁהָא בֵּין בִּרְכָהָא, וְגָעַת גּוֹעָה בָּתַר גּוֹעָה, וְקוּדְשָׁא בְּרִיךְ הוּא שָׁמַע קָלָהּ, וְאִתְמְלֵי רַחֲמִין, וְחָס עַל עָלְמָא. וְהִיא נַחֲתַת מֵרֵישׁ טוּרָא, וְרָהֲטַת, וּטְמִירַת גַּרְמָהָא. וְכָל שְׁאָר חֵיוָתָא אֲבַתְרָהָא רָהֲטִין, וְלָא מַשְׁכְּחִין לָהּ. הה"ד, כְּאַיָּל תַּעֲרוֹג עַל אֲפִיקֵי מָיִם. מַאי עַל אֲפִיקֵי מָיִם. עַל אֲפִיקֵי מַיִם מֵהַנְהוּ דְאִתְיְבָשׁוּ, וְעָלְמָא צָחֵי עַל מַיָּא, כְּדֵין תַּעֲרוֹג.

697. And when the world is in need of rain, all the other animals collect near her, and she goes up to the top of a high mountain, puts her head between her knees, and cries out with one long cry after another. And the Holy One, blessed be He, hears her voice, and is overcome by mercy and has pity on the world. And she comes down from the top of the mountain, and runs to hide herself. And all the other animals run after her, but do not find her. This is as it is written: "As the hart pants after the water brooks." What is the meaning of "the water brooks"? This refers to those water brooks that have dried up, and the world is thirsty for water. Then she "pants."

698. בְּשַׁעֲתָא דְאִתְעַבְּרַת, אַסְתִּימַת, כֵּיוָן דְמָטָא זִמְנָא לְמֵילַד, גָּעַאת וְרָמַאת קָלִין, קָלָא בָּתַר קָלָא, עַד שַׁבְעִין קָלִין, כְּחוּשְׁבַּן תֵּיבִין דְּיַעַנְךָ יְיָ' בְּיוֹם צָרָה, דְאִיהִי שִׁירָתָא דְעוּבָּרְתָּא דָא. וְקוּדְשָׁא בְּרִיךְ הוּא שָׁמַע לָהּ, וְזַמִּין לְגַבָּהּ. כְּדֵין אָפִיק חַד חִוְיָא רַבְרְבָא, מִגּוֹ טוּרֵי חָשׁוֹךְ וְאָתֵי בֵּין טוּרִין, פּוּמֵיהּ מְלַחֲכָא בְּעַפְרָא, מָטֵי עַד הַאי אַיָּל, וְאָתֵי וְנָשִׁיךְ לָהּ בְּהַהוּא אֲתַר, תְּרֵי זִמְנֵי.

698. When she conceives, she is closed up, but when the time comes for her to give birth, she shouts and cries out, cry after cry, up to seventy shouts, as the number of words in the psalm: "Hashem will answer you in the day of trouble" (Tehilim 20:2), which is the song of this pregnant one. And the Holy One, blessed be He, hears her, and arranges HER SALVATION for her. And then a certain large serpent emerges from the mountains of darkness, and comes between the mountains, its mouth licking the dust and it reaches this hart and comes and bites it twice in the same place.

699. זִמְנָא קַדְמָאָה נָפִיק דְּמָא, וְאִיהִי לָחִיךְ. זִמְנָא תִּנְיָינָא, נָפִיק מַיָּיא וְשָׁתוּ כָּל אִינּוּן בְּעִירָן דִּי בְּטוּרַיָּיא, וְאִתְפְּתָחַת וְאוֹלִידַת. וְסִימָנָךְ וַיַּךְ אֶת הַסֶּלַע בְּמַטֵּהוּ פַּעֲמָיִם. וּכְתִיב וַתֵּשְׁתְּ הָעֵדָה וּבְעִירָם.

699. On the first occasion, blood comes OUT OF HER, and the serpent licks it. On the second occasion water comes out, and all those animals of the mountains drink, and she herself is opened and gives birth. And this you may derive from the verse: "and with his rod he smote the rock twice, and water came forth abundantly, and the congregation drank, and their beasts also" (Bemidbar 20:11).

700. בְּהַהוּא זִמְנָא דְקוּדְשָׁא בְּרִיךְ הוּא חָס עָלָה עַל עוֹבָדָא דְּנָחָשׁ דָּא. מַה כְּתִיב, קוֹל יְיָ' יְחוֹלֵל אַיָּלוֹת וַיֶּחֱשׂוֹף יְעָרוֹת וְגוֹ', קוֹל יְיָ' יְחוֹלֵל אַיָּלוֹת, אִינּוּן חַבְלִין וְצִירִין, לְאַתְּעָרָא אִינּוּן שַׁבְעִין קַלִּין. מִיָּד וַיֶּחֱשׂוֹף יְעָרוֹת, לְאַתְּעָרָא הַהוּא נָחָשׁ, וּלְאִתְגַּלְּיָיא הַהִיא חַיָּה בֵּינַיְיהוּ לְמֵיהַךְ. וּבְהֵיכָלוֹ, מַאי וּבְהֵיכָלוֹ. בְּהֵיכָלוֹ דְקוּדְשָׁא בְּרִיךְ הוּא, כָּל אִינּוּן אָכְלוּסִין, פַּתְחִין וְאַמְרִין כָּבוֹד. מַאי כָּבוֹד. בָּרוּךְ כְּבוֹד יְיָ' מִמְּקוֹמוֹ.

700. The Holy One, blessed be He, has pity on her because of what the serpent did, as it is written: "The voice of Hashem makes the hinds to calve, and strips the forests bare; and in His temple everyone speaks of his glory" (Tehilim 29:9). "The voice of Hashem makes the hinds to calve" refers to the pangs and pains that give rise to those seventy shouts, AS ABOVE. And then follows "and strips the forests bare" in order to awaken that serpent, and reveal the animal to go amongst them. "and in His temple": What does this mean? It refers to the temple of the Holy One, blessed be He, WHICH IS MALCHUT, in which all those multitudes THAT ARE IN THE WORLDS OF BRIYAH, YETZIRAH, AND ASIYAH open and say: Glory! What is meant by glory? It refers to "Blessed be the glory of Hashem from His place" (Yechezkel 3:12), WHICH IS MALCHUT THAT IS CALLED 'THE GLORY OF HASHEM'.

A Synopsis

We hear about the number of years before the hind will give birth to the redemption, and we hear that two Messiahs will be revealed to

the world. Then the Torah sages who suffered pangs as though they were in labor will be respected and honored, and the wicked will be judged above and below.

רעיא מהימנא

701. וְאִי תֵּימָא דְלֵע' תָּחִיל וּלְב' שְׁנִין אוֹלִידַת, בָּתַר אֶלֶף וּמָאתָן, כְּחוּשְׁבַּן רע"ב. הָא כְּתִיב בְּטֶרֶם תָּחִיל יָלָדָה. וְרָזָא דְמִלָּה, וְהָיָה טֶרֶם יִקְרָאוּ וַאֲנִי אֶעֱנֶה עוֹד וְגו'. וּמַאי בְּטֶרֶם. אֶלָּא קֹדֶם דְּיִשְׁתַּלִּימוּ, שִׁבְעִין וּתְרֵין שְׁנִין, בָּתַר אֶלֶף וּמָאתָן, אִינּוּן חֲבָלִים דְּיוֹלֵדָה, יִתְגַּלְּיָין ב' מְשִׁיחִין בְּעָלְמָא. וּבְהַהוּא זִמְנָא וּבְהֵיכָלוֹ כֻּלּוֹ אוֹמֵר כָּבוֹד, וְהָא אוֹקְמוּהָ כָּבוֹד חֲכָמִים יִנְחָלוּ.

Ra'aya Meheimna (the Faithful Shepherd)

701. (THE BEGINNING OF THE ARTICLE IS MISSING.) One might suggest that after seventy YEARS she will feel THE PAINS OF THE BIRTH PANGS and in two years she will give birth TO THE REDEMPTION, one thousand and two hundred years after THE DESTRUCTION OF THE TEMPLE, THAT IS TO SAY, AFTER THE END OF THE FIFTH MILLENIUM, WHICH IS ALL DESTRUCTION, AND A FURTHER TWO HUNDRED YEARS INTO THE SIXTH MILLENIUM, AND SEVENTY YEARS FOR THE BIRTH PANGS, AND TWO YEARS FOR THE BIRTH ITSELF, coming to the year 272 IN THE SIXTH MILLENIUM. But it is written: "Before she travailed, she brought forth" (Yeshayah 66:7). And the secret of the matter is contained in the verse: "And it shall come to pass, that before they call, I will answer" (Yeshayah 65:24). And what is the meaning of before? HE ANSWERS, before the completion of the seventy years and the two years following the passing of one thousand and two hundred years, WHERE THESE 72 YEARS ARE the birth pangs, two Messiahs will be revealed to the world. And at that time: "and in His temple everyone speaks of His glory." And it has already been taught: "The wise shall inherit glory" (Mishlei 3:35). IN OTHER WORDS: "AND IN HIS TEMPLE EVERYONE SPEAKS OF HIS GLORY," THE MEANING OF WHICH IS THAT THE GLORY OF THE WISE WILL BE THROUGHOUT HIS TEMPLE.

702. בְּהַהִיא שַׁעֲתָא, אִלֵּין מָארֵי תּוֹרָה יְהוֹן נִכְבָּדִים. אִלֵּין דִּסְבִילוּ

כַּמָּה חֲבָלִים וְצִירִין כַּיּוֹלֵדָה, וַהֲווֹ מְבוּזִין בֵּין עַמֵּי הָאָרֶץ, יְהוֹן
נִכְבָּדִים. וּמִיַּד יְיָ׳ לַמַּבּוּל יָשָׁב, לְרַשִׁיעַיָא. אֵין מַבּוּל, אֶלָּא דִּינִין
דְּמַבּוּל. כְּגַוְונָא דְּנִפְתָּחוּ מַעְיְינוֹת תְּהוֹם וַאֲרוּבוֹת הַשָּׁמַיִם נִפְתְּחוּ בְּיוֹמֵי
טוֹפָנָא, אוֹף הָכָא יִתְעָרוּן דִּינִין לְגַבַּיְיהוּ עֵילָּא וְתַתָּא, עַד דְּלֵית סוֹף
וְתַכְלִית, וְכָל בִּזּוּיִין וּקְלָנָא, דְּעָבְדוּ אוּמִין עכו״ם דְּעָלְמָא, לְשֵׁם יְהֹוָה
וּלְעַמֵּיהּ, וְכַמָּה חֵרוּפִין דִּסְבִילוּ יִשְׂרָאֵל מִנַּיְיהוּ עַל שֵׁם יְיָ׳, מִכֻּלְּהוּ
נָטִיל נוּקְמָא קוּדְשָׁא בְּרִיךְ הוּא, וְעַל דָּא אִתְקְרֵי, נוֹקֵם יְיָ׳ וְנוֹטֵר וּבַעַל
חֵמָה לְגַבַּיְיהוּ.

702. And at that time, those Torah sages will be respected, those who suffered pangs and travails as a woman in labor, and who were despised by the ignorant; they will be honored. And immediately: "Hashem sat enthroned at the flood" (Tehilim 29:10) on account of the wicked. Flood here symbolizes Judgments of the flood, when "were all the fountains of the great deep broken open, and the windows of heaven were opened" (Beresheet 7:11), at the time of the Flood. So, too, THEN Judgments will rise over them, OVER THE WICKED, above and below, with no end FOR THEIR JUDGMENTS. And every contempt and disgrace shown by the idolatrous nations of the world towards Hashem and His people and the many insults that Yisrael suffered from them for the sake of Hashem's Name – for all of them the Holy One, blessed be He, will exact vengeance, and therefore, as far as they are concerned, "Hashem revenges, and is full of wrath" (Nachum 1:2) towards them.

105. The holiday of Pesach

A Synopsis
We are told that the redemption will take place on the fourteenth day of the month of Nissan.

703. וּבַחֹדֶשׁ הָרִאשׁוֹן, מַאן רִאשׁוֹן. דָּא נִיסָן. תַּמָּן אוֹלִידַת הַהִיא חַיָּה, לְקַיֵּים מַה דְּאוֹקְמוּהָ מָארֵי מַתְנִיתִין, בְּנִיסָן נִגְאֲלוּ וּבְנִיסָן עֲתִידִין לְהִגָּאֵל. וּבִי"ד דִּילֵיהּ, וַיֹּאמֶר כִּי יָד עַל כֵּס יָהּ, תַּמָּן אוֹמֵי לְאַעְבְּרָא מֵעָלְמָא זַרְעָא דְּעֵשָׂו עֲמָלֵקַיִּים, בְּהַהוּא זִמְנָא מִשְׁכוּ וּקְחוּ לָכֶם צֹאן לְמִשְׁפְּחֹתֵיכֶם וְשַׁחֲטוּ הַפָּסַח. מִשְׁכוּ׃ מָשַׁךְ יָדוֹ אֶת לוֹצְצִים.

703. "And on... the first month" (Bemidbar 28:16). HE ASKS: What is meant here by the first month? AND ANSWERS: It is Nissan, which is when that animal gave birth TO THE LIGHTS OF THE REDEMPTION, in accord with the teaching of the sages of Mishnah: In the month of Nissan they were redeemed, and in the month of Nissan they will be redeemed. And this is with His hand (Heb. *yad* = fourteen), ON HIS FOURTEENTH, ACCORDING TO THE SECRET OF THE VERSE: "for he said, because Yah has sworn (lit. 'put a hand') by His throne" (Shemot 17:16), when He swore to remove the seed of Esau, the Amalek, from the world. At that time: "Draw out and take lambs according to your families, and kill the passover" (Shemot 12:21), WHERE THE MEANING OF "draw out" (Heb. *mishchu*) is as in the verse: "he stretched out (Heb. *mashach*) his hand with scorners" (Hoshea 7:5).

704. בְּהַהוּא זִמְנָא, כֹּה אָמַר יְיָ' לָרוֹעִים הַפּוֹשְׁעִים בִּי. וְאוֹמֵר, וְאֶל אַדְמַת יִשְׂרָאֵל לֹא יָבֹאוּ. וְאִלֵּין אִינּוּן רוֹעִים דְּעָנָא, פַּרְנָסֵי דָּרָא. וּבְג"ד אִתְּמַר עֲלַיְיהוּ, הִנֵּה אָנֹכִי מְפַתֶּיהָ וְהוֹלַכְתִּיהָ הַמִּדְבָּרָה. וְנִשְׁפַּטְתִּי אִתְּכֶם וְגוֹ', כַּאֲשֶׁר נִשְׁפַּטְתִּי אֶת אֲבוֹתֵיכֶם דְּקָטִיל לוֹן בְּמַכַּת חֹשֶׁךְ.

ע"כ רעיא מהימנא

704. At that time, thus said Hashem: to the rulers who transgressed against Me: "neither shall they enter into the land of Yisrael" (Yechezkel 13:9), and

this refers to the shepherds of the flock, the supporters of the generation. Wherefore it is said about them: "Therefore, behold, I will allure her, and bring her into the wilderness" (Hoshea 2:16). "and there will remonstrate with you... As I remonstrated with your fathers" (Yechezkel 20:35-36), NAMELY, whom He killed in the plague of darkness.

End of Ra'aya Meheimna

A Synopsis
Rabbi Shimon explains to Rabbi Elazar how the upper days, the Sfirot of Zeir Anpin, will be drawn to the lower days, to the Sfirot of Malchut. On the fourteenth day the animal, Malchut, will give birth to the lights of the Redemption and the serpent will depart. Then Malchut will be sanctified on high and will be called 'Glory'.

705. וּבַחֹדֶשׁ הָרִאשׁוֹן, מַאן חֹדֶשׁ הָרִאשׁוֹן. דָּא אִיהוּ חֹדֶשׁ, דְּהַאי חַיָּה אִתְגַּלְיָיא בֵּיהּ וְאִתַּתְקָפַת בֵּיהּ, וְנָפְקָא לְעָלְמָא בְּאַרְבְּעָה עָשָׂר יוֹם. בְּאַרְבְּעָה עָשָׂר, אִלֵּין שְׁאַר חֵיוָותָא, דְּאִינּוּן י' י' לְכָל סְטָר, בְּד' סִטְרִין דְּעָלְמָא. וּבִסְפָרִי קַדְמָאֵי, אִיהוּ י', וְחַד לְכָל סְטָר לְאַרְבַּע סִטְרִין, וְאִינּוּן אַרְבַּע עָשָׂר. כֵּיוָן דְּאִינּוּן אַרְבַּע, מִתְחַבְּרָאן וּמִתְתַּקְּנָן עִם אִינּוּן עֲשַׂר דִּבְסִטְרָא דִּימִינָא, כְּדֵין י"ד, בְּחֶדְוָה לְאִתְתַּקְּנָא חַיָּה דָּא בְּתִקּוּנָהָא.

705. "And on...the first month" (Bemidbar 28:16). HE ASKS: What is meant by the first month? AND ANSWERS: This is the month in which that animal, NAMELY, MALCHUT, is revealed in and strengthened by and goes forth into the world, NAMELY, EMERGES FROM HER CLOSURE, IN THE SECRET OF THE VERSE: "AND STRIP THE FORESTS BARE" (TEHILIM 29:9) on the fourteenth day. The fourteen days refer to the remaining animals, NAMELY, CHESED AND GVURAH, TIFERET AND MALCHUT OF ZEIR ANPIN, THAT ILLUMINATE WITHIN MALCHUT, for they are ten in each direction, SINCE CHESED, GVURAH, TIFERET AND MALCHUT, ARE THE FOUR DIRECTIONS at the four corners of the world, NORTH, SOUTH, EAST AND WEST, EACH ONE OF WHICH IS COMPOSED OF TEN SFIROT. And in the early writing IT IS STATED that she, MALCHUT, is ten, and that one SFIRAH OF CHESED, GVURAH, TIFERET AND MALCHUT, is in each of the four directions OF THE WORLD, making fourteen. And since these four, CHESED,

GVURAH, TIFERET AND MALCHUT, join in and are established with the ten THAT ARE IN MALCHUT from the right-hand side, this makes the fourteenth day OF THE MONTH for the fixing of this animal, WHICH IS MALCHUT, with all her establishment, with rejoicing.

706. ר' אֶלְעָזָר אָמַר, וַדַּאי הָכִי הוּא. וְת"ח, כְּתִיב מִשְׁכוּ וּקְחוּ לָכֶם צֹאן וְגוֹ', מִשְׁכוּ, מַאי מִשְׁכוּ. כְּמַאן דְּמָשִׁיךְ מֵאֲתָר אַחֲרָא, לַאֲתָר דָּא. מְשֹׁכוּ יוֹמִין עִלָּאִין לְגַבֵּי יוֹמִין תַּתָּאִין. יוֹמִין עִלָּאִין אִינוּן שס"ו, כְּחוּשְׁבַּן מִשְׁכוּ. יוֹמִין תַּתָּאִין, זִמְנִין דְּאִינוּן שנ"ה, וּבְזִמְנָא, דְּאִתְנַהֲרָא סִיהֲרָא בְּאַשְׁלְמוּתָא, סְלִיקוּ לְמֶהֱוֵי אִינּוּן יוֹמִין שס"ה, כְּחוּשְׁבַּן מִשְׁכוּ חָסֵר חַד.

706. Rabbi Elazar said: "Of course, that is how it is, but come and see, It is written: "Draw out and take lambs..." What is the meaning of "Draw out"? AND REPLIES: IT IS TO BE UNDERSTOOD as one who draws something from another place to this place, namely, draw out the upper days, WHICH ARE THE SFIROT OF ZEIR ANPIN, to the lower days, TO THE SFIROT of MALCHUT. The upper days OF ZEIR ANPIN number 366, as in the numerical value of "Draw out" (Heb. *mishchu*), NAMELY, THE NUMBER OF DAYS IN A SOLAR YEAR, WHICH IS ZEIR ANPIN. The lower days OF MALCHUT are usually 355 days in a year, (Heb. *shanah* = 355). But when the moon, WHICH IS MALCHUT, shines at its fullest, the number of its days rises to be 365 days, AS THE SOLAR YEAR, WHICH IS ZEIR ANPIN, namely, as the numerical value of "*mishchu*," less one.

707. מְשֹׁכוּ יוֹמִין עִלָּאִין לְגַבֵּי יוֹמִין תַּתָּאִין, לְמֶהֱוֵי כֻּלְּהוּ כַּחֲדָא בַּחֲבוּרָא חֲדָא. וּמַאן מָשִׁיךְ לוֹן. אִינוּן עֲשַׂר דְּלִסְטַר יְמִינָא, דִּכְתִיב בְּעָשׂוֹר. בְּעָשׂוֹר, בַּעֲשָׂרָה מִבָּעֵי לֵיהּ, מַאי בְּעָשׂוֹר. אֶלָּא ט' אִינוּן לְכָל סְטָר, וּנְקוּדָה חֲדָא דְּאַזְלָא בְּאֶמְצָעִיתָא. כְּגַוְונָא דָּא, וְהַהִיא נְקוּדָה, אַשְׁלִימַת לְעֶשֶׂר. וע"ד בְּעָשׂוֹר, כְּמָה דְּאִתְּמַר זָכוֹר וְשָׁמוֹר. לְשַׁמּוּשָׁא בְּעֶשְׂרָה, אִינוּן יוֹמִין תֵּשַׁע, בְּהַהוּא נְקוּדָה. לַחֹדֶשׁ הַזֶּה, יוֹמִין דְּלִסְטַר יְמִינָא, בְּגִין לְאִתְחַבְּרָא זֹאת בָּזֶה, לְמֶהֱוֵי כֹּלָּא חַד.

-164-

707. Draw the upper days OF ZEIR ANPIN to the lower days OF MALCHUT, so that they will be one, all joined together. And who draws them? Tese are, the ten OF MALCHUT when she is on the right side, THAT IS CHESED. For it is written: "on the tenth day (Heb. *be'asor*)" (Shemot 12:3), NAMELY, MALCHUT WHEN SHE IS ON THE RIGHT SIDE. HE ASKS, IT IS WRITTEN AS "*be'asor*," when the verse should have used the more common *be'asarah* (lit. 'the tenth day'); what is be'asor? HE ANSWERS, there are nine in each direction with one point that goes in the middle, thus: ⦂⸫, and this point completes the ten SFIROT. This is why it is written "*be'asor*," just as it is written: "Remember (Heb. *zachor*)" (Shemot 20:8) and "Keep (Heb. *shamor*)" (Devarim 5:12), NAMELY, THE FORM OF THE INFINITIVE ABSOLUTE OF THE VERB, THE MEANING OF *BE'ASOR* THUS BEING to use the ten IN SUCH A WAY that these nine days WILL USE that point. "of this month" (Shemot 12:3), WHICH IS NISSAN, ALLUDES TO CHESED, TO SHOW THAT THESE days THAT ARE DRAWN DOWN will be on the right side, WHICH IS CHESED in order to combine *zot* (lit. 'this', feminine), WHICH IS MALCHUT, with *zeh* (lit. 'this', masculine), WHICH IS ZEIR ANPIN, for it all to be one.

708. וּבְזִמְנָא דְּאִינוּן ד׳ אִתְקְשָׁרוּ לד׳ סִטְרִין בַּהֲדַיְיהוּ. כְּדֵין אוֹלִידַת הַהוּא חַיָּה וְחִוְיָא אָזִיל לֵיה וּבְהַהוּא זִמְנָא מְקַדְּשִׁין לְעֵילָא לְהַאי חַיָּה וְקָרַאן לָה כָּבוֹד. וּכְדֵין אִתְקַדָּשׁ מוֹעֲדָא. מַה דְּלָא הֲוָה עַד הַשְׁתָּא, וּכְעַן קָרַאן לָה כָּבוֹד, הֲדָא הוּא דִכְתִיב וּבְהֵיכָלוֹ כֻּלוֹ אוֹמֵר כָּבוֹד.

708. And when these four DAYS THAT FOLLOW THE TENTH OF THE MONTH join up with the four directions, SOUTH, NORTH, EAST AND WEST, WHICH ARE THE SECRET OF CHESED AND GVURAH, TIFERET AND MALCHUT, and combine with them, WITH THE TEN DAYS, then that animal, WHICH IS MALCHUT, gives birth to THE LIGHTS OF THE REDEMPTION, and the Serpent departs. And at that time that animal is sanctified on high, and is called "Glory," and then the festival is sanctified. This had not been the case previously, but now, IN THE FESTIVAL, she is called "glory," as it is written: "and in His temple everyone speaks of His glory."

A Synopsis

The Faithful Shepherd says that the explanation given is insufficiently clear and requires more illumination. He tells the

rabbis that "on the tenth day" means the nine Sfirot are in all directions, and that they parallel the nine months of a pregnant woman's period of gestation. He talks about "remember" and "keep" and "glory," and enumerates the numerology associated with this lesson.

רעיא מהימנא

709. אָמַר רַעְיָא מְהֵימָנָא, מִלִּין אִלֵּין סְתִימִין, וְצָרִיךְ לְמִפְתַּח לוֹן לְגַבֵּי חַבְרַיָּיא, דְּמַאן דְּסָתִים לוֹן גְּנִיזִין דְּאוֹרַיְיתָא, אִיהוּ מְצַעֵר לוֹן. דְּלָרַשִּׁיעַיָּא נְהוֹרִין דְּרָזִין, אִתְחֲזָרַן לוֹן חֲשׁוֹכִין. וְאִיהוּ מָתְלָא לְמָמוֹנָא דְּאִיהוּ גָּנִיז, מַאן דְּחָפַר לֵיהּ, עַד דְּגָלֵי לֵיהּ, וְלָאו אִיהוּ דִּילֵיהּ, אִתְהַדָּר בְּסוּכְלְתָנוּתֵיהּ בַּחֲשׁוֹכָא וְקַבְלָא. וּלְמַאן דְּאִיהוּ דִּילֵיהּ, נָהִיר לֵיהּ. וּבְג״ד, אִית לב״נ לְגַלָּאָה רָזִין סְתִימִין דִּבְאוֹרַיְיתָא.

Ra'aya Meheimna (the Faithful Shepherd)

709. The Faithful Shepherd said: These matters THAT ARE STATED ABOVE, IN THE PRECEDING PARAGRAPH, are insufficiently clear and they have to be explained for the friends, for whoever hides the secrets of the Torah from them, saddens them, for the lights of the secrets are darkness for the wicked. And it is like silver that is hidden away. If one digs until he discovers it, but it is not his, it becomes like darkness and gloom in his mind, while for one to whom it belongs, it illuminates on him. This is the reason why a person should reveal the hidden secrets of the Torah TO THE FRIENDS.

710. בֶּעָשׂוֹר: ט׳ אִינּוּן לְכָל סְטָר, לָקֳבֵל ט׳ יַרְחִין דְּיוֹלֵדָה, בְּחוּשְׁבַּן א״ח. מַאן יוֹלֶדֶת. ד׳ מִן אֶחָד. א״ח, אִיהוּ ט׳, לְד׳ סְטְרִין דְּאָת ד׳, וְאִינּוּן אַרְבָּעִים. א״ח זָכוֹר, ד׳ שָׁמוֹר. הָא אַרְבְּעִין וּתְרֵין.

710. "on the tenth day" (Shemot 12:3) means that the nine Sfirot are in all directions, paralleling the nine months of a pregnant woman's period of gestation, which is the same as the numerical value of Aleph Chet of one (Heb. *Echad* -Aleph Chet Dalet). Who is the woman with child? She is the Dalet of *echad*. Aleph Chet (= nine) are the nine SFIROT in the four

directions of the letter Dalet (= four), and they are forty. Aleph Chet CORRESPOND TO "Remember," WHICH IS ZEIR ANPIN, while Dalet CORRESPONDS TO "Keep," WHICH IS MALCHUT, AND TOGETHER WITH THEM, they are 42.

711. אִשְׁתְּאַר כָּבוֹד, דְּאִתְּמַר בֵּיהּ בשכמל"ו. וְאִיהוּ כָּבוֹד ל"ב, ד' זִמְנִין לְכָל סְטָר דְּאָת ד', הֲרֵי ס"ד לְד' סְטְרִין, רנ"ו. וְאוֹקְמוּהָ, כָּבוֹד לְעֵילָא, ל"ב לְתַתָּא. ובג"ד מְיַיחֲדִין בְּכָל יוֹמָא תְּרֵין זִמְנִין, דְּאַמְרָן בְּהוּ תְּרֵין זִמְנִין כָּבוֹד, דְּאִיהוּ ס"ד. וּתְרֵין זִמְנִין ד' ד' מִן אֶחָ"ד, הֲרֵי ע"ב. הֲרֵי ד' דְּאֶחָ"ד, שְׁלִימוּ דְּמ"ב שְׁמָהָן. וּשְׁלִימוּ דְע"ב שְׁמָהָן. ובג"ד אַמְרִין בְּמִזְמוֹר לְדָוִד מִי זֶה מֶלֶךְ הַכָּבוֹד יְיָ' עִזוּז וְגִבּוֹר. וּבְזִמְנָא תִּנְיָינָא מִי הוּא זֶה מֶלֶךְ הַכָּבוֹד.

ע"כ רעיא מהימנא

711. This leaves us with "glory," as it is said: "Blessed be the name of the glory of His kingdom forever and ever." And this is glory (Heb. *kavod* = 32) and heart (Heb. *lev* = 32), THE SUM OF WHICH IS 64. And there are four directions to this letter Dalet, 64 to the four sides, which comes to 256. And it has been taught: Glory above and heart below, and for this reason, the recital of the unity is said twice daily, in which we say 'glory' twice, which amounts to 64. Add to this the two Dalet's of *echad*, and we have 72. And so the Dalet of *echad* completes the 42-letter Names and also completes the 72-letter Names. And this is why it is said in 'A Psalm of David': "Who is this King of glory? Hashem strong and mighty" (Tehilim 24:8), and again: "Who is this King of glory? Hashem of hosts, He is the King of glory" (Ibid.10).

End of Ra'aya Meheimna

A Synopsis
We are told how the Temple is sanctified.

712. מַאן הֵיכָלוֹ. דָּא הֵיכָל עִלָּאָה פְּנִימָאָה, דְּתַמָּן מִתְקַדְּשָׁא כֹּלָּא. תַּמָּן מְקַדְּשִׁין לְמַאן דְּחָזֵי לְאִתְקַדְּשָׁא. הֵיךְ מְקַדְּשִׁין לֵיהּ בְּהַהוּא

הֵיכְלָא. בְּקַדְמֵיתָא אִתְפְּתָחוּ תַּרְעִין, וְחַד מַפְתְּחָא סְתִימָא, אַתְקִין
וּפָתַח תַּרְעָא חַד, לִסְטַר דָּרוֹם, כְּדֵין עָאל כַּהֲנָא רַבָּא בְּהַהוּא פִּתְחָא,
וְאִזְדָּרַז בְּהֵימְיָינוֹי, וְתִקּוּנוֹי. וְאִתְעַטַּר בְּעִטְרָא דִּקְדוּשָׁה וּלְבִישׁ חוּשְׁנָא
וְאֵפוֹדָא, וּמְעִילָא דְּשִׁבְעִין זַגִּין וְרִמּוֹנִין, דְּאִינוּן פַּעֲמוֹן זָהָב וְרִמּוֹן.
וְצִיץ נֵזְרָא דְּקוּדְשָׁא עַל מִצְחֵיה, דְּאִתְקְרֵי צִיץ נֵזֶר הַקֹּדֶשׁ, וְאִתְקְשַׁט
בְּד' בִּגְדֵי זָהָב, וּבְד' בִּגְדֵי לָבָן. וְעַל הַהוּא צִיץ מ"ב אַתְוָון מְלַהֲטָן
בֵּיה, וּמְנַצְצָן עֲלֵיה, וְנָהִיר כָּל הַהוּא הֵיכְלָא בִּנְהוֹרִין עִלָּאִין.

712. IT IS WRITTEN: "AND IN HIS TEMPLE EVERYONE SPEAK OF HIS GLORY" (TEHILIM 29:9). HE ASKS: What is meant by "His temple?" AND HE ANSWERS: This refers to the inner upper temple, where everything, NAMELY, BINAH, is sanctified. There whoever is fitting for sanctification is sanctified. How is that temple sanctified? HE ANSWERS THAT initially the gates are opened BY DA'AT. HE EXPLAINS HIS WORDS: One concealed key, NAMELY, DA'AT, fixed and opened one gate on the south side, WHICH IS THE SECRET OF THE RIGHT COLUMN. Then the High Priest, WHICH IS CHESED, enters into that opening and hurries with his girdle, WHICH IS THE SECRET OF MALCHUT, and his implements, NAMELY, THE FOUR GARMENTS OF AN ORDINARY PRIEST, NAMELY, MITRE, TUNIC, GIRDLE, AND BREECHES, WHICH CORRESPOND TO THE FOUR LETTERS OF ADONAI, WHICH IS MALCHUT. SUBSEQUENTLY, he is adorned with a diadem of holiness, and puts on a breastplate and efod and a robe of seventy bells and pomegranates, which are "a golden bell and pomegranate" (Shemot 28:34). And the plate of the holy crown on his forehead is called 'the plate of the holy crown', NAMELY, THE YUD OF YUD HEI VAV HEI. And he was embellished with the four garments of gold and with the four garments of white, WHICH CORRESPOND TO THE EIGHT LETTERS IN THE NAMES OF YUD HEI VAV HEI AND ADONAI, and on that plate 42 letters sparkle, NAMELY, THE 42-LETTER NAME, and the whole of that temple shines with upper lights.

713. אִסְתָּחַר הַהוּא מַפְתְּחָא, וּפָתַח סִטְרָא אַחֲרָא דִּבְסְטַר צָפוֹן, כְּדֵין
עָאל לֵוִי, מַעֲשְׂרָא דְּיַעֲקֹב, דְּאַפְרִישׁ לְקוּדְשָׁא בְּרִיךְ הוּא. וְכִנּוֹר דְּעֶשֶׂר
נִימִין עִמֵּיה, וְאִתְעַטַּר בְּעִטְרוֹי, וּכְדֵין אִסְתָּחַר מַפְתְּחָא, וּפָתַח בְּהַהוּא
הֵיכְלָא חַד תַּרְעָא, הַהוּא תַּרְעָא דְּקַיְימָא בְּאֶמְצָעִיתָא, עַמּוּדָא דִּלְסְטַר

מִזְרָח עָאל וְאִתְעַטָּר בְּשַׁבְעִין עִטְרִין, וְאִתְעַטָּר בְּאַרְבַּע אַתְוָון, דְּאִינּוּן
תְּרֵיסָר. וְאִתְעַטָּר בְּגִלּוּפִין דְּמָאתָן וְע׳ אֶלֶף עָלְמִין, וְאִתְעַטָּר בְּעִטְרִין
דְּסַיְיפֵי עָלְמָא עַד סַיְיפֵי עָלְמָא, בְּכַמָּה לְבוּשֵׁי יְקָר, בְּכַמָּה עִטְרִין
קַדִּישִׁין.

713. And that key, WHICH IS THE SECRET OF DA'AT, AS ABOVE, turned and opened another side OF BINAH, to the north. Then Levi, WHICH IS THE SECRET OF GVURAH AND THE LEFT COLUMN, entered, and he is the tithe of Jacob, whom he set aside OUT OF HIS SONS for the Holy One, blessed be He, and with him the ten-stringed lyre, WHICH IS THE SECRET OF THE TEN SFIROT OF THE LEFT COLUMN. And he is crowned with diadems, NAMELY, THE MOCHIN OF THE UPPER THREE SFIROT WHICH ARE CALLED 'DIADEMS'. And then the key turned yet again and opened a gate in that temple, that gate that stands in the center, namely, the pillar that is on the eastern side, WHICH IS TIFERET, THE CENTRAL COLUMN. It, NAMELY, TIFERET enters, and is adorned IN THAT GATE with seventy diadems, WHICH ARE THE SECRET OF THE 72 NAMES. And it is adorned with four letters, which are twelve, NAMELY, WITH THE TWELVE PERMUTATIONS OF THE FOUR LETTERS OF YUD HEI VAV HEI. AND THESE ARE THE SECRET OF CHESED AND GVURAH, TIFERET AND MALCHUT, IN EACH ARE THREE COLUMNS. And it is adorned with engravings of two hundred and seventy thousand worlds. And it is crowned with diadems THAT SHINE from one end of the world to the other, NAMELY, IN MALCHUT THAT IS CALLED 'WORLD', and in a number of valuable garments and a number of holy diadems.

714. אִסְתְּחַר הַהוּא מַפְתְּחָא, וּפָתַח לֵיהּ כָּל תַּרְעִין גְּנִיזִין, וְכָל תַּרְעִין
דִּקְדוּשִׁין טְמִירִין, וְאִתְקַדָּשׁ בְּהוּ, וְקַיְּימָא תַּמָּן כְּמַלְכָּא. מִתְבָּרֵךְ בְּכַמָּה
בִּרְכָאן, מִתְעַטָּר בְּכַמָּה עִטְרִין. כְּדֵין נַפְקֵי כֻּלְּהוּ בְּחַבּוּרָא חֲדָא,
מִתְעַטְּרָן בְּעִטְרַיְיהוּ כַּדְקָא יָאוֹת. כֵּיוָן דְּנַפְקֵי אִתְּעַר לֵיהּ בְּקִשּׁוּטוֹי.

714. That key, WHICH is DA'AT, AS ABOVE, turned once again and opened all the concealed gates and all the hidden holy gates, and ZEIR ANPIN is sanctified in them, and stands there as King. THAT IS, FROM THE ASPECT OF MALCHUT, WHICH IS IN THE CENTRAL COLUMN OF BINAH, He is

there blessed with a number of blessings and crowned with a number of diadems. Then all of them issue forth FROM BINAH TO THEIR PLACE IN ZEIR ANPIN. AND ALL OF THEM ISSUE FORTH, joined together, and are crowned with their diadems as is fitting. Once they have left BINAH FOR THE PLACE OF ZEIR ANPIN, they awaken ZEIR ANPIN SO THAT HE WILL PUT on His adornments.

715. וְהַאי חַיָּה אִתְּעָרָא, וְאַזְעִירַת גַּרְמָה, מִגּוֹ רְחִימוּ דְשִׁירָתָא, הֵיךְ אַזְעִירַת גַּרְמָה מִגּוֹ רְחִימוּ דְשִׁירָתָא, אַזְעָרַת גַּרְמָה זְעֵיר זְעֵיר, עַד דְּאִתְעֲבֵידַת נְקוּדָה חֲדָא. כֵּיוָן דְּאִיהִי אַזְעִירַת גַּרְמָה, כְּדֵין כְּתִיב, וַיֵּלֶךְ אִישׁ מִבֵּית לֵוִי וַיִּקַּח אֶת בַּת לֵוִי. בַּת לֵוִי וַדַּאי, מִסִּטְרָא דִשְׂמָאלָא. הֵיאַךְ אָחִיד לָה. אוֹשִׁיט שְׂמָאלָא תְּחוֹת רֵישֵׁהּ מִגּוֹ חֲבִיבוּ.

715. And this animal, NAMELY, MALCHUT, awakens and contracts herself out of love of the song. And how does she diminish herself? Out of love of the song she contracts herself bit by bit until it becomes just a point. And since she has contracted herself, it is then written: "And there went a man of the house of Levi" (Shemot 2:1), WHICH IS THE SECRET OF THE HOLY ONE, BLESSED BE HE: "and took to wife a daughter of Levi" (Ibid.), WHICH IS MALCHUT. She is certainly CALLED "a daughter of Levi," because she is from the left side. How does he hold her? He puts his left hand under her head, out of love, NAMELY, THE LEFT SIDE OF ZEIR ANPIN BECOMES THE UPPER THREE SFIROT OF MALCHUT, AND ARE REFERRED TO AS HEAD, THIS BEING IN THE SECRET OF THE VERSE: "HIS LEFT HAND IS UNDER MY HEAD" (SHIR HASHIRIM 8:3).

716. וְאִי תֵּימָא, כֵּיוָן דְּאִיהִי נְקוּדָה חֲדָא, אֵיךְ יָכִיל לְאַחֲדָא בִּנְקוּדָה זְעֵירָא. אֶלָּא לְגַבֵּי עֵילָא, כָּל מַה דְּהוּא מִלָּה זְעֵירָא, דָּא תּוּשְׁבַּחְתָּא, וְדָא עִלּוּיָיא וְרַב בִּרְבוּ עִלָּאָה. מִיַּד כַּהֲנָא רַבָּא אִתְּעַר לָהּ, וְאָחִיד לָהּ, וְחָבִיק לָהּ, דְּאִלּוּ הֲוַות רַבְרְבָא, לָא יַכְלִין לְאַחֲדָא כְּלָל. אֲבָל כֵּיוָן דְּאַזְעִירַת גַּרְמָה, וְאִיהִי נְקוּדָה חֲדָא, כְּדֵין אֲחִדִין בָּהּ, וְסַלְּקִין לָהּ לְעֵילָא, כֵּיוָן דְּסַלְּקִין לָהּ, וְיָתְבָא בֵּין תְּרֵין סִטְרִין אִלֵּין, כְּדֵין הַהוּא עַמוּדָא דְּקַיְימָא בְּאֶמְצָעִיתָא, אִתְחַבַּר בַּהֲדָהּ בְּחֲבִיבוּ דִּנְשִׁיקִין, בִּרְחִימוּ דְּחִבּוּרָא חֲדָא. כְּדֵין וַיִּשַּׁק יַעֲקֹב לְרָחֵל, בִּרְחִימוּ דִּנְשִׁיקִין

מִתְדַּבְּקָן דָּא בְּדָא, בְּלָא פֵּרוּדָא, עַד דְּנַקְטָא נַפְשָׁא דְעֲנוּגִין כַּדְקָא
יָאוּת.

716. And you might well ask that, since she is NOW a small point, how could
ZEIR ANPIN unite with a small point? AND HE ANSWERS THAT as
mentioned above, the smaller a thing is the more praiseworthy it is, and this
is a virtue, and she is really supremely large, FOR, WHEN SHE IS SMALL, the
High Priest immediately awakens for her, WHICH IS CHESED OF ZEIR
ANPIN who holds and embraces her. Had she been large, Zeir ANPIN AND
MALCHUT would not have been able to unite at all, but, since she contracted
herself and is a small point, THE SFIROT OF ZEIR ANPIN can hold her, and
raise her up on high, BETWEEN THE TWO ARMS OF ZEIR ANPIN, NAMELY,
CHESED AND GVURAH. And after they have raised her up, she sits between
these two sides, NAMELY CHESED AND GVURAH, and then the pillar that
stands in the center, NAMELY TIFERET, WHICH IS THE CENTRAL COLUMN,
joins with her in a love of kisses, a love of perfect union. And then: "And
Jacob," THAT IS, ZEIR ANPIN, "kissed Rachel," WHO IS MALCHUT
(Beresheet 29:11), for with the love of kisses, they cleave to each other
without separation, until she receives a Soul of delights as is fitting.

717. בְּשַׁעֲתָא דְּנַקְטָא נַפְשָׁא דְעֲנוּגִין כַּדְקָא יָאוּת, וּבַעְיָא לְפַקְדָא
לְחֵילָהָא, מִתְכַּנְּשִׁין כֻּלְּהוּ, וְקַרְיָין לָהּ מִגּוֹ הֵיכָלָא קַדִּישָׁא, כְּבוֹד כָּבוֹד
כָּבוֹד. בְּהֵיכָלָא קַדִּישָׁא אַבָּא וְאִמָּא, פַּתְחֵי וְאָמְרֵי מְקוּדָשׁ מְקוּדָשׁ.
כְּדֵין יַרְחָא אִתְקַדַּשׁ כַּדְקָא יָאוּת. וּבַחֹדֶשׁ הָרִאשׁוֹן,
רִאשׁוֹן וַדַּאי, וע"ד מִשְׁכוּ וְגוֹ'. וע"ד בֶּעָשׂוֹר לַחֹדֶשׁ הַזֶּה, דְּאִתְחַבַּר
סִיהֲרָא בְּשִׁמְשָׁא, וּמָה דַּהֲוַת נְקוּדָה חֲדָא, כַּד נַחְתָּא אִתְפְּשַׁט זְעֵיר
זְעֵיר, וְאִתְמַלְּיָיא, וְאִתְעֲבֵידַת ה', מַלְיָיא מִכָּל סִטְרִין, מִתְקַדְּשָׁא כַּדְקָא
יָאוּת.

717. When she receives a Soul of delights, as is fitting, and she wants to visit
her hosts, they all gather together and call her: Glory, glory, glory from the
holy temple OF ABA AND IMA. And in the holy temple itself, Aba and Ima,
NAMELY, CHOCHMAH AND BINAH, open by saying: Sanctified, sanctified!
IN OTHER WORDS THEY EMANATE TO MALCHUT FROM THEIR LIGHTS
WHICH ARE CALLED 'HOLINESS'. Then the month, WHICH IS MALCHUT, is

sanctified properly. And it is then written: "And on...the first month" (Bemidbar 28:16), for it is certainly the first. And it is therefore THEN WRITTEN ABOUT HER: "AND ON...THE FIRST MONTH." And therefore, SCRIPTURE SAYS: "Draw out and take you lambs..." (Shemot 12:21), THE MEANING OF WHICH IS: DRAW DOWN THE UPPER DAYS OF ZEIR ANPIN TO MALCHUT, and it is therefore WRITTEN: "On the tenth day of this month" (Ibid. 3), THE MEANING OF WHICH IS THAT the moon, WHICH IS MALCHUT, has become joined to the sun, WHICH IS ZEIR ANPIN, NAMELY, THAT THE NINE SFIROT OF ZEIR ANPIN WILL USE AND ILLUMINATE IN MALCHUT. And whereas she was a single point AFTER THE CONTRACTION, when she descended, she now expands bit by bit and fills out and becomes the FINAL Hei OF YUD HEI VAV HEI, which is full OF EMANATION from all FOUR directions and is properly sanctified.

A Synopsis

The Faithful Shepherd adds information about how the moon, Malchut, becomes full and is joined to the sun.

רעיא מהימנא

718. אִסְתְּחַר הַהוּא הֵיכָלָא, וּפָתַח תַּרְעָא אַחֲרָא דִּסְטָר דָּרוֹם בְּשַׁבְעִין וּתְרֵין עִטְרִין. לְבָתַר אַפְתַּח תַּרְעָא תְּלִיתָאָה, לְסְטַר מִזְרָח, בְּחַמְשִׁין נְהוֹרִין, דְּחַמְשִׁין תַּרְעִין דְּבִינָה. לְבָתַר אַפְתַּח תַּרְעָא אַחֲרָא דִּלְסְטַר מַעֲרָב, בְּע"ב עִטְרִין, וְכֻלְּהוּ רמ"ח בְּחוּשְׁבַּן תֵּיבִין דְּפָרְשִׁיָּין דק"ש. וּמַה דִּבְקַדְמֵיתָא הַהִיא חַיָּה הֲוַת זְעֵירָא, בְּהַהוּא זִמְנָא אִתְרַבִּיאַת, הֲדָא הוּא דִּכְתִיב, מְלֹא כָל הָאָרֶץ כְּבוֹדוֹ, דְּאִיהוּ כָּבוֹד עִלָּאָה וְתַתָּאָה.

Ra'aya Meheimna (the Faithful Shepherd)

718. (THE BEGINNING OF THE ARTICLE IS MISSING). That temple turned and opened another gate on the south side, NAMELY, IN THE RIGHT COLUMN, with 72 diadems, WHICH IS THE SECRET OF THE NAME OF 72 THAT ILLUMINATES IN THE RIGHT COLUMN. Later it opens a third gate on the eastern side, WHICH IS THE CENTRAL COLUMN, with fifty lights of the fifty gates of Binah. Next it opens another gate on the western side, WHICH IS THE SECRET OF MALCHUT in the 72 diadems OF THE NAME OF 72, and all the 248 CHASSADIM, being the number of words in the sections of the

reading of Sh'ma. And whereas this animal, WHICH IS MALCHUT, was initially small, at that time, HAVING RECEIVED 72 DIADEMS AND 248 CHASSADIM, she grows, which is as is written: "the whole earth is full of His glory" (Yeshayah 6:3), which is the upper glory and the lower glory, ALL OF WHICH MALCHUT RECEIVES WITH THE DECLARATION OF THE UNITY IN THE READING OF SH'MA.

719. כַּד מָטֵי לְחַ"י עָלְמִין, דְּבֵיה חַ"י בִּרְכָאן דִּצְלוֹתָא, וּפָתַח בֵּיה אֲדֹנָי שְׂפָתַי תִּפְתָּח וּפִי יַגִּיד תְּהִלָּתֶךָ. כְּדֵין עַמּוּדָא דְּאֶמְצָעִיתָא, אִתְחַבַּר בַּהֲדָהּ בִּחֲבִיבוּ דִּנְשִׁיקִין דְּשִׂפְוָון, וְאִינּוּן נֶצַח וְהוֹד, דְּלָשׁוֹן אִיהוּ צַדִּיק בֵּינַיְיהוּ. לְשׁוֹן לְמוּדִים בְּהַהוּא זִמְנָא, וַיִּשַּׁק יַעֲקֹב לְרָחֵל, כְּדֵין קָרָאן לְהַהִיא חַיָּה, כָּבוֹד כָּבוֹד. אַבָּא וְאִימָּא, מְקוּדָּשׁ מְקוּדָּשׁ. כְּדֵין יַרְחָא אִתְקַדְּשָׁא כַּדְקָא יָאוּת, כְּדֵין וּבַחֹדֶשׁ הָרִאשׁוֹן רִאשׁוֹן וַדַּאי.

719. When one reaches the eighteen (Heb. *chai* = living) worlds, in which are the eighteen blessings of the prayer, NAMELY, IN THE AMIDAH PRAYER, which one starts with "Adonai, open my lips; and my mouth shall rehearse Your praise" (Tehilim 51:17), then the Central Column, WHICH IS ZEIR ANPIN, joins with her with affectionate kisses of the lips, WHICH ARE NETZACH AND HOD; with the tongue, which is the Righteous, THAT IS YESOD, between them IN THE SECRET OF the tongue of the learned. At that time "And Jacob kissed Rachel" (Beresheet 29:11), WHERE JACOB IS ZEIR ANPIN AND RACHEL IS MALCHUT, and then that animal, MALCHUT, is called 'Glory, glory'; and Aba and Ima say 'Sanctified, sanctified'. THAT IS, ABA AND IMA EMANATE TO HER THEIR LIGHTS THAT ARE CALLED 'HOLINESS', and then the month, WHICH IS MALCHUT, is properly sanctified. And she is then CALLED "And on...the first month" (Bemidbar 28:16), first without a doubt.

720. וּכְדֵין מִשְׁכוּ. וע"ד בְּעֶשְׂוֹר לַחֹדֶשׁ הַזֶּה, דְּאִתְחַבַּר סִיהֲרָא קַדִּישָׁא בְּשִׁמְשָׁא. דְּאִתְּמַר בֵּיה, כִּי שֶׁמֶשׁ וּמָגֵן יְיָ' אֱלֹהִים. וּמַה דַּהֲוַת נְקוּדָה זְעֵירָא, אִתְמַלְּאַת בְּסִיהֲרָא, וּכְדֵין אִיהִי הַחֹדֶשׁ מָלֵא. וְסִיהֲרָא אִתְמַלְּיָיא מָלֵא כָּל הָאָרֶץ כְּבוֹדוֹ. בְּקַדְמֵיתָא חָסֵר, וּכְעַן בִּשְׁלִימוּ.

ע"כ רעיא מהימנא

720. And then: "Draw out" THE UPPER DAYS OF ZEIR ANPIN TO MALCHUT, which is why IT IS WRITTEN: "On the tenth day of this month" (Shemot 12:3), THE MEANING OF WHICH IS THAT THE NINE DAYS OF ZEIR ANPIN SHINE TOWARDS MALCHUT, NAMELY, that the holy moon, WHICH IS MALCHUT, is joined to the sun, WHICH IS ZEIR ANPIN, about which it is said: "For Hashem Elohim is a sun and a shield" (Tehilim 84:12). And whereas MALCHUT was a small point, she filled out as the FULL moon, and then the month is full, NAMELY, the moon, WHICH IS MALCHUT, is full, and she is: "the whole earth is full of His glory." Initially she was lacking, but now she is complete, FULL.

End of Ra'aya Meheimna

A Synopsis

Rabbi Chiya learns that the Paschal sacrifice is a lamb because a lamb was the idol and deity of the Egyptians, and it was hard for the Egyptians to see their idol tied and held prisoner and sacrificed in the fire. In this way the Egyptians saw the power of the God of Yisrael. Rabbi Elazar turns the conversation to the prohibition against eating leavened bread, and we learn that anyone who eats leavened bread on Pesach is met with death, and he dies in this world and in the World to Come.

721. ר' חִיָּיא פָּתַח, בְּאַרְבָּעָה עָשָׂר יוֹם לַחֹדֶשׁ פֶּסַח וְגוֹ'. אִימְרָא דְּאִיהוּ פִּסְחָא אֲמַאי. אֶלָּא דַּחֲלָא דְּמִצְרָאֵי, וֶאֱלָהָא דִּלְהוֹן, הֲוָה אִמְרָא. בְּגִין דְּמִצְרָאֵי פַּלְחִין לְמַזַּל טָלֶה, וּבג"כ פַּלְחִין לְאִימְרָא. ת"ח, כְּתִיב הֵן נִזְבַּח אֶת תּוֹעֲבַת מִצְרַיִם. מַאי תּוֹעֲבַת מִצְרַיִם. וְכִי עַל דְּשַׂנְאִין לֵיהּ, כְּתִיב תּוֹעֲבַת מִצְרַיִם. אֶלָּא דַּחֲלָא דְּמִצְרָאֵי, וֶאֱלָהָא דִּילְהוֹן, אִקְרֵי תּוֹעֲבַת מִצְרַיִם. כְּמָה דִּכְתִיב, כְּתוֹעֲבֹת הַגּוֹיִם, דַּחֲלָא דִּשְׁאַר עַמִּין.

721. Rabbi Chiya opened by quoting: "And on the fourteenth day of the first month is the Pesach (Passover)" (Bemidbar 28:16). HE ASKS: Why is the paschal sacrifice a lamb? HE ANSWERS, the Egyptians worshipped the lamb, which was one of their deities, for they worshipped the constellation Aries. Come and see: It is written: "for we shall sacrifice the abomination of Egypt" (Shemot 8:22). What is meant by "the abomination of Egypt?" Could it be that because it is hateful to them it is called "the abomination of Egypt?" On

the contrary, it is called "the abomination of Egypt" because it is the Egyptians' idol and their deity. It is similarly written: "the abominations of those nations" (Devarim 18:9), THE MEANING OF WHICH IS the idol of these nations.

722. ת"ח חָכְמְתָא דְּיוֹסֵף, דִּכְתִּיב וּמִקְצֵה אֶחָיו לָקַח חֲמִשָּׁה אֲנָשִׁים, וְאוֹלִיף לוֹן לְמֵימַר, אַנְשֵׁי מִקְנֶה הָיוּ עֲבָדֶיךָ. וְכִי מַלְכָּא דַּהֲוָה שַׁלִּיט עַל כָּל אַרְעָא, וְאַבָּא לְמַלְכָּא, עָבֵיד כְּדָא, וְעָבֵיד לַאֲחוֹי וְיִשַּׂנְאוּן לְהוֹן, וְלָא יַחְשְׁבוּן לְהוֹן. אֶלָּא וַדַּאי תּוֹעֲבַת מִצְרַיִם, דַּחֲלָא וֶאֱלָהָא דִּילְהוֹן אִקְרֵי הָכִי, וע"ד כְּתִיב, הֵן נִזְבַּח אֶת תּוֹעֲבַת מִצְרַיִם.

722. Come and see the wisdom of Joseph, as is written: "And he took some of his brothers, five men" (Beresheet 47:2), and he taught them to say "Your servants are shepherds" (Ibid. 3). And would a king who was ruler over the country and who was like a father to the king have done such a thing to his brothers to make THE EGYPTIANS hate them and not show them consideration? – IF YOU HOLD THE VIEW THAT THE ABOMINATION OF THE EGYPTIANS IS EVERY SHEPHERD, WHICH MEANS HATED BY THE EGYPTIANS. But in reality the abomination of the Egyptians is what their idol and their deity was called. Therefore is it written: "For we shall sacrifice the abomination of Egypt" (Shemot 8:22) MEANING THEIR DEITY.

723. אָמַר יוֹסֵף, כָּל מֵיטַב מִצְרַיִם הִיא אֶרֶץ רַעְמְסֵס, וְהַהִיא אַרְעָא אַפְרִישׁוּ לְדַחֲלָא דִּלְהוֹן, לְרַעְיָא וּלְמֵיהַךְ בְּכָל עִנּוּגִין דְּעָלְמָא. וְכָל מִצְרָאֵי חֲשִׁיבוּ לְאִינּוּן דְּרָעָאן לְדַחֲלֵיהוֹן, כְּדַחֲלֵיהוֹן. אֲעָבֵיד לְאַחַי דְּיַרְתּוּן הַהִיא אַרְעָא, וְיִסְגְּדוּן לוֹן מִצְרָאֵי, וְיַחְשְׁבוּן לוֹן כַּדְקָא יָאוּת. וְהַיְינוּ דִּכְתִּיב כִּי תּוֹעֲבַת מִצְרַיִם כָּל רוֹעֵה צֹאן, מְחַשְּׁבִין לוֹן כְּדַחֲלֵיהוֹן.

723. Joseph said, All the best of Egypt is the land of Rameses, and this part of the country they set aside for their idol, NAMELY, THE FLOCKS, for them to be pastured and go THERE to their hearts' delight. And all the Egyptians considered those who tended their idols as themselves idols. HE SAID: I shall arrange it so that my brothers inherit that country, and the Egyptians shall

bow down to them, and will accord them proper treatment, and this is what is written: "for every shepherd is an abomination to the Egyptians" (Beresheet 47:34). Which is FOR THIS REASON, they should treat them as their deity.

724. א״ר יוֹסֵי, וְהָא תָּנֵינָן כְּמָה דְּאִתְפְּרַע קוּדְשָׁא בְּרִיךְ הוּא מֵאִינוּן דְּפַלְחֵי לַע״ז, הָכִי אִתְפְּרַע מֵע״ז מַמָּשׁ, וְכִי יוֹסֵף עָבֵיד לַאֲחוֹי ע״ז. א״ל, לָא עָבֵיד יוֹסֵף לַאֲחוֹי ע״ז, אֶלָּא עָבֵיד לוֹן לְשַׁלְטָאָה עַל ע״ז דִּילְהוֹן, וּלְאַכְפְּיָא ע״ז דִּילְהוֹן תְּחוֹת יְדַיְיהוּ, וּלְרַדָּאָה לוֹן בַּמַּקֵּל. אָמַר יוֹסֵף, אִי יִשְׁלְטוֹן אַחַי עַל ע״ז דִּילְהוֹן, כ״ש דְּיִשְׁלְטוֹן עַל גַּרְמַיְיהוּ, וּבג״כ אוֹתִיב לוֹן בְּמֵיטַב אַרְעָא, וְאַשְׁלִיט לוֹן עַל כָּל אַרְעָא.

724. Rabbi Yosi said: Haven't we learned, just as the Holy One, blessed be He, punishes idolaters, so will He punish idolatry itself? If this is so, why did Joseph make his brothers into idols, THAT THE EGYPTIANS SHOULD BOW DOWN TO THEM AS THOUGH THEY WERE DEITIES? He replied to him: Joseph did not make his brothers into idols but into rulers over the idolatry of the Egyptians, subdue their idolatry under the hand OF HIS BROTHERS, and smite it with the rod. Joseph said: If my brothers control their idolatry, how much more will they rule over them themselves, which is why he settled them in the best of the country and made them rulers over all the land.

725. וע״ד אָמְרָא דְּאִיהוּ פֶּסַח אֲמַאי. אֶלָּא דַּחֲלָא דְּמִצְרָאֵי, וֶאֱלָהָא דִּילְהוֹן הֲוָה אִימְרָא. אָמַר קוּדְשָׁא בְּרִיךְ הוּא, מִבְּעֲשׂוֹר לַחֹדֶשׁ סִיבוּ דַּחֲלָא דִּילְהוֹן דְּמִצְרָאֵי, וְתִפְשׂוּ לֵיהּ, וִיהֵא אָסוּר וְתָפִישׁ בְּתְפִישָׁה דִּילְכוֹן, יוֹמָא חַד וּתְרֵין וְג׳, וּבְיוֹמָא ד׳, אַפִּיקוּ לֵיהּ לְדִינָא, וְאִתְכְּנָשׁוּ עֲלֵיהּ.

725. And so, why is the paschal sacrifice a lamb? THE ANSWER IS because a lamb was the idol and deity of the Egyptians. The Holy One, blessed be He: 'From the tenth of the month, take the fear of the Egyptians, capture and bind it and let it be imprisoned and hold it in your keeping one day, and two, and three days, and on the fourth day carry out its sentence, and assemble over it'.

726. וּבְשַׁעְתָּא דְמִצְרָאֵי הֲווֹ שַׁמְעִין קָל דַּחֲלָא דִּילְהוֹן, דְּתָפִישׂ בִּתְפִישָׂה דְּיִשְׂרָאֵל, וְלָא יַכְלִין לְשֵׁזָבָא לֵיהּ, הֲווֹ בָּכָאן, וַהֲוָה קַשְׁיָא עֲלַיְיהוּ, כְּאִילּוּ גַּרְמַיְיהוּ אִתְעֲקִידוּ לִקְטָלָא. אָמַר קוּדְשָׁא בְּרִיךְ הוּא, יְהֵא תָּפִישׂ בִּרְשׁוּתַיְיכוּ, יוֹמָא בָּתַר יוֹמָא, אַרְבָּעָה יוֹמִין, בְּגִין דְּיֶחֱמוּן יָתֵיהּ תָּפִישׂ, וּבְיוֹמָא ד' אַפִּיקוּ לֵיהּ לִקְטָלָא, וְיֶחֱמוּן לֵיהּ מִצְרָאֵי הֵיךְ אַתּוּן עַבְדִּין בֵּיהּ דִּינָא, וְדָא קַשְׁיָא לְהוֹ מִן כָּל מַכְתְּשֵׁי דְּעָבֵד לוֹן קוּדְשָׁא בְּרִיךְ הוּא, אִינּוּן דִּינִין דְּיַעַבְדוּן בְּדַחֲלֵיהוֹן.

726. And when the Egyptians heard the voice of their idol which was being held by Yisrael, and they were unable to rescue it, they cried and it was as difficult for them as though they themselves had been tied up for the kill. The Holy One, blessed be He said: 'Let it be in your possession day after day for four days, so that THE EGYPTIANS may see it bound and imprisoned, and on the fourth day, bring it out to be killed and let the Egyptians see how you enact judgment on it.' And this, NAMELY, THESE JUDGMENTS THAT THEY PERFORMED ON THEIR IDOL, was harder for them to bear than all the plagues that the Holy One, blessed be He, brought on them.

727. לְבָתַר דַּיְינִין לֵיהּ בְּנוּרָא, דִּכְתִיב פְּסִילֵי אֱלֹהֵיהֶם תִּשְׂרְפוּן בָּאֵשׁ. אָמַר קוּדְשָׁא בְּרִיךְ הוּא, אַל תֹּאכְלוּ מִמֶּנּוּ נָא. דְּלָא יֵימְרוּן בִּרְעוּתָא וּבְתִיאוּבְתָּא דְּדַחֲלָנָא, אַכְלִין לֵיהּ הָכִי. אֶלָּא אַתְקִינוּ לֵיהּ צָלִי, וְלָא מְבוּשָׁל, דְּאִלּוּ מְבוּשָׁל יְהֵא טָמִיר, וְלָא יֶחֱמוּן לֵיהּ, אֶלָּא תִּקּוּנָא דִּילֵיהּ דְּיֶחֱמוּן לֵיהּ הָכִי מוֹקְדָא בְּנוּרָא, בְּגִין דְּרֵיחֵיהּ נוֹדֵף.

727. Subsequently, they cast it into the fire, as it is written: "and burn their carved idols with fire" of their deities (Devarim 7:5). The Holy One, blessed be He said: "Eat not of it raw" (Shemot 12:9) so that THE EGYPTIANS will not say: They were so desirous of, and had such a longing for our idol that they ate it INSUFFICIENTLY ROASTED. But it was decreed that it should be eaten roasted and not boiled, for had it been boiled it would have been covered UNDER THE WATER IN THE PAN, and they would not have seen it, but the way to deal with it is that they should see it thus being burnt in the fire, since its odor then spreads FAR AND WIDE.

728. וְתוּ רֵישֵׁיה עָלֵיה כָּפוּף עַל קַרְסוּלוֹי, דְּלָא יֵימְרוּן דְּחַיָּה, אוֹ מִלָּה אַחֲרָא הוּא, אֶלָּא דְּיִשְׁתְּמוֹדְעוּן לֵיה, דְּאִיהוּ דַּחֲלָא דִּלְהוֹן. וְתוּ, דְּלָא יֵיכְלוּן לֵיה. בְּתִיאוּבְתָּא, אֶלָּא עַל שַׂבְעָא, אֹרַח קְלָנָא וּבִזְיוֹן. וְתוּ, עֶצֶם לֹא תִשְׁבְּרוּ בוֹ, אֶלָּא דְּיֶחֱמוּן גַּרְמוֹי רָמָאן בְּשׁוּקָא, וְלָא יֵיכְלוּן לְשֵׁזָבָא לֵיה. וְעַ"ד כְּתִיב, וּבֵאלֹהֵיהֶם עָשָׂה ה' שְׁפָטִים. דִּינִין סַגִּיאִין. תּוּ וּמַקֶּלְכֶם בְּיֶדְכֶם, וְלָא חַרְבָּא וְרוֹמְחָא וּשְׁאַר מָאנֵי קְרָבָא.

728. Moreover, its head bent to its legs so that they should not say that it was some animal or other thing, but that they should recognize it as their idol. Moreover, it was not to be eaten out of lust, but on a full stomach by way of disgrace and contempt. Moreover, "neither shall you break a bone of it" (Ibid. 46), but they should see its bones cast into the marketplace and be unable to rescue it. For this reason it is written: "Upon their Elohim also Hashem executed judgments" (Bemidbar 33:4), that is, many judgments. Moreover, "and your staff in your hand" (Shemot 12:11), but not a sword, spear, nor any other instrument of war, IN ORDER TO DEMONSTRATE THAT YOU ARE NOT AFRAID OF THEM.

729. אָמַר ר' יְהוּדָה, הָא אוֹקְמוּהָ, דְּמִצְרָאֵי פַּלְחֵי לְמַזַּל טָלֶה, וּבְג"כ פַּלְחִין לְאִימְרָא. א"ר יוֹסֵי, אִי הָכִי, טָלֶה יִפְלְחוּן, וְלָא אִימְרָא. א"ל, בְּלָא פַּלְחִין, אֶלָּא מַזַּל טָלֶה נָחִית וְסַלִּיק בְּטָלֶה וְאִימְרָא, וּבְג"כ פַּלְחִין לְכֹלָּא. א"ל הָכִי שְׁמַעְנָא, דְּכָל בְּעִירָא רַבָּא דַּחֲלָא דִּלְהוֹן הֲוָה, וְעַ"ד קָטִיל קוּדְשָׁא בְּרִיךְ הוּא כָּל בְּכוֹר בִּבְהֵמָה. וְהָא אִתְּמַר דְּאִלֵּין אִינוּן דַּרְגִּין דִּלְעֵילָּא, דְּאִקְרוּן הָכִי.

729. Rabbi Yehuda said: We have already learned that the Egyptians worshipped the constellation of Aries, which is why they worshipped the lamb. Rabbi Yosi said: If that is so, they should have worshipped a ram, A BABY RAM, rather than a lamb. He answered him: They worshipped them all. But the constellation of Aries ascends and descends, SOMETIMES APPEARING as a ram and AT OTHERS like a LARGE lamb, for which reason they worshipped them all. He said to him: What I have heard is that every large animal was an idol for them, which is why the Holy One, blessed be He, killed all the firstborn of the cattle. And we have already learned that these

were the grades on high: NAMELY, UPPER SPIRITUAL FORCES OF
IMPURITY, which are so called 'FIRSTBORN OF CATTLE', AND THAT WAS
WHY THEY WORSHIPPED THEM.

730. א"ר אֶלְעָזָר, כְּתִיב כָּל מַחְמֶצֶת לֹא תֹאכֵלוּ, וּכְתִיב לֹא יֵאָכֵל
חָמֵץ. אֶלָּא דָּא דְּכַר, וְדָא נוּקְבָּא. אר"ש, אֶלְעָזָר בְּרִי, בְּדָא כְּתִיב לֹא
תֹאכֵלוּ, וּבְדָא כְּתִיב לֹא יֵאָכֵל, אֲמַאי לָא כְּתִיב לֹא תֹאכֵלוּ. אֶלָּא,
נוּקְבָּא דְּאִיהִי אַסְטִיאַת אָרְחָהָא, בְּאַזְהָרָה וַדַּאי, דְּכַר דְּאִיהוּ אָחִיד
בְּחוּטָא דְּדַכְיוּ יַתִּיר, בְּבַקָּשָׁה. וְעַל דָּא כְּתִיב, לֹא יֵאָכֵל, לֹא תֹאכֵלוּ.

730. Rabbi Elazar said: It is written: "You shall eat nothing leavened" (Heb.
machmetzet) (Shemot 12:20), and: "no leavened bread shall be eaten" (Heb.
chametz) (Shemot 13:3). WHAT IS THE DIFFERENCE BETWEEN
'MACHMETZET' AND 'CHAMETZ'? The latter is masculine, while the former is
feminine. Rabbi Shimon said: Elazar, my son, in the former case it is written,
"You shall eat nothing" while in the latter case it is written, "no... shall be
eaten." Why in the latter case, does it not say: "You shall eat no LEAVENED
BREAD"? HE ANSWERS THAT with the female, who MUCH MORE corrupts
her ways, THE STATEMENT is by way of warning: "YOU SHALL EAT
NOTHING." BUT IN THE CASE OF the male OF THE KLIPOT, who is more
inclined to grasp a thread of purity THAN THE FEMALE, THE STATEMENT IS
by way of request: "NO...SHALL BE EATEN," WHICH IS NOT THE
LANGUAGE OF WARNING OR COMMAND. This is why it is written IN THE
ONE CASE "no...shall be eaten," AND IN THE OTHER CASE "You shall eat
nothing."

731. א"ל אַבָּא, וְהָא כְּתִיב לֹא תֹאכַל עָלָיו חָמֵץ. א"ל, אַסְגֵּי תָּבִין
יְתִירִין לִיקָרָא לְקָרְבְּנָא. אֲבָל בְּקַדְמֵיתָא בְּבַקָּשָׁה לֹא יֵאָכֵל. אֲבָל
לְבָתַר בְּאַזְהָרָה, לֹא תֹאכְלוּ, דְּהוּא קַשְׁיָא מִתַּרְוַויְיהוּ. מַחְמֶצֶת מ"ט.
בְּגִין דְּרֵיחָא דְּמוֹתָא אִית תַּמָּן. חָמֵץ, דְּכַר. מַחְמֶצֶת, נוּקְבָּא. רַגְלֶיהָ
יוֹרְדוֹת מָוֶת, בְּרֵישָׁא וְסֵיפָא דְּתֵיבָה, תִּשְׁכַּח לָהּ. וּבְגִין דָּא מַאן דְּאָכִיל
חָמֵץ בְּפֶסַח, אִיהוּ אַקְדִּימַת לֵיהּ מוֹתָא, וְלִינְדַע דְּמִית הוּא בְּעָלְמָא
דֵין, וּבְעָלְמָא דְּאָתֵי, כְּתִיב וְנִכְרְתָה הַנֶּפֶשׁ הַהִיא.

731. He said to him: But father, it is also written: "You shall eat no leavened bread with it" (Devarim 16:3), NAMELY, THE LANGUAGE OF WARNING IS ALSO USED FOR *CHAMETZ*, WHICH IS THE MALE OF THE KLIPAH. He replied: In honor of the sacrifice, Scripture uses many extra words, AND THEREFORE SAYS: "YOU SHALL EAT NO LEAVENED BREAD WITH IT." But initially IT WAS SAID ABOUT *CHAMETZ*, "no leavened bread shall be eaten," WHICH is THE LANGUAGE of request. But subsequently, ABOUT *MACHMETZET*, a warning IS USED: "You shall eat nothing," for THE FEMALE OF THE KLIPOT is the most hardened of the two of them, OF THE MALE AND FEMALE OF THE KLIPAH. What is the reason for *machmetzet* BEING SO CALLED? It is because there is a smell of death there. *Chametz* ALLUDES TO the male AND HAS THEREFORE NO ALLUSION TO DEATH, but *machmetzet* is female. AND IT IS WRITTEN: "Her feet go down to death" (Mishlei 5:5). THUS, the first and last letters of the word *MACHMETZET* ARE MEM AND TAV THAT spell DEAD (HEB. *MET* - MEM TAV). Thus she, THE FEMALE, greets anyone who eats leavened bread on Pesach with death, and it should be known that he dies in this world and in the World to Come, as it is written: "even that soul shall be cut off" (Shemot 12:19).

732. מַצָּה אֲמַאי אִתְקְרִיאַת מַצָּה. אֶלָּא הָכִי תָּנֵינָן, שַׁדַּי: בְּגִין דְּאָמַר לְעוֹלְמוֹ דַּי, דְּיֹאמַר לְצָרוֹתֵינוּ דַּי. אוֹף הָכִי מַצָּה, בְּגִין דְּקָא מְשַׁדֵּד דִּמְבָרְחַת לְכָל סִטְרִין בִּישִׁין, וְעָבֵיד קְטָטָה בְּהוּ, כְּגַוְונָא דְּשַׁדַּי דִּמְזוּזָה, דִּמְבְרִיחַ לְשֵׁדִים וּמַזִּיקִים דְּתַרְעָא, אוֹף הָכִי אִיהִי מַבְרְחַת לוֹן מִכָּל מִשְׁכְּנֵי קְדוּשָׁה, וְעָבֵיד מְרִיבָה וּקְטָטָה בְּהוּ. כד"א, מַסָּה וּמְרִיבָה. ע"ד כְּתִיב מַצָּה. וְהָא מַסָּה בְּסָמֶךְ אִיהוּ. אֶלָּא תַּרְגּוּמוֹ דְּמַסָּה, אִיהוּ מְצוּתָא.

732. Why is unleavened bread called 'matzah'? It is as we have learned, Shadai, WHICH IS INTERPRETED as MEANING, May He who (Heb. *she*) said to His world Enough (Heb. *dai*), say to our troubles Enough, NAMELY, MAY HE CHASE AWAY FROM US JUDGMENTS AND TROUBLES. Matzah is likewise, for it subdues and subjugates; namely, it chases away the evil ones of all sides and makes a quarrel with them, just as the name Shadai of the mezuzah chases away the evil spirits and demons that are at the gate. So, too, MATZAH chases them away from all the dwellings of holiness, and makes a quarrel (Heb. *merivah*) and a fight with them, as it is written: "Masah and Merivah" (Shemot 17:7), and therefore the name is written as matzah. HE ASKS, but masah is spelled with a Samech, AND NOT WITH A TZADIK? HE

ANSWERS THAT the Aramaic translation of Masah is matzuta. HENCE MATZAH IS SPELLED WITH TZADIK.

A Synopsis

The Faithful Shepherd talks about the ten plagues and about God's intention to punish all the rulers of Egypt because they misled mankind and made themselves divine. He examines the reason why unleavened bread was to be eaten for seven days, and he brings in the factors of the seven Sfirot and the seven planets and the seven blessings.

רעיא מהימנא

733. אָמַר רַעְיָא מְהֵימָנָא, כְּגוֹן לִישָׁנָא דְּאִיהוּ מַקֵּל לְכָל אַנְשֵׁי בֵּיתֵיהּ, וְאִיהוּ לִישָׁנָא דְּאָת ו', וְאִיהוּ מַטֶּה דְּבֵיהּ עֲשַׂר אוֹתִיּוֹת, וּבֵיהּ מְחָא קוּדְשָׁא בְּרִיךְ הוּא עַל יְדוֹי י' מְחָאן. וּבְגִין דְּכָל מְחָאן הֲוֹו מִסִּטְרָא דְּה' ה', ר' עֲקִיבָא אוֹמֵר, מְנַיִן שֶׁכָּל מַכָּה וּמַכָּה שֶׁהֵבִיא הַקָּדוֹשׁ בָּרוּךְ הוּא עַל הַמִּצְרִים בְּמִצְרַיִם הָיְתָה שֶׁל חָמֵשׁ מַכּוֹת וְכוּ', אֱמֹר מֵעַתָּה וְכוּ'. וְאָת ה' סַלְקָא בָּאת י' לְחַמְשִׁין מְחָאן, חָמֵשׁ זְמָנִין חַמְשִׁין, אִינּוּן ר"ן. וּבְג"ד, וְעַל הַיָּם לָקוּ ר"ן מַכּוֹת.

Ra'aya Meheimna (the Faithful Shepherd)

733. The Faithful Shepherd said: Just as the tongue is a rod over all members of the household, FOR HE CHASTISES THEM WITH HIS TONGUE, WHICH IS THE SAME FOR THEM AS THOUGH HE HAS CHASTISED THEM WITH A ROD; and as the tongue is the secret of the letter Vav, WHICH IS ZEIR ANPIN THAT IS CALLED YUD HEI VAV HEI, and is a rod in which are ten letters; FOR YUD HEI VAV HEI, WHEN SPELLED OUT FULLY WITH ALEPHS, HAS TEN LETTERS YUD-VAV-DALET, HEI-ALEPH, VAV-ALEPH -VAV, HEI-ALEPH and with it the Holy One, blessed be He, smote them with ten plagues through it; and since all the plagues were from the side of the two Hei's OF THE YUD HEI VAV HEI, THEREFORE Rabbi Akiva says: How do we know that each plague that the Holy One, blessed be He, brought down on the Egyptians in Egypt consisted of five plagues? We should deduce from this that... And the letter Hei (whose numerical value is

five) times the letter Yud (whose numerical value is ten) gives fifty plagues, and Hei times fifty is 250, which is why at the sea they were smitten with 250 plagues.

734. אָמַר יוֹסֵף, כָּל מֵיטַב אֶרֶץ מִצְרַיִם רַעְמְסֵס הִיא, וְהַהִיא אַרְעָא אַפְרִישׁוּ לְדַחֲלָן דִּלְהוֹן, לְרַעְיָא וּלְמֵיהַךְ בְּכָל עִנּוּגִין דְּעָלְמָא. וְכָל מִצְרָאֵי חָשִׁיבוּן לְאִינּוּן דְּרָעָן לְדַחֲלֵיהוֹן, כִּדְחֲלֵיהוֹן. וְדָא שָׁאִיל יוֹסֵף מִפַּרְעֹה, לְשַׁלְטָאָה אֲחוֹי עַל דַּחֲלָן דְּמִצְרָאֵי, דְּאִתְכַּפְיָין תְּחוֹת יְדֵיהּ, כְּעַבְדִּים בָּתַר מַלְכֵּיהוֹן, לְמֶהֱוֵי כֻּלְּהוּ מִתְכַּפְיָין תְּחוֹת שֵׁם יְיָ' מִסִּטְרַיְיהוֹן, וְלָא שַׁלִּיט בְּעָלְמָא אֶלָּא שֵׁם יְדֹוָד. וְאִתְכַּפְיָין כָּל מְמָנָן תְּחוֹת יְדֵיהּ.

734. Joseph said, the best of the land of Egypt, which is Rameses – and this is the land that they set aside for their idol to pasture in to its heart's content. And all the Egyptians considered those who tend their idols as themselves idols. And this is why Joseph requested from Pharaoh THE LAND OF RAMESES TO TEND THEIR FLOCKS, in order to place his brothers in control over the deities of Egypt, so that they should be subjugated under them as slaves under their king, and that all of them should be subjugated under the Name of Yud Hei Vav Hei on their part, and that none should rule in the world excepting the Name of Yud Hei Vav Hei, and that all the appointed chieftains should also be subjugated to Him.

735. וּלְאַחֲזָאָה לוֹן, דְּאִיהוּ עָתִיד לְאִיתְפָּרְעָא מִנְּהוֹן, הה"ד, וּבְכָל אֱלֹהֵי מִצְרַיִם אֶעֱשֶׂה שְׁפָטִים אֲנִי יְדֹוָד. כַּד מַטְעַיִין לִבְרַיָּין וְעָבְדִין גַּרְמַיְיהוּ אֱלוֹהוּת. וּבְגִין דְּטָלֶה מְמָנָא דִּילֵיהּ, אִיהוּ רַב עַל כָּל מְמָנָן דֶּאֱלֹהִים אַחֵרִים, מָנֵי קוּדְשָׁא בְּרִיךְ הוּא לְיִשְׂרָאֵל, וְיִקְחוּ לָהֶם אִישׁ שֶׂה לְבֵית אָבוֹת שֶׂה לַבָּיִת, וְאַשְׁלִיט לוֹן עֲלֵיהּ, וְתַפְשֵׂי לֵיהּ תָּפִישׂ בִּתְפִישָׂה דִּלְהוֹן יוֹמָא וּתְרֵין וּתְלַת. וּלְבָתַר דָּא אַפִּיקוּ לֵיהּ לְדִינָא לְעֵינֵי כָּל מִצְרָאֵי, לְאַחֲזָאָה דֶאֱלָהָא דִּלְהוֹן בִּרְשׁוּ דְיִשְׂרָאֵל לְמֶעְבַּד בֵּיהּ דִּינָא.

735. And to show them that He will in the future punish them, as it is written: "and against all the Elohim of Egypt I will execute judgments: I am

Hashem" (Shemot 12:12), because they mislead mankind and make themselves divine; and since the appointee of the ram is greater than the appointees of the other Elohim, the Holy One, blessed be He, commanded Yisrael: "They shall take to them every man a lamb, according to the house of their fathers, a lamb for a house" (Ibid. 3); and He gave them control over it, and they took hold of it as they did for one day, and for two and three days, and subsequently they brought it out for judgments before the eyes of all Egypt, to demonstrate that their deity is at Yisrael's disposal to punish it.

736. בג״ד, אַל תֹּאכְלוּ מִמֶּנּוּ נָא וּבָשֵׁל מְבוּשָׁל בַּמַּיִם כִּי אִם צְלִי אֵשׁ רֹאשׁוֹ עַל כְּרָעָיו וְעַל קִרְבּוֹ, לְמֶהֱוֵי דָן בְּאֵשׁ צָלִי, וּמָנֵי לְזַרְקָא לְגַרְמֵיהּ דִּילֵיהּ בְּשׁוּקָא בְּבִזְוּי. וּבג״ד, וְעֶצֶם לֹא תִשְׁבְּרוּ בוֹ. וּמָנֵי לְיוֹמָא ד׳, בָּתַר דַּהֲוָה תָּפִישׂ ג׳ יוֹמִין קָשׁוּר, לְמֶעְבַּד בֵּיהּ דִּינָא. וְדָא קַשְׁיָא לוֹן מִכָּל מַכְתְּשִׁין דְּמָחָא לוֹן קוּדְשָׁא בְּרִיךְ הוּא, עַל יְדָא דְּרַעְיָא מְהֵימְנָא. וְלֹא עוֹד, אֶלָּא הַמְּנֵי דְּלָא לְמֵיכַל לֵיהּ בְּתִיאוּבְתָּא. וּמִיַּד דְּחָמָאן גַּרְמוֹי בְּשׁוּקָא, וְלָא יַכְלִין לְשֵׁזָבָא לֵיהּ, דָּא קַשְׁיָא לוֹן מִכֹּלָּא. וְלֹא עוֹד, אֶלָּא דְּאִתְמַר בְּהוּ, וּמַקֶּלְכֶם בְּיֶדְכֶם, לְאִתְכַּפְיָיא כָּל דַּחֲלָן דְּמִצְרָאֵי, תְּחוֹת יְדַיְיהוּ. וּבְגִין דְּאִינְהוּ בְּכוֹרוֹת מִמָּנָן, כְּתִיב וַיְיָ׳ הִכָּה כָל בְּכוֹר.

736. Therefore it is written: "Eat not of it raw, nor boiled at all in water, but roast with fire; its head with its legs, and with its entrails" (Shemot 12:9), so that it should be punished in the roasting fire. And He commanded that its bones be cast with contempt into the marketplace, wherefore it is written: "Neither shall you break a bone of it" (Ibid. 46). And He commanded that on the fourth day, after it had been bound for three days, judgment be enacted upon it. And this was harder for them than all the plagues with which the Holy One, blessed be He, smote them through the Faithful Shepherd. Furthermore, He commanded that it not be eaten with appetite, BUT WITH A FULL STOMACH. And immediately on their seeing its bones in the marketplace and being unable to rescue it, this was the most difficult thing for them. Furthermore, it is said about them: "and your staff in your hand" (Ibid. 11), to subdue all the idols of Egypt under their hands. And since their Elohim are the firstborn of the chieftains, it is written: "Hashem smote all the firstborn" (Ibid. 29).

737. בָּתַר כָּל דָּא כְּתִיב, לֹא יֵאָכֵל חָמֵץ שִׁבְעַת יָמִים תֹּאכַל עָלָיו
מַצּוֹת לֶחֶם עוֹנִי. וּכְתִיב כָּל מַחְמֶצֶת לֹא תֹאכֵלוּ. אָמְרוּ רַעְיָא מְהֵימָנָא,
אֲמַאי מָנֵי דְּלָא לְמֵיכַל חָמֵץ שִׁבְעַת יוֹמִין, וּלְמֵיכַל בְּהוֹן מַצָּה. וַאֲמַאי
לֹא יֵאָכֵל, וַאֲמַאי לֹא תֹאכֵלוּ. אֶלָּא ז' כֹּכְבֵי לֶכֶת וְאִינוּן: שצ"ם
חנכ"ל. וְאִינוּן מִסִּטְרָא דְּטוֹב וָרָע, נְהוֹרָא דִּלְגוֹ מַצָּה. קְלִיפָה דִּלְבַר
חָמֵץ. וְאִינוּן חָמֵץ דְּכַר מַחְמֶצֶת נוּקְבָא.

737. And after all this, it is written: "no leavened bread (Heb. *chametz*) shall be eaten" (Shemot 13:3), "seven days you shall you eat unleavened bread (Heb. *matzot*) with it, the bread of affliction" (Devarim 16:3). And it is written: "You shall eat nothing leavened (Heb. *machmetzet*)" (Shemot 12:20). The Faithful Shepherd said: Why did He command not to eat leavened bread for seven days, but to eat on them unleavened bread (Heb. *matzah*)? And why IN ONE CASE is it written: "no...shall be eaten," while in THE OTHER CASE it is written: "You shall eat nothing"? AND HE ANSWERS, there are seven planets, namely Saturn, Jupiter, Mars, Sun, Venus, Mercury, and Moon. And they are from the side of good and evil, for the light that is within is *matzah*, while the Klipah that is on the outside is *chametz*. And the *chametz* is masculine, while *machmetzet* is feminine, AND THEY ARE MALE AND FEMALE OF THAT SAME KLIPAH THAT IS ON THE OUTSIDE. AND ABOUT THE MALE OF THE KLIPAH, WHICH IS NOT THAT GRAVE, IT IS SAID: "NO...SHALL BE EATEN," BUT ABOUT THE FEMALE OF THE KLIPAH, WHICH IS A SERIOUS MATTER, IT IS SAID: "YOU SHALL EAT NOTHING."

738. מַצָּה דִּלְגוֹ שְׁמוּרָה. וְאִינוּן, שֶׁבַע הַנְּעָרוֹת הָרְאוּיוֹת לָתֶת לָהּ
מִבֵּית הַמֶּלֶךְ. וְאִתְּמַר עֲלַיְיהוּ, וּשְׁמַרְתֶּם אֶת הַמַּצּוֹת. מַצָּה אִיהִי
שְׁמוּרָה לְבַעְלָהּ, דְּאִיהוּ ו'. וּבֵיהּ אִתְעֲבֵיד מִצְוָה.

738. The *matzah* that is within THE SEVEN ABOVE-MENTIONED PLANETS is guarded FROM THE KLIPOT, which are "and the seven maidens who were chosen to be given her, out of the king's house" (Ester 2:9). And about them it is said: "And you shall observe (guard) the (commandment of) unleavened bread" (Shemot 12:17). *Matzah* is guarded FROM THE KLIPOT, for her husband, who is Vav, NAMELY, ZEIR ANPIN, WHICH IS THE SECRET OF

THE VAV OF YUD HEI VAV HEI. And *MATZAH* (MEM TZADIK HEI), with it, THE VAV, becomes *mitzvah* (Eng. 'a precept' - Mem Tzadik Vav Hei).

739. וּמַאן דְּנָטִיר לָהּ לְגַבֵּי יָהּ, דִּגְנִיזִין בְּמ"ץ מִן מַצָּה, וְאִינּוּן. י"ם ה"ץ. וּמְנֵי קוּדְשָׁא בְּרִיךְ הוּא לְבָרֵךְ לָהּ שֶׁבַע בִּרְכוֹת לֵיל פֶּסַח, דְּאִינּוּן שֶׁבַע הַנְּעָרוֹת דִּילָהּ, שצ"ם חנכ"ל. וּמְנֵי לְאַעְבְּרָא מִנְּהוֹן חָמֵץ וּמַחְמֶצֶת, דְּאִינּוּן עֲנָנִים חֲשׁוֹכִין דִּמְכַסְּיָין עַל נְהוֹרִין, דְּשִׁבְעָה כֹּכְבֵי לֶכֶת, דְּאִתְּמַר בְּהוֹן וַתָּבֹאנָה אֶל קִרְבֶּנָה וְלֹא נוֹדַע כִּי בָאוּ אֶל קִרְבֶּנָה וּמַרְאֵיהֶן רַע, חָשׁוּךְ כַּאֲשֶׁר בַּתְּחִלָּה. דְּכָל כַּךְ חֲשׁוֹכָא דַעֲנָנִין דִּלְהוֹן, דְּלָא יַכְלִין נְהוֹרִין לְאַנְהָרָא לְהוֹן, וּבְגִין דָּא וְלֹא נוֹדַע כִּי בָאוּ אֶל קִרְבֶּנָה.

ע"כ רעיא מהימנא

739. And he who guards it for Yud-Hei, that are hidden in the Mem Tzadik of *matzah*, FOR, ACCORDING TO THE ATBASH CIPHER, WHERE THE FINAL LETTER, TAV, IS SUBSTITUTED FOR THE FIRST LETTER, ALEPH, AND THE PENULTIMATE LETTER, SHIN, FOR THE SECOND LETTER, BET, Yud is Mem, Hei is Tzadik, AS THE MEM OF *MATZAH* IS REPLACED BY YUD, AND THE TZADIK OF MATZAH IS REPLACED BY HEI, THIS THEREFORE BEING THE SECRET OF YUD-HEI, HIDDEN IN MEM TZADIK OF *MATZAH*. And the Holy One, blessed be He, commanded that MALCHUT be blessed with seven blessings on the Eve of Pesach, namely, her seven maidens, WHICH ARE CALLED 'Saturn', 'Jupiter', 'Mars', 'Sun', 'Venus', 'Mercury', and 'Moon'. And He commanded that THE KLIPOT, WHICH ARE *chametz* (lit. 'leavened bread') and *machmetzet* (lit. 'anything leavened') be removed from them, for they are dark clouds that cover the lights of the seven planets, about which it was saaid: "and when they had eaten them up, it could not be known that they had eaten them; but they were still ill-favored," namely, darkness, "as at the beginning." (Beresheet 41:21). For the darkness of their clouds is so STRONG that the lights THAT ARE IN THE SEVEN PLANETS are unable to illuminate to them, and for this reason: "it could not be known that they had eaten them."

End of Ra'aya Meheimna

106. "Rebuke the wild beast of the reed grass"

A Synopsis

Rabbi Shimon explains the meaning of the wild beast and the reed grass. He says that the reed is the head over all the kingdoms and in the future God will break it like a reed.

740. רִבִּי שִׁמְעוֹן פָּתַח וְאָמַר, גְּעַר חַיַּת קָנֶה עֲדַת אַבִּירִים בְּעֶגְלֵי עַמִּים. גְּעַר חַיַּת, דָּא חַיָּה דְּאִתְאָחַד בָּה עֵשָׂו. קָנֶה: תָּנֵינָן, דְּבְיוֹמָא דְּנָסַב שְׁלֹמֹה מַלְכָּא בַּת פַּרְעֹה, בָּא גַּבְרִיאֵל, נָעַץ קָנֶה בְּיַמָּא רַבָּא, וְעָלֵיהּ אִתְבְּנֵי קַרְתָּא דְרוֹמִי. מַאי קָנֶה. דָּא דְּכוּרָא דְּהַאי חַיָּה בִּישָׁא, דְּאִית לֵיהּ סִטְרָא זְעֵירָא בְּאַחְדוּתָא דִקְדוּשָׁה. וְדָא אִיהוּ קָנֶה, דְּנָעִיץ בְּיַמָּא רַבָּא. וּבְג"כ אִיהוּ שַׁלְטָא עַל עָלְמָא, וְעַל שׁוּלְטָנוּ דָּא כְּתִיב, קָנֶה וָסוּף קָמֵלוּ. קָנֶה, שׁוּלְטָנוּתָא וְרֵאשׁ לְכָל מַלְכָּוָון. תּוּ קָנֶה, דְּזַמִּין קוּדְשָׁא בְּרִיךְ הוּא לְתַבְּרָא לֵיהּ כְּקָנֶה דָּא.

740. Rabbi Shimon opened with: "Rebuke the wild beast of the reed grass, the company of the bulls with the calves of the peoples" (Tehilim 68:31). "Rebuke the wild beast" refers to that beast on to which Esau held. "Reed grass" is as we have learned, for on the day that Solomon married the daughter of Pharaoh, Gabriel came and stuck a reed in the sea, and the city of Rome was built on it. What is "reed?" It is the male of that wicked animal ONTO WHICH ESAU HELD, which has a small part in the unity of holiness, namely the reed that GABRIEL stuck into the great sea. And for this reason it rules the world, and about this rule it is written: "the reeds and rushes shall wither" (Yeshayah 19:6). "Reed" is the regime and head over all kingdoms, and furthermore IT IS FOR THIS REASON CALLED "reed," since in the future the Holy One, blessed be He, is going to break it as a reed.

741. ת"ח, בְּמִצְרַיִם אִיהִי שַׁלְטָא, וּמְנָה נַפְקוּ כַּמָּה שִׁלְטָנִין לְזַנַּיְיהוּ, וְכֹלָא בְּרָזָא דְּחָמֵץ, כֵּיוָן דְּתַבָּר לָהּ קוּדְשָׁא בְּרִיךְ הוּא, אַפִּיק חָמֵץ וְאָעִיל מַצָּה. בְּמָה. בְּחוּטָא זְעֵירָא מִכֹּלָא, תָּבַר ח' חָמֵץ, וְאִתְעֲבֵיד מַצָּה. אִינוּן אַתְוָון. אֶלָּא דְּתָבַר ח' דְּהַאי חַיָּה, דְּאִקְרֵי חָמֵץ. וע"ד

אִקְרֵי חַיַּת קָנֶה, דְּנוֹחַ לְאִתְבְּרָא כְּקָנֶה דָּא. בְּמָה אִתְּבַר. בְּחוּטָא זְעֵירָא כְּנִימָא, תָּבַר ח' וְאִתְעֲבַר מֵאֵיתָנָה, וַהֲוָה מַצָּה. וְע"ד כְּתִיב, גְּעַר חַיַּת קָנֶה, גָּעַר בָּהּ קוּדְשָׁא בְּרִיךְ הוּא, וְאִתְּבַר ח' חָמֵץ, וְאִתְעֲבֵיד ה'.

741. Come and see: In Egypt THAT "WILD BEAST OF THE REED GRASS" rules, and a number of different types of regime issue from it. And they all are in the secret of *chametz*. Since the Holy One, blessed be He, broke it, He removed the *chametz* (lit. 'leavened bread') and introduced *matzah* (lit. 'unleavened bread'). What did He use TO BREAK IT? With the smallest and thinnest thread, He broke the letter Chet of *chametz* (Chet Mem Tzadik). Thus it is called "the wild beasts of the reed grass" because it is as easy to break as is reed. With what was it broken? It was with a thread small as a hair that He broke the Chet and removed it from its former state and it became *matzah*. Therefore it is written: "Rebuke the wild beast of the reed grass," for the Holy One, blessed be He, rebuked it, and the Chet of *chametz* was broken and became a Hei.

742. וְזַמִּין קוּדְשָׁא בְּרִיךְ הוּא. לְתַבְּרָא לֵיהּ לְהַהוּא קָנֶה, כְּגַוְונָא דָּא, יִתְבַּר רַגְלֵיהּ דְּק' מִקָּנֶה, וְיִשְׁתְּאַר הִנֵּה. הִנֵּה יְיָ' אֱלֹהִים בְּחָזָק יָבֹא וּזְרוֹעוֹ מוֹשְׁלָה לוֹ הִנֵּה שְׂכָרוֹ אִתּוֹ וּפְעוּלָּתוֹ לְפָנָיו. מַאי וּפְעוּלָּתוֹ. דָּא פֹּעַל דְּהַהִיא ק' דְּיִתְבַּר לָהּ, וְאִיהִי פְּעוּלָה לְפָנָיו, אִיהוּ יַעֲבַר רַגְלֵיהּ, וִיהֵא הִנֵּה רִאשׁוֹן לְצִיּוֹן הִנֵּה הִנָּם וְגוֹ'.

742. And in the future the Holy One, blessed be He, will break that reed as follows: He will break off the foot of the Kof of *kaneh* (lit. 'reed'), so *hineh* (lit. 'behold' - Hei Nun Hei) will remain, AS IS WRITTEN: "Behold, Adonai Elohim will come with might, and His arm shall rule for Him: behold, His reward is with Him, and His hire before Him" (Yeshayah 40:10). What is the meaning of "and His hire"? This is the operation on that letter Kof, "and His hire before Him," for He will remove the foot of the Kof OF *KANEH* (KOF NUN HEI), making it into *hineh*. "A harbinger to Zion will I give: Behold (Heb. *hineh*), behold them" (Yeshayah 41:27).

A Synopsis

Rabbi Shimon says that Esau is Rome that is attached to the reed
that Gabriel stuck in the great sea; the reed is also called leavened

bread. When the Redemption comes God will break that reed and the Temple will be revealed in the world. The Faithful Shepherd compares the two Temples to the pupils of the eye that are clouded. He talks about the two Messiahs and looks forward to the day when the rule of Rome will be broken.

רעיא מהימנא

743. רְבִּי שִׁמְעוֹן פָּתַח וְאָמַר, גְּעַר חַיַּת קָנֶה עֲדַת אַבִּירִים בְּעֶגְלֵי עַמִּים. גְּעַר חַיַּת קָנֶה, דָּא קָנֶה דְּאִתְאֲחַד בֵּיהּ עֵשָׂו, דְּאִיהִי קַרְתָּא דְּרוֹמִי רַבְּתָא, דְּנָעַץ גַּבְרִיאֵל קָנֶה בְּיַמָּא רַבָּא, וּבְנוּ עֲלֵיהּ כְּרַךְ גָּדוֹל דְּרוֹמִי. קָנֶה דְּחָמֵץ. וְכַד יֵיתֵי פוּרְקָנָא לְיִשְׂרָאֵל, יִתְבַּר לֵיהּ. הה"ד גְּעַר חַיַּת קָנֶה עֲדַת. וּמִתְעַבַּר מִיַּד חָמֵץ מֵעָלְמָא. מַחְמֶצֶת דִּילֵיהּ רוֹמִי. וְיִתְגַּלְיָא מַצָּה בְּעָלְמָא, דְּאִיהִי בֵּי מַקְדְּשָׁא דְּבַיִת רִאשׁוֹן וּבַיִת שֵׁנִי.

Ra'aya Meheimna (the Faithful Shepherd)

743. Rabbi Shimon opened with the verse: "Rebuke the wild beast of the reed grass, the company of the bulls with the calves of the peoples." "Rebuke the wild beast of the reeds" refers to a reed, to which is attached Esau, which is the great city of Rome, that Gabriel stuck as a reed in the great sea – WHICH IS A SECRET OF THE REED ATTACHED TO MALCHUT THAT IS CALLED 'THE GREAT SEA', and on it a large city, Rome was built, WHICH IS THE SECRET OF THE KINGDOM OF ESAU. And this is a reed that is CALLED '*chametz*' (lit. 'leavened bread'). When the Redemption comes to Yisrael, He will break THAT REED, as it is written: "Rebuke the wild beast of the reed grass, the company," and the *chametz* THAT IS DRAWN DOWN FROM THE REED is immediately removed from the world, WITH its *machmetzet*, NAMELY, ITS FEMALE, which is THE CITY Rome, and *matzah* (lit. 'unleavened bread') will be revealed in the world, for this is the Temple, the First Temple and the Second Temple, WHICH ARE BINAH AND MALCHUT.

744. אָמַר ר"מ, דְּאִינּוּן לָקֳבֵל בַּת עַיִן יָמִין, וּבַת עַיִן שְׂמָאל. וְאִינּוּן לָקֳבֵל רוֹמִי רַבְּתִי, רוֹמִי זְעֵירָא. לָקֳבֵל תְּרֵין עֲנָנִין, דִּמְכַסְיָין עַל בַּת עֵינָא יְמִינָא וּשְׂמָאלָא. וְאִינּוּן לָקֳבֵל שְׂאוֹר וְחָמֵץ. וְעַד דְּאִלֵּין יִתְבַּעֲרוּן

מֵעָלְמָא בַּל יֵרָאֶה וּבַל יִמָּצֵא חַד מִנַּיְיהוּ, בַּיִת רִאשׁוֹן וְשֵׁנִי לָא יִתְגַּלְיָין בְּעָלְמָא.

744. The Faithful Shepherd said: They, THE FIRST TEMPLE AND THE SECOND TEMPLE, correspond to the pupil of the right eye and the pupil of the left eye, and they correspond to the large and small Rome, corresponding to the two clouds that cover the pupils of the right EYE and of the left EYE. They, in turn, correspond to leaven and leavened bread. And as long as these are not removed from the world, not to be seen or not to be found, the First Temple and the Second Temple are unable to be revealed in the world.

745. וְאַסְוָותָא דַּעֲנָנָא עֵינָא, דְּאַחֲשִׁיךְ לְבַת עֵינָא יָמִין וּשְׂמֹאל, מַה יְהֵא אַסְוָותָא דִלְהוֹן. מָרָה דְּעֶגְלָא. וְהַיְינוּ שָׁם יִרְעֶה עֵגֶל וְשָׁם יִרְבָּץ. שָׁם יִרְעֶה עֵגֶל, דָּא מָשִׁיחַ בֶּן יוֹסֵף, דְּאִתְּמַר בֵּיהּ בְּכוֹר שׁוֹרוֹ הָדָר לוֹ. וְשָׁם יִרְבָּץ, דָּא מָשִׁיחַ בֶּן דָּוִד. חַד אַעֲבָר רוֹמִי רַבָּתִי. וְחַד אַעֲבָר רוֹמִי זְעֵירְתָּא. דְּמִיכָאֵל וְגַבְרִיאֵ"ל לְקַבְלַיְיהוּ אִינּוּן.

745. And what healing will there be for the clouds that darken the pupils of the right and left eyes? What will be their remedy? This is the gall of a calf, as it is written: "there shall the calf feed, and there shall he lie down" (Yeshayah 27:10). "There shall the calf feed" refers to Messiah son of Joseph, about whom it is said: "His firstling of his herd, grandeur is his" (Devarim 33:17), WHICH IS THE SECRET OF THE FACE OF OX FROM THE LEFT SIDE. "and there shall he lie down" refers to Messiah son of David. One, NAMELY, MESSIAH SON OF DAVID, removes the large Rome, and the other, NAMELY MESSIAH SON OF JOSEPH, removes the small Rome; and corresponding to them are Michael and Gabriel, WHERE MICHAEL CORRESPONDS TO MESSIAH SON OF DAVID AND GABRIEL TO MESSIAH SON OF JOSEPH.

746. וּבְגִין דָּא ח', דְּאִיהוּ חוּטָא זְעֵירָא, תָּבַר לָהּ, וְיֵיעוּל ה' בְּאַתְרָהָא. דִּבְקַדְמֵיתָא קָנֶה וְסוֹף קָמֵלוּ. קָנֶה שֻׁלְטָנוּתָא דְּרוֹמִי, וְסוֹף לְכָל מַלְכִין, דְּעָתִיד קוּדְשָׁא בְּרִיךְ הוּא לְתַבְּרָא לֵיהּ. גְּעַר חַיַּת קָנֶה, גְּעַר חַיָּה בִּישָׁא, ח' מִן חָמֵץ, וְאִתְבַּר רַגְלֵיהּ מִן מַחְמֶצֶת, דְּאִתְּמַר בָּהּ רַגְלֶיהָ יוֹרְדוֹת מָוֶת. וְעוֹד גְּעַר חַיַּת קָנֶה, יַתְבַּר רֶגֶל קוֹף מִן קָנֶה, וְיִשְׁתְּאַר הֵ"ה. מִיָּד

הִנֵּה יְיָ׳ אֱלֹהִים בְּחָזָק יָבֹא, רֹאשׁוֹן לְצִיּוֹן הִנֵּה הִנָּם וְלִירוּשָׁלַם מְבַשֵּׂר אֶתֶּן. הִנֵּה׃ ס׳ בָּתַר אֶלֶף וּמָאתָן.

746. And hence the Chet, which is a thin thread, is broken, and is replaced with a Hei, TURNING THE *CHAMETZ* (CHET MEM TZADIK) INTO *MATZAH* (MEM TZADIK HEI). For initially, "The reeds and rushes (Heb. *suf*) shall wither." 'Reeds' refers to the rule of Rome, which is an end (Heb. *sof*) for all the kings, and which in the future the Holy One, blessed be He, will break. "Rebuke the wild beast of the reed grass" means rebuking the wicked beast, which is the Chet of *chametz*, and the foot of the Chet of *machmetzet* is broken, of which it is said: "Her feet go down to death" (Mishlei 5:5). Moreover: "Rebuke the wild beast of the reed grass" means that He will break the foot of the Kof of *kaneh* (Kof Nun Hei), and *hineh* (Eng. 'behold' - Hei Nun Hei) remains. Immediately: "Behold, Adonai Elohim will come with might..." and: "A harbinger to Zion will I give: Behold, behold them (Heb. *hineh hinam*); and to Jerusalem a messenger of good tidings." THE NUMERICAL VALUE OF '*hineh*' is sixty; NAMELY, SIXTY YEARS after the year 1200, THE VERSES QUOTED ABOVE WILL BE FULFILLED, AS IS CLARIFIED BELOW.

107. Four redemptions

A Synopsis

Rabbi Shimon talks about the number of years until the redemption and the gathering in of the exiles, and we learn that there will be four redemptions. Explanation is made of the associated gematria and of the role of the four beasts of the chariot.

747. וְאָמַר בּוּצִינָא קַדִּישָׁא, כָּל הַנֶּפֶשׁ לְבֵית יַעֲקֹב שִׁשִּׁים וָשֵׁשׁ. שִׁשִּׁים, לְאַתְעֲרוּתָא דִּמְשִׁיחַ רִאשׁוֹן. וָשֵׁשׁ, לְאַתְעֲרוּתָא דִּמְשִׁיחַ שֵׁנִי. אִשְׁתְּאָרוּ ו' שָׁנִים לְעֶ"ב, לְקַיֵּים בְּהוּ, שֵׁשׁ שָׁנִים תִּזְרַע שָׂדֶךָ וְשֵׁשׁ שָׁנִים תִּזְמוֹר כַּרְמֶךָ וְאָסַפְתָּ אֶת תְּבוּאָתָה, דְּאִתְּמַר קֹדֶשׁ יִשְׂרָאֵל לַיְיָ' רֵאשִׁית תְּבוּאָתֹה.

747. And the holy luminary said: "All the souls that came with Jacob...were 66" (Beresheet 46:26). Sixty is for the awakening of the first Messiah, and six is for the awakening of the second Messiah, and this leaves six years to go until the number 72, WHICH IS WHEN THE REDEMPTION WILL TAKE PLACE, NAMELY, ONE THOUSAND YEARS, WHICH IS THE WHOLE OF THE FIFTH MILLENIUM THAT IS DESTRUCTION THROUGHOUT, AND 272 YEARS INTO THE SIXTH MILLENIUM, to establish therein the verse: "Six years you shall sow your field, and six years you shall prune your vineyard, and gather in its fruit" (Vayikra 25:3); NAMELY, TWICE SIX AFTER ONE MILLENIUM AND SIXTY YEARS IS THE TIME TO "GATHER IN ITS FRUIT" NAMELY, THE INGATHERING OF THE EXILES, FOR YISRAEL IS CALLED 'FRUIT', as it is said: "Yisrael is holy to Hashem, the firstfruits of His increase" (Yirmeyah 2:3).

748. אִם כֵּן, מַה כְּתִיב לְעֵיל רָנּוּ לְיַעֲקֹב שִׂמְחָה. אֶלָּא אַרְבַּע גְּאוּלוֹת עֲתִידִין לְמֶהֱוֵי, לָקֳבֵל אַרְבַּע כּוֹסוֹת דְּפֶסַח. בְּגִין דְּיִשְׂרָאֵל מְפוּזָרִין בְּאַרְבַּע פִּנּוּת עָלְמָא, וְאִינּוּן דִּיהוֹן רְחוֹקִין מְאוּמִין, אַקְדִּימוּ לְרָנּוּ. וְתִנְיָינִין, לְשִׁתִּין. וּתְלִיתָאִין, לְשִׁתִּין וָשִׁית. וּרְבִיעָאִין לְעֶ"ב.

748. HE ASKS: If it is so, THAT THE REDEMPTION IS TO BE IN THE 1272ND YEAR, what is the intent of the verse: "Sing (Heb. *ronu* = 256) with

gladness for Jacob" (Yirmeyah 31:6), WHICH WOULD SEEM TO IMPLY THAT THE REDEMPTION WILL BE IN THE 1256TH YEAR? HE ANSWERS THAT there are to be four redemptions corresponding to the four cups of wine at Pesach, AND THEY ARE THE SECRET OF CHOCHMAH AND BINAH, TIFERET AND MALCHUT, since Yisrael are scattered into the four directions of the world, WHICH ARE THE SECRET OF CHOCHMAH AND BINAH, TIFERET AND MALCHUT, and those who are among the nations that are far away, will be REDEEMED early, in the one thousand 256th YEAR. The next group WILL BE REDEEMED in the 1260TH YEAR; the third GROUP in the 1266TH YEAR; and the fourth GROUP in the YEAR 1272ND YEAR.

749. וּפוּרְקָנִין אִלֵּין, יֶהוֹן בְּאַרְבַּע חֵיוָן, בְּשֵׁם יְדֹוָד דְּרָכִיב עָלַיְיהוּ. הה״ד כִּי תִרְכַּב עַל סוּסֶךָ מַרְכְּבוֹתֶיךָ יְשׁוּעָה. דִּלְקָבְלַיְיהוּ, יִתְעַר לְתַתָּא אַרְבַּע דְּגָלִין, וּתְרֵיסָר שְׁבָטִין. בְּרָזָא דַּיְדֹוָד מֶלֶךְ, יְדֹוָד מָלָךְ, יְדֹוָד יִמְלוֹךְ לְעוֹלָם וָעֶד. תְּרֵיסָר אַתְוָון אִינּוּן, לְקָבֵל תְּרֵיסָר שְׁבָטִין, וי״ב אַנְפִּין דִּתְלַת אֲבָהָן, דְּאִתְּמַר עָלַיְיהוּ הָאָבוֹת הֵן הֵן הַמֶּרְכָּבָה. וְאִינּוּן עֲשַׂר שְׁבָטִין, אֶלֶף שְׁנִין. תְּרֵין שְׁבָטִין, מָאתָן שְׁנִין. ומי״ב אַתְוָון, תַּלְיָין ע״ב שְׁמָהָן, דְּאִינּוּן ע״ב שְׁנִין, בָּתַר אֶלֶף וּמָאתָן.

749. And these redemptions will be with the four living creatures OF THE CHARIOT: LION, OX, EAGLE AND MAN, in the name of Yud Hei Vav Hei that rides on them, as it is written: "that You ride upon Your horses, Your chariots of salvation" (Chavakuk 3:8). In correspondence them will awaken below four standards and twelve tribes, in the secret OF THE THREE YUD HEI VAV HEI'S IN: 'Hashem reigns; Hashem reigned; Hashem will reign forever and ever'. There are here twelve letters, corresponding to the twelve tribes, and the twelve faces of the three patriarchs, NAMELY, THE THREE COLUMNS OF CHESED, GVURAH AND TIFERET, about whom it has been said: The patriarchs are the Chariot, FOR THE FOUR LIVING CREATURES ARE IN THE CHARIOT, THE FACE OF LION, OX, EAGLE, AND MAN. AND EACH HAS THE THREE COLUMNS CHESED, GVURAH AND TIFERET, MAKING TWELVE FACES. And these ten tribes ALLUDE to a thousand years, while the other two tribes ALLUDE to two hundred years, and from the twelve letters OF THE THREE YUD HEI VAV HEI'S are suspended the 72 Names. FOR THERE ARE TWELVE LETTERS IN EACH SFIRAH OF CHESED, GVURAH, TIFERET, NETZACH, HOD AND YESOD OF ZEIR ANPIN, AND

TWELVE MULTIPLIED BY SIX ARE 72. And these 72 are the years after one thousand and two hundred years. AND FROM THIS IS THE ALLUSION THAT THE REDEMPTION WILL COME AFTER 1272 YEARS, AS ABOVE. AND IT SHOULD BE UNDERSTOOD THAT ALL THE APOCALYPTIC DATES MENTIONED IN THE ZOHAR IMPLY THAT THAT IS A FAVORABLE TIME FOR YISRAEL TO REPENT, AND THAT THEIR REDEMPTION IS DEPENDENT ON THEIR REPENTANCE.

750. וְאִינּוּן כ״ד, לְכָל חַיָּה מִתְּלַת חֵיוָן. כ״ד רָזָא דִילֵיהּ, וְקָרָא זֶה אֶל זֶה וְאָמַר. וְאִינּוּן תְּלַת כִּתּוֹת, מָן כ״ד צוּרוֹת. כַּת אַחַת אוֹמֶרֶת קָדוֹשׁ, וְכַת תִּנְיָינָא אוֹמֶרֶת קָדוֹשׁ, וְכַת תְּלִיתָאָה אוֹמֶרֶת קָדוֹשׁ. מִיַּד אִתְּעַר שְׂמָאלָא בְּמ״ב אַתְוָון, דְּעָבֵד דִּינָא בַּעֲמָלֵק.

750. And they, THE 72 NAMES, allot 24 to each of the three holy living creatures CHESED, GVURAH, TIFERET, WHICH IS TO SAY AS FOLLOWS: IF ONE DIVIDES THE 72 NAMES BETWEEN THE SIX SFIROT CHESED, GVURAH, TIFERET, NETZACH, HOD AND YESOD, THERE WILL BE TWELVE IN EACH SFIRAH, AS ABOVE; BUT IF ONE DIVIDES THE 72 BETWEEN THE THREE SFIROT CHESED, GVURAH AND TIFERET ONLY, THERE WILL BE 24 IN EACH SFIRAH, FOR 3 X 24 = 72. And the secret of 24 is: "And one called to the other and said" (Yeshayah 6:3), they being three groups OF ANGELS, EACH CONSISTING of 24 forms, where the first group says "Holy," and the second group says "holy," and the third group says "holy." AND ALL OF THIS IS IN THE ILLUMINATION OF THE 72 NAMES, FOR THE THREE GROUPS TOGETHER COME TO 72. The left immediately awakens with 42 letters, NAMELY, THE 42-LETTER NAME, that executes judgment on Amalek.

108. "A bird's nest"

A Synopsis
This section talks about the sages of the Torah, the sages of the Mishnah, the people of Yisrael, priests and Kabbalists. We hear that during the exile prayer was decreed instead of sacrifices.

751. כִּי יִקָּרֵא קַן צִפּוֹר לְפָנֶיךָ בַּדֶּרֶךְ מָארֵי מִקְרָא. בְּכָל עֵץ, מָארֵי מִשְׁנָה. דְּאִינּוּן כְּאֶפְרוֹחִים, דִּמְקַנְּנִין בְּעַנְפֵי אִילָנָא. אִית דְּאַמְרֵי, בְּכָל עֵץ, אִלֵּין יִשְׂרָאֵל. דְּאִתְּמַר בְּהוּ, כִּי כִימֵי הָעֵץ יְמֵי עַמִּי. אוֹ עַל הָאָרֶץ, אִלֵּין מָארֵי תוֹרָה, דְּאִתְּמַר בְּהוּ, עַל הָאָרֶץ תִּישָׁן וְחַיֵּי צַעַר תִּחְיֶה וּבַתּוֹרָה אַתָּה עָמֵל. אֶפְרוֹחִים: אִלֵּין פִּרְחֵי כְּהוּנָה. אוֹ בֵּיצִים: אִלֵּין דְּזָן לוֹן קוּדְשָׁא בְּרִיךְ הוּא מִקַּרְנֵי רְאֵמִים וְעַד בֵּיצֵי כֵנִים. וְהָאֵם רוֹבֶצֶת עַל הָאֶפְרוֹחִים, בְּזִמְנָא דַּהֲווֹ קְרֵבִין קָרְבְּנִין. מַה כְּתִיב לֹא תִקַּח הָאֵם עַל הַבָּנִים.

751. "If a bird's nest chance to be before you in the way" (Devarim 22:6). "In the way" refers to the sages of the Bible, "in any tree" to the sages of the Mishnah, who are as young birds nestling in the branches of the tree. And some say that "in any tree" (Ibid.) refers to Yisrael about whom it is said: "for as the days of a tree shall the days of My people be" (Yeshayah 65:22); or that "on the ground" refers to the sages of the Torah, about whom it is said: 'Sleep on the ground and live a life of suffering while you toil in the Torah'. "Young ones" (Devarim 22:6)) refers to young priests, and "eggs" (Ibid.) are those whom the Holy One, blessed be He, nourishes from buffalo's horns to louse's eggs THAT IS TO SAY, INCLUDING EVERYTHING, FROM THE SMALLEST TO THE LARGEST. "And the mother sitting upon the young" (Ibid.) is the time when sacrifices used to be offered. What is written THEN? "You shall not take the mother bird together with the young" (Ibid.). THAT IS TO SAY: DO NOT BREAK UP THE UNION OF THE MOTHER, WHO IS THE SHECHINAH, WITH THE YOUNG, WHO ARE YISRAEL.

752. חָרֵב בֵּי מַקְדְּשָׁא, וּבָטְלוּ קָרְבְּנִין, מַה כְּתִיב, שַׁלֵּחַ תְּשַׁלַּח אֶת הָאֵם. וְגָלוּ הַבָּנִים, וְהַיְינוּ וְאֶת הַבָּנִים תִּקַּח לָךְ, מִסִּטְרָא דָּא דְּאָת ו', דְּאִיהוּ עוֹלָם אָרוֹךְ דְּאִתְּמַר בֵּיהּ לְמַעַן יִיטַב לָךְ וְהַאֲרַכְתָּ יָמִים, לְעוֹלָם

שֶׁכֻּלּוֹ אָרוֹךְ.

752. After the destruction of the Temple and the annulment of the sacrifices, what is written? "but you shall surely let the mother go" (Ibid. 7), WHERE THE MOTHER IS THE SHECHINAH, and the young have been exiled, namely, "and take the young to you" (Ibid.). FOR THE KABBALISTS ARE CALLED 'YOUNG','for they are from the side of the letter Aleph that is inserted in the spelling of the letter Vav FULLY SPELLED OUT AS VAV-ALEPH-VAV OF YUD HEI VAV HEI, which is a long world, FOR THIS LETTER ALEPH THAT IS INSERTED IN THE FULL SPELLING VAV-ALEPH-VAV, IS DRAWN DOWN FROM BINAH, WHICH IS THE SECRET OF THE WORLD TO COME, WHICH IS A WORLD THAT IS THROUGHOUT LONG, about which it is said: "that it may be well with you, and that you may prolong your days" (Ibid.) in the world that is altogether long.

753. וּבַאֲתָר דְּקָרְבְּנִין, תַּקִּינוּ צְלוֹתִין, וּמְצַפְצְפִין בְּקָלִין דְּשִׁירִין. בְּקוֹל דק״ש, לְגַבֵּי עַמּוּדָא דְּאֶמְצָעִיתָא דְּאִיהוּ לְעֵילָא. דְּהָא אִימָא וּבְרַתָּא בְּגָלוּתָא, וּמִיָּד דְּנָחִית, קַשְׁרִין לֵהּ בִּבְרַתָּא, דְּאִיהִי יַד כֵּהָה, לְמֶהֱוֵי קָשִׁיר ו' עִם ה', בְּשִׁית סְפִירָאן. מִיָּד מְלַחֲשִׁין לְגַבֵּי חָכְמָה, בָּרוּךְ שֵׁם כְּבוֹד מַלְכוּתוֹ לְעוֹלָם וָעֶד.

753. AND IN THE EXILE, prayer was decreed instead of sacrifices, AND YISRAEL raised their voices with the sound of the songs, the reading of Sh'ma, WHICH ASCENDS to the Central Column that is on high, NAMELY, ZEIR ANPIN, for the mother and the daughter, WHICH ARE BINAH AND MALCHUT, are in exile, FOR INASMUCH AS MALCHUT IS PART OF BINAH, TO THAT EXTENT BINAH IS ALSO IN EXILE, and immediately on ZEIR ANPIN's descent, He is joined with the daughter, WHICH IS MALCHUT, that is called 'dim hand', in order to connect Vav, WHICH IS ZEIR ANPIN, with Hei, WHICH IS MALCHUT in six Sfirot, FOR THE READING OF SH'MA IS THE DRAWING DOWN OF THE SIX INTERMEDIATE SFIROT OF GREATNESS TO ZEIR ANPIN AND MALCHUT. Immediately, 'Blessed be the name of the glory of His kingdom forever and ever' is whispered to Chochmah, FOR IT IS THE SECRET OF THE UNIFICATION OF MALCHUT, TO WHICH BOUNTY IS THEN DRAWN DOWN FROM CHOCHMAH.

109. The four passages in the Tefilin and the reading of Sh'ma

A Synopsis

After a description of the four sections of the Tefilin we hear that the prayer, the Sh'ma, is the crown on the head of Zeir Anpin, because Sandalfon ties all the prayers together and makes them into a crown. The assertion is made that the Shechinah is God's tabernacle, His table, His candelabra, His ark and His altar.

754. אֶחָ"ד כָּבוֹ"ד, גִי' מ"ה מִן חָכְמָה. דְּנָחִית לֵיהּ לְגַבֵּי אִמָּא, וּמִיַּד דְּנָחִית, קַשְׁרִין לֵיהּ עַמָּא בְּקִשּׁוּרָא דִּתְפִילִין דְּרֵישָׁא. ובג"ד בְּאַרְבַּע פָּרְשִׁיָּין דִּתְפִילִין, קַדֶּשׁ לִי, חָכְמָה. וְהָיָה כִּי יְבִיאֲךָ, בִּינָה. שְׁמַע יִשְׂרָאֵל תִּפְאֶרֶת, כָּלִיל ו' סְפִירָן, בְּשִׁית תֵּיבִין. וְהָיָה אִם שָׁמוֹעַ, מַלְכוּת, יַד כֵּהָה. צְלוֹתָא כֶּתֶר כ' עַל רֵישֵׁיהּ, אֵין קָדוֹשׁ כַּיְדֹוָד, דְּסַנְדַּלְפוֹן קוֹשֵׁר כָּל צְלוֹתִין, וְעָבֵיד לוֹן כֶּתֶר.

754. The NUMERICAL VALUE OF 'one' (Heb. *echad*), THE FINAL WORD OF THE FIRST LINE OF THE SH'MA YISRAEL, together with THE NUMERICAL VALUE OF 'glory' (Heb. *kavod*), FROM 'BLESSED BE THE GLORY OF THE NAME OF HIS KINGDOM FOR EVER AND EVER', add up to Mem Hei of Chochmah (Chet Caf Mem Hei). For CHOCHMAH is brought down to Ima, and immediately on the descent OF CHOCHMAH TO IMA, the people bind it with the knot of the head Tefilin. And for this reason, the four sections of the Tefilin are: "Sanctify to me" (Shemot 13:1-10), which is Chochmah; "And it shall be when Hashem shall bring you into the land" (Shemot 13:11-16), which is Binah; "Hear, O Yisrael" (Devarim 6:4-9), which is Tiferet, consisting of six Sfirot in the six words OF THE SH'MA; "And it shall come to pass, if you hearken" (Devarim 11:13-21), which is Malchut that is CALLED 'a dim hand'. The prayer is Keter (lit. 'crown'), namely, a crown on the head OF ZEIR ANPIN, IN THE SECRET OF THE VERSE: "There is none holy as Hashem" (I Shmuel 2:2), WHERE THE LETTER CAF (MEANING 'AS') ALLUDES TO KETER, because Sandalfon ties all the prayers together and makes them into a crown.

755. בְּהַהוּא זִמְנָא צָרִיךְ לְסַדְּרָא פָּתוֹרָא לִסְעוּדָתָא דְּמַלְכָּא, וּמַשְׁכְּנָא וּמְנַרְתָּא וַאֲרוֹנָא וּמַדְבְּחָא, וְכָל מִינֵי שִׁמּוּשָׁא דְּבֵיתָא דְּמַלְכָּא. וְלָאו

בָּתַר פָּתוֹרָא אַזְלֵינָן דְּלָאו עוֹבָדָא דְקוּדְשָׁא בְּרִיךְ הוּא, דְּלָא אַזְלֵינָן אֶלָּא בָּתַר פָּתוֹרָא דְּאִיהוּ עוֹבָדֵי יְדוֹי דְקוּדְשָׁא בְּרִיךְ הוּא, דְּאִיהוּ שְׁכִינְתֵּיה. מִשְׁכָּן דִּילֵיה, פָּתוֹרָא דִּילֵיה, מְנַרְתָּא דִּילֵיה, אֲרוֹנָא דִּילֵיה, מַדְבְּחָא דִּילֵיה, אִיהִי כְּלִילָא מִכָּל מָאנֵי שִׁמּוּשָׁא לְמַלְכָּא עִלָּאָה.

755. At that time the table has to be prepared for the King's banquet, and the tabernacle and candelabra and the ark and the altar and all sorts of utensils of the King's house have to be arranged. And we do not refer to just any table that is not made by the Holy One, blessed be He, for we are referring to none other than the table which is made by the Holy One, blessed be He, which is His Shechinah. And THE SHECHINAH is ZEIR ANPIN's tabernacle, His table, His candelabra, His ark, His altar, for She, THE SHECHINAH, consists of all the utensils of the Supernal King, WHO IS ZEIR ANPIN.

110. The shewbread which is the twelve faces

A Synopsis

We learn about the sacrifices that are made by fire, and about the correspondence between the show-bread and the twelve countenances of the three Holy Beasts. The Faithful Shepherd uses the analogy of the oven in which the bread is baked to show the role of the Shechinah, and says that there is clean fine flour in the bread of the Torah. In reference to the wood that is burned in the offering he tells us that the name given to the sages of Torah is "trees of holiness."

756. אִינְהוּ אִינּוּן דִּמְתַקְּנֵי חַמְרָא וְנַהֲמָא דְמַלְכָּא עִלָּאָה, דְּאִתְּמַר בְּהוּ אֶת קָרְבָּנִי לַחְמִי לְאִשַּׁי, דְּלֵית לְקָרְבָא לֵיה לְגַבֵּיה אֶלָּא אִלֵּין דְּאִתְקְרִיאוּ אִשֵּׁי יְיָ. ובג"ד אֶת קָרְבָּנִי לַחְמִי לְאִשַּׁי. דְּעָלֵיה אִתְּמַר, לְכוּ לַחֲמוּ בְלַחְמִי. וְאִתְקְרֵי לֶחֶם הַפָּנִים, דְּאִינּוּן י"ב אַנְפִּין, יְבָרֶכְךָ יהוה, יָאֵר יהוה, יִשָּׂא יהוה, תְּרֵיסַר אַנְפִּין דִּתְלַת חֵיוָן.

756. Those WHO ARE CALLED 'CHILDREN', WHO ARE MENTIONED ABOVE, are the ones who arrange the wine and bread of the supernal King, ZEIR ANPIN, and about them it is said: "My offering, the provision of My sacrifices made by fire" (Bemidbar 28:2). For only those that are called 'the fire offerings of Hashem' may be offered to Him, and it is therefore WRITTEN: "My offering, the provision of My sacrifices made by fire." For it is said about it: "Come, eat of my bread" (Mishlei 9:5), and they are called 'the shewbread' (lit. 'the bread of the countenances'), there being twelve countenances THAT ARE ALLUDED TO IN THE THREE YUD HEI VAV HEI'S: "Hashem bless you... Hashem make His face to shine... Hashem lift up His countenance..." (Bemidbar 6:24-26), AND THERE ARE THUS TWELVE THAT CORRESPOND TO THE twelve countenances of three holy living creatures.

757. מַאי לֶחֶם דְּאִלֵּין פָּנִים. דָּא נַהֲמָא דְאָדָם, דְּאִיהוּ יו"ד ה"א וָא"ו ה"א. וְאִית לֵיה נַהֲמָא בְּאַרְבַּע אַנְפִּין, דְּאִינּוּן אַרְבַּע אַתְוָון יְדֹוָ"ד. הַאי נַהֲמָא דְפָתוֹרָא דְמַלְכָּא, אִיהוּ סֹלֶת נְקִיָּה.

757. What is the bread of these twelve countenances? It is the bread of man, who is THE SECRET OF YUD HEI VAV HEI, FULLY SPELLED WITH

ALEPH'S, THUS Yud-Vav-Dalet, Hei-Aleph, Vav-Aleph-Vav, Hei -Aleph,
WHICH IS THE NUMERICAL EQUIVALENT OF MAN (HEB. *ADAM* = 45).
AND THEY ARE TWELVE IN THE SECRET OF THE THREE YUD HEI VAV
HEI'S, WHICH MEAN THE THREE COLUMNS, IN EACH OF WHICH IS ONE
YUD HEI VAV HEI, MAKING A TOTAL OF TWELVE LETTERS, AS ABOVE.
And He has bread in four faces, which are the four letters of Yud Hei Vav
Hei, THAT INCLUDE TWELVE FACES, AS ABOVE. This bread of the King's
table is clean fine flour, THAT CONTAINS NO CHAFF OR STRAW, WHICH
ARE JUDGMENTS.

758. כְּבִשָׁן דִּילֵיהּ, דְּאוֹפֶה בֵּיהּ נַהֲמָא, שְׁכִינְתָּא. תַּמָּן אִתְבְּשַׁל
וְאִשְׁתְּלִים. וּבג״ד, אֵין בּוֹצְעִין אֶלָּא מֵאֲתָר דְּגָמַר בִּשׁוּלָא. כְּגַוְונָא
דִּשְׁלִימוּ דְּפֵרֵי, אִיהוּ גְּמַר בִּשׁוּלוֹ. וְהַאי אִיהוּ אֲדֹנָי, גְּמַר וּשְׁלִימוּ
דַּיְדֹוָד, דְּאִיהוּ לֶחֶם הַפָּנִים. אֲדֹנָי, כְּבִשָׁן דִּילֵיהּ. דְּאִיהִי כְּבוּשָׁה תְּחוֹת
בַּעְלָהּ. וּבְגִינָהּ אִתְּמַר, וְהַר סִינַי עָשַׁן כֻּלּוֹ מִפְּנֵי אֲשֶׁר יָרַד עָלָיו יְיָ׳
בָּאֵשׁ וַיַּעַל עֲשָׁנוֹ כְּעֶשֶׁן הַכִּבְשָׁן. וְלֹא כְּכִבְשָׁן דְּאֵשׁ דְּהֶדְיוֹט, אֶלָּא
כְּכִבְשָׁן, דְּבֵיהּ כָּבֵשׁ רַחֲמָיו לְעַמֵּיהּ, כַּד מְצַלִּין וּבָעוֹן בָּעוּתִין, כֵּן
יִכְבְּשׁוּ רַחֲמֶיךָ אֶת כַּעַסְךָ. וּבֵיהּ כִּבְשֵׁי דְרַחֲמָנָא לָמָה לָךְ.

758. His oven, in which he bakes the bread, is the Shechinah, for THE
BREAD cooks and is completed there. And this is why one should not start
cutting the bread other than at the point where its cooking was completed,
namely, it is similar to the perfection of a fruit that has reached full ripeness.
And this is Adonai, WHICH IS MALCHUT, which is completion and
perfection of Yud Hei Vav Hei, WHICH IS ZEIR ANPIN, which is the
shewbread (lit. 'bread of the faces'), NAMELY, THE TWELVE COUNTENANCES
MENTIONED ABOVE WHICH ARE IN ZEIR ANPIN. Adonai is ZEIR ANPIN's
oven AND COMPLETES HIM. AND SHE IS CALLED 'A FURNACE' (HEB.
KIVSHAN) because she is subdued (Heb. *KEVUSHAH*) under Her husband,
and for Her it is said: "And Mount Sinai smoked in every part, because
Hashem descended upon it in fire: and the smoke thereof ascended like the
smoke of a furnace" (Shemot 19:18). "Furnace" here does not MEAN as an
ordinary furnace, but rather that in which He applies (Heb. *kovesh*) His
mercy to His people when they pray and present their supplications. AND SO
IS IT SAID: 'May Your mercy suppress (Heb. *yichbeshu*) your anger'. And IT

WAS SAID of it: What do you have to do with the secrets (Aramaic *kivshei*) of the Merciful One?

759. וּבְנַהֲמָא דְאוֹרַיְיתָא, אִית סֹלֶת דְּיָהַב לֵיהּ מַלְכָּא, לְאִינוּן דְּאִתְּמַר עֲלַיְיהוּ, כָּל יִשְׂרָאֵל בְּנֵי מְלָכִים. מֵיכְלָא דְצַדִיקַיָּא. וְאִית נַהֲמָא דְאוֹרַיְיתָא, דְּאִיהוּ פְּסוֹלֶת, לְאִינוּן עַבְדִין וּשְׁפָחוֹת, דְּבֵי מַלְכָּא. וּבְגִּ"ד בְּמַטְרוֹנִיתָא אִתְּמַר וַתָּקָם בְּעוֹד לַיְלָה וַתִּתֵּן טֶרֶף לְבֵיתָהּ וְחֹק לְנַעֲרוֹתֶיהָ, דְּאִינוּן מָארֵי מַתְנִיתִין. וּבְגִּ"ד אִתְּמַר בְּמֵיכְלָא דְּמַלְכָּא, וַעֲשִׂירִית הָאֵיפָה סֹלֶת וַדַּאי, וְדָא יוֹ"ד מִן אֲדֹנָי, אִיהִי עֲשִׂירִית. וְדָא סֹלֶת דְּמֵיכְלָא דְּמַלְכָּא אִשְׁתְּכָחַת.

759. And in the bread of the Torah there is CLEAN fine flour, which the King gives to those about whom it is said: 'All Yisrael are the children of kings', NAMELY, HE GIVES IT TO THOSE WHO ARE CALLED 'CHILDREN', for it is the food of the righteous. And there is also bread of the Torah that is waste matter and which is given to the servants and handmaids of the King's house, WHO ATTEND TO THE HORSES AND RIDERS OF THE KING'S HOUSE. And for this reason it is said about the Queen: "She rises also while it is yet night, and gives food to her household, and a portion to her maidens" (Mishlei 31:15), who are the sages of the Mishnah. And this is why it is said about the food of the King: "and a tenth part of an efah of flour" (Bemidbar 28:5). FINE FLOUR, certainly; while THE TENTH PART OF AN EFAH is Yud (whose numerical value is ten) of Adonai, which is certainly tenth, and it follows that this fine flour is the food of the King, AS ABOVE.

760. קוּם בּוּצִינָא קַדִּישָׁא, אַנְתְּ וְרִבִּי אֶלְעָזָר בְּרָךְ, וְרִבִּי אַבָּא, וְרִבִּי יְהוּדָה, וְרִבִּי יוֹסֵי, וְרִבִּי חִיָּיא, וְרִבִּי יוּדָאי, לְתַקְּנָא דּוֹרוֹנָא לְמַלְכָּא, וּלְקָרְבָא כָּל אֵבָרִין, דְּאִינוּן יִשְׂרָאֵל, קָרְבְּנִין לְקוּדְשָׁא בְּרִיךְ הוּא הַהוּא דְּאִתְקְרֵי נְשָׁמָה, לְגַבֵּי אֵבָרִים שְׁכִינְתָּא קַדִּישְׁתָּא, אֵשׁ שֶׁל גָּבוֹהַּ. דְּאָחִיד בְּעֵצִים, דְּאִתְקְרִיאוּ עֲצֵי הָעוֹלָה, דְּאִינוּן עֵץ הַחַיִּים וְעֵץ הַדַּעַת טוֹב וָרָע. עֲצֵי הַקֹּדֶשׁ אִתְקְרִיאוּ, אִינוּן מָארֵי תוֹרָה, דְּאִתְאַחֲדַת בְּהוֹן אוֹרַיְיתָא, דְּאִתְּמַר בָּהּ הֲלֹא כֹה דְבָרִי כָּאֵשׁ נְאָם יְיָ'.

760. THE FAITHFUL SHEPHERD SAID: Rise up, holy luminary, you and Rabbi Elazar, your son, together with Rabbi Aba, Rabbi Yehuda, Rabbi Yosi, Rabbi Chiya and Rabbi Yudai, to prepare a gift for the King, THE HOLY ONE, BLESSED BE HE, to make a sacrifice of all the limbs, which are Yisrael, so that they should be sacrificial offerings to the Holy One, blessed be He. And those who are called 'the Soul' OF YISRAEL ARE OFFERED to the limbs of the holy Shechinah, NAMELY, TO THE SFIROT OF MALCHUT, WHICH IS CALLED 'fire OF the Most High'. AND THIS FIRE is attached to the pieces of wood that are called "the wood (lit. 'tree') of the burnt offering" (Beresheet 22:6), namely, the Tree of Life, WHICH IS ZEIR ANPIN, and the Tree of Knowledge of Good and Evil, WHICH IS MALCHUT. Trees of holiness are the name given to the sages of Torah, for the Torah is attached to them, of which it is said: "Is not My word like a fire? says Hashem" (Yirmeyah 23:29).

111. "My offering, the provision of My sacrifices made by fire"

A Synopsis

We are told that Yisrael offers the Torah to God, and the Torah is His bread and His wine and His meat; the Torah is holy flesh that descends from heaven. This explains the meaning of "My offering, the provision of My sacrifices made by fire."

761. וְאִתְּמַר בָּהּ, עוֹלָה לַיְיָ', קָרְבָּן לַיְיָ', אִשֶּׁה לַיְיָ', וְאִתְּמַר אֶת קָרְבָּנִי לַחְמִי לְאִשַּׁי. וְהָא כְּתִיב דְּלֵית לְקָרְבָא קָרְבָּן אֶלָּא לַיְיָ', מַאי נִיהוּ, אֶת קָרְבָּנִי לַחְמִי לְאִשַּׁי. אֶלָּא אָרְחָא, דְּמַאן דְּקָרִיב דּוֹרוֹנָא, לְמִקְרַב לֵיהּ לְמַלְכָּא, וּלְבָתַר אִיהוּ פָּלִיג לֵיהּ, לְמַאן דְּבָעֵי. אוֹף הָכִי יִשְׂרָאֵל, מַקְרִיבִין אוֹרַיְיתָא לְקוּדְשָׁא בְּרִיךְ הוּא, דְּאִיהוּ לַחְמוֹ, וְאִיהוּ יֵינוֹ, וְאִיהוּ בְּשָׂר דִּילֵיהּ, וְאִתְּמַר בָּהּ, עֶצֶם מֵעֲצָמַי וּבָשָׂר מִבְּשָׂרִי. בְּשַׂר קֹדֶשׁ, דְּאוֹקְמוּהָ עָלָהּ מָארֵי מְתִיבְתָּאן, בִּבְשָׂר הַיּוֹרֵד מִן הַשָּׁמַיִם עַסְקִינָן.

761. It is said ABOUT MALCHUT: "a burnt offering to Hashem" (Bemidbar 28:11), "an offering to Hashem" (Vayikra 27:9), "a sacrifice made by fire to Hashem" (Bemidbar 28:6), and it is said: "My offering, the provision of My sacrifices made by fire" (Ibid. 2). And has it not already been written: Sacrifices must be offered to none other than Hashem? What, therefore, is the meaning of "My offering, the provision of My sacrifices made by (also: 'to') fire"? HE ANSWERS, one who offers a gift does so by custom for the king, and the king distributes it to whomever he pleases. Yisrael, likewise, offers the Torah, WHICH IS MALCHUT, to the Holy One, blessed be He, that is His bread and His wine and His meat. And it is said about it, ABOUT THE TORAH, WHICH IS MALCHUT, "bone of my bones, and flesh of my flesh" (Beresheet 2:23). And this is holy flesh, about which the head of the Yeshivah taught: We are talking about flesh that descends from heaven.

112. Fine flour, average flour and waste matter

A Synopsis
Moses says that God gives His finest food to those He loves who are on the side of the Tree of Life; He gives His average food to the angels, or sages of Mishnah; and he gives the waste food to the evil spirits and demons.

762. קוּדְשָׁא בְּרִיךְ הוּא מַאי עָבֵיד מֵהַהוּא דּוֹרוֹנָא. לְמַלְכָּא דְּאָכִיל עַל פָּתוֹרָא. דְּקַרְבִין עַל פָּתוֹרֵיה מִכָּל מִין וָמִין, סֹלֶת, וּבֵינוֹנִי, וּפְסוֹלֶת. וְאִיהוּ פָּלִיג מִפָּתוֹרֵיה, לְכָל מָארֵי סְעוּדָתָא, לְכָל חַד כַּדְקָא יָאוֹת, עַל יְדֵי מְמָנָן דִּילֵיה. וּמֵהַהוּא נַהֲמָא, דְּאִיהוּ סֹלֶת, דְּמַלְכָּא אָכִיל, אִיהוּ מָנֵי לְמֵיהַב לְאִינוּן דִּרְחִימִין גַּבֵּיה. הַה״ד, אֶת קָרְבָּנִי לַחְמִי לְאִשַּׁי רֵיחַ נִחֹחִי. דְּהַיְינוּ אִשֵּׁי יְיָ׳ וְנַחֲלָתוֹ יֹאכֵלוּן הַאי אִיהוּ מִסִּטְרָא דְּאִילָנָא דְּחַיֵּי. אֲבָל מִסִּטְרָא דְּעֵץ הַדַּעַת טוֹב וָרָע, מַנֵי לְמֵיהַב בֵּינוֹנִי, לְמַלְאָכִים. וּפְסוֹלֶת לַשֵּׁדִין וּמַזִּיקִין, דְּאִינוּן מְשַׁמְּשִׁין לְסוּסְוָון וּלְפָרָשִׁיִּין דְּמַלְכָּא.

762. What does the Holy One, blessed be He, do with this gift? HE IS like a king who eats at his own table, and every type is served at the table: fine flour, medium flour, and waste matter, and he distributes from his table to all those sitting at the banquet, through his appointees, to each one as befits him. He commands that bread made out of fine flour that the king eats be given to those he loves who are near to him as it is written: "My offering, the provision of My sacrifices made by fire, for a sweet savor to Me" (Bemidbar 28:2), namely: "the offerings of Hashem made by fire, and His dues shall they eat" (Devarim 18:1). And THIS FOOD is from the side of the Tree of Life AND IS, THEREFORE, CLEAN FINE FLOUR, WITHOUT ANY WASTE MATTER AT ALL. But from the side of the Tree of Knowledge of Good and Evil, IN WHICH THERE IS WASTE MATTER, which is the average flour, He commanded to be given to the angels, while the waste matter HE GIVES to the evil spirits and demons who serve the horses and riders of the King.

763. וְאוֹף הָכִי דְּפָרְשִׁין דְּמַלְכָּא, הֲווֹ מָארֵי מִשְׁנָה, דְּאִינוּן כְּמַלְאָכִים. מְשַׁמְּשִׁין לוֹן שֵׁדִים יְהוּדָאֵי, דְּאִינוּן רְשִׁימִין בְּאוֹת שַׁדַּי, וְאִית שֵׁדִין

וּמַזִּיקִין מִסְטְרָא דִּמְסָאֲבוּ, דְּאִתְקְרִיאוּ שֵׁדִים עכו״ם. וְזֶה לְעוּמַת זֶה עָשָׂה הָאֱלֹהִים.

763. And here, too, THE MEDIUM FLOUR IS GIVEN to the King's horsemen, namely the sages of Mishnah, who are as the angels, and their servants are the Jewish spirits (Heb. *shed* - Shin Dalet) marked by the sign of Shadai, NAMELY WITH THE LETTERS SHIN DALET OF SHADAI (SHIN-DALET-YUD). And there are also evil spirits and demons from the side of impurity that are called 'idol-worshipping spirit', for "The Elohim has made the one as well as the other" (Kohelet 7:14).

764. וּבְגִין דָּא אָמְרוּ מָארֵי מַתְנִיתִין, דְּאִינּוּן ג׳ מִינִין מִינַּיְיהוּ, חַד מִין דִּלְהוֹן כְּמַלְאֲכֵי הַשָּׁרֵת. וּמִין תִּנְיָינָא, כִּבְנֵי אָדָם. וּמִין תְּלִיתָאי, כִּבְעִירָן. וְאִית בְּהוֹן חַכִּימִין בְּאוֹרַיְיתָא דִּבְכְתַב וְדִבְעַל פֶּה. אִתְקְרֵי יוֹסֵף שִׁידָא, עַל שֵׁם דְּאוֹלִיד לֵיהּ שֵׁד. וְלָאו לְמַגָּנָא אָמְרוּ מָארֵי מַתְנִיתִין, אִם הָרַב דּוֹמֶה לְמַלְאַךְ יְיָ׳ צְבָאוֹת תּוֹרָה יְבַקְשׁוּ מִפִּיהוּ. וְאַשְׁמְדָאי מַלְכָּא, הוּא וְכָל מִשְׁפַּחְתֵּיהּ, הָא אוּקִימְנָא דְּאִינּוּן שֵׁדִין יְהוּדָאִין, דְּאִתְכַּפְיָין בְּאוֹרַיְיתָא, וּבִשְׁמָהָן דְּאוֹרַיְיתָא.

764. And for this reason the sages of the Mishnah said: There are three kinds of them, OF THE SPIRITS OF THE JEWS. One kind are like ministering angels, the second kind are like human beings and the third kind are like animals, and some of them are scholars in the Written Law and the Oral Law. And he who is called 'Joseph the spirit' is so called because he was sired by a spirit. And it was not for nothing that the sages of the Mishnah said: If the rabbi is similar to an angel of Hashem Tzva'ot, let them seek Torah from his mouth. FOR THE SAGES OF THE MISHNAH ARE LIKE ANGELS. And Asmodeus, the king OF THE SPIRITS, and all his family are, it has been taught, Jewish spirits, for they were subdued by the Torah and the names of the Torah.

765. וּבְנֵי אַהֲרֹן, בְּגִין דַּעֲרִיכוּ קָרְבְּנֵהוֹן, בְּגִין דָּא אִתְעֲנָשׁוּ, דְּכֻלְּהוּ קָרְבְּנִין אע״ג דְּאִתְקְרִיבוּ לְגַבֵּי מַלְכָּא, אִיהוּ פָּלִיג לוֹן לְכָל חַד כַּדְקָא חֲזֵי. וְנָטַל לְחוּלָקֵיהּ מַה דְּאִתְחֲזֵי לֵיהּ.

765. And because the sons of Aaron arranged their sacrifices, this is why they were punished, for even though all the sacrifices are offered to the King, THE KING distributes them to each one, as befits him, and takes for Himself what befits Him.

End of Ra'aya Meheimna

113. Shavuot

A Synopsis

We learn that the Torah depends on the river issuing forth from Eden.

766. וּבְיוֹם הַבִּכּוּרִים בְּהַקְרִיבְכֶם מִנְחָה חֲדָשָׁה וְגוֹ'. אָמַר רִבִּי אַבָּא, יוֹם הַבִּכּוּרִים, מַאן יוֹם. דָּא נָהָר הַיּוֹצֵא מֵעֵדֶן, דְּאִיהוּ יוֹמָא מֵאִינּוּן בְּכוֹרִין עִלָּאִין. וְדָא אִיהוּ דְּאוֹרַיְיתָא תַּלְיָא בֵּיהּ, וְאִיהוּ אַפִּיק כָּל רָזִין דְּאוֹרַיְיתָא. וּבְגִין דְּאִיהוּ אִילָנָא דְּחַיֵּי, פְּרִי אִילָנִין אִצְטְרִיכוּ לְאַיְיתָאָה.

766. "Also on the day of the firstfruits, when you bring a new meal offering to Hashem" (Bemidbar 28:26). Rabbi Aba said: It is written "the day of the firstfruits," but what does "day" refer to? HE ANSWERS THAT this is a river issuing forth from Eden, NAMELY, ZEIR ANPIN, which is a day of those upper firstfruits, NAMELY YUD HEI, ABA AND IMA, WHO ARE CALLED 'FIRSTFRUITS'. And upon it the Torah depends, NAMELY, ZEIR ANPIN, and He brings forth all the secrets of the Torah, and because He is the Tree of Life, the fruit of the tree has to be brought.

A Synopsis

Moses says that Yisrael is the firstfruits for God of all the nations in the world. He tells us that Vav is the river that comes out of Eden, and that when the river comes out then all the secrets of the Torah also come out. Moses talks about the six Sfirot that are called the primordial years of the creation of the world; because the six Sfirot preceded the world and all the creatures, they are called firstfruits. Man is called the firstborn son after the name of the sign of the covenant that is Yud. Lastly the Faithful Shepherd tells us that the Torah is called 'glory' and anyone who studies Torah is called a king.

רעיא מהימנא

767. וּבְיוֹם הַבִּכּוּרִים בְּהַקְרִיבְכֶם מִנְחָה חֲדָשָׁה וְגוֹ'. רִבִּי אַבָּא אָמַר, יוֹם הַבִּכּוּרִים אִינּוּן בִּכּוּרִים עִלָּאִין דְּאוֹרַיְיתָא. הה״ד, רֵאשִׁית בִּכּוּרֵי אַדְמָתְךָ תָּבִיא וְגוֹ'. אָמַר ר״מ, כְּגַוְונָא דִּבְכוֹרִים לְאִמְּהוֹן, אוֹף הָכִי

אִתְקְרִיאוּ פֵּירוֹת בִּכּוּרִים, דְּפֵירוֹת דְּאִילָנִין, כִּבְכּוּרָה בַּתְּאֵנָה, הָכִי יִשְׂרָאֵל קַדְמוֹנִים וּבִכּוּרִים לְקוּדְשָׁא בְּרִיךְ הוּא, מִכָּל אוּמִין דְּעָלְמָא, הה"ד קֹדֶשׁ יִשְׂרָאֵל לַיהו"ד וְגוֹ'. וּבג"ד אִתְּמַר בְּהוֹן, תָּבִיא בֵּית יְהֹוָה אֱלֹהֶיךָ. וּבְגִין דָּא אוּמִין עכו"ם, דְּאִתְּמַר בְּהוֹן וַיֹּאכְלוּ אֶת יִשְׂרָאֵל בְּכָל פֶּה. יֶאְשָׁמוּ רָעָה תָּבֹא אֲלֵיהֶם.

Ra'aya Meheimna (the Faithful Shepherd)

767. "Also on the day of the firstfruits, when you bring a new meal offering to Hashem." Rabbi Aba said: "the day of the firstfruits" refers to the upper firstfruits of the Torah, NAMELY, ABA AND IMA, as it is written: "The first of the firstfruits of your land you shall bring" (Shemot 23:19). The Faithful Shepherd said, Just as the firstborn to their mother, so are the firstfruits of the tree called, "the first ripe fruit in the fig" (Hoshea 9:10). So, too, are Yisrael the first-ripe and the firstfruits for the Holy One, blessed be He, of all the nations of the world, as it is written: "Yisrael is holy to Hashem..." (Yirmeyah 2:3). For this reason it is said about them, ABOUT THE FIRST FRUITS THAT ALLUDE TO YISRAEL: "you shall bring to the house of Hashem your Elohim" (Shemot 23:19), NAMELY, THAT THEY SHOULD MERIT COMPLETE REDEMPTION. And because of what it is said about the idolatrous nations: "and they devour Yisrael with open mouth" (Yeshayah 9:11); IT IS ALSO SAID ABOUT THEM: "ALL THAT DEVOUR HIM shall be held guilty; evil shall come upon them" (Yirmeyah 2:3).

768. אוֹף הָכִי ו' דְּכָלִיל שִׁית סְפִירָאָן, וְאִיהוּ בֵּן י"ד, אִתְקְרֵי בְּכ"ר. וְכָל עַנְפִין דְּנָפְקִין מִנֵּיהּ דִּבְהוֹן רָאשִׁין, אִתְקְרִיאוּ בִּכּוּרִים. ו' אִיהוּ נָהָר, מֵאִינּוּן בִּכּוּרִים עִלָּאִין, וְהַהוּא נָהָר נָפִיק מֵעֵדֶן. וְדָא אִיהוּ דְּאוֹרַיְיתָא תַּלְיָיא בֵּיהּ. וְכַד נָפִיק נַפְקֵי כָּל רָזִין דְּאוֹרַיְיתָא, וּבְגִין דְּאִיהוּ אִילָנָא דְּחַיֵּי אוֹרַיְיתָא, הֲדָא הוּא דִּכְתִּיב, עֵץ חַיִּים הִיא לַמַּחֲזִיקִים בָּהּ. וּפִקּוּדִין דִּילָהּ לְאִיבָּא פְּרִי דְּאִילָנִין, אִצְטְרִיכוּ לְאַיְיתָאָה.

768. And so, too, Vav, WHICH IS ZEIR ANPIN, that includes six Sfirot, and which is the son of Yud-Hei, WHICH ARE ABA AND IMA THAT ARE CALLED

'FIRSTFRUITS', is called 'a firstfruit'. And all the branches that come out from it and in which there are heads, THE LEVELS WHICH CONTAIN THE UPPER THREE SFIROT THAT ARE TERMED HEAD, are called 'firstfruits'. Vav is a river of those upper firstfruits, BEING ZEIR ANPIN, and this is the river that comes out of Eden, WHICH IS YUD HEI, and it is on this that the Torah is dependent. And when it comes out AND IS REVEALED then all secrets of the Torah come out because it is both the Tree of Life and the Torah, as it is written: "She is a Tree of Life to those who lay hold on her" (Mishlei 3:18). And the precepts OF ZEIR ANPIN, WHO IS THE TORAH, are like the buds of the fruit of the tree that have to be brought TO THE HOUSE OF HASHEM.

769. אָמַר רַעְיָא מְהֵימָנָא וְאִי תֵּימְרוּן אֲמַאי בִּכּוּרִים, דְּלְהוֹן אִתְקְרִיאוּ מִנְחָה חֲדָשָׁה, מְשִׁית יַרְחִין לְשִׁית יַרְחִין. וּמִבַּר נָשׁ דְּאִתְּמַר בֵּיהּ כִּי הָאָדָם עֵץ הַשָּׂדֶה לְתִשַׁע יַרְחִין, אוֹ לְשִׁבְעָה. וּבְעֵירָא אוֹף הָכִי, שַׁבְעַת יָמִים יִהְיֶה תַּחַת אִמּוֹ וּמִיּוֹם הַשְׁמִינִי וָהָלְאָה יֵרָצֶה לְקָרְבַּן אִשֶּׁה לַיהֹוָה, לְקָרְבָּא קָרְבָּנָא קֳדָם יְיָ'. וְעוֹד סְפִירָאן, בְּהוֹן שֵׁם יְהֹוָה, וְכָל כִּנּוּיִין דִּילֵיהּ, אֲמַאי אִתְקְרִיאוּ בְּשֵׁם חַיָּון.

769. The Faithful Shepherd said, You might ask: Why are the firstfruits, that are called "a new meal offering" (Bemidbar 28:26), TO BE FOUND ON THE TREE for periods of six months? THAT IS, DURING THE SIX MONTHS OF THE WINTER AND AUTUMN THEY ARE ON THE TREE AS A FETUS IN ITS MOTHER'S WOMB, AND FROM WHEN THEY START GROWING UNTIL THEY ARE FULLY RIPE ANOTHER SIX MONTHS PASS. WHAT IS THE REASON FOR THIS TAKING SIX MONTHS? And again, about man it is said: "for is the tree of the field a man" (Devarim 20:19). WHAT IS THE REASON FOR HIS HAVING a nine or seven-month GESTATION PERIOD? And it is also SAID about cattle: "then it shall be seven days under its dam; and from the eighth day and thenceforth it shall be accepted for an offering made by fire to Hashem" (Vayikra 22:27), namely, to be offered as a sacrifice before Hashem. AND WHAT IS THE REASON FOR THE SEVEN DAYS BEING REQUIRED? Furthermore, why are the Sfirot, in which are the Name of Yud Hei Vav Hei and all His appellations, called by the names of the living creatures, NAMELY, LION, OX, EAGLE AND MAN?

770. אֶלָּא מִנְחָה חֲדָשָׁה בְּאֹרַח רָזָא , דָּא שְׁכִינְתָּא. מְשִׁית יַרְחִין לְשִׁית

יַרְחִין, אִינּוּן שִׁית סְפִירָאן, דְּאִתְקְרִיאוּ שָׁנִים קַדְמוֹנִיּוֹת לִבְרִיאַת
עָלְמָא, דְּאִינּוּן שִׁיתָא אַלְפֵי שְׁנִין הֲוֵי עָלְמָא, מִסִּטְרָא דְּאִימָּא עִלָּאָה.
וּמִסִּטְרָא דְּאִימָּא תַּתָּאָה, אִתְקְרִיאוּ יַרְחִין. וּבְגִין דְּקָדְמוּ לְעָלְמָא, וְכָל
בִּרְיָין, אִתְקְרִיאוּ בִּכּוּרִים.

770. HE ANSWERS, however, "a new meal offering" is to be understood by way of mystery, AND ITS MEANING is the Shechinah. From six months to six months THAT THE FRUITS ARE GESTATING ON THE TREE refers to the six Sfirot CHESED, GVURAH, TIFERET, NETZACH, HOD AND YESOD which are called 'the primordial years of the creation of the world', which are the secret of the six thousand years that the world has been in existence, AND THEY ARE CALLED 'YEARS' from the aspect of supernal Ima, WHICH IS BINAH, while from the aspect of lower Ima, WHICH IS MALCHUT, they are called 'months'. And because these SIX SFIROT preceded the world and all the creatures, they are called 'firstfruits', AND THIS IS THE SECRET WHY THE FRUIT OF THE TREE ARE FIRSTFRUITS OF SIX MONTHS, FROM THE TIME THEY START GROWING UNTIL THEY ARE FULLY RIPE, NAMELY, CORRESPONDING TO CHESED, GVURAH, TIFERET, NETZACH, HOD AND YESOD FROM THE ASPECT OF MALCHUT.

771. וּשְׁכִינְתָּא מִנְחָה חֲדָשָׁה, מִסִּטְרָא דְּחַיָּה, דְּאִתְּמַר בָּהּ וּדְמוּת
פְּנֵיהֶם פְּנֵי אָדָם. וְאִיהוּ תֵּשַׁע לְחֻשְׁבּוֹן זְעֵיר דַּחֲנוֹךְ. אִיהוּ בַּר נָשׁ
דְּאִתְיְילִיד לְתֵשַׁע יַרְחִין דְּעוּבָּרָא, דְּאִיהִי עֲשִׂירָאָה. וּבְדָא כָּלִיל
מִכֻּלְּהוּ, וְאִתְקְרֵי בֶּן בּוּכְרָא, עַל שֵׁם אוֹת בְּרִית, דְּאִיהוּ י', טִפָּה
קַדְמָאָה דְּאִתְמְשַׁךְ מִנֵּיהּ זֶרַע יוֹרֶה כַּחֵץ. דְּאִיהוּ ו', וְאִיהוּ י', סָלִיק עַל
ו', כְּאִיבָּא דְּסָלִיק עַל עַנְפָּא דְּאִילָנָא.

771. And the Shechinah, which is "a new meal offering" is from the aspect of the living creature, about whom it is said "As for the likeness of their faces, they had the face of a man" (Yechezkel 1:10), THAT IS THE NINE MONTHS OF GESTATION. FOR THE NUMERICAL VALUE OF 'MAN' (HEB. *ADAM*) is nine in the small calculation of Enoch, FOR ACCORDING TO THE SECRET OF THE SMALL NUMBER, WHICH PERTAINS TO METATRON, WHO IS CALLED 'ENOCH', THE VALUE OF THE LETTERS IS CONSIDERED ONLY AS A NUMBER OF UNITS, SUCH THAT THE LETTER MEM WILL BE ONLY

FOUR, AND SO, TOO, TAV WILL BE ONLY FOUR, AND SO ON, SO THAT THE NUMERICAL VALUE OF ADAM IS NINE. And this is THE SECRET OF man, who is born after nine months of gestation. AND THE BORN MAN is the tenth TO THEM and is thereby included in all TEN SFIROT. And MAN is called 'the firstborn son', after the name of the sign of the covenant, WHICH IS YESOD, which is Yud, NAMED AFTER the first drop drawn out of him, seed shot as an arrow, FROM WHICH MAN IS BORN. AND EVERY DROP IS CALLED 'YUD', BECAUSE IT INCLUDES YUD SFIROT. And YESOD is Vav (numerical value of six) AND IS THE DROP, being Yud that rises over Vav, WHICH IS YESOD, just as the fruit rises over the branch of the tree. AND BECAUSE THERE ARE THREE UPPER SFIROT, WHICH ARE THE SECRET OF FIRSTFRUITS, IN THE TEN SFIROT, MAN IS THEREFORE CALLED 'A FIRSTBORN SON'.

772. וְאע״ג דְּכַמָּה עַנְפִין אִית בְּאִילָנָא, וְכַמָּה תְּאֵנִים עֲלַייהוּ, אִינוּן דְּאַקְדִּימוּ בְּקַדְמֵיתָא, אִתְקְרִיאוּ בִּכּוּרִים. אִלֵּין אִינוּן רֵישִׁין דְּכֻלְּהוּ. כְּגַוְונָא דִּלְהוֹן אִתְּמַר שְׂאוּ שְׁעָרִים רָאשֵׁיכֶם. שְׂאוּ מָרוֹם עֵינֵיכֶם וּרְאוּ מִי בָרָא אֵלֶּה. שְׂאוּ אֶת רֹאשׁ כָּל עֲדַת בְּנֵי יִשְׂרָאֵל.

772. And although there are many branches on the tree, on which are a number of figs, those THAT RIPEN first at the beginning are called 'firstfruits'. And these are the 'heads' of all of them, and on a parallel with them it is said: "Lift up your heads, O you gates" (Tehilim 24:7), THE MEANING OF WHICH IS AS: "Lift up your eyes on high, and behold who has created these?" (Yeshayah 40:26); and also: "Take the sum (lit. 'Lift the head') of all the congregation of the children of Yisrael" (Bemidbar 1:2).

773. שְׂאוּ שְׁעָרִים רָאשֵׁיכֶם. שְׁעָרִים אִלֵּין, אִינוּן חַמְשִׁין תַּרְעִין דְּבִינָה. דְּאִיהִי מְתִיבְתָּא דִּלְעֵילָּא. וּשְׂאוּ פִּתְחֵי עוֹלָם, דִּמְתִיבְתָּא תַּתָּאָה, דְּכָל מַאן דְּאִשְׁתְּדַל בְּאוֹרַיְיתָא לְסוֹף מִתְנַשֵּׂא. הה״ד, אִם נָבַלְתָּ בְהִתְנַשֵּׂא. וְאוֹקְמוּהָ מָארֵי מַתְנִיתִין, כָּל הַמְנַבֵּל עַצְמוֹ עַל דִּבְרֵי תוֹרָה, לְסוֹף מִתְנַשֵּׂא, וְיָבֹא מֶלֶךְ הַכָּבוֹד, וְלֵית כָּבוֹד אֶלָּא תוֹרָה.

773. "Lift up your heads, O you gates." Gates here are the fifty gates of Binah, which are the Heavenly Yeshivah. "and be lifted up, you everlasting

doors" refers to the doors of the Earthly Yeshivah, WHICH IS MALCHUT, for everyone who engages in the Torah is, at the end, lifted, as it is written: "If you have done foolishly in lifting yourself up" (Mishlei 30:32). And the sages of the Mishnah taught: Whoever abases himself (acts foolishly) for words of the Torah will, in the end, be exalted. And this is the meaning of "and the King of glory shall come in" (Tehilim 24:7), for there is no glory apart from the Torah.

774. מֵהָכָא, מַאן דְּיָלִיף אוֹרַיְיתָא דְּאִתְקְרִיאַת כָּבוֹד, אִקְרֵי מֶלֶךְ. וְלָא תֵּימָא בְּהַהוּא עָלְמָא דְּאָתֵי וְלָא יַתִּיר, אֶלָּא מֶלֶךְ בִּתְרֵין עָלְמִין, בְּדִיּוּקְנָא דְּמָארֵיהּ. וּבְגִין דָּא כָּפוּל פְּסוּקָא תְּרֵין זִמְנִין, חַד מִי זֶה מֶלֶךְ הַכָּבוֹד. תִּנְיָינָא מִי הוּא זֶה מֶלֶךְ הַכָּבוֹד. שְׂאוּ שְׁעָרִים רָאשֵׁיכֶם, מַאי רָאשֵׁיכֶם תְּרֵין זִמְנִין. אִינּוּן חֵיוָן דְּמֶרְכַּבְתָּא עִלָּאָה, וְחֵיוָן דְּמֶרְכַּבְתָּא תַּתָּאָה.

ע"כ רעיא מהימנא

774. It follows that whoever learns Torah, which is called 'glory', is himself called 'a king', FOR IT IS WRITTEN "AND THE KING OF GLORY SHALL COME IN." And it should not be said that he is a king in the World to Come and no more than that, for he is a king in both the worlds, in the image of his Master. And this is why the verse comes twice: "Who is this king of glory?" (Ibid. 8) and "Who is this king of glory?" (Ibid. 10), WHICH INDICATES BOTH THE WORLDS, THIS WORLD AND THE WORLD TO COME. The verse "Lift up your heads, O you gates" appears twice. What is the meaning of "your heads"? HE ANSWERS THAT on the one occasion they refer to the living creatures of the heavenly Chariot, WHICH IS ABOVE THE CHEST OF ZEIR ANPIN; and on the other occasion they refer to the living creatures of the lower Chariot THAT ARE IN MALCHUT.

End of Ra'aya Meheimna

A Synopsis
Rabbi Shimon explains the meaning of "lift up your heads, O you gates." We learn that God sanctifies all the festivals and makes sure that all the hosts of heaven become sanctified along with the children of Yisrael, in one unity.

775. רִבִּי שִׁמְעוֹן פָּתַח קְרָא וְאָמַר, שְׂאוּ שְׁעָרִים רָאשֵׁיכֶם וְגוֹ'. הַאי קְרָא אוֹקְמוּהָ וְאִתְּמַר. אֲבָל שְׂאוּ שְׁעָרִים רָאשֵׁיכֶם, אִלֵּין אִינוּן תַּרְעִין עִלָּאִין, תַּרְעִין דְּסָכְלְתָנוּ עִלָּאָה. וְאִינוּן חַמְשִׁין תַּרְעִין. רָאשֵׁיכֶם, אִינוּן רָאשִׁים מַאן אִינוּן. אֶלָּא, כָּל חַד וְחַד, אִית לֵיהּ רֵישָׁא לְאִתְפַּשְּׁטָא וּלְמֵיעַל דָּא בְּדָא, וּלְאִתְכַּלְלָא דָּא בְּדָא.

775. Rabbi Shimon unraveled a verse, saying: "Lift up your heads, O you gates..." This verse has been taught and we have learned it. "Lift up your heads, O you gates," these are the upper gates, the gates of upper understanding, and they are fifty in number. "your heads." What heads does this refer to? HE ANSWERS THAT each one, NAMELY, EACH GATE, has a head to be unclothed and enter into one another and to be incorporated within each other.

776. אַשְׁכַּחְנָא בְּסִפְרָא דַּחֲנוֹךְ, שְׂאוּ שְׁעָרִים, אִלֵּין אִינוּן תַּרְעִין דִּלְתַּתָּא מֵאֲבָהָן, וְאִינוּן תְּלָתָא בַּתְרָאִין. רָאשֵׁיכֶם: אִלֵּין אִינוּן רָאשֵׁי אַלְפֵי יִשְׂרָאֵל, וְאִינוּן אֲבָהָן עִלָּאֵי, וְאִינוּן רָאשִׁין דְּאִינוּן תַּרְעִין. וּבְגִין אִלֵּין דְּאִינוּן אוֹפַנִּים, דְּסָחֲרָן וְנַטְלִין לוֹן עַל כַּתְפַּיְיהוּ, אַמְרֵי שְׂאוּ שְׁעָרִים רָאשֵׁיכֶם, שְׂאוּ לְמַאן. לְרָאשֵׁיכֶם. דְּאִינוּן רָאשִׁין עֲלַיְיכוּ, וְשָׁלְטָנִין עֲלַיְיכוּ. וְהִנָּשְׂאוּ פִּתְחֵי עוֹלָם. אִלֵּין אִמָּהָן וְאַרְבַּע אִינוּן דִּלְתַתָּא.

776. I found in the Book of Enoch: "Lift up your heads, O you gates." These are the gates that are below the patriarchs, NAMELY, BELOW CHESED, GVURAH AND TIFERET, WHICH ARE CALLED 'PATRIARCHS', and they are the three last SFIROT, NAMELY NETZACH, HOD AND YESOD. "your heads" are the heads of the thousands of Yisrael, and they are the upper patriarchs, NAMELY CHESED, GVURAH AND TIFERET, WHICH, AT THE TIME OF GREATNESS, BECOME CHOCHMAH, BINAH AND DA'AT, and they are the heads of those gates. And for the sake of these, NETZACH, HOD AND YESOD, which are the Ofanim that encompass and bear them on their shoulders, it is said: "Lift up your heads, O gates." Lift up whom? Your heads, for they, CHESED, GVURAH AND TIFERET, are heads over you and have control over you. "and be lifted up, you everlasting doors" (Tehilim

24:7): These are the matriarchs, and they are four who are below, NAMELY CHESED, GVURAH, TIFERET AND MALCHUT, THAT ARE IN MALCHUT, WHERE SARAH IS CHESED, RIVKAH IS GVURAH, LEAH IS TIFERET AND RACHEL IS MALCHUT.

777. וְיָבֹא מֶלֶךְ הַכָּבוֹד, דָּא מַלְכָּא עִלָּאָה דְּכֹלָּא, דְּאִיהוּ מֶלֶךְ מֵהַהוּא כָּבוֹד, דְּנָהִיר לְסִיהֲרָא, וּמַאן אִיהוּ. יְיָ' צְבָאוֹת. וַיָּבֹא, לְאָן אֲתָר. לְמֵיעַל אוֹרַיְיתָא בַּאֲרוֹנָא, בְּחִבּוּרָא חֲדָא, כַּדְקָא יָאוּת. וְכֵיוָן דְּהַאי עָאל לְאַתְרֵיהּ, כְּדֵין אוֹרַיְיתָא עָאל בַּאֲרוֹנָא. וְאִתְחַבַּר חִבּוּרָא חֲדָא, אוֹרַיְיתָא עִלָּאָה, בְּאוֹרַיְיתָא דִּבְעַל פֶּה, מִתְחַבְּרוּ לְפָרְשָׁא מִילִין סְתִימִין.

777. "and the king of glory shall come in": This is the supernal King over all, NAMELY, ZEIR ANPIN, WHICH INCLUDES CHESED, GVURAH, TIFERET, NETZACH, HOD AND YESOD, for He is King of that same glory because He gives light to the moon, WHICH IS MALCHUT, THAT IS CALLED 'GLORY'. And who is this? It is "Hashem Tzva'ot" (Ibid. 10), NAMELY, ZEIR ANPIN, WHO IS SO CALLED. "shall come" (Ibid. 7). HE ASKS, To what place HE "SHALL COME"? AND HE ANSWERS, to bring the Torah, WHICH IS ZEIR ANPIN, into the Ark, WHICH IS MALCHUT, in one union as is fitting. For after the former has entered His place, NAMELY, AFTER ZEIR ANPIN HAS UNITED WITH MALCHUT, WHICH IS HIS PLACE, IT IS THEN CONSIDERED THAT the Torah, WHICH IS AN ASPECT OF ZEIR ANPIN, has entered the Ark, WHICH IS AN ASPECT OF MALCHUT. And they have become joined together in one union, the upper Torah WHICH IS AN ASPECT OF ZEIR ANPIN with the Oral Torah, WHICH IS AN ASPECT OF MALCHUT, for they join together in order to interpret hidden matters, NAMELY, TO REVEAL THE SECRETS OF THE TORAH TO THE RIGHTEOUS.

778. אֵימָתַי. בְּשָׁבוּעוֹתֵיכֶם. לְמִנְיָינָא דְּאַתּוּן מוֹנִין. דִּבְכָל שַׁעֲתָא דְּיִשְׂרָאֵל עַבְדִּין חוּשְׁבָּנִין לְיַרְחִין וְזִמְנִין, קוּדְשָׁא בְּרִיךְ הוּא אַתְקִין תֵּיבָה גּוֹ אִינּוּן רְקִיעִין, וְאַעֲבַּר כָּרוֹזָא, הָא בְּנֵי לְתַתָּא, קַדִּישׁוּ יַרְחָא, קַדִּישׁוּ זִמְנָא, אִתְקַדָּשׁוּ כֻּלְּכוּ לְעֵילָּא. וְעָבֵיד לְכָל חֵילֵי דִּבִשְׁמַיָּא, דְּמִתְקַדְּשִׁין כַּחֲדָא בְּעַמָּא קַדִּישָׁא, וְכֻלְּהוּ נַטְרֵי כַּחֲדָא, נְטִירָא חֲדָא,

וְעַל דָּא בְּשָׁבוּעוֹתֵיכֶם, לְמִנְיָינָא דְּאַתּוּן מוֹנִין אִינּוּן שֶׁבַע שַׁבָּתוֹת.

778. HE ASKS: When IS THIS UNITY MADE? AND HE ANSWERS: ABOUT THIS IT IS WRITTEN: "ALSO ON THE DAY OF THE FIRSTFRUITS, WHEN YOU BRING A NEW MEAL OFFERING TO HASHEM in your feast of weeks" (Bemidbar 28:26). AND THE MEANING OF IT is according to your reckoning. For whenever Yisrael make calculations regarding the new moons and festivals, the Holy One, blessed be He, sets an Ark within the heavens, NAMELY, ONE THAT IS LIKE THE LECTERN ARK OF THE READER, and passes a proclamation: 'My sons on earth have sanctified the month (or) have sanctified the festival. Sanctify yourselves, all of you in heaven.' And He sees to it that all the hosts of the heavens become sanctified as one with the holy people and they all keep one observance ON THE DAY THAT YISRAEL DETERMINED ON EARTH. Therefore IT IS WRITTEN: "in your...weeks," namely, according to your reckoning of these seven weeks.

114. "But you shall surely let the mother go"

A Synopsis

Rabbi Shimon uses the analogy of the mother bird brooding over her chicks to show how Yisrael must count seven weeks and thereby draw down seven Sfirot.

779. וּכְדֵין מָשִׁיךְ קוּדְשָׁא בְּרִיךְ הוּא, מְשִׁיכוּ דְּשֶׁבַע דַּרְגִּין לְתַתָּא, בְּהַהוּא דַּרְגָּא דְּאִתְאֲחַד בְּהוּ, בְּאִינּוּן שֶׁבַע שַׁבָּתוֹת. וְאִי תֵּימָא, וְהָא שִׁיתָּא אִינּוּן וְלָא יַתִּיר. אֶלָּא כְּדֵין אִימָא יָתְבָא עַל אֶפְרוֹחִין, וְאִשְׁתְּכָחַת רְבִיעָא עָלַיְיהוּ. וַאֲנָן מְפַרְחִין לָהּ, וְנַטְלִין אִינּוּן שִׁית בְּנִין. בְּהַאי דַּרְגָּא דִּלְתַתָּא, לְקַיְּימָא דִּכְתִיב, שַׁלֵּחַ תְּשַׁלַּח אֶת הָאֵם וְאֶת הַבָּנִים וְגוֹ'.

779. And then the Holy One, blessed be He, draws down seven grades to that grade, NAMELY, MALCHUT, which unites with them, with those seven weeks, WHICH ARE THE SECRET OF CHESED, GVURAH, TIFERET, NETZACH, HOD, YESOD AND MALCHUT. And should you suggest that there are six grades, and no more, NAMELY CHESED, GVURAH, TIFERET, NETZACH, HOD AND YESOD, FOR MALCHUT IS THE ONE THAT RECEIVES FROM THEM AND IS NOT PART OF THE RECKONING, HE ANSWERS: Then mother, NAMELY, BINAH, is sitting upon the young, WHICH ARE CHESED, GVURAH, TIFERET, NETZACH, HOD, YESOD AND MALCHUT, and is to be found brooding over them. BINAH is sent to fly away FROM THEM, and we take those six young ones, NAMELY CHESED, GVURAH, TIFERET, NETZACH, HOD AND YESOD, with the grade that is below them, NAMELY, MALCHUT, to fulfill the verse: "but you shall surely let the mother go, and take the young to you" (Devarim 22:7), WHERE THE MOTHER IS BINAH AND THE YOUNG ARE CHESED, GVURAH, TIFERET, NETZACH, HOD, YESOD AND MALCHUT. AND WE THEREFORE COUNT SEVEN WEEKS, DRAWING DOWN SEVEN SFIROT, NAMELY, MALCHUT ALSO, AND HAVING DRAWN DOWN MALCHUT ALSO, WE DRAW DOWN CHESED, GVURAH, TIFERET NETZACH, HOD AND YESOD TO INCLUDE THEM IN MALCHUT.

115. Yisrael know how to hunt good game

A Synopsis

Rabbi Hamnuna Saba continues the analogy and tells how Malchut, as though a chick, is coaxed out from under the Mother, Binah, with soft little prayers. Then Malchut stays with Yisrael, and the other Sfirot, like more small birds, fly out to Yisrael as well. We learn that one cannot pursue the Mother, Binah, for she is inconceivable.

780. רַב הַמְנוּנָא סָבָא אָמַר, בְּהַאי יוֹמָא, לָא נַטְלִין יִשְׂרָאֵל אֶלָּא חָמֵשׁ בְּנִין, וְאִינּוּן חֲמִשָּׁה חוּמָשֵׁי תּוֹרָה. וְאִי תֵּימָא שִׁית אִינּוּן. אֶלָּא שְׁבַע אִינּוּן, בְּחַד צְפַר דְּאִשְׁתְּכַח בֵּין גַּדְפָהָא דְּאִימָא. וְיִשְׂרָאֵל, יַדְעֵי לְמֵיצָד צֵידָא טָבָא, רַבָּא וְיַקִּירָא. מָה עָבְדֵי. מַפְּקֵי מִתְּחוֹת גַּדְפָהָא דְּאִמָּהָא, הַהוּא צִפּוֹרָא, בִּלְחִישׁוּ דְּפוּמָא מְלַחֲשׁוּ לְגַבָּה, לְחִישׁוּ בָּתַר לְחִישׁוּ.

780. Rav Hamnuna Saba said: On that day Yisrael takes only five sons, which are the five books of the Torah, NAMELY, CHESED, GVURAH, TIFERET, NETZACH AND HOD OF ZEIR ANPIN, WHICH ARE THE FIVE PARTS OF ZEIR ANPIN, WHO IS CALLED 'TORAH'. And should you object, saying that the Sfirot are six in number, FOR THERE IS ALSO YESOD, HE ANSWERS, the truth really is that there are seven, together with a certain bird, WHICH IS MALCHUT, and they are thus between the wings of mother, WHICH IS BINAH. AND THE REASON WHY HE THOUGHT INITIALLY THAT THERE WERE ONLY FIVE GRADES, CHESED, GVURAH, TIFERET, NETZACH AND HOD, IS THAT THERE ARE IN ESSENCE ONLY FIVE GRADES WITH YESOD AND MALCHUT THAT ARE INCLUSIVE OF THOSE FIVE GRADES, AND CONTAINING NOTHING NEW. And Yisrael know how to hunt for good and valuable game. What do they do? They draw out that bird, WHICH IS MALCHUT, from under the wings of mother with soft little sounds from the mouth that they whisper to her, one after the other, NAMELY, WITH MANY PRAYERS.

781. וְהַהוּא צְפּוֹרָא דְּחָיִישׁ לְאִינּוּן לְחִישִׁין, וּלְאִינּוּן קַלִּין, דְּקָא מְלַחֲשֵׁי לְגַבָּה. וְאע"ג דְּאִיהִי תְּחוֹת גַּדְפֵּי אִמָּהָא, זָקִיף רֵישָׁא וְאִסְתַּכְּלַת לְגַבֵּי הַהוּא לְחִישׁוּ דְּקָלָא, וּפַרְחַת לְגַבַּיְיהוּ, וְנַפְקַת מִתְּחוֹת

גַּדְפָּהָא דְּאִימָּא. כֵּיוָן דְּיִשְׂרָאֵל נַטְלֵי לָהּ, אַתְקִיפוּ בָּהּ, וְלַחֲשִׁין לָהּ,
וְקַשְׁרִין לָהּ בְּקִשּׁוּרָא דְּלָא תִּפְרַח וְתֵזִיל. מִיַּד נַטְלֵי לָהּ יִשְׂרָאֵל בְּהַהוּא
קִשּׁוּרָא, וְאִיהִי בָּעָאת לְמִפְרַח וּלְמֵיזַל, וְלָא יָכִילַת לְמֵיזַל לָהּ.

781. And that bird, sensing those whispers and the sounds that they voice to
her under their breath, even though she is under the wings of mother, she
raises her head and looks out at the whispering voices and flies out to them,
emerging from under the wings of mother. So Yisrael takes her and holds
her, whispering to her and tying her with a knot so that she will not fly off
and leave. Yisrael immediately catch her in this knot, and the bird wants to
fly off and leave them but is unable to do so.

782. וּבְעוֹד דְּהִיא קְשִׁירָא בִּידַיְיהוּ, אִינּוּן מְלַחֲשֵׁי בְּקַלֵּיהוֹן, וְאִיהִי
מְצַפְצְפָא בַּהֲדַיְיהוּ, וּפַרְחַת לְעֵילָּא, וְנַחֲתַת. וְכָל אִינּוּן בְּנִין דִּתְחוֹת
גַּדְפֵּי אִמְּהוֹן, כֵּיוָן דְּשַׁמְעֵי הַהוּא צִפְצָפָא דְּאֲחַתְהוֹן, וּלְחִישׁוּ דְּהַהוּא
קָלָא, מִיַּד נַפְקֵי מִתְּחוֹת גַּדְפָּהָא דְּאִמְּהוֹן, וּפַרְחֵי לְגַבֵּי הַהוּא צִפּוֹרָא,
וְיִשְׂרָאֵל נַטְלֵי לוֹן, וְאַחֲדֵי בְּהוּ. וְאִלְמָלֵא הַהוּא צִפּוֹרָא דְּקָא אַחֲדֵי
בְּקַדְמֵיתָא, אִינּוּן לָא פַרְחֵי לְגַבַּיְיהוּ לְעָלְמִין, וְלָא יַכְלִין לְאַחֲדָא בְּהוּ.

782. And while she is still bound in the hands OF YISRAEL, they whisper
their sounds, and she chirps with them, and flies up and down. And all those
sons who are under the wings of their mother, NAMELY, CHESED,
GVURAH, TIFERET, NETZACH, HOD AND YESOD OF ZEIR ANPIN, when
they hear that chirping of their sister, MALCHUT, and the whisper of that
sound FROM YISRAEL, they immediately emerge from under the wings of
their mother and fly towards that bird, WHICH IS MALCHUT, and Yisrael
take them and unite with them. And had it not been for that bird, with which
they were attached initially, they, CHESED, GVURAH, TIFERET, NETZACH,
HOD AND YESOD, would never have flown to them, and they would not
have been able to unite with them.

783. הֵיךְ צָדִין צֵידָה דְּהַאי צִפְּרָא קַדִּישָׁא. מַתְקְנִין לְקַמָּא מֵיכְלָא
יַקִּירָא בְּחֶדְוָוה, וְכָל עִנּוּגִין, וְעָאלִין לְבֵי כְּנִשְׁתָּא וּלְבֵי מִדְרָשָׁא,
וּמְצַפְצְפָן לְגַבָּהּ בְּקַל לְחִישׁוּ כַּדְקָא יָאוּת. וְאִיהִי דְּמִטַּמְּרָא תְּחוֹת

-217-

גַּדְפָּהָא דְּאִימָא, זַקְפַת רֵישָׁא, וְחָמְאת פָּתוֹרִין מְתַקְּנָן, וְצִפְצוּפִין לְגַבָּה כַּדְקָא יָאוֹת. נָפְקַת וּפַרְחַת לְגַבַּיְיהוּ כְּמָה דְּאִתְּמַר, וּבָה אֲחִדִין כָּל אִינּוּן בְּנִין.

783. How does one catch this holy bird? This is done by preparing before her valuable food with rejoicing, and all sorts of delights, and attending the synagogue and the school-house, and chirping at her in a whispering voice, as is fitting. And she, THE BIRD, who is hiding under the wings of Mother, raises her head and looks at the prepared tables, with the chirping which is for her sake, NAMELY, THE PRAYERS, as is fitting, and she emerges FROM UNDER THE WINGS OF MOTHER, and flies to them, as we have learned, and all those sons, NAMELY CHESED, GVURAH, TIFERET, NETZACH, HOD AND YESOD OF ZEIR ANPIN, hold on to her.

784. וּמְשַׁלְחִין לְהַהוּא דִּרְבִיעָא עָלַיְיהוּ וְאַזְלַת. בְּגִין דְּהָא מִן רְקִיעָא שְׁבִיעָאָה וּלְעֵילָּא, בְּמִכּוּסֶה מִמְּךָ אַל תִּדְרוֹשׁ. שָׁלַח לֵיהּ, דְּלָא תִיכוֹל לְאַדְבְּקָה וע"ד כְּתִיב, שַׁלֵּחַ תְּשַׁלַּח וְגוֹ'.

784. And they send the one who is sitting over them, NAMELY, MOTHER, WHICH IS BINAH, WHICH IS SITTING OVER CHESED, GVURAH, TIFERET, NETZACH, HOD, YESOD AND MALCHUT, and she goes off. Because from the seventh heaven, WHICH IS CHESED, and above, NAMELY, THE UPPER THREE SFIROT, do not expound what is hidden from you. THEREFORE, send her away, THAT IS, THE MOTHER, WHICH IS BINAH, WHICH IS ONE OF THE UPPER THREE SFIROT, for you will not be able to catch her. About this, Scripture says: "You shall surely let the mother go, and take the young to you" (Devarim 22:7), THE MEANING OF WHICH IS THAT YOU SHOULD NOT TRY TO PURSUE BINAH, FOR SHE IS NOT CONCEIVABLE. BUT THE YOUNG, NAMELY CHESED, GVURAH, TIFERET, NETZACH, HOD, YESOD AND MALCHUT, WHICH ARE CONCEIVABLE, YOU MAY TAKE TO YOU.

785. מִקְרָא קֹדֶשׁ, דָּא קְרִיאָה וְצִפְצוּפָא, דְּעַבְדִּין לְהַהוּא צִפֳּרָא קַדִּישָׁא בְּקַדְמֵיתָא. וְכֵיוָן דְּאַחֲדִין בָּהּ שְׁאַר יוֹמִין, אִקְרוּן מִקְרָאֵי קֹדֶשׁ. הַאי צִפֳּרָא אִקְרֵי קֹדֶשׁ, דִּכְתִיב, כִּי קֹדֶשׁ הִיא לָכֶם. וּבְגִין דְּאִיהִי קֹדֶשׁ, אִיהִי קָרְאָה לְכוּלְּהוּ וְאַתְיָין לְגַבָּה. וּבְגִין כָּךְ אִקְרוּן מִקְרָאֵי קֹדֶשׁ.

785. "you shall have a holy gathering (lit. 'calling')" (Bemidbar 28:26). This is the calling and chirping, NAMELY, THE PRAYERS, that we utter for that holy bird, WHICH IS MALCHUT, at the beginning. SUBSEQUENTLY, since the remaining days CHESED, GVURAH, TIFERET, NETZACH, HOD AND YESOD, hold on to her, they are called 'holy callings' IN THE PLURAL. FOR this bird is called 'holy', as it is written: "for it (she) is holy to you" (Shemot 31:14), WHICH IS SAID ABOUT MALCHUT. And because she is holy, she calls to all of them, CHESED, GVURAH, TIFERET, NETZACH, HOD AND YESOD, and they come to her, which is why they are called 'holy callings'.

786. אִיהִי קָרְאָה, וְיִשְׂרָאֵל מְצַפְצְפָן בַּהֲדָה, וְקַרְאָן אוֹף הָכִי. וְעַל דָּא אִינּוּן אַתְיָין לְגַבַּיְיהוּ, וְאַחֲדֵי בְּהוּ. בְּגִין כָּךְ אֵלֶּה מוֹעֲדֵי יְיָ' מִקְרָאֵי קֹדֶשׁ אֲשֶׁר תִּקְרְאוּ אוֹתָם. מִקְרָאֵי קֹדֶשׁ, בְּצִפְצוּפָא דִּלְהוֹן, וּבְהַהוּא צִפְּרָא קַדִּישָׁא קֹדֶשׁ, דְּקָרָא לוֹן.

786. And she calls TO CHESED, GVURAH, TIFERET, NETZACH, HOD AND YESOD, and Yisrael chirp along with her, and they, too, call, and they therefore come to them and unite with them. This is why IT IS WRITTEN: "These are the feasts of Hashem, holy gatherings (callings), which you shall proclaim (call)" (Vayikra 23:4). AND THEY ARE CALLED 'holy callings' AFTER their chirping, AND AFTER that holy bird, WHICH IS holy, that calls them.

116. "A bird's nest"

A Synopsis

The Faithful Shepherd says that the bird is the Shechinah, the nest
is the Temple and the chicks are Yisrael. When Yisrael sinned and
the Temple was destroyed the Shechinah went away. We are told
about the six orders of the Mishnah, the six words of the Sh'ma
Yisrael, the sages of the Bible, and the Kabbalists – and in all these
Moses emphasizes the role and importance of prayer and intention.

רַעְיָא מְהֵימָנָא

787. אָמַר רַעְיָא מְהֵימָנָא, מִלִּין אִלֵּין, כַּמָּה סְתִימִין אִינּוּן, לְמַאן דְּלָא
יָדַע, וְגַלְיָין לְמַאן דְּיָדַע בְּהוּ. וַדַּאי הַהוּא צִפּוֹרָא אִיהוּ שְׁכִינְתָּא. קֵן
דִּילָהּ, דָּא בֵּי מַקְדְּשָׁא. וְיִשְׂרָאֵל אִינּוּן אֶפְרוֹחִין, דְּאִימָּא יָתְבָא עֲלַיְיהוּ.
הה"ד, וְהָאֵם רוֹבֶצֶת עַל הָאֶפְרוֹחִים, וְאִינּוּן מָארֵי מִשְׁנָה, דְּפַרְחִין
בְּפִקּוּדִין דִּילָהּ. אוֹ בֵּיצִים, אִינּוּן מָארֵי מִקְרָא.

Ra'aya Meheimna (the Faithful Shepherd)

787. The Faithful Shepherd said: How obscure these matters are for one who
does not know them, and how transparent for one who does! Certainly that
bird is the Shechinah and her nest is the Temple, WHERE THE SHECHINAH
RESTED. And Yisrael are the young ones, upon whom the mother, WHICH IS
THE SHECHINAH, sits. Scripture says: "and the mother bird sitting upon the
young, OR UPON THE EGGS" (Devarim 22:6). This refers to the sages of the
Mishnah, who fly with her precepts. "or upon the eggs" refers to the sages of
the Bible.

788. וּבְזִמְנָא דְּחָבוּ יִשְׂרָאֵל, וְאִתְחָרִיב בֵּי מַקְדְּשָׁא, מַה כְּתִיב. שַׁלֵּחַ
תְּשַׁלַּח אֶת הָאֵם, הה"ד, וּבְפִשְׁעֵיכֶם שֻׁלְּחָה אִמְּכֶם. וְאִינּוּן מָארֵי שִׁיתָא
סִדְרֵי מִשְׁנָה כְּתִיב בְּהוּ, וְאֶת הַבָּנִים תִּקַּח לָךְ. דְּאִינּוּן שִׁית, מִסִּטְרָא
דְּשִׁית בְּנִין דְּתִתְחוֹת אִימָּא עִלָּאָה, דְּאִינּוּן בְּשִׁית תֵּיבִין דְּק"ש. אוֹ בְּשִׁית
סִדְרֵי מִשְׁנָה, אֶחָד הַמַּרְבֶּה וְאֶחָד הַמַּמְעִיט וּבִלְבַד שֶׁיְּכַוֵּין לִבּוֹ לַשָּׁמַיִם.

וְקַשְׁרִין לוֹן בְּקִשְׁרִין דִּתְפִלִּין, עַל רֵישָׁא וְעַל דְרוֹעָא.

788. But when Yisrael sinned, and the Temple was destroyed, what is written? "but you shall surely let the mother go" (Ibid. 7), BEING THE SHECHINAH. This is as it is written: "And for your transgressions was your mother sent away" (Yeshayah 50:1). And about the sages of the six orders of the Mishnah, it is written: "and take the young to you" (Devarim 22:7), These are the six ORDERS, from the side of the six sons CHESED, GVURAH, TIFERET, NETZACH, HOD AND YESOD, which are under upper mother, WHICH IS BINAH, and which are alluded to in the six words of the reading of Sh'ma Yisrael, or in the six orders of the Mishnah. It is all the same, whether (a man offers) much or little, if only he directs his mind towards Heaven, NAMELY, TO UNITE MALCHUT WITH ZEIR ANPIN WHO IS CALLED 'HEAVEN', and binds it with the knot of the Tefilin on the head and on the arm.

789. וּבְמַאי נַטְלִין בְּנִין בְּכַמָּה צְפְצוּפִין דְּקַלִּין דְּק"ש. וּלְבָתַר לַחֲשִׁין בְּלִחִישׁוּ בִּצְלוֹתָא דַחֲשַׁאי, לְגַבֵּי אִימָּא וּבְרַתָּא, וְאִינּוּן ה' ה', וְנָחֲתִּין לְגַבֵּיהּ ו', בְּקֶשֶׁר דִּילֵיהּ דְּאִיהוּ יוּ"ד. וְשַׁרְיָא ה' עִלָּאָה, עַל ו', תְּפִלִּין עַל רֵישֵׁיהּ. ה זְעֵירָא, נָחַת לְגַבֵּי י', דְּאִיהוּ קֶשֶׁר דְּה' עִלָּאָה, עַל רֹאשׁ ו', וְאִיהוּ ו', קֶשֶׁר עִמָּהּ בְּה' דְּיָד כֵּהָה.

789. With what do the sons take? With many chirps of the sounds of the reading of Sh'ma Yisrael? And afterwards they secretly whisper the silent prayer, NAMELY, THE AMIDAH PRAYER to the Mother, WHICH IS BINAH, and to the daughter, WHICH IS MALCHUT. And these are Hei Hei, FORM MOTHER IS THE FIRST HEI OF YUD HEI VAV HEI AND THE DAUGHTER IS THE LAST HEI. And they descend to the Vav, WHICH IS ZEIR ANPIN, with His knot, which is the Yud OF YUD HEI VAV HEI, NAMELY, CHOCHMAH. And supernal Hei, WHICH IS BINAH, rests upon the Vav, WHICH IS ZEIR ANPIN, THIS BEING THE SECRET OF the Tefilin over his head. And the small Hei, WHICH IS MALCHUT, descends to Yud OF THE YUD HEI VAV HEI, which is the knot of the upper Hei that is on the head of the Vav. FOR THIS IS THE SECRET OF ABA, WHICH IS YUD OF YUD HEI VAV HEI, WHO ESTABLISHED THE DAUGHTER, WHICH IS MALCHUT. And this Vav, WHICH IS ZEIR ANPIN, is connected with her in the Hei of a dim hand,

NAMELY, THE KNOT OF THE HAND TEFILIN. AND THIS IS IN SUCH A WAY
THAT THE YUD OF YUD HEI VAV HEI, WHICH IS THE SECRET OF THE
KNOT OF THE HEAD TEFILIN, WHICH IS THE SECRET OF IMA ON THE
HEAD OF THE VAV AND IS THE KNOT OF THE HAND TEFILIN, WHICH IS
MALCHUT, IS WITH THE DIM HAND OF ZEIR ANPIN.

790. וּבג"ד, אֶפְרוֹחִים מִסִּטְרָא דְּאָת ו', כָּלִיל ו' סִדְרֵי מִשְׁנָה. אוֹ
בֵּיצִים, אִלֵּין. מָארֵי מִקְרָא, דְּאִתְּמַר עָלַיְיהוּ, בֶּן ה' שָׁנִים לְמִקְרָא, וְדָא
ה'. בְּנִין מִסִּטְרָא דְּבֶן יָ"ה, אִלֵּין מָארֵי קַבָּלָה. עָלַיְיהוּ אִתְּמַר לֹא תִקַּח
הָאֵם עַל הַבָּנִים.

790. And for this reason, 'the young ones' are from the side of the letter
Vav, which includes the six orders of the Mishnah, NAMELY CHESED,
GVURAH, TIFERET, NETZACH, HOD AND YESOD. "or upon the eggs"
refers to the sages of the Bible, WHICH IS MALCHUT, THE FINAL HEI OF
THE YUD HEI VAV HEI. And it is said about them: At Hei (= five) years old,
one is fit for the study of Scripture, and this is MALCHUT, WHICH IS Hei.
'The young' refers to the side of the son of Yud Hei, NAMELY, ZEIR ANPIN,
WHICH HAS THE UPPER THREE SFIROT FROM YUD HEI, and these are the
Kabbalists, about whom it is said: "you shall not take the mother bird
together with the young" (Devarim 22:6).

117. Moses' bride

A Synopsis

We learn that the sages of Kabbalah are also called the sages of the Talmud, and that study is divided into three parts: one-third study of the Torah, one-third study of the Mishnah and one-third study of the Talmud. The Faithful Shepherd explains how it is permitted to interpret the secrets of the Torah by expanding and restricting the meanings of certain words. In this way the sages can piece together the inner meanings, just as a tailor pieces together the cloth for a suit. Moses concludes by speaking about the seven lights of the candelabrum and the seven blessings of the Sh'ma.

791. וּמָארֵי קַבָּלָה, אִינּוּן מָארֵי תַּלְמוּד. וְאִתְּמַר עָלַיְיהוּ, וְשִׁנַּנְתָּם. וְאוּקְמוּהָ מָארֵי מַתְנִיתִין, אַל תִּקְרֵי וְשִׁנַּנְתָּם, אֶלָּא וְשִׁלַּשְׁתָּם, דְּאִינּוּן שְׁלִישׁ בְּמִקְרָא, שְׁלִישׁ בַּמִּשְׁנָה, שְׁלִישׁ בַּתַּלְמוּד. וְרָזָא דְמִלָּה, כִּי יִקָּרֵא קַן צִפּוֹר לְפָנֶיךָ בַּדֶּרֶךְ, בְּמָארֵי מִקְרָא. וְעָשִׂיתָ מְנוֹרַת זָהָב טָהוֹר. הָא אוּקְמוּהָ, וְעָשִׂיתָ מְנוֹרַת, כְּלָל. זָהָב, פְּרָט. מִקְשָׁה, כְּלָל. וְכַמָּה מִקְרָאִין מָארֵי מַתְנִיתִין, אִינּוּן מַרְבִּין וּמְמַעֲטִין, כְּגוֹן רִיבָּה וּמִיעֵט. אוֹף הָכִי, מַרְבִּין, אַל תִּקְרֵי מַה. אֶלָּא מֵאָה. אוֹף הָכִי, אַל תִּקְרֵי וְשִׁנַּנְתָּם, אֶלָּא וְשִׁלַּשְׁתָּם. וְדַרְשִׁינָן מִנֵּיהּ, שְׁלִישׁ בְּמִקְרָא, שְׁלִישׁ בַּמִּשְׁנָה, שְׁלִישׁ בַּתַּלְמוּד. כִּדְאִיתָא בְּקִדּוּשִׁין.

791. And the sages of Kabbalah are the sages of the Talmud, and it is said about them: "and you shall teach them diligently (Heb. *veshinantam*)" (Devarim 6:7). And the sages of the Mishnah taught: Do not read *veshinantam* (lit. repeat them twice) but *Veshilashtam* (lit. repeat them thrice) namely, a third in the Torah, a third in the Mishnah, and a third in the Talmud. And the secret of the matter is: "If a bird's nest chance to be before you in the way" (Devarim 22:6): "in the way" refers to the sages of the Torah, "IN ANY TREE" TO THE SAGES OF THE MISHNAH, AND "OR ON THE GROUND" TO THE SAGES OF THE TALMUD, NAMELY, A THIRD IN TORAH, A THIRD IN MISHNAH, AND A THIRD IN TALMUD. AND ONE NEED NOT BE SURPRISED THAT THE SAGES CHANGED THE WORD *VESHINANTAM* INTO *VESHILASHTAM*, FOR ON THE VERSE "And you shall make a candlestick of pure gold" (Shemot 25:31), they taught: "And you

shall make a candlestick " is a general proposition, "of gold" is a particular proposition, and "of beaten work" is a general proposition. And there are likewise a number of verses where the sages of the Mishnah expand or restrict THE MEANING, according to THE PRINCIPLES OF amplification and diminution, and there are also cases WHERE A LETTER is added, AS WHEN IT IS SAID: Do not read 'mah': (Eng. 'what' - Mem Hei) but 'me'ah' (Eng. 'one hundred' - Mem Aleph Hei). And so it is WHEN WE SAY: Do not read *veshinantam* but *veshilashtam*, and we deduce from this: a third in the Torah, a third in the Mishnah, and a third in the Talmud, as said in tractate Kidushin.

792. אוף הָכִי, בְּיוֹם כַּלַּת מֹשֶׁה, כַּלָּת דַּרְשִׁינָן בֵּיהּ. אִי תֵּימָא דְּדַרְשֵׁינָן לוֹן מִנְּהוֹן. כֵּיצַד מֵאַלְפָּא בֵּיתָא, וְלָא מֵעַצְמָן דְּאִינּוּן לֵית לוֹן רְשׁוּ, לְאוֹסָפָא, וְלָא לְמִגְרַע אוֹת מִנֵּיהּ, אוֹ לְאַחְלָפָא אָת דָּא בְּאָת אַחֲרָא. הָא כְּתִיב כַּלּוֹת מָלֵא בְּאוֹרַיְיתָא. מַאן יָהִיב לוֹן רְשׁוּת לְמִגְרַע אוֹת מִנֵּיהּ, דְּהוּא ו', הָא לָא אִית הָכָא מִלָּה דְּאִתְחַלִּיף בְּאַלְפָּא בֵּיתָא. אֶלָּא עַל אִלֵּין תֵּיבִין חֲסֵרִין, דְּאִינּוּן מְלֵאִים. וּמְלֵאִים, דְּאִינּוּן חֲסֵרִים. וְעַל כָּל פֵּירוּשִׁין דְּיַכְלִין לְמֶעְבַּד לְקַשְׁטָא כַּלָּה בְּתַכְשִׁיטִין דִּילָה, קוּדְשָׁא בְּרִיךְ הוּא מָנֵי לְמֶעְבַּד, כְּמָה דְּיֵימְרוּן, וּלְמֶהֱוֵי מַאֲמִין לוֹן, הה"ד עַל פִּי הַתּוֹרָה אֲשֶׁר יוֹרוּךְ.

792. So, too: "And it came to pass on the day that Moses had finished (Heb. *kalot*)" (Bemidbar 7:1), which we interpret as though it were written the bride of (Heb. *kalat*) MOSES. And lest you think that we have this exegesis from them, namely, from THE LETTERS OF the alphabet IN THE WORD, WHERE 'KALOT' IS THE SAME AS 'KALAH', without themselves ADDING ANYTHING for it is not permitted to add or take away a letter from it, nor to substitute one letter for another. If this be so, then in the Torah it is written with the full spelling *kalot*: (Caf Lamed Vav Tav) WITH A VAV. Who, then, gave permission to take away one letter from it, namely the Vav AND TO INTERPRET IT as *KALAT* (CAF LAMED Tav)? There is here no case of exchanging in alphabet EXCHANGE, SUCH AS THE ATBASH CIPHER. BUT RATHER THE VAV HAS BEEN REMOVED FROM THE WORD, AND IT HAS BEEN EXPOUNDED AS CAF LAMED TAV, WRITTEN WITHOUT VAV. But certain words that are written in the abbreviated spelling ARE EXPOUNDED

as though written out in full, and other WORDS that are written out in full are (expounded) as though written out in the abbreviated form. About these and about all sorts of explanations that can be made to embellish the bride, WHICH IS THE TORAH, in her ornaments, the Holy One, blessed be He, commanded us to do as they say, and to trust them, as it is written: "according to the sentence of the Torah which they shall teach you" (Devarim 17:11).

793. לְאוּמָן דְּחָתַךְ מָאנֵי לְבוּשִׁין דְּמַלְכוּתָא, וְעָבֵד מִנְהוֹן חֲתִיכָן סַגִּיאִין, אִינוּן דְּיַדְעִין אַתְרִין דְּחָסְרִין אִלֵּין חֲתִיכוֹת, אוֹ אִלֵּין דְּמִשְׁתַּאֲרִין, אִינוּן מְתַקְּנִין אִינוּן לְבוּשִׁין, וְשָׁוְיָן אִינוּן חֲתִיכוֹת דְּאִתּוֹסְפָן, בַּאֲתָר דִּמְעוּטִין, וַחֲתִיכוֹת דְּאִינוּן מְעַטִּין, מוֹסִיפִין עֲלַיְיהוּ, וְהַאי אִיהוּ עַל פִּי הַתּוֹרָה אֲשֶׁר יוֹרוּךָ.

793. THE MATTER MAY BE LIKENED to a tailor who has cut cloth in order to make royal garments, and has made many pieces from them. Those who know the places where those pieces are missing AND ARE FAMILIAR WITH the pieces which remain will be able to make the garments, for the pieces that have been collected together are placed where they are missing, and pieces that are too small are added to. And this is the true meaning of the verse: "according to the sentence of the Torah which they shall teach you."

794. וְאִי תֵּימָא, אִי כַּךְ הוּא, מַאי אִיהוּ דְּלִזְמְנִין טָעֵי חַד מִנַּיְיהוּ, וְיֵימָא הַדְרֵי בִּי. אֶלָּא עַד דְּיַעַבְדֵי הוֹרָאָה מֵהַהִיא מִלָּה דְּחוֹלְקִין עֲלָהּ, יָכִיל הַהוּא דְּאַקְשֵׁי עֲלָהּ, לְמֵימַר הַדְרֵי בִּי. דְּלָא כָּל מְפָרְקֵי תַּכְשִׁיטִין דְּכַלָּה, יַדְעִין בַּחֲתִיכוֹת לְאָן אַזְלָן, עַד דְּיְהֵא פָּסַק עַל בּוּרְיֵיהּ, פְּרוּקִין דַּהֲלָכוֹת עַל בּוּרְיַיְיהוֹן.

794. And you might well ask that, if this is so, what about the case where one of them occasionally makes a mistake and says: I recant. HE ANSWERS, before issuing instructions concerning that matter about which there is a difference of opinion, the one who poses the difficulty can say: I withdraw. For not all those who make the parts of a bride's ornaments know where each piece goes, until the ruling is made, AND PRIOR TO WHEN resolutions to the arguments of the Halachot have been given.

795. מְנוֹרָה, שֶׁבַע בּוֹצִינִין דִּילָהּ, אֶת שֶׁבַע הַנְּעָרוֹת הָרְאוּיוֹת לָתֶת לָהּ מִבֵּית הַמֶּלֶךְ. לָקֳבֵל שי"ן דִּתְלַת רָאשִׁין ש. ושי"ן דְּאַרְבַּע רָאשִׁין דִּתְפִילִין . וְאִינּוּן לָקֳבֵל ז' בִּרְכָאן דק"ש, דְּאִינּוּן בַּשַׁחַר מְבָרֵךְ שְׁתַּיִם לְפָנֶיהָ וְאַחַת לְאַחֲרֶיהָ, וּבָעֶרֶב מְבָרֵךְ שְׁתַּיִם לְפָנֶיהָ וּשְׁתַּיִם לְאַחֲרֶיהָ. לְבָתַר, כַּהֲנָא רַבָּא בַּעֲבוֹדָה, דִּמְשַׁמֵּשׁ בְּכַנְפֵי מִצְוָה, פַּעֲמוֹנִים וְרִמּוֹנִים, אִינּוּן קְשָׁרִין וְחוּלְיָין וְצִיץ תְּפִילִין, מִתַּמָּן וְאֵילָךְ וְעָשִׂיתָ מִזְבֵּחַ מִקְטַר קְטֹרֶת.

795. The candlestick has seven lights, WHICH ARE THE SECRET OF THE VERSE "and the seven maidens who were chosen to be given her, out of the king's house" (Ester 2:9), and they correspond to the three-headed Shin and the four-headed Shin, ש, of the Tefilin, NAMELY, TO THE SEVEN HEADS OF THE TWO SHINS TOGETHER. And these correspond to the seven blessings of the reading of Sh'ma, namely: In the morning two blessings are said before it and one after, and in the evening, two blessings are said before and two after. And subsequently THE PRECEPT IS WRITTEN that the High Priest at the Temple Service has to serve with the wings of the precept, namely bells and pomegranates, which are as the knots and links of the fringes and the plate WHICH IS AS the Tefilin. From that point on it is written: "And you shall make an altar for the burning of incense" (Shemot 30:1).

118. "And you shall offer a sacrifice made by fire for a burnt offering"

A Synopsis

The Faithful Shepherd says that all sacrifices for burnt offerings must correspond to the sins committed, and he tells us what these are. We learn that all sacrifices are not equal, and that a distinction must be made between one holiness and another that is lower.

796. פָּתַח רַעְיָא מְהֵימְנָא, וְאָמַר, כְּתִיב בְּפַרְשָׁתָא דָא, וְהִקְרַבְתֶּם אִשֶׁה עוֹלָה לַיְיָ׳. וְאוֹקְמוּהָ, דְּעוֹלָה לָאִשִׁים. ובג״כ סָמַךְ עוֹלָה לְאִשֶׁה. וְעוֹד אוֹקְמוּהָ, דְּלֵית עוֹלָה אַתְיָא אֶלָא עַל הִרְהוּר הַלֵב.

796. The Faithful Shepherd began by saying: It is written "And you shall offer a sacrifice made by fire for a burnt offering to Hashem" (Bemidbar 28:19), and it has already been taught that a burnt offering is committed to the flames, ALL OF IT BEING BURNT BY FIRE, and this is why the two expressions "an offering made by fire" and "a burnt offering" are placed next to each other. And it has also been taught: A burnt offering is due only as an expiation for sinful contemplation of the heart.

797. וַדַּאי, כָּל קָרְבְּנִין לָא אַתְיָין, אֶלָא לְכַפְּרָא. כָּל קָרְבְּנָא וְקָרְבְּנָא, עַל כָּל אֶבְרִין דב״נ, כְּפוּם הַהוּא חֵטָא דְּהַהוּא אֵבֶר. עַל טִפִּין דְּמוֹחָא, עוּגוֹת מַצוֹת כִּי לֹא חָמֵץ. אִי זָרִיק טִפִּין קַדְמָאִין, קֹדֶם דְּאַחְמִיצוּ, בַּאֲתָר דְּלָאו דִּילֵיה. וְעַל אִלֵּין דְּאַחְמִיצוּ, וְזָרִיק לוֹן בַּאֲתָר דְּלָא אִצְטְרִיךְ, צָרִיךְ לְאַיְיתָאָה עָלַיְיהוּ לֶחֶם חָמֵץ, וְאִינוּן לַחְמֵי תוֹדָה הָכִי הֲווֹ, מִנְּהוֹן חָמֵץ, וּמִנְּהוֹן מַצָה.

797. Without doubt the purpose of all the sacrifices is only for the making of atonement, with each sacrifice making atonement for man's limbs according to the sin he committed with that limb. For drops of marrow, NAMELY, THE SIN OF WASTING SEED, HE BRINGS "unleavened cakes...for it was not leavened" (Shemot 12:39); namely, if he discharged initial drops before they acidify in a place that does not belong to him, NAMELY, WITHOUT A FORBIDDEN WOMAN IN WHOM THE DROPS ACIDIFY. And regarding those that acidified, which in discharged in a place where he should not have,

NAMELY, IN A WOMAN FORBIDDEN TO HIM WHERE THE DROPS BECOME ACID (HEB. *CHAMETZ*), he has to bring leavened bread, and thus were the loaves of thanksgiving offerings: some were leavened and others were unleavened.

798. פָּרִים מִסִּטְרָא דְדִינָא, כְּבָשִׂים וְאֵילִים וְעַתּוּדִים וְעִזִּים. בְּגִין דְּאִינּוּן אַנְפֵּי דְּשׁוֹר, כֻּלְּהוּ שְׁחִיטָתָן בַּצָּפוֹן, וְקִבּוּל דָּמָן בִּכְלֵי שָׁרֵת בַּצָּפוֹן. שְׁחִיטָה וְקַבָּלָה וּזְרִיקָה כֻּלָּם בַּצָּפוֹן. לְבַסְּמָא מִדַּת הַדִּין, דְּאָתֵי לְבֵית דִּין מִסִּטְרָא דִּגְבוּרָה. בֵּית דִּין הַגָּדוֹל מִסִּטְרָא דִּגְבוּרָה, דְּתַמָּן בִּינָה. בֵּית דִּין הַקָּטָן, מִסִּטְרָא דְּמַלְכוּת. וְכָל אִינּוּן שׁוֹפְכֵי דָמִים לְמִצְוָה, אִינּוּן מִסִּטְרָא דִּגְבוּרָה.

798. Bullocks are from the side of Judgment. LIKEWISE, sheep and rams and he-goats and goats ARE ALL FROM THE SIDE OF JUDGMENT, because they are 'the face of ox,' AS IT IS SAID: "THE FACE OF AN OX ON THE LEFT SIDE" (YECHEZKEL 1:10), WHICH IS THAT OF JUDGMENT. All of them were slaughtered on the north side and their blood was received in a vessel of ministry on the north side. The slaughtering, the receipt, and tossing (of the blood) were all on the north side, WHICH IS THE LEFT SIDE, in order to sweeten AND MITIGATE the attribute of Judgment, which comes to the court from the side of Gvurah. The Great Law-court is from the side of Gvurah, where Binah is, while the Small Law-court is from the side of Malchut. And all those who shed blood in fulfillment of a precept are from the side of Gvurah.

799. וּמַה דְּאוֹקְמוּהָ, עוֹלַת שַׁבָּת בְּשַׁבַּתּוֹ וְלָא בְּשַׁבָּת אָחֳרָא, בְּגִין דְּעָבַר יוֹמוֹ בָּטֵל קָרְבָּנוֹ. דְּקָרְבָּן דּוֹחָה שַׁבָּת, וְאַדְלִיק אֵשׁ בְּשַׁבָּת, בְּגִין דְּאִיהוּ אֶשָּׁא קְדוֹשָׁה. דְּכָל אֵשׁ דְּקָרְבְּנִין אִיהוּ קֹדֶשׁ, וְשַׁבָּת קֹדֶשׁ, אֲחִידָן דָּא בְּדָא.

799. And the teaching that "the burnt offering of every Shabbat" (Bemidbar 28:10) must be offered on that Shabbat, and not on any other is because if the day has passed, the offering lapses, AND CANNOT BE MADE UP ON ANOTHER SHABBAT. The offering of the sacrifice takes precedence over

Shabbat, and fire may be kindled on the Shabbat because it is holy fire, for the fire that is used for offering all the sacrifices is holy, and this holy fire and the holy Shabbat take hold of each other.

800. אֲבָל אֵשׁ דְּחוֹל, אָסִיר לְאַחֲדָא לֵיהּ בַּקֹּדֶשׁ, וּבְג"ד מָנֵי לוֹן לְיִשְׂרָאֵל, לֹא תְבַעֲרוּ אֵשׁ בְּכֹל מוֹשְׁבוֹתֵיכֶם בְּיוֹם הַשַּׁבָּת. דְּהַאי אִיהוּ כִּלְאַיִם דְּטוֹב וָרָע. וּבְשַׁבָּת דְּשַׁלְטָא אִילָנָא דְּחַיֵּי, דְּלֵית בֵּיהּ תַּעֲרוֹבֶת, וְחוּלִין דִּטְהָרָה אָסִיר לְעָרְבָא בְּאֵשׁ דִּקְדוּשָׁה. כָּל שֶׁכֵּן חוּלִין דְּטוּמְאָה, דְּאָסִיר לְעָרְבָא לוֹן בִּקְדוּשָׁה. אוֹף הָכִי כָּל קָרְבָּנִין, אִתְקְרִיאוּ בְּשַׂר קֹדֶשׁ. וְכָל קָרְבָּנִין דְּכָל מִין, אִית בְּהוֹן חוּלִין דִּטְהָרָה, וְאִית בְּהוֹן קֹדֶשׁ וְקֹדֶשׁ הַקֳּדָשִׁים.

800. But profane fire may not be combined with the holy, NAMELY WITH THE SHABBAT, which is why He commanded Yisrael: "You shall kindle no fire throughout your habitations on the Shabbat day" (Shemot 35:3), for this would be tantamount to mixing good and bad, FOR on the Shabbat the Tree of Life is in control, and there is no mixture OF GOOD AND BAD in it. And secular objects that pertain to purity may not be mixed with the fire of holiness, and how much more so may the secular objects that pertain to impurity not be mixed with holiness. So, too, all the sacrifices are called "holy flesh" (Yirmeyah 11:15), and all the sacrifices of every type contain secular things of purity, and they contain holiness, and the holy of holies.

801. וְרָזָא, דְּאִית הֶפְרֵשׁ בֵּין קֹדֶשׁ לְקֹדֶשׁ, הה"ד, וְהִבְדִּילָה הַפָּרֹכֶת לָכֶם בֵּין הַקֹּדֶשׁ וּבֵין קֹדֶשׁ הַקֳּדָשִׁים. אוֹף הָכָא אֶשּׁוֹת דְּקָרְבָּנִין, לָאו אִינּוּן שָׁוִין. דְּאֵשׁ שֶׁל גָּבוֹהַּ מְקוּדָשׁ מֵאֵשׁ דְּקֹדֶשׁ דִּלְתַתָּא. דְּאִתְקְרֵי אֵשׁ עֲצֵי הַקֹּדֶשׁ, אוֹ אֵשׁ בְּשַׂר הַקֹּדֶשׁ. וְאֶשָּׁא דְּקוּדְשָׁא, אִית בֵּיהּ הַפְרָשָׁה לְבֵין אֵשׁ הֶדְיוֹט. אַף עַל גַּב דְּאוֹקִמוּהָ עָלֵיהּ, דְּמִצְוָה לְהָבִיא מִן הַהֶדְיוֹט, אַף עַל גַּב דְּאִית אֵשׁ דְּקוּדְשָׁא, דְּכָל חַד צָרִיךְ לְאַתְרֵיהּ.

801. And the secret of the matter is that a distinction is to be made between one king of holiness and another, as it is written: "and the veil shall be for you as a division between the holy place and the holy of holies" (Shemot

26:33). Here, too, the fires of the offering are not equal, for the fire that is higher is holier than the holy fire below, which are called 'the fire of the holy wood' or 'the fire of the holy flesh'. And there is distinction between holy fire and ordinary fire THAT IS BROUGHT TO THE ALTAR, even though it has been taught that it is a positive precept to bring of the ordinary FIRE even when there is holy fire ON THE ALTAR, for each has to have its own place.

802. יִשְׂרָאֵל אִמְתִּילוּ לְהַאי. דְּהָא יִשְׂרָאֵל בִּכְלָל אִתְקְרִיאוּ מְלָכִים כְּמָה דְאוֹקְמוּהָ, כָּל יִשְׂרָאֵל בְּנֵי מְלָכִים. אֲבָל כַּד הֲווֹ עָאלִין לְבֵי מַקְדְּשָׁא, כָּל חַד שַׁרְיָיא בְּאַתְרֵיה, כִּדְקָא יָאוֹת לֵיה. אוֹף הָכִי כָּל קָרְבְּנִין לָאו אִינּוּן שָׁוִין, דְּאַף עַל גַּב דִּבְכוּלְּהוּ כְּתִיב קָרְבָּן לַיְיָ׳, אִיהוּ פָּלִיג כֹּלָּא כָּל חַד וְחַד כִּדְקָא יָאוֹת. וְרָזָא דָא, אִשְׁתְּמוֹדַע בְּפָרֵי הֶחָג, דַּהֲווֹ קְרִיבִין לוֹן יִשְׂרָאֵל קֳדָם יְיָ׳.

802. Yisrael are likened to this, for Yisrael as a rule is called 'kings', as it has been taught: All Yisrael are the children of kings. But when they entered the Temple, each one went to his own place, THE PRIESTS BY THEMSELVES, THE LEVITES BY THEMSELVES, AND YISRAEL BY THEMSELVES. Similarly, with regard to the sacrifices, although about each one it is written "a sacrifice to Hashem," they are not equal, for He, THE HOLY ONE, BLESSED BE HE, distributes everything, each as is fitting to him. And the secret of the matter can be learned from the bullocks of Sukkot (holiday of the Booths) that Yisrael used to offer before Hashem, AND HE DISTRIBUTED THEM FOR THE SUSTENANCE OF THE SEVENTY NATIONS.

119. "Also on the day of the firstfruits"

A Synopsis

Rabbi Shimon tells Moses that it is through Moses' deeds that the Shechinah is renewed in the prayers of the patriarchs. He goes on to speak about the renewal that takes place during the prayers of the Festival of Weeks. His exposition includes a discussion of the numerical value of "all" (Heb. *kol*), the sea of the Torah, and Malchut that is the end of all the seas. The numbers seven and fifty are emphasized.

803. אָמַר בּוֹצִינָא קַדִּישָׁא, קוּם רַעְיָא מְהֵימְנָא מִשְּׁנָתָךְ, דְּאַנְתְּ וַאֲבָהָן יְשֵׁנֵי עָפָר אִתְקְרוּן, דְּעַד כְּעַן הֲוֵיתוּן מִשְׁתַּדְּלִין בְּאוֹרַיְיתָא, בְּאִינוּן יְשֵׁנִים בַּמִּשְׁנָה, דְּאִתְּמַר בְּהוֹן עַל הָאָרֶץ תִּישָׁן. וּבְיוֹם הַבִּכּוּרִים בְּהַקְרִיבְכֶם מִנְחָה חֲדָשָׁה לַיהוָה. אַתּוּן אִינוּן בִּכּוּרִים דִּשְׁכִינְתָּא, וּבְעוֹבָדִין דִּלְכוֹן, אִיהִי אִתְחַדְּשַׁת בִּצְלוֹתִין דַּאֲבָהָן בְּכָל יוֹמָא. דְּאוֹקְמוּהָ מָארֵי מַתְנִיתִין, תְּפִלּוֹת כְּנֶגֶד אָבוֹת תִּקְנוּם. וּבק"ש דְּאָמַר רַעְיָא מְהֵימְנָא שְׁמַע יִשְׂרָאֵל, וְאוֹקְמוּהָ כָּל הַקּוֹרֵא ק"ש בְּכָל יוֹם, כְּאִלּוּ הוּא מְקַיֵּים וְהָגִיתָ בּוֹ יוֹמָם וָלַיְלָה.

803. Said the holy luminary, NAMELY RABBI SHIMON: Arise, O Faithful Shepherd, from your sleep, for you and the patriarchs are called 'those that sleep in the dust', for until now you have engaged in the Torah with those who sleep at the Mishnah, about whom it is said: 'and on the ground shall you sleep'. And it is said: "Also on the day of the firstfruits, when you bring a new meal offering to Hashem" (Bemidbar 28:26). You are the firstfruits of the Shechinah, and through your deeds THE SHECHINAH is renewed by the prayers of the patriarchs each day, for the sages of the Mishnah taught: The prayers were ordained corresponding to the patriarchs; and by the reading of Sh'ma. For the Faithful Shepherd, NAMELY, MOSES, said: "Hear O Yisrael" (Devarim 6:4); and it has been taught: everyone who recites the Sh'ma every day, it is as if he established; "but you shall meditate therein day and night" (Yehoshua 1:8).

804. וַדַּאי בִּצְלוֹתִין דִּלְכוֹן, בִּקְרִיאַת שְׁמַע דִּלְכוֹן, שְׁכִינְתָּא אִיהִי אִתְחַדְּשַׁת קַמֵּיהּ דְּקוּדְשָׁא בְּרִיךְ הוּא. ובג"ד, וְהִקְרַבְתֶּם מִנְחָה חֲדָשָׁה

לֵיהֲוָה. בִּצְלוֹתִין דְּאִינּוּן בַּאֲתַר דְּקָרְבְּנִין. בְּאָן קָרְבְּנִין דְּצְלוֹתִין אִיהִי
מִתְחַדֶּשֶׁת. בְּשָׁבוּעוֹתֵיכֶם. דְּהַיְינוּ שָׁבוּעוֹת, דְּבֵיהּ מַתַּן תּוֹרָה, וְאִתְקְרֵי
חֲמִשִּׁים יוֹם לָעוֹמֶר. וּבֵיהּ שִׁבְעָה שָׁבוּעוֹת, מִסְּטְרָא דְּהַהוּא דְּאִתְּמַר
בֵּיהּ, שֶׁבַע בַּיּוֹם הִלַּלְתִּיךָ, וְאִיהִי מַלְכוּת כַּלָּה. כְּלִילָא מִשְּׁבַע סְפִירָן,
כְּלִילָא בַּבִּינָה, דְּאִיהִי אִתְפַּשְּׁטַת בָּהּ ה' סְפִירָאן לַחֲמִשִּׁין.

804. Certainly, through your prayer and in your reading of Sh'ma, the Shechinah is renewed before the Holy One, blessed be He, and this is why it is said: "And you shall present a new meal offering to Hashem" (Vayikra 23:16), namely, by the prayers which are instead of sacrifices. But in which sacrifices, NAMELY prayers, is She renewed? "In your (feast of) weeks" (Bemidbar 28:26), namely, Shavuot, which is when the Torah was given, and which is called 'fifty days' of the counting of the Omer, and which comprises seven weeks, from the side of the one about whom it is said: "Seven times a day I praise You" (Tehilim 119:164), which is Malchut, which is CALLED 'a bride', and is composed of the seven Sfirot CHESED, GVURAH, TIFERET, NETZACH, HOD, YESOD AND MALCHUT, and is a part of Binah, which spreads out in five Sfirot CHESED, GVURAH, TIFERET, NETZACH AND HOD into fifty.

805. יְסוֹד כָּל, כָּלוּל מֵאִלֵּין חֲמִשִּׁין. כָּל"ה. כָּל ה: כָּ"ל ה'. כְּלִילָא מֵחֲמִשִּׁים,
כֻּלְּהוּ נִבְלָעִים בְּגוֹ חֲמִשִּׁים, חָכְמָה דְּאִיהִי, י' עִלָּאָה, מוּבְלַעַת בְּגוֹ
חֲמִשִּׁין. ה' זִמְנִין עֶשֶׂר. ה' בִּינָה. י' חָכְמָה. י' עֶשֶׂר זִמְנִין ה' הַיְינוּ חֲמִשִּׁין
וּבְחוּשְׁבָּן כָּ"ל. וּבְחוּשְׁבָּן יָ"ם. וְאִיהוּ יַם הַתּוֹרָה. מְקוֹרָא דִּילֵיהּ כֶּתֶר,
דְּלֵית לֵיהּ סוֹף. שְׁאָר סְפִירָאן, אִתְקְרִיאוּ עַל שְׁמָהּ שִׁבְעַת יָמִים.
וּמַלְכוּת יַם סוֹף, סוֹף דְּכָל יָמִים.

805. Yesod, WHICH IS CALLED 'All' (Heb. *kol*), WHOSE NUMERICAL VALUE IS FIFTY, is ALSO composed of these fifty, NAMELY, CHESED, GVURAH, TIFERET, NETZACH AND HOD, EACH OF WHICH IS COMPOSED OF TEN, AND MALCHUT IS CALLED 'bride' (Heb. *kalah* - Caf Lamed Hei), THE LETTERS OF WHICH CAN BE READ AS: *kol* (Caf Lamed) Hei (having the numerical value of five), NAMELY, five SFIROT composed of fifty. Each of them is enclosed within the fifty. Chochmah, which is upper Yud is

enclosed within the fifty, for Hei times Yud EQUAL FIFTY, WHERE Hei is Binah and Yud is Chochmah, AND THERE ARE YUD HEI IN CHOCHMAH, WHICH, WHEN MULTIPLIED BY EACH OTHER, MAKE FIFTY, AND THERE ARE YUD HEI IN BINAH; AND WHEN Yud is MULTIPLIED by Hei, the result is fifty, and this is the numerical value of the word "All" (Heb. *kol*), AS ABOVE, and the numerical value of the word Sea (Heb. *yam*), FOR BINAH IS CALLED 'SEA', WHOSE NUMERICAL VALUE AMOUNTS TO FIFTY. And the reference is to the Sea of the Torah, WHERE FROM BINAH, WHICH IS CALLED 'SEA', EMERGES THE TORAH, WHICH IS ZEIR ANPIN. Its origin is Keter, which is infinite. The remaining Sfirot, NAMELY, CHESED, GVURAH, TIFERET, NETZACH, HOD, YESOD AND MALCHUT, are named after it: seven seas, AND THE NUMERICAL VALUE OF THE WORD SEA IS FIFTY, IT FOLLOWS THAT IN EACH OF THEM THERE IS FIFTY. And Malchut IS CALLED 'the reed' (Heb. *suf*) sea BECAUSE IT IS the end (Heb. *sof*) of all the seas.

806. וּבג"ד דְּאִינּוּן חַמְשִׁין שֶׁבַע שָׁבוּעוֹת, מִנְחָתָם שְׁלֹשָׁה עֶשְׂרוֹנִים, וּשְׁנֵי עֶשְׂרוֹנִים. חֲמֵשׁ, דְּאִינּוּן חֲמֵשׁ זִמְנִין עֲשַׂר. הה"ד, וּמִנְחָתָם סֹלֶת בְּלוּלָה בַשֶּׁמֶן שְׁלֹשָׁה עֶשְׂרוֹנִים לַפָּר הָאֶחָד וּשְׁנֵי עֶשְׂרוֹנִים לָאַיִל הָאֶחָד עִשָּׂרוֹן עִשָּׂרוֹן לַכֶּבֶשׂ הָאֶחָד לְשִׁבְעַת הַכְּבָשִׂים. וְשִׁבְעַת הַכְּבָשִׂים, לָקֳבֵל שֶׁבַע שַׁבָּתוֹת תְּמִימֹת תִּהְיֶינָה. כָּל חַד עִם שִׁית יוֹמִין דִּילֵיהּ.

806. And because EACH ONE OF the seven weeks is fifty, AS ABOVE: "and their meal offering... three tenth measures for one bullock, two tenth measures for one ram" (Bemidbar 28:28), making altogether five TENTH MEASURES, which are five times ten, FOR EACH TENTH MEASURE IS TEN, AND FIVE TENTH MEASURES ARE FIFTY. This is the meaning of the verse: "and their meal offering of flour mingled with oil, three tenth measures for one bullock, two tenth measures for one ram, a tenth measure for one lamb, for the seven lambs." The seven lambs correspond to "seven complete Shabbatot shall there be" (Vayikra 23:15), AND THESE ARE SEVEN MALCHUTS, FOR MALCHUT IS CALLED 'SHABBAT', and each one has six days with it, NAMELY: CHESED, GVURAH, TIFERET, NETZACH, HOD AND YESOD AND THEY, WITH THE DAY OF SHAVUOT, COME TO FIFTY.

120. Yom Kippur

A Synopsis

The Zohar tells us that Yom Kippur is from the Tree of Life, where no evil has any part. On that day even those people who are under a sentence of judgment are forgiven. We hear about the difference between vows and oaths, and about the iniquities of Yisrael that are purified or whitened through repentance. We learn that on Yom Kippur a Shofar raises up a voice for freedom. There are three grades of worship on that day: thought, speech and deed.

807. וּבֶעָשׂוֹר לַחוֹדֶשׁ הַשְּׁבִיעִי, דְּאִיהוּ תִּשְׁרֵי. מִקְרָא קֹדֶשׁ יִהְיֶה לָכֶם, דָּא יוֹם הַכִּפּוּרִים. דְּאִיהוּ עֲשִׂירִי י', כָּלִיל מְעַשְׂרֵת יְמֵי תְּשׁוּבָה. וְתַקִּינוּ בֵּיהּ ה' צְלוֹתִין, לְחַבְּרָא עִם ה'. מַאי מִקְרָא קֹדֶשׁ. לְאַפְרְשָׁא לֵיהּ מִשְּׁאַר יוֹמִין, דְּאִית בְּהוּ פּוּלְחָנָא דְּחוֹל. וּבְגִין דָּא, כָּל מְלֶאכֶת עֲבוֹדָה לֹא תַעֲשׂוּ.

807. "And you shall have on the tenth day of this seventh month" which is the month of Tishrei, "a holy gathering" (Bemidbar 29:7), which is Yom Kippur, which is the tenth, which is Yud, and these are the Ten Days of Repentance, and five prayer services were ordained for it in order to join the Yud with the Hei, NAMELY, CHOCHMAH WITH BINAH. What is the meaning of "holy gathering"? It is to differentiate it from other days when secular work is permitted which is why scripture says: "you shall not do any work" (Ibid.).

808. דְּיוֹמִין דְּאִית בְּהוֹן מְלֶאכֶת חוֹל, אִינוּן מִסְּטְרָא דְּעֵץ הַדַּעַת טוֹב וָרָע. דְּאִתְהַפַּךְ מִמַּטֶּה לְנָחָשׁ, וּמִנָּחָשׁ לְמַטֶּה. לְכָל חַד כְּפוּם עוֹבְדוֹי, וְדָא מְטַטְרוֹן מַטֶּה, נָחָשׁ, סָמָאֵל. אֲבָל בְּהַאי יוֹמָא דְּאִיהוּ יוֹם הַכִּפּוּרִים דְּאִתְקְרֵי קֹדֶשׁ, שַׁלְטָא אִילָנָא דְּחַיֵּי, דְּלָא אִשְׁתְּתַּף עִמֵּיהּ שָׂטָן וּפְגַע רָע. וּמִסְּטְרֵיהּ לֹא יְגוּרְךָ רָע. וּבְגִין דָּא, בֵּיהּ נַיְיחִין עַבְדִּין בְּאִילָנָא דְּחַיֵּי, וּבֵיהּ נַפְקָן לְחֵירוּת, בֵּיהּ נַפְקֵי מִשִּׁלְשׁוּלֵיהוֹן.

808. And those days on which secular work may be done are from the side of the Tree of Knowledge of Good and Evil, that turned from a rod into a

serpent and from a serpent back into a rod, for each person according to his deeds, and this Metatron is rod, while Samael IS serpent. But on this day, which is Yok Kippur that is called 'holy', the Tree of Life is in control, and no devil nor evil spirit joins with it, and from its side "nor shall evil dwell with You" (Tehilim 5:5), BUT IT IS THROUGHOUT GOOD. And this is why in it, in the Tree of Life, the slaves find rest and go out to freedom, and emerge from their chains.

809. אִינּוּן דְּאִית עָלַיְיהוּ גְּזַר דִּין, בְּנֶדֶר וּבִשְׁבוּעָה, וּבְגִין דָּא תַּקִּינוּ לְמֵימַר בֵּיהּ, כָּל נִדְרֵי וְאִיסָרֵי וְכוּ', כּוּלְּהוֹן יְהוֹן שְׁבִיתִין וּשְׁבִיקִין לָא שְׁרִירִין וְלָא קַיָּימִין. וּבְגִין דָּא נֶדֶר דִּידָן״ד, דְּאִיהוּ תִּפְאֶרֶת. וּשְׁבוּעָה דַּאֲדֹנָי, דְּאִיהוּ מַלְכוּת. דְּעַבְדוּ עַל גָּלוּתָא דִּלְהוֹן, בְּחָכְמָה וּבִינָה יְהוֹן שְׁבִיקִין וּשְׁבִיתִין לָא שְׁרִירָן וְלָא קַיָּימִין, וְנִסְלַח לְכָל עֲדַת בְּנֵי יִשְׂרָאֵל. דְּחֶסֶד אִיהוּ מַיִם. גְּבוּרָה אֵשׁ. תִּפְאֶרֶת אֲוִיר. וּבְגִין דָּא אוּקְמוּהָ מָארֵי מַתְנִיתִין, הֶתֵּר נְדָרִים פּוֹרְחִים בַּאֲוִיר.

809. Those over whom there is a verdict, A VERDICT NOT TO BE CHANGED under vow or oath, it was decreed for this reason that the following shall be recited: "All vows (Aramaic *Kol nidrei*), bonds...they shall all of them be released and annulled. They shall not be binding, nor shall they have any power." BUT THE VERDICT SHALL BE VOIDED FROM THEM. And this is why the vow is in the name of Yud Hei Vav Hei, which is Tiferet, while the oath is in the name of Adonai, which is Malchut, for they caused their own exile BY THEIR SINS. AND NOW, by means of Chochmah and Binah, 'they will be released and annulled; they shall not be binding, nor shall they have any power'. "And all the congregation of the children of Yisrael shall be forgiven" (Bemidbar 15:26). Chesed is water, Gvurah is fire, and Tiferet is air, AND SINCE THE VOWS ARE IN TIFERET, WHICH IS AIR, the sages of the Mishnah therefore taught: release from vows hovers in the air, FOR THE RELEASE FROM CHOCHMAH AND BINAH HOVERS IN THE AIR, WHICH IS TIFERET, AND FROM THERE ANNULS THE VOW.

810. וּבְגִין דִּשְׁבוּעָה מִמַּלְכוּת, דְּאִיהִי לְתַתָּא מִינֵיהּ. אוּקְמוּהָ, נְדָרִים עַל גַּבֵּי שְׁבוּעוֹת עוֹלִים. וְעוֹד אוּקְמוּהָ, כָּל הַנִּשְׁבַּע כְּאִילּוּ נִשְׁבַּע בַּמֶּלֶךְ עַצְמוֹ. וְכָל הַנּוֹדֵר כְּאִילּוּ נוֹדֵר בְּחַיֵּי הַמֶּלֶךְ. הַמֶּלֶךְ עַצְמוֹ, אֲדֹנָי. חַיֵּי

הַמֶּלֶךְ, יְדוֹנָ"ד. וּבְגִין דָּא כִּי יִדּוֹר נֶדֶר לַיְדוֹנָ"ד.

810. And since the oath is from Malchut, which is below the vow WHICH IS TIFERET, they taught that vows are higher than oaths, and they also taught: Everyone who swears an oath is as though he swears on the king himself, and everyone who vows a vow is as though he does so on the life of the king himself. The King himself REFERS TO Adonai, WHICH IS MALCHUT. The life of the King REFERS TO Yud Hei Vav Hei, WHICH IS ZEIR ANPIN, FROM WHOM THE LIFE FLOWS TO THE KING, WHICH IS MALCHUT. And for this reason, IT IS WRITTEN: "If a man vow a vow to Hashem" (Bemidbar 30:3), WHICH IS ZEIR ANPIN.

811. וְאוֹף הָכִי אִית רָזָא אַחֲרָא, חַיֵּי הַמֶּלֶךְ, חָכְמָה. הה"ד הַחָכְמָה תְּחַיֶּה בְעָלֶיהָ. כָּל הַנּוֹדֵר בַּיְהֹוָה, דְּאִיהוּ תִּפְאֶרֶת. כְּאִילּוּ נוֹדֵר בַּחָכְמָה, דְּאִיהוּ יוֹ"ד הֵ"א וָא"ו הֵ"א, חַיֵּי הַמֶּלֶךְ. וְכָל הַנִּשְׁבַּע בַּאדֹנָי, כְּאִילּוּ נִשְׁבַּע בַּמֶּלֶךְ עַצְמוֹ. עַצְמוֹ דָּא אִימָּא עִלָּאָה, כְּאִילּוּ נִשְׁבַּע בָּהּ, דְּאִיהִי עֶצֶם הַשָּׁמַיִם לָטֹהַר. מִסִּטְרָא דְחֶסֶד, עֶצֶם מֵעֲצָמַי. וּבָשָׂר מִבְּשָׂרִי, מִסִּטְרָא דִגְבוּרָה, דָּא מַלְכוּת. וּבְחָכְמָה דְּאִיהִי חַיֵּי תִּפְאֶרֶת, אִיהוּ סָלִיק לְאִתְקְרֵי אָדָם, הה"ד כְּתִפְאֶרֶת אָדָם.

811. And even thus, there is another secret: The life of the King refers to Chochmah, as it is written: "wisdom gives life to those who have it" (Kohelet 7:12). THEREFORE everyone who vows on Yud Hei Vav Hei, which is Tiferet, it is as if he vowed upon Chochmah OF ZEIR ANPIN, which is YUD HEI VAV HEI FULLY SPELLED WITH ALEPH'S, THUS: Yud-Vav-Dalet, Hei-Aleph, Vav-Aleph-Vav, Hei-Aleph, which is the life of the King, WHICH IS THE LIFE OF ZEIR ANPIN. And everyone who swears an oath on Adonai is as though he swore on the King himself. This is because himself (Heb. *atzmo*) is supernal Ima, NAMELY, BINAH, AND IT IS as though he had sworn on her, namely, on "as it were the very (Heb. *etzem*) heaven for clearness" (Shemot 24:10), NAMELY, THE MOCHIN OF MALCHUT. For from the aspect of Chesed, MALCHUT IS CALLED "bone (Heb. *etzem*) of my bones" (Beresheet 2:23). But from the aspect of Gvurah, Malchut is called "and flesh of my flesh" (Ibid.), and in Chochmah, which is the life of Tiferet, NAMELY, ITS MOCHIN, it, TIFERET, rises up to be called 'man', WHICH IS

45 IN NUMERICAL VALUE, as it is written: "the beauty (Tiferet) of a man" (Yeshayah: 44:13). FOR TIFERET IS CALLED 'MAN' WHEN IT HAS THE MOCHIN OF CHOCHMAH, WHICH IS THE SECRET OF WHY HE IS CALLED BY YUD HEI VAV HEI FULLY SPELLED WITH ALEPH'S, THAT HAS THE NUMERICAL VALUE OF 45.

812. וְאִתְּמַר בְּיוֹם הַכִּפּוּרִים. וְעִנִּיתֶם אֶת נַפְשׁוֹתֵיכֶם. וּבֶעָשׂוֹר לַחֹדֶשׁ הַשְּׁבִיעִי הַזֶּה תְּעַנּוּ אֶת נַפְשׁוֹתֵיכֶם. תַּקִּינוּ בֵּיהּ ה' עִנּוּיִים, בְּגִין דְּתִתְלַבֵּן ה' זְעֵירָא בְּה' עִלָּאָה, דְּאִיהוּ ה' צְלוֹתִין. לְקַיֵּים בְּיִשְׂרָאֵל, אִם יִהְיוּ חֲטָאֵיכֶם כַּשָּׁנִים כַּשֶּׁלֶג יַלְבִּינוּ. וְהַאי אִיהוּ רָזָא דְּלָשׁוֹן שֶׁל זְהוֹרִית, בְּגִין דְּכָל חוֹבִין דְּיִשְׂרָאֵל מָטוּן לְגַבֵּי מַלְכוּת. וּתְשׁוּבָה דְּאִיהִי בִּינָה, מְלַבֶּנֶת לוֹן. בְּגִין דְּאִתְּמַר בָּהּ, הַשּׁוֹכֵן אִתָּם בְּתוֹךְ טוּמְאוֹתָם. וְד' בִּגְדֵי לָבָן, וְד' בִּגְדֵי זָהָב לְמַלְבַּשׁ, יְאָהֲדֹוָנָהִי.

812. And it is said about Yom Kippur: "and you shall afflict your souls" (Bemidbar 29:7) AND ALSO: "in the seventh month, on the tenth day of the month, you shall afflict your souls" (Vayikra 16:29). And five afflictions were decreed for it, so that small Hei, WHICH IS MALCHUT, should be purified in upper Hei, WHICH IS BINAH, OF WHOSE LEFT COLUMN, THE AFFLICTIONS ARE DRAWN, which are five prayers, to establish in Yisrael: "though your sins be like scarlet, they shall be as white as snow" (Yeshayah 1:18). And this is the secret of the crimson colored strip, WHICH WAS TIED TO THE DOOR OF THE SANCTUARY FROM INSIDE, WHICH, WHEN THE HE-GOAT REACHED THE WILDERNESS, TURNED WHITE. All the iniquities of the House of Yisrael reach to Malchut; and Repentance, which is Binah, purifies (whitens) them, for it is written about it, ABOUT MALCHUT: I AM HASHEM "that remains among them in the midst of their uncleanness" (Vayikra 16:16). And the four garments of white and the four garments of gold for apparel are THE SECRET OF Yud-Aleph-Hei-Dalet-Vav-Nun-Hei-Yud, WHICH IS THE COMBINATION OF THE LETTERS OF YUD HEI VAV HEI AND THOSE OF ADONAI. FOR THE FOUR GARMENTS OF WHITE ARE THE SECRET OF THE FOUR LETTERS OF YUD HEI VAV HEI WHILE THE FOUR GARMENTS OF GOLD ARE THE SECRET OF THE FOUR LETTERS OF ADONAI.

813. וְתַקִּינוּ לִתְקוֹעַ שׁוֹפָר בְּיוֹם הַכִּפּוּרִים, לְסַלְּקָא קוֹל דְּאִיהוּ ו',

לְחֵרוּת. דְּאִתְּמַר בָּהּ, בְּכָל צָרָתָם לוֹ צָר, בָּא', וּבוֹ', קְרֵי וּכְתִיב. וַעֲבוֹדַת יוֹם הַכִּפּוּרִים אִיהִי בַּאֲרִיכוּת, וְאִיהִי כְּלִילָא מִתְּלַת דַּרְגִּין, בְּמַחֲשָׁבָה דִבּוּר וּמַעֲשֶׂה.

813. And it was decreed that a Shofar be sounded on Yom Kippur, to raise up a voice, which is Vav OF YUD HEI VAV HEI, NAMELY, ZEIR ANPIN, to freedom, WHICH IS BINAH, about which it is said: "In all their affliction He was afflicted (or: 'there was affliction for (Heb. *lo*) him')" (Yeshayah 63:9). 'LO' IS with Aleph and Vav, THAT IS, in how it is pronounced and written, FOR IT IS SPELLED WITH ALEPH (NO), ALTHOUGH PRONOUNCED WITH VAV (FOR HIM). FOR "IN ALL THEIR AFFLICTION" ALLUDES TO FIVE AFFLICTIONS AND THE JUDGMENTS WHOSE SOURCE IS IN BINAH, IN ITS LEFT COLUMN. AND IN THE SECRET OF THE SHOFAR BLOWING, ZEIR ANPIN IS ALSO RAISED UP THERE TO BINAH, AND THIS IS WHY THERE ARE TWO VERSIONS OF THE TEXT, AS WRITTEN AND AS READ, WITH AN ALEPH AND WITH A VAV, WHERE THE ALEPH ALLUDES TO BINAH, IN THE SECRET OF TEACH (HEB. *ALEPH*) BINAH, AND THE VAV ALLUDES TO ZEIR ANPIN THAT ASCENDED TO BINAH. And worship on Yom Kippur is conducted at length and comprises three grades: thought, speech, and deed.

121. The holiday of Sukkot

A Synopsis

We are reminded of the origin of this Festival dating from the time when Yisrael were led out of Egypt. The size and construction of the Tabernacle is described, and the point is made that the shadow cast by the roof is not an ordinary shadow but is really the protection cast over the soul. There are seven letters that incorporate the shape of a shelter or tabernacle: Bet, Gimel, Dalet, Caf, Pe, Resh and Tav. The seven planets are said to correspond to these letters, and many other analogies are drawn by means of the number seven. We hear about the meaning, composition and purpose of the lulav, and why the lulav is taken in the right hand and the Etrog in the left. Next we hear that the Patriarchs, together with Moses, Aaron, David and Solomon, all come to Rabbi Shimon and bless him and praise his light. Rabbi Shimon begins talking about the seventy bullocks that Yisrael used to sacrifice during the seven days of Sukkot – one less bullock every day. He says that the clue to this decrease is found in the fact that the ark came to rest in the seventh month, when the waters were continually receding. In the same way the sins of Yisrael decrease and so too do the number of accusers. The purpose of Noah's ark and the purpose of the Sukkah are the same – to give protection. The Shechinah protects all those who keep the sign of the Covenant.

814. בַּחֲמִשָּׁה עָשָׂר יוֹם לַחֹדֶשׁ הַשְּׁבִיעִי וְגוֹ', דְּאִיהִי תִּשְׁרֵי, מִקְרָא קֹדֶשׁ יִהְיֶה לָכֶם כָּל מְלֶאכֶת עֲבוֹדָה לֹא תַעֲשׂוּ וְחַגּוֹתֶם אוֹתוֹ חַג לַיְיָ' שִׁבְעַת יָמִים וְגוֹ'. בַּחֲמִשָּׁה עָשָׂר, מִסִּטְרָא דִּי"ה. וְחַגּוֹתֶם אוֹתוֹ, דָּא אוֹת ו', עַמּוּדָא דְּאֶמְצָעִיתָא. שִׁבְעַת יָמִים, מִסִּטְרָא דְּבַת שֶׁבַע, דְּאִיהִי מַלְכוּת. אֲבָהָן, וְרַעְיָא מְהֵימָנָא, וְאַהֲרֹן, דָּוִד וּשְׁלֹמֹה, הָא אִינּוּן שֶׁבַע, לְקָבֵל שֶׁבַע סְפִירָאן. אֲנָא בָּעֵינָא לְתַקְנָא לְכוֹן סֻכָּה, דְּאִיהִי אִימָּא עִלָּאָה, לְסַכְּכָא עֲלַיְיהוּ, כְּאִמָּא עַל בְּנִין.

814. "And on the fifteenth day of the seventh month," which is Tishrei, "you shall have a holy gathering; you shall do no servile work, and you shall keep a feast to Hashem seven days" (Bemidbar 29:12). On the fifteenth day means from the side of Yud Hei, NAMELY, CHOCHMAH AND BINAH. "and you shall keep a feast"; THIS IS THE LETTERS OF the letter Vav, which is the

Central Pillar, NAMELY, ZEIR ANPIN. Seven days is from the side of Bathsheba (the daughter of seven), which is Malchut WHICH IS THE LAST HEI. The patriarchs, WHICH ARE CHESED, GVURAH AND TIFERET, and the Faithful Shepherd WHO IS NETZACH, and Aaron WHO IS HOD, and David WHO IS MALCHUT, and Solomon (Heb. *shlomo*), WHO IS YESOD THAT IS CALLED '*SHALOM*' (ENG. 'PEACE'), are seven, corresponding to seven Sfirot. I want to construct for you a Sukkah, which is supernal Ima, who will provide a shelter over them, OVER THE SEVEN SFIROT, as the mother over the young.

815. וּבְגִין ז׳ סְפִירָאן אָמַר קְרָא, כִּי בַסֻּכּוֹת הוֹשַׁבְתִּי אֶת בְּנֵי יִשְׂרָאֵל, בְּמַפְּקָנוּתְהוֹן מֵאַרְעָא דְמִצְרַיִם, בְּז׳ עֲנָנֵי כָבוֹד. סוּכָּה בְּאָת ו׳, אִיהוּ בְּרָזָא דִּתְרֵין בְּנִין, יְדֹוָד אֲדֹנָי. וְהָכִי סָלִיק סוּכָּ״ה בְּחוּשְׁבָּן יְאָהְדֹוָנָהִי. תְּרֵין כְּרוּבִים, דְּהֵם סוֹכְכִים בְּכַנְפֵיהֶם עַל הַכַּפֹּרֶת וּפְנֵיהֶם אִישׁ אֶל אָחִיו.

815. And on account of the seven Sfirot, Scripture said: "I made the children of Yisrael to dwell in booths, when I brought them out of the land of Egypt" (Vayikra 23:43), namely, with seven clouds of glory, WHICH ARE THE SECRET OF SEVEN SFIROT. *Sukkah* (Eng. 'booth' or 'tabernacle') WHEN SPELLED with a letter Vav, is in the secret of the two young, OVER WHOM BINAH PROVIDES A SHELTER, NAMELY, Yud Hei Vav Hei and Adonai, NAMELY, ZEIR ANPIN AND MALCHUT, for the numerical value of *Sukkah* amounts to Yud-Aleph-Hei-Dalet-Vav-Nun-Hei-Yud, FOR *SUKKAH* (SAMECH VAV CAF HEI) CONSISTS OF THE LETTERS CAF VAV, WHICH HAVE THE SAME NUMERICAL VALUE AS THE LETTERS OF YUD HEI VAV HEI, AND THE LETTERS SAMECH HEI, WHICH HAVE THE SAME NUMERICAL VALUE AS ADONAI. AND THEY ARE THE SECRET OF the two Cherubs who are "overspreading the covering with their wings, and their faces shall look one to another" (Shemot 25:20), WHO ARE THE SECRET OF ZEIR ANPIN AND MALCHUT.

816. וְאִית עֲשָׂרָה טְפָחִים בַּכְּרוּבִים מִתַּתָּא לְעֵילָא, מֵרַגְלֵיהוֹן עַד רֵישֵׁיהוֹן, וּמֵרֵישֵׁיהוֹן וְעַד רַגְלֵיהוֹן, וְשַׁרְיָין עַל טֶפַח דְּאִיהוּ י׳. וַעֲשָׂרָה עֲשָׂרָה מֵעֵילָא לְתַתָּא, וּמִתַּתָּא לְעֵילָא, הַיְינוּ יוֹ״ד. וּבְג״כ, שִׁעוּרָא

דְּסֻכָּה אָמְרוּ רַבָּנָן, לֹא פָּחוֹת מֵעֲשָׂרָה, וְלֹא לְמַעְלָה מֵעֶשְׂרִים. סֻכָּה הָעֲשׂוּיָה כְּכִבְשָׁן מִסְּטְרָא דְּאִימָא, עָלָה אִתְּמַר, וְהַר סִינַי עָשַׁן כֻּלּוֹ מִפְּנֵי אֲשֶׁר יָרַד עָלָיו יְיָ׳ בָּאֵשׁ וַיַּעַל עֲשָׁנוֹ כְּעֶשֶׁן הַכִּבְשָׁן. וְכֹלָּא חַד.

816. And the Cherubs, WHO ARE MALE AND FEMALE, are ten handbreadths from bottom to top, NAMELY, TEN SFIROT OF RETURNING LIGHT, from their feet to their heads, AND TEN SFIROT OF DIRECT LIGHT from their heads to their feet, and they rest on a handbreadth, which is THE SECRET OF Yud. THEY THEREFORE CONTAIN ten from top to bottom and ten from bottom to top, NAMELY, THE TEN SFIROT OF DIRECT LIGHT AND THE TEN SFIROT OF RETURNING LIGHT, and this is Yud-Vav-Dalet, WHOSE NUMERICAL SUM IS TWENTY. And this is why the sages ruled that the size of a *Sukkah* should be not less than ten and not more than twenty. A *Sukkah* that is built in the shape of a furnace is from the side of Ima, WHICH IS JUDGMENT, about which it is said: "And Mount Sinai smoked in every part, because Hashem descended on it in fire: and the smoke of it ascended like the smoke of a furnace" (Shemot 19:18), and it is all one.

817. וְסֻכָּה תִּהְיֶה לְצֵל יוֹמָם, דְּסִכּוּךְ בְּעֵינָן. וְסִכּוּךְ אִתְעָבֵיד לַצֵּל. דְּאִתְּמַר בֵּיהּ, בְּצֵל שַׁדַּי יִתְלוֹנָן. וְלֹא בְּצֵל סֻכַּת הֶדְיוֹט, דְּאַגִּין עַל גּוּפָא מִשִּׁמְשָׁא. אֶלָּא צֵל לְאַגָּנָא עַל נִשְׁמְתָא. בְּצִלּוֹ חִמַּדְתִּי וְיָשַׁבְתִּי. אֲשֶׁר אָמַרְנוּ בְּצִלּוֹ נִחְיֶה בַגּוֹיִם. צֵל עִם ם׳, אִיהִי צֶלֶם. דְּאִתְּמַר בֵּיהּ, אַךְ בְּצֶלֶם יִתְהַלֶּךְ אִישׁ. ם׳ סְתוּמָה אִית לָהּ אַרְבְּעָה דְּפָנוֹת.

817. "And there shall be a tabernacle for a shadow in the daytime" (Yeshayah 4:6). This is because a roof is required, and this casts a shadow, about which it is said: "shall abide under the shadow of Shadai" (Tehilim 91:1). And the meaning is not to the shadow cast by an ordinary Sukkah that protects the body from the sun, but to the shadow that casts a protection over the Soul. THIS IS IN THE SECRET OF THE VERSE "I sat down under its shadow with great delight" (Shir Hashirim 2:3) and "Of Whom we said: 'Under His shadow we shall live among the nations'" (Eichah 4:20). The word *tzel* (lit. 'shadow') with a final letter Mem added to it forms the word *tzelem* (Eng. 'image'), WHERE *TZEL* IS THE SECRET OF THE ROOFING MATERIAL AND THE FINAL MEM IS THE SECRET OF THE FOUR

SIDE-WALLS OF THE SUKKAH, and it is said: "Surely every man walks in a vain show (Heb. *tzelem*)" (Tehilim 39:7). Closed Mem has four sides to it, WHICH ARE THE SECRET OF THE FOUR SIDE-WALLS OF THE SUKKAH.

818. וּמַה דְּאוּקְמוּהָ שְׁתֵּים כְּהִלְכָתָן וּשְׁלִישִׁית אֲפִילוּ טֶפַח. וּלְמַ"ד שְׁלֹשָׁה כְּהִלְכָתָן וּרְבִיעִית אֲפִילוּ טֶפַח. וְאִינּוּן בְּגִין דָּא, תְּרֵין, תְּלַת, אַרְבַּע, הָא תֵּשַׁע, טֶפַח אִיהִי עֲשִׂירָאָה, לְאַשְׁלְמָא כָּל חֶסְרוֹן. וּבְגִין דָּא, שִׁיעוּר סֻכָּה לָא פָּחוּת מֵעֶשֶׂר, דְּאִיהִי מַלְכוּת, עֲשִׂירָאָה דְּכָל דַּרְגִּין. וְלָא לְמַעְלָה מֵעֶשְׂרִין, דְּאִיהִי כ', כֶּתֶר עֶלְיוֹן, דְּלָא שַׁלְטָא בֵּיהּ עֵינָא. כָּבוֹד עִלָּאָה, עֲלֵיהּ אָמַר מֹשֶׁה, הַרְאֵנִי נָא אֶת כְּבוֹדֶךְ, וְאָתִיב לֵיהּ קוּדְשָׁא בְּרִיךְ הוּא, לֹא תוּכַל לִרְאוֹת אֶת פָּנָי. וְלֵית כָּבוֹד, בְּלָא כ'.

818. And with regard to the teaching: Two according to the regulations, and a third of even a handbreadth; and of him who says three according to the regulations, and a fourth of even a handbreadth: that is because OF THE THREE MEASUREMENTS, two, three, four, which TOGETHER MAKE nine, WHERE TWO ARE CHOCHMAH AND BINAH, THREE ARE CHESED, GVURAH AND TIFERET, AND FOUR ARE NETZACH, HOD, YESOD AND MALCHUT. And the handbreadth MENTIONED WITH THE TWO OR WITH THE THREE is the tenth, NAMELY, MALCHUT, that makes up every shortage. And this is why the size of a Sukkah is not less than ten, referring to Malchut, which is the tenth of all the Sfirot, and not more than twenty, which is Caf (the numerical value of which is twenty), THAT ALLUDES TO upper Keter, which is further than the eye can see AND IS UNFATHOMABLE. This is that upper glory, about which Moses said: "I pray You, show me Your glory" (Shemot 33:18), to which the Holy One, blessed be He, responded: "you can not see My face" (Ibid. 20), and there is no glory (Heb. *kavod*) without Caf.

819. וּבְגִין דָּא שָׁעֲרוּ מָארֵי מַתְנִיתִין לְקַבְּלַיְיהוּ, סֻכָּה הָעֲשׂוּיָה כְּמָבוֹי, מִסְּטְרָא דְּאָת ב', כְּמִין גַּא"ם, מִסְּטְרָא דְּאָת ג', כְּמִין צְרִיף, מִסְּטְרָא דְּאָת ד'. וְשֶׁבַע אַתְוָון אִינּוּן, בַּג"ד כְּפַר"ת. כ', כְּבִשְׁןָ. ב', בּוּרְגָּנִין. וּשְׁאַר סֻכּוֹת. וְכֻלְּהוּ רְמִיזֵי לְגַבֵּי מָארֵי מַתְנִיתִין. וְלֵית לְאַרְכָא בְּהוֹן.

819. And for this reason the sages of the Mishnah viewed as corresponding to them: a Sukkah made like an alleyway, which is from the side of the letter Bet, and in the shape of a right angle, which is from the side of the letter Gimel, and like a hut which is from the side of the letter Dalet. And these seven letters Bet, Gimel, Dalet, Caf, Pe, Resh and Tav WHICH ARE DOUBLED BY THE ADDITION OF A DAGESH (A DOT) IN THEM, ALLUDE TO THE SEVEN SFIROT CHESED, GVURAH, TIFERET, NETZACH, HOD, YESOD AND MALCHUT, NAMELY, DUE TO THE ASPECT OF JUDGMENT THAT IS IN THEM. AND THEY ARE THE INITIAL LETTERS THAT ALLUDE TO THE SEVEN SUKKAHS MADE INVALID, BECAUSE OF THE JUDGMENT THAT IS IN THEM. Caf ALLUDES TO A SUKKAH MADE like a furnace (Heb. *kivshan*), AND Bet TO A SUKKAH that is a wayside station (Heb. *burganin*), and THE OTHER LETTERS to the remaining INVALID Sukahs, all of which are referred to by the sages of the Mishnah, SUCH AS THE SUKKAH OF FRUIT (HEB. *PEROT*) WATCHMEN, THE SUKKAH OF SHEPHERDS (HEB. *RO'IM*), OR THE SUKKAH OF SAMARITANS (HEB. *KUTIM*), and there is no need to prolong the discussion on them.

820. וְאִינּוּן לְקַבְלַיְיהוּ שִׁבְעָה כֹּכְבֵי לֶכֶת, וְאִינּוּן דְּכַר וְנוּקְבָּא. וּבְגִין דָּא אִתְקְרִיאוּ ז' כְּפוּלוֹת. כְּגוֹן שִׁבְעָה שַׁרְגִּין דִּמְנַרְתָּא, דְּאִתְּמַר בָּהּ שֶׁבַע בַּיּוֹם הִלַּלְתִּיךָ. הָכִי שִׁבְעָה וְשִׁבְעָה מוּצָקוֹת. הָכִי שִׁבְעָה סְפִירָאן כְּפוּלוֹת. וְשִׁבְעָה יוֹמֵי בְּרֵאשִׁית לְתַתָּא, שִׁבְעָה לְעֵילָּא, אֵין כָּל חָדָשׁ תַּחַת הַשָּׁמֶשׁ.

820. And corresponding to them, TO THE SEVEN LETTERS BET, GIMEL, DALET, CAF, PE, RESH AND TAV are the seven planets, and they are male and female, FOR WHEN THESE SEVEN LETTERS ARE WEAK THEY ARE OF THE MALE AND WHEN THEY ARE STRONG (WITH A DAGESH) THEY ARE OF THE FEMALE. And they are therefore called 'the seven double letters' and are like the seven candles of the candelabrum, WHICH ARE THE SECRET OF THE SEVEN SFIROT CHESED, GVURAH, TIFERET, NETZACH, HOD, YESOD AND MALCHUT, and it is said about it: "Seven times a day I praise You" (Tehilim 119:164). And so IT IS SAID: "and seven pipes to the seven lamps, which were upon the top of it" (Zecharyah 4:2), WHICH ARE THE SECRET OF THE SEVEN DOUBLE LETTERS, NAMELY, THE SEVEN LETTERS IN THEIR WEAK FORM AND THE SEVEN LETTERS IN THEIR STRONG FORM, and likewise, the seven Sfirot are double, CONTAINING

SEVEN OF JUDGMENT AND SEVEN OF MERCY. And so, too, are the seven days of Creation below, NAMELY, THE SEVEN SFIROT OF MALCHUT, WHICH HAVE A *DAGESH* WITH JUDGMENTS, and the seven above, NAMELY, THE SEVEN SFIROT OF ZEIR ANPIN, WHICH ARE WEAK IN JUDGMENTS. FOR ABOUT THE SEVEN SFIROT THAT ARE BELOW, IT IS SAID: "and there is nothing new under the sun" (Kohelet 1:9), FOR ALL INNOVATIONS COME FROM THE SUN, NAMELY THE SEVEN SFIROT OF ZEIR ANPIN AND NOT FROM UNDER THE SUN, BY WHICH IS MEANT THE SEVEN SFIROT OF MALCHUT.

821. לוּלָב דָּא צַדִּיק. דְּדָמֵי לְחוּט הַשִּׁדְרָה, דְּבֵיהּ ח"י חוּלְיָין, לָקֳבֵל ח"י נְעְנוּעִין דְּלוּלָב. וְאִינּוּן לָקֳבֵל ח"י בִּרְכָאן דִּצְלוֹתָא. לָקֳבֵל שְׁמֹנָה עָשָׂר אַזְכָּרוֹת, דְּהָבוּ לַיְיָ' בְּנֵי אֵלִים. לָקֳבֵל שְׁמֹנָה עָשָׂר אַזְכָּרוֹת דְּק"ש. וְנַעֲנוּעַ לְשִׁית סִיטְרִין, בְּחוּשְׁבַּן ו'. תְּלַת נְעְנוּעִין בְּכָל סְטְרָא, אִינּוּן ח"י.

821. Lulav is the Righteous, NAMELY, YESOD, for the Lulav is like the spinal chord that contains eighteen vertebrae, corresponding to the eighteen shaking movements with the Lulav. And they correspond to the eighteen blessings of the Amidah prayer, and they correspond to the eighteen mentions, NAMELY, THE NAMES OF YUD HEI VAV HEI, in "Ascribe to Hashem, O you mighty" (Tehilim 29:1), and the eighteen times that the Name is mentioned in the reading of Sh'ma. And the Lulav is shaken in six directions: SOUTH, NORTH, EAST, UP, DOWN AND WEST, which makes six, and it is shaken three times in each direction, MAKING a total of eighteen.

822. לוּלָב בְּיָמִין, כָּלִיל שִׁשָּׁה דְּאִינּוּן ג' הֲדַסִּין, גְּדוּלָּה גְּבוּרָה תִּפְאֶרֶת. וְדַמְיָין לִתְלַת גַּוְונֵי עֵינָא. ב' בַּדֵּי עֲרָבוֹת, נֶצַח וְהוֹד. וְדַמְיָין לִתְרֵין שִׁפְוָון. לוּלָב, יְסוֹד, דּוֹמֶה לַשִּׁדְרָה. דְּבֵיהּ קִיּוּם דְּכָל גַּרְמִין. וְעָלֵיהּ אָמַר דָּוִד, כָּל עַצְמוֹתַי תֹּאמַרְנָה יְיָ' מִי כָמוֹךָ. אֶתְרוֹג, מַלְכוּת, דּוֹמֶה לְלִבָּא. דְּבֵיהּ הַרְהוּרִין.

822. The lulav IS TAKEN in the right HAND, and is comprised of six, namely three myrtle branches, CORRESPONDING TO Greatness, Gvurah, and Tiferet,

and they are like the three colors in the eye, WHICH ARE WHITE, RED, AND GREEN. And the two willow twigs are Netzach and Hod, and they are similar to the two lips. The Lulav IS Yesod and is like the spinal column that supports all the bones and about which David said: "All my bones shall say, Hashem, who is like You" (Tehilim 35:10). And the Etrog is Malchut and is like the heart, in which are thoughts.

823. וְנִעְנוּעִין דְּהַלֵּל, אִינּוּן מְשׁוּתָּפִין בְּנַעֲנוּעִין דִּנְטִילַת לוּלָב, וְאִינּוּן ח״י בְּאָנָא. ח״י ח״י, בְּהוֹדוּ תְּחִלָּה וָסוֹף. ח״י דִּנְטִילַת לוּלָב, הֲרֵי ע״ב. וּבְגִין דָּא לוּלָב בְּחוּשְׁבַּן ח״ס, וְד׳ מִינִין דְּלוּלָב, הָא חֶסֶד, דְּרוֹעָא יְמִינָא. וּבְגִין דָּא תַּקִּינוּ לוּלָב בַּיָּמִין, לְסִטְרָא דְּחֶסֶד. אֶתְרוֹג לְסִטְרָא דִּגְבוּרָה, לִשְׂמָאלָא לְבָּא. וּבְגִין דָּא אֶתְרוֹג הַדּוֹמֶה לַלֵּב, תַּקִּינוּ לְמֶהֱוֵי בְּיַד שְׂמָאל. כְּמָה דְּאוּקְמוּהָ, לוּלָב בַּיָּמִין, וְאֶתְרוֹג בִּשְׂמָאלוֹ. אִינּוּן לָקֳבֵל זָכוֹר וְשָׁמוֹר. וּמַאן נָטִיל תַּרְוַוייְהוּ. עַמּוּדָא דְּאֶמְצָעִיתָא. לוּלָב בִּימִינֵיהּ, וְאֶתְרוֹג בִּשְׂמָאלֵיהּ.

823. And the shakings of the Halel are common to the shakings of the taking up of the Lulav, and there are eighteen SHAKINGS at "Save us, Hashem, we pray You" (Tehilim 118:25), eighteen each at the first and last "O, give thanks" (Ibid. 1 and 29), and eighteen at the taking up of the Lulav, making a total of 72 SHAKINGS. And this is why the numerical value of Lulav, which is 68, together with the four kinds of the Lulav, COMES TO 72, and this is the same as the numerical value of Chesed, which is the right arm. And this is why it was decreed that the Lulav be taken in the right hand, which is the side of Chesed, and the Etrog in the side of Gvurah, in the left, CORRESPONDING TO the heart. And this is why it was decreed that the Etrog, which is like the heart, be held in the left hand, as it has been taught: Lulav in the right hand and Etrog in the left, corresponding to 'Remember' and 'Keep'. And who is the one taking both LULAV AND ETROG is the Central Column, MEANING ZEIR ANPIN. The Lulav is his right, the Etrog is his left.

824. אָתוּ אֲבָהָן, וְרַעְיָא מְהֵימְנָא, וְאַהֲרֹן וְדָוִד וּשְׁלֹמֹה, וּבָרִיכוּ לֵיהּ, וְאָמְרוּ לֵיהּ, אַנְתְּ בּוּצִינָא קַדִּישָׁא, וְחַבְרַיָּיא דִּילָךְ דְּאִינּוּן שִׁית, לָקֳבֵל אִינּוּן ז׳. וְאַנְתְּ בּוּצִינָא קַדִּישָׁא נֵר מַעֲרָבִי בְּאֶמְצַע, דְּכָל שִׁית נֵרוֹת

נְהִרִין מִנָּךְ. בְּכָל חַד אִתְּמַר בֵּיהּ, נֵר יְיָ' נִשְׁמַת אָדָם. וְרַעְיָא מְהֵימְנָא נָהִיר בָּךְ, וְאַנְתְּ בְּחַבְרַיָּיא דִּילָךְ, וְכֹלָּא חַד, בְּלָא פְּרוֹדָא כְּלַל. וּמִתַּמָן וְאֵילָךְ מִתְפַּשְּׁטִין עַנְפִּין לְכָל מָארֵי חָכְמְתָא, אַשְׁלִים מִלִּין דַּחֲבוּרָא קַדְמָאָה דִּילָךְ לְאַעְטְרָא לוֹן.

824. The patriarchs came with the Faithful Shepherd and Aaron, David and Solomon and blessed him, RABBI SHIMON, saying to him: You, holy luminary, and your friends, who are six in number, correspond to these seven SFIROT, and you, the holy luminary, are a western light in the middle of the six lights that illuminate from you. And about each one it is said: "The soul of man is the candle of Hashem" (Mishlei 20:27). And the Faithful Shepherd illuminates in you, and you in your friends and all of you are one, without any separation whatsoever. And from there and onwards, the branches, NAMELY, THE ILLUMINATIONS, spread out, to all masters of wisdom. Complete what you are saying in the first compilation part, to crown them.

825. פָּתַח בּוּצִינָא קַדִּישָׁא וְאָמַר, מַיִם רַבִּים לֹא יוּכְלוּ לְכַבּוֹת אֶת הָאַהֲבָה וְגו'. מַאי בּוּז. יוֹמָא תִּנְיָינָא, וְיוֹמָא שְׁתִיתָאָה, וְיוֹמָא שְׁבִיעָאָה דְּסוּכּוֹת. דִּבְהוֹן הֲווֹ מְנַסְּכִים מַיִם וְיַיִן.

825. The holy luminary began by quoting: "Many waters cannot quench love…IT WOULD BE UTTERLY SCORNED" (Shir Hashirim 8:7). What is the meaning of "IT WOULD BE UTTERLY scorned"? This refers to the second day, the sixth day, and the seventh day of Sukkot on which libations of water and wine were poured out.

826. דְּשֶׁבַע יוֹמִין דְּסוּכּוֹת, בְּהוֹן הָיוּ מַקְרִיבִין יִשְׂרָאֵל שִׁבְעִים פָּרִים, לְכַפְּרָא עַל שַׁבְעִין מְמָנָן, בְּגִין דְּלָא יִשְׁתְּאַר עָלְמָא חָרוּב מִנַּיְיהוּ. הה"ד, וּבַחֲמִשָּׁה עָשָׂר יוֹם וְהִקְרַבְתֶּם עוֹלָה אִשֵּׁה לְרֵיחַ נִיחֹחַ לַיְיָ' פָּרִים בְּנֵי בָקָר שְׁלֹשָׁה עָשָׂר תְּמִימִים. וּבַיּוֹם הַשֵּׁנִי פָּרִים י"ב. וּבַיּוֹם הַשְּׁלִישִׁי י"א. וּבַיּוֹם הָרְבִיעִי עֲשָׂרָה. וּבַיּוֹם הַחֲמִישִׁי פָּרִים תִּשְׁעָה. וּבַיּוֹם הַשִּׁשִּׁי פָּרִים שְׁמֹנָה. וּבַיּוֹם הַשְּׁבִיעִי שִׁבְעָה. וְכֻלְּהוּ שַׁבְעִין. וּבְכָל יוֹמָא הֲווֹ חֲסֵרִים. אֲמַאי חֲסֵרִים.

826. During the seven days of Sukkot, Yisrael used to sacrifice seventy bullocks to make atonement for the seventy ministers OF THE SEVENTY NATIONS, so that the world would not remain destroyed because of them. And this is what the verse says: "And on the fifteenth day... you shall offer a burnt offering, a sacrifice made by fire, of a sweet savor to Hashem: thirteen young bullocks...without blemish" (Bemidbar 29:12-13). And on the second day twelve, and on the third day eleven bullocks, and on the fourth day ten, and on the fifth day nine bullocks, and on the sixth day eight bullocks, and on the seventh day seven. And all TOLD, THERE are seventy bullocks, each day one less being presented. HE ASKS, Why was there a reduction?

827. אֶלָּא הָכָא קָא רָמִיז, וַתָּנַח הַתֵּיבָה בַּחֹדֶשׁ הַשְּׁבִיעִי. וּמַה הָתָם בִּימֵי טוֹפָנָא, וְהַמַּיִם הָלְכוּ הָלוֹךְ וְחָסוֹר. אוּף הָכִי בְּתִשְׁרֵי, דְּאִיהוּ יַרְחָא שְׁבִיעָאָה, דְּבֵיהּ כַּמָּה פְּקוּדִין, רֹאשׁ הַשָּׁנָה וְיוֹם הַכִּפּוּרִים, סֻכָּה וְלוּלָב אֶתְרוֹג, מִינִין דְּלוּלָב שׁוֹפָר. שְׁכִינְתָּא עִלָּאָה שַׁרְיָיא עַל יִשְׂרָאֵל, דְּאִיהִי תְּשׁוּבָה, סוּכָּה. אֶתְרוֹג, וְקוּדְשָׁא בְּרִיךְ הוּא דְּאִיהוּ לוּלָב. מִיַּד וְהַמַּיִם הָיוּ הָלוֹךְ וְחָסוֹר, מִתְמַעֲטִין חוֹבִין דְּיִשְׂרָאֵל, אוּף הָכִי מִתְמַעֲטִין מְמָנָן דְּאִינּוּן מַלְאֲכֵי חַבָּלָה, דִּמְמָנָן עֲלַיְיהוּ, דְּדַמְיָין לְמֵי טוֹפָנָא. כְּמָה דְּאוֹקְמוּהָ, עָשָׂה עֲבֵרָה אַחַת קָנָה לוֹ קַטֵּיגוֹר אֶחָד. בְּהַהוּא זִמְנָא דְּמִתְמַעֲטִין חוֹבִין, מִתְמַעֲטִין פָּרִים דִּלְהוֹן, מִתְמַעֲטִין מְמָנָן דְּע׳ אוּמִין, מִתְמַעֲטִין ע׳ אוּמִין, מִתְמַעֵט טוּבָא דִּלְהוֹן.

827. AND HE ANSWERS THAT THE VERSE here gives us a hint. "And the ark rested in the seventh month" (Beresheet 8:4), WHICH IS TISHREI. And just as then in the days of the Flood, when the waters decreased continually, so also here, in Tishrei, which is the seven month, in which there are a number of precepts, Rosh Hashanah and Yom Kippur, Sukkah, Lulav and Etrog, the kinds of the Lulav and Shofar. FOR THEN the upper Shechinah rests on Yisrael, and this is Repentance, NAMELY, BINAH THAT IS CALLED 'REPENTANCE', AND IS THE SECRET OF Sukkah, Etrog, WHICH IS MALCHUT, and Lulav, that is the Holy One, blessed be He, NAMELY, ZEIR ANPIN. Immediately "And the waters decreased continually" (Ibid. 5), for the sins of Yisrael become less. So, too, the angels of destruction who are appointed over them, OVER THE INIQUITIES, become less, FOR THE INIQUITIES are similar to the waters of the Flood, as has been taught: He

that commits one transgression, gets for himself one accuser. And at the time that the iniquities become less, their bullocks are reduced in number, the appointees over the seventy nations are reduced, the seventy nations diminish, and their goodness becomes less.

828. תֵּיבַת נֹחַ, מְנֵי קוּדְשָׁא בְּרִיךְ הוּא, לְאַעֲלָא עִמֵּיה שְׁנַיִם שְׁנַיִם שִׁבְעָה שִׁבְעָה זָכָר וּנְקֵבָה, לְקָרְבָּנָא, לְאַגָּנָא עַל נֹחַ, וְעַל כָּל אִינוּן דְּעָאלִין עִמֵּיה לַתֵּיבָה. אוֹף הָכִי אִלֵּין דִּמְנַטְּרִין חַגִּין וּזְמַנִּין, דְּאִינוּן יָמִים טוֹבִים, שְׁנַיִם שְׁנַיִם שִׁבְעָה שִׁבְעָה, שְׁנַיִם שְׁנַיִם תְּרֵין יוֹמִין דר"ה, וּתְרֵין יוֹמִין דְּשָׁבוּעוֹת, וּבְגִין דְּאִינוּן תְּרֵין מִנַּיְיהוּ בְּסָפֵק, הָא אִית שְׁנֵי יְמֵי הַפּוּרִים בְּאַתְרַיְיהוּ. שִׁבְעָה שִׁבְעָה, ז' יוֹמִין דְּפֶסַח, ז' יוֹמִין דְּסוּכּוֹת. נֹחַ לָקֳבֵל יוֹם הַשַּׁבָּת, וְהַאי אִיהוּ מִכָּל הַחַי.

828. And the Holy One, blessed be He, commanded Noah to take into the ark two and two, seven and seven, male and female, to be a sacrifice to protect Noah and all those who went into the ark with him. So, too, those who observe festivals and seasons, which are feast days, are two and two, seven and seven. Two and two refers to the two days of Rosh Hashanah and the two days of Shavuot, and because there are two OF SHAVUOT because of doubt, therefore, there are two days of Purim in their stead. Seven and seven refer to the seven days of Pesach, and the seven days of Sukkot. Noah corresponds to the Shabbat day, and this is the meaning of what is written: "of every living (Heb. *chai* = eighteen) thing" (Beresheet 6:19), BECAUSE TWO + TWO + SEVEN + SEVEN = EIGHTEEN, WHICH IS *CHAI*.

829. סֻכָּה קָא אֲגִינַת עֲלַייהוּ דְּיִשְׂרָאֵל, הה"ד וְסֻכָּה תִּהְיֶה לְצֵל יוֹמָם מֵחֹרֶב. סֻכָּה קָא אֲגִינַת. מַה תֵּיבַת נֹחַ לְאַגָּנָא, אוֹף הָכִי סֻכָּה לְאַגָּנָא. וְעוֹד מִכָּל הַחַי, ח"י בִּרְכָּאן דִּצְלוֹתָא, מֵאִינוּן ט' ט', בִּרְכָתָא דְּמִינִין בָּהּ אִשְׁתְּלִימוּ י' סְפִירָאן מֵעֵילָא לְתַתָּא, וּמִתַּתָּא לְעֵילָא. וְאִיהוּ לָקֳבֵל נֹחַ.

829. The Sukkah protects Yisrael, as it is written: "And there shall be a tabernacle for a shadow in the daytime from the heat" (Yeshayah 4:6).

THUS, the Sukkah gives protection. Just as the purpose of Noah's ark was to give protection, so is the Sukkah to give protection. Again: "of every living (Heb. *chai* = eighteen) thing," where *chai* is the eighteen blessings of the prayer, which SUB-DIVIDE INTO two groups of nine each. AND WITH the blessing concerning the heretics, the ten Sfirot are completed, FOR THIS MAKES TEN TOGETHER WITH THE FIRST NINE, AND AGAIN TOGETHER WITH THE LAST NINE. And they correspond to the ten Sfirot OF DIRECT LIGHT that is from above downwards, and the ten Sfirot OF RETURNING LIGHT that is from below upwards. And this corresponds to Noah, WHICH IS TO SAY THAT THE EIGHTEEN BLESSINGS OF THE PRAYER CORRESPOND TO THE EIGHTEEN OF NOAH, NAMELY, TWO AND TWO, SEVEN AND SEVEN, WHICH ADD UP TO EIGHTEEN.

830. וְעוֹד מִכָּל הַחַי, שְׁכִינְתָּא אֲגִינַת עַל אִלֵּין דְּנַטְרִין י׳, אוֹת שַׁבָּת בִּתְחוּמָא דִּילֵיהּ, דְּאִיהוּ ח׳ אֲלָפִים, תְּרֵין אַלְפִין לְכָל צַד. וְעוֹד, מִכָּל הַחַי, אִלֵּין דְּנַטְרִין י׳ אוֹת בְּרִית, דְּאִיהוּ בְּח׳ יוֹמִין, דְּאִתְּמַר עֲלַיְיהוּ, וּבַיּוֹם הַשְּׁמִינִי יִמּוֹל בְּשַׂר עָרְלָתוֹ. וְעוֹד, מִכָּל הָחַי, אִלֵּין דְּנַטְרִין אוֹת י׳, תְּפִלִּין בִּתְמַנְיָיא פָּרְשִׁיָּין.

830. Again: "of every living thing." This means that the Shechinah protects all those who keep the Yud, which is the sign of the Shabbat, in its limits, namely, eight thousand CUBITS, NAMELY, two thousand in each direction. AND THE YUD OF THE SIGN OF THE SHABBAT AND THE CHET (= EIGHT) OF THE LIMITS ARE CHET YUD: *CHAI*, LIVING. Again: "of every living thing." This means those who keep the sign of the covenant, which is Yud, which is at the eighth day, about which it is said: "And in the eighth day the flesh of his foreskin shall be circumcised" (Vayikra 12:3). AND THE YUD OF THE SIGN OF THE COVENANT AND THE CHET OF THE EIGHT DAYS FORM *CHAI*. Again: "of every living thing" refers to those who observe the sign of the Tefilin, which is Yud, AND IN WHICH ARE eight passages, THUS: CHET YUD: *CHAI*.

831. שְׁכִינְתָּא דְּאִיהִי סוּכָּה, אֲגִינַת עֲלַיְיהוּ, וּפְרִישַׁת גַּדְפָּאָה עֲלַיְיהוּ, כְּאִמָּא עַל בְּנִין, וּבְגִין דָּא תַּקִּינוּ לְבָרְכָא, הַפּוֹרֵס סוּכַּת שָׁלוֹם עָלֵינוּ. וּבְגִין דָּא בְּיַרְחָא שְׁבִיעָאָה, דְּבֵיהּ כָּל פִּקּוּדִין אִלֵּין, מַיִם רַבִּים לֹא

יוּכְלוּ לְכַבּוֹת אֶת הָאַהֲבָה. עִם יִשְׂרָאֵל בַּאֲבוּהוֹן שֶׁבַּשָּׁמַיִם. וְלֵית מַיִם רַבִּים, אֶלָּא כָּל אוֹמִין וּמְמָנָן דִּלְהוֹן. אִם יִתֵּן אִישׁ, דְּאִיהוּ סָמָאֵל, כָּל מַה דְּאִית לֵיהּ בְּעָלְמָא דֵין, בְּגִין דְּיִשְׁתַּתַּף בְּאִלֵּין פִּקּוּדִין עִם יִשְׂרָאֵל, בּוֹז יָבוּזוּ לוֹ.

831. The Shechinah, which is the Sukkah, protects them and spreads Her wings over them, as does the mother bird over the young. And this is why the text of the prayer was worded: 'who spreads the tabernacle of peace over us'. And for this reason, in the seventh month, which contains all these precepts, "Many waters cannot quench love" (Shir Hashirim 8:7) of Yisrael for their Father who is in Heaven. And there is no meaning to "many waters" except all the nations and their ministers. And if a man, this being Samael, give all that he possesses in this world in order to join in partnership with Yisrael in these precepts, "it would be utterly scorned" (Ibid.).

122. Shmini Atzeret

A Synopsis

Rabbi Shimon explains about the small banquet on the eighth day that he says is from the aspect of Malchut. He answers his son's query as to why the banquet for Yisrael was from the lower Shechinah but the banquet for all seventy nations was from the upper Mother, Binah.

832. וּבַיּוֹם הַשְּׁמִינִי עֲצֶרֶת פַּר אֶחָד אַיִל אֶחָד, הָא אוּקְמוּהָ מָארֵי מַתְנִיתִין, לְמַלְכָּא דְּזַמִּין אוּשְׁפִּיזִין, לְבָתַר דְּשָׁלַח לוֹן, אָמַר לְאִלֵּין בְּנֵי בֵּיתָא דִּילֵיהּ, אֲנָא וְאַתּוּן נַעֲבֵיד סְעוּדָה קְטַנָּה. וּמַאי עֲצֶרֶת. כמד"א, זֶה יַעְצוֹר בְּעַמִּי, וְלֵית עֶצֶר אֶלָּא מַלְכוּת. מִסִּטְרָא דִּשְׁכִינְתָּא עִלָּאָה, עָבֵיד סְעוּדָתָא רַבְרְבָא, וּמִסִּטְרָא דְּמַלְכוּתָא, סְעוּדָתָא זְעֵירָא. וְנוֹהֲגִין לְמֶעְבַּד יִשְׂרָאֵל עִמָּהּ חֶדְוָה, וְאִתְקְרִיאַת שִׂמְחַת תּוֹרָה. וּמְעַטְּרָן לס"ת בְּכֶתֶר דִּילֵיהּ, רֶמֶז ס"ת לְתִפְאֶרֶת, שְׁכִינְתָּא עֲטֶרֶת תִּפְאָרֶת.

832. "On the eighth day you shall have a solemn assembly...one bullock, one ram" (Bemidbar 29:35-36). The sages of the Mishnah have already taught that the matter is to be likened to the case of a king who invites guests to his house, and after he has sent them on their way, says to the members of his household: Let us, you and I, make a small banquet. And what is the meaning of "solemn assembly" (Heb. *atzeret*)? It is as is written: "this one shall reign (Heb. *ya'atzor*) over My people" (I Shmuel 9:17). And there is no reign apart from Malchut. FOR from the aspect of upper Shechinah, WHICH IS BINAH, he made the large banquet, but he made the small banquet from the aspect of Malchut. And Yisrael make joy with her, and she is called 'Simchat Torah', (lit. 'the Rejoicing of the Torah') (holiday on which we dance with the Torah). And the scrolls of the Torah have their crowns placed on them, alluding to the fact that the scroll of the Torah is Tiferet, while the Shechinah is ITS CROWN, NAMELY, the crown of Tiferet.

833. אָמַר ר' אֶלְעָזָר, אַבָּא, אֲמַאי מִסִּטְרָא דְּאִמָּא עִלָּאָה, זַמִּין לְכָל מְמָנָן דְּכָל אוּמִין, וּמִסִּטְרָא דִּשְׁכִינְתָּא תַּתָּאָה, לָא זַמִּין אֶלָּא לְאוּמָה יְחִידָה, לְקַבֵּל פַּר יְחִידָה.

833. Rabbi Elazar asked, Father, why is it that from the side of supernal Ima, WHICH IS BINAH, He invited all the appointees of all the nations, NAMELY, WITH THE SEVENTY BULLOCKS, REFERRED TO ABOVE, and from the side of the lower Shechinah, He invited only a solitary nation, corresponding to the one bullock? SHOULD IT NOT HAVE BEEN THE OTHER WAY AROUND, WITH YISRAEL RECEIVING FROM SUPERNAL IMA, AND THE MINISTERS OF THE NATIONS FROM MALCHUT?

834. אָמַר לֵיהּ בְּרִי, שַׁפִּיר שָׁאֵילַת. בְּגִין דְּמַלְכוּת אִיהִי רְמִיזָא לִבְרַתָּא, דְּאִיהִי צְנוּעָה בְּבֵית אָבִיהָ וְאִמָּה. וְאִיהִי אֲרוּסָה וְלָא נְשׂוּאָה. לָאו אוֹרַח אַרְעָא, לְמֵיכַל עִם אוֹשְׁפִּיזִין. אֲבָל אִימָּא דְּהִיא נְשׂוּאָה, אוֹרַח אַרְעָא אִיהוּ בָּתַר דְּמִזְמִין בַּעְלָהּ אוֹשְׁפִּיזֵי, לְמֵיכַל עַל פָּתוֹרָא עִם בַּעְלָהּ. וְאִי אִינוּן אוֹשְׁפִּיזִין נוּכְרָאִין, לָא אַכְלֵי עִמְּהוֹן, לָא אַבָּא, וְלָא אִמָּא, וְכָל שֶׁכֵּן בְּרַתָּא. וּבְגִין כָּךְ בִּסְעוּדָתָא דְּשַׁבְעִין מְמָנָן, לָא אִשְׁתְּתַּף לְמֵיכַל עִמְּהוֹן, חַד מִן מָארֵי מַלְכָּא, בְּגִין דְּאִינוּן נוּכְרָאִין. אָמַר לֵיהּ וַדַּאי כְּעַן אִתְיַישְּׁבַת מִלָּה בְּלִבָּאי, עַל בּוּרְיֵיהּ.

834. He replied: My son, that is a good question that you have asked, and the answer is: Because Malchut alludes to a daughter who is modest in the house of her father and mother, and she is engaged but not married, THEREFORE, it is not customarily considered proper that she should eat with the guests. But as for the mother, who is married, HERE it is the customary way that when her husband invites guests, she should eat WITH THE GUESTS, at the table with her husband. And if they are foreign guests, then no one eats with them, neither father nor mother, and certainly not the daughter, WHO IS MALCHUT. And this is the reason why at the banquet for the seventy ministers not one of the members of the King's household joins in to eat with them, because they are foreigners. He said: Surely the matter has now been settled in my thoughts correctly.

123. Explanations about Malchut

A Synopsis

Rabbi Shimon tells us that the Shechinah ascends to the place she came from, Infinity, as a result of the burnt offerings. She takes the Sfirot up with her to provide a sweet aroma for God and then descends bringing atonement for Yisrael's sins with her. Rabbi Shimon says that all the grades ascend and descend in her. We learn why Malchut is called 'peace offerings' and why everything is included in Malchut. She is Chochmah and Binah and Tiferet. We also hear of the twelve commandments that are included in her.

835. עוֹלַת תָּמִיד, דָּא שְׁכִינְתָּא, דִּסְלִיקַת לְעֵילָּא בְּהַהוּא דַּרְגָּא, דְּאִתְּמַר בָּהּ עֶרֶב וָבוֹקֶר בְּכָל יוֹם תָּמִיד, וְאוֹמְרִים פַּעֲמַיִם שְׁמַע יִשְׂרָאֵל. וְאִיהִי סְלִיקַת בְּעַמּוּדָא דְּאֶמְצָעִיתָא, דְּאִיהוּ תָּדִיר עִמָּהּ בְּלָא פְּרוּדָא כְּלָל.

835. The daily burnt offering (Heb. *olat tamid*) is the Shechinah which always (Heb. *tamid*) ascends (Heb. *olah*) on that grade about which it is said: 'Evening and morning, every day, twice each and every day, saying Sh'ma Yisrael'. And She ascends in the Central Pillar, WHICH IS ZEIR ANPIN, who is with Her always, without any separation at all.

836. וּלְאָן סְלִיקַת. לְאֲתַר דְּאִתְגְּזָרַת מִתַּמָּן, דְּאִיהוּ אֵין סוֹף, וְאִיהוּ גְּבוֹהַּ מִכָּל סְפִירָאן. וּבג"ד אוּקְמוּהָ. עוֹלָה כֵּלָּה לַגְּבוֹהַּ סַלְקָא. וְכַד אִיהִי סְלִיקַת, אֲחִידָן בָּהּ כָּל סְפִירָן, וְאִינּוּן סַלְקִין עִמָּהּ. וּמַאי סְלִיקוּ דִּילָהּ. לְרֵיחַ נִיחֹחַ, לְמֵיהַב רֵיחָא טָבָא קֳדָם יְיָ', וּלְבָתַר אִתְּמַר בָּהּ, וַיֵּרֶד מֵעֲשׂוֹת הַחַטָּאת וְהָעוֹלָה. נַחְתַת מַלְיָא כַּפָּרָה מִכָּל חוֹבִין דְּיִשְׂרָאֵל.

836. But whence does She ascend? To the place from which She was derived, which is Infinity, and She is then higher than all the Sfirot, which is why it was taught: The whole of the burnt offering ascends to the Most High. And as She ascends, all the other Sfirot are attached to Her, and ascend with her. What is the meaning of this ascent of Hers TO INFINITY? It

-253-

is to provide a sweet savor, to give a good savor before Hashem. And afterwards it is said about Her: "and came down from offering the sin offering, and the burnt offering" (Vayikra 9:22), namely, She descends FROM INFINITY, full of atonement over all of Yisrael's sins.

837. וְהָא סְלִיקוּ דִּילָהּ אִיהוּ, בְּעַמוּדָא דְּאֶמְצָעִיתָא. אוֹף הָכִי נְחִיתוּ דִּילָהּ אִיהוּ בֵּיהּ, וְכָל חַיָּילִין דִּילָהּ, וּבְגִין דָּא אִקְרֵי סֻלָּם, דְּבֵיהּ כָּל כְּנוּיִין סַלְקִין וְנַחְתִּין, דְּאִינוּן תַּלְיָין מִן יְדֹוָד. וּבְג״ד, כָּל קָרְבְּנִין וְעָלָוָון אִינוּן לַיְדֹוָד. וְאִתְקְרִיאַת קָרְבָּן, עַל שֵׁם דְּאִתְקְרִיבוּ בָּהּ כָּל כְּנוּיִין לַיְדֹוָד.

837. And Her ascent is with the Central Pillar, WHICH IS ZEIR ANPIN, and so also is Her descent, and that of all Her hosts, in it. And for this reason She is called 'a ladder' for all the appellatives; NAMELY, ALL THE GRADES ascend and descend in Her, suspended from the Name Yud Hei Vav Hei, WHICH IS ZEIR ANPIN, and thus all the sacrifices and all the burnt offerings are to Yud Hei Vav Hei. And She is called 'a sacrifice' because all the appellatives draw near, through Her, to Yud Hei Vav Hei, WHICH IS ZEIR ANPIN.

838. וּבְגִין דָּא אִתְּמַר עָלָהּ, קָרְבָּנוֹ קַעֲרַת כֶּסֶף אַחַת. לֵית דַּרְגָּא דְּאִתְקְרִיב לְגַבֵּי יְדֹוָד, פָּחוּת מִנָּהּ. וְלֵית צְלוֹתָא וּפִקּוּדָא מִכָּל פִּקּוּדִין דְּאוֹרַיְיתָא, וְכָל קָרְבְּנִין וְעָלָוָון, דְּאִינוּן לְבַר מִנָּהּ. בְּכָל דַּרְגִּין דִּסְפִירָאן לָא מִתְקַבְּלָן קֳדָם יְדֹוָד, לְבַר מִנָּהּ. וּבְגִין דָּא אִתְּמַר עָלָהּ, בְּזֹאת יָבֹא אַהֲרֹן אֶל הַקֹּדֶשׁ. וּבְג״ד אָמַר נָבִיא, כִּי אִם בְּזֹאת יִתְהַלֵּל הַמִּתְהַלֵּל.

838. And for this reason it was said about Her: "and his offering was one silver dish" (Bemidbar 7:13), NAMELY MALCHUT. For there is no grade that can draw near to Yud Hei Vav Hei without MALCHUT, and there is no prayer, nor precept of any of the precepts that are in the Torah or any of the sacrifices and burnt offerings that are outside OF MALCHUT. And in all the grades that are in the Sfirot, none is received before Yud Hei Vav Hei without her, which is why it was said about her: "Thus (lit. 'with this' (Heb. zot, feminine)) shall Aaron come into the holy place" (Vayikra 16:3), WHERE

MALCHUT IS CALLED 'ZOT'. And for this reason the prophet said: "But let him that glories glory in this (zot)" (Yirmeyah 9:23).

839. אִיהִי שְׁלָמִים, שְׁלִימוּ דִּשְׁמָא דִּידוֹד, בְּכָל דַּרְגָּא וְדַרְגָּא. אִיהִי ה'. אֲדֹנָי. י' דִּידוֹד. אִיהִי ה' מִן אֱלֹהִים. אִיהִי ה' מִן אֶהְיֶה. י' מִן שַׁדַּי. סוֹף דְּכָל הֲוָיָה וְכִנּוּי. וּבְג״ד אִתְּמַר בַּהּ, סוֹף דָּבָר הַכֹּל נִשְׁמָע אֶת הָאֱלֹהִים יְרָא וְאֶת מִצְוֹתָיו שְׁמוֹר. אִיהִי סוֹף מֵעֲשֶׂר סְפִירָאן, יַם סוֹף. שְׁלִימוּ דְּעֶלְאִין וְתַתָּאִין. אִיהוּ תַּרְעָא לְאַעֲלָא לְכָל חָכְמְתָא, לְכָל כִּנּוּי וַהֲוָיָה, וּלְאַעֲלָא בְּכָל סְפִירָה וּסְפִירָה, יְדִיעָה דְּכֹלָּא. וּפָחוּת מִינָהּ, לֵית רְשׁוּ לְשׁוּם בְּרִיָּה, לְאַשְׁגָּחָא לְשׁוּם יְדִיעָה בָּעוֹלָם. עֲלָהּ אִתְּמַר, זֶה הַשַּׁעַר לַיְיָ' צַדִּיקִים יָבֹאוּ בוֹ.

839. And she, MALCHUT, is CALLED 'peace offerings' (Heb. shelamim) because she is the completion (Heb. shlemut) of the Name Yud Hei Vav Hei in each and every grade. She is Hei OF YUD HEI VAV HEI; she is Adonai; she is the Yud of Yud Hei Vav Hei; she is the Hei of Elohim; she is the Hei of Eheyeh. She is the Yud of Shadai: (Shin-Dalet-Yud); she is the end of every Yud Hei Vav Hei and appellative, wherefore it is said about her: "The end of the matter, when all is said and done: Fear Elohim and keep His commandments" (Kohelet 12:13). She is the end (Heb. sof) of the ten Sfirot and is called 'Yam Suf' (Eng. 'the reed sea'). She is the completion of the upper beings and of the lower beings; she is the gate by which one has to enter for all wisdom and for every appellative and Yud Hei Vav Hei and for entering into each and every Sfirah. She is the knowledge of everything, and without NAMELY MALCHUT no creature has permission to look into any knowledge that is in the world. About her it is said: "this is the gate of Hashem, into which the righteous shall enter" (Tehilim 118:20).

840. אִיהוּ שֵׁם מ״ב אַתְוָון, דִּבְהוֹן אִתְבְּרִיאוּ עֶלְאִין וְתַתָּאִין. אִיהִי אִתְקְרִיאַת עַיִן מִסִּטְרָא דִּימִינָא, הִנֵּה עֵין יְדוָד אֶל יְרֵאָיו. וְאִתְקְרִיאַת אֹזֶן מִסִּטְרָא דִּשְׂמָאלָא, הַטֵּה אֱלֹהַי אָזְנְךָ וּשֲׁמָע. וְאִתְקְרִיאַת רֵיחַ מִסִּטְרָא דְּעַמּוּדָא דְּאֶמְצָעִיתָא. וְאִתְקְרִיאַת פֶּה, מִגַּרְמָהּ. הה״ד פֶּה אֶל פֶּה אֲדַבֶּר בּוֹ.

840. She, MALCHUT, is the 42-letter Name, NAMELY, THE FOUR LETTERS OF YUD HEI VAV HEI, THE TEN LETTERS OF IT BEING FULLY SPELLED, AND THE 28 LETTERS OF THE FULL SPELLING FULLY SPELLED. THIS AMOUNTS TO 42 LETTERS, AND MALCHUT IS THE SECRET OF THE FINAL HEI'S THAT ARE IN THE 42-LETTER NAME, through which the upper and lower beings were created. She is called 'eye' from the right side, WHICH IS THE CHOCHMAH IN HER, AS IT IS WRITTEN: "Behold, the eye of Hashem is upon those who fear Him" (Tehilim 33:18); and she is called 'ear' from the left side, WHICH IS THE BINAH IN HER, AS IT IS WRITTEN: "O my Elohim, incline Your ear, and hear" (Daniel 9:18). And from the aspect of the Central Pillar, WHICH IS THE TIFERET IN HER, she is called 'smell,' while from her own aspect, WHICH IS MALCHUT, she is called 'mouth,' as it is written: "With him I speak mouth to mouth" (Bemidbar 12:8).

841. אִתְקְרִיאַת פְּקוּדָא קַדְמָאָה אָנֹכִי, מִסְטְרָא דְּכֶתֶר, דְּאִיהוּ אַיִ"ן מֵאֱלֹהֵינוּ. אָנֹכִי בֵּיהּ כ', כֶּתֶר. וּבֵיהּ אַיִן. וְכֶתֶר אִתְקְרֵי מִסְטְרָא דְּאִימָּא עִלָּאָה. דְּאִדְכַּר לְגַבַּהּ חַמְשִׁין זִמְנִין יְצִיאַת מִצְרַיִם בְּאוֹרַיְיתָא. וְאִיהִי בַּ"ת מִן בְּרֵאשִׁית, דְּכָלִילָא עֲשַׂר אֲמִירָן, מִסְטְרָא דְּחָכְמָה בַּת י', בְּחָכְמָה יָסַד אֶרֶץ. בְּאַבָּא יָסַד בְּרַתָּא. וְאִיהוּ נָתִיב לֹא יְדָעוֹ עָיִט, דְּכָלִיל לַ"ב נְתִיבוֹת, דְּאִינּוּן לַ"ב אֱלֹהִים מִסְטְרָא דְּאִימָּא עִלָּאָה, דְּאִתְקְרֵי כָּבוֹד. וְכַד אִתְכְּלִילָן בְּבְרַתָּא, אִתְקְרֵי לַ"ב. וּבְגִין דָּא כְּבוֹד לְעֵילָא, לַ"ב לְתַתָּא.

841. And she is called 'the first commandment', "I am (Heb. *anochi*)" (Shemot 20:2), NAMELY, THE BEGINNING OF THE DIVINE REVELATION, from the aspect of Keter, that is in her, which is Ayin (Eng. 'nought'), NAMELY, THE LETTERS ALEPH YUD NUN from 'our Elohim' (Aleph-Lamed-Hei-Yud-Nun-Vav), FOR KETER IS CALLED 'NOUGHT' IN THE SENSE OF ABSENCE OF CONCEPTION. 'anochi' (Aleph Nun Caf Yud) contains the letter Caf that stands for Keter and Aleph Yud Nun (Heb. *ayin*). And Keter is so called from the aspect of supernal Ima, for whom the Exodus from Egypt is mentioned fifty times in the Torah, CORRESPONDING TO THE FIFTY GATES OF BINAH, AND KETER OF MALCHUT IS IN BINAH. And she is a daughter (Heb. *bat* - Bet Tav) from "In the beginning" (Heb. *Beresheet* Bet Resh Aleph Shin Yud Tav), which includes all of the ten sayings BY WHICH THE WORLD WAS CREATED. And from the aspect of

Chochmah, she is the daughter of Yud, AS IT IS SAID: "by wisdom founded the earth" (Mishlei 3:19), NAMELY, MALCHUT, WHICH IS CALLED 'EARTH', for Aba, WHICH IS CHOCHMAH, founded the daughter, WHICH IS MALCHUT. And she is "a path which no bird of prey knows" (Iyov 28:7), which is comprised of 32 paths, namely the 32 Names of Elohim from the aspect of supernal Ima that is called 'glory' (Heb. *kavod* = 32). And when they are included in the daughter, WHICH IS MALCHUT, MALCHUT is called heart (Heb. *lev* = 32), and this is why there is glory above and a heart below.

842. וִי' דִּבְרָן אִתְיְיהִיבוּ. חָמֵשׁ בְּלוּחָא חֲדָא, וַחֲמֵשׁ בְּלוּחָא תִּנְיָינָא. אִיהִי כָּלִיל לוֹן, ה' מִכֶּתֶר עַד גְּבוּרָה. וְה' מֵעַמוּדָא דְּאֶמְצָעִיתָא, עַד בְּרַתָּא. וְאִינוּן ה' ה'. וְכִי אִית לְמַלְּלָא בַּעֲשָׂרָה פִּיוֹת. אֶלָּא כָּלִיל לוֹן בְּבַת יְחִידָה י' וְאִתְעֲבִידוּ כֻּלְּהוּ חֲדָא. אוֹף הָכִי ו', אִתְקְרֵי קוֹל, וְלָא אִשְׁתְּמוֹדְעִין בֵּיהּ, עַד דְּאִשְׁתָּתַּף עִם דִּבּוּר. וּבְגִין דָּא, קוֹל דְּבָרִים אַתֶּם שׁוֹמְעִים.

842. And the Ten Commandments were given on two tablets, five on each, and MALCHUT includes them, for they are the five SFIROT from Keter to Gvurah, and the five SFIROT from the Central Pillar, WHICH IS TIFERET to the daughter, WHICH IS MALCHUT. And they are twice Hei. HE ASKS: IF THE TEN COMMANDMENTS ARE FROM THE TEN SFIROT, is it then possible to speak with ten mouths, WITH EACH SFIRAH SPEAKING WITH ITS OWN SPECIAL MOUTH? HE ANSWERS, He included all TEN COMMANDMENTS in the only daughter, WHICH IS MALCHUT, and all of them became one. THUS, THE TEN COMMANDMENTS BECAME INCORPORATED WITHIN MALCHUT. And so it is that Vav, WHICH IS TIFERET, that is called 'voice', cannot be perceived until it joins with speech, WHICH IS MALCHUT. And this is why IT IS WRITTEN: "you heard the voice of the words" (Devarim 4:12), WHERE VOICE ALLUDES TO ZEIR ANPIN AND WORDS TO MALCHUT.

843. אִיהִי פִּקּוּדָא תִּנְיָינָא מִסְטְרָא דִּגְבוּרָה, יִרְאָה בְּחוּשְׁבָּן. וּרְמִיזָא בְּמִלַּת בְּרֵאשִׁית, יָרֵא בֹּשֶׁת. וְאוֹקְמוּהָ, מַאן דְּלֵית לֵיהּ בֹּשֶׁת פָּנִים, וַדַּאי דְּלָא עָמְדוּ אֲבָהָתוֹי עַל טוּרָא דְּסִינַי.

843. She, MALCHUT, is the second commandment from the side of Gvurah, which is the same numerical sum as for the word *Yir'ah*, (Eng. 'fear') FOR

THEY BOTH HAVE THE NUMERICAL VALUE OF 216. And this is intimated in the word *Beresheet* (Eng. 'In the beginning'), WHOSE LETTERS, REARRANGED, SPELL: *Yere boshet* (Eng. 'fearful of shame'), and it has been taught: Whoever has no modesty, certainly his forefathers were not present on Mount Sinai.

844. אִיהִי פְּקוּדָא תְּלִיתָאָה, דְּאִתְקְרֵי אַהֲבַת חֶסֶד. הה״ד אַהֲבַת עוֹלָם אֲהַבְתִּיךְ עַל כֵּן מְשַׁכְתִּיךְ חָסֶד. אַהֲבָה כְּלִילָא מֵאֲבָהָן, דְּאִתְקְרֵי בְּהוֹן בַּכֹּל מִכֹּל כֹּל. וְרָזָא דְּמִלָּה, זָכַרְתִּי לָךְ חֶסֶד נְעוּרַיִךְ אַהֲבַת כְּלוּלוֹתָיִךְ.

844. She is the third commandment, which is called 'love of Chesed', as it is written: "I have loved you with an everlasting love: therefore I have remained true to you (with Chesed)" (Yirmeyah 31:2). Love, WHICH IS MALCHUT, is composed of the patriarchs, and in their contexts is called: '*bakol*' (Eng. 'in all'), '*mikol*' (Eng. 'of all'), '*kol*' (Eng. 'all'), WHICH IS MALCHUT THAT IS CALLED *KOL* (ENG. 'ALL'). ABOUT ABRAHAM IT IS SAID: "AND HASHEM HAD BLESSED ABRAHAM IN ALL THINGS" (BERESHEET 24:1); AND ABOUT ISAAC IT IS WRITTEN: "AND I HAVE EATEN OF ALL" (BERESHEET 27:33); AND ABOUT JACOB: "BECAUSE I HAVE ALL" (BERESHEET 33:11). And the secret of the matter is the verse: "I remember in your favor, the devotion (Chesed) of your youth, your love as a bride" (Yirmeyah 2:2), WHICH IS SAID ABOUT MALCHUT.

845. וְאִיהִי פְּקוּדָא רְבִיעָאָה, יִחוּד, מִסִּטְרָא דְּעַמּוּדָא דְּאֶמְצָעִיתָא, שְׁמַע יִשְׂרָאֵל. וְאִיהִי כ״ה כ״ה אַתְוָון, עִמֵּיהּ בְּשִׁית תֵּיבִין, דְּאִינּוּן שְׁמַע יִשְׂרָאֵל. וּבְגִינָהּ אָמַר אַבְרָהָם נֵלְכָה עַד כ״ה וְנִשְׁתַּחֲוֶה. כ״ה תֹּאמַר לְבֵית יַעֲקֹב.

845. And she is the fourth commandment, which is the unity from the aspect of the Central Pillar, NAMELY, THE UNIFICATION OF Sh'ma Yisrael. That is 25 (Caf Hei) plus 25 letters with Him, WITH ZEIR ANPIN, NAMELY, 25 LETTERS OF SH'MA YISRAEL, WHICH IS ZEIR ANPIN, PLUS 25 LETTERS OF 'BLESSED BE THE NAME OF THE GLORY OF HIS KINGDOM FOREVER AND EVER', WHICH IS MALCHUT, that are in the six words of Sh'ma Yisrael, WHICH ARE SIX SFIROT of ZEIR ANPIN. And for her sake,

Abraham said: "...will go yonder (Heb. *coh* Caf Hei) and prostrate ourselves" (Beresheet 22:5), AND ALSO: "Thus (Heb. *coh*) shall you say to the house of Jacob" (Shemot 19:3).

846. אִיהוּ א״ח, עַמּוּדָא דְּאֶמְצָעִיתָא, וְאִיהִי ד', שְׁלִימוּ דְּיִחוּדָא דִּילֵיהּ, לְאַשְׁלְמָא בֵּיהּ אֶחָד. א״ח, כָּלִיל ט' סְפִירָאן, דְּאִינּוּן א' אֵין סוֹף. ח' תְּמַנְיָא סְפִירָאן, מֵחָכְמָה עַד יְסוֹד. ד' מַלְכוּת, קוֹצָא דִּילָהּ, בָּהּ אִשְׁתְּלִימוּ לַעֲשָׂרָה, דְּאִינּוּן יוֹ״ד הֵ״א וָא״ו הֵ״א. ד' כְּלִילָא מֵד' אַתְוָון יְדֹוָ״ד.

846. And He, ZEIR ANPIN, is Aleph Chet OF ECHAD: (ENG. 'ONE' - ALEPH CHET DALET), which is the Central Pillar, while she, MALCHUT, is the Dalet OF *ECHAD*. She is the completion of His unity, perfecting in Him THE SECRET OF one. Aleph Chet (= nine) OF *ECHAD* include nine Sfirot, namely: Aleph is Infinity, NAMELY, KETER, and the Chet (= eight) Sfirot from Chochmah to Yesod. The Dalet OF *ECHAD* is Malchut, with the tip OF THE DALET ALLUDING TO YESOD. In her, IN MALCHUT, the Sfirot are completed to ten, which are THE TEN LETTERS Yud-Vav-Dalet, Hei-Aleph, Vav-Aleph-Vav, Hei-Aleph. The Dalet (= four) OF *ECHAD* is comprised of the four letters of Yud Hei Vav Hei.

847. פְּקוּדָא חֲמִישָׁאָה, וְהָגִיתָ בּוֹ יוֹמָם וָלַיְלָה. אִיהִי אוֹרַיְיתָא דִּבְכְתַב מִסִּטְרָא דְּחֶסֶד. וְאוֹרַיְיתָא דִּבְעַל פֶּה מִסִּטְרָא דִּגְבוּרָה. דִּבְהוֹן חָכְמָה וּבִינָה. כְּמָה דְּאוּקְמוּהָ מָארֵי מַתְנִיתִין, הָרוֹצֶה לְהַחְכִּים יַדְרִים. לְהַעֲשִׁיר יַצְפִּין. וְעַמּוּדָא דְּאֶמְצָעִיתָא כָּלִיל תַּרְוַויְיהוּ, וּבְגִין דָּא אִתְקְרֵי שָׁמַיִם, כָּלִיל אֵשׁ וּמַיִם, אֵשׁ דִּגְבוּרָה, וּמַיִם דְּחֶסֶד.

847. The fifth commandment is: "but you shall meditate therein day and night" (Yehoshua 1:8). She, MALCHUT, is the Written Torah from the side of Chesed and the Oral Torah from the side of Gvurah, in which Chochmah and Binah are, FOR AT THE TIME OF GREATNESS, CHESED ASCENDS AND BECOMES CHOCHMAH, WHILE GVURAH ASCENDS AND BECOMES BINAH. This is as the sages of the Mishnah taught: He who wants to be wise shall turn south and he who wants to be rich shall turn north, WHERE THE

MEANING OF RICH IS IN KNOWLEDGE AND UNDERSTANDING. And the Central Pillar, WHICH IS TIFERET, incorporates both of them, THE RIGHT AND THE LEFT, and for this reason is called 'heavens' (Heb. *shamayim)* for it includes fire (Heb. *esh*) and water (Heb. *mayim*). Fire is Gvurah and water is Chesed.

848. וּבְגִין דָּא כֶּתֶר, דְּאִיהִי כַּף, עֲשָׂרָה עֲשָׂרָה הַכַּף בְּשֶׁקֶל הַקֹּדֶשׁ. דְּאִינּוּן יה״ה, תְּלַת אַתְוָון, אִתְעֲבֵידוּ כַּף, עַל ו'. וְהַיְינוּ כְּנֶגֶד כֶּתֶר תּוֹרָה, ו' הַיְינוּ ס״ת, כַּף עֲטָרָה עַל רֵישֵׁיהּ. וְכֹלָּא יְדֹנָ״ד, כ״ו בְּחוּשְׁבַּן.

848. And for this reason, Keter, which is Caf, is the secret of the verse: "weighing ten shekels apiece (Heb. *kaf*), after the shekel of the sanctuary" (Bemidbar 7:86), NAMELY, TEN SFIROT FROM ABOVE DOWNWARDS AND TEN SFIROT FROM BELOW UPWARDS, which is Yud-Hei-Hei, three letters that become Caf, NAMELY, KETER, over Vav WHICH IS ZEIR ANPIN, and correspond to *Keter Torah*, (lit. 'the crown of the Torah'). For the Vav is the scroll of the Torah, and the Caf, WHICH IS YUD-HEI-HEI, is the diadem over its head. And all of it together, NAMELY, YUD-HEI-HEI WITH VAV, is Yud Hei Vav Hei whose numerical value is Caf Vav (= 26), WHERE THE CAF IS THE SECRET OF KETER OVER THE VAV.

849. פִּקּוּדָא שְׁתִיתָאָה, אִיהִי תְּפִלָּה שֶׁל יַד, בִּדְרוֹעָא שְׂמָאלָא. וּמִסִּטְרָא דִּגְבוּרָה ה' דְּיַד כֵּהָה, מִכֶּתֶר וְעַד גְּבוּרָה, ה' סְפִירָאן, וְאִינּוּן תְּפִילִין דְּרֵישָׁא דְּעַמּוּדָא דְּאֶמְצָעִיתָא. וְאִיהִי קֶשֶׁר תְּלַת רְצוּעוֹת, דְּאִינּוּן נֵצַח הוֹד יְסוֹד.

849. The sixth commandment OF MALCHUT is the hand Tefilin, WHICH IS TO BE PLACED on the left arm, WHICH IS GVURAH, and from the side of Gvurah it is the Hei of the dim hand, WHICH IS MALCHUT. AND THEREFORE THE HAND TEFILIN, WHICH IS MALCHUT, MUST BE PLACED ON THE LEFT ARM, WHICH IS GVURAH OF ZEIR ANPIN. And from Keter to Gvurah there are five Sfirot, and they are THE ASPECT OF the head Tefilin of the Central Pillar, WHICH IS ZEIR ANPIN. FOR FROM KETER TO GVURAH IS THE ASPECT OF THE HEAD TEFILIN, FOR THEY ARE ZEIR ANPIN, AND BELOW GVURAH THEY ARE THE HAND TEFILIN, FOR THEY

ARE MALCHUT. And she, MALCHUT, is the knot of the three straps, namely Netzach, Hod and Yesod; NAMELY, SHE IS THE KNOT OF THE TWO STRAPS OF THE HEAD, WHICH ARE NETZACH AND HOD, AND THE KNOT OF THE ONE STRAP OF THE HAND TEFILIN, WHICH IS YESOD. AND IT FOLLOWS THAT SHE IS THE KNOT OF THE THREE STRAPS.

850. וְאִיהִי פִּקוּדָא שְׁבִיעָאָה, מִצְוַת צִיצִית, כָּלִיל תְּכֵלֶת וְלָבָן, דִּינָא וְרַחֲמֵי. בְּנוּרָא, אֶשָּׁא חִוַּורָא לָא אָכִיל. תְּכֵלָא, אָכִיל וְשָׁצֵי, וַתֹּאכַל אֶת הָעוֹלָה. חִוָּור מִימִינָא, תְּכֵלֶת מִשְּׂמָאלָא, עַמּוּדָא דְּאֶמְצָעִיתָא, יְחוּד בֵּין תַּרְוַויְיהוּ, יָרוֹק. בְּגִין דָּא אוֹקְמוּהָ מָארֵי מַתְנִיתִין, מֵאֵימָתַי קוֹרִין אֶת שְׁמַע בְּשַׁחֲרִין מִשֶּׁיַּכִּיר בֵּין תְּכֵלֶת לְלָבָן. וּבְגִין דָּא תַּקִּינוּ פָּרָשַׁת צִיצִית, לְמִקְרֵי לָהּ בְּיִחוּדָא.

850. And she is the seventh commandment, which is the precept of Tzitzit (the fringes), comprised of blue and white, which are Judgment and Mercy. In the flame OF THE CANDLE, the white fire does not devour WHAT IS UNDER IT, FOR IT IS ATTACHED ONLY TO THE BLUE FIRE THAT IS UNDER IT, BUT the blue fire OF THE CANDLE IS ATTACHED TO THE WICK AND THE OIL, AND IT devours and destroys WHAT IS UNDER IT, FOR THE WHITE FIRE IS CHESED AND THE BLUE FIRE IS JUDGMENT. AND ABOUT THE BLUE FIRE, WHICH IS JUDGMENT, IT IS SAID: "and consumed the burnt offering" (I Melachim 18:38). For the white is from the right and the blue from the left, while the Central Pillar, which is the unity of the two of them, OF THE RIGHT SIDE AND THE LEFT SIDE, is green. For this reason the sages taught: From what time in the morning may the Sh'ma be recited? As soon as one can distinguish between blue and white, NAMELY, AS SOON as ONE CAN DISTINGUISH BETWEEN CHESED AND JUDGMENT, FOR ONE HAS TO UNITE THEM IN THE CENTRAL COLUMN, THIS BEING THE SECRET OF THE READING OF SH'MA YISRAEL. And this is why it was decreed that the section about the fringes be included in the unity OF THE READING OF SH'MA YISRAEL, BECAUSE ITS PRECEPT IS TO BE FULFILLED WITH WHITE AND BLUE, WHICH HAVE TO BE BROUGHT TOGETHER IN THE READING OF SH'MA YISRAEL.

851. וְאִיהִי פִּקוּדָא תְּמִינָאָה, מְזוּזָה. שְׁכִינְתָּא אִתְקְרִיאַת מְזוּזָה, מִסִּטְרָא דְּעַמּוּדָא דְּאֶמְצָעִיתָא, דְּאַתְוָון דִּידוֹ"ד. וּמִסִּטְרָא דְּצַדִּיק, רָזָא

דִּבְרִית, אִתְקְרֵי שַׁדַּי. שַׁדַּי חוֹתָמָא דְּמַלְכָּא, דְּאִיהוּ יְדוָד.

851. And she is the eighth commandment, which is mezuzah. The Shechinah is called 'mezuzah' from the aspect of the Central Pillar, NAMELY, ZEIR ANPIN, which is the letters of Yud Hei Vav Hei, and from the aspect of the Righteous, WHICH IS YESOD, which is the secret of the covenant that is called 'Shadai'. Shadai is the seal of the King, who is Yud Hei Vav Hei. THEREFORE THERE IS A YUD HEI VAV HEI INSIDE THE MEZUZAH, CORRESPONDING TO THE CENTRAL PILLAR, AND THE WORD SHADAI ON THE OUTSIDE OF THE MEZUZAH, CORRESPONDING TO YESOD.

852. פְּקוּדָא תְּשִׁיעָאָה, שְׁכִינְתָּא אִתְקְרִיאַת אוֹת בְּרִית, מִסְטְרָא דְּצַדִּיק יְסוֹד עוֹלָם. זֹאת אוֹת הַבְּרִית. בֵּינִי, עַמּוּדָא דְּאֶמְצָעִיתָא, וּבֵין בְּנֵי יִשְׂרָאֵל, נֶצַח הוֹד. אוֹת, דָּא צַדִּיק. הִיא, דָּא שְׁכִינְתָּא. כִּי שֵׁשֶׁת יָמִים עָשָׂה יְיָ' אֶת הַשָּׁמַיִם, מִכֶּתֶר עַד עַמּוּדָא דְּאֶמְצָעִיתָא. דְּלֵית שִׁית בְּכָל אֲתָר, אֶלָּא מִסְטְרָא דְּאָת ו'. וְלֵית שְׁבִיעִי, אֶלָּא מִסְטְרָא דְּאָת י', עֲטָרָה עַל רֵישֵׁיהּ חָכְמָה עִלָּאָה. אוֹת הוּא. חָכְמָה תַּתָּאָה, אוֹת הִיא.

852. The ninth commandment is the Shechinah, which is called 'the sign of the covenant' from the aspect of the Righteous, the Foundation of the World, WHICH IS YESOD, as it is written: "This (Heb. *zot*) is the token of the covenant" (Beresheet 9:17). *ZOT* REFERS TO THE SHECHINAH AND SHE IS "THE TOKEN OF THE COVENANT." AND IT IS WRITTEN: "IT IS A SIGN BETWEEN ME AND THE CHILDREN OF YISRAEL FOR EVER: FOR IN SIX DAYS HASHEM MADE THE HEAVEN AND THE EARTH, AND ON THE SEVENTH DAY HE RESTED, AND WAS REFRESHED" (SHEMOT 31:17). "between Me," the Central Pillar, WHICH IS ZEIR ANPIN, "and the children of Yisrael," Netzach and Hod, TERMED THE CHILDREN OF YISRAEL. "Sign" refers to the Righteous, NAMELY, YESOD. "is (fem.)" refers to the Shechinah. "for in six days Hashem made the heaven" NAMELY, from Keter to the Central Pillar, WHICH IS TIFERET, THIS BEING THE SIX SFIROT, KETER, CHOCHMAH, BINAH, CHESED, GVURAH AND TIFERET, for whenever six is mentioned it is only from the aspect of the letter Vav, WHICH IS TIFERET. HERE, TOO, THE SIX DAYS REFER TO TIFERET, TOGETHER WITH THE FIVE SFIROT THAT PRECEDE IT, AND WHICH IT INCLUDES. BUT FROM TIFERET AND DOWNWARDS IT IS NO LONGER THE ASPECT OF

ZEIR ANPIN, BUT RATHER THE ASPECT OF MALCHUT. And there is no seventh, other than from the aspect of the letter Yud, WHICH IS MALCHUT, WHICH IS a diadem on the head OF ZEIR ANPIN IN THE SECRET OF THE VERSE "A VIRTUOUS WOMAN IS A CROWN TO HER HUSBAND" (MISHLEI 12:4). AND SHE IS THEN IN THE ASPECT OF supernal Chochmah AND IS CALLED "It is a sign," in the masculine form. AND WHEN MALCHUT IS lower Chochmah SHE IS CALLED "It is a sign," in the feminine form. AND THIS IS WHY THE WRITTEN TEXT IS "It is A SIGN," WITH A VAV, NAMELY, IN THE MASCULINE FORM, ALTHOUGH IT IS POINTED WITH THE VOWEL 'I' SHOWING IT IS TO BE READ IN THE FEMININE FORM.

853. וְתַקִּינוּ לְמִגְזַר לִתְמַנְיָא, דְּאִינּוּן ח', מִן חָכְמָה עַד יְסוֹד. לְקַבְּלָא בְּהוֹן י' זְעֵירָא, לְסַלְקָא לָהּ עַד כֶּתֶר, לְמֶהֱוֵי עֲטָרָה עַל רֵאשֵׁיהוֹן. וְתַקִּינוּ לְשַׁוְוֵיא לַעֲרְלָה בְּמָנָא דְּעַפְרָא, לְקַיֵּים וְנָחָשׁ עָפָר לַחְמוֹ.

853. And circumcision was decreed for the eighth, namely the eight SFIROT from Chochmah to Yesod, to receive in them the small Yud, WHICH IS MALCHUT, and to elevate her to Keter, for her to be a diadem over the heads OF THE EIGHT SFIROT. And it was decreed that the foreskin be placed in a vessel with dust, in order to fulfill the verse "and dust shall be serpent's food" (Yeshayah 65:25).

854. פִּקּוּדָא עֲשִׂירָאָה, וְשָׁמְרוּ בְּנֵי יִשְׂרָאֵל אֶת הַשַּׁבָּת. שְׁכִינְתָּא אִתְקְרִיאַת שַׁבָּת, מִסִּטְרָא דִּתְלַת דַּרְגִּין עִלָּאִין דְּאִינּוּן שׁ', ג' כִּתְרִין: כֶּתֶר, חָכְמָה, וּבִינָה. וְאִיהִי בַּת, רְבִיעָאָה לוֹן. שִׁית יוֹמִין, מֵחֶסֶד עַד יְסוֹד, בְּהוֹן תַּעֲשֶׂה מְלָאכָה, בְּגִין דְּבִנְיָינָא מַתְחִיל מֵחֶסֶד, הה"ד עוֹלָם חֶסֶד יִבָּנֶה. אֲבָל מִבִּינָה וּלְעֵילָּא, אִיהִי מְנוּחָה וְעֹנֶג וּשְׁבִיתָה לְכָל עוֹבָדָא.

854. The tenth commandment OF MALCHUT is: "Wherefore the children of Yisrael shall keep the Shabbat" (Shemot 31:16). The Shechinah is called 'Shabbat', from the aspect of the three upper grades, namely Shin, WHICH ALLUDES to the three Sfirot: Keter, Chochmah and Binah. And MALCHUT is daughter and is fourth to these. "Six days" (Shemot 31:15) REFERS TO THE SIX SFIROT from Chesed to Yesod, NAMELY, CHESED, GVURAH,

TIFERET, NETZACH, HOD AND YESOD, on which work may be done, because the building OF THE WORLD commences with Chesed, as it is written: "The world is built by love (lit. 'Chesed')" (Tehilim 89:3). But from Binah and upwards, NAMELY, IN THE FIRST THREE SFIROT, there is rest and pleasure and cessation from all work.

855. פִּקוּדָא חַד סָר, אִיהִי אִתְקְרִיאַת צְלוֹתָא דְּשַׁחֲרִית מִנְחָה עַרְבִית, מִסְטְרָא דִּתְלַת אֲבָהָן, וְאִיהִי תְּפִלַּת כָּ״ל פֶּ״ה, לֵית כָּל, אֶלָּא צַדִּיק דִּכְתִּיב כִּי כֹל בַּשָּׁמַיִם וּבָאָרֶץ, וְתִרְגֵּם יוֹנָתָן בֶּן עוּזִיאֵל, דְּאָחִיד בִּשְׁמַיָּא וּבְאַרְעָא. פֶּ״ה כְּחוּשְׁבַּן מִילָה. וּמַה בְּרִית בֵּיה מִתְיַחֲדִין דְּכַר וְנוּקְבָּא דִּלְתַתָּא, אוֹף בַּיְסוֹד, מִתְיַיחֵד חָתָן וְכַלָּה דִּלְעֵילָא, הוּא חַי עָלְמִין כָּלִיל חַ״י בִּרְכָאן, הה״ד בְּרָכוֹת לְרֹאשׁ צַדִּיק.

855. The eleventh commandment THAT IS IN MALCHUT is called 'the Shacharit, Minchah and Arvit (morning, afternno and evening) prayers', from the aspect of the three patriarchs, NAMELY CHESED, GVURAH AND TIFERET. It is the prayer of every (Heb. *kol*) mouth (Heb. *peh*), NAMELY, MALCHUT CLEAVING TO YESOD, FOR PRAYER IS MALCHUT AND EVERY MOUTH IS YESOD. For the word *kol* (Eng. 'all' or 'every') only means the Righteous, WHICH IS YESOD, as it is written: "for all that is in heaven and on earth" (I Divrei Hayamin 29:11), which Yonatan Ben Uziel translated (into Aramaic) as "that takes hold of heaven and earth," NAMELY, YESOD THAT IS ATTACHED TO HEAVEN AND EARTH THAT ARE ZEIR ANPIN AND MALCHUT. *Peh* (= 85) has the same numerical value as *milah* (Eng. 'circumcision') and just as man and woman below unite by the covenant, so, too the bride and bridegroom above come together in Yesod, THEY BEING ZEIR ANPIN AND MALCHUT. YESOD is the life (Heb. *CHAI* = eighteen) of the worlds, because it includes the eighteen blessings OF THE AMIDAH PRAYER, as it is written: "Blessings are upon the head of the just" (Mishlei 10:6).

856. וּבג״ד, כָּל הַכּוֹרֵעַ כּוֹרֵעַ בְּבָרוּךְ וְכָל הַזּוֹקֵף זוֹקֵף בַּשֵּׁם. דָּא שְׁכִינְתָּא, בְּשֵׁם דִּידוֹ״ד, בֵּיה צָרִיךְ לְזַקְפָא שְׁכִינְתָּא. הַהִיא דְּאִתְּמַר בָּהּ, נָפְלָה לֹא תוֹסִיף קוּם בְּתוּלַת יִשְׂרָאֵל, ע״י דַּרְגָּא אַחֲרָא, וּבג״ד בַּיוֹם הַהוּא אָקִים אֶת סֻכַּת דָּוִד הַנּוֹפֶלֶת. הַהוּא דְּאִתְּמַר בֵּיה, יְדוֹ״ד זוֹקֵף

בְּפוּפִים.

856. And for this reason when one bows one should bow at 'Blessed,' WHICH IS THE SECRET OF YESOD, and when returning to the upright position, one should do so (at the mention of) the Name. This is the Shechinah in the Name of Yud Hei Vav Hei, with which the Shechinah has to be stood upright, the same about whom it is said: "The virgin of Yisrael is fallen; she shall no more rise" (Amos 5:2) BY HERSELF, but she shall by another grade, NAMELY, YUD HEI VAV HEI, NAMELY, ZEIR ANPIN, and for this reason: "On that day I will raise up the tabernacle of David that is fallen" (Amos 9:11); and the reference is to Him, about whom it is said: "Hashem raises those who are bowed down" (Tehilim 146:8), AND, THEREFORE, WHEN RETURNING TO THE UPRIGHT POSITION, ONE SHOULD DO SO AT THE NAME.

857. פְּקוּדָא תְּרֵיסָר, אִיהִי אִתְקְרִיאַת חַג הַמַּצוֹת, וְחַג הַשָּׁבוּעוֹת, וְחַג הַסֻּכּוֹת, מִסִּטְרָא דְּג' אֲבָהָן. ור"ה מִסִּטְרָא דִּילָהּ, דִּינָא דְּמַלְכוּתָא דִּינָא. וְאִית דְּיֵימָא, פֶּסַח דְּרוֹעָא יְמִינָא. שָׁבוּעוֹת, מַתַּן תּוֹרָה, דְּאִתְיְיהִיבַת בְּמַדְבְּרָא, דְּאִיהוּ מְמָנָא עֲלֵיהּ שׁוֹר, מִסִּטְרָא דִּגְבוּרָה. סֻכּוֹת וַיַּעֲקֹב נָסַע סֻכּוֹתָה. פְּקוּדָא תְּלֵיסַר, ק"ש.

857. The twelfth commandment THAT IS IN MALCHUT is called 'the Festival of matzot' and 'the Festival Shavuot' and 'the Festival of Sukkot', from the aspect of the three patriarchs, WHO ARE CHESED, GVURAH AND TIFERET; and Rosh Hashanah is the aspect of MALCHUT herself, WHICH IS THE SECRET OF, 'The law of the government (Malchut) is the law'. There is also the opinion that THE HOLIDAY OF Pesach is the right arm, NAMELY, CHESED; Shavuot, IS THE TIME WHEN the Torah was given in the wilderness, where the appointee OVER THE WILDERNESS is an ox from the side of Gvurah. SHAVUOT THUS IS GVURAH. Sukkot IS TIFERET AS IT IS SAID: "And Jacob journeyed to Sukkot" (Beresheet 33:17), JACOB BEING TIFERET. AND IN ALL OTHER PLACES, THE AUTHOR SAYS THAT PESACH IS CHESED, SUKKOT IS GVURAH, AND SHAVUOT IS TIFERET. The thirteenth commandment THAT IS IN MALCHUT is the reading of Sh'ma.

124. Explanations of the Holy Names and appelations

A Synopsis

Rabbi Shimon tells us the names that are applied to the Endless Light, and says that these names are a result of the creation of those creatures who can apply those names to Him. His name changes depending on the actions of those in the world; for the righteous He has the attribute of Mercy and for the wicked He has the attribute of Judgment – thus His name can be Yud Hei Vav Hei or Adonai. He is therefore called after the quality of each generation and each person, but He Himself has no specific quality or name. Rabbi Shimon says that the soul is not found in any one part of the body but is in the whole body; in just this way God is found everywhere in the world. Every single one of His names testifies that He is Master of all the worlds. We hear that every person in Yisrael inherits a world according to his level on high, as each and every righteous person has a world for himself. Lastly Rabbi Shimon concludes that the soul is like God only insofar as it rules over all parts of the body, but not in any other respect.

858. וְאִית לְמִנְדַּע, דְּאִיהוּ אִתְקְרֵי חָכָם בְּכָל מִינֵי חָכְמוֹת. וּמֵבִין, בְּכָל מִינֵי תְּבוּנוֹת. וְחָסִיד, בְּכָל מִינֵי חֲסָדִים. וְגִבּוֹר, בְּכָל מִינֵי גְּבוּרוֹת. וְיוֹעֵץ, בְּכָל מִינֵי עֵצוֹת. וְצַדִּיק, בְּכָל מִינֵי צְדָקוֹת. וּמֶלֶךְ, בְּכָל מִינֵי מַלְכוּת. עַד אֵין סוֹף. עַד אֵין חֵקֶר. וּבְכָל אִלֵּין דַּרְגִּין, בְּחַד אִקְרֵי רַחֲמָן. וּבְחַד אִקְרֵי דַּיָּין. וְהָכִי בְּכַמָּה דַּרְגִּין, עַד אֵין סוֹף. אִי הָכִי שִׁנּוּי אִית, בֵּין רַחֲמָן לַדַּיָּין. אֶלָּא קוֹדֶם דְּבָרָא עָלְמָא, אִתְקְרֵי הוּא בְּכָל אִלֵּין דַּרְגִּין, עַל שֵׁם בִּרְיָין דַּהֲווֹ עֲתִידִין לְהִבָּרְאוֹת, דְּאִי לָאו בִּרְיָין דְּעָלְמָא, אֲמַאי אִתְקְרֵי רַחוּם דַּיָּין, אֶלָּא עַל שֵׁם בִּרְיָין דַּעֲתִידִין.

858. And it should be known that THE ENDLESS LIGHT is called 'Wise One in all sorts of wisdom', and 'Understanding One in all sorts of understanding', and 'Pious One in all sorts of piety', and 'Mighty One in all sorts of might', and 'Counselor in all sorts of counsel', and 'Righteous in all sorts of righteousness', and 'King in all sorts of kingship', to infinity and immeasurably. And in all these grades, in one He is called 'Merciful One' and in another He is called 'Judge', and so on in a number of grades until infinity. HE ASKS, if so, it implies that there is a difference between Merciful One

and Judge. AND HE ANSWERS, yet before He created the world, He was called by all these grades after the names of the creatures of the world, that were destined to be created. And if not AFTER the creatures of the world, why should He have been called 'Merciful One', 'Judge', FOR THERE WOULD HAVE BEEN NONE FOR HIM TO SHOW MERCY TO. Thus HE WAS INDEED SO CALLED only after the creatures that were in the future to be created, BUT THERE IS NOT, HEAVEN FORBID, ANY CHANGE IN HIM HIMSELF.

859. וּבְג״ד, כָּל שְׁמָהָן, אִינוּן כִּנּוּיִין דִּילֵיהּ. עַל שֵׁם עוֹבָדִין דִּילֵיהּ. כְּגַוְונָא דָא, בָּרָא נִשְׁמְתָא, בְּדִיּוּקְנָא דִּילֵיהּ, דְּאִתְקְרִיאַת עַל שֵׁם פְּעוּלוֹת דִּילָהּ, בְּכָל אֵבֶר וְאֵבֶר דְּגוּפָא, דְּאִתְקְרֵי עָלְמָא זְעֵירָא. כְּגַוְונָא דְּמָארֵי עָלְמָא, אִתְנְהִיג בְּכָל בִּרְיָין. וּבְכָל דָּרָא, כְּפוּם עוֹבָדוֹי. כָּךְ נִשְׁמְתָא, כְּפוּם עוֹבָדוֹי דְּכָל אֵבֶר וְאֵבֶר. הַהוּא אֵבֶר דְּעָבֵיד בֵּיהּ פִּקּוּדָא, אִתְקְרֵי נִשְׁמְתָא, לְגַבֵּי חֶמְלָה וְחִסְדָּא חִנָּא וְרַחֲמֵי. וּבְהַהוּא אֵבֶר דְּעָבֵיד בֵּיהּ עֲבֵירָה, אִתְקְרֵי נִשְׁמְתָא לְגַבֵּי, דִּינָא וְחֵימָה וְכָעַס. אֲבָל לְבַר מִן גּוּפָא, לְמַאן תְּהֵא חֶמְלָה, אוֹ אַכְזָרִיּוּת.

859. And for this reason, all the Names are appellatives of Him, after His deeds. In such a way He created the soul in His likeness, which is so named following its actions in each of the parts of the body, which is itself called 'a small world'. Just as the Master of the Universe behaves with each creature in each generation according to its deeds, so also is the soul according to the deeds of each part. That same part of the body with which he observes a precept is called 'soul' because of compassion, loving-kindness, grace and mercy THAT ARE ACTIVATED IN HIS BODY. And that part of his body with which he commits a transgression is called 'soul' for judgment and wrath and anger THAT ARE ACTIVE IN HIS BODY. But outside the body, for whom can there be compassion or cruelty BECAUSE OF THE DEEDS OF THE BODY?

860. אוֹף הָכִי מָארֵי עָלְמָא, קֹדֶם דְּבָרָא עָלְמָא, וּבָרָא בִּרְיָין דִּילֵיהּ, לְמַאן אִתְקְרֵי רַחוּם וְחַנּוּן אוֹ דַּיָּין. אֶלָּא כָּל שְׁמָהָן דִּילֵיהּ, אִינוּן כִּנּוּיִין, וְלָא אִתְקְרֵי בְּהוֹן, אֶלָּא עַל שֵׁם בִּרְיָין דְּעָלְמָא, וּבְג״ד, כַּד מָארֵי דָרָא אִינוּן טָבִין, אִיהוּ אִתְקְרֵי לְגַבַּיְיהוּ, יְהֹו״ה בְּמִדַּת רַחֲמִים.

וְכַד מָארֵי דָרָא אִינּוּן חַיָּיבִין, אִתְקְרֵי אֲדֹנָ״י בְּמִדַּת הַדִּין. לְכָל דָּרָא,
וּלְכָל בַּ״נ, כְּפוּם מִדָּה דִּילֵיהּ. אֲבָל לָאו דְּאִית לֵיהּ מִדָה וְלָא שֵׁם יְדִיעַ.

860. So, too, for whom could the Master of the Universe have been called
'Merciful One', 'Gracious One' or 'Judge' prior to His creating the world
and His creating His creatures? Thus all His names are but appellations, and
He is so called only after the creatures of the world. Thus, when the
members of the generation are good, namely, He is for them called Yud Hei
Vav Hei in the attribute of Mercy. But when the members of the generation
are wicked, He is for them called 'Adonai' in the attribute of Judgment. For
He is CALLED after the quality of each generation and of each person, but He
Himself has no SPECIFIC quality and no specific name.

861. כְּגַוְונָא דִּסְפִירָאן, דְּכָל סְפִירָה אִית לָהּ שֵׁם יְדִיעַ, וּמִדָּה, וּגְבוּל,
וּתְחוּם. וּבְאִלֵּין שְׁמָהָן מָארֵי עָלְמָא אִיהוּ אִתְפְּשַׁט, וְאַמְלִיךְ בְּהוֹן,
וְאִתְקְרֵי בְּהוֹן, וְאִתְכַּסֵּי בְּהוֹן, וְדָר בְּהוֹן, כְּנִשְׁמָתָא לְגַבֵּי אֵבָרִים דְּגוּפָא.
וּמַה רִבּוֹן עָלְמִין, לֵית לֵיהּ שֵׁם יְדִיעַ וְלָא אֲתַר יְדִיעַ, אֶלָּא בְּכָל סִטְרָא
שׁוּלְטָנוּתֵיהּ. אוּף הָכִי לֵית לָהּ לְנִשְׁמָתָא שֵׁם יְדִיעַ, וְלָא אֲתַר יְדִיעַ,
בְּכָל גּוּפָא אֶלָּא בְּכָל סְטַר שׁוּלְטָנוּתֵיהּ, וְלֵית אֵבָר פָּנוּי מִנָּהּ.

861. Consider the Sfirot, where each Sfirah has a specific name, quality,
border, and field. The Master of the Universe spreads throughout these
names and rules by them and is called after them and is clothed in them and
lives amongst them as a soul within the parts of the body. And just as the
Master of the Worlds has no specific name and no specific place, but His rule
is in all directions IN THE WORLD, so also the soul has neither name nor
place anywhere in the body, but its rule is in every direction, and there is no
part of the body that is vacated of it.

862. וּבְג״ד, לֵית לְרַשְׁמָא לָהּ בְּחַד אֲתַר, דְּאִי לָאו הָא חָסֵר
שׁוּלְטָנוּתָא בִּשְׁאַר אֵבָרִים. וְלָא לְאִתְקְרֵי לָהּ בִּשְׁמָא חַד, אוֹ בִּתְרֵין, אוֹ
בַּג׳. לְמֵימַר דְּאִיהִי חָכְמָה מִבִּינָה, וְאִית לָהּ דַּעַת, וְלָא יַתִּיר. דְּאִי
עָבֵיד הָכִי, הָא חָסֵר לָהּ מִשְׁאַר דַּרְגִּין.

862. And for this reason, no one place IN THE BODY should be noted as that OF THE SOUL, for, otherwise, IF ONE PLACE IS SO NOTED it would follow that its rule is lacking in the remaining parts of the body. Nor is it to be called by one, two, or even three names, saying that it is Chochmah and from Binah, that it has Da'at, and no more, for if one does this, IT WOULD FOLLOW THAT it lacks the other grades.

863. כ״ש לְמָארֵי עָלְמָא, דְּלֵית לְרַשְׁמָא לֵיהּ בַּאֲתָר יְדִיעַ, אוֹ לְאִתְקְרֵי לֵיהּ בִּשְׁמָהָן, אוֹ לְשַׁנָּאָה לֵיהּ בְּהוֹן, אוֹ לְשַׁלְּשָׁא לֵיהּ כְּגוֹן דַּרְגָּא דִּמְרַכַּבְתָּא, דְּאִתְּמַר בָּהּ קְדוּשָׁה לְךָ יְשַׁלֵּשׁוּ, דְּכָל דַּרְגִּין דְּכָל מַרְכְּבוֹת דִּילֵיהּ, אִינוּן מְשׁוּלָשִׁים, כְּגוֹן הָאָבוֹת הֵן הֵן הַמֶּרְכָּבָה, דְּאִינוּן דְּמוּת אַרְיֵה שׁוֹר נֶשֶׁר, דְּאִינוּן מֶרְכָּבָה לְאָדָם. דְּאִתְּמַר עֲלֵיהּ, וּדְמוּת פְּנֵיהֶם פְּנֵי אָדָם. וּמִסִּטְרָא דְּנוּקְבָא, אִינוּן שַׁלְטִין עַל אָדָם, וְנוּקְבָא אִיהִי מֶרְכָּבָה לְגַבַּיְיהוּ. וּבְג״ד אִתְּמַר לְךָ יְשַׁלֵּשׁוּ.

863. And this is even truer with respect to the Master of the Universe, to whom no place should be ascribed nor specific name attributed, nor should He be doubled or tripled IN THEM, namely, the grade of the Chariot, in which it is said, 'They thrice ascribe holiness to You', since all the grades of all His Chariots are tripled, as in "the patriarchs, they are the Chariot," namely the likeness of lion, ox and eagle. For they are a Chariot for man, and it is said of them: "As for the likeness of their faces, they had the face of a man" (Yechezkel 1:10). And from the aspect of the Female, they, LION, OX, EAGLE, rule over man, WHICH IS THE NAME OF THE FEMALE, and the Female is a Chariot for LION, OX, EAGLE. And this is why it is said about her "They thrice ascribe holiness to You."

864. וְאוֹף הָכִי אַתְוָון, דְּאִינוּן אַנְפִּין דְּחֵיוָן, מְשׁוּלָשִׁין, כְּגַוְּונָא דָּא: יד״ו. הו״י. וה״י. ה׳ רְבִיעָאָה, קְדוּשָׁה לְךָ יְשַׁלֵּשׁוּ. אִיהִי שְׁלָמִים דְּכֻלְּהוּ, לְאַשְׁלָמָא בְּכֻלְּהוּ שֵׁם יְדֹו״ד. אֲבָל לְמָארֵיהּ דְּכֹלָּא, לֵית לְשַׁלְּשָׁא בֵּיהּ בִּשְׁמָהָן, וְלָא בְּאַתְוָון, אֶלָּא אִיהוּ אִתְקְרֵי בְּכָל שְׁמָהָן, וְלֵית לֵיהּ שֵׁם יְדִיעַ. וְכָל שֵׁם וְשֵׁם אַסְהִיד עֲלֵיהּ, דְּאִיהוּ אָדוֹן כָּל עָלְמִין. אַסְהִיד עֲלֵיהּ אֲדֹנָי.

864. Similarly, the letters YUD-HEI-VAV, that ALLUDE TO the faces of the living creatures, LION, OX AND EAGLE, are tripled, thus: Yud-Hei-Vav, Hei-Vav-Yud, and Vav-Hei-Yud. Hei is a fourth FOR THEM AND IS THE SECRET OF "They thrice ascribe holiness to You," AS ABOVE. It is the peace offerings (Heb. *shelamim*) of all of them, for in all of them it completes (Heb. *mashlemet*) in them all the Name of Yud Hei Vav Hei. But neither names nor letters must be tripled for the Master of All, for He is called by all the names and has no one specific name, and every single name testifies about Him that He is Master of all the worlds, AND THE NAME Adonai testifies about Him.

865. דְּאִית בַּ"נ, דְּיָרִית ג' מֵאָה וְעֶשֶׂר עָלְמִין, הה"ד, לְהַנְחִיל אוֹהֲבַי יֵשׁ. כְּפוּם דַּרְגָּא דִּילֵיהּ, דְּאִתְקְרֵי יֵשׁ מֵאַיִן. וְדָא חָכְמָה עִלָּאָה. וְאִית בַּ"נ דְּלָא יָרִית אֶלָּא עָלְמָא חַד, כְּפוּם דַּרְגָּא דִּילֵיהּ, כְּמָה דְּאוֹקְמוּהָ, כָּל צַדִּיק וְצַדִּיק יֵשׁ לוֹ עוֹלָם בִּפְנֵי עַצְמוֹ. וְהָכִי יָרִית עָלְמִין כָּל בַּ"נ מִיִּשְׂרָאֵל, כְּפוּם דַּרְגָּא דִּילֵיהּ לְעֵילָא. אֲבָל לְמָארֵי עָלְמָא, לֵית לִרְשָׁמָא לֵיהּ עָלְמִין בְּחוּשְׁבָּן, אֶלָּא כָּל אָדוֹן כָּל עָלְמִין, וַאֲדנַ"י קָא סָהִיד עֲלֵיהּ.

865. And there is a person who inherits three hundred and ten worlds, as it is written: "That I may cause those that love Me to inherit substance (Heb. *yesh* = 310)" (Mishlei 8:21). THIS IS according to the level OF CHOCHMAH that is called 'something out of nothing', FOR KETER IS CALLED 'NAUGHT' AND CHOCHMAH, 'SUBSTANCE THAT IS DRAWN OUT OF NAUGHT', and this is upper Chochmah. And there is also the person who only inherits one world, according to his level as has been taught: Each and every righteous man has a world for himself. Likewise every person in Yisrael inherits a world according to his level on high, but there is no recording of a world for the Master of the Universe, for He is the Master (Heb. *adon*) of all the worlds, as the name Adonai testifies about Him.

866. אוֹף הָכִי יְהוֹ"ה, מִנֵּיהּ תַּלְיָיא כָּל הֲוָיִין, וְאִיהוּ וְכָל הֲוָיִין דִּילֵיהּ, סָהֲדִין עַל מָארֵי עָלְמָא, דְּאִיהוּ הֲוָה קֹדֶם כָּל הֲוָיִין. וְאִיהוּ בְּתוֹךְ כָּל הֲוָיָה. וְאִיהוּ לְאַחַר כָּל הֲוָיָה. וְדָא רָזָא, דְּסָהֲדִין הֲוָיִין עֲלֵיהּ, הָיָה, הֹוֶה, וְיִהְיֶה.

866. Likewise with the Name Yud Hei Vav Hei, on which all existences depend, and He and all His existences testify about the Master of the Universe that He pre-existed all existences, that He is within every existence, and that He will be after all existences. And this is the secret that the beings testify about Him, that He was, is, and will be.

867. דִּינָא, בְּהִפּוּךְ אַתְוָון אֲדֹנָ"י. וּבְגִ"ד אָמְרוּ רַזַ"ל, דִּינָא דְּמַלְכוּתָא דִּינָא. שֵׁם אֵ"ל סָהִיד עַל מָאֵרי דְּכֹלָּא, דְּלֵית יְכוֹלֶת לְכָל שֵׁם, וַהֲוָיָה וְדַרְגָּא. כָּל שֶׁכֵּן לִשְׁאַר בִּרְיָין, פְּחוּת מִנֵּיה. הֲדָא הוּא דִּכְתִּיב, כְּלָא חֲשִׁיבִין וּכְמִצְבְּיֵהּ עָבֵיד בְּחֵיל שְׁמַיָא וְגוֹ'. אֱלֹהִי"ם, סָעִיד עַל אֱלָהוּת דִּילֵיהּ, דְּאִיהוּ אֱלֹהִי"ם וֵאלֹהֵי הָאֱלֹהִים, וְאִיהוּ אֱלוֹהַּ עַל כֹּלָּא, וְלֵית אֱלוֹהַּ עָלֵיהּ. צְבָאוֹ"ת, סָהִיד עָלֵיהּ כִּדְכְתִיב, וּכְמִצְבְּיֵיהּ עָבֵיד בְּחֵיל שְׁמַיָא. שַׁדַּ"י, סָהִיד עָלֵיהּ, דְּכַד אִיהוּ אָמַר לְעוֹלָם דִּי עָמַד בִּתְחוּמֵיהּ, וְלָא אִתְפְּשַׁט יַתִּיר. וְאוּף לְמַיָּא וְרוּחָא וְאֶשָׁא.

867. *Dina* (Eng. 'judgment') is composed of the letters of Adonai, re-arranged. And for this reason, our teachers of blessed memory said: The law of the government is the law (Heb. *dina*). The name El testifies about the Master of All, that no name, Yud Hei Vav Hei, grade, and certainly none of the other creatures has any ability apart from Him. And this is as is written: "and all the inhabitants of the earth are reputed as nothing: and He does according to His will in the host of heaven..." (Daniel 4:32). Elohim testifies to His Divinity, that He is the Elohim, and the Elohim of Elohim, and He is Eloha over all, and there is no Eloha above Him. *Tzva'ot* (Eng. 'Hosts') testifies about Him, as it is written: "He does according to His will in the host of heaven." Shadai (Shin-Dalet-Yud) testifies about Him that (Heb. *she*), when He said to the world "Enough" (Heb. *dai*), THE WORLD stopped within its limits and did not expand any more. Likewise, to the water, wind, and fire HE SAID: "ENOUGH."

868. וְאוּף הָכִי, כָּל הֲוָיָה, וְשֵׁם, סָהֲדִין עָלֵיהּ. דְּכַד הֲוָה אִיהוּ יָחִיד קוֹדֶם דְּבָרָא עָלְמָא, אֲמַאי הֲוָה אִיהוּ צָרִיךְ לְאִתְקְרֵי בִּשְׁמָהָן אִלֵּין, אוֹ בִּשְׁאַר כִּנּוּיִין, כְּגוֹן רַחוּם וְחַנּוּן אֶרֶךְ אַפַּיִם וְגוֹ', דַּיָּין אַמִּיץ חָזָק. וְסַגִּיאִין בְּכָל אִינוּן שְׁמָהָן וְכִנּוּיִין, אִתְקְרֵי עַל שֵׁם כָּל עָלְמִין וּבִרְיָין

דִּלְהוֹן, לְאַחֲזָאָה שׁוּלְטָנוּתֵיהּ עֲלַיְיהוּ.

868. Likewise, every Yud Hei Vav Hei and every name testify about Him, for when He was alone, before He created the world, why did He need to be called by these names or by the other appellatives, such as Merciful One, Gracious one, Long-suffering, Judge, Mighty, Strong? There are many such names that are so coined after all the worlds and the creatures in them in order to show that His rule is over them.

869. אוּף הָכִי נִשְׁמְתָא, עַל שׁוּלְטָנוּתָא דְּכָל אֵבָרִים דְּגוּפָא, אַמְתִּיל לָהּ לְגַבֵּיהּ. לָאו דְּאִיהִי אַדְמְיָא לֵיהּ אִיהִי בְּעַצְמָהּ, דְּהוּא בָּרָא לָהּ, וְלֵית לֵיהּ אֱלוֹהַּ עֲלֵיהּ דְּבָרָא לֵיהּ. וְעוֹד, נִשְׁמְתָא אִית לָהּ כַּמָה שְׁנוּיִים וּמִקְרִים וְסִבּוֹת, דְּאִתְקְרִיאוּ לָהּ. מַה דְּלָאו הָכִי לְמָארֵי כֹּלָּא. וּבְגִ"ד הִיא אַדְמְיָא בְּשָׁלְטָנוּתָא דִּילָהּ עַל כָּל אֵבְרֵי גוּפָא, אֲבָל לָא בְּמִלָּה אַחֲרָא.

869. And it is likewise with the soul, WHICH, IN THE ASPECT OF its rule over all the parts of the body, is likened to Him. JUST AS HE IS RULER OVER ALL THE WORLDS, SO IS THE SOUL RULER OVER ALL PARTS OF THE BODY, but it is not meant to say that the soul is like Him in its essence, for it was He who created it, while HE has no Elohim above Him who created Him. Furthermore there are a number of differences and incidents and causes that happen to the soul, which is not the case for the Master of All. For this reason, the soul is like Him only respecting its rule over all parts of the body, but not in any other respect.

125. The reading of Sh'ma Yisrael and the Tefilin

A Synopsis
Rabbi Shimon rearranges the letters in Sh'ma, Shem and Echad to teach us about God as witness and about the reason for the four compartments of the Tefilin.

870. וְעוֹד, שְׁמַע יִשְׂרָאֵל, שֵׁם ע' רַבָּתִי, ד' מִן אֶחָ"ד רַבָּתִי, הַיְינוּ ע"ד, בֵּין שֵׁ"ם מִן שְׁמַע, א"ח מִן אֶחָ"ד. עֵד יְיָ' בָּכֶם. וְעַל כָּל אֶחָד וְאֶחָד דִּמְיַחֵד אוֹתוֹ בָּעוֹלָם. וְעַל כֵּן אָמַר דָוִד, אָנֹכִי אֶשְׂמַח בַּיְיָ', שֵׂ"מ מִן שְׁמַע, א"ח מִן אֶחָ"ד, הֲרֵי אֶשְׂמַח.

870. Furthermore, *Sh'ma* (Eng. 'Hear' Shin Mem Ayin) Yisrael: CONSISTS OF THE LETTERS OF *shem* (Eng. 'name' - Shin Mem) and great Ayin. Similarly, Dalet of *echad*: (Eng. 'one' - Aleph Chet Dalet) is written large, AND THESE TWO LARGE LETTERS spell '*ed*' (Eng. 'witness' - Ayin Dalet). Thus, between the Shin Mem of *Sh'ma*, WHICH IS MALCHUT THAT IS CALLED 'NAME', and the Aleph Chet of *echad*, WHICH IS ZEIR ANPIN, ARE THE LARGE LETTERS AYIN DALET, WHICH ARE THE SECRET OF THE VERSE: "Hashem is witness (Heb. *ed*) against you" (I Shmuel 12:5). AND SO HE IS INDEED A WITNESS over each and every one who proclaims His unity in the world. And therefore David said: "I will rejoice (Heb. *esmach* - Aleph Sin Mem Chet) in Hashem" (Tehilim 104:34) and the Shin Mem of *Sh'ma*, WHICH IS MALCHUT, together with the Aleph Chet of *Echad*, WHICH IS ZEIR ANPIN, spell '*esmach*'. AND THIS IS THE SECRET OF THE UNITY OF ZEIR ANPIN AND MALCHUT, FROM THE ASPECT OF GREATNESS, FOR MALCHUT, FROM THE ASPECT OF GREATNESS, IS CALLED 'NAME' (HEB. *SHEM* - SHIN MEM).

871. וְעוֹד. ד' רַבָּתִי, ד' בָּתֵּי תְּפִילִין, דִּמְנַח לְהוֹן א"ח, וְאִתְעַטָּר בְּהוּ, וְאִינּוּן פְּאֵר עַל רֵישֵׁיהּ. וְאִינּוּן יהה"ו, י' עֲטָרָא עַל ה', דְּאִיהִי בְּרַתָּא, וְהַיְינוּ יָדֹו"ד בְּחָכְמָה יָסַד אָרֶץ, אַבָּא יָסַד בְּרַתָּא. ה', אִמָּא עִלָּאָה, עֲטָרָה עַל ו', דְּאִיהוּ בְּרָא, וְהַיְינוּ כּוֹנֵן שָׁמַיִם בִּתְבוּנָה. בְּאִמָּא כּוֹנֵן בְּרָא. וְהַאי אִיהוּ דְּעוֹלָם הַבָּא אֵין בּוֹ לֹא אֲכִילָה וְלֹא שְׁתִיָּה, אֶלָּא צַדִּיקִים יוֹשְׁבִים וְעַטְרוֹתֵיהֶם בְּרָאשֵׁיהֶם.

871. Furthermore, the large letter Dalet (whose numerical value is four) OF *ECHAD* ALLUDES TO THE four compartments of the Tefilin that Aleph Chet OF *ECHAD*, WHICH IS ZEIR ANPIN, puts on, and with which he is adorned, and they are an ornament on his head. And they are THE SECRET OF THE COMBINATION Yud-Hei-Hei-Vav. The Yud, WHICH IS CHOCHMAH, is a diadem on Hei, which is the daughter, NAMELY, MALCHUT. Thus, "Hashem by wisdom founded the earth" (Mishlei 3:19), for Aba, WHICH IS THE SECRET OF CHOCHMAH, founded the daughter, WHICH IS MALCHUT, THAT IS CALLED 'EARTH'. THE SECOND Hei OF THE COMBINATION YUD-HEI-HEI-VAV is Supernal Ima, which is a diadem on the Vav, which is the son, NAMELY, ZEIR ANPIN, as we read: "by understanding (Heb. *Tevunah*) He established the heaven" (Ibid.), FOR ZEIR ANPIN, WHO IS CALLED 'HEAVENS', RECEIVES THE MOCHIN FROM TEVUNAH, NAMELY, SUPERNAL IMA, for Ima established the son. Thus, in the World to Come, WHICH IS BINAH, there is no eating and no drinking, but the righteous sit with their diadems on their heads. THE RIGHTEOUS HERE ARE ZEIR ANPIN, WHO HAS A DIADEM ON HIS HEAD, FROM BINAH THAT IS CALLED 'THE WORLD TO COME'.

126. Two arrangements of the four passages of the Tefilin

A Synopsis

The Tefilin are said to be the Mochin, and Rabbi Shimon describes all the parts of the phylacteries and their meaning in terms of the Sfirot and the Holy Names of God and the letters of the alphabet. Lastly Rabbi Shimon tells us what Rabbi Akiva had to say about the flowing light that is never interrupted and that comes from Infinity.

872. וּבְרַתָּא אִיהִי תְּפִלָּה שֶׁל יַד, כֶּהָ״ה. י׳ קֶשֶׁר דִּילֵיהּ. ה׳ עִלָּאָה אִימָּא, תְּפִלִּין דְּרֵישָׁא עַל רֹאשׁ תִּפְאֶרֶת. תְּפִלִּין דִּילֵיהּ, כְּסֵדֶר יְדֹוָ״ד, דְּאִיהוּ קַדֶּשׁ לִי. וְהָיָה כִּי יְבִאֲךָ. שְׁמַע. וְהָיָה אִם שָׁמוֹעַ. אֲבָל בְּעָלְמָא דְּאָתֵי, הֲוָיוֹת בְּאֶמְצַע, דְּאִינּוּן ה׳ ה׳. וּבְג״ד אָמַר הַנָּבִיא, בְּזֹאת יִ״תְהַלֵּל הַ״מִתְהַלֵּל הַ״שֵׂכֵּל וְ״יָדֹעַ אוֹתִי כִּי אֲנִי יְדֹוָ״ד. וּבְג״ד אוֹקְמוּהָ מָארֵי מַתְנִיתִין, דְּאִית בְּרֵישָׁא אֲתָר, לְאָנָחָא תְּרֵי זוּגֵי דִּתְפִלֵּי. וְדָא זָכֵי לִתְרֵין פִּקוּדִין, דְּאוֹקְמוּהָ עֲלַיְיהוּ, לֹא כָּל אָדָם זוֹכֶה לִשְׁתֵּי שׁוּלְחָנוֹת.

872. And the daughter, WHICH IS MALCHUT, is the Tefilin of the dim hand. Yud is its knot. Upper Hei, namely, Ima, is the head Tefilin on the head of Tiferet. Its Tefilin, NAMELY, ITS MOCHIN, are according to the order Yud Hei Vav Hei, which is "Sanctify to Me" (Shemot 13:1-10), YUD. "And it shall be when Hashem shall bring you into the land" (Shemot 13:11-16) IS HEI; "Hear, O Yisrael" (Devarim 6:4-9) IS VAV; and "And it shall come to pass, if you will hearken diligently" (Devarim 11:13-21) IS THE FINAL HEI. THIS ORDER IS FOR THE TEFILIN OF THE HEAD OF ZEIR ANPIN. But in the World to Come, WHICH IS BINAH, THE TEFILIN, NAMELY, THE MOCHIN THAT SHE RECEIVES, the order is that Yud Hei Vav Hei's, which are Hei Hei, are in the center. THAT IS, YUD FIRST, WHICH IS "SANCTIFY TO ME"; AND THE VAV OF "HEAR" IN THE END; "AND IT SHALL BE WHEN HASHEM SHALL BRING YOU INTO THE LAND"; "AND IT SHALL COME TO PASS, IF YOU WILL HEARKEN DILIGENTLY," THAT IS HEI-HEI, ARE IN THE MIDDLE. And on this the prophet said: "but let him that glories glory in this, that he understands and knows Me, that I am Hashem" (Yirmeyah 9:23), WHERE THE INITIAL LETTERS SPELL YUD-HEI-HEI-VAV. And this is why the sages of the Mishnah taught: There is room on the head to lay two pairs of Tefilin. And such a one merits to observe two

precepts, about which it has been taught: Not everyone merits to enjoy two
tables.

873. י' חָכְמָה. ה' בִּינָה. ו' עַמּוּדָא דְּאֶמְצָעִיתָא. ה' מַלְכוּת קַדִּישָׁא.
רֵישָׁא דְּאִתְעַטָּר בְּאַרְבַּע אַתְוָון, דָּא כֶּתֶר רִיהֲטָא דְּרֵישָׁא דְּאַסְחַר לוֹן,
וְכַסֵּי לוֹן. אַהֲבָה חֶסֶד ק"ש, דְּשַׁקִּילָא לְאוֹרַיְיתָא, דְּאִתְיְיהִיבַת מִימִינָא.
תְּפִלִּין עֹז, מִשְּׂמָאלָא דִּגְבוּרָה. עַמּוּדָא דְּאֶמְצָעִיתָא, כָּלִיל כֹּלָּא, כַּנְפֵי
דְּמִצְוָה, נֶצַח וְהוֹד, תְּכֵלֶת וְלָבָן. מְזוּזָה רָשִׁים שַׁדַּי, צַדִּיק. וּשְׁכִינְתָּא
תַּרְעָא דִּמְזוּזָה, זֶה הַשַּׁעַר לַיְדֹו"ד.

873. IN THE FOUR SECTIONS OF THE HEAD TEFILIN, the Yud, WHICH IS
THE SECTION "SANCTIFY TO ME," is Chochmah. The Hei, WHICH IS THE
SECTION "AND IT SHALL BE WHEN HASHEM SHALL BRING YOU INTO THE
LAND," is Binah. Vav, WHICH IS THE SECTION "HEAR, O YISRAEL," is the
Central Pillar. And the Hei, WHICH IS THE SECTION "AND IT WILL COME
TO PASS, IF YOU WILL HEARKEN DILIGENTLY," is holy Malchut. The head
that is crowned with these four letters is Keter, which is the circumference of
the head that comprises THE TEFILIN THAT ARE THE MOCHIN and covers
them. The reading of Sh'ma is love, Chesed, and is equivalent to the Torah
that was given on the right. The Tefilin, CALLED 'strength', are on the left
side, which is Gvurah. The Central Pillar, WHICH IS TIFERET, includes
everything, FOR IT COMPRISES CHESED AND GVURAH. The wings of the
precept, WHICH ARE THE TZITZIT (THE FRINGES), in which are blue and
white, are Netzach and Hod. The Mezuzah, ON WHICH IS recorded the name
Shadai, is the Righteous, NAMELY, YESOD, and the Shechinah is the gate
onto which the Mezuzah is affixed, ABOUT WHICH IT IS WRITTEN: "this is
the gate of Hashem" (Tehilim 118:20).

874. וְעוֹד ש' תְּלַת רְצוּעוֹת. ד' קֶשֶׁר שֶׁל תְּפִילִין מֵאֲחוֹרוֹי. י' קֶשֶׁר
דִּתְפִלִּין דְּיָד. וּבְגִין דָּא שַׁדַּ"י מִלְבַר, יְדֹו"ד מִלְּגוֹ, דְּאִיהִי ד' פַּרְשִׁיָּין.
דְּד' רָאשִׁין, רֶמֶז לְאַרְבַּע בָּתֵּי דִּתְפִלִּין. שַׁדַּי אוֹת דִּילֵיהּ, עוֹלֶה
מְטַטְרוֹן.

874. Furthermore, the THREE-HEADED LETTER Shin is the three straps, THE
TWO OF THE HEAD TEFILIN AND THE ONE OF THE HAND TEFILIN. Dalet

is the knot of the HEAD Tefilin at the back OF THE HEAD, while Yud is the knot of the hand Tefilin. TOGETHER THEY SPELL SHADAI. This is why Shadai is written on the outside OF THE TEFILIN, while Yud Hei Vav Hei is inside THE TEFILIN, for it is the four sections THEREIN. The four-headed letter Shin ש alludes to the four compartments of the Tefilin. Shadai is His, ZEIR ANPIN's, sign, and amounts to the same NUMERICAL VALUE as Metatron.

875. וְעוֹד. י׳ חָכְמָה קַדֶּשׁ לִי. ה׳ בִּינָה, וְהָיָה כִּי יְבִיאֲךָ. ו׳ שְׁמַע, שִׁית תֵּיבִין, רְמִיזָא לְשִׁית סְפִירָן, שִׁית עַנְפִין דְּאִילָנָא, דְּכָלַל לוֹן תִּפְאֶרֶת. ה׳ וְהָיָה אִם שָׁמוֹעַ מַלְכוּת. אִלֵּין אִינּוּן דְּרֵישָׁא, דְּאִיהוּ כֶּתֶר, כ׳, אֵין קָדוֹשׁ כַּיְיָ׳ כִּי אֵין בִּלְתֶּךָ.

875. Again: Yud, Chochmah, is the section "Sanctify to me." Hei, Binah, is the section "And it shall be when Hashem brings you into the land." Vav is the Sh'ma, IN WHICH THERE ARE six words: "HEAR, O YISRAEL, HASHEM OUR ELOHIM, HASHEM IS ONE" (DEVARIM 6:4), alluding to the six Sfirot which are six branches of the tree which Tiferet includes. The LAST Hei is THE SECTION "And it will come to pass, if you will hearken diligently" which is Malchut. These are THE MOCHIN of the head, FOR THE HEAD, which is Keter, IS THE SECRET OF THE LETTER CAF, IN THE SECRET OF THE VERSE: "There is none holy as (Heb. *Caf*) Hashem..." (I Shmuel 2:2), WHERE THE LETTER CAF (ENG. 'AS') IN THE EXPRESSION "AS HASHEM" IS KETER OF ZEIR ANPIN.

876. שַׁדַּי, רָמִיז רְצוּעֵי וּבָתֵּי וְקִשְׁרֵי דִּתְפִלִּין מִלְּבַר. אוֹף הָכִי בַּמְּזוּזָה, יְדוֹ״ד מִלְּגוֹ, שַׁדַּ״י מִלְּבַר, דְּאַרְבַּע רָאשִׁין, עִם ד׳, רָמִיז לְד׳ בָּתֵּי, וּלְקֶשֶׁר תְּפִלִּין מֵאָחוֹר, ד׳ כְּפוּלָה. אוֹף הָכִי ש׳ כְּפוּלָה, י׳ קֶשֶׁר דְּיָד כֵּהָה, דְּאִיהוּ בֵּיתָא חֲמִישָׁאָה. ד׳ דְּשַׁדַּ״י, אִיהוּ מוֹחָא, דְּאוֹקְמוּהָ עֲלֵיהּ, בִּמְקוֹם שְׁמוֹחוֹ שֶׁל תִּינוֹק רוֹפֵס בּוֹ. וְדָא תִּינוֹק יוֹנֵק מִשְׁדֵי אִמּוֹ, שַׁדַּי.

876. Shadai alludes to the straps, compartments, and knots of the Tefilin from the outside, FOR SHIN OF SHADAI ALLUDES TO THE THREE STRAPS, TWO OF THE HEAD AND ONE OF THE HAND. DALET OF SHADAI ALLUDES TO THE FOUR COMPARTMENTS OF THE HEAD TEFILIN, AND ALSO TO THE

KNOT OF DALET THAT IS BEHIND THE HEAD. YUD OF SHADAI ALLUDES TO THE KNOT OF THE HAND TEFILIN. The same holds for the Mezuzah, there being Yud Hei Vav Hei on the inside and THE NAME Shadai on the outside. The four-headed letter Shin 𝕎, with the Dalet OF SHADAI alludes to the four compartments and to the knot of HEAD Tefilin behind the HEAD, WHICH HAS THE SHAPE OF a double Dalet. Likewise, there is a double Shin, ONE ON THE RIGHT SIDE OF THE COMPARTMENT AND ONE ON THE LEFT SIDE OF THE COMPARTMENT. Yud OF SHADAI is the knot OF THE TEFILIN of the dim hand, which is the fifth compartment: THAT IS TO SAY THAT WITH THE FOUR COMPARTMENTS OF THE HEAD TEFILIN THE FIFTH COMPARTMENT IS THAT OF THE HAND TEFILIN. Dalet of Shadai is the brain, about which it has been taught: the place on the head where a baby's brain is seen to pulsate, and this is a baby suckling from the breasts (Shin Dalet Yud) OF ITS MOTHER, NAMELY, FROM Shadai.

877. תְּפִלִּין דְּמָארֵי עָלְמָא, כֶּתֶר. וּמַאי נִיהוּ כֶּתֶר דְּמָארֵי עָלְמָא. יְדֹנָ"ד. דְּאִיהוּ: י' חָכְמָה. ה' בִּינָה. ו' תִּפְאֶרֶת. כָּלִיל שִׁית סְפִירִין. ה' מַלְכוּת. וּבְגִ"ד וּמִי כְעַמְּךָ כְּיִשְׂרָאֵל כִּי מִי גוֹי גָּדוֹל אֲשֶׁר לוֹ אֱלֹהִים קְרוֹבִים אֵלָיו, כַּיְיָ' אֱלֹהֵינוּ בְּכָל קָרְאֵנוּ אֵלָיו. אַרְבַּע קְרָאֵי, כֻּלְּהוּ רְשִׁימִין בְּךָ, רָזָא דְאָת כ': י' י'. דְּאִיהִי י' י' מִן יְאָהֲדֹוָנָהי, עֲשָׂרָה עֲשָׂרָה הַכַּף בְּשֶׁקֶל הַקֹּדֶשׁ, כ' מִן כֶּתֶר, כְּלִילָא מֵעֲשַׂר סְפִירָאן, כְּלִילָן מֵעֵילָא לְתַתָּא, וּמֵעֲשַׂר סְפִירָאן מִתַּתָּא לְעֵילָא.

877. The Tefilin of the Master of the Universe are Keter. And what is the crown of the Master of the Universe? It is Yud Hei Vav Hei; namely, the Yud OF YUD HEI VAV HEI is Chochmah, Hei is Binah, and Vav is Tiferet, which includes the six Sfirot CHESED, GVURAH, TIFERET, NETZACH, HOD AND YESOD. The FINAL Hei is Malchut, NAMELY, TEN SFIROT. And this is the reason "And what one nation in the earth is like (Heb. *ke* - Caf) Your people, like Yisrael" (II Shmuel 7:23); "For (Heb. *ki* - Caf Yud) what great nation is there so great, that has Elohim so near to them, as (Heb. *ke* - *Caf*) Hashem our Elohim is in all things that we call upon Him for?" (Devarim 4:7); AND ALSO THE VERSE, MENTIONED ABOVE: "THERE IS NONE HOLY AS HASHEM" (I SHMUEL 2:2). All THESE four verses have marked in them the letter Caf, and the secret of the letter Caf (whose numerical value is twenty) is Yud Yud (the numerical value of each being ten), NAMELY THE

YUD AT THE BEGINNING AND THE YUD AT THE END OF THE
COMBINATION Yud-Aleph-Hei-Dalet-Vav-Nun-Hei-Yud. AND THIS IS THE
INNER MEANING OF THE VERSE "weighing ten shekels apiece (Eng. 'ten
ten'), after the shekel of the sanctuary" (Bemidbar 7:86), NAMELY, the *Caf*
of Keter, that is composed of ten Sfirot, AS ABOVE, and they comprise TEN
SFIROT OF DIRECT LIGHT, from above downwards, and ten Sfirot OF
RETURNING LIGHT, which are upwards from below.

‏878. וְאִלֵּין אִינּוּן, וְהַמַּיִם אֲשֶׁר מֵעַל הַשָּׁמָיִם, מַיִם עֶלְיוֹנִים זְכָרִים, מַיִם‏
‏תַּחְתּוֹנִים נְקֵבוֹת. וְעָלַיְיהוּ אָמַר ר' עֲקִיבָא לְתַלְמִידָיו, כְּשֶׁתַּגִּיעוּ לְאַבְנֵי‏
‏שַׁיִשׁ טָהוֹר, אַל תּאמְרוּ מַיִם מַיִם, שֶׁמָּא תִסְתַּכְּנוּ בְּנַפְשְׁכֶם. דְּלָאו אִינּוּן‏
‏מַיִם כְּמַשְׁמָעָן. אֶלָּא אִיהוּ אוֹר נוֹבֵעַ. וּבְגִין דָּא, אִדְמוּ לְמַיִם נוֹבְעִים.‏
‏וְהַאי נְהוֹרָא לֵית לֵיהּ פְּסַק, וְלא קִצּוּץ, וּפֵרוּד. וּבְגִין דְּאִינּוּן מִכֶּתֶר,‏
‏אִתְקְרִיאָן שֶׁאֵין לָהֶם סוֹף, דְּכֶתֶר אֵין סוֹף אִתְקְרֵי.‏

‏ע"כ רעיא מהימנא‏

878. And these TWENTY SFIROT, OF DIRECT LIGHT AND OF RETURNING
LIGHT, are THE SECRET OF THE VERSE "waters that are above the heavens"
(Tehilim 148:4), which are the male upper waters, NAMELY, THE TEN
SFIROT OF DIRECT LIGHT, WHILE "THE WATERS WHICH WERE UNDER
THE FIRMAMENT" (BERESHEET 1:7) ARE the female lower waters,
NAMELY THE TEN SFIROT OF RETURNING LIGHT. And Rabbi Akiva said to
his pupils about them: When you reach the stones of pure marble, do not say:
Water, water, lest you endanger your souls. For it is not water as is usually
understood, NAMELY, CHASSADIM, but 'flowing light'; NAMELY, IT IS
ALSO COMPOSED OF CHOCHMAH THAT IS CALLED 'LIGHT', AND FROM
THE ASPECT OF CHASSADIM, IT IS 'FLOWING'. This is why it was likened
to flowing water. And this light is never interrupted, nor is it cut off, nor
divided. And because it is from Keter, it is called 'infinite WATER', for Keter
is called the Endless Light.

End of Ra'aya Meheimna

127. Shavuot

A Synopsis

Rabbi Shimon says that burnt offerings are not required during Shavuot because Yisrael have already observed the days of purity and the Other Side now has no hold over them. Shavuot belongs to the Tree of Life and not to the Tree of Knowledge of Good and Evil.

879. וְהִקְרַבְתֶּם עוֹלָה לְרֵיחַ נִיחֹחַ לַיְיָ'. ת"ח, בְּפֶסַח כְּתִיב, וְהִקְרַבְתֶּם אִשֶּׁה עוֹלָה לַיְיָ'. וְהָכָא לָא כְּתִיב אִשֶּׁה, אֶלָּא וְהִקְרַבְתֶּם עוֹלָה. מ"ט. יוֹמָא דָא, יוֹמָא דְּעַיְילַת כַּלָּה לְחוּפָּה אִיהוּ. וְיִשְׂרָאֵל מָנוּ יוֹמִין דְּדַכְיוּ. יוֹמִין וְשָׁבוּעִין, וְאִתְכְּלִילוּ וְעָאלוּ בְּיוֹמִין דְּדַכְיוּ. וְהִיא נַפְקַת מִכָּל סִטְרָא בִּישָׁא, וְנַטְרַת יוֹמֵי דַּכְיוּ כַּדְקָא חֲזֵי. וְרָזָא דָא, מַלְכָּא טַעַם בְּתוּלָה טָעִים. בג"כ לָא כְּתִיב בֵּיהּ אִשֶּׁה, דְּהָא אַחֲרָא לָא קָרִיב לְמַשְׁכְּנָא, וְהָא אִתְרַחַק מִתַּמָּן. וע"ד אִשִּׁים לָאו הָכָא, וְלָאו אִצְטְרִיכוּ לְהָכָא, וְיִשְׂרָאֵל מְרַחֲקָן אִינוּן מִן סִטְרָא בִּישָׁא. א"ר אַבָּא, עֲדַיִין צְרִיכִין אֲנָן לִפְתָחָא דָא לְמִפְתַּח.

879. "And you shall offer the burnt offering for a sweet savor to Hashem" (Bemidbar 28:27). Come and see, About Pesach it is written: "You shall offer a sacrifice made by fire for a burnt offering to Hashem" (Ibid. 19). Yet here it is not written 'a sacrifice made by fire' but "And you shall offer the burnt offering." What is the reason for this? AND HE ANSWERS, the reason is that this day OF SHAVUOT is a day on which the bride enters the wedding canopy; NAMELY, MALCHUT ENTERS THE WEDDING CANOPY WITH ZEIR ANPIN, and Yisrael COME from THE COUNTING OF the days and weeks of purity, and are taken in and enter into THESE days of purity, NAMELY, THE SECRET OF THE SEVEN DAYS CHESED, GVURAH, TIFERET, NETZACH, HOD, YESOD AND MALCHUT, IN EACH ONE OF WHICH ARE CHESED, GVURAH, TIFERET, NETZACH, HOD, YESOD AND MALCHUT, MAKING A TOTAL OF 49 DAYS. And she, MALCHUT, has emerged from the aspect of everything bad, NAMELY, THEY NO LONGER HAVE ANY HOLD OVER HER, and has observed the days of purity as fitting, NAMELY, THE 49 DAYS OF THE COUNTING. And this is the secret of the king who tasted the taste of a virgin. IN OTHER WORDS, THE SECRET OF THE VERSE "A VIRGIN, NEITHER HAD ANY MAN KNOWN HER" (BERESHEET 24:16), IF THE

MATTER BE DISCLOSED, IS THAT NO ONE OF THE OTHER SIDE HAD ANY HOLD OVER HER. And this is why it is not written about it 'a sacrifice made by fire', for no other came close to the Sanctuary, WHICH IS MALCHUT, and THE OTHER PARTY has already been removed from there. Thus there are not, nor is there any need for, offerings made by fire in this case, for Yisrael have removed themselves from the Evil Side. Rabbi Aba said: We still have to open this gate.

880. אר״ש, אֲרִימִית יְדַי בִּצְלוֹ לְמַאן דְּבָרָא עָלְמָא, וְרָזָא דָא, אַשְׁכְּחָן בְּסִפְרֵי קַדְמָאֵי, אִשִּׁים אִינּוּן בְּאֶמְצָעִיתָא, וְאַתְיָין בְּסִטְרָא דָא וּבְסִטְרָא דָא, אִדַּבְּקוּ בְּאִילָנָא דְּדַעַת טוֹב וָרָע, אִדַּבְּקָן בְּרָע, וְאִדַּבְּקָן בְּטוֹב. וּבג״כ, בִּשְׁאַר יוֹמִין כְּתִיב בְּהוּ אִשֵּׁה עוֹלָה. אֲבָל בְּהָנֵי יוֹמָא, דְּאִילָנָא דְּחַיֵּי קַיְּימָא, וְלָא אַחֲרָא, לֵית אֲנָן צְרִיכִין לְאִשֶּׁה, וְלָא אִצְטְרִיךְ לְמֶהֱוֵי תַּמָּן. וְיוֹמָא דָא, יוֹמָא דְּאִילָנָא דְּחַיֵּי אִיהוּ, וְלָא דְּדַעַת טוֹב וָרָע. וּבג״ד, וְהִקְרַבְתֶּם עוֹלָה לְרֵיחַ נִיחֹחַ לַיְיָ', וְלָא אִשֵּׁה לַיְיָ' עוֹלָה. וְעוֹלָה, לְשׁוֹן עוֹלָה, כְּמָה דְּאִתְּמַר, וְהָא אִתְעַרְנָא מִלֵּי דְּפָרִים בְּנֵי בָקָר, וְכָל הַהוּא קָרְבָּן.

880. Rabbi Shimon said: I lifted up my hands in prayer to Him who created the world and found this secret in the works of the early masters: Offerings made by fire are in between THE GOOD AND THE EVIL, and they come on this side and on that side, for they are attached to the Tree of Knowledge of Good and Evil, AND ARE, THEREFORE, attached to both the bad and to the good. For this reason, on the other days, it is written: "a sacrifice made by fire for a burnt offering" FOR THEY CONTAIN JUDGMENTS AND HAVE A HOLD ON THE TREE OF KNOWLEDGE OF GOOD AND EVIL. But on these days when the Tree of Life and no other is to be found, NAMELY, ON SHAVUOT, we do not need an offering made by fire, and it does not have to be there, for this day OF SHAVUOT belongs to the Tree of Life and not the Tree of Knowledge of Good and Evil. This is why SCRIPTURE SAYS: "And you shall offer the burnt offering for a sweet savor to Hashem" (Bemidbar 28:27), and not 'a sacrifice made by fire to Hashem for a burnt offering'. And THE MEANING OF 'burnt offering' (Heb. olah) is derived from ascent, FOR IT ASCENDS (HEB. OLAH) TO THE MOST HIGH ONE, as we have learned. And we have already clarified these matters IN THE COMMENTARY about one-year old bullocks and the whole of that offering.

128. Rosh Hashanah

A Synopsis
Rabbi Shimon uses the story of Isaac and Jacob and Esau to illustrate the meaning of the two days of Judgment and the need for the burnt offering.

881. וּבַחֹדֶשׁ הַשְּׁבִיעִי, כְּמָה דְּאִתְּמַר, יוֹמָא דר״ה, דִּינָא דְּכָל עָלְמָא, דִּינָא תַּקִּיפָא, וְדִינָא רַפְיָא. וַעֲשִׂיתֶם עוֹלָה, וְהִקְרַבְתֶּם מִבָּעֵי לֵיהּ, כִּשְׁאַר כָּל יוֹמִין, מַאי וַעֲשִׂיתֶם. אֶלָּא בְּיוֹמָא דָא, וַעֲשֵׂה לִי מַטְעַמִּים כְּתִיב. כַּמָּה מַטְעַמִּים וְתַבְשִׁילִים עָבְדוּ יִשְׂרָאֵל בְּהָנֵי יוֹמֵי, בְּעוֹד דִּמְקַטְרְגָא אָזִיל לְפַשְׁפְּשָׁא בְּחוֹבִין דְּעָלְמָא. וע״ד לָא כְּתִיב וְהִקְרַבְתֶּם, אֶלָּא וַעֲשִׂיתֶם עוֹלָה. וְלָא אִשֵּׁה עוֹלָה. וְכֵן בְּכָל שְׁאַר יוֹמִין, לָא כְּתִיב אִשֵּׁה, דְּלֵית לוֹן חוּלָקָא בְּכָל הָנֵי יוֹמֵי. כ״ש בְּהַאי יוֹמָא, דַּאֲנָן עַבְדִּין מַטְעַמִּים וְתַבְשִׁילִים בְּלָא דַּעְתָּא דְּסִטְרָא אַחֲרָא, דְּהָא יִצְחָק מְשַׁדֵּר לֵיהּ לָצוּד צֵידָה דְּחוֹבִין דִּבְנֵי עָלְמָא, וּלְאַיְיתָאָה לְגַבֵּיהּ.

881. "And in the seventh month, ON THE FIRST DAY OF THE MONTH" (Bemidbar 29:1). This is as we have learned, that Rosh Hashanah is the Day of Judgment for the whole world: stringent Judgment ON THE FIRST DAY and lenient judgment ON THE SECOND DAY. HE ASKS: IT IS WRITTEN, "And you shall make a burnt offering" (Ibid. 2), whereas it should have been written: 'And you shall offer a burnt offering', as on all the other days. What is the meaning of "And you shall make?" AND HE ANSWERS, on this day OF ROSH HASHANAH it is written: "and make me savory food" (Beresheet 27:4), WHICH IS WHAT ISAAC SAID TO ESAU, WHO IS THE ACCUSER. And during these days Yisrael makes many savory foods and dishes, NAMELY, BY PRECEPTS AND PRAYERS, while the accuser goes to search for the sins of the world, TO MAKE THEM INTO SAVORY FOODS FOR THE PROSECUTION. It is therefore not written: 'And you shall offer a burnt offering', but: "And you shall make a burnt offering," NAMELY, MAKE AND PREPARE SAVORY FOODS. And it is not WRITTEN: 'a sacrifice made by fire to Hashem for a burnt offering'. Also on all the other festival days, in which days there is no part FOR THE OTHER SIDE, it is not written 'a sacrifice made by fire' AS IN SHAVUOT AND YOM KIPPUR, and certainly not on this day, on which we make savory foods and dishes without the knowledge of the Other Side, for

he had been sent by Isaac to hunt game that is the iniquities of men, and to bring them to him.

882. וּבְעוֹד דְּאִיהוּ אָזִיל, יִשְׂרָאֵל נַטְלֵי עֵיטָא בְּרִבְקָה, וְעַבְדִין כָּל אִינוּן פּוּלְחָנִין, כָּל אִינוּן צְלוֹתִין, מְזַמְּנֵי שׁוֹפָר וְתַקְעִין לֵיהּ, בְּגִין לְאַתְעָרָא רַחֲמֵי. וְהָא אוֹקִימְנָא, וַיָּבֵא לוֹ יַיִן וַיֵּשְׁתְּ, דְּאָתֵי מֵרָחוֹק, מִגּוֹ אֲתָר דְּחַמְרָא עַתִּיקָא, וְשָׁתֵי. וְאַטְעִים לֵיהּ, וְחַדֵּי. וְאַחַר כַּךְ מְבָרֵךְ לֵיהּ בְּכַמָּה בִּרְכָאן, וְאַעֲבַּר עַל חוֹבוֹי. מַה כְּתִיב, וַיְהִי אַךְ יָצוֹא יָצָא יַעֲקֹב וְעֵשָׂו אָחִיו בָּא מִצֵּדוֹ, טָעִין מִכַּמָּה טוֹעֲנֵי כְּמָה דְּאִתְּמַר, וְהָא אוֹקִימְנָא מִלָּה.

882. And while he is yet on the way, Yisrael takes advice from Rivkah and do all these rituals and all the prayers, and prepare a Shofar and sound it in order to awaken Mercy. And we have already learned: "and he brought him wine, and he drank" (Beresheet 27:25), for he came from afar, FROM BINAH, from that place where the wine is old. And he drank, found it delicious, and rejoiced. And after that ISAAC, WHO IS THE LEFT COLUMN, blessed him with a number of blessings and removed his iniquities. It is then written: "and Jacob was yet scarce gone out from the presence of Isaac his father, and Esau his brother came in from his hunting" (Beresheet 27:30), namely, he was carrying with him a number of burdens OF INIQUITIES, as has been stated, and we have already learned these matters.

883. וּבג״כ אִיהוּ יוֹמָא דִּיבָבָא, וְקָרְבְּנָא אִיהוּ עוֹלָה. אַיִל אֶחָד, כְּמָה דְּאִתְּמַר, בְּגִין אֵילוֹ דְּיִצְחָק. וּשְׂעִיר עִזִּים אֶחָד לְחַטָּאת, שׁוֹחַד לְסַמָּאֵל לְכַפָּרָה אַנְפּוֹי, בְּהַהוּא בְּכִיָּה דְּאִיהוּ בָּכֵי בְּהַאי יוֹמָא, כֵּיוָן דְּחָמֵי דְּלָא אִתְעֲבֵיד רְעוּתֵיהּ, וְהָא לְמַגָּנָא צַד צֵידָה. כְּמָה דְּאִתְּמַר. כְּגַוְונָא דָא יוֹמָא דְּכִפּוּרֵי, וְהָא כְּתִיב בפ׳ אֱמוֹר.

883. And this is why it is a day of the T'ruah SOUND OF THE SHOFAR, and the sacrifice is a burnt offering. One ram is, as we have learned, because of the ram of Isaac. The one kid of the goats for a sin offering is a bribe to Samael, to make atonement before him for having wept on that day when he realized that his will had not been done and he had gone hunting for nothing. as we have learned. This is similar on Yom Kippur, as written in the portion of Emor.

129. Sukkot

A Synopsis
Rabbi Aba and Rabbi Elazar talk about the third day of Sukkot,
employing the analogy of the ark landing on Mount Ararat and the
waters receding.

884. וּבַחֲמִשָּׁה עָשָׂר יוֹם וְגוֹ'. ר' אַבָּא פָּתַח, וַתָּנַח הַתֵּיבָה בַּחֹדֶשׁ
הַשְּׁבִיעִי וְגוֹ', ת"ח, כָּל הָנֵי יוֹמִין, אַזְלַת אִימָא עַל בְּנַיָּיא, בְּגִין דְּלָא
יִשְׁלוֹט סִטְרָא אַחֲרָא עָלַיְיהוּ, וּבְגִין לְשֵׁזָבָא לוֹן. כֵּיוָן דְּאִשְׁתְּזִיבוּ בְּנָהָא,
וְהָא יַתְבִין בַּסֻּכּוֹת, מִתְנַטְרִין בִּנְטוּרָא. יוֹמָא קַדְמָאָה, וְיוֹמָא תִּנְיָינָא,
פַּקְדַת לוֹן לְיִשְׂרָאֵל, לְמֶעְבַּד סְעוּדָתָא לִמְמָנָן דִּשְׁאַר עַמִּין, וְאִיהִי לָא
שַׁרְיָא תַּמָּן. בְּיוֹמָא תְּלִיתָאָה, דְּאִיהוּ י"ז לַחֹדֶשׁ, שָׁרִיאַת לְמִשְׁרֵי
עָלַיְיהוּ. הה"ד, וַתָּנַח הַתֵּיבָה בַּחֹדֶשׁ הַשְּׁבִיעִי בְּשִׁבְעָה עָשָׂר יוֹם לַחֹדֶשׁ
עַל הָרֵי אֲרָרָט, טוּרִין דְּכָל לְוָוטִין וּמְרָדִין שָׁרְיָאן בְּגַווַיְיהוּ.

884. "And on the fifteenth day of the seventh month" (Bemidbar 29:12).
Rabbi Aba began by quoting: "And the ark rested in the seventh month"
(Beresheet 8:4). Come and see: Throughout these days, FROM YOM KIPPUR
TO SUKKOT, the Mother, WHICH IS THE SHECHINAH, hovers over the
children, WHO ARE YISRAEL, in order that the Other Side should not have
control OVER YISRAEL, and in order to save them. After the children have
been saved and are sitting in their booths (Heb. *sukkot*), they are guarded
with the protection OF MOTHER, WHICH IS THE SHECHINAH. On the first
and second days OF THE HOLIDAY OF SUKKOT, She commanded Yisrael to
make a feast for the ministering angels of the other nations, NAMELY THE
SEVENTY BULLOCKS FOR THE SEVENTY MINISTERS, and She does not
dwell there WITH THEM. On the third day, which is the seventeenth day of
the month, THE SHECHINAH begins to rest on them. And this is the meaning
of the verse: "And the ark rested in the seventh month, on the seventeenth
day of the month, upon the mountains of Ararat," WHERE THE ARK IS THE
SECRET OF THE SHECHINAH, AND THE MOUNTAINS OF ARARAT ARE the
mountains in the midst of which rest all the curses and all the punishments,
WHICH ARE THE APPOINTEES OF THE NATIONS.

885. אָמַר רַבִּי אֶלְעָזָר, יוֹמָא קַדְמָאָה דְּחַג, לָא שַׁרְיָא עָלַיְיהוּ, וְלָא

יוֹמָא תִּנְיָינָא, אֶלָּא יוֹמָא תְּלִיתָאָה, דְּאוֹסִיף וְגָרַע שַׁרְיָא עֲלַיְיהוּ, אוֹסִיף אַתְוָון, וְגָרַע קָרְבְּנִין. דִּכְתִּיב עַשְׁתֵּי עָשָׂר וְגוֹ'. וְהָכִי אִתְחֲזֵי לְרַע עַיִן, בְּגִין דְּיוֹמָא קַדְמָאָה וְיוֹמָא תִּנְיָינָא חֶדְוָה דִּבְנָהָא, וְאִינּוּן מְפַלְגֵּי עֲדָאָן לוֹן. מִיּוֹמָא תְּלִיתָאָה וּלְהָלְאָה, דְּאִיהִי שַׁרְיָא עֲלַיְיהוּ, מַה כְּתִיב. וְהַמַּיִם הָיוּ הָלוֹךְ וְחָסוֹר עַד הַחֹדֶשׁ הָעֲשִׂירִי בָּעֲשִׂירִי בְּאֶחָד לַחֹדֶשׁ נִרְאוּ רָאשֵׁי הֶהָרִים וְהַמַּיִם הָיוּ הָלוֹךְ וְחָסוֹר, אִלֵּין קָרְבְּנִין, דְּאַזְלִין וּמִתְמַעֲטִין. וּכְמָה דְּאִינּוּן מִתְמַעֲטִין, הָכִי נָמֵי אִתְמְעַט טוּבָא דִּלְהוֹן.

885. Rabbi Elazar said: On the first day of Sukkot, MALCHUT does not rest on them, ON THE MINISTERS OF THE SEVENTY NATIONS, nor on the second day; but only on the third day, which decreases by addition, does She rest on them, adding letters and decreasing in sacrifices, as it is written: "Eleven (Heb. *ashtei asar*) bullocks" (Bemidbar 29:20), which is appropriate for the evil eye. For on the first day and the second day there is rejoicing of the children, and Yisrael distributes booty to them, TO THE APPOINTEES OF THE NATIONS. From the third day and onwards, when MALCHUT rests upon them, what is written? "And the waters decreased continually until the tenth month; in the tenth month, on the first day of the month, were the tops of the mountains seen" (Beresheet 8:5). "And the waters decreased continually"; these are the sacrifices that are continually reduced, and as they become fewer in number so does their goodness become less.

130. The water libation

A Synopsis

Rabbi Shimon explains about the contraction as the waters receded and the relevance to the water libation during the second, sixth and seventh days of Sukkot. He compares the mountains of Ararat to the mountains of darkness and the curses of the Other Side, that gradually become visible as the waters recede. We hear about the sacrifices of the rams and lambs and bullocks and their effect on the seventy heathen nations for whom they are offered. Lastly we are reminded how Yisrael break through all the Klipot to find joy on the eighth day of assembly, Shmini Atzeret. In this the Other Side has no part.

886. אר״ש, אֶלְעָזָר, ת״ח, מִיּוֹמָא תְּנְיָינָא שָׁרִיאוּ מַיָּיא לְאִתְחֲזָאָה, כֵּיוָן דְּשָׁרִיאוּ מַיִם, מִיּוֹמָא תְּלִיתָאָה אִיהִי שַׁרַת עֲלַיְיהוּ, וְאִינּוּן מַיִם לָא הֲווֹ יַדְעֵי בַּבְלָאֵי, אֲמַאי רְשִׁימִין הָכָא, דְּהָא טוּבָא דְיִשְׂרָאֵל לָא הֲוֵי בַּאֲתָר דִּמְעוּטָא, אֶלָּא בַּאֲתָר דְּרִבּוּיָיא. וּבְגִין דְּאִלֵּין מַיִין דִּרְשִׁימִין הָכָא אִתְמַעֲטָן, אָתֵי קְרָא לְאַשְׁמְעִינָן דִּכְתִיב, וְהַמַּיִם הָיוּ הָלוֹךְ דְּאִינּוּן טוּרֵי לְוָטִין, הָיוּ הָלוֹךְ וְחָסוֹר טוּבָא דִּלְהוֹן, וּנְגִידוּ דְּאָנְגִּיד עֲלַיְיהוּ, הָיוּ הָלוֹךְ וְחָסוֹר, וּבְגִין דְּאִינּוּן מַיִם דִּלְהוֹן הוּא, לָא אִתְחַבְּרָן אַתְוָון, דְּלָא יִתְחַבַּר טוּבָא דִּלְהוֹן, אֶלָּא זְעֵיר זְעֵיר.

886. Rabbi Shimon said, Elazar, come and see: From the second day, the waters began to appear, NAMELY, THE LIBATION OF WATER ON THE ALTAR BEGAN. FOR ITS PURPOSE WAS ALSO TO DRAW DOWN LIVELIHOOD AND SUBSISTENCE FOR THE OTHER SIDE. "AND IF HE BE THIRSTY, GIVE HIM WATER TO DRINK" (MISHLEI 25:21): THIS WATER IS THE WATER THAT IS MENTIONED HERE FOR LIBATION ON THE DAYS OF SUKKOT. And after the water had begun, AND THE OTHER SIDE AND THE SEVENTY NATIONS HAD RECEIVED PLENTY, THEY THEN GREW IN STRENGTH, AND from the third day MALCHUT rested on them. And the Babylonians did not know why these waters are mentioned here IN CONNECTION WITH SUKKOT, THAT IS TO SAY THAT THEY DID NOT KNOW THAT THEIR PURPOSE WAS TO PROVIDE SUBSISTENCE TO THE NATIONS OF THE WORLD, for the

goodness of Yisrael does not lie where there is contraction, NAMELY, IN THE BULLOCKS OF SUKKOT THAT ARE REDUCED IN NUMBER, but in a place of expansion. And since these waters that are mentioned here decrease, TOGETHER WITH THE BULLOCKS OF SUKKOT, Scripture comes to inform us that it is written: "And the waters..." (Beresheet 8:5). That is, the waters that are known from the days of Sukkot are the ones that are mentioned among the sacrifices. FOR ON THE SECOND DAY IT IS SAID THAT ABOUT THE SACRIFICES IS "THEIR DRINK OFFERINGS (HEB. *VENISKEIHEM*)" (BEMIDBAR 29:18), THE LAST LETTER OF WHICH IS MEM. AND ON THE SIXTH DAY, IT IS SAID, "AND ITS DRINK OFFERINGS" (HEB. *UNSACHEIHAH*)" (IBID. 31), WITH YUD. AND ON THE SEVENTH DAY "AFTER THE ORDINANCE (Heb. *KEMISHPATAM*)" (IBID. 33), THE LAST LETTER OF WHICH IS MEM. AND THESE THREE LETTERS TOGETHER SPELL *MAYIM* (ENG. 'WATERS' - MEM YUD MEM), FROM WHICH IT FOLLOWS THAT THERE IS AN ALLUSION TO THE WATER LIBATION IN THE TORAH. For they, THE SACRIFICES, are mountains of curses that continually decrease, and their goodness, and the emanation that is drawn down on them "decreased continually" (Beresheet 8:5). And because these waters belong to them, TO THE NATIONS AND TO THE OTHER SIDE, the letters MEM YUD MEM were not joined together AND THE WORD DID NOT APPEAR EXPLICITLY WRITTEN IN THE TORAH. BUT THE LETTERS ARE SCATTERED, WITH MEM BEING IN "AND THEIR DRINK-OFFERINGS'" THE YUD IN "AND ITS DRINK-OFFERINGS," AND THE FINAL MEM IN "AFTER THE ORDINANCE," AS ABOVE. And the purpose of this is so that their goodness should not be joined, but BE little by little.

887. אֲבָל לְיִשְׂרָאֵל, דְּאִינּוּן מְקוּדְשָׁא בְּרִיךְ הוּא, מַה כְּתִיב. וְדוֹרְשֵׁי יְיָ' לֹא יַחְסְרוּ כָל טוֹב. רֵישֵׁיהּ דִּקְרָא, כְּפִירִים רָשׁוּ וְרָעֵבוּ, אִלֵּין מְמָנָן דִּשְׁאָר עַמִּין. וְדוֹרְשֵׁי יְיָ', אִלֵּין יִשְׂרָאֵל, לֹא יַחְסְרוּ כָל טוֹב, אִלֵּין אַזְלִין וְאִסְתַּלָּקוּ לְעֵילָא לְעֵילָא. וּבְג"כ, טוּבָא דִּלְהוֹן דְּאִינּוּן מַיִם, הָיוּ הָלוֹךְ וְחָסוֹר. עַד הַחֹדֶשׁ הָעֲשִׂירִי. דָּא טֵבֵת, דְּהָא כְּדֵין יְמֵי הָרָעָה הֲווֹ, וְאִתְעֲרַת הַהִיא רָעָה וְאִתְתַּקְפַת, וְכַלָּה קַדִּישָׁא לָא אַנְהִירַת מִגּוֹ שִׁמְשָׁא, כְּדֵין נִרְאוּ רָאשֵׁי הֶהָרִים, אִלֵּין אִינּוּן הֲרֵי חֲשׁוֹכָא, טוּרִין דִּלְוָטִין אִתְחֲזוּן וְאִתְתַּקְפוּ, וְעַבְדִין בִּישִׁין בְּעָלְמָא.

887. But regarding Yisrael, who are from the Holy One, blessed be He, WHO IS THE CENTRAL COLUMN, what is written? "but they who seek Hashem

shall not want any good thing" (Tehilim 34:11). The first half of this verse is: "The young lions lack, and suffer hunger" (Ibid.). The young lions are the appointees of the other nations. They that seek Hashem are Yisrael, who will not lack all good things because they continually ascend higher and higher, FOR ONE MAY PROMOTE TO A HIGHER DEGREE OF SANCTITY BUT NOT DEMOTE. For this reason, their good, THAT OF THE NATIONS AND OF THE OTHER SIDE, which are waters, "decreased continually until the tenth month" (Beresheet 8:5), which is the month of Tevet, for then are the days of evil, FOR THE MONTHS OF TEVET AND SHEVAT ARE THE PERIOD OF JUDGMENT AND ARE CALLED 'THE DAYS OF EVIL'. And this evil awakens and grows stronger, and the holy bride, WHICH IS MALCHUT, does not illuminate from the midst of the sun, NAMELY, IS SEPARATED FROM THE SUN, WHICH IS ZEIR ANPIN. And then the tops of these mountains became visible, THAT IS THE JUDGMENTS OF THE LEFT SIDE THAT ARE DRAWN DOWN WITH THE BULLOCKS OF SUKKOT, namely, those mountains of darkness and mountains of curses that appear and grow stronger and do evil things in the world.

888. בְּיוֹמִין אִלֵּין, אִשֶּׁה בְּהַאי עוֹלָה, דְּהָא כְּדֵין הָנֵי אִשִּׁים אָכְלֵי חוּלָקֵהוֹן. שַׁבְעִים פָּרִים אִלֵּין, אִינּוּן לָקֳבֵל שַׁבְעִים מְמָנָן, דְּשַׁלְטוּ עַל שַׁבְעִין עַמִּין. וְסַלְקִין בְּיוֹמָא קַדְמָאָה, וְנַחְתֵּי בְּכָל יוֹמָא וְיוֹמָא, וְאִקְרוּן פָּרִים מְנַגְחִין בְּיוֹמִין דִּלְהוֹן. אֵילִם, אַרְבֵּיסַר, תְּרֵין בְּכָל יוֹמָא אִינּוּן י"ד יְהֹוָ"ה. יְדָא דְּשַׁלִּיטָא עֲלַיְיהוּ תָּדִיר, בְּכָל יוֹמָא וְיוֹמָא. אַמְרִין בְּנֵי שָׁנָה, מִנְיָינָא דִּלְהוֹן ח"ץ.

888. About these days OF THE HOLIDAY OF SUKKOT IT IS WRITTEN: "a sacrifice made by fire" (Bemidbar 29:13) regarding THEIR burnt offering, NAMELY THE WORDS, "AND YOU SHALL OFFER A BURNT OFFERING FOR A SACRIFICE MADE BY FIRE" (IBID.). For then these offerings made by fire, devour their portions, namely, those seventy bullocks corresponding to the seventy appointees who rule over the seventy nations. AND THEIR NUMBER is greatest on the first day and decreases with each passing day. And they are called 'goring bullocks' on their days. Fourteen rams. (THE TEXT HERE IS MISSING, BUT SHOULD READ AS FOLLOWS: "TWO RAMS, AND FOURTEEN LAMBS OF THE FIRST YEAR" (BEMIDBAR 29:13).) The two RAMS on each day are fourteen Yud Hei Vav Hei, AS SEVEN TIMES TWO IS FOURTEEN. And this refers to the hand (Heb. yad = fourteen) that controls them

continually, every day. And the total number of the lambs of the first year is 98, FOR SEVEN TIMES FOURTEEN EQUALS 98.

889. וְאִי תֵּימָא אִי הָכִי, רַע עַיִן הֲוֵינָן לְגַבַּיְיהוּ. אִין, דְּהָא כְּתִיב, כִּי גֶחָלִים אַתָּה חוֹתֶה עַל רֹאשׁוֹ. אֲבָל אֲנַן לָא יַהֲבִינָן אֶלָּא בְּחֶדְוָותָא, דְּלֵית בְּיוֹמֵי שַׁתָּא, חֶדְוָותָא, כְּאִלֵּין יוֹמִין. וּבְגִין דַּאֲנַן יָהֲבִין בְּטוּב לִבָּא, וּבְחֶדְוָותָא דִּרְעוּתָא, אִתְהַפָּךְ עָלַיְיהוּ גֶחָלִים עַל רֵישֵׁיהוֹן, גּוֹמְרִין מְלַהֲטָן, דְּחֶדְוָותָא דִּילָן, עַבְדֵי לוֹן בִּישׁ. י"ד, ע', וחצ. כַּךְ סַלְקִין בְּחוּשְׁבָּנָא דִּילְהוֹן.

889. And you might ask: If so, IF WE OFFER FOURTEEN RAMS SO THAT THE HAND (HEB. *YAD* = FOURTEEN) OF YUD HEI VAV HEI WILL RULE; AND IF WE OFFER 98 LAMBS, WHICH IS A BAD OMEN, FOR IT CORRESPONDS TO THE 98 CURSES IN THE ADMONITION AND ALSO IT IS SAID THAT 'TILL A DART (HEB. *CHETZ* = 98) STRIKE THROUGH HIS LIVER' then are we not being evil-eyed towards them, FOR HE SAYS TO HIM: 'EAT AND DRINK, SAYS HE TO HIM; BUT HIS HEART IS NOT WITH HIM'? HE ANSWERS: Yes, for it is written: "IF YOUR ENEMY BE HUNGRY, GIVE HIM BREAD TO EAT, AND IF HE BE THIRSTY, GIVE HIM WATER TO DRINK: for you shall heap coals of fire upon his head" (Mishlei 25:21-22). But we give only out of rejoicing, for throughout the whole year, there is no rejoicing like that on these days OF SUKKOT. And since we give out of the goodness of our hearts, in rejoicing and willingly, OUR GIFTS to them turn into coals of fire on their head, burning coals, for our rejoicing affects them badly, namely, the fourteen RAMS, seventy BULLOCKS, and 98 LAMBS, which is their sum total OF SACRIFICES, WHERE THE FOURTEEN RAMS INDICATE THE HAND OF YUD HEI VAV HEI THAT CONTROLS THEM, AND THE SEVENTY BULLOCKS IN THEIR DECREASING PROGRESSION TEACH THAT THEIR GOODNESS WILL CONTINUALLY DECREASE, WHILE THE 98 LAMBS TEACH ABOUT THE 98 CURSES THAT REST ON THEM; OR IN OTHER WORDS: 'A DART STRIKE THROUGH THEIR LIVER'.

890. וְכָל דָּא אִיתֵּימָא מַאן יָהִיב לָן לְאַקְרָבָא עָלַיְיהוּ, דִּלְמָא אִינוּן לָא בָּעָאן כָּל דָּא. אֶלָּא לֵית חֶדְוָוה לְכָל אִינוּן מִמְּנָן, בְּכָל אִינוּן תּוֹרִים אֵילִים וְאָמְרִין כְּהַנֵּי, בְּשַׁעְתָּא דְּיִשְׂרָאֵל יַהֲבֵי לוֹן סְעוּדָתִין אִלֵּין. וְעִם

כָּל דָּא לָא מִתְקַרְבוּ כְּלָא, אֶלָּא לְקוּדְשָׁא בְּרִיךְ הוּא בִּלְחוֹדוֹי, וְאִינוּן מִתְקַרְבֵי תַּמָּן, וְאִיהוּ פָּלִיג לוֹן. וְעַל דָּא כְּתִיב, אִם רָעֵב שׂוֹנַאֲךָ הַאֲכִילֵהוּ לֶחֶם, אִלֵּין אִינוּן קָרְבְּנִין דְּחַג. וְאִם צָמֵא הַשְׁקֵהוּ מָיִם, אִלֵּין מַיִם דִּרְשִׁימִין הָכָא בְּיוֹמֵי דְּחַג. וּבְיוֹמָא תְּנַיְינָא, וּבְיוֹמָא שְׁתִיתָאָה וּשְׁבִיעָאָה, וְסִימָן בּוֹ״ז יָבוּזוּ לוֹ.

890. And regarding all this, but you might ask: Who asked us to sacrifice for them, FOR THE APPOINTEES OF THE SEVENTY NATIONS? Perhaps they are not interested in our doing so? But all of these appointees have no such rejoicing as at that time which they have with all these bullocks and rams and lambs that Yisrael offer to them at these banquets. Nevertheless, nothing is offered except to the Holy One, blessed be He alone, while they, THE APPOINTEES, come close and the Holy One, blessed be He, distributes to them. And about this it is written: "If your enemy be hungry, give him bread to eat," where bread refers to the festival offerings; and in "and if he be thirsty, give him water to drink," water refers to that water that is marked TO BE POURED OUT IN A LIBATION on the days of Sukkot, on the second, sixth, and seventh days. And this is derived from, "it would be utterly scorned (Heb. *boz* - Bet Vav Zayin)" (Shir Hashirim, 8:7), WHERE THE NUMERICAL VALUES OF THE LETTERS BET, VAV, AND ZAYIN ARE TWO, SIX AND SEVEN, RESPECTIVELY.

891. מַיִם רַבִּים לֹא יוּכְלוּ לְכַבּוֹת אֶת הָאַהֲבָה, אִלֵּין אִינוּן מַיִם, דִּי מְנַסְּכֵי יִשְׂרָאֵל, בְּחֶדְוָה וּבִרְחִימוּ דְקוּדְשָׁא בְּרִיךְ הוּא, דִּכְתִיב וּשְׁאַבְתֶּם מַיִם בְּשָׂשׂוֹן. וּנְהָרוֹת לֹא יִשְׁטְפוּהָ, אִלֵּין אִינוּן נַהֲרֵי דְּאֲפַרְסְמוֹנָא דַכְיָא, דְּכֻלְּהוּ דַּכְיֵי וּמִתְקַשְּׁרֵי בִּרְחִימוּ דָא. אִם יִתֵּן אִישׁ אֶת כָּל הוֹן בֵּיתוֹ בְּאַהֲבָה בּוֹז יָבוּזוּ, דָּא סַמָאֵל, בְּאַהֲבָה דְּיִשְׂרָאֵל, לְמֶהֱוֵי לֵיהּ חוּלָקָא בַּהֲדַיְיהוּ, בְּאִינוּן מַיִם דִּרְשִׁימִין הָכָא בְּפָרְשָׁתָא, דִּכְתִיב אִם יִתֵּן אִישׁ אֶת כָּל הוֹן בֵּיתוֹ בְּאַהֲבָה בּוֹז יָבוּזוּ, סִימָנָא דְּאִינוּן מַיִם בּוֹ״ז, יָבוּזוּ לוֹ וַדַּאי, דְּהָא כֻּלְּהוּ אִתְחֲשִׁיבוּ לְגַבָּן, חֶרֶשׂ נִשְׁבָּר, דְּלֵית לֵיהּ תִּקְּנָה לְעָלְמִין.

891. "Many waters cannot quench love" (Ibid.) this refers to the waters that Yisrael pour out in libation out of rejoicing and love for the Holy One,

blessed be He, as it is written: "Therefore with joy shall you draw water" (Yeshayah 12:3). "nor can the floods drown it" (Shir Hashirim 8:7). These are the floods of the pure balsam, NAMELY, THE EIGHTEEN RIVERS OF PLENTY THAT ARE DRAWN DOWN FROM YESOD OF BINAH. For all of them cleave to, and form a bond with, this love. "if a man would give all the substance of his house, it would be utterly scorned " (Ibid.). This refers to Samael; and he gives "for love" (Ibid.) of Yisrael, namely, so that he should have a portion with them in these waters about which it is written in this section: "if a man would give all the substance of his house for love, it would be utterly scorned (Heb. boz)," which is a mnemonic for these waters THAT ARE POURED OUT ON THE SECOND (BET), SIXTH (VAV), AND SEVENTH (ZAYIN) DAYS. It would certainly be scorned, for all the substance OF SAMAEL is considered for us as a broken potsherd that can never be repaired.

892. מַיִם דִּלְהוֹן אִתְפְּלִיגוּ בְּיוֹמִין בּוֹ"ז, אִשְׁתָּאֲרוּ שְׁאַר יוֹמִין, דְּאִינּוּן חֲמִישִׁי רְבִיעִי שְׁלִישִׁי, וְסִימָן, חֶרֶ"שׁ אֶת חַרְשֵׁי הָאֲדָמָה, וְלֵית לוֹן תִּקּוּנָא בַּהֲדָן, וְלָא לְעָלְמִין. וְאִי תֵּימָא בּוֹז יָבוּזוּ לוֹ כְּתִיב. הָתָם כִּי לֹא בָזָה וְלֹא שִׁקַּץ עֱנוּת.

892. HE EXPLAINS HIS WORDS: The water OF SAMAEL, THE OTHER SIDE AND THE NATIONS, is distributed on the days of boz (Bet Vav Zayin). This leaves the other days, namely, the fifth, fourth, and third days of Sukkot, ON WHICH THERE IS NO WATER LIBATION. The mnemonic for this: He ploughed (Heb. charash - Chet Resh Shin) the furrows of the land, WHERE THE LETTERS OF CHARASH STAND FOR CHAMISHI (LIT. 'FIFTH'), REVI'I (LIT. 'FOURTH') AND SHLISHI (LIT. 'THIRD'), ON WHICH DAYS THERE IS NO LIBATION OF WATER, and they have no correction through us, nor indeed forever. FOR JUST AS THEY HAVE NO CORRECTION ON THE FIFTH, FOURTH, AND THIRD DAYS, SO THEY NEVER WILL HAVE ANY CORRECTION. And should you wish to point that it is written "it would be utterly scorned," WHEREAS, ACCORDING TO THE ABOVE, IT SHOULD HAVE BEEN WRITTEN 'IT WOULD NOT BE UTTERLY SCORNED', NAMELY, THAT THEY DO NOT WANT THE SCORN (SECOND, SIXTH, AND SEVENTH), WHICH IS THE SUBSTANCE OF SAMAEL, HE THEN RESPONDS: Elsewhere IT IS WRITTEN: "For He has not despised (scorned) nor abhorred the affliction of the afflicted" (Tehilim 22:25).

‎893. יוֹמָא קַדְמָאָה מַאי עָבֵיד לֵיהּ. אֶלָּא לָא אִקְרֵי רִאשׁוֹן, וְלָא אִקְרֵי ‎אֶחָד, אֶלָּא חֲמִשָּׁה עָשָׂר סְתָם, בְּלָא רְשׁוּמָא כְּלַל. אֲבָל שִׁירוּתָא ‎דְּרִשִׁימוּ דְּמַיִין, מִיּוֹם שֵׁנִי הֲוֵי. וְהָכִי אִתְחֲזֵי, בְּגִין דְּלֵית טוֹב בַּשֵּׁנִי, ‎וּבְג״כ, לָא רָשִׁים רִאשׁוֹן וְלָא אֶחָד כְּלַל, וַהֲוֵי בִּסְתָם, וְשָׁרֵי רְשִׁימוּ ‎דְּיוֹמִין, בְּיוֹם שֵׁנִי. וְאִתְפְּלָגוּ מַיִם בְּבו״ז, וְאִשְׁתָּאֲרוּ בְּיוֹמִין חֵר״ש, כְּמָה ‎דְּאִתְּמַר, וְכֹלָּא כַּדְקָא יֵאוֹת.

893. HE ASKS: What about the first day OF SUKKOT?, HE THINKS THE SECOND, SIXTH, AND SEVENTH (HEB. *BOZ*) DAYS ARE CONSIDERED THOSE OF THE WATER LIBATION, AND THE FIFTH, FOURTH AND THIRD (HEB. *CHARASH*) DAYS ARE FREE OF THE LIBATION OF WATER, BUT HE DOES NOT MENTION THE FIRST DAY OF THE FESTIVAL AT ALL. HE ANSWERS, THE FIRST DAY is not called either 'first' nor 'one', but IS CALLED simply "the fifteenth day" (Bemidbar 29:12). No special mention is made of it BECAUSE THERE IS NOTHING SPECIAL ABOUT IT TO MENTION, but the water libation is first mentioned on the second day, and this is how it should be. BECAUSE ON THIS DAY A PORTION IS GIVEN TO THE OTHER SIDE, IT IS FITTING THAT THIS SHOULD BE ON THE SECOND DAY, for about the second day IT WAS not SAID: 'THAT IT WAS good'. This is why he does not mention the first or one day at all, but just simply IS THE FIFTEENTH DAY, and the first mention of the days, and the renewal of the days, begins on the second day. And the water is distributed on the second, sixth and seventh days, and there is no libation of water on the fifth, fourth or third days, as we have learned – and it all falls into place.

‎894. זַכָּאָה חוּלָקֵהוֹן דְּיִשְׂרָאֵל, דְּיַדְעֵי לְאַעֲלָאָה לְגוֹ מוֹחָא דְּאֱגוֹזָא. ‎וּבְגִין לְמֵיעָאל לְגוֹ מוֹחָא, מִתְבָּרִין קְלִיפִין אִלֵּין, וְעָאלִין. מַה כְּתִיב ‎לְבָתַר כָּל הַאי. בַּיּוֹם הַשְּׁמִינִי עֲצֶרֶת תִּהְיֶה לָכֶם. לְבָתַר דְּתַבְרוּ כָּל הָנֵי ‎קְלִיפִין, וְתַבְרוּ כַּמָּה גְּזִיזִין, וְכַמָּה נְחָשִׁים קָטְלוּ, וְכַמָּה עֲקְרַבִּים דַּהֲווֹ ‎לוֹן בְּאִינוּן טוּרֵי דַּחֲשׁוֹכָא, עַד דְּאַשְׁכָּחוּ אֲתָר דִּישׁוּבָא, וְקַרְתָּא ‎קַדִּישָׁא, מַקְּפָא שׁוּרִין סְחוֹר סְחוֹר, כְּדֵין עָאלוּ לְגַבָּהּ, לְמֶעְבַּד נַיְיחָא ‎תַּמָּן, וּלְמֶחֱדֵי בָהּ. וְהָא אוֹקִימְנָא מִלָּה.

894. Happy is the portion of Yisrael, who know how to enter the kernel of the nut; NAMELY, HOLINESS IS LIKE THE KERNEL OF A NUT THAT IS SURROUNDED BY SHELLS, and in order to get into the kernel, they break off these shells THAT SURROUND IT, and enter. What is written subsequently? "On the eighth day you shall have a solemn assembly" (Bemidbar 29:35). For after they break through all these Klipot and break down a number of forces and kill a number of serpents and a number of scorpions, which were there in wait for them in those mountains of darkness, until they managed to find the place of settlement and a holy city WHICH IS THE HOLY MALCHUT, surrounded by walls on all sides, they then entered it ON THE EIGHTH DAY OF ASSEMBLY (HEB. *SHMINI ATZERET*) to give it satisfaction there, and rejoice in it. And we already explained the matter.

895. וְדָא אִיהוּ עֲצֶרֶת, כְּנִישׁוּ. אֲתָר דְּמִתְכְּנַשׁ כֹּלָּא לְגַבָּהּ. תִּהְיֶה לָכֶם, וְלָא לְאַחֲרָא, לְמֶחְדֵּי אַתּוּן בְּמָארֵיכוֹן, וְאִיהוּ בַּהֲדַיְיכוּ. וְעַל דָּא כְּתִיב, שִׂמְחוּ בַיְיָ' וְגִילוּ צַדִּיקִים וְהַרְנִינוּ כָּל יִשְׁרֵי לֵב.

895. And this is "a solemn assembly," THE MEANING OF WHICH IS a gathering, NAMELY MALCHUT, for she is a place where everything gathers, FOR SHE IS A RECEPTACLE FOR ALL THE HIGHER LUMINARIES. "you shall have," namely you and nobody else shall have, FOR THE OTHER SIDE HAVE NO PART OF IT, but it is you who rejoice with your Master, and He with you. And on this it is written: "Be glad in Hashem and rejoice, O you righteous: and shout for joy, all you who are upright in heart" (Tehilim 32:11).

Matot

Name of Articles

Page No.

1. The world is maintained by two colors only   296

1. The world is maintained by two colors only

A Synopsis

Rabbi Yehuda and Rabbi Yitzchak talk about the wise-hearted women that spin and work with their hands, and from this they derive that those women combine Judgment and Mercy. We hear that Rabbi Elazar said that every woman is considered Judgment until she marries a man of Yisrael, who is compassion, and thus Judgment and Mercy are joined together. The rabbis explain why it is forbidden for men to have intercourse with women from the other nations. We hear that God called the souls of Yisrael Chesed so that the world would never be without love. From this it is clear that anyone who destroys Chesed will not exist in the World to Come. Matot ends with a reference to levirate marriage, where the childless man's brother restores Chesed to the world.

1. וְכָל הַטַּף בַּנָּשִׁים אֲשֶׁר לָא יָדְעוּ מִשְׁכַּב זָכָר. תַּמָּן תָּנֵינָן, א״ר יְהוּדָה, אֵין הָעוֹלָם מִתְנַהֵג אֶלָּא בִּתְרֵי גְּווֹנִין, דְּאָתוּ מִסְטַר אִתְּתָא דְּאִשְׁתְּכָחַת חַכִּימַת לִבָּא. הה״ד, וְכָל אִשָּׁה חַכְמַת לֵב בְּיָדֶיהָ טָווּ וַיָּבִיאוּ מַטְוֶה אֶת הַתְּכֵלֶת וְאֶת הָאַרְגָּמָן. וּמַאי מַתְיִין. אֶת הַתְּכֵלֶת וְאֶת הָאַרְגָּמָן, גַּווֹנִין דִּכְלִילָן בְּגוֹ גְּווֹנֵי.

1. "But all the women children that have not known man by lying with him" (Bemidbar 31:18). In relation to this, we learned that Rabbi Yehuda said the world is maintained by two colors only, WHITE AND RED – NAMELY CHASSADIM AND CHOCHMAH OF THE LEFT that come from the aspect of the wise-hearted woman. Hence, it says, "and all the women that were wise-hearted did spin with their hands, and brought that which they had spun, both of blue, and of purple" (Shemot 35:25). What did they bring? THE SCRIPTURE SAYS blue and purple, which are colors contained within colors; THAT IS, THERE ARE TWO MAIN COLORS – WHITE AND RED – AND BLUE AND PURPLE COLORS ARE INCLUDED WITHIN THESE TWO COLORS.

2. הֲדָא הוּא דִּכְתִיב, דָּרְשָׁה צֶמֶר וּפִשְׁתִּים וַתַּעַשׂ בְּחֵפֶץ כַּפֶּיהָ. וּכְתִיב בְּיָדֶיהָ טָווּ, מַאי טָווּ. אָמַר רִבִּי יְהוּדָה, טָווּ בְּדִינָא, טָווּ בְּרַחֲמֵי. א״ר יִצְחָק, אֲמַאי אִתְקְרִיא אִשָּׁה. אָמַר לֵיהּ דִּכְלִילָא בְּדִינָא, וּכְלִילָא בְּרַחֲמֵי.

2. This is the meaning of: "she seeks wool and flax, and works willingly with her hands" (Mishlei 1:13), SINCE WOOL PERTAINS TO THE RIGHT AND MERCY, AND FLAX TO THE LEFT AND JUDGMENT. It is also written: "did spin with their hands." What is "spin"? Rabbi Yehuda says: They spin with Judgment and they spin with Mercy; THAT IS, THEY INTERLACE RIGHT AND LEFT WITH EACH OTHER, AND THE JUDGMENTS OF THE LEFT ARE SWEETENED BY THE MERCY OF THE RIGHT. Rabbi Yitzchak said: Why is a woman (Heb. *ishah*) so called, WHICH IS DERIVED FROM FIRE (HEB. *ESH*)? He said to him: She contains Judgment and Mercy. SHE IS THEREFORE CALLED 'ISHAH', THE LETTERS OF *ESH-HEI*, *ESH* BEING JUDGMENT AND *HEI* MERCY.

‎3. ת״ח, דא״ר אֶלְעָזָר, כָּל אִתְּתָא בְּדִינָא אִתְקַרְיָא, עַד דְּאַטְעָמָא טַעֲמָא דְרַחֲמֵי. דְּתַנְיָא, מִסְטְרָא דב״ג, אָתֵי חִוָּורָא. וּמִסְטְרָא דְּאִתְּתָא, אָתֵי סוּמָקָא. טַעֲמָא אִתְּתָא מֵחִוָּורָא, וְחִוָּורָא עָדִיף.

3. Come and behold. Rabbi Elazar said: Every woman is considered to be of Judgment, SINCE THEY ARE ROOTED IN THE LEFT COLUMN. IT IS SO until she tastes the taste of Mercy – THAT IS, MARRIES A MAN – AS A MALE IS ROOTED IN THE RIGHT COLUMN, WHICH IS CHESED AND MERCY. We learned that it is from the side of the man that white is produced, SUCH AS THE BONES OF THE FETUS, FOR HE IS OF MERCY. From the side of the woman comes the red OF THE FETUS, THE RED OF FLESH AND SINEW, WHICH ARE OF JUDGMENT. When a woman tastes of the white – THAT IS, WHEN SHE IS MARRIED TO A MAN – white is more predominant in her, THOUGH HER ROOT IS THE RED.

‎4. ות״ח אֲמַאי אֲסִירָן נְשֵׁי שְׁאַר עַמִּין, דְּיַדְעֵי מִשְׁכְּבֵי דְכוּרָא. מִשּׁוּם דְּתַנֵּינָן, אִית יְמִינָא, וְאִית שְׂמָאלָא. יִשְׂרָאֵל, וּשְׁאַר עַמִּין. וג״ע, וְגֵיהִנָּם. עָלְמָא דָא, וְעָלְמָא דְּאָתֵי. יִשְׂרָאֵל לְקָבְלֵי דְּרַחֲמֵי, וּשְׁאַר עַמִּין לְקָבְלֵי דְּדִינָא. וּתְנָן, אִתְּתָא דְּאַטְעֲמָא טַעֲמָא דְּרַחֲמֵי, רַחֲמֵי נַצְחָא. אִתְּתָא דְּטַעֲמָא טַעֲמָא דְּדִינָא, דִּינָא בְּדִינָא אִתְדַּבְּקַת, וַעֲלַיְיהוּ אִתְקְרֵי וְהַכְּלָבִים עַזֵּי נֶפֶשׁ לֹא יָדְעוּ שָׂבְעָה.

4. Come and behold: this is why women of the other nations, who know man by lying with him, are forbidden to be wed. We have learned that there is right – CHESED – and left – JUDGMENT – which are Yisrael and the other nations, AND ALSO the Garden of Eden, ON THE RIGHT, and Gehenom, ON THE LEFT. This world is ON THE LEFT and the World to Come is ON THE RIGHT. The children of Yisrael correspond to Mercy, ON THE RIGHT, and the other nations to Judgment, ON THE LEFT. We have learned that when a woman has a taste of Mercy – THAT IS, WHEN SHE MARRIES ONE OF THE MEN OF YISRAEL – Mercy overpowers JUDGMENT AND SHE TURNS INTO MERCY. When a woman has a taste of Judgment – THAT IS, WHEN SHE MARRIES A FOREIGNER WHO PERTAINS TO JUDGMENT, AS MENTIONED – Judgment cleaves to Judgment. THE JUDGMENT IN THE WOMAN ADHERES TO THE JUDGMENT IN THE FOREIGNER. It is written of them: "the dogs are insolently greedy, they never have enough" (Yeshayah 56:11).

5. וְעַל דָּא תְּנֵינָן, הַנִּבְעֶלֶת לעכו"ם קְשׁוּרָה בּוֹ כַּכֶּלֶב. מַה כַּלְבָּא תַּקִּיפָא בְּרוּחֵיהּ חֲצִיפָא. אוֹף הָכָא דִּינָא בְּדִינָא, חֲצִיפָא בְּכֹלָּא. הַנִּבְעֶלֶת לְיִשְׂרָאֵל, תְּנֵינָן, כְּתִיב וְאַתֶּם הַדְּבֵקִים בַּה' אֱלֹהֵיכֶם חַיִּים כֻּלְּכֶם הַיּוֹם. מ"ט. מִשּׁוּם דְּנִשְׁמָתָא דְּיִשְׂרָאֵל, אַתְיָיא מֵרוּחָא דֶּאֱלֹהִים חַיִּים. דִּכְתִיב כִּי רוּחַ מִלְפָנַי יַעֲטוֹף, מַשְׁמַע דִּכְתִיב מִלְפָנַי. וּבג"כ, אִתְּתָא דְּהִיא בְּתוּלְתָּא, וְלָא אִתְדַּבְּקַת בְּדִינָא קַשְׁיָא דִּשְׁאַר עַמִּין, וְאִתְדַּבְּקַת בְּיִשְׂרָאֵל, רַחֲמֵי נַצְחָא וְאִתְבְּשָׂרַת.

5. In relation to this, we have learned that a woman who is married to a foreigner is attached to him like a dog. Just as a dog has a strong impudent spirit, she WHO IS MARRIED TO A FOREIGNER is also most impudent, WHEN Judgment CLEAVES to Judgment. We learned that she who is married to one of the children of Yisrael, it says OF HER: "but you that did cleave to Hashem your Elohim are alive every one of you this day" (Devarim 4:4). What is the reason thereof? The soul of Yisrael comes from the spirit of living Elohim, as written: "but the spirit...should faint (also: 'envelop') before Me" (Yeshayah 57:16). This is understood from the phrase, "before Me," WHICH MEANS FROM BEFORE THE SHECHINAH, NAMELY FROM ZEIR ANPIN CALLED 'LIVING ELOHIM'. Therefore, in a virgin woman, who does not cleave to the Harsh Judgment of the other nations, AS MENTIONED

ABOVE, but cleaves to Yisrael, WHICH IS OF MERCY, Mercy is more powerful, and she is corrected FROM THE JUDGMENT IN HER.

6. וְת״ח, כְּתִיב אָמַרְתִּי עוֹלָם חֶסֶד יִבָּנֶה. מַאי חֶסֶד. הוּא חַד מִכִּתְרֵי עִלָּאֵי דְמַלְכָּא, דְנִשְׁמָתָא דְיִשְׂרָאֵל קָרָא לָהּ קוּדְשָׁא בְּרִיךְ הוּא חֶסֶד. עַל תְּנַאי דְיִתְבְּנֵי, וְלָא יִשְׁתֵּיצֵי חֶסֶד מֵעָלְמָא. מַשְׁמַע דִכְתִיב יִבָּנֶה. בְּג״כ תָּנֵינָן, מַאן דְּשֵׁצֵי חֶסֶד מֵעָלְמָא, אִשְׁתֵּיצֵי הוּא לְעָלְמָא דְאָתֵי. וְעַל דָא כְּתִיב, לֹא תִהְיֶה אֵשֶׁת הַמֵּת הַחוּצָה, בְּגִין לְמֶעְבַּד חֶסֶד עִם מִיתָא. וְאִתְעֲבֵיד בִּנְיָינָא, דִכְתִיב עוֹלָם חֶסֶד יִבָּנֶה.

6. Come and behold. It is written: "for I have said, 'The world is built by Chesed'" (Tehilim 89:3). What is Chesed? HE ANSWERS: It is one of the King's supernal Sfirot, NAMELY THE HIGHEST OF THE LOWER SEVEN SFIROT. For the Holy One, blessed be He, named the soul of Yisrael Chesed, on the condition that it would build CHESED. Thus, Chesed will never cease. This is derived from the phrase, "is built," WHICH REFERS TO CHESED THAT WILL BE BUILT. We have therefore learned that he who causes Chesed to cease in the world will perish in the world to come. Hence, it is written: "the wife of the dead shall not marry abroad to a stranger" (Devarim 25:5), in order to do kindness (Chesed) with the dead man, so that he will be built and established, as it is written, "the world is built by Chesed" (Tehilim 89:3).